# Using

# Microsoft® Word 2000

*Jane Calabria*

*Dorothy Burke*

*Rob Kirkland*

A Division of Macmillan Computer Publishing, USA
201 W. 103rd Street
Indianapolis, Indiana 46290

## Contents at a Glance

# Using Microsoft® Word 2000

ISBN: 0-7897-1854-5

Library of Congress Catalog No.: 98-86982

01 00 99    6 5 4 3 2 1

First printing: May 1999

Interpretation of the printing code: the rightmost double-digit number is the year of the book's printing; the rightmost single-digit number, the number of the book's printing. For example, a printing code of 99-1 shows that the first printing of the book occurred in 1999.

**Executive Editor**
Jim Minatel

**Acquisitions Editor**
Don Essig

**Development Editor**
Melanie Palaisa

**Technical Editor**
Bill Bruns

**Managing Editor**
Thomas F. Hayes

**Copy Editor**
Kate Givens

**Indexer**
Julie Bess

**Proofreader**
Tricia Sterling

**Cover Designer**
Dan Armstrong

**Book Designer**
Ruth Harvey

**Layout Technician**
Cyndi Davis-Hubler

# Contents

# About the Authors

**Jane Calabria** has authored 13 Macmillan Computer Publishing books on the topics of Microsoft Windows (95 and 98), Word, Excel, and PowerPoint as well as Lotus Notes and Domino. She and her husband, Rob Kirkland, own Stillwater Enterprises, Inc., a consulting firm located near Philadelphia, PA, and are preeminent authors, speakers, and trainers on the topic of Lotus Notes and Domino, and conduct national training sessions and seminars. Jane has coauthored many books with Dorothy Burke. Their books include: the *Certified Microsoft Office User Exam Guides*(s) for *Word 97, Excel 97, and PowerPoint* 97. Jane and Dorothy have also authored the *Microsoft Works 6-in-1, Microsoft Windows 95 6-in-1, Microsoft Windows 98 6-in-1*, and the predecessor to this book, *Using Microsoft Word 97* (Third Edition).

**Rob Kirkland** is a Certified Lotus Notes Instructor (CLI), a Certified NetWare Engineer (CNE), and a Microsoft Certified Product Specialist (MCPS) for Windows NT. With Jane Calabria, he is coauthor of the *Professional Developers Guide to Domino* and is a contributing author of several Que books including *Using Windows NT Workstation, Intranet Publishing, Running a Perfect Intranet*, and *Intranet HTML*. Rob began his computer teaching career as a word processing and desktop publishing guru. Today, Rob also teaches Lotus Notes, Novell NetWare, Windows NT, numerous application programs, and hardware management. As a consultant, he sets up networks, designs applications, and subdues unruly hardware and software. In his spare time, Rob picked up a law degree.

**Dorothy Burke** is a Certified Lotus Notes Instructor (CLI) and teaches Domino system administration and application development. She has been an independent consultant and trainer since 1988. Dorothy has contributed to several MCP books, including *Special Edition Using PowerPoint 97, Easy Lotus Notes R5*, and along with Jane Calabria, has coauthored seven books on the topics of Lotus Notes and Domino, Microsoft Windows and Microsoft Word, Excel, and PowerPoint. As a trainer, Dorothy teaches word processing, desktop publishing, operating systems, spreadsheets, and graphics programs, as well as Lotus Notes and Domino. As a consultant, Dorothy works with Lotus Notes and Domino, developing applications for Notes and Web clients.

# Dedication

*To Christina Manieri, thank you for your invaluable assistance with this project. May your future be as bright as your smile. Love always and forever.*

# Acknowledgments

What is it like to write a book without Melanie Palaisa, Development Editor? It's like using a computer without a keyboard. We are thrilled to be working with Mel again and we thank her for everything she has taught and continues to teach us.

Thanks also to the "Que East" team: Janet Crawford and Carol Manieri for their late hours, research, keystroking, food breaks, Boggle breaks, and exercise demands.

We had some special technical assistance and support in this edition, and we'd like to thank Barbara Anderson, of Interfusion Inc., Merchantville, NJ for her contribution of figures throughout this book and Filza Potapova for her assistance with the multilingual aspects of Word 2000. We welcome them both to our team and look forward to working with them on other projects.

A special thanks to John Pierce and Jim Minatel for their long hours and dedication to this series and in particular, to this team of authors. We really like the look and feel of this new series and the Using series has become one of our favorites.

And a *huge* thanks to technical editor Bill Bruns, for keeping us in sync with the new features of Word 2000. Bill's networking and support experience is a real value to this edition.

# Tell Us What You Think!

As the reader of this book, *you* are our most important critic and commentator. We value your opinion and want to know what we're doing right, what we could do better, what areas you'd like to see us publish in, and any other words of wisdom you're willing to pass our way.

As the Executive Editor for the General Desktop Applications team at Que Publishing, I welcome your comments. You can fax, email, or write me directly to let me know what you did or didn't like about this book—as well as what we can do to make our books stronger.

*Please note that I cannot help you with technical problems related to the topic of this book, and that due to the high volume of mail I receive, I might not be able to reply to every message.*

When you write, please be sure to include this book's title and author as well as your name and phone or fax number. I will carefully review your comments and share them with the author and editors who worked on the book.

Fax:      317.581.4663

Email:    office@mcp.com

Mail:     Executive Editor
          General Desktop Applications
          Que Publishing
          201 West 103rd Street
          Indianapolis, IN 46290 USA

We first started using Microsoft Word when it was still in version 1.1. It was a DOS-based program in those days—graphical user interfaces like the Macintosh and Windows didn't exist yet. At that time Word was a pioneering program, unique among word processors in its treatment of characters, paragraphs, and pages as discrete objects—each having its own properties. Word's object orientation made it uniquely easy to use for the creation of great-looking, highly formatted documents. Clearly, Microsoft was on to something when it came up with this word processor because now virtually all programs designed for laying out pages or editing and formatting text have adopted the same paradigm that we first encountered in Word 1.1.

Over the years we have learned, used, taught, and written about many other software programs. For awhile, when WordPerfect dominated the world of computerized word processing, we hardly thought about Word. But Word had impressed us because of its power and ease of use and we found ourselves returning to it again and again. With each revision, it became more powerful, more relevant, and easier to use. Now it has become our preferred word processing program. It is our great pleasure to present the latest version of Word to you.

Microsoft has long developed Word with an eye to three things:

- Power. Microsoft wants you to be able to use Word to do anything that can be done with words.

- Ease of use. Microsoft wants it to be so easy that you don't hesitate to do it just because it is too much effort. It wants it to be so easy that the process doesn't distract you from your ultimate goal of communication with words.

- Ease of learning. Microsoft wants Word to be easy to master so that you don't hesitate to try tasks simply because you have never done so.

One of a programmer's most difficult challenges is to add power while retaining ease of use and ease of learning in a program. Microsoft has never lost sight of these goals. As a result, not only has Word gained new features with each new release, but its existing features have become easier to use. Also, some of the new features—for example, wizards and the Office Assistant—have had the sole purpose of making it easy for you to discover and begin using Word's power.

That is our goal too. We want you to get your word processing done quickly, efficiently, and painlessly. We'll help you to quickly discover the power of Word. We'll help you to quickly learn the tools that Word provides. We'll show you the easiest and most efficient ways of using those tools. In the end, we hope you will feel the same excitement we feel about Word and the same pleasure that we feel in having mastered a powerful set of tools.

## Why This Book?

Have you ever purchased a *Using* book from Que? The *Using* books have proven invaluable to readers as both learning guides and as references for many years. The *Using* series is an industry leader, and has practically become an industry standard. We encourage and receive feedback from readers all the time and we consider and implement their suggestions whenever possible.

*Using Microsoft Word 2000* incorporates fresh new ideas and approaches to the *Using* series. This book is not a compiled authority on all the features of Word. Instead, it is a streamlined, conversational approach for using Word productively and efficiently. New features include the following:

- Improved index to help you find information the first time you look! What do you call tasks and features? As we wrote, we anticipated every possible name or description of a task that we've heard people call it. For example, if you wanted to know how to include artwork in your letterhead, where do you look? Should you check the index for art, clip art, scanned images, graphics, letterhead, or pictures? The answer is *yes*—check the index for any of those terms and you will find your answer on the first pass.

- Real-life answers. Throughout the book you will find *our* real-life examples and experiences. We recommend when to use tables versus tabs versus columns. We tell you why you don't want to create a database with a field containing first names and last names. We even suggest when wizards save you time and when you might be more productive creating your own documents from scratch. After all, we've been there and done that! We understand that *how* to perform a task is only one question you may have, and perhaps the bigger questions are *why* and *what for*?

- Relevant information written just for you! We have carefully scrutinized which features and tasks to include in this book and have included those that apply to your everyday use of Word. We have also included those tasks and skills required to pass the Microsoft Office Use Specialist® exams.

  We realize that very few people use as much as 50% of Word's capabilities. Our experience tells us that there are two reasons for this:

- Time. You can't spare the time from work to attend classes on Word 97. You don't have the time at work to explore every nook and cranny of the software. And, when you do need to perform a task that is new to you, you need to get it done quickly.

- Need. Why invest in material that teaches you how to perform tasks you will never need to perform? Word is a powerful (and potentially complex) software program. But your work does not involve powerful, complex word processing tasks? Will it ever? Why spend time on features you don't need?

- Reference or Tutorial. You can learn to quickly perform a task using step-by-step instructions, or you can investigate the why and wherefore of a task with our discussions preceding each task.

- Wise Investment. Pay the right price for the right book. We won't waste your valuable bookshelf real estate with redundant or irrelevant material, nor do we assume you "know it all" or need to "know it all." Here is what you need, when you need it, how you need it, with an appropriate price tag.

- Easy-to-find procedures. Every numbered step-by-step procedure in the book has a short title explaining exactly what it does. This saves you time by making it easier to find the exact steps you need to accomplish a task.

- Cross referencing, to give additional, related information. We've looked for all the tasks and topics that are related to a topic at hand and referenced those for you. So, if you need to look for coverage that leads up to what you are working on, or if you want to build on the new skill you just mastered, you have the references to easily find the right coverage in the book.

- Side note elements with quick-read headlines save you time. Often, we'll want to give you a little tip or note about how to make something work best. Or we'll need to give you a warning about a problem you may encounter. By giving these side notes precise titles that explain their topic and by placing them in the margins, we make each one easy to skip if you don't need it and easy to find the topic of if you want to read it.

## Who Should Use This Book

Anyone who uses Word and needs to accomplish a specific task, solve a problem, or wants to learn a technique that applies to something they need to get done. Basically, anyone who

- Has basic Windows skills but is new to Word.
- Uses Word 97, but wants to become more proficient in Word 2000.
- Uses Word at work.
- Uses Word at home.

- Needs to create special documents, such as newsletters or letterheads.
- Wants to manage small databases and mailing lists, such as club memberships or client lists.

If you are preparing for the Microsoft Office User Specialist Exam, you'll find that this book covers all the tasks required for the exam, but is not limited to the exam topics. We include many topics and tasks here that we feel are important and applicable to using Microsoft Word at work, with material beyond the scope of the Microsoft exams. If you have experience with Word and you want to study for the Word exam, we recommend you read Que's *Microsoft Word 97 Exam Guide* (ISBN 0-7897-1290-3).

This book is not for you if you have never used a Windows-based computer program. In that case, we recommend you read *Sams Teach Yourself Microsoft Word 2000 in 24 Hours*. This book is also not for you if your goal is to learn everything there is to know about Word 2000. In that case, we recommend you read *Special Edition Using Microsoft Word 2000*.

# How This Book Is Organized

*Using Microsoft Word 2000* has task-oriented, easy-to-navigate tutorials and reference information presented in a logical progression from simple to complex tasks. It covers features of the program you use in your daily work. Features are explained thoroughly. Examples come from real-life experiences. You can work through the book lesson by lesson or you can find specific information when you need to perform a job quickly.

*Using Microsoft Word 2000* is divided into eight parts:

### Part I: Introduction to Word 2000

This is fundamental information for those who are new to Word 2000. You learn the basics of word processing, how to find help and how to install or upgrade to Word 2000, as well as some of the new features of Word 2000.

## Part II: Use Everyday Word Processing Techniques

More fundamentals are found here including managing files, using spell check and grammar check, and navigating text. You also learn inside information and tips and tricks for working more productively. So, even if you're familiar with previous versions of Word, Part II can help you work more efficiently.

## Part III: Increase Productivity

This section can take you from someone who knows how to use Word to someone who uses Word to their advantage! Learn how tables help you to organize and lay out information in a document, work with lists, apply styles, and get control over your text and paragraph alignment, breaks, and spacing.

## Part IV: Create Professional Documents

Formatted pages using sections, outlines, columns, and templates are what differentiate between amateur and professional-looking documents. Here, you learn to produce great-looking documents quickly and efficiently.

## Part V: Incorporate Data and Objects from Other Sources

No man is an island and no software product today is a standalone product! Learn how to integrate data from other programs into your Word documents, and how to insert graphics, special characters, drawings, and WordArt. Show off your skills and add impact to your reports with charts!

## Part VI: Use Word at Work—Real World Solutions

Here, we apply the skills you've learned to document-oriented tasks. When you need to manage workgroup documents and learn how to do this without hopping from chapter to chapter, this is your one-stop shopping. Master the creation of documents using wizards, which may be intuitive, but are only the beginning of document creation, not the finished product. Manage long documents, design custom forms, and turn your skills into a real-world solution. Also learn about Word's new multilingual features and how best to make them work for you.

### Part VII: Use Word with the Internet

Word 2000 is a real Internet tool and here you learn how to apply Word's Internet features to your Internet needs. Use Word as your email editor and create Web documents and forms.

### Part VIII: Automate, Customize, and Fine-Tune

Write macros to automate your word processing tasks and learn to use wizards to create elaborate documents. Learn how to customize Word features.

Be sure to make use of the tearout card inside the book's cover. Tear this out and take it with you wherever you use Word. It contains some of the most common information you'll need that isn't easy to remember.

# Conventions Used in This Book

Commands, directions, and explanations in this book are presented in the clearest format possible. The following items are some of the features that will make this book easier for you to use:

- Menu and dialog box commands and options. You can easily find the onscreen menu and dialog box commands by looking for bold text like you see in this direction: Open the **File** menu and click **Save**.

- Hotkeys for commands. The underlined keys onscreen that activate commands and options are also underlined in the book as shown in **File** and **Save**.

- Combination and shortcut keystrokes. Text that directs you to hold down several keys simultaneously is connected with a plus sign (+), such as Ctrl+P.

- Graphical icons with the commands they execute. Look for icons like this in text and steps. These indicate buttons onscreen that you can click to accomplish the procedure.

- Cross references. If there's a related topic that is a prerequisite to the section or steps you are reading, or a topic that builds further on what you are reading, you'll find the cross reference to it after the steps or at the end of the section like this:

**SEE ALSO**

➤ *To learn more about setting font options, see page 74*

- Glossary terms. For all the terms that appear in the glossary, you'll find the first appearance of that term in the text in *italics* along with its definition.

- Sidebars. Information related to the task at hand, or "inside" information from the author, is offset in sidebars that don't interfere with the task at hand and make it easy to find this valuable information. Each of these sidebars has a short title to help you quickly identify the information you'll find there. You'll find the same kind of information in these that you might find in notes, tips, or warnings in other books, but here the titles should be more informative.

Your screen may look slightly different from some of the examples in this book. This is due to various options during installation and because of hardware setup.

# Introduction to Word 2000

# CHAPTER

# 1

# Install or Upgrade to Word 2000

This chapter tells you how to install or upgrade to the Microsoft Word component of Office 2000. If Word 2000 is already installed on your computer and you are new to Word, you can skip this chapter and move to Chapter 3, "Get Acquainted with Word." If Word is installed on your computer but you are new to this version, consider skipping this chapter and moving to Chapter 2, "What's New in Word 2000."

# Before You Install

Before you begin installation, back up important data files. If you don't know how to back up files, see "Back Up Data Files" in Chapter 8, "Protect Your Files and Control File Access."

Many people purchase Word 2000 as part of the Microsoft Office 2000 suite of applications, which also includes such applications as Excel, PowerPoint, and Access. If you are installing Word as part of Microsoft Office 2000, you have the option of installing all of the Office applications or some of the applications. You need to decide which applications you want (or need) to install before you begin.

To install Word as part of Microsoft Office, your system must meet the following requirements:

**What's an X86?**

X86 computers use Intel's 80486 (the "486") or successor processors or processors that are compatible with Intel processors. Examples include the following: 486, Pentium, Pentium Pro, Celeron, Pentium II, and Cyrix chips. Predecessors of the 486 (8088, 80286, 80386) are not included in this X86 list because Windows 95 and Windows NT 4.x will not run on them.

- The operating system on your computer must be Windows 95, Windows 98, or Windows NT Workstation 4.0 with Service Pack 3. In this example, we install on a PC running Windows 98.

- Your computer must be at least an x86-compatible PC that meets the minimum requirements to run Windows 98 or Windows NT Workstation 4.0 (here, we install Office on a Windows 98 machine). Microsoft recommends a 90MHz Pentium or better with at least 32MB RAM. To check the system specifications for your computer, click **Start** and then choose **Settings**, **Control Panel**. Double-click the System icon. The information you need to check is on the **General** tab of the System Properties dialog box (see Figure 1.1). Click **OK** to close the box.

- Your hard disk should have 250MB of available space. To quickly see the amount of free disk space on your computer, double-click the My Computer icon on your desktop and then select the icon for your hard disk. In Windows 98 the amount of free disk space displays on the left side of the window or in the Status bar at the bottom of the window (see Figure 1.2). In Windows NT and Windows 95 the amount of free disk space appears in the Status bar at the bottom of the window.

FIGURE 1.1

The System Properties dialog box indicates the operating system, type of processor, and the amount of RAM found on your system.

FIGURE 1.2

When you highlight your C: drive in the My Computer window, a pie chart illustrating the amount of free and used disk space appears on the left of the window.

**1** Free disk space

**2** Free disk space on Status bar

**What if I don't want to install all of Office?**

Even if you don't meet the hard disk space requirements for installing the entire Office suite, you may have sufficient space to install Word. However, you should meet the other requirements in order for Word to function smoothly (such as the proper operating system and required RAM).

- Windows NT users need 4MB of free Registry space available. To check the amount of free Registry space you have, click **Start** and then choose **Settings**, **Control Panel**. Double-click the System icon. Click the **Performance** tab. Under Virtual Memory, click the **Change** button. In the Registry Size section (see Figure 1.3), compare the amounts of **Current Registry Size** and **Maximum Registry Size**. If the difference between them is less than 4MB, increase the maximum Registry size so that it is at least 4MB greater than the current Registry size. Choose **OK**.

FIGURE 1.3

The difference between the Current Registry Size and the Maximum Registry Size in Windows NT must be at least 4MB.

**Network installation options**

Although installing Word directly from a CD onto your computer is the easiest method, there are other options for setting up the program, particularly in situations where your computer is connected to a network. One option is that the installation CDs are installed on a network file server. This would allow you to install Word on your computer across the network rather than from a CD. Also, if a shared version of Word has been installed on a network file server, you can install Word on your computer without having to copy all the files onto your hard disk. Consult your network administrator before installation to see how to set up Word on your computer.

- If you plan on installing International Support for additional languages, you need an extra 50MB of hard disk space available for each language interface you want to install.
- You must have a CD-ROM drive.

**SEE ALSO**

➤ *To back up files, see page 147*

➤ *For more information on the language capabilities of Word 2000, see page 676*

# Install from Scratch

You must close all application programs running on your computer before you begin installation. Then insert the Office 2000 CD into your CD-ROM drive.

**Perform a New Install**

1. Click **Start** and choose **Run**.

2. In the Open text box, type `D:\Setup.exe` (substitute the letter for your CD-ROM drive if your drive is not D:).

   *Or*

   Click **Browse**. Double-click My Computer and then right-click the icon for your CD-ROM drive. Choose **Open**, and then double-click Setup.exe.

3. Choose **OK**.

4. When the Welcome to Microsoft Office 2000 screen appears, enter your name in the **User Name** text box. Enter your initials in the **Initials** box, and then type the name of your company or organization in the **Organization** box. This data becomes the user information that automatically appears when signing your name to comments, creating faxes and letters using wizards, and making revisions.

5. In the **CD Key** boxes, enter the CD Key number that appears on the back of the Office 2000 CD case. Then click **Next**. (If you are installing across the network, contact your network administrator to obtain the key number.)

6. A confirmation of the information you entered in the last screen appears. If this is incorrect, click **Back** and return to the previous screen to change it. Otherwise, read the license agreement and select **I Accept the Terms in the License Agreement** to continue with the installation. Click **Next**.

7. Click **Install Now** to install the most frequently used features of Office. (If Word is the only part of Office 2000 you want to install, click **Customize**, then deselect everything but Word and the options of Word that you want to install. To do this, click the drive icon for each non-Word component and choose Not Available from the drop-down menu. To choose Word components, click the plus sign (+) next to the drive icon for Word, then click the drive icons of each component and choose from the drop-down menu.)

8. When the installation is finished, a dialog box appears indicating that the setup was completed successfully. Choose **OK**.

**Automatic installation startup**

In many cases, inserting the Office 2000 CD will cause the Office Setup program to run automatically. If this happens to you, skip to step 4 of the installation instructions. If the setup program does not run automatically, begin at step 1.

**Locate your CD key**

You need your CD key number to register your copy of Word. Locate the CD key number on the back of the CD jewel case. You also need an Internet connection to run the Register Wizard. If you do not have an Internet connection, fill out the registration card that came with your copy of Office 2000 and send it by snail mail. To learn how to connect your PC to the Internet, you might want to refer to Que's *Windows 98 6-in-1* or *Windows 95 6-in-1*.

9. You now need to restart your computer. Click **Yes** in the next dialog box to restart your computer.

10. After your computer reboots, you may start Microsoft Word.

The first time you run any of the applications in Office you will be prompted to register your copy. Follow the directions in the Registration Wizard to register online (if your modem is connected), via email or telephone (click **More Options** to make those choices), or by clicking **Next** to move to the next step in the process. To complete your registration at a later time, click **Register Later**.

# Upgrade from an Older Version of Word

If you have a previous version of Word installed you don't have to worry about losing all your custom settings and templates. The installation program detects previous versions and preserves any customized settings you have made. We still recommend that you back up data files before beginning the upgrade process. Also, close any other applications that you have open before you insert the Office 2000 CD into your CD-ROM drive.

### Upgrade to Office or Word 2000

1. Click **Start** and choose **Run**. (If the setup program begins automatically when you insert the CD, skip to step 4.)

2. In the **Open** text box, type D:\Setup.exe (substitute the letter for your CD-ROM drive if your drive is not D:).

   *Or*

   Click **Browse**. Double-click **My Computer** and then double-click the icon for your CD-ROM drive. Select Setup.exe and then click **Open**.

3. Choose **OK**.

4. When the Welcome to Microsoft Office 2000 screen appears, your name and organization may already appear on the screen because they were detected by the setup program. If they are not there or are incorrect, enter your name in the **User Name** text box. Enter your initials in the **Initials** box,

and then type the name of your company or organization in the **O̲rganization** box. This data becomes the user information that automatically appears when signing your name to comments, creating faxes and letters using wizards, and making revisions.

5. In the **CD K̲ey** boxes, enter the CD Key number that appears on the back of the Office 2000 CD case. Then click **N̲ext**.

6. A confirmation of the information you entered in the last screen appears. If this is incorrect, click **B̲ack** and return to the previous screen to change it. Otherwise, read the license agreement and select **I A̲ccept the Terms in the License Agreement** to continue with the installation. Click **N̲ext**.

7. Click **I̲nstall Now** to install the most frequently used features of Office. The setup program will detect the components of Office that you currently have installed and will update them.

8. When the installation is finished, a dialog box appears saying that the setup was completed successfully. Choose **OK**.

9. Click **Y̲es** in the next dialog box to restart your computer.

10. After your computer reboots, you may start Microsoft Word.

# What's New
# in Word 2000

Read about new features in Word 2000

Learn where to find coverage in this book

Microsoft's goal in this version is to make Word the easiest way to create email, Web, or print documents anywhere in the world. The new features added in Word 2000 are directed at the following areas:

- Web-centered document creation
- Rich email creation
- Personalization based on patterns of use
- Support for international users

# Web-Related Features

With the proliferation of intranets and greater use of the Internet to conduct business, users want to be able to use the familiar tools of Word to create Web documents or pages. They don't want to be forced to learn Web-authoring programs. Users also want to be able to save Word documents in HTML format and then convert HTML documents back into Word without loss of formatting. To help users do this, Word has added the following features:

- *Preserved Formatting*. When existing documents are saved as HTML and then reopened, none of Word's formatting will be lost (except versioning and passwords).
- *Improved Web Page Wizard*. The Web Page Wizard gives you an easy and quick way to create Web pages and multiple-page Web sites.
- *Browser Compatibility*. Some lower versions of Web browsers are unable to view certain Web pages. In Word you can turn off features that are not supported by these older browsers so the Web pages you design can be viewed by anyone.
- *Web Layout View*. This new view replaces the old Online Layout view and makes it easier to create, edit, and view Web pages.
- *Improved Web Page Preview*. You can preview your Web pages in your default browser, even if you haven't saved them yet.

- *Frames.* Adding frames to Web sites simplifies navigation, and you can add a table of contents for your Web site in a frame.

- *Table of Contents in Frames.* Several options have been added to the table of contents function so you can use it for online tables and put them in frames.

- *Themes.* Themes set up consistency between your Web pages to unify a site.

- *Improved Hyperlink Interface.* It's easier to create, edit, follow, and remove hyperlinks in documents.

- *Improved Table Formatting.* Several online table formatting options have been added to support nesting tables, AutoFit, floating tables, new border formatting, and formats designed for the Web.

- *Improved Picture Support.* HTML-style alignment is now supported for pictures and other inserted objects.

- *Improved Horizontal Lines.* Word supports horizontal lines with full HTML functionality.

**SEE ALSO**

➤ *To learn more about creating Web documents, see page 592*

➤ *Learn more about frames and designing Web pages, page 606*

# Email-Related Features

Word 97 introduced the ability to send email messages directly from Word. Word 2000 takes this ability a couple of steps further with the following features:

- *Email Editor for Microsoft Outlook.* In Outlook, you set an option to use Word 2000 as your email editor.

- *Customized Stationery.* You can choose your own font settings, backgrounds, and themes for your email.

- *Improved AutoSignature.* You can send messages and add custom signatures.

**SEE ALSO**

➤ *Learn more about configuring and using Word as an email editor, page 570*

# International Features

Word 2000 provides an easy and powerful way for users outside the United States to create Web, email, and print documents.

- *Single Executable Version*. Except for Thai, Vietnamese, and Indian, Word 2000 combines all language versions into one single executable, making available features that were specific to only some countries in previous versions.
- *Language Settings*. Users can set the language settings in the application without affecting the operation of Word. This makes it possible for Word users to travel to other countries and still work in their own language.
- *Proofing Tools*. Users can install proofing tools for their language of preference.
- *Language AutoDetect*. Word automatically detects the language users type in, so tools such as spelling and grammar checking adjust to accommodate the preferred language.
- *Multiple AutoCorrect Listings*. Word makes it possible to have multiple AutoCorrect lists to support several users with different preferred languages.
- *Asian Languages*. Word users can now type in Japanese, Korean, and Chinese even though they are using Western operating systems. Plus, new features have been added and several were improved to support these language groups.

SEE ALSO
➤ *Learn more about installing the Language Pack for Microsoft Office, page 676*

# General Features

Additional features have been added and improved to make working in Word simpler and more efficient. Some of these upgraded features include:

- *Click and Type*. When you are in the Page Layout or Web Layout views, move your cursor anywhere on the page and double-click. Then just start typing.

- *Print Zoom*. You are now able to scale your document page size when you are ready to print. You may also print several pages on one sheet of paper.

- *Improved View Choices*. Word 2000 has reduced the number of views to Normal, Web Layout, Print Layout, and Outline.

- *Multiple Item Clipboard*. Office 2000 now has the Office Clipboard, which lets you collect several items and store them on the Clipboard so you can paste them out together.

- *Personalized Menus*. The menu commands that you access most often appear prominently on the menus. To see less frequently used commands, you have to expand the menu.

- *Improved Tables*. Your tables can include other tables (nesting tables), can have text wrap around the tables (floating tables), can be positioned as you want them, and can display integrated header rows. You'll be able to grab tables and move them or resize them.

- *Improved Table Tool*. The table drawing tool supports drawing on text, splitting text, adding rows and columns outside of a table, converting paragraph borders to tables, and creating diagonal cell borders. Plus, erasing borders is easier.

- *Improved Graphics in Tables*. Text wraps around the graphics in table cells. Graphics behave as they do outside the table.

- *24-Bit Color*. Borders, text, and shadings can be set to any 24-bit color.

- *Improved WordArt*. Your WordArt objects can be floating or inline. They can be used for bullets and banners.

- *Improved ClipArt Gallery*. The ClipArt Gallery now has more pictures and an easier-to-use interface.

- *Picture Bullets*. Now you can use graphics as your bullets in a document.

- *Improved Bullets and Numbering*. Multilevel bulleted and numbered lists are now the default.

- *Improved AutoCorrect*. AutoCorrect is now intelligent. It looks for obvious spelling mistakes even if they aren't in the AutoCorrect list and corrects them as you type.

- *Improved Spelling and Grammar Checker*. New words have been added to the dictionary, and the grammar checker is now less likely to incorrectly mark text.
- *Working with Older Versions*. Word 2000 has the capability to turn off features not found in earlier versions, in case you're sharing files with users who still have older versions of Word.

# PART

# *II*

# Use Everyday Word Processing Techniques

# Get Acquainted with Word

Start and close Word and Word documents

Create a basic document

Use menus, keyboard commands, and toolbar icons to work efficiently

Get help on Word from built-in help or Microsoft's Web site

# Understand Word

Microsoft Word 2000 is a word processing program designed for Windows 98 and Windows NT 4.0 and later. Word can integrate information with other Microsoft Office products such as Excel and PowerPoint. For example, you can create a document in Word and send the document's outline to PowerPoint.

Word is a powerful program and it is the most popular word processing program today. Word includes capabilities to create charts, drawings, and databases within documents (such as those used in mail merges). Word also has the capability to link to charts, drawings, and databases that were created in other programs.

Files you create in Word can be mailed, saved, or converted to other file formats so that you can open them in other programs. Files can also be saved as HTML documents for use on and distribution over the Internet.

Microsoft Word files are called *documents* and by default, filenames are given the extension of .doc. When you save a report you want to name "First Quarter Budget," Word will assign the file extension of .doc so that the full filename of your report becomes First Quarter Budget.doc.

This chapter reviews the basics of Word. The following sections are filled with reminders and refreshers on the fundamental elements of Word.

**SEE ALSO**

➢ *To learn more about charts, see page 445*

➢ *To learn about creating drawings, see page 422*

➢ *For information on databases and mail merge, see page 482*

➢ *For information on linking Word information to other programs, see page 405*

➢ *To learn about creating HTML and Internet documents, see page 592*

# Start Word 2000

Word 2000 can be started in several different ways. The method that you use depends on your personal preference and your system configuration. One way to start Word is by locating the

Word program on the Windows Start menu and clicking the program icon.

If you have Office 2000 installed, you can start Word from the Office toolbar (if you elected to display the Office toolbar when you start Windows). You can also start Word by choosing the **Start** menu and then selecting either **New Office Document** or **Open Office Document**. If you choose **New Office Document**, the New Document dialog box appears. Click the **General** tab and choose **Blank Document**. You are now ready to begin working in your new document. To start Word and work on an existing document, click **Start** and select **Open Office Document**. From the files listed in the Open Office Document dialog box, select the one that you want to edit and choose **Open**.

When the document you want to edit is one on which you recently worked, you can open that document and Word by clicking Start and then choosing **Documents** from the menu. Select the document you want from the submenu that appears.

You might have a Word shortcut on your desktop and you can start Word by clicking the Shortcut button ▣.

If you do not have a shortcut to Word set up, you can create one.

### Set Up a Word Shortcut

1. Locate the Word Program file by clicking the **Start** button and then choosing **Find**. Then select the **Files or Folders** option.

2. The Find: All Files dialog box appears. In the **Named** field, type Winword.exe. If you know that the program files for Word are located on a drive other than C:, choose the other drive in the **Look In** field. If you have multiple hard disks and don't know which one to search, you can search them all by choosing **My Computer** in the **Look In** field.

3. Click the **Find Now** button. When Windows is finished searching, the Word file appears in the dialog box as shown in Figure 3.1.

**Turning off the Office toolbar**

To turn off the Microsoft Office toolbar, right-click the toolbar (the toolbar itself, not the buttons on the toolbar) and click Exit. Choose **Yes** or **No** to display the toolbar the next time you start your computer. To view the toolbar again, select the Microsoft Office Shortcut bar from your **Start** menu's list of programs.

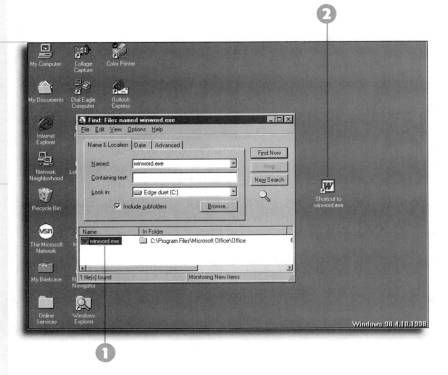

FIGURE 3.1

Add a Word shortcut to your desktop by dragging the Winword.exe file onto the desktop.

**1** Drag from here…

**2** …to here.

**Don't see the Formatting toolbar?**

To display the Formatting toolbar, go to the **View** menu and select **Toolbars**. From the **Toolbars** submenu select **Formatting**. Also, your screen may have other toolbars showing or they may be arranged in a different order. Alternatively, you can right-click the menu and select **Formatting** from the pop-up menu.

4. To add the shortcut to your desktop, click and drag the Winword.exe file to your desktop.

5. As you release your mouse, the icon changes from a file icon to a shortcut icon.

6. Close the dialog box.

7. To change the name of the shortcut from "Shortcut to winword.exe" to "Word 2000" (or whatever name you want to assign), right-click the icon and choose **Rename** from the shortcut menu. Type the text you want to identify the icon and then press Enter.

# Work in the Word Workspace

Word contains elements that are common in other Windows programs—Title bar, Menu bar, Status bar, scrollbars, Minimize button, Restore/Maximize button, Close button, and Control button. Depending on your default setup, you also might see the Standard toolbar and a Formatting toolbar.

You should have a basic understanding of Windows and of these elements to use Word 2000 effectively. Figure 3.2 shows the major elements of the Word window.

To do almost anything in Word 2000 (except the actual writing), you must use a command. Commands can be invoked in three different ways:

- Menu. Select a command from a menu.
- Toolbar. Click an icon in a toolbar or on a scrollbar.
- Keyboard shortcuts. Use a key combination.

## Use Personalized Menus

You can navigate a menu with a mouse or the keyboard. Menus are personalized in Word 2000. When you first click on a menu item, you see only the most frequently used list of menu items. As you use a menu, only the items that you use most often are immediately displayed on the menu.

To access a command in the menu using the mouse, click the menu name (such as **File**). Because of the adaptive menu feature, you may not see all items available in the menu. To expand the menu, either hold your mouse on the menu bar selection for a second, or click the arrows located at the bottom of the menu. You can also double-click the menu to see more options.

To access a menu using the keyboard, hold down the Alt key and press the underlined letter.

Shortcut menus are available by right-clicking your mouse. These menus are *context sensitive*; that is, they will change depending upon the item selected or the task you are performing. For example, when you select text and then right-click it, you will see a menu to change the font, add bullets and numbers, cut, copy, and so forth. If you right-click inside of text without selecting it first, the menu does not include copy and paste.

SEE ALSO

➤ *To learn how to cut, copy, and paste using shortcut menus, see page 63*

➤ *To learn more about text formatting, see page 73*

➤ *To add bullets and numbering, see page 224*

FIGURE 3.2

Basic elements of the Word window.

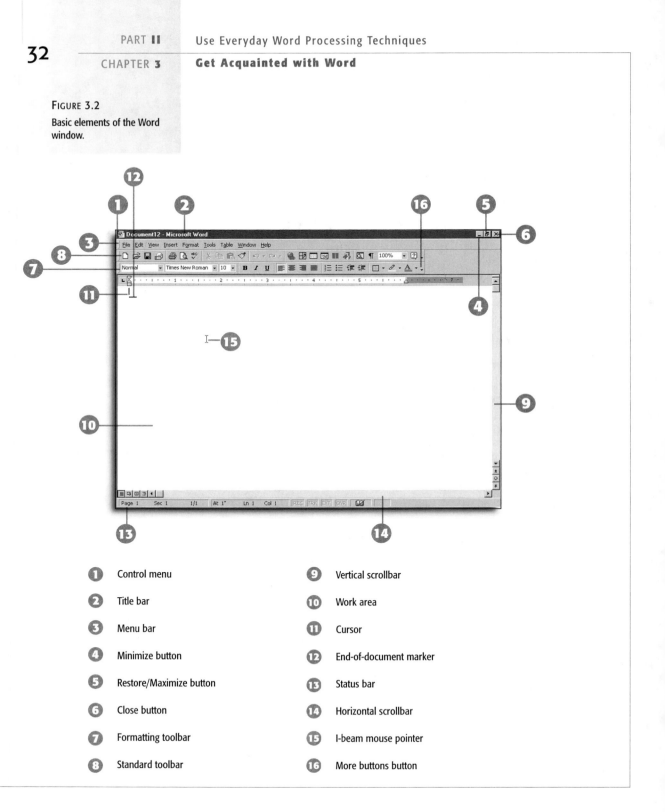

| | | | |
|---|---|---|---|
| **①** | Control menu | **⑨** | Vertical scrollbar |
| **②** | Title bar | **⑩** | Work area |
| **③** | Menu bar | **⑪** | Cursor |
| **④** | Minimize button | **⑫** | End-of-document marker |
| **⑤** | Restore/Maximize button | **⑬** | Status bar |
| **⑥** | Close button | **⑭** | Horizontal scrollbar |
| **⑦** | Formatting toolbar | **⑮** | I-beam mouse pointer |
| **⑧** | Standard toolbar | **⑯** | More buttons button |

## Manage Toolbars

To activate a toolbar item, click its icon on the toolbar. If you are unsure of an icon's purpose, point to it and wait briefly. A *ScreenTip* displays the name of the tool.

Toolbars contain the most commonly used commands. Toolbars available in Word contain sets of related commands, such as the toolbar for Formatting, which contains font, font size, bold, italic, and so forth. New in this version of Word are personalized toolbars; that is, toolbars that change depending upon your usage of commands. This helps to keep the onscreen display of icons at a minimum, reducing screen clutter. You can tell whether all of the items on a toolbar are displayed by the absence or presence of the More Buttons button ⧉ on the right of the toolbar (see Figure 3.2).

If you click the More Buttons button ⧉, you will see the **Add or Remove Buttons** menu. Click that menu and a full set of available options for your toolbar is displayed along with the corresponding icon. Once you select an item from the Add or Remove Buttons list, that icon will appear on your toolbar so that you don't have to dig into the menu system again.

When you first start using Word, you may want to make some changes to the toolbars by adding or deleting buttons. This is a simple process, but if you need additional instructions, refer to Chapter 31, "Customize and Fine-Tune Word."

## Save Time with Keyboard Shortcuts

*Keyboard shortcuts* are keystrokes that activate a command directly. Keyboard shortcuts are not Alt plus a key to open the menu; they are keystrokes that bypass the menu. Keystrokes that you use to open a menu, such as Alt plus a key, are referred to as *accelerator keys*.

Word can help you to become familiar with keyboard shortcuts by displaying the shortcut keys in the ScreenTips boxes that appear when you point at an icon on a toolbar. To activate the ScreenTips feature, go to the **Tools** menu and select **Customize**. In the Customize dialog box, click the **Options** tab. In this tab, select the **Show S̲hortcut Keys in ScreenTips** check box.

**Work more efficiently with keyboard shortcuts**

We encourage you to use the keyboard techniques as much as possible. Push yourself to do it. The mouse is a crutch. Use the Alt key to open the menus and the arrow keys or hotkeys to navigate them. Use the keyboard shortcuts whenever they are available.

The basic tasks you need to create letters are used in many types of documents. The following section walks you through how to create a basic Word document so that you may review the basics of working with Word documents.

**SEE ALSO**

➤ *To learn more about keyboard shortcuts, see page 54*

➤ *To learn more about positioning and customizing toolbars, see pages 638 and 640*

➤ *To learn more about customizing Word defaults, see page 650*

# Create and Save a Basic Document

When you first start Word, a new, blank document is displayed ready for you to begin typing. Here's a quick refresher and a list of reminders regarding how to enter text, dates, and time. The basics of editing, saving, and closing documents also are covered:

- The blinking vertical line represents your cursor position, or insertion point (see Figure 3.2). Whatever you type appears at the insertion point. The horizontal line is the end-of-document marker.

- The word wrap function fits text within the margins. You only need to use the Enter key when you want to start a new line or a new paragraph.

- You can insert a date (instead of typing a date) by choosing **Date and Time** from the **Insert** menu. The Date and Time dialog box appears as shown in Figure 3.3. Select the date format you want and click **OK**. By inserting a date in this way, the date becomes part of your document text. If you click the **Update Automatically** option in the Date and Time dialog box, the date is inserted as a field and is automatically updated each time you print or open your letter.

- Consider turning on Word's **Show/Hide** option, which displays nonprinting characters, such as paragraph marks. Using this option, you can easily see where you have placed unnecessary spaces, where tabs were used instead of spaces, and where line and paragraph breaks are. Throughout this book, you will find that nonprinting characters display whenever you work in Word. To display these characters, click the Show All button ¶ on the Standard toolbar.

**Caution: Automatic update**

If the date of your document is important, do *not* choose to automatically update. The date will change with future printings and the document will appear to have been composed on a date other than its original date.

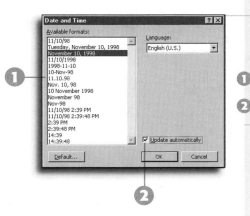

- If you make a mistake while typing, use the Backspace key to erase characters to the left of your cursor one at a time. You can also delete text by pressing the Delete key. This deletes characters one at a time to the right of your cursor position. Another way to delete text is by selecting a word and pressing the Delete key. To replace existing text with new text, select the text you want to replace and begin typing your new text.

- To save your document, click the Save button 🔲 on the Standard toolbar. The Save As dialog box appears as shown in Figure 3.4. Name your document by typing a name in the **File Name** field. It is likely that your default settings will save this document in a file folder called My Documents. (If you are familiar with Windows and want to save to a different folder, select where you want to save the file and click the **Save** button.)

- To print your document, you can view it in Print Preview mode or you can print without previewing. To view the document before printing, click the Print Preview button 🔲 on the Standard toolbar. Figure 3.5 shows a letter as viewed in Print Preview mode. To print directly from Print Preview, click the Print button 🖨 on the toolbar. To return to your document, click the Close button. To print without previewing, click the Print button 🖨 on the Standard toolbar.

FIGURE 3.4

Choose a filename and location to save your letter.

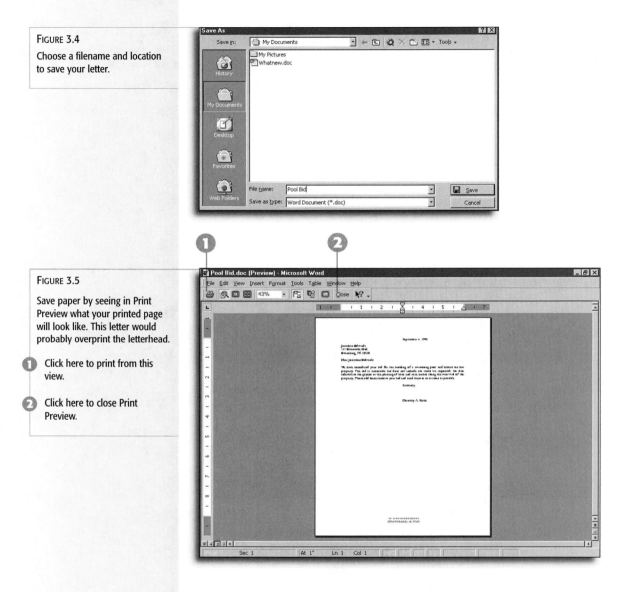

FIGURE 3.5

Save paper by seeing in Print Preview what your printed page will look like. This letter would probably overprint the letterhead.

**1** Click here to print from this view.

**2** Click here to close Print Preview.

- To close your letter, click the Close button ☒ on the menu bar. You also can close a letter by selecting the **File** menu, and then choosing **Close**.

**SEE ALSO**

➤ *For more information about Date and Time fields, see page 473*

➤ *To learn more about using fields in document merging, see page 484*

➤ *To learn more about saving documents and folders and file management, see page 137*

➤ *To learn more about printing and Print Preview mode, see page 260*

# Use Office Assistant to Create Documents

The Office Assistant is a cartoon that appears as one of several characters—for example, a paper clip (named Clippit) or a small dog (named Rocky)—and is usually present when you first open Word. The default character is Clippit. Throughout this book, you may see several different Office Assistants displayed in the figures. If the Office Assistant is not visible, choose **Microsoft Word Help** from the **Help** menu or press F1.

## Create a Letter

When you begin typing a letter, a balloon may appear next to the Office Assistant that offers to help you create the letter (see Figure 3.6). This is prompted by the word "Dear" followed by a name and a colon or comma. Once you type "Dear John:" and press the Spacebar, the Office Assistant appears ready to assist you in writing your letter. Select **Get Help with Writing the Letter** to have the Office Assistant help you.

The Office Assistant opens the Letter Wizard (see Figure 3.7) and offers information or hints about how to choose the options in the dialog box.

### Create a Letter Using a Wizard

1. To automatically insert a date in your letter, check the **Date Line** option. From the drop-down list box, select a format for the date.

2. From the **Choose a Page Design** drop-down list, select a look for your letter—Professional, Contemporary, Elegant, or Normal.

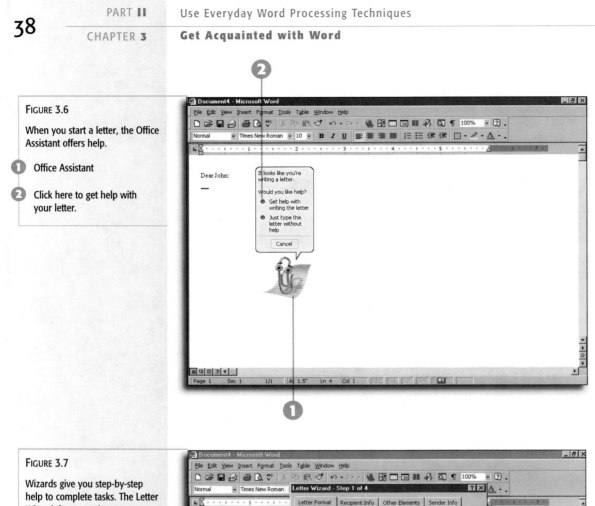

FIGURE 3.6

When you start a letter, the Office Assistant offers help.

**1** Office Assistant

**2** Click here to get help with your letter.

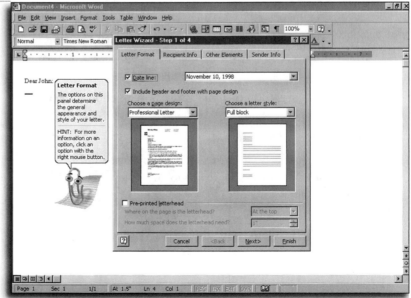

FIGURE 3.7

Wizards give you step-by-step help to complete tasks. The Letter Wizard, for example, automates the process of creating a letter.

**3.** When you select a page design other than Normal or Current, the Wizard automatically selects the **Include Header and Footer with Page Design** option. The header and footer contain the return address information in these designs, as well as the page number if you have more than one page. If you don't want those items to appear, deselect the option.

**4.** From the **Choose a Letter Style** drop-down list, select how you want the paragraphs to indent—Full Block, Modified Block, or Semi-Block. If you aren't sure what these selections mean, choose one and a sample appears in the preview window.

**5.** Select **Pre-Printed Letterhead** if you plan to print your letter on stationery. When you select this option, specify the position of the letterhead by making a selection from the **Where on the Page Is the Letterhead?** Drop-down list and enter the size of the letterhead (in inches) in the **How Much Space Does the Letterhead Need?** text box.

**6.** Click **Next** to continue entering information to build your letter (clicking **Back** in the Wizard takes you to the previous step). If you are using Outlook and are maintaining an Address Book in that application, you can click the Address Book button to use a name and address listed there. Otherwise, type a name in the **Recipient's Name** box (or select one you used previously). Enter the recipient's address in the **Delivery Address** box, pressing Shift+Enter each time you want to start a new line.

**7.** Under Salutation, select the type of greeting you want to use—**Informal**, **Formal**, **Business**, or **Other**. A suggested salutation appears in the text box, but you can select or enter another greeting. Click **Next**.

**8.** To add other elements to your letter, such as a subject line, select the appropriate option. Then select or enter text for that element.

**9.** Enter the name and address of anyone who should receive a carbon copy, or select carbon copy recipients from your Address Book. Click **Next**.

10. Enter your name or the name of the sender into the **Sender's Name** box (or select one). Then enter a **Return Address** (select **Omit** if the return address is preprinted).

11. Enter or select a **Complimentary Closing** and any elements you want included in the closing.

12. Click **Finish** to add all the elements to your letter and close the Letter Wizard.

13. **Type Your Text Here** is selected in the letter. Start typing the body of your letter, and your text will replace the highlighted text.

14. The Office Assistant asks whether you want to do more and offers to help make an envelope or a mailing label. If you need to go back and change some item in the Letter Wizard, that is another option offered by the Office Assistant. Click the option you want, or choose **Cancel** whether you need no further assistance.

15. Print and save the letter (if you attempt to close the letter without saving it, the Office Assistant will ask whether you want to save it).

## Create a Memo

The Office Assistant can't always guess what you want to do, although it does stand by to help you as needed. To see the Office Assistant balloon, click the Office Assistant once. To get help creating a memo, do the following:

### Create a Memo Using Office Assistant

1. In the text box, type memo and press Enter.

2. Click **Create a Memo** in the balloon (see Figure 3.8).

3. A Help window appears. Click in that window to bring it to the foreground so you can read it. The window has a list of instructions for opening the Memo Wizard, which will help you create your memo. You can leave this window on the screen for as long as you need it, minimize it so you can refer to it later, or click the Close button in the upper-right corner to close it.

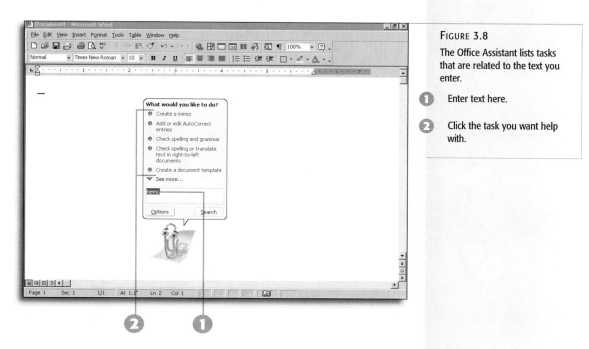

FIGURE 3.8

The Office Assistant lists tasks that are related to the text you enter.

**1** Enter text here.

**2** Click the task you want help with.

**4.** To create the memo, click in the document window. Then choose the **File** menu and select **New**.

**5.** When the New dialog box appears (see Figure 3.9), click the **Memo** tab.

**6.** Select the Memo Wizard icon and choose **OK**.

FIGURE 3.9

The New dialog box lists available wizards to help create common documents.

7. Follow the instructions in the Memo Wizard to set up your memo. Click **Next** to continue to the next step; click **Back** to return to the previous step. When you're finished selecting options, choose **Finish**. The Office Assistant will prompt you as you work through the wizard to help you choose a memo style and select options.

8. When the memo document first appears, there are areas in the document where **Click Here and Type** text appears. Click each of those areas and enter the appropriate text.

9. To fax or email your memo, click **Send the Memo to Someone** in the Office Assistant balloon. Otherwise, click **Cancel** to close the Office Assistant balloon.

10. Save and print your memo. The Office Assistant will prompt you to save the document if you close it without saving it first.

# Find Help

Word has onscreen help and, like all Microsoft products, additional help can be found by searching Microsoft Web sites. Help can be accessed in several ways, as described in the following list:

- Get interactive help by asking the Office Assistant. (Choose the **Help** menu and select **Microsoft Word Help** or press F1.)

- Get a Help window where you ask a question of the Answer Wizard, view an index of help topics, or see a list of help topics. (Choose the **Help** menu and select **Microsoft Word Help** or press F1, if the Office Assistant is turned off.)

- Find the definition of a screen element by using the What's This? feature. (Choose the **Help** menu and select **What's This?** or press Shift+F1 or click the Microsoft Word Help icon [?] on the Standard toolbar.)

- Reveal a ScreenTip by pointing at an onscreen object.

- Access online support and view frequently asked questions by visiting a Microsoft Web site. This method requires an Internet connection. (Choose the **Help** menu and select **Office on the Web**.)

The purpose of each help method differs slightly. If you know where to go in the help databases to find something, or you want to find all the information on a given help topic, you can browse the **Contents** tab in the Help window.

If you know the name of a feature, you can search the **Index** tab for it in the Help window.

If you don't know the name of a feature or its location in the help databases, you can do a full-text search. You can do this in two different places—in the **Answer Wizard** tab in the Help window, or in the Office Assistant.

If you want to know what some item on the screen is supposed to do, point at it with the mouse pointer. For some items, a Help Tip pops up and tells you about the object. If that doesn't happen, click the object using What's This? help. A more comprehensive explanation will pop up.

If all else fails, you can go to Microsoft's Web site where you can look up information in the Microsoft Office Frequently Asked Questions (FAQ) page. You also can seek help directly from Microsoft support personnel.

## Browse Help Contents

If you know exactly where to go in Help to find the information you need, or you want to research a topic thoroughly, Help Contents is for you. Access Help Contents by choosing the **Help** menu and selecting **Microsoft Word Help**. If the Office Assistant is turned off, the Help window appears. Click the **Contents** tab on the left window pane.

The Contents tab displays categories of information. When you double-click a category or click the small plus sign (+) to the left of it, the category expands to display an indented list of either related subcategories or help topics, as shown in Figure 3.10.

**Turning off the Office Assistant**

To turn off the Office Assistant for an entire Word session, click **Options** in the Assistant balloon (if the balloon isn't visible, click the Assistant). Then deselect the option **Use the Office Assistant** on the **Options** tab and choose **OK**.

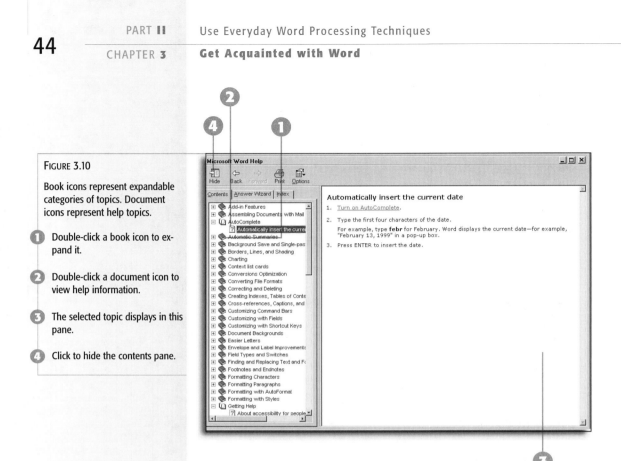

FIGURE 3.10

Book icons represent expandable categories of topics. Document icons represent help topics.

**1** Double-click a book icon to expand it.

**2** Double-click a document icon to view help information.

**3** The selected topic displays in this pane.

**4** Click to hide the contents pane.

**Seeing help topics**

Can't read the full title of a Help topic? Just point to the topic and hold the pointer there briefly. The full text of the topic appears as a pop-up. Alternatively, drag the divider between the window panes to the right.

When you double-click a Help topic, the Help topic opens in the window pane to the right of the Help window. To have this window float on top of all the other screen windows so that you can (if you want) keep the help topic information open for reference while you work, click the Hide icon. Help articles may contain a labeled screen, a series of step-by-step instructions, or an explanation of a concept (see Figure 3.11).

A Help topic that instructs you to carry out some task typically opens as narrow windows on the right side of your screen so that you can leave them open while you work. Some help topics include a **Show Me** button that, when clicked, indicates the menu or dialog box you need to access to perform the action you are querying. One or more **For More Information** buttons also may appear. These buttons open more detailed Help topic windows. Finally, clicking text highlighted by underlining and colored green displays a definition of the highlighted term.

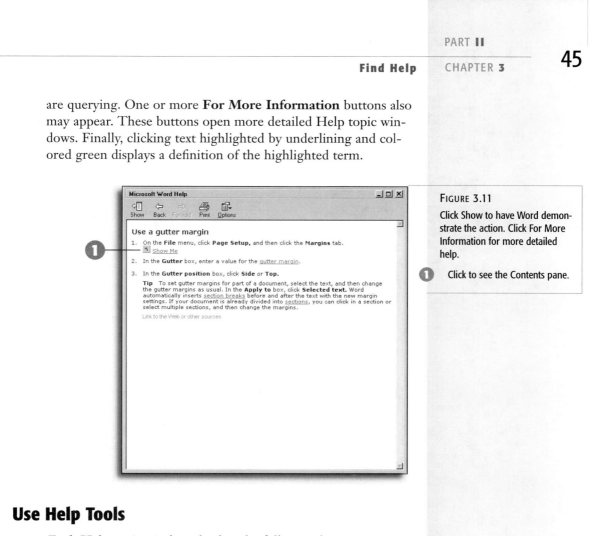

FIGURE 3.11
Click Show to have Word demonstrate the action. Click For More Information for more detailed help.

**1** Click to see the Contents pane.

## Use Help Tools

Each Help topic window also has the following buttons:

- **Show/Hide Tabs**. Expands or collapses the Help window so you can see the Contents pane or hide it.

- **Back**. Displays the previously viewed Help topic (if applicable).

- **Forward**. Displays the next topic (if you've gone back through a series of topics you already opened).

- **Print**. Prints the current Help topic.

- **Options**. Displays a menu that includes the actions of the other buttons (**Show/Hide Tabs**, **Back**, **Forward**, and **Print**) plus **Refresh** to refresh the topic and **Stop** to stop accessing a Web Help topic.

## Browse the Help Index

If you know the name of a Word feature, you can locate all references to that feature in the Help Index. The index, available on the **Index** tab of the Help window, presents a list of all the topics found that match the keyword you type or select (see Figure 3.12). Enter the first characters of a word into the **Type Keywords** field. As you type each character, the list in the **Or Choose Keywords** list scrolls closer and closer to the item you are typing. If you type a word that does not appear in the index, the index list scrolls past the point where your word should have appeared. If that happens, just backspace and type another word.

If, for example, you type the word print in the **Type Keywords** box, the **Or Choose Keywords** list scrolls to the first word beginning with "p" when you type the letter p, then scrolls to the first word beginning with "pr" when you type the r, and so on. In general, the most efficient way to use the index is to type enough of the word you are looking for to get to that vicinity of the index, and then scroll through that part of the list looking for promising entries.

After you type or select the keyword you want, click **Search**. A set of related topics appears in the **Choose a Topic** box. Select the one you want. To search for another topic, click **Clear** and begin again.

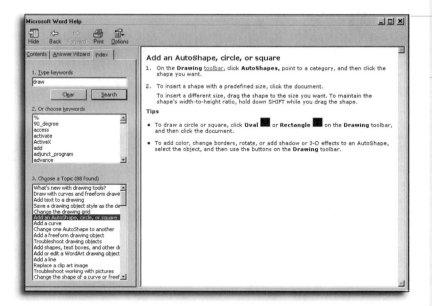

FIGURE 3.12
Use the Index tab to find specific
words and phrases in Help.

## Use the Answer Wizard

Word Help actually has two search features—the **Answer Wizard** tab, located in the Help window, and the Office Assistant. Answer Wizard uses a full-text index to enable you to search for any word that appears in the help database. This differs from the Help Index (described in the previous section of this chapter), which only lists words that appear in help topic titles. The advantage of using the **Answer Wizard** panel over the **Index** is that you might find relevant topics because you searched for a term that was significant but did not appear in the title of the help topic. That's why we recommend that you use the **Index** if you know the name by which Word refers to a topic, and use the **Answer Wizard** feature (or Office Assistant, described in the next section), when you aren't sure how Word refers to a topic.

The **Answer Wizard** tab contains a text box and a topic list as shown in Figure 3.13. To search, enter a word, phrase, or question in the **What Would You Like to Do?** text box. Click the **Search** button, and a list of related topics appears in the **Select Topic to Display** box. Double-click a topic from the list to display that information in the Help Topic pane.

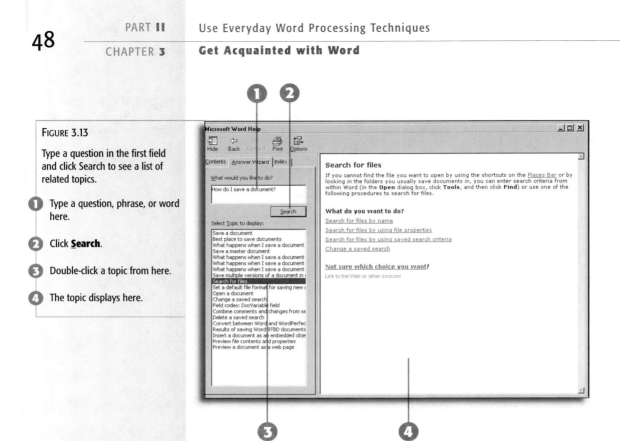

FIGURE 3.13

Type a question in the first field and click Search to see a list of related topics.

**1** Type a question, phrase, or word here.

**2** Click **Search**.

**3** Double-click a topic from here.

**4** The topic displays here.

## Search with Office Assistant

The Office Assistant can be amusing, helpful, and annoying. It uses what Microsoft calls *IntelliSense natural-language technology*, which means that it can interpret questions you pose to it, and it can anticipate what kinds of help you may need and offer that help unbidden—based on what you are doing in your document. One of Office Assistant's more helpful features is its search feature, which you access by popping up the balloon that asks **"What would you like to do?"**

If the Office Assistant is currently visible on your screen, click it to reveal the **"What would you like to do?"** balloon. If the Office Assistant isn't visible on your screen, press F1 (or choose **Microsoft Word Help** from the **Help** menu) to pop it up. The **"What would you like to do?"** balloon will pop up, too (see Figure 3.14).

**Office Assistant not there?**

If you turned the Office Assistant off so you could work with the Help window, choose **Show the Office Assistant** from the **Help** menu to reactivate it.

FIGURE 3.14

Type a word, phrase, or question in the Office Assistant bubble text box to get advice or help. Here, "Rocky" is the chosen Office Assistant.

1 Type keywords here.

2 Click **Search**.

Enter any word, phrase, sentence, or question in the text field of the balloon, and then press Enter. The IntelliSense search engine tries to figure out from what you typed what help topics you might be looking for. The search engine pops up a list of help topics. You can select a help topic that you want by clicking it. A Help Topics window opens for the topic that you choose.

As a demonstration of how the Office Assistant search engine works, enter the word keystroke in the balloon, and then press Enter. The list of topics that pops up should include the item "Shortcut Keys." Click that item and the Shortcut Keys Help Topic window pops up. Browse through it; this window contains a list of links to categories of Help topics concerning shortcut keys for specific Word functions.

## Optimize the Office Assistant

The Office Assistant can be very helpful. If you are finding that you don't agree, that it's either not helpful or is way too intrusive, you should try to optimize it to your liking before you give up on it. The Office Assistant can do a lot of other things beside search for help topics. It also can display the following things:

- Suggested Help. The Office Assistant can guess what help you might look for based on what you are doing. So, when you click the Office Assistant, the help topics appear even though you haven't entered a query.

- Tips. If the Office Assistant thinks you could be doing something more efficiently, it offers to tell you so by displaying a light bulb icon. If the Office Assistant is

---

**No Office Assistant?**

Run **Setup for Microsoft Office** or **Microsoft Word** and select the Office Assistant as an installation option. Close Word and access the Control Panel by choosing the **Start** menu and selecting **Settings**. Then select **Control Panel** from the submenu. Double-click the Add/Remove Programs icon. Choose Microsoft Office or Microsoft Word and follow the instructions as the wizard guides you through setup.

currently visible on your screen, the light bulb appears in its window. If it is not currently visible, the light bulb appears in the toolbar as part of the Office Assistant icon. Click the light bulb to pop up the tip.

- Messages. If something happens that the Office Assistant thinks you would like to know about, it pops up a message onscreen, either in a balloon or in a message box. If, for example, Word cannot AutoSave your document (say, because you are low on disk space), Office Assistant pops up a message that AutoSave was postponed.

If Office Assistant is not doing these things for you, or if it is and you find them unbearably annoying, you can change the Office Assistant options. Click the Office Assistant to pop up its balloon, and then choose **Options** in the balloon to open the Office Assistant dialog box with the **Options** panel displayed (see Figure 3.15). Set the options as desired—don't be afraid to experiment with them, and remember to use What's This? help to get an explanation of any unclear item in the dialog box—then close the dialog box and see if the Office Assistant behaves more to your liking.

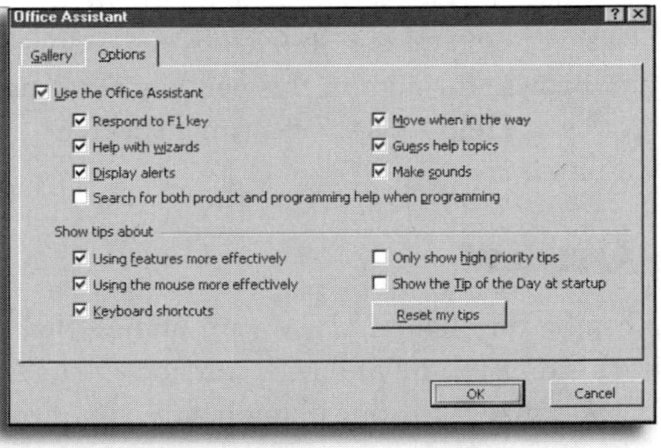

**That Office Assistant is underfoot!**

If you find that the Office Assistant is in your way, even though you can drag it anywhere on the screen, make sure that **Move When in the Way** is checked as one of the Office Assistant options.

FIGURE 3.15

Change the behavior of the Office Assistant here. Click the Gallery tab to select a different Office Assistant.

**A Gallery of Characters**

If you prefer to change to one of the other Office Assistant characters, click **Options** in the Office Assistant balloon, click the **Gallery** tab, and then click **Back** or **Next** to view the available characters. When you find one you want to use, choose **OK**. If you don't find a character you like in the Gallery, search the Microsoft Web site for more.

## Learn About Screen Objects

If you want to know what a particular icon, label, or other object is in the Microsoft Word window or in a dialog box, you can find out in two different ways. First, in the Word window, point at any object on the screen. After a second or so, the name of the object might pop up. This alone may be enough to tell you what the object is for. If not, or if no name pops up at all, try using What's This? help. Either press Shift+F1 or choose **What's This?** from the **Help** menu. Your mouse pointer will change to an arrow and a question mark . With this pointer click any object on the screen. A balloon usually pops up with a description of the object (see Figure 3.16).

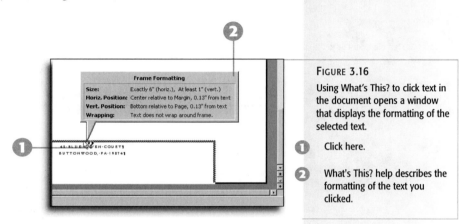

**FIGURE 3.16**

Using What's This? to click text in the document opens a window that displays the formatting of the selected text.

**1** Click here.

**2** What's This? help describes the formatting of the text you clicked.

Depending on what you point at, the question mark pointer may disappear after you click an object. If it disappears, then you are back in normal pointer mode and you can continue working or, if you want help on another screen object, you have to press Shift+F1 again. Alternatively, if the pointer remains in What's This? mode (question mark in mouse pointer) and you want to turn off that mode, you can press Esc, and the mouse pointer returns to normal.

In a dialog box, you can right-click an object to pop up a menu that has the entry **What's This?** in it, and then click **What's This?** to display the pop-up Help window. Alternatively, click the icon in the upper-right corner of the dialog box, and then click an object in the dialog box (see Figure 3.17).

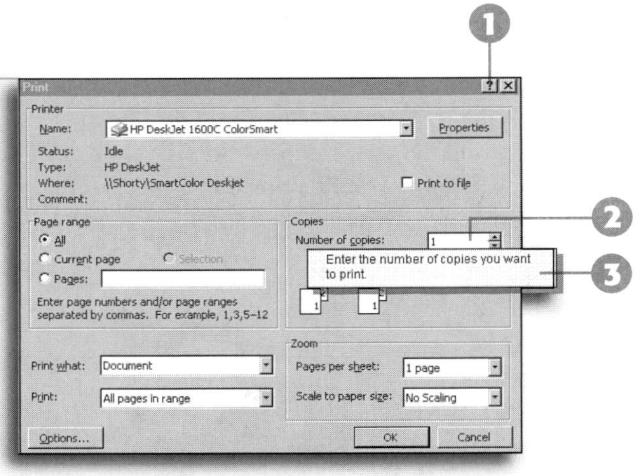

**FIGURE 3.17**

Using What's This? in this dialog box opened a window offering more detailed instructions about the **Number of Copies** field.

**1** Click here.

**2** Then click an element of the dialog box…

**3** …to see help about the item you clicked.

## Get Help from the Office Web Site

If you have a connection to the World Wide Web and you feel a need to seek help directly from Microsoft (or if you just want to take a short break to surf the Web), you can reach the Office Web site directly from within the **Help** menu. Open the **Help** menu and then select **Office on the Web** to open your browser and connect to the Office Web site.

At the Office Web site, you can search a library of technical notes for topics relevant to your problem, or you can submit a query directly to Microsoft support. You can see what updates are available for Word (and other Microsoft programs) and download them if they look helpful.

Like many other companies, Microsoft is making greater and greater use of the World Wide Web to provide support to users of its products. If you don't have access to the World Wide Web yet, this may be just the excuse you need to finally obtain Web access.

# Navigate, Select, and Edit Text and Documents

Move quickly from place to place in your documents

Cut, copy, and paste text efficiently

Correct mistakes with Undo and Redo

**Scrolling through your document**

When you use the vertical scrollbar to move up or down through your document, keep in mind that the entire scrollbar represents the entire document and not just one page. If you drag the scroll box, a pop-up text box appears as you drag. The pop-up Word tells you what page you are scrolling past and the main headings you are passing (if you are using Word's default heading styles–Heading 1, Heading 2, and so forth).

# Use Efficient Navigation and Selection Techniques

Word is designed to make writing easy. You can compose, navigate, edit, and format your text effortlessly thanks to Word's sophisticated navigation and selection tools. By becoming aware of the full range of tools available to you, you can learn to get the most out of your time writing in Word.

A glance at the tables in the following pages might suggest that you will never be able to remember them all and, in fact, most people start out using only the basic techniques. As you become more proficient, gradually add more efficient techniques to your word processing skills.

## Use the Go To Feature

Navigation—getting from one place in your document to another—is quick when you only want to move your cursor a couple of lines or characters. Use the arrow keys for short navigation trips. The vertical scrollbar helps you when you want to move longer distances, but it isn't accurate and it doesn't move the cursor.

When you know the contents of your document, it's much faster to navigate the document using Word's Go To feature. This feature works well when you know which of the following you wish to navigate to:

- The page number you want
- The number of pages to move backward or forward from the current position of the cursor
- The section in your document you want to see (you need to know the number of how many sections before or after your cursor position it is)
- The line to move to (helpful if you have used line numbering or know how many lines forward or backward you want to go)
- The bookmark
- The comment (you must know the reviewer's name)

- The footnote or endnote (you must know the number)
- The field (by name)
- The table (if you know the table number)
- The graphic (especially if you have assigned figure numbers)
- The equation (you must know the number)
- The object (you must know the name)
- The heading (you must enter the heading number)

You need to have numbers assigned to many of these items in order to quickly find them. However, in many cases, knowing the relative position (number of such items in relation to your current cursor position) works just as well.

To activate the Go To feature do one of the following:

- Choose **Edit** from the menu and then select **Go To**.
- Press Ctrl+G
- Press F5

Once the Go To feature is activated, the Find and Replace dialog box opens (see Figure 4.1) with the **Go To** tab already selected. Select the type of item you want to go to from the **Go to what?** list. Then, in the text box on the right, enter the required information (a number or name) needed to find the item you want. Choose **Go To**.

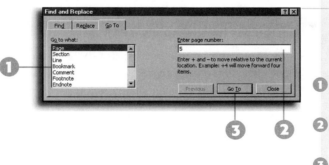

**FIGURE 4.1**

You may navigate to any spot in your document by using the Go To feature.

1. Select the item you want to find.

2. Enter name, number, or relative position.

3. Click here to move your cursor to the item.

The dialog box remains open, ready for the command to seek another item or the **Next** or **Previous** item. When you have finished using the dialog box, choose **Close**.

After you have used the Go To feature, the two browsing buttons at the bottom of the vertical scrollbar become Go To buttons (see Figure 4.2). Depending on what item you were previously seeking, the up browse button will go to the previous instance of the item and the down browse button will go to the next instance.

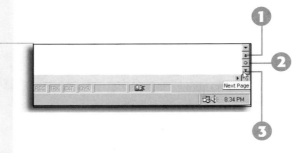

FIGURE 4.2

The browse buttons become Go To buttons after you use the Go To feature.

1 Previous Go To

2 Select Browse Object

3 Next Go To

**Finding text**

When you know the text you want to find within a document (as opposed to the page number, bookmark, and so forth) use Word's "Find Text" feature. See the section "Find Text" in Chapter 6, "Use Proofing Tools" for information on how to locate text within your document.

The browse buttons don't remain constant, however. If you do a Find and Replace, the browse buttons switch to Find Previous and Find Next. Or, if you go to a different type of item, the browse buttons will only seek that new item.

To use the browse buttons as Go To buttons again, click the Select Browse Object button and choose Go To ⟶ . This opens the Find and Replace dialog box to the **Go To** tab so you look for another item.

**SEE ALSO**

➤ *To learn more about sections, see page 286*

➤ *To learn more about bookmarks, see page 563*

➤ *To learn more about footnotes and endnotes, see page 319*

➤ *To learn more about comments, see page 513*

➤ *To learn more about finding text, see page 110*

# Navigate and Select with Keystrokes

As you become more experienced using Word, you'll appreciate eliminating the need to reach for the mouse, thus increasing your productivity.

Although expedient navigation is a timesaving technique, text selection is a *required* technique for efficient word processing. Many features of Word require that you select text before employing the feature. You *must*, for example, select text to cut, copy, delete, or move it. To add a word to your custom dictionary or to use the thesaurus, you must first select the word (see Figure 4.3). Table 4.1 lists the most frequently used keystroke combinations for navigating and selecting text.

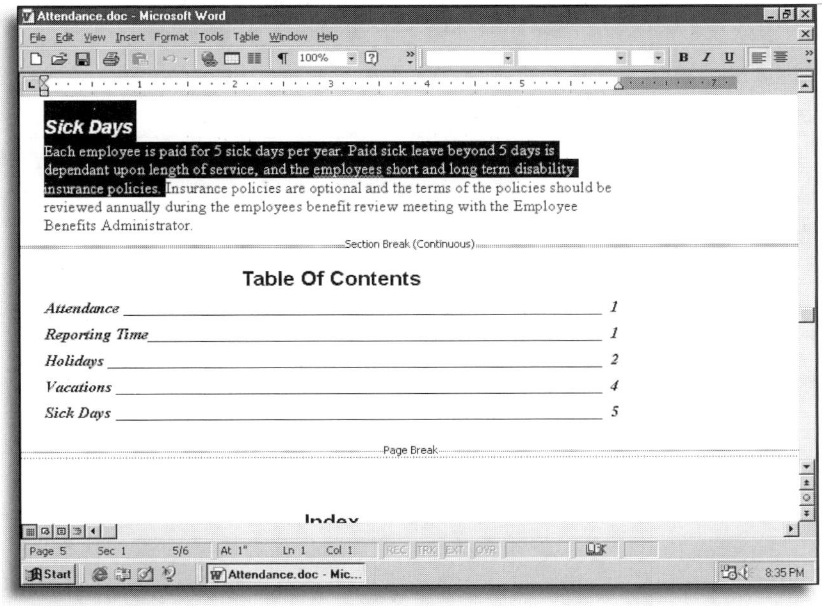

**FIGURE 4.3**
Selected text appears highlighted in black on your screen.

TABLE 4.1   **Key combinations for navigating a document and selecting text**

| To Move by a: | Direction: | Keystrokes to Move: | Keystrokes to Select: (Note: Selection works from insertion point.) |
| --- | --- | --- | --- |
| **Word** | Right | Ctrl+Right arrow | Shift+Ctrl+ Right arrow |
| *To select entire words, place the insertion point at the beginning of the word.* | | | |
| | Left | Right, or end | Shift+ Ctrl+Left arrow |
| *To select entire words, place the insertion point at the end of the word.* | | | |
| **Line of Text** | Down | Down arrow | Shift+End |
| *To select an entire line, place the insertion point at the beginning of the line.* | | | |
| | Up | Up arrow | Shift+Home |
| *To select an entire line, place the insertion point at the end of the line.* | | | |
| **Paragraph** | Down | Ctrl+Down arrow | Shift+Ctrl+ Down arrow |
| *To select an entire paragraph, place the insertion point at the beginning of the paragraph.* | | | |
| | Up | Ctrl+Up arrow | Shift+Ctrl+ Up arrow |
| *To select an entire paragraph, place the insertion point at the end of the paragraph.* | | | |
| **Screen** | Down | Page Down | Shift+Page Down |
| *To select an entire screen, place the insertion point at the beginning of the screen.* | | | |
| | Up | Page Up | Shift+Page Up |
| *To select an entire screen, place the insertion point at the end of the screen.* | | | |

| To Move by a: | Direction: | Keystrokes to Move: | Keystrokes to Select: (Note: Selection works from insertion point.) |
| --- | --- | --- | --- |
| **Page** | Down | Ctrl+Page Down | Shift+Ctrl+ Page Down |

*To select an entire page, place the insertion point at the beginning of the screen.*

| | Up | Ctrl+Page Up | Shift+Ctrl+ Page Up |
| --- | --- | --- | --- |

*To select an entire page, place the insertion point at the end of the page.*

| **Document** | Down | Ctrl+End | Shift+Ctrl+ End |
| --- | --- | --- | --- |

*To select an entire document, place the insertion point at the beginning of the document.*

| | Up | Ctrl+Home | Shift+Ctrl+ Home |
| --- | --- | --- | --- |

*To select an entire document, place the insertion point at the end of the document.*

*To select an entire document, press Ctrl+A.*

To deselect text (turn off the selection highlighting), move your cursor or click elsewhere in the document.

At times, you make a selection and then realize you should have selected more text. The minute you move your cursor or click anywhere else in your document, the highlighting on your selection turns off. To continue selecting, press F8 or hold down the Shift key and then move your cursor to the end of the text you want selected. When you use F8, you have to press ESC to stop the selection process if you don't perform an operation on the selected text.

Some navigational keystroke shortcuts can be found in the menu system, such as Find and Select All (see Figure 4.4), but a complete list can be found in the Help menu by searching for "keystroke shortcuts" and selecting "Find text and navigate through documents."

**Type where you want**

Typing begins at the cursor insertion point. By positioning the cursor, you are able to add text anywhere in your document. In previous versions of Word, you had to add spaces, tabs, or carriage returns to type in whitespace—unused space below your insertion point. Word 2000 offers a new feature, Click-n-Type, which now makes it possible to type in any whitespace on your document. All you need to do is double-click anywhere in whitespace and begin typing. One caveat: you must be in Print Layout view or Web Layout view to take advantage of this new feature.

FIGURE 4.4

To select an entire document, press Ctrl+A, as described in the **Edit** menu.

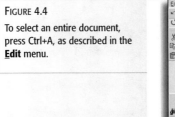

**More help on keystrokes**

Use ScreenTips to help you learn keyboard shortcuts. From the **Tools** menu, choose **Customize**. Click the **Options** tab. Then select **Show Shortcut Keys in ScreenTips** and choose **Close**. Keyboard shortcuts will appear in the ScreenTip information when you point at a toolbar button.

**SEE ALSO**

➤ *To learn about selecting text within a table, see page 173*

➤ *To learn about selecting text while in Outline view, see page 315*

As you can see in Table 4.1, selecting text is just an extension of moving the insertion point. You use the same techniques as you do when navigating text, but you add the Shift key to your keystroke combination.

## Select Text with the Mouse

If keyboard combinations don't do it for you, or you can't break the habit of reaching for the mouse, consult Table 4.2 for mouse techniques. Clicking the mouse is faster and more accurate than dragging the mouse. This section shows you several techniques for using mouse clicks to select text.

Did you know that double-clicking inside of a word selects the word? Also, place your mouse in the left margin of a document and when the pointer changes to an arrow, click:

- Once to select a line
- Twice to select a paragraph
- Three times to select the entire document—triple-clicking within a paragraph selects an entire paragraph

Click again anywhere in the document to deselect lines, paragraphs, or text.

TABLE 4.2   **Mouse text selection techniques**

| To Select | Position Your Mouse | Do This |
|---|---|---|
| **Any amount of text** | At the beginning of the text | Drag to the end of the text. |
| | Click at the beginning of the text | Hold down Shift and click at the end of the text. |
| **A word** | Anywhere in the word | Double-click the word. |
| **Multiple words** | In the first word | Double-click the word, hold down the mouse key, and drag. |
| **A line** | In the left margin of the line | Click. |
| **A sentence** | Anywhere in the sentence | Hold down Ctrl and then click. |
| **Multiple sentences** | Anywhere in the sentence | Ctrl+click then drag. |
| **A paragraph** | In the left margin of the paragraph | When the pointer changes to an arrow, double-click. |
| | Anywhere in the paragraph | Triple-click. |
| **Multiple paragraphs** | Anywhere in the paragraph | Triple-click. First hold down the mouse key and then drag. |
| | In a left margin of the first or last paragraph | When the pointer changes to an arrow, drag the mouse up or down. |
| **An entire document** | In the left margin of the document | When the pointer changes to an arrow, triple-click. |

**Check your default settings for word selection**

When you use the drag method to select words, Word automatically selects whole words as you drag. If you prefer to disable this feature, choose the **Tools** menu and select **Options**, and click the **Edit** tab. Deselect **When Selecting, Automatically Select Entire Word**.

**See what you're editing**

Word can magnify or reduce your view of the page to help you see the text you're selecting and editing. Click the down arrow next to the Zoom tool on the Standard toolbar (the Zoom tool is the box with the percentage in it). A list of percentages displays, plus some options such as Page Width. Choose 100% to see your text in a size closest to the way it will appear on a printed page. Any percentages larger than 100% will magnify the text; percentages smaller than 100% will reduce the view. This magnification does not affect the final look of the document.

**The Cut and Copy commands replace the Clipboard contents**

Each time you cut or copy, the new selection replaces the contents of the Clipboard. If you are pasting information, be certain to complete your paste before you cut or copy again.

SEE ALSO
> *Learn how to select graphics with the mouse, see page 370*

# Edit Text

When you edit text you begin to see the importance of efficient text-selection techniques. Many editing functions are performed on selected text, such as cut, copy, move, and delete. Table 4.3 describes Word's editing tools, the shortcut keys for each, and the toolbar icons for each. The following are a few of the many tools provided by Word to help you edit text:

- *Cut, copy,* and *paste,* are actions that involve the Clipboard. Cutting and copying items places the items on the Clipboard and pasting items places the contents of the Clipboard in to your document. *Items* can be text, graphics, tables, and any object that can be selected in a Word document. Cut, copy, and paste can be performed with the mouse or with keystroke combinations. Use cut, copy, and paste when you need to move or reuse text.

- *Move* is an action associated with the mouse—no keystroke combinations are dedicated for moving text. However, if you cut and paste items using keystroke combinations, you have effectively moved text with keystroke combinations.

- *Insert mode* describes the program mode that adjusts spacing when you add new text to a document.

- *Overtype mode* replaces existing text with your new text. Insert mode is the default mode.

- *Delete* is an action you should reserve for text you want to permanently remove. Deleted text is not placed in the Windows Clipboard. You can delete text with either mouse techniques or keystroke combinations.

- *Undo* and *Redo* are internal to Word and do not involve the Windows Clipboard. With the **Undo** and **Redo** commands, you can reverse tasks that you have performed.

TABLE 4.3   **Text-editing techniques (select text before trying these techniques)**

| | Cut | Copy | Paste | Move | Delete | Undo | Redo |
|---|---|---|---|---|---|---|---|
| **Keyboard shortcuts** | Ctrl+X | Ctrl+C | Ctrl+V | Ctrl+X then Ctrl+V | Back-space or Delete | Ctrl+Z | Ctrl+Y |
| **Menu commands** | Edit, Cut | Edit, Copy | Edit, Paste | Edit, Copy then Edit, Paste | Edit, Clear | Edit, Undo | Edit, Redo |
| **Toolbar icon** | | | | then | | | |
| **Right-mouse click** | Select Cut. | Select Copy. | Select Paste. | Select Cut, then Paste. | Select Cut. | | |
| **Mouse technique** | | Select text, hold down the mouse button+Ctrl and drag. | | Select text, then drag. | | | |

## Cut, Copy, and Paste Text

The **Cut** command removes text and places the text in the Windows Clipboard. Text must be selected before you can use the **Cut** command. After selecting the text, press Ctrl+X or right-click and choose **Cut** from the pop-up menu (see Figure 4.5).

**Where did I leave off?**

When you edit text and move your cursor from place to place within the document, it's easy to lose sight of the last spot where you made a change. This is also true when you open a document that you were working on earlier and you can't remember where you stopped. Press Shift+F5 to return to the last text change you made.

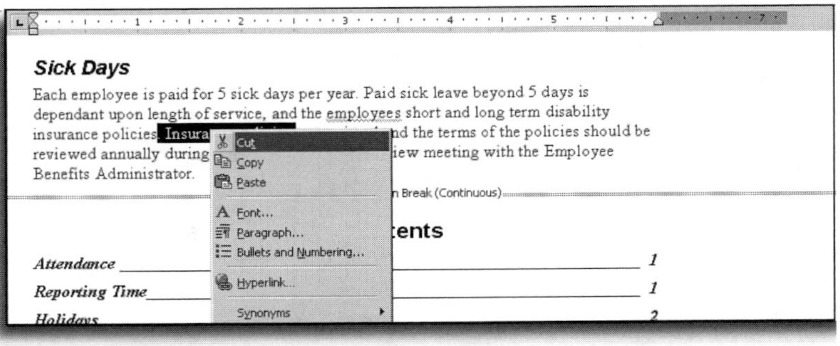

FIGURE 4.5

Right-click for the convenient pop-up menu—also called the *context menu*. The **Cut** option is active only after you have selected text.

*Sick Days*

Each employee is paid for 5 sick days per year. Paid sick leave beyond 5 days is dependant upon length of service, and the employees short and long term disability insurance policies Insura... ...nd the terms of the policies should be reviewed annually during ...iew meeting with the Employee Benefits Administrator.

- Cut
- Copy
- Paste
- A  Font...
- Paragraph...
- Bullets and Numbering...
- Hyperlink...
- Synonyms

**Three basic editing keystrokes**

If you aren't a fan of shortcut keys, so be it. But, if you memorize just these six, you'll find your productivity increases: Ctrl+X to cut, Ctrl+V to paste, Ctrl+Z to undo, Ctrl+C to copy, Ctrl+S to save, and Ctrl+P to print.

**Warning: Check for selected text before pasting**

Selected text will be replaced with the contents of the Windows Clipboard when you choose **Paste**, meaning that you could inadvertently overwrite important text in your document. You can use **Undo** if you inadvertently paste text. The replacement of text in this way is the default setting in Word. Should you want to disable this setting, choose the **Tools** menu and select **Options**. Then in the Options dialog box click the **Edit** tab. Deselect the **Typing Replaces Selection** option.

The **Copy** command copies the selected text and places the text in the Windows Clipboard. The same methods used to cut text are used when copying text. Select the text and press Ctrl+C, or right-click and choose **Copy** from the pop-up menu. The **Paste** command inserts the contents of the Windows Clipboard into your document at your insertion point. Check your insertion point before pasting and press Ctrl+V or right-click and choose **Paste**.

If the contents of the Clipboard are empty, **Paste** is not an available option. To copy and paste in the same mouse movement, select text and hold down the Ctrl key as you drag it to a new location. Word copies the highlighted text and inserts it in the new location. When you copy and paste using this method, the cursor appears with a + sign while dragging.

**Cut**, **Copy**, and **Paste** commands are also found in the **Edit** menu and on the standard toolbar.

## Move Text

Moving text is a function of the mouse—unless you use the keystrokes for **Cut** (Ctrl+X) and **Paste** (Ctrl+V). To move text with the mouse:

### Move Text Using the Mouse

1. Select the text you want to move.
2. Point to the middle of the selected text.
3. Hold down your mouse button and drag the text. As you drag, the mouse pointer displays a small box around its tail.

**4.** A vertical line appears above your pointer (see Figure 4.6). This line acts as the insertion point. Move the insertion point to your desired position on the document and release the mouse button.

**Sick Days**

Each employee is paid for 5 sick days per year. Paid sick leave beyond 5 days is dependant upon length of service, and the employees short and long term disability insurance policies. Insurance policies are optional and the terms of the policies should be reviewed annually during the employees benefit review meeting with the Employee Benefits Administrator.

FIGURE 4.6

The drag-and-drop method enables you to see the *from* and *to* positions of selected text if you are moving within a screen.

❶ Selected text

❷ Move to here

## Move Multiple Text Entries with Spike

If you need to move text from one place to another, most of the time you will use the Windows **Cut** and **Paste** commands or Word's drag-and-drop method. But Word does provide another, specialized method for moving text—the AutoText Spike entry.

The *Spike* is like the Windows Clipboard, in that it stores text for you temporarily while you move it. But it is different from the Clipboard in that it can store multiple text entries. You append each item to the Spike, in the order you want them to appear. Then you paste them as a group in to a new location. You can paste the same group again and again. They remain in the Spike until you empty it, and you must empty the Spike to add a different set of items to it.

Moving text to a new screen or page

We find the drag-and-drop method of moving text inconvenient if we are moving text far from its original location. In that case, we prefer to use the **Cut** and **Paste** commands.

- *Adding text to the Spike.* To move selected text to the Spike, press Ctrl+F3. Do the same for each subsequent item you want to add to the Spike, being careful to do it in the order you want the text to appear when you paste out the group.

- *Inserting the Spike's contents without emptying it.* Position your insertion point where you want to put the contents. Open the **Insert** menu and select **AutoText**. Then select **AutoText** from the submenu. From the list below **Enter AutoText Entries Here**, select **Spike**, and then choose **Insert**. Alternately you may enter the word spike where you want its contents to appear, then press F3.

■ *Inserting the Spike's contents and emptying the Spike.* With your insertion point in the position where you want the Spike's contents to appear, press Ctrl+Shift+F3. This inserts the Spike's contents at the insertion point and empties the Spike.

An example of a use for the Spike would be the assembly of a contract from a library of boilerplate paragraphs. You could scroll through the library and collect the paragraphs you want onto the Spike, then change to a new document and empty the Spike. All the spiked paragraphs would appear there in the order that they were spiked. Another example would be the assembly of a list of items from a larger list. Say you have a directory of names and you want to address a memo to a subset of them. You could scroll through the directory, adding names of addressees to the Spike, and then empty the Spike into the addressee field of the memo.

## Insert Text

No menu command or special instructions are needed to add new text to a document. The generic term for adding new text is *insert*; however, this term should not be confused with the menu choice **Insert**, which is used when you need to insert AutoText and other objects.

**SEE ALSO**

➤ *To learn more about using the AutoText feature to create a list of frequently used words, text, and formatting, see page 131*

➤ *For more information about inserting graphics, see page 367*

➤ *For more information about inserting page numbers, see page 302*

➤ *To learn about inserting tables, see page 165*

To add new text to your document, place your cursor at the insertion point and type. Text to the right of your insertion point moves as you type, allowing the required space you need for your new text. This is the default mode of all word processing programs, and it's called *Insert mode*.

Insert mode is the preferred mode for most people. However, there may be times when you want to replace large blocks of text. In these instances you can switch to *Overtype mode*.

To switch to Overtype mode, double-click the grayed-out OVR button located on the status bar.

When the OVR button is displayed in black text, Overtype mode is active. To turn off Overtype mode, double-click the OVR icon again. When the button is gray, Overtype mode is disabled.

## Delete Text

There are several ways to remove unwanted text from your documents:

- *Delete.* Press the Delete key to remove the character to the right of your cursor. Hold down the key to continue deleting. If you have text selected, pressing Delete will remove that text.

- *Backspace.* Press the Backspace key to remove the character to the left of your cursor. Hold it down to continue deleting. Use Ctrl+Backspace to remove the word to the left of the cursor. If you have text selected, pressing Backspace will remove that text.

- *Clear.* Select the text you want to remove and then select **Clear** from the **Edit** menu.

- *Cut.* Select the text you want to remove and then select **Cut** from the **Edit** menu. This places the selected text in the Windows Clipboard, but you don't have to paste it back into your document.

## Undo and Redo

What happens when you paste or move text to the wrong place in your document? Or if you delete text that you didn't mean to delete? Word provides a few ways to undo what you have done. Choose the **Edit** menu and select **Undo**, or press Ctrl+Z, to reverse your last command.

You also can view a list of the most recent changes you have made to your document, allowing you to undo several steps by clicking the arrow key located next to the Undo button. To reverse an undo action, click the Redo button on the toolbar. Figure 4.7 shows a list of recent actions.

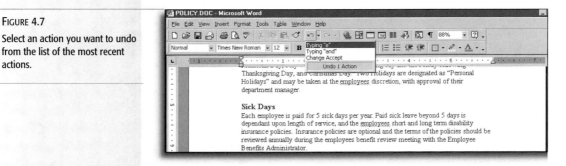

## Copy Multiple Items with Office Clipboard

When you are copying items within Microsoft Office applications, the Windows Clipboard and the Office Clipboard are available to you. The Office Clipboard is a new feature allowing you to copy up to 12 items at a time and paste them into an Office program. Note the differences between the Office Clipboard and the Windows Clipboard:

- The *Windows Clipboard* allows you to cut, copy, or paste one item or block of text to and from any Windows-based software program.

- The *Office Clipboard* allows you to copy (collect) up to 12 items, or blocks of text from any Office 2000 product (such as Word 2000 or Excel 2000) and paste them into any Office 2000 product. It can then be pasted in the same order in which they were copied, or any order or combination.

The Office Clipboard keeps track of what you collected and lets you paste any of the items into Office applications. This feature is called *Collect and Paste*.

For example, if you are preparing an annual report, you can copy a chart from Excel 2000 and a drawing from PowerPoint 2000 into your Word document. You can avoid having to take the extra steps of going first to Excel, copying the chart, switching to Word, pasting the chart, and then repeating a similar operation with PowerPoint. How much simpler it would be to copy each of the items first and then paste them individually or all at one time into Word.

To work with the Office Clipboard, right-click any toolbar and select **Clipboard**. The Clipboard toolbar appears (see Figure 4.8).

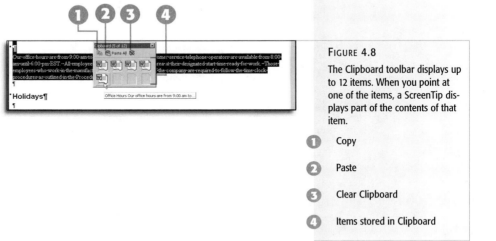

FIGURE 4.8

The Clipboard toolbar displays up to 12 items. When you point at one of the items, a ScreenTip displays part of the contents of that item.

1　Copy

2　Paste

3　Clear Clipboard

4　Items stored in Clipboard

Use the **Edit, Copy** command, Ctrl+C, or the Copy icon 🖺 to copy a selected item to the Office Clipboard (this also copies it to the Windows Clipboard). An icon representing the item appears on the Clipboard toolbar. When you make another selection (from any Office program) and copy it, that item is also added to the Office Clipboard. The same item is also stored in the Windows Clipboard, but the first item is dropped from the Windows Clipboard. The difference is that the Office Clipboard stores both items and up to 10 more.

To paste an item from the Office Clipboard to your document, click the icon that represents the item you want to paste. To paste all of the items at one location in your document, click the Paste All icon 🖺. The position of your cursor determines where the pasted items go.

Clear all the items from the Office Clipboard by clicking the Clear Clipboard icon 🖺. Click **Close** to close the Clipboard toolbar.

**End window clutter**

The one drawback of keeping several windows open at the same time is that it may reduce the speed at which Word works, as windows use computer resources and memory. Always close any documents when you are finished working with them by choosing **Close** from the **File** menu.

# Switch Between Documents

As in previous versions, Word 2000 allows you to open more than one document at a time. This makes it easy for you to work in one document while referring to another or to gather pieces of several documents into a final document. With your current document open, all you have to do is create a new document or open another existing document. You don't have to close the one you're working on. A feature that is new in Word 2000 is the ability to switch documents by using the taskbar.

Once you have several documents open, switch between them in one of the following ways:

- Use the **Window** menu. The menu lists each of the documents you currently have opened. Documents are listed by their filenames, unless you haven't saved them. In that case they are listed as Document1, Document2, and so forth. Just select the name of the document you want to view.

- The Windows taskbar. A button appears on the taskbar for each document you have open. The buttons display the name or number of the document. Just click on the button for the document you want to see.

- Press Alt+Tab. Each document is a window, and Alt+Tab is the keyboard shortcut for switching between windows. It works for documents, plus any other windows you may have open.

To see two or more documents on the screen at one time, open the **Window** menu and choose **Arrange All**, as shown in Figure 4.9. This not only makes it convenient when referring to text in a second document, but you can use the drag-and-drop method to move text between documents. You drag the selected text from one window to the other.

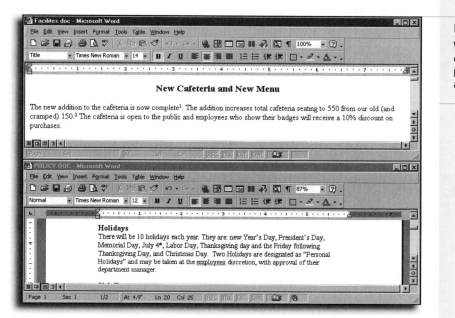

FIGURE 4.9

When you have two documents open, choosing **Arrange All** displays one document window above the other.

# Change the Appearance of Text

Format text with different fonts and sizes as well as bold, italic, and underline

Copy text formatting quickly and efficiently

Bring text to life onscreen with animation

# Format Text

Writing consists of two main activities—composing/editing text and formatting text. When you compose text or edit it, you create and refine content. When you format text, you make the content presentable. You make it readable. You may argue that the most important task is the creation of the content, and I might agree. But formatting is also of vital importance because, if people won't or cannot read what you wrote, you might as well not have wasted your time writing it.

Chapter 4, "Navigate, Select, and Edit Text and Documents," discussed the features of Word that help you to create and refine content. This and later chapters discuss formatting.

Word has always divided formatting into four categories:

- *Character formatting*. How individual characters look.
- *Paragraph formatting*. How individual paragraphs look.
- *Page formatting*. How pages look.
- *Section formatting*. How major divisions of a document look.

This chapter discusses character formatting. The other types of formatting are discussed in later chapters. Character formatting includes the following characteristics of text:

- Font (or typeface)
- Type size
- Type style

**SEE ALSO**

➤ *Learn how to format paragraphs, page 209*
➤ *See how to format pages and sections, page 286*

When you format characters, you choose a font (typeface), a size, and one or more character styles.

# Choose a Font

Fonts are identified by their names and are typically classed according to certain general characteristics shared by all fonts. These include whether the font has serifs and whether it is proportional or monospaced. The default Windows fonts (and therefore the most commonly used fonts in Windows programs) are Arial, Times New Roman, and Courier New.

*Serifs* are the short lines that appear at the ends of the main strokes of individual characters (see Figure 5.1). A font whose characters have serifs is a *serif* font. A font without serifs is a *sans serif* font. Courier and Times New Roman are *serif* fonts. Arial is a *sans serif* font.

Serif fonts are considered to be easier to read than sans serif fonts and therefore are favored for body text. Sans serif fonts are generally cleaner looking than serif fonts, and are favored for headlines. Sans serif fonts are also easier to read on some computer screens than serif fonts, and therefore may be the default font for body text in some programs such as Web browsers.

A *monospace font* or *nonproportional font* is one in which all characters are displayed or printed in a uniform width. For example, the letter "i" is the same width as the letter "m," even though "m" requires more vertical strokes than "i." A *proportional font* is one in which each character is only as wide as it needs to be. Arial and Times New Roman are proportional fonts. Courier (Courier New and all forms of Courier) is a monospace font.

**Watch out for "font du jour" syndrome**

Be prudent in your formatting options. It is a generally accepted rule of desktop publishing that no more than three fonts should be used within a document.

**FIGURE 5.1**

Fonts in this example are all 18 point. The short "finishing" strokes on the ends of the characters in Courier and Times New Roman but not Arial are *serifs*. The characters in Courier are of uniform width.

Fonts can also be described according to how they are stored and rendered (*bitmap* or *raster* fonts, *vector* fonts, and *TrueType* fonts). Fonts can also be described according to what device they are intended for (*screen* or *display* fonts and *printer* fonts).

All fonts (except the ones on the old daisy-wheel printers) are bitmaps when we look at them onscreen or on paper. That is, if you look really closely, you can see that they are just arrays of dots. Bitmap fonts are stored in the computer that way as well. That is, every character of each font is stored as an array of dots.

Vector and TrueType fonts, on the other hand, are stored in the computer as mathematical descriptions of the shapes of their characters. The characters don't become bitmaps until they are rendered.

Storing the fonts as TrueType fonts is much more efficient than storing them as bitmaps. With bitmap fonts you have to store a copy of each character for each size that you want to display/ print the character. This can take up a lot of disk space and, as a result, if you have any bitmap fonts on your computer you probably only have them in a few sizes—typically 8-, 10-, 12-, 14-, 18-, and 24-point.

With vector and TrueType fonts you only have to store one outline of each character. The rendering engine can generate a bitmap of almost any size from the stored outline. You can also rotate the characters. You can't do that with bitmap fonts.

Bitmap and vector fonts are usually device dependent. That means that a given bitmap or vector font is designed to be displayed on a computer screen or printed on a particular make and model of printer.

TrueType fonts are usually not device dependent. The TrueType rendering engine can generate bitmaps for the screen and for any printer.

You really don't have to worry about these things. Windows usually takes care of all the messy details for you. You tell it what kind of printer you have and it figures out which fonts you can use. You tell Word 2000 which printer you plan to use (in the Print dialog box—File, Print in the menu), and only that printer's fonts and the TrueType fonts will appear in Word 2000's font lists. When you choose a font in Word 2000, you can tell which kind of font it is by the symbol that appears to the left of the font name. The symbol for TrueType fonts looks like "TT". The symbol for printer fonts is a picture of a printer.

If you choose a printer font, it probably will not have a corresponding screen font. Windows will substitute one of its own, built-in screen fonts. The result is that what you see on the screen will only be an approximation of what will print out. The line lengths will be the same, but the characters may look different.

Also, some printer fonts may be bitmap fonts while others may be vector fonts. The only reason why you care is that you may have limited font sizes available to you if you choose a bitmap printer font. You can usually tell when you have chosen a bitmap printer font because there will be fewer choices in the list of sizes.

Choose a font using the Formatting toolbar or menus.

To choose a font before you type, position your cursor at the point from which you want to affect the font change. Then select a Font on the Formatting toolbar. To change the font of existing text, select the text and right-click your mouse. From the shortcut menu, choose **Font**. The Font dialog box appears (see Figure 5.3). Click the **Font** tab. Scroll the Font box and click the name of the font you want.

---

**Which type of font should I use: TrueType or Printer?**

There are two advantages to TrueType fonts: onscreen accuracy and portability. There is one potential advantage to printer fonts: printing speed.

TrueType generates both screen and printer fonts, so the onscreen representation of your document will probably be truer to the printed version than if you use a printer font. If you send your document to someone else, it will print the same on their printer as on yours, if you use TrueType fonts; it might not print the same if you use printer fonts.

But, you might find on some printers that your document prints faster if you use resident printer fonts, because you don't have to wait for Windows to render the TrueType characters and download them to your printer.

**Displaying the Formatting toolbar**

If your Formatting toolbar does not show up (see Figure 5.2), click the **View** menu, and select **Toolbars**. Then select **Formatting** from the submenu.

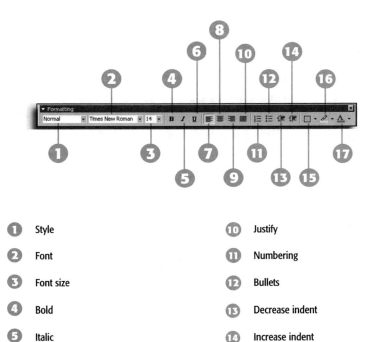

| 1 | Style | 10 | Justify |
|---|-------|----|---------|
| 2 | Font | 11 | Numbering |
| 3 | Font size | 12 | Bullets |
| 4 | Bold | 13 | Decrease indent |
| 5 | Italic | 14 | Increase indent |
| 6 | Underline | 15 | Outside border |
| 7 | Align left | 16 | Highlight |
| 8 | Center | 17 | Font color |
| 9 | Align right | | |

Alternatively, select a font by clicking the Font Name drop-down list on the Formatting toolbar (refer to Figure 5.2), or by clicking the **Fo̲rmat** menu, and selecting **Font**.

If you choose a font *before* you type your text, the font change is in effect for the rest of the document until and unless you change the font. If you select text before you choose a font, the font change applies to that selected text only, unless what you select includes the last paragraph mark in the document, in which case anything you add to the end of the document appears in that font.

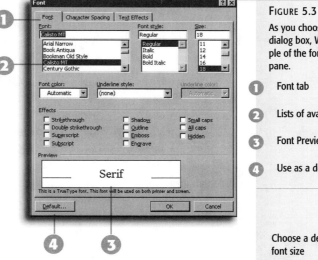

**SEE ALSO**
➤ *For more information on templates, see page 344*

## Choose a Size

Word measures fonts by their height, not by characters per inch. Word measures height by points (there are 72 points per inch); and the larger the number of points the bigger the type.

To choose a font size for text not yet typed, position your cursor at the point from which you want to affect the font size.

**FIGURE 5.3**

As you choose a font in the Font dialog box, Word displays a sample of the font in the Preview pane.

❶ Font tab

❷ Lists of available fonts

❸ Font Preview

❹ Use as a default font

**Choose a default font and font size**

Word's default font and font size for a new blank document is Times New Roman, 12 point. To make another font and/or font size the default font for Word, click the **Default** button located in the Font dialog box (see Figure 5.3) after making your font selection. The default font is associated with your current template and will affect all future documents created with that template.

To choose a font size for existing text, select the text. The quickest way to change size is to click the Size drop-down list on the Formatting toolbar. Click the size of the font you desire. Alternatively, you can right-click your mouse and choose **Font**, or select the **Format** menu and choose **Font**.

Some fonts are scalable. That means they will print or display at any size that you choose within some range of sizes. For example, if you need to squeeze a certain amount of text onto a single page, you might find that 11.5 points is the largest possible size that lets you do that. A scalable font would let you use that size. Nonscalable fonts are available only in discrete sizes, for example, 8 points, 10 points, 12 points, 14 points, 18 points, and 24 points. In this example, you would have to choose 10 point text to fit all the text on the page.

When you select a scalable font, if you want a size other than those listed, you can type the font size you want in the Font Size box.

To determine whether a font is scalable, consult the Font dialog box. Right-click some text and choose **Font**. The Font dialog box appears. A description of the font appears under the Preview pane as shown in Figure 5.4. Select a different font in the dialog box, and the information regarding the font will change accordingly. If it says it is a TrueType font, it is a scalable font. Other scalable fonts include PostScript fonts and some printer fonts.

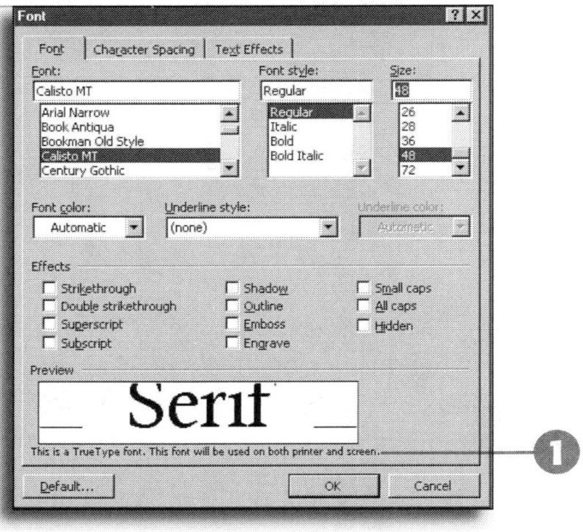

FIGURE 5.4

Font information tells you the relationship between the screen font and the printed font.

**1** Find additional font information here.

Scalable fonts include scalable printer fonts and TrueType fonts. TrueType fonts are scalable to any font size. Several TrueType fonts are automatically installed when Windows is installed on your system. Depending on your printer, you might see scalable printer fonts as an option.

## Choose a Style

Font style options in Word include Regular (also known as Roman, as in Times Roman), *Italic*, **Bold**, and ***Bold Italic.*** Style selection can be made before or after typing text. Although Word does not classify underlining as a *style* per se, most people think of underlining as an alternative to boldfacing and italicizing; so I mention underlining here as well.

Bold, italic, and underlining are used to emphasize text. It is generally accepted that italicizing a word is the preferred method for emphasizing text within paragraphs and bold is reserved for titles or headings. Using underlining for emphasis is passé; don't do it.

To apply a font style for text that has not yet been typed, position your cursor where you want the style to begin. Use shortcut keystrokes or toolbar buttons to apply a style:

- **Bold**. Press Ctrl+B or click the Bold icon ▣.
- *Italic*. Press Ctrl+I or click the Italic icon ▣.
- <u>Underline</u>. Press Ctrl+U or click the Underline icon ▣.

You can use these font styles in any combination. To apply a font style for existing text, select the text and click the toolbar icons.

You can also select font styles in the **Style** box of the Font Properties box. Styles are displayed in the Preview section of the dialog box as you select them.

Like fonts and font sizes, styles are toggle keys; that is the style will stay in effect for all text until you turn off the style. To disable a style, click the indented button on the formatting toolbar.

**Using styles for emphasis**

Professional typesetters always used italic for emphasis. Because most of us can easily print and display italic with modern printers and computers, we too should use italic. Only use underlining, boldface, or all CAPS if your printer can't produce italic.

## Underline Text

In other word processing programs, underline is categorized as a font *style*. Microsoft assigns underline its own category style, perhaps because Word provides so many underlining options.

You can underline a word, a string of text, a paragraph, or an entire document. Like bold and italic, you can turn on underlining before you type or apply underlining to existing text. Use the Underline icon [U] on the Formatting toolbar for single under-line. To turn off underlining, click the icon again.

To underline existing text, select the text and click the Underline icon on the Formatting toolbar.

The Underline icon underlines empty spaces if you select a block of text before clicking it. You can change the options to underline words only by accessing the Font dialog box.

On the **Font** tab of the Font dialog box, use the drop-down menu in the Underlining box to choose an underlining option. As you select underlining options they are displayed in the Preview pane (see Figure 5.5).

**When and how to apply formatting**

I prefer to write first, format later. That way I can stay focused on one thing at a time. I also prefer to use keystrokes rather than the mouse to apply formatting, because it's faster.

**Keystrokers**

There is a keyboard shortcut for underlining words only. It is Ctrl+Shift+W. You should also use this underline format when you don't want to underline tabs (especially helpful for underlining headings for tabbed columns). Try Ctrl+Shift+D for double underlining (useful in underlining final totals for balance sheets).

FIGURE 5.5

As you select underlining options, they are displayed in the Preview pane of the Font dialog box.

**1** Click here to select underlining options.

**2** Preview options here.

Figure 5.6 displays some underlining options. Options range from double underline to double wavy underline and include a number of dashed and dotted lines along the way. You can even change the color of the underline to be different from the text color by choosing one from the **Underline Color** drop-down list in the Font dialog box.

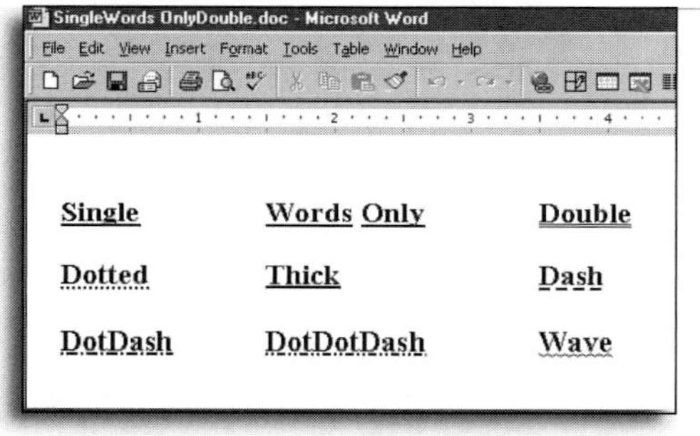

**FIGURE 5.6**
These examples show some of Word's available underlining options.

## Choose a Color

Like all other text formatting features, you can choose a different text color for a single word, a string of text, a paragraph, or an entire document. The default font color is set at *Automatic.* The Automatic color setting sets black as the color of text. However, if you shade a paragraph, with formatting of 80 percent or greater, Automatic changes the text color to white for readability purposes.

**SEE ALSO**

➤ *To shade a paragraph, see page 89*

Use the Font Color icon on the Formatting toolbar for quick color selection. To apply color to text you have not yet typed, click the Font Color icon ▣ on the Formatting toolbar and then type your text. To apply color to existing text, select the text, and then click the Font Color icon.

If you need more colors than the choices provided from the Formatting toolbar, use the Font dialog box. Right-click your mouse and choose **Font** from the menu. Click the **Font Color** drop-down list to select a color. Colors are displayed in the Preview section of the dialog box as you select them. When you have selected a color, click **OK**.

**Don't choose black as a text color**

Choosing black as a text color disables the built-in formatting features of Automatic.

Like other font features, color selection stays in effect until and unless you select another color or reset to Auto.

## Choose Font Effects

Font effects can be selected in the Font dialog box. If you find that you frequently use font effects, you may want to customize your toolbar by adding an icon for font effects.

**SEE ALSO**

➤ *To learn to customize toolbars, see page 640*

To apply effects, select the text and choose your options in the Font dialog box. Alternatively, choose your options in the Font dialog box, type the text, and then disable the options in the Font dialog box when you are finished.

To view the Font dialog box, right-click and select **Font** from the pop-up menu or click the **Format** menu, and select **Font**. Table 5.1 describes the font effects available in the Effects section of the Font dialog box. Figure 5.7 demonstrates those effects.

### Capitalization

Oops! You forgot to turn off the Caps Lock key? AutoCorrect automatically detects that the first letter of your sentence is in lowercase and the remainder is in uppercase and switches it to the proper case. If you deliberately want to change the case of the text you typed, select the text and choose **Change Case** from the **Format** menu and select the type of capitalization you want—sentence case, lowercase, uppercase, title case, or toggle case (the options are displayed in the case). To quickly change the case of selected text from uppercase to lowercase or vice versa, press Shift+F3 as many times as needed to cycle through uppercase, lowercase, and title case.

### Some effects look better than others

The shadow, outline, emboss, and engrave effects do not display well onscreen or at small point sizes. These are best used for printed documents in titles, headings, or on large fonts.

TABLE 5.1    **Font effects**

| Effect | Description |
|---|---|
| Strikethrough | Draws a line through the text. |
| Double Strikethrough | Draws a double line through the text. |
| Superscript | Changes the font to a smaller font size (if available) and raises the font above the baseline. |
| Subscript | Changes the font to a smaller font size (if available) and lowers the font below the baseline. |
| Shadow | Places a shadow beneath and to the right of characters. |
| Outline | Displays the inner and outer lines of each character. Not available for all fonts. |
| Emboss | Makes characters appear raised off the page. |
| Engrave | Makes characters appear depressed into the page. |
| Small caps | Changes all lowercase letters to capital letters and reduces their size. |

| Effect | Description |
|---|---|
| <u>A</u>ll caps | Changes all lowercase letters to capitals. |
| <u>H</u>idden | Hides text. |

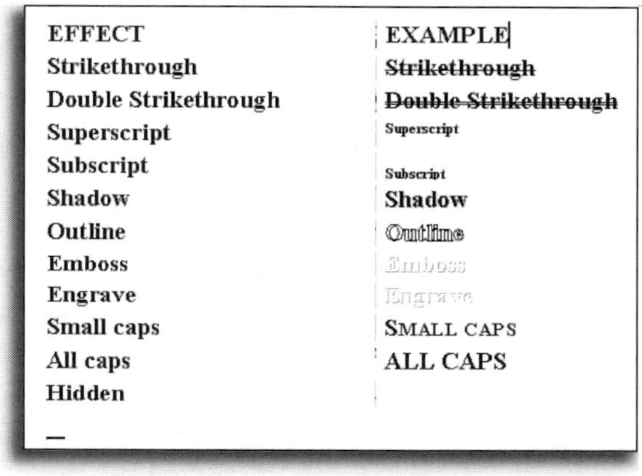

| EFFECT | EXAMPLE |
|---|---|
| Strikethrough | ~~Strikethrough~~ |
| Double Strikethrough | ~~Double Strikethrough~~ |
| Superscript | Superscript |
| Subscript | Subscript |
| Shadow | Shadow |
| Outline | Outline |
| Emboss | Emboss |
| Engrave | Engrave |
| Small caps | SMALL CAPS |
| All caps | ALL CAPS |
| Hidden | |

FIGURE 5.7

Font effects can dramatically change a document's appearance.

**SEE ALSO**

➤ *To learn more about AutoCorrect and capitalization, see page 118*

# Repeat Formatting

Applying formatting options may take several steps. Word provides shortcuts for repeat formatting. They include the following:

- Using Find to locate text and Replace to replace text with formatted text
- AutoCorrect and AutoText to apply formatting options
- Creating styles that include the formatting options you want to apply
- Using the Edit menu to repeat formatting selections
- Using Format Painter to repeat formatting selections

You should use the **<u>E</u>dit** menu and the **Format Painter** if you occasionally need to repeat formatting options on a small document. If your work frequently involves special formatting, you should consider creating styles, using AutoText, or using AutoCorrect.

**SEE ALSO**

➤ *To learn how to create styles and apply automatic formatting, see page 251*

➤ *To create formatted AutoCorrect and AutoText entries, or to replace text with formatted text, see page 116*

## Repeat Formatting with Menu Commands

When you apply a formatting option, Word keeps track of those options and the **Edit** menu displays the last formatting option that you applied. For example, as soon as you apply color to a word, view the **Edit** menu and you find **Undo Font Color** and **Repeat Font Color** as menu selections. This is useful for repeating formatting options that do not otherwise have shortcut keystrokes. Keep in mind, however, that the **Edit** menu tracks only your last action. If you bold and underline a word, only the underline action appears in the **Edit** menu. Additionally, as soon as you type new text, formatting options are replaced by typing options. Using the Format Painter is a more accurate way of repeating formatting options and saves you time.

## Use Format Painter

The Format Painter 🖌 enables you to copy formatting from a selected object or text and apply it to other objects or text within your document. For example, you may have words within your document that you want to appear in subscript and small caps; SUCH AS THIS. To apply subscript and small caps, you must select the text and access the Font dialog box, click **Subscript** and click **Small Caps**. This can be labor intensive. Alternatively, you can apply the formatting to one word or phrase then use the Format Painter to apply the same formatting to other words or phrases. This saves time and keystrokes. Additionally, you can use the Format Painter to quickly apply formatting to one word or phrase, or you can toggle it on to use it for many words or phrases, then turn it off when you are done.

**Apply Formatting to Text with Format Painter**

**1.** Click once inside the text whose formatting you want to copy.

**2.** Click the Format Painter ![icon] on the Standard toolbar. Your mouse pointer turns into a paintbrush.

**3.** Select the text to which you want to apply the formatting:

- To apply the formatting to only one word or object, you click once inside the word or click the object. You don't need to drag over the word or object.

- To apply the formatting to an entire paragraph, select the paragraph by clicking in the margin.

- To apply the formatting to several words or objects, you must drag the mouse over the words or objects to select them.

When you release the mouse button, the formatting is applied to the new text and your pointer returns to normal appearance.

When you use the Format Painter to apply formatting, that new formatting overrides all the current formatting for that text. For example, if you use the Format Painter to copy bold and red color attributes from existing text, then you apply these attributes to text that currently is in italic, the text becomes bold and red but loses the italic. If you want to have the text in italic too, you must apply the italic again.

# Animate Text

Animated text can bring a document to life on the screen. However, you should know that animated text features will not convert to HTML if you are creating a document for the Web. Of course, animated text can't translate to the printer, so text animation features should be reserved for documents that will be read online and in Word.

**Keep Format Painter on**

To keep the Format Painter on and repeat formatting throughout your document, double-click on the **Format Painter** ![icon]. The Format Painter stays active so that you can continue to format non-adjacent text. When you are finished, press the **Esc** key or click the **Format Painter** icon again to deactivate it.

**Apply Animation Effects to Text**

1. Select the text you want to animate.

2. Right-click the text and choose **Font** from the pop-up menu.

3. The Font dialog box appears. Click the **Text Effects** tab (see Figure 5.8).

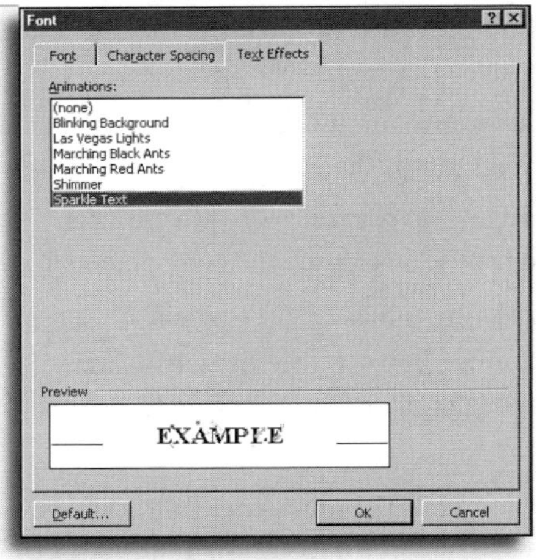

FIGURE 5.8

As you select animation effects, they appear in the **Preview** window.

4. Choose an effect from the **Animations** list. Click **OK** to close the dialog box and apply the animation effect to your text.

Other character formatting techniques in Word include character spacing, scaling, kerning, and character styles. Character spacing, scaling, and kerning are covered in *Special Edition Using Microsoft Word 97 Best Seller Edition* published by Que.

SEE ALSO

➤ *Learn more about creating HTML pages on page 604*

➤ *Learn how to apply character styles on page 92*

# Apply Shading and Borders

A great way to emphasize headlines, captions, and other important text is to apply a border or shading to that text. Borders and shading can also separate a piece of text from the rest of the text on a page, such as a sidebar story in a newsletter.

### Apply Borders and Shading

1. Carefully select the text to which you want to apply borders or shading. What you select determines what gets shaded/bordered. The rules are as follows:

   * If you don't select any text, the results affect the entire paragraph in which the insertion point appears.

   * If you select text within a single paragraph, but the paragraph mark itself is not included in the selection, the results affect only the selected text.

   * If you select text included in more than one paragraph (so that at least one paragraph mark is included in the selection), the results affect all the paragraphs in which any of the selected text resides.

   You *can* override these rules in the Borders and Shading dialog box, however.

2. Open the **Format** menu, and select **Borders and Shading** to display the Borders and Shading dialog box.

3. Click the **Borders** tab to work with border options (see Figure 5.9).

   * Under Setting, click one of the preset border options. Select **None** to remove all borders from the selected paragraph(s), **Box** to insert a box border around the selected paragraph(s), and **Shadow** to insert a box border around the selected paragraph(s) and apply preset shadow formatting to the border. Select **3-D** to insert a box border around the selection and apply preset 3D border formatting. Choose **Custom** to create a border using the options you click in the Preview window. When you choose any of these settings, the current selections in **Style**, **Color**, and **Width** apply to the borders.

- From the **Style** list, select the type of line you want to use for the border, including dotted, dashed, and wavy lines.

- Click the **Color** drop-down list to select a color to apply to the border.

- From the **Width** drop-down list, choose the thickness of the border line from 1/4-point to 6 points.

- In the Preview box, click the individual border lines or use the border line buttons to apply or remove borders or change the attributes of a particular border (select the attributes first and then add the border).

- From the **Apply To** drop-down list, select whether to apply the border to just the selected text or to the whole paragraph(s).

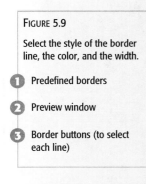

FIGURE 5.9

Select the style of the border line, the color, and the width.

❶ Predefined borders

❷ Preview window

❸ Border buttons (to select each line)

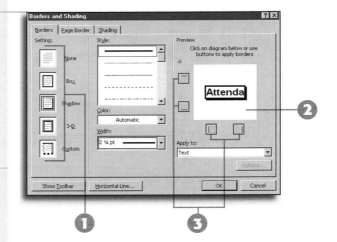

**4.** Select the **Shading** tab to choose shading options (see Figure 5.10).

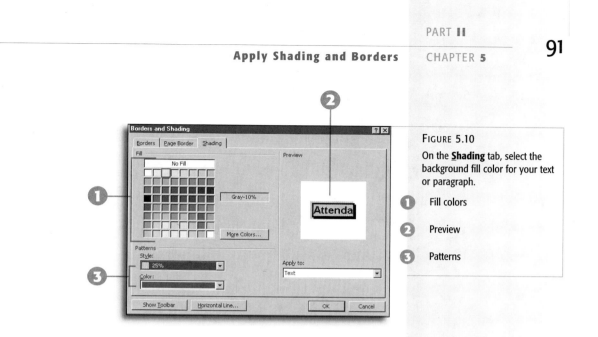

FIGURE 5.10

On the **Shading** tab, select the background fill color for your text or paragraph.

1️⃣ Fill colors

2️⃣ Preview

3️⃣ Patterns

- Under **Fill**, select the color or shade of gray with which you want to fill the selection. Click **More Colors** to see a larger selection of colors.

- From the **Patterns Style** drop-down list, choose a shading percentage for the color you selected under **Fill** or a pattern of lines such as Lt Horizontal or Dk Trellis.

- If you selected a pattern of lines, select the **Color** of the lines from the drop-down list. The Fill color then becomes the background color for the pattern.

- From the **Apply To** drop-down list select whether to apply the shading options to just the selected text or to the whole Paragraph(s).

  **5.** Click **OK**.

To quickly choose shading colors, border line styles, border line colors, and border line widths, use the Tables and Borders toolbar. Click the **View** menu, and select **Toolbars**. From the submenu, select **Tables and Borders** 🔲 to display the toolbar, or choose Tables and Borders on the Standard toolbar.

Select the text to which you want to add borders and shading, and then click the appropriate button on the toolbar. Table 5.2 lists the buttons on the toolbar that apply to borders and shading. Figure 5.11 shows the full toolbar.

**Effective use of patterns with text**

When using patterns behind text, make the pattern small, the color light, and the text big and bold.

TABLE 5.2   **The Tables and Borders toolbar buttons**

| Button | Description |
|---|---|
| **Line Style** | Sets the style of the border lines (dotted, dashed, wavy, double, and so on) |
| **Line Weight** | Sets the thickness of the border lines |
| **Border Color** | Sets the color of the border lines |
| **Borders** | Specifies where the border appears (top, bottom, left, right, or box) |
| **Shading Color** | Sets the color of the background shading for the paragraph (you cannot specify the percentage) |

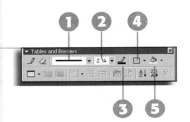

FIGURE 5.11

Border and shading options appear on the Tables and Borders toolbar.

1 Line style

2 Line weight

3 Border color

4 Border options

5 Shading color

# Assign Character Styles

Styles are sets of formatting attributes that you can apply to text in your document. Typically styles are applied to whole paragraphs and allow you to use preset formatting for headings, captions, numbered paragraphs, and so forth. However, Character styles are useful when you find yourself using the Format Painter over and over again to apply character formatting.

Character styles add to the current formatting of text. For example, if the text is 12-point Arial italic and your character style applies bold and strikethrough, the text to which you apply the character style will be 12-point Arial bold, italic, and strikethrough.

### Assign a Character Style

1. To apply a style to existing text, select the text to which you want to assign the style. If you want to apply a style as you are entering new text, place your insertion point where you want the newly styled text to appear.

2. Choose a style from the Style list on the Formatting toolbar. When you click the down arrow next to the Style box, you see each style name displayed in the style's font. An underlined "a" indicates a character style (see Figure 5.12).

3. Click the name of the style you want to use to apply the style to the selected text.

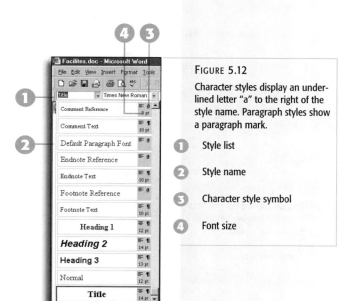

FIGURE 5.12

Character styles display an underlined letter "a" to the right of the style name. Paragraph styles show a paragraph mark.

1. Style list

2. Style name

3. Character style symbol

4. Font size

When you want to remove the character style from selected text, apply the character style Default Paragraph Font. The text reverts to the formatting defined in the paragraph style assigned to the paragraph in which the selected text is located.

### Create a Character Style

1. Open the **Format** menu and choose **Style**.

2. Choose **New**.

3. Type a name for the new style in the **Name** box (see Figure 5.13).

4. Choose **Character** from the **Style Type** box.

5. Choose **Format** and then **Font** to set the style's attributes from the Font dialog box. Choose **OK**.

6. (Optional) To add a border or shading to the new character font, choose **F<u>o</u>rmat** and then **<u>B</u>order** to open the Borders and Shading dialog box. Make your selections and then choose **OK**.

7. Choose **OK** to close the New Style dialog box.

8. Choose **<u>A</u>pply** to apply the new style to current text. Choose **Close** to save the new style definition without assigning it to any text.

Creating a character style is easiest when you select text first, apply the font attributes you want in the new style, and then follow steps 1–5 above. You won't have to select any formatting, so skip to steps 7–8 to finish creating the style.

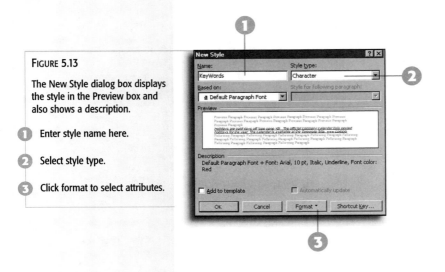

F<small>IGURE</small> 5.13

The New Style dialog box displays the style in the Preview box and also shows a description.

1 Enter style name here.

2 Select style type.

3 Click format to select attributes.

**SEE ALSO**
➤ *To learn more about creating, modifying, and assigning styles, see page 238*

# Use Proofing Tools

Correct spelling errors for individual words or an entire document

Check for correct grammatical usage and correct errors

Replace words with synonyms or antonyms from the thesaurus

Find and replace text and formatting

Automate common word and phrase entry and corrections with AutoText and AutoCorrect

# Run Spell Check

Spell check is useful because everyone makes typos, even if you consider yourself to be a good speller. Word's spell check is especially easy to use because it operates while you type and flags errors the moment you make them.

As you type, Word continuously checks your spelling and flags any suspect words with a wavy red underline. You might notice as you type, toward the right end of the status bar, a little book icon with turning pages. That's the spell checker at work. When you stop typing, the pages stop turning and the book has either a red "x" or a red check mark on it. The "x" means that, somewhere in your document, a spelling (or grammar) flag is unresolved. The check mark means that all flags are resolved.

Even though Word may flag a word for spelling, the word isn't necessarily misspelled. Word flags a word for spelling if the word doesn't appear in Word's spelling dictionary, or in the personal dictionary to which Word adds entries that you flag as correct spellings, or in any custom dictionary you might be using. If a correctly spelled word doesn't appear in any of those dictionaries, Word will assume it is incorrect and flag it.

Other times Word fails to flag a word even though, in the context in which it is used, the word is misspelled. Word, for example, would not flag the word *merry* as a misspelling in the following sentence: "He wants to merry her." You still need to proofread your work.

## Spell Check a Flagged Word

You can either stop and correct errors flagged by Word immediately, or you can wait and correct them later. To correct a word flagged by the automatic spell checker, right-click the word. A menu pops up. Suggested replacement words (if there are any) appear in the pop-up menu, as well as commands for dealing with the misspelling (see Figure 6.1).

---

**Spell check doesn't work?**

If Word doesn't seem to be catching your spelling errors, your language option may be set incorrectly or the spelling checker is turned off. Open the **Tools** menu and select **Language**. In the Language dialog box select the **Set Language** option. In the **Mark Selected Text As** list, make sure the language you are using is the one selected (a check mark appears in front of the selected language). A common problem lies with languages that have different spellings for different countries or usages (such as English(US) or English(UK). Also, make sure the **Do Not Check Spelling or Grammar** option is deselected.

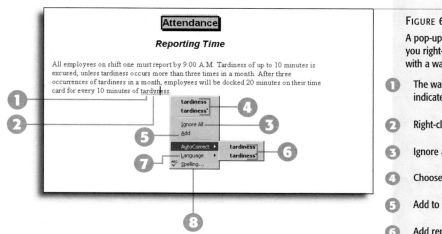

FIGURE 6.1

A pop-up menu appears when you right-click a word marked with a wavy red underline.

1   The wavy red underline indicates a misspelling

2   Right-click here

3   Ignore all occurrences

4   Choose replacement word

5   Add to custom dictionary

6   Add replacement work to AutoCorrect

7   Select a different language

8   Start Spell Check

The choices in the pop-up menu and their uses are as follows:

- Click the appropriate replacement word to replace the word with one of the suggestions.

- Click **Ignore All** to ignore all occurrences of that spelling of the word in the document.

- Click **Add** to add the word to your custom dictionary.

- Click **AutoCorrect** to add the misspelling to the AutoCorrect list, and then select the proper replacement spelling from the submenu that appears.

- Click **Language** to switch to another language dictionary (if you have another one installed) or to select a different language setting.

- Click **Spelling** to start a regular spell check as discussed in the next section.

**SEE ALSO**

➤ *Learn how to create a custom dictionary, page 101*

➤ *Learn more about AutoCorrect, page 118*

➤ *Learn more about using other languages, page 676*

## Check an Entire Document or Selected Block of Text

Instead of correcting spelling as you type, you can correct the whole document at once. You may prefer to wait until after you've finished composing the document to take care of such chores as spell checking. Maybe you don't want to be distracted from writing, so you disable automatic spell checking. Or you might conclude that it's more efficient to spell check the whole document in a single pass (so that, for example, you can have Word correct every instance of a misspelled word with one command, rather than having to correct each instance individually).

When you do a manual spell check, Word checks the document beginning at the location of your insertion point. After the spell checker reaches the end of the document, a dialog box appears asking if you want to continue from the beginning. When you choose to have the spell checker continue, it checks the remainder of the document and finishes when it reaches the original position of your insertion point.

To check only a portion of a document, select the text you want to check before starting the spell checker. Word checks the selected text from beginning to end.

You can start the spell checker in one of three ways:

- Select the **Tools** menu and choose **Spelling and Grammar**.
- Press F7.
- Choose the Spelling and Grammar button ![abc] on the Standard toolbar.

When the Spelling and Grammar dialog box appears (see Figure 6.2), make sure the **Check Grammar** check box is clear if you only want to check spelling. If this option is selected, the checker also checks for grammar errors (which are covered later in the "Check Grammar" section of this chapter).

When spell checker finds a word in the document that has no match in the spelling or custom dictionaries, it displays the word and its surrounding text in the **Not in Dictionary** box. The suspect word appears in red. (The word is also selected and highlighted in the body of the document.) In the **Suggestions** box is a list of possible correct spellings for the highlighted word. You can then do one of the following:

- Select the appropriate replacement word in the **Suggestions** box and choose **Change** to use one of the suggested replacements.

- If none of the suggested replacements is appropriate, correct the word manually by editing it in the **Not in Dictionary** box. Then choose **Change**.

- Choose **Change All** to replace this and all other instances of the word in the document with either the manual correction you made or with one of the suggested replacement words. Note: This corrects all instances of a particular misspelling of a word, but does not correct different misspellings of the same word.

- Choose **Ignore** to leave the word unchanged in the document.

- Choose **Ignore All** to ignore this and all other instances of the word in the document.

- Choose **Add** to add the word to the custom dictionary.

- Choose **AutoCorrect** to add the misspelling and its correction to the AutoCorrect list. Then, if this misspelling appears in later documents, Word automatically corrects your spelling as you type. To learn more about AutoCorrect, refer to the section, "Define and Modify AutoCorrect Entries," later in this chapter.

- Choose **Cancel** to terminate the spell check process without finishing the entire document or selection.

Spell check stops at each suspect word in the document or selection, and you have the same alternatives for each misspelling. When the entire document or selection has been checked, Word displays a message stating that spell check is complete. Choose **OK** to return to your document.

## Set Spell Check Options

If you don't want to deal with spelling while you enter text, you can either hide the spell check marks while you work, or turn off automatic spell checking entirely. You can also control how spell checker works by setting options.

To see what spell check options are available, to hide the spell check marks, or to turn off automatic spell checking, you must display the Spelling and Grammar Options dialog box. You can do this in two ways. Either choose the **Options** button when the Spelling dialog box is open, or from the **Tools** menu choose **Options**, and then select the **Spelling & Grammar** tab (see Figure 6.3).

To hide the spell check marks while you work, click **Hide Spelling Errors in this Document**. To turn automatic spell checking off, deselect **Check Spelling as You Type**. Other options you can set include the following:

- **Always Suggest Corrections**. Turn this off if you have a slow computer.

- **Suggest from Main Dictionary Only**. When checked, only the main dictionary is checked and Word does not search other dictionaries.

---

**Interrupt the spell check whenever you want**

Sometimes spell check highlights a word and you notice that you need to edit other words around it. If so, just click in the document and make your changes. Spell check suspends its operation when you click in the document. When you finish editing, choose the **Resume** button in the Spelling and Grammar dialog box to resume the spell check.

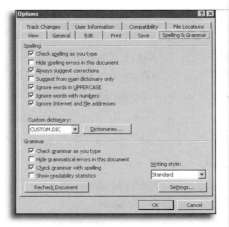

FIGURE 6.3

**The Spelling & Grammar** tab of the Options dialog box displays the name of your custom dictionary.

- **Ignore Words in UPPERCASE**. When this option is selected, Word ignores acronyms.

- **Ignore Words with Numbers**. When this option is selected, Word ignores words with numbers.

- **Ignore Internet and File Addresses**. When this option is selected, Word ignores URLs and filenames.

## Create and Edit a Custom Dictionary

When you spell check your document, you have the option to add new words to the Custom.dic dictionary file provided by Word. You can add proper names and terminology you use frequently that are not contained in Word's standard spelling dictionary. When you are performing a spell check of your document and Word finds one of these terms for the first time, choose **Add** in the Spelling and Grammar dialog box to add that word to the custom dictionary. If such a word is marked by the automatic spell check, right-click the word and click **Add** in the pop-up menu that appears.

If you add a misspelled word to the custom dictionary by mistake, you can edit the word or delete it from the custom dictionary. Also, when you have a list of names or words you need to add to the dictionary, you can add them all at once, instead of waiting for the words to appear in a document.

Misspelled words in the custom dictionary

Before you add a word to the custom dictionary, make sure that it is spelled correctly. If you add a misspelled word to the custom dictionary, Word will never detect the misspelled word in the future. To correct the situation, you have to edit the word in the custom dictionary.

### Add, Edit, and Delete Words in a Custom Dictionary

1. From the **Tools** menu, select **Options**.

2. When the Options dialog box appears, click the **Spelling & Grammar** tab (see Figure 6.3).

3. Choose **Dictionaries**.

4. From the list of custom dictionaries (see Figure 6.4), select the one you want to edit. Be careful not to clear its check mark.

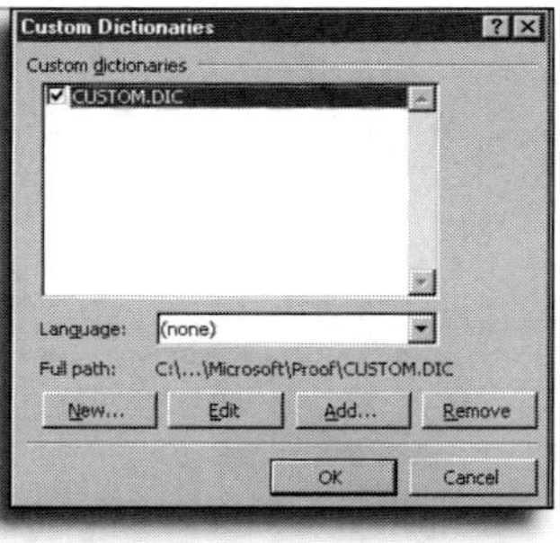

FIGURE 6.4

In the Custom Dictionaries dialog box, select the dictionary in which you want to add, delete, or edit entries.

5. Choose **Edit**. A warning appears saying that Word will turn off the automatic spelling and grammar checking. Choose **OK** to continue.

6. The dictionary document opens (see Figure 6.5). Make your additions, deletions, and corrections to the listed entries. Press Enter after each added word so that every word is on a separate line. If you need to search for a word, use the **Find** command on the **Edit** menu, or sort the list alphabetically, if you prefer, by opening the **Table** menu and selecting sort.

FIGURE 6.5

The dictionary file is a Word document with a list of words, each on a separate line.

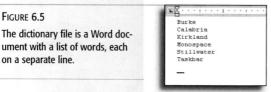

**7.** After making your changes and additions, save the document and close it.

**8.** To reactivate the automatic spell checker, from the **Tools** menu select **Options**. Select the **Spelling & Grammar** tab from the Options dialog box (refer to Figure 6.3). Click **Check Spelling as You Type** to place a check mark in the box. Click **OK**.

Where Microsoft Word 2000 stores the Custom.dic dictionary depends on your operating system. Under Windows 98 without user profiles, Word stores it in the *systemroot*\Application Data\Microsoft\Proof folder (where *systemroot* is your Windows directory). Under Windows NT or Windows 98 with user profiles, Word stores it in the *systemroot*\Profiles\*profilename*\ Application Data\Microsoft\Proof folder (where *profilename* is your logon name). Word allows you to use other custom dictionaries, such as legal or medical dictionaries, that contain words often used in your business or profession. You must specify the location of these dictionaries and then activate them for use.

### Selecting Additional Custom Dictionaries

**1.** From the **Tools** menu, select **Options**.

**2.** Select the **Spelling & Grammar** tab in the Options dialog box (refer to Figure 6.3).

**3.** Choose **Dictionaries**.

**4.** In the Custom Dictionaries dialog box (refer to Figure 6.4), choose **Add**.

**5.** Enter the name of the dictionary file in the **File Name** box of the Create Custom Dictionary dialog box (see Figure 6.6) or click the name of the file in the list of files.

**6.** Choose **OK**.

**7.** From the **Tools** menu, select **Options** and then select the **Spelling & Grammar** tab in the Options dialog box.

**8.** Choose **Dictionaries**.

**9.** The name of the new dictionary is listed in the **Custom Dictionaries** box. Click the check box in front of the file-name to place a check mark there.

---

**Quick access to spelling and grammar options**

Right-click the Spelling and Grammar icon on the Status bar and choose **Options**.

---

**What are user profiles?**

In Windows, a user profile is a Windows configuration customized for the use of a single logon user. User profiles are stored in the Profiles folder, located in your Windows folder. User profiles include all the things personal to a user regarding the configuration of Windows—such things as the background color, pattern, and wallpaper of your screen, your screen saver settings, the arrangement of icons on your Windows desktop, the choices available in your Start menu, and your personal data folders.

Windows NT always uses user profiles. Windows 98 does not use them unless you tell it to. You only need to tell it to use profiles if more than one person uses the computer.

To enable user profiles in Windows 98, choose **Settings**, **Control Panel** in the Start menu. Then double-click **Passwords** to open the Password Properties dialog-box. Go to the **User Profiles** tab and select "**Users Can Customize Their Preferences and Desktop Settings**...".

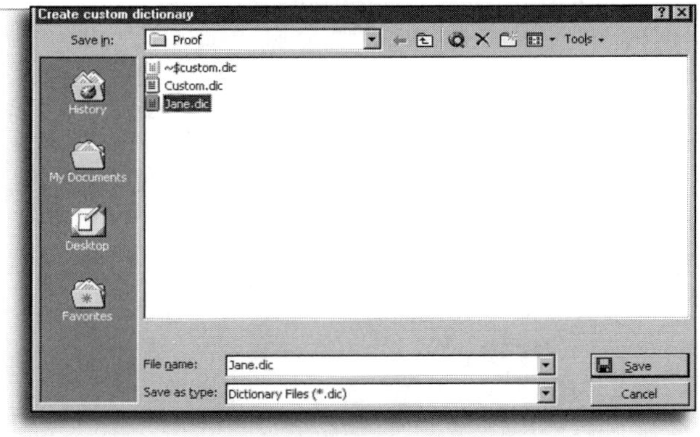

FIGURE 6.6

Select the location and name of the custom dictionary or enter the name of the dictionary in the **File Name** box.

10. Choose **OK**. Then choose **OK** in the Options dialog box. The next time you spell check your document, Word will also check the new custom dictionary.

SEE ALSO
➤ *Learn more about sorting lists, page 222*

## Share Custom Dictionaries

In certain industries, particularly medical and engineering, it is useful to share custom dictionary entries by distributing the dictionaries to others via email or network access. One person in the office, for example, can invest the time to create a dictionary of terms or acronyms, even names of clients. They can then save the custom dictionary as described in the preceding steps. The dictionary file can then be mailed to others, or access to it can be provided via a network. Individual users who receive the dictionary through email or from a network should save it to their Word dictionaries folder. The default directory for Word dictionaries is C:\Program Files\Common Files\Microsoft Shared\Proof. Users can then activate the custom dictionary by including it in the **Custom Dictionaries** list.

### Adding a New Custom Dictionary

1. Open the **Tools** menu and select **Spelling & Grammar**.
2. Click the **Options** button in the Spelling and Grammar dialog box, and then click the **Dictionaries** button.

3. In the Custom Dictionaries dialog box, click the **Add** button.

4. Select the new dictionary from the Proof folder and click **OK**.

Word now uses this new dictionary in conjunction with the user's own custom dictionary. If preferred, users can open the new dictionary file and copy all entries into their own custom dictionary. The advantage of keeping a separate dictionary is that the custom dictionaries can be disabled or enabled at any time by removing or adding their check marks in the **Custom Dictionaries** list. Another advantage of keeping the dictionary separate is that it enables the dictionary to be replaced (if the dictionary administrator has additions or corrections) without affecting any entries they may have saved in their own custom dictionary.

# Run Grammar Check

Word's grammar check reviews your grammar as you write, just as spell check reviews spelling as you write. As spell check flags suspect spelling with a wavy red underline, grammar check flags suspected grammatical problems with a wavy green underline. You can either check grammar flags on the spot, or you can wait until you have finished writing and check all flags in one pass— just like you can with spell check.

Grammar check is a more complex tool than spell check. Spell check just compares words against its spelling dictionary and flags them if they are not in the dictionary. Grammar check reviews your writing using a mass of rules to flag a wide variety of problems, including punctuation, capitalization, and style problems.

The importance of this fact is that grammar check is even less accurate than the spell check. It doesn't catch every problem. It sometimes flags text that is grammatically accurate. It flags ungrammatical text but then identifies the wrong grammar problem. You should carefully scrutinize grammar flags before accepting Word's opinion. If you find that Word repeatedly misidentifies a particular kind of problem, don't hesitate to turn

**Grammar check isn't perfect**

Word's grammar check is a useful tool, but it's not intelligent. It just follows rules. Don't assume that grammar check catches every error and don't assume every solution it offers is any better than yours, or even correct. Grammar check certainly cannot check to see if you actually wrote what you meant to write. It is no substitute for careful writing, editing, and proofreading.

off that type of grammar checking. To turn off grammar check settings go to the **Tools** menu and select **Options**. In the Options dialog box select the **Spelling & Grammar** tab, and then select **Settings**.

## Correct a Single Grammar Error

You can correct a single flagged grammar error by right-clicking the green-underlined text. A pop-up menu appears, as shown in Figure 6.7. The pop-up menu offers the following choices:

- Click the suggested "grammatically correct" replacement, which is the first choice on the pop-up menu.
- Click **Ignore** to ignore the possible error and to make the wavy line disappear.
- Click **Grammar** to start a regular grammar check.
- Click **About this Sentence** to get a brief explanation of the grammar involved.

FIGURE 6.7

To quickly correct grammatical errors, right-click the flagged word(s) and choose a correction from the pop-up menu.

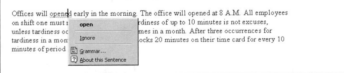

## Check an Entire Document or Selected Block of Text

You may prefer to write first and check all grammar and spelling later. That way, if grammar check flags things repeatedly that you consider to be acceptable, you can choose **Ignore All** once and grammar check will not flag it again—and you save time. In that case, you can run a grammar check when you are ready by starting grammar check. If you have selected a block of text, grammar check only checks grammar within the selection. Otherwise, it checks the whole document. You can start grammar check in one of these ways:

- From the **Tools** menu, select **Spelling & Grammar**.
- Press F7.
- Choose the Spelling & Grammar button  on the Standard toolbar.

The Spelling and Grammar dialog box appears and Word now works its way through either the whole document or the selected text, searching for errors. Note that it checks for both grammar and spelling errors. Each time Word locates a phrase with a suspected grammatical error, it highlights the phrase in the body of the document and displays the phrase and its surrounding text in the Spelling and Grammar dialog box (see Figure 6.8). The suspect phrase appears in green text in the dialog box. A description of the problem appears at the top of the dialog box and sometimes the Office Assistant displays a more detailed description of the problem. The **Suggestions** box lists any suggested fixes.

**Grammar check isn't working**

Make sure the **Check grammar** option is checked in the Spelling and Grammar dialog box.

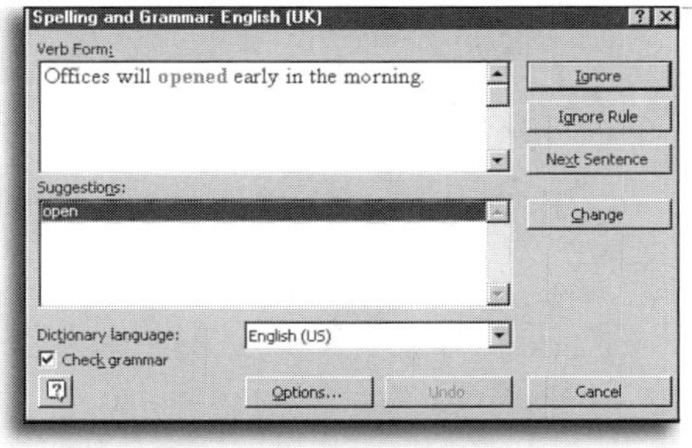

FIGURE **6.8**

The suspected grammar error is marked in green with a description of the error appearing in the pop-up menu.

Make any of the following choices with respect to each suspected grammar error:

- Select one of the suggested fixes in the **Suggestions** list box and then choose **Change**.
- Edit the text to correct the error and then choose **Change**.
- Choose **Ignore** to ignore this instance of the problem.
- Choose **Ignore All** to ignore this instance and all other instances of the problem in the document.
- Choose **Ignore Rule** to ignore this rule of grammar while checking this document.

- Choose **Next Sentence** to go on to the next sentence and ignore the current problem.
- Choose **Close** (x) or **Cancel** to stop grammar check and close the dialog box.
- Choose **Options** to set options for how grammar check works.

Unless you close the dialog box, Word continues to check each possible spelling and grammar error throughout the document. Each time you have the same set of choices. A message box appears when the spelling and grammar checking is complete. Choose **OK** to return to your document.

## Set Grammar Checking Options

If you don't want to deal with grammar issues while you are entering text, you can either hide the grammar check marks while you work or you can turn off automatic grammar checking entirely. You also can control how grammar check works by setting options.

To see what grammar check options are available, to hide the grammar check marks, or to turn off automatic grammar checking, display the Spelling and Grammar Options dialog box. You can do this in two ways. Either choose the **Options** button when the Grammar dialog box is open, or from the **Tools** menu choose **Options**, and then choose the **Spelling & Grammar** tab in the Options dialog box.

To hide the grammar check marks while you work, click **Hide Grammatical Errors in This Document**. To turn automatic grammar checking off, deselect **Check Grammar as You Type**. Other options you can set include whether you want Word to check your grammar at the same time as it checks your spelling, whether you want to see readability statistics at the end of the grammar check, and writing style.

Readability statistics tell you the grade-level in school that a theoretical reader must have attained to read what you have written. In general, if you use big words and long sentences, you are writing to a more educated audience.

The **W**riting Style option (standard, formal, casual, or technical) determines what set of grammatical rules grammar check uses. You may also select a custom writing style, in which case you may select which grammar and style options you want checked. To turn a particular kind of grammar checking on or off, choose the **T**ools menu and select **O**ptions. In the Options dialog box select the **Spelling & Grammar** tab and then choose **Se**t**tings**.

# Consult the Thesaurus

Word includes a thesaurus to help you find *synonyms* (words with similar meanings) and *antonyms* (words with opposite meanings) for words in your document. Using the thesaurus not only helps your vocabulary, but gives you alternatives to using the same word over and over again throughout your text. Use the thesaurus as follows:

### Finding Alternate Words with Thesaurus

1. Place the insertion point in the word that you want to look up in the thesaurus. (If the insertion point appears between words, the thesaurus automatically selects the word preceding the insertion point.)

2. From the **T**ools menu, choose **L**anguage. Then select **T**hesaurus on the menu. Alternatively, press Shift+F7. The Thesaurus dialog box opens (see Figure 6.9).

3. Choose the options you want:

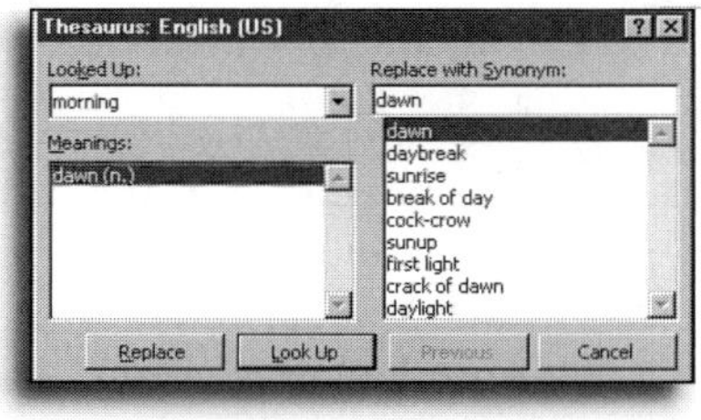

**How many spaces between sentences?**

The general rule is: Use one space between sentences if you are writing with a proportional font, such as Arial or Times; use two spaces between sentences if you are writing with a non-proportional font, such as Courier. Word's grammar check can check the number of spaces between sentences for you. To set up grammar check to check spacing, go to Grammar Settings. (From the **Tools** menu select **Options**. In the Options dialog box select the **Spelling & Grammar** tab and then **Se**t**tings**. Then select the **Spaces Between Sentences** option.)

**A quick synonym search**

Position your cursor in any properly spelled word and right-click for a list of synonyms.

FIGURE 6.9

Click the **Look Up** button if you want to find a synonym for another word.

- If Word provides *synonyms* for the looked up word, you can choose the meaning of the word as you are using it. After you choose a synonym you can either replace your word with the chosen synonym or look up synonyms for the synonym.

- If Word provides *antonyms* for the looked up word, you can choose one. After you choose an antonym you can either replace your word with the chosen antonym or you can look up synonyms for the antonym.

- Sometimes Word provides a list of similar words to the looked up word. You can choose a similar word, and then choose a meaning and a synonym for the similar word.

- Sometimes Word is unable to provide synonyms, antonyms, or related words for a looked up word. When this happens, Word displays an alphabetical list of words spelled similar to the looked up word. You can choose a word from the alphabetical list, then choose a synonym, antonym, or related word for the chosen word.

- You can enter another word in the **Looked Up** field or pick a word in the list of synonyms, and then choose **Look Up** to find synonyms for your new word.

- If you have looked up synonyms for synonyms, you can go back to a previous synonym by choosing **Previous**.

## Find and Replace Text

Someday you might need to find a particular word or phrase in a document, such as the name of a person in a contract document. Or you might need to replace every instance of underlining with italic. You could do it manually, but you don't have to because Word has a versatile tool—Find and Replace—that can find or replace text, formatting, and special characters (such as tab markers). Specifically, Find and Replace can find and/or replace the following things:

- *Text strings*. Either strings of text embedded in words, or discrete words or whole phrases.

- *Text strings with formatting*. Strings of text that are formatted a particular way, such as underlining.

- *Formatting*. Font formatting options, such as underlining and bold, that are not necessarily associated with words or text.

- *Styles*. Find all instances of a named style or replace one named style with another.

- *Special characters*. Tab markers, forced line breaks, non-breaking spaces, non-breaking hyphens, whitespace, and so on.

**SEE ALSO**

➤ *For information about styles, see page 237*

## Find Text

When you activate the Find feature, Word normally searches the entire document to find each occurrence of the text. To limit the scope of the search, select the text you want to search through before starting Find, and Find only searches through the selected text.

To activate Find, do one of the following:

- Open the **Edit** menu and select **Find**.
- Press Ctrl+F.
- Click the Select Browse Object icon ▣ in the vertical scrollbar (see Figure 6.10), then, in the pop-up menu click the Find icon 🔍.

The Find and Replace dialog box appears (see Figure 6.11), and the **Find** tab should already be selected.

FIGURE 6.10

Click the Select Browse Object icon located on the scrollbar to view the Find and Replace dialog box.

 Find icon

**2** Select the Browse Object icon

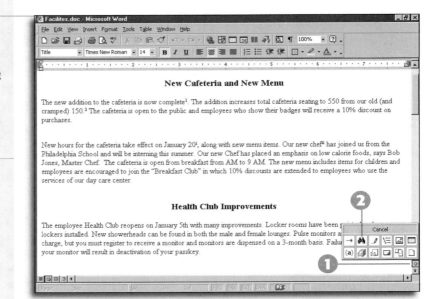

FIGURE 6.11

Enter the word or phrase you are seeking in the **Find What?** box.

## Search for Text

1. Type the text that you are seeking in the **Find What?** text box. This word or phrase is also referred to as the *search string*.

2. Choose the **More** button (if necessary) to specify search options, as explained in the section "Define Search Options," later in this chapter.

3. Choose **Find Next**. Find looks through the document for text that matches your search string. When it finds matching text, Word highlights the text in the document and stops. The Find and Replace dialog box remains onscreen.

**4.** Choose **Find Next** if you want to continue the search for another instance of the search string. Click **Cancel** or press Esc to close the dialog box and return to the document. The text in the document is still highlighted.

When Word finishes searching the entire document, or if it couldn't find the search string in the document, a dialog box displays a message to that effect. Choose **OK** to continue working in the document.

When you open the Find and Replace dialog box a second time during the same session of Word, the previous search string (if any) still displays in the **Find What?** text box. This makes it easy to repeat the previous search.

If you exit the Find and Replace dialog box, you can quickly jump to the next or previous occurrence of the search string text in your document by clicking on the Next Find/Go To or Previous Find/Go To buttons on the vertical scrollbar (as shown in Figure 6.12).

**Using the Select Browse Object icon**

The Find/Go To and Previous Find/Go To buttons display the next or previous item currently selected in the **Select Browse Object** menu. This could be footnotes, endnotes, comments, sections, and so forth. The default selection is a page, in which case these buttons work like a page up or page down button. When page is the current selection, the buttons appear in black. When any other item is selected, the buttons appear in blue. To reset the buttons so that they work as page up or page down, click the Select Browse button and choose the **Browse By Page** option in the pop-up menu.

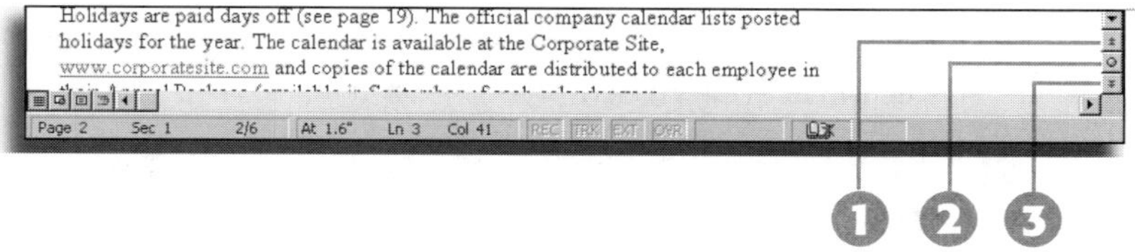

Holidays are paid days off (see page 19). The official company calendar lists posted holidays for the year. The calendar is available at the Corporate Site, www.corporatesite.com and copies of the calendar are distributed to each employee in

Page 2   Sec 1   2/6   At 1.6"   Ln 3   Col 41   REC TRK EXT OVR

**FIGURE 6.12**

Use the Find/Go To buttons to find text without opening the Find and Replace dialog box.

**1** Previous/Find Go To

**2** Select Browse Object

**3** Next/Find Go To

## Replace Text

In addition to finding text in your document, Word's Replace feature can replace your search string with new text. To replace text, do one of the following:

- From the **Edit** menu, select **Replace**.
- Press Ctrl+H.
- Click the Select Browse Object icon ⊙ in the vertical scrollbar, then, in the pop-up menu, click the Find icon 🔍 .

When the Find and Replace dialog box appears, select the **Replace** tab if it is not already selected (see Figure 6.13).

### Replace Text

1. Type the text you want to replace in the **Find What?** text box. You can leave this field blank but only if you want to search for formatting only. However, you have to search for something.

2. Type the text you want to replace it with in the **Replace With** text box. If you search for text and leave this field blank, you are in effect telling Word to delete all instances of the search string.

3. Choose the **More** button (if necessary) to specify search options as explained in the next section of this chapter.

4. Choose **Find Next** to locate and highlight the first occurrence of text that matches your search string.

5. Then do one of the following:

   • Choose **Replace** to replace the text matching the search string with the replacement text and then locate the next occurrence of the search string in your document.

   • Choose **Find Next** to leave the text matching the search string unchanged and to locate the next occurrence of the search string.

   • Choose **Replace All** to replace all text in the entire document that matches the search string with the replacement text.

6. Choose **Cancel**. Alternatively, press **Esc** to close the Find and Replace dialog box and return to your document.

When Word has finished searching through the document and has replaced all occurrences of the search text or can't find any further occurrences, a message box appears. Click **OK** to return to your document.

# Define Search Options

Unless you change the options, Find locates the search string even if it's in a different case or is part of another word. The search string "ten", for example, finds "ten", "TEN", "often", and so on. You can narrow your search with Word's search options by choosing **More** in the Find and Replace dialog box (it doesn't matter if you have the **Find** tab or the **Replace** tab selected). When you do, the dialog box expands to offer additional options (see Figure 6.14); choose **Less** to shrink the dialog box.

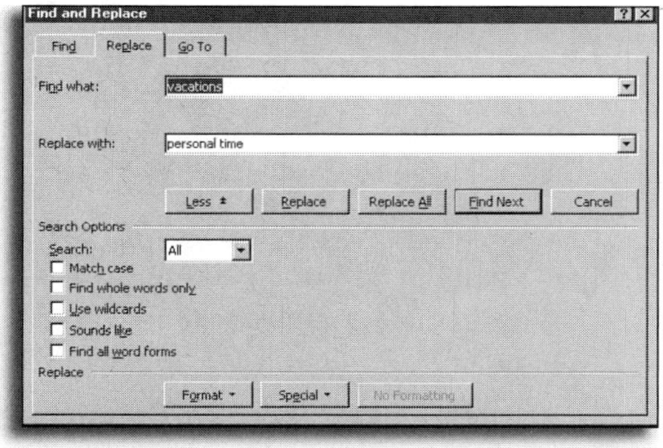

FIGURE 6.14

Choose **More** to expand the Find and Replace dialog box and to display options to narrow your search.

The following options are available in the Find and Replace dialog box:

- Click **Match Case** to require an exact match for uppercase and lowercase letters. When selected, "Ten" only matches "Ten" and not "ten" or "TEN".

- Click **Find Whole Words Only** to avoid finding text that is part of another word. Then, "ten" matches only "ten" and not "often", "attention", and so on. This is especially important if you plan to use the **Replace All** feature of **Find and Replace**, which will replace every instance of the **Find What** string with the **Replace With** string without consulting you.

**Using wildcards**

You can use * in the middle of a search string, but you may find a lot more words than you bargained for. For example, a search for s*t could produce "set," "sat," "sent," "suit," "suet," "spot," "sweet," "sweat," "sentient," "sentiment," and who knows what else. If you know exactly how many characters should be replaced by the wildcard, use ? instead, like this: s??t, which would find "sent," "suit," "suet," and "spot," but not "set," "sat," "sweet," "sweat," "sentient," "sentiment," or any other word that is not four letters in length.

- Click **Use Wildcards** to use * and ? wildcards in the search string. You use the * wildcard to match any sequence of zero or more characters and the ? wildcard to match a single character. The search string "ca?" would match "car," "can," but not "came" or "catch." The search string "ca*" would match "came," "catch," "canter," and so on.

- Click **Sounds Like** to find homonyms—words that sound similar to the search string. For example, "fare" would match "fair."

- Click **Find All Word Forms** to find alternate forms of the search string, such as "came" or "coming" to match "come." You can't use this option if you selected the **Use Wildcards** option.

To determine what part of the document you want to search, click the **Search** drop-down arrow and select one of the following:

- Select **All** to search the entire document. Word searches from the insertion point to the end of the document, then from the beginning of the document back to the insertion point.

- Select **Down** to search from the insertion point to the end of the document. Word searches from the insertion point to the end of the document then asks you if it should continue searching from the top of the document back to the insertion point.

- Select **Up** to search from the insertion point to the beginning of the document. Word searches from the insertion point to the beginning of the document, then asks you if it should continue searching from the end of the document back to the insertion point.

## Find and Replace Formatting Options

Find and Replace is able to find and replace text with specified formatting, such as replacing underlining with italics. Suppose, for example, that you want to replace a bolded word with bold and italic. Instead of searching for every instance of the word and manually applying italics, you can search for the bolded occurrences of the word and replace them with bold and italic. Use this method to find and replace character attributes, paragraph formatting, and styles.

**Find and Replace Text with Specified Formatting**

1. Open the **E**dit menu and choose **R**eplace.

2. In the **Fi**n**d What?** text box, type the word or phrase you want to replace. If you want to find only those bolded occurrences of the word, click the **Fo**rmat button, choose **F**ont and in the **Font Sty**le box select **Bold**. Otherwise, skip to step 3.

3. Click once in the **Replace Wi**th text box to activate it. If you want to change only the formatting of text, you don't have to retype the text here and you can skip to step 4. If you are replacing the text with new text, type the new text in the **Replace Wi**th box.

4. Click the **Fo**rmat button to select formatting options. Choose **F**ont and select the formatting options you want. Note that the effects options all have gray check marks as shown in Figure 6.15. By default, these options are all selected—each and every one of them—even though they appear to be grayed out. To find or replace text that is only bold and italic, you must deselect the effect options that do not apply and reselect those that do. Reselecting changes the check mark to black.

5. Click **F**ind **N**ext to find each occurrence of your search, and **R**eplace to replace it. Alternatively, click **Replace A**ll to replace all occurrences of the word in your document.

To find formatting of text, but not the text itself, leave the **Fi**n**d What?** and **Replace Wi**th text boxes empty, but choose the formatting options for each. In this way, you can replace formatting on any word, not just specific words.

**Be very careful with formatting options**

Word remembers the last search that you performed, including formatting options. Formatting can be applied to text you want to find and text you want to replace. Be certain to select the **Fi**n**d What?** or **Replace Wi**th text boxes *before* you click the **Fo**rmat button. To clear formatting options, click the **No Formatting** button as shown in Figure 6.14. It's a good idea to clear the formatting before beginning each new search.

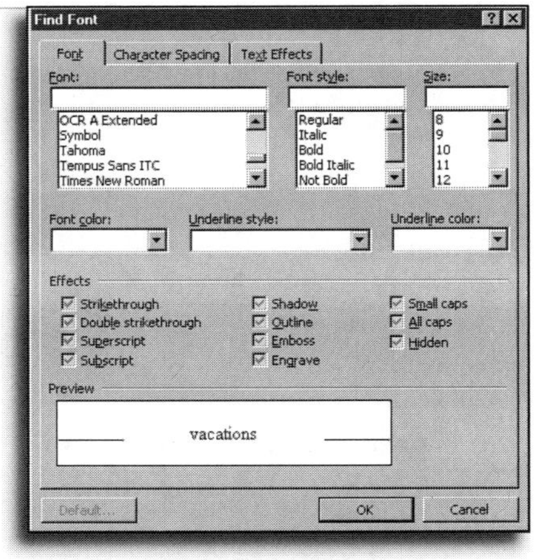

FIGURE 6.15

When you select **Font** as the formatting type, the Find Font dialog box appears.

FIGURE 6.15

When you select **Font** as the formatting type, the Find Font dialog box appears.

## Find and Replace Special Characters

Word can find and replace characters that don't appear on your keyboard such as paragraph marks, column breaks, non-breaking spaces, tabs, graphics, and so on.

To find or replace one of the special characters or a graphic, open the Find and Replace dialog box. Click in the **Find What?** or **Replace With** box. Choose **Special** to select from a pop-up list of unusual characters or graphics. (To search for regular spaces, press the Spacebar in the **Find What?** text box.) A code appears in the box that represents the item. Then conduct your Find and Replace as usual.

# Define and Modify AutoCorrect Entries

AutoCorrect is a handy feature of Microsoft Word that automatically corrects common typing, capitalization, and spelling errors for you, as you type. It also enables you to type shortcuts that AutoCorrect replaces with the full text, such as typing MS and having AutoCorrect replace it with Microsoft. Although Word has a number of default AutoCorrect entries, you can add your own common misspellings and shortcuts.

AutoCorrect only checks whole words, so if you type adn, Word won't replace it with and until you press the Spacebar, period, or some other key that indicates the word is complete.

AutoCorrect is also a useful tool for applying formatting options. In a business letter, for example, you might want your company name to always appear in a certain font and size, regardless of the font you are using for the letter. By creating an AutoCorrect entry of your company name with formatting options, you eliminate the need to format while you type, or to run search and replace when you are finished with the letter.

## Replace Text As You Type

You can add new entries to AutoText during a spell check (see the "Run Spell Check" section at the beginning of this chapter), or in the AutoCorrect dialog box. After an entry has been added to the AutoCorrect list, corrections (or formatting options) are applied to the word at the time you type it and after you press the Spacebar at the end of the word.

To see how AutoCorrect works with its default entries, type the characters adn. When you press the Spacebar, Word corrects your typo to and. With some special characters, Word does not wait until you press the Spacebar. For example, to create a registered trademark, ®, type (r). When you press the right parenthesis, the registered trademark replaces your text. If you don't want the trademark, but really want (r), press the Backspace key immediately after you type the right parenthesis and before you press the Spacebar.

### Add AutoCorrect Entries Without Formatting

1. From the **Tools** menu, select **AutoCorrect** to open the AutoCorrect dialog box (see Figure 6.16). Click the **AutoCorrect** tab if it's not already selected.

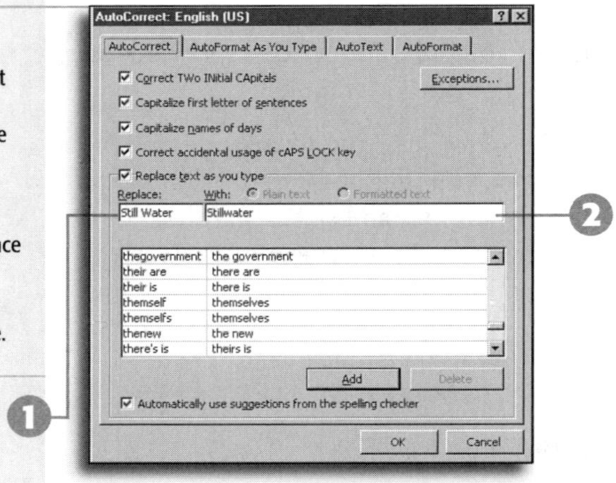

FIGURE 6.16

Define or modify AutoCorrect entries by typing the misspelling or shortcut text in the **Replace** box and the text to replace it in the **With** box.

**1** Type text you want to replace here.

**2** Type replacement text here.

2. Click **Replace Text as You Type** to place a check mark there, if it isn't already checked.

3. In the **Replace** box, enter the text you want AutoCorrect to automatically replace for you, such as your initials or a word you commonly misspell.

4. Click **Plain Text** if it is not selected to insert text without formatting options.

5. Choose **Add**. If the text in the **Replace** box is already listed, choose **Replace** to replace the existing replacement text with the text you entered in the **With** box.

6. Choose **OK**.

Test your new AutoCorrect entry by typing the word in a document and pressing the Spacebar.

### Add New AutoCorrect Entries with Formatting

1. Type the text in your document and format it.

2. Select the text. To store paragraph formatting with your entry, include the paragraph mark at the end of the text, in your selection.

3. From the **Tools** menu, select **AutoCorrect**. The AutoCorrect dialog box appears (see Figure 6.17).

4. In the **Replace** text box, type a name for the AutoCorrect entry (an abbreviation, or the entire word or phrase).

5. Click **Formatted Text**.

6. To save the entry and close the dialog box, click **Add**.

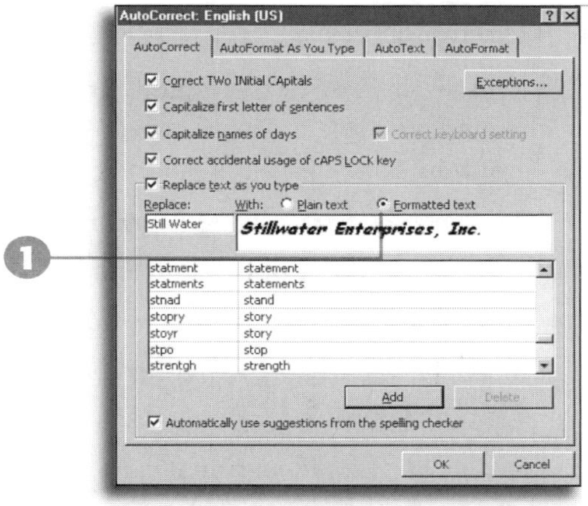

**FIGURE 6.17**

Formatted AutoCorrect entries display their formatting in the AutoCorrect dialog box.

1 Click here for **Formatted Text**.

# Change How Word Handles Capitalization

By default, AutoCorrect handles common capitalization problems. For example, it capitalizes the first letter of the first word in a sentence. Word also corrects or changes the following:

- Two initial capitals. If you do not release the Shift key quickly enough and your word contains two initial capital letters, word changes the second letter to lowercase.

- Days of the week. Word capitalizes days of the week.

- Accidental use of Caps Lock key. If you accidentally leave the Caps Lock key on, Word switches uppercase letters to lowercase and vice versa.

In most cases, the Word default settings for handling capitalization work well. However, there are exceptions. Two areas in which you may find exceptions are the use of abbreviations that contain periods and the use of two initial capitals. For example, you can abbreviate included, including, or inclusive using "incl" followed by a period. But if this abbreviated word appears in the middle of a sentence, whatever immediately follows it will be capitalized by Word. Word views the period as the end of a sentence. What if your company name is "IBeam"? Word's default settings change the company name to "Ibeam." When you encounter these situations, you have two choices: disable the first letter of sentence or two initial caps options, or create exceptions to those rules.

To disable any of the capitalization settings, open the **Tools** menu and select **AutoCorrect**. Deselect the capitalization option.

### Create Exceptions to Word Capitalization Settings

1. Open the **Tools** menu and choose **AutoCorrect**.
2. Click the **Exceptions** button (see Figure 6.18).
3. The AutoCorrect Exceptions dialog box appears, as shown in Figure 6.18.
   - To add an initial caps exception (such as IBeam), click the **INitial CAps** tab and type your exception in the **Don't Correct** text box.
   - To add an abbreviated word that includes a period (such as incl.) click the **First Letter** tab and type the word with it's period in the **Don't Capitalize After** text box (see Figure 6.18).
4. Click **OK** to return to the AutoCorrect dialog box.
5. Click **OK** to return to your document.

To modify the AutoCorrect entries, do one of the following:

- Select an AutoCorrect entry and choose **Delete** to delete it from the list.
- Select an entry that you want to modify, edit the text in the **With** text box, and choose **Replace**.

Choose **OK** to accept your changes and to close the Auto-Correct dialog box. Choose **Cancel** to close the dialog box without saving your changes.

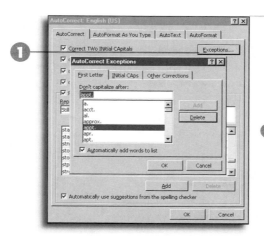

FIGURE 6.18

In the AutoCorrect Exceptions dialog box, you can specify which words you don't want automatically followed by a capital letter or which words are exceptions to the two-initial caps rule.

**①** **Exceptions** button

# Create and Insert AutoText

AutoCorrect stores frequently used text or graphics that *automatically* replace designated text entries. AutoText (called the *Glossary* in older versions of Word) also keeps frequently used text and graphics for you but only inserts them in the document when you call for them—not automatically. For example, you could store your company logo as an AutoText entry and insert it in your document when you press the appropriate keys. AutoText is also useful for abbreviating entries of larger bodies of text, such as addresses or frequently used boilerplate paragraphs.

### Creating an AutoText Entry

**1.** Select whatever text and/or graphics you want to include in the AutoText entry. Be sure to include the paragraph marker in the selection if you want the text's paragraph formatting to be part of the entry.

**2.** On the **Insert** menu, select **AutoText**. Then select the option **New**. You can also press Alt+F3, or choose **New** on the AutoText toolbar. The Create AutoText dialog box appears (see Figure 6.19).

---

**Using the AutoText toolbar**

If you use AutoText frequently, you may find it convenient to have the AutoText toolbar displayed. From the **View** menu select **Toolbars**. Then select **AutoText**.

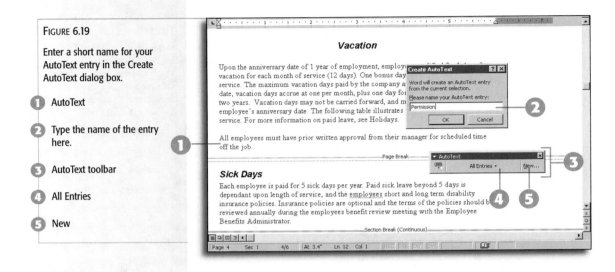

**3.** Accept the entry name that automatically appears or enter
your own in the **Please Name Your AutoText Entry** text
box.

**4.** Choose **OK**.

AutoText entries can be inserted into your documents in several
different ways:

- Type the name of the AutoText entry and then press F3.

- From the **Insert** menu, select **AutoText**. Then select the
desired entry from the submenu.

- Choose the middle button on the AutoText toolbar to see a
list of available AutoText entries. If the current text style is
Normal, this button is labeled **All Entries**. Otherwise, the
button has the name of the current paragraph style (see
Figure 6.20). Then select the entry you want from the list
that appears.

- When AutoComplete is enabled (as explained later in this
section), Word displays a matching AutoText entry in a small
pop-up menu next to the insertion point when you have
typed enough of the AutoText entry name to identify the
entry, as shown in Figure 6.21. Press F3 or Enter to insert
the entire entry. To ignore it, keep typing.

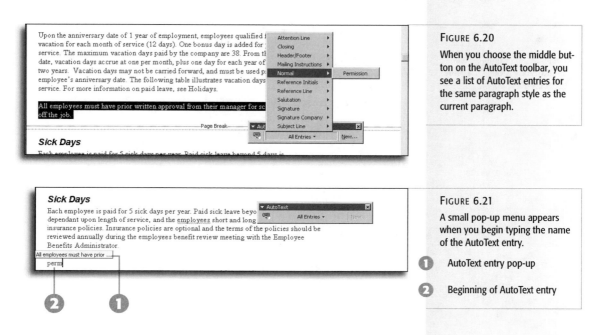

**FIGURE 6.20**
When you choose the middle button on the AutoText toolbar, you see a list of AutoText entries for the same paragraph style as the current paragraph.

**FIGURE 6.21**
A small pop-up menu appears when you begin typing the name of the AutoText entry.

① AutoText entry pop-up

② Beginning of AutoText entry

**SEE ALSO**
➤ *To learn more information about paragraph styles, see page 241*

As mentioned previously, the AutoText list displays only those entries that match the current paragraph style, unless the current style is Normal. To display all entries, regardless of style, hold down the Shift key while clicking the AutoText toolbar or choose **AutoText** from the **Insert** menu.

### Activate the AutoComplete Option

**1.** On the **Insert** menu, select **AutoText** and then select **AutoText...** from the submenu, or choose AutoText  on the AutoText toolbar to open the AutoText dialog box. You also can select the **Tools** menu and then choose **Auto-Correct**. Then click the **AutoText** tab to open the dialog box (see Figure 6.22).

FIGURE **6.22**

Enable the AutoComplete feature of AutoText by clicking the **Show AutoComplete** option.

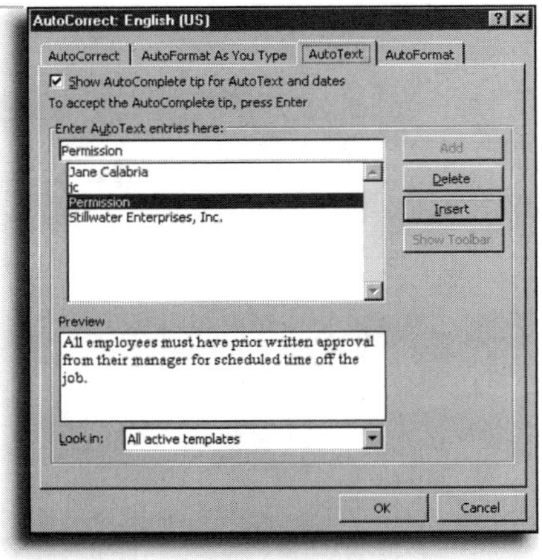

2. Click **Show AutoComplete Tip for AutoText and Dates** to place a check mark there.

3. Choose **OK**.

When you want to remove an AutoText entry from the AutoText dialog list, open the AutoText dialog box (as described in step 1).

Select the entry you want to remove from the list, and then choose **Delete**. Choose **OK**.

# Manage Files

Find and open an existing file

Create folders to organize and store your documents

Rename your documents

Save your documents in formats acceptable to other applications or other versions of Word

Use the summary data Word stores with your file

# Know the Open and Save As Dialog Box Options

The Open and Save As dialog boxes are designed to help you locate and manipulate files. In that way, they are like the Windows Explorer and they incorporate many features of the Windows Explorer. You can frequently save yourself the trouble of opening the Windows Explorer by just going to the Open or Save As dialog box instead.

Some of the features available in the Open and/or Save As dialog boxes include the following:

- Standard file management tools, such as delete, rename, cut, copy, paste files or folders, create new folders, print files, send files to various destinations (floppy disk, mail recipient, My Briefcase), create shortcuts, and map network drives.

- Add files to Zip files (if you have installed WinZip).

- Select multiple files with the Shift and Ctrl keys, and then perform file management (such as **Open**, **Print**, **Cut**, **Copy**, **Delete**, or **Create Shortcut**) on all of them at once.

- Open files in a variety of ways, including **Open Read-Only** and **Open as Copy**.

- Open files located on FTP servers on the Internet or an intranet, and save files to FTP servers.

- View files in several different ways with the Views button—List, Details, Properties, and Preview.

- Sort files by name, file type, size, or date modified.

- View the contents of multiple folders in one view, either sorted by name, file type, size, or data modified, or grouped by folder.

- View the properties or preview the contents of files.

You can reach the various functions available in the Open and Save As dialog boxes in three ways (see Figure 7.1):

- Right-click a file, folder or blank space to pop up a menu of commands. Some of the commands vary, depending on whether you are in the Open or Save As dialog box and whether you right-click a file or folder.

- Click the buttons across the top of the Open and Save As dialog boxes.
- Click the **Tools** button to drop down a menu of commands. The commands vary depending on whether you are in the Open or Save As dialog box.

FIGURE 7.1

Clicking **Tools** in the Open and Save As dialog boxes displays a menu of things you can do to files and folders other than opening or saving them.

# Open Recently Used Files

There are several ways to find and open a Word document. You can use the Most Recently Used list in the **File** menu, use the Open dialog box and name the file you want to open, search the document summary information as described in this chapter, or use Windows 95 methods such as the **Start** menu or Explorer.

The best method for finding and opening an existing Word document depends on your circumstances. If you have worked on the document recently, you can probably pick the filename from a Most Recently Used list of files. When you know the name and location of a file, you can use a method that allows you to enter that information. In cases where you can't find the file in a list and can't remember the filename or location, you can use a search tool to locate the file.

The easiest method for finding and opening a file is usually to use one of the Most Recently Used (MRU) lists, found either in the **Documents** submenu of the **Start** menu or in the Word **File** menu (see Figure 7.2). These lists contain the names of the last few files you have saved (the number of files in each list varies). To access a file from this list, click the filename (alternatively, press the number of the document). Provided you have not moved the file from its original location (disk and folder), renamed it, or deleted it Word automatically opens the file.

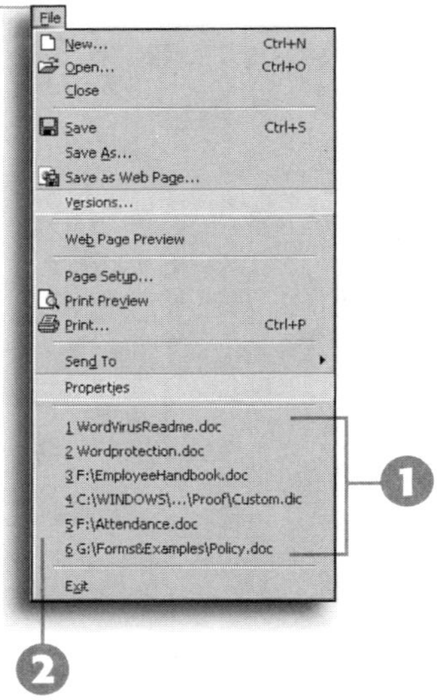

FIGURE 7.2

By default, Word lists only four files on the MRU list but you can change this, as you can see from this figure. To change the number of files that appear in the MRU, open the **Tools** menu and select **Options**.

**1** Click file here...

**2** ...or press a file number on the keyboard.

To change the number of files that appear in Word's MRU, access the Options dialog box. You can display as many as nine filenames or disable the MRU by removing the check mark next to the Most Recently Used file list.

### Change How Many Files are Listed in the Most Recently Used Files List

1. Choose **Tools**, and then select **Options** from the menu.

2. Click the **General** tab of the Options dialog box (see Figure 7.3).

3. Use the arrow keys (spinners) in the **Entries** box to indicate the number of files you would like to see listed in the MRU list (you can set a maximum of 9).

   To disable the MRU, remove the check mark next to **Recently Used File List**.

4. Click **OK**.

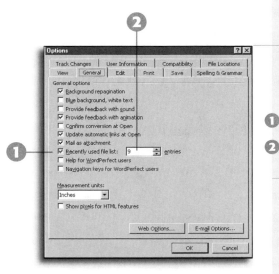

FIGURE 7.3

Display up to nine filenames in the Most Recently Used list of the **File** Menu.

1 Disable/Enable here

2 Use arrow keys to increase/decrease number of files here

# Open Files Not Found in the Most Recently Used List

It's very possible that you need to open a file that does not appear in the Most Recently Used list. This could be a file that you haven't accessed recently, or one that was created with another program, such as WordPerfect.

To open a file, choose **File**, then select **Open** from the menu or click the Open icon 🖻 on the Standard toolbar. The Open dialog box appears as shown in Figure 7.4. The file list displays all Word documents found in the current folder (documents with the file extension .doc). The current folder is identified in the **Look In** box. Folders are represented by Folder icons. Documents have Page icons.

FIGURE 7.4

From the Open dialog box you can preview, search for, and open files.

1. File list

2. Folder icon

3. Document icon

4. Look in list box

5. Previous folder

6. Up one level button

7. Preview pane

8. File name list box

9. Files of type list box

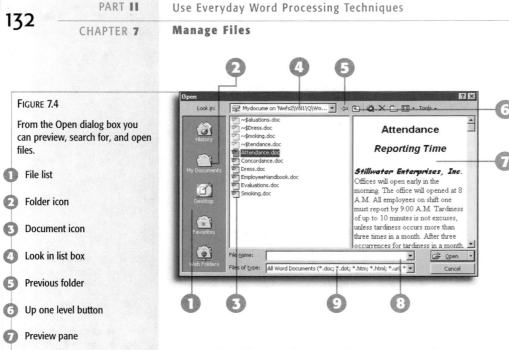

**Viewing your files**

The files and folders in the file list of the Open and Save As dialog boxes can be viewed in one of four displays by choosing the **Views** button ⊞. **List** is a simple list of the file or folder names next to their icons. **Details** illustrates the name, size, type, and last date modified for the files and folders. **Properties** displays the file or folder properties for the selected item. **Preview** shows the beginning text (or picture) of the selected file.

The following list describes options and actions you take in the Open dialog box:

- To open a file, click the filename and click **Open**. Alternatively, double-click a filename or click the filename and press Enter. If you know the exact name of a file, type the filename in the **File Name** box.

- To open a file in Read-only mode, right-click it, and then choose **Open Read-Only** from the menu that appears. Alternatively, select the file and then click the down arrow next to the **Open** button and select **Open Read-Only**.

- To open a copy of a file, right-click the file or select the file and click the down arrow next to the **Open** button, and then choose **Open as Copy** from the menu that appears. The file appears in a window titled **Copy of [*filename*]**.

- To preview a file, click the filename; then click the **Views** button ⊞. Select **Preview** from the menu. The file appears in the preview pane.

- To navigate through folders, click the **Up One Level** button, or double-click a folder to open it. To locate a folder not found in the file list, click the drop-down arrow in the

Look **In** box, and select another folder. To go back to a folder you opened previously, click the **Previous Folder** button ⟵. The most frequently used folders—History, My Documents, Desktop, Favorites, and Web Folders—are displayed on the left of the dialog box; click a button to open that folder.

- To see a list of files other than Word documents, click the drop-down arrow in the **Files of Type** box and select the types of files you want to view. Select **All Files** if you are unsure of a file type.

- If you want frequent quick access to a file or folder, select it and then select **Add to Favorites** from the **Tools** menu. That adds a shortcut for the file or folder to the Favorites folder. Later you can quickly locate the shortcut by clicking **Favorites** 🗀 on the left side of the dialog box.

You can also open Word files from My Computer or Windows Explorer by double-clicking the file. This starts the Word program and opens the file.

## Perform File Searches

If you need to search for files based on their properties or by using the same search criteria repeatedly, you can use Word's Advanced Find feature to define complex searches and to save searches for re-use later. Open the Find dialog box (see Figure 7.5) by clicking **Tools** in the Open dialog box and selecting **Find**.

In the Find dialog box you can define searches based on multiple search criteria. If you made entries in any of the **File Name** or **Files of Type** fields in the Open dialog box before you chose **Find**, those entries appear in the Find dialog box's list of search criteria.

You can delete those search criteria by selecting them and choosing Delete. You can clear all the search criteria by choosing **New Search**. You can retrieve a previously saved set of search criteria by choosing **Open Search**. You can add search criteria by filling

**Where are the file extensions?**

If the file extensions aren't displayed, select **Folder Options** from the **View** menu, click the **View** tab, and then deselect **Hide File Extensions for Known File Types**. If you're using Windows 95, open the Windows Explorer. Select the **View** menu and then choose **Options**. Deselect **Hide File Extensions for Known File Types**. Click **OK**.

in the fields in the **Define More Criteria** section. Choose **And** or **Or**, choose a **Property**, choose a **Condition**, and (depending on the property and condition you chose) optionally enter a **Value**. Then choose **Add to List**. Use **And** if you want to find files that meet the criteria in the **Find Files That Match These Criteria** box plus match the conditions you set for more criteria. Use **Or** if you want to find files that either meet one set of criteria or the other set.

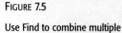

FIGURE 7.5

Use Find to combine multiple search criteria to locate files.

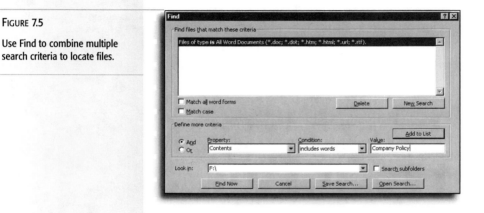

As an example for searching with conditions, let's say you need to find any documents that concern the ABC Company. Because you had All Word Documents selected in the Files of Type dialog box, that criteria is already entered in the **Find Files That Match These Criteria** box. Select **And**, choose **Contents** from the **Property** list, select **Includes Words** as the **Condition**, and enter ABC Company as the **Value**. Word will then search for all files that mention ABC Company.

Enter the pathname of the folder through which Word should search in the **Look In** field. Check **Search Subfolders** if you want Word to look in subfolders. Check **Match All Word Forms** and **Match Case** to further refine your search.

If you think you will want to reuse the search, choose **Save Search** and give the search a name. Otherwise choose **Find Now** to return to the Open dialog box and have Word conduct the search. Word returns the search results in the Open dialog box.

# Use Different Methods to View Files

By default, the folders and then the files in the file list appear in alphabetical order by filename. There are times, however, when it would be easier to find the files you need if the file list were in a different order.

To change the order of the list, click the **Views** button [icon], select **Arrange Icons**, and make one of the following choices:

- **By** **N**ame displays the list in alphabetical order by folder or filename.
- **By** **T**ype displays the list in alphabetical order by file extension.
- **By** **Si**ze displays the list in order by the size of the file (in bytes), from smallest to largest.
- **By** **D**ate displays the files in order based on the date the file was last modified.

If you are viewing the files using the Details view (click **Views** [icon] and select **Details**), the filename, size, type, and modified date appear for each file. Click the column header to sort the files again based on the information in that column. For instance, clicking **Modified** sorts the files by last date modified. That normally puts the oldest files last. To reverse the date order, click the header again to list the files with the oldest shown first. This same method works with the other headers too.

# Speed Up Saves with Fast Saves and Background Saves

If your file is large, saving it can take several seconds, even more on a slow computer. This can be a real distraction to a writer on a roll, trying to get her thoughts into words. Word lets you alleviate the distraction with two features that speed up saves—fast saves and background saves.

The alternative to a full save is a fast save. When Word does a fast save, it only saves changes you have made since the last save;

it appends the changes to the end of the previously saved copy of the file. When Word does a full save, it resaves the whole document, replacing the disk copy entirely with the copy in memory. As you can imagine, a fast save is potentially much faster than a full save. The downside is that the file keeps getting bigger as successive edits keep getting appended to the end of the file. If you activate fast saves, Microsoft recommends that you turn off fast saves at the end of each session, then do one last save. (You can also leave Fast Saves on and use Save **A**s and save the file to the same filename which will do a full save without requiring you to turn Fast Saves off.) This is a full save and it shrinks the file back to its minimum size. We recommend that you stay away from fast saves.

Activate fast saves by opening the Options dialog box (choose **Tools**, and then select **Options**) to the **Save** tab, and choose **Allow _F_ast Saves**.

You can also activate background saves—choose **Allow Background Saves** on the **Save** tab of the Options dialog box. If background saving is active, when you tell Word to save a document, it does so in the background. This allows you to continue working on the document while Word is saving it (Word only saves the changes you made before commanding it to save). The problem with background saving is that Word needs processor time and memory to accomplish it. If your computer has a slow processor or is low on RAM, background saves will tax it so heavily that you may not be able to work anyway until after Word finishes saving the document.

## Change Document Names

When you're working with a saved document or file, you might need to rename it. Typically you do this when you want to create a document that is similar to an existing one. You open the original document and save it to a different name. Then your modifications are made in the new file and the original file remains intact. For example, you created a welcome letter for a new client and saved it with the client's name. Now you want to send a similar letter to another new client. Open the original letter and save it with a new name so your changes won't affect the original, make your modifications to the new file, print it (if you need to), and save it.

### Saving a File with a Different Filename

1. Click **File**, and then select **Save As** on the menu. The Save As dialog box appears (see Figure 7.6).

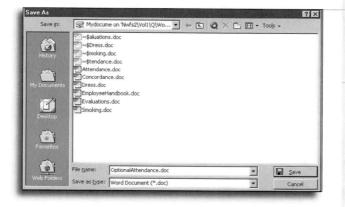

FIGURE 7.6

Replace the name of the file with the new name and then choose **Save**.

2. The current document name appears in the **File Name** text box. The name is highlighted, so typing the new filename automatically replaces the current filename.

3. (Optional) To save the document in a different folder or on a different drive, select the folder and/or drive from the **Save In** list box.

4. Choose **Save**. The document is saved with the new name (it appears on the Word title bar) but the original file still exists under its original name.

**SEE ALSO**

➤ *Save successive versions of the same document, page 520*

# Save Files in Different File Formats

When you're sharing files with others, on your office network or through email or Internet mail, you may need to save the document in a format the recipient can use with his version of Word or with another word processing program.

### Saving a File in a Different Format

1. With your document open, click **File**, and then select **Save As** on the menu.

2. When the Save As dialog box opens (see Figure 7.7), enter the name you want to give the file in the **File Name** box. If you're converting the file to another version of Word (that uses the same .doc file extension as Word 97), you may want to give the file a different name than your current document so that you don't overwrite your original Word 97 document.

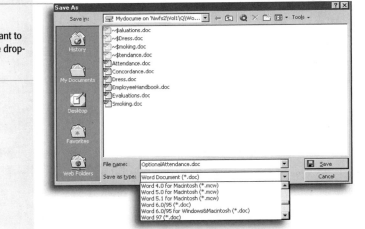

FIGURE 7.7

Select the file format you want to use from the **Save as Type** drop-down list.

3. From the **Save In** box, select the drive and folder where you want to store the file.

4. Select the file format in which you want to save the file from the **Save as Type** drop-down list. Use **Word 6.0/95** to exchange files with users of Microsoft Word 6.0 or 7.0 for Windows 95 (users of Word 97 should be able to read your files without changing the format). Select **Web Page** to save the document as a Web-ready page for your Internet or intranet Web site. (If the word processor file format you

need isn't listed, ask the person who will be opening the file to tell you what formats his word processor can accept, such as Text Only or Rich Text Format.)

**5.** (Optional) If others will be opening the document in Word and you think they might not have the TrueType fonts that you used, you can embed copies of the fonts in the document, so that the other users will open the documents using the fonts you chose. To do this, choose **Too**l**s**, **General Options** in the Save As dialog box. This opens the Save dialog box, where you can select **Embed TrueType Fonts**. If you only used 32 or fewer characters of some fonts, you can also choose **Embed Chara**c**ters in Use Only**. This will minimize the increase in the size of your document that embedding the fonts will cause.

**6.** Choose **Save** to convert your document to the format you have chosen.

If you are creating pages for your Internet or intranet Web site, the formatting instructions in the document must be in Hypertext Markup Language (HTML). Word converts documents to HTML for you when you follow the preceding steps. However, if you only need to save your file in HTML format and don't need to convert a file you already saved as a Word document, you should use the following steps.

### Saving a Document in HTML Format

**1.** With the document open, click the **File** menu, and then select **Save as Web Pa**g**e** on the menu to open the Save As HTML dialog box (see Figure 7.8).

**2.** Enter a name for the document in the **File Name** box. The HTML file extension is automatically added to the filename. The **Save as Type** automatically displays **Web Page** as the file format.

**3.** From the **Save In** drop-down list, select the drive and folder where you want to store the file.

**4.** Choose **Save**.

---

**Word 6.0/Word 95 file sizes**

When you save a file in the Word 6.0/Word 95 format, the file you save can be significantly larger than the original Word 2000 file. Also, if you work with huge documents or many graphics in Word 2000, you will have to break documents over 32MB into smaller pieces to save them in Word 6.0/ Word 95.

FIGURE 7.8

In the Save As dialog box, the Web Page file format is automatically selected.

**SEE ALSO**

➤ *For more information on HTML documents, see page 603*

# View Document Properties

Word keeps a set of information, called *properties*, about each document you create. Document properties contain information such as filename, location and size of the file, and summary and statistical information. Word gathers and maintains much of the information automatically. Some of it you add yourself, either because Word makes you (for example, the filename) or optionally (for example, the summary information). In fact, you can record just about any information about a document that you think might be useful to you later. Document properties are useful for a variety of reasons:

- You can keep a library of Word documents organized
- You can locate lost documents
- You can analyze the contents of a document using document properties
- You can track the history of a document through document properties

### Viewing a Document's Properties

1. With the document open, click the **File** menu, and then select **Properties** to open the Properties dialog box (see Figure 7.9).

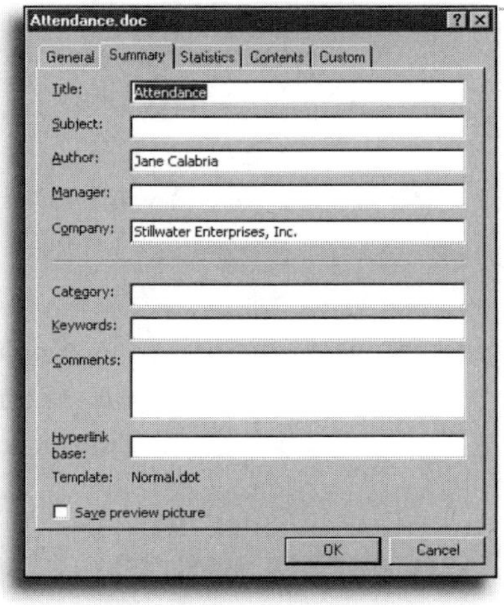

FIGURE 7.9
Word stores information about your document in the Properties dialog box.

2. Click the tab that contains the information you want to see:

- **General**. Information on this tab includes the filename and location, the type of file, the size (in bytes), and the created, modified, and last accessed dates.

- **Summary**. Although you can modify the data on this tab, Word supplies a title, the author's name, and the author's company. You can add a subject, a manager, a document category, keywords to help find the document when you're searching for it, a hyperlink base (the generalized location that all your hyperlinks in the document have in common), and the name of the template on which the document is based. If **Save Preview Picture** is checked, an image of the first page of the document appears in the Open dialog box when you select the document.

- **Statistics**. From the Statistics tab you can learn who saved the document last, what revision this version of the document is, how much time was involved when the document was last edited, and how many pages, paragraphs, lines, words, and characters there are in the document.

- **Contents**. This tab lists the headings in the document, but only if you selected **Save Preview Picture** on the **Summary** tab.

- **Custom**. Use this tab to create your own properties that you want to track. You must give each custom property a name, assign a type, and enter a value for the property.

3. When you have finished viewing the properties, choose **OK** to accept any changes you made or choose **Close** to close the dialog box without saving changes.

# Find a Document Using Summary Information

The Document Summary collects important information about each document such as the document author and title. You can search for a document on the basis of Document Summary information or incorporate the Document Summary information into the document itself. To incorporate Document Summary information into the document, you add to the document fields whose content is derived from the Document Summary. For example, add fields that automatically place the author's name and the document filename in the footer.

### Inserting Document Summary Field Codes in a Document

1. Position your insertion point where you want the field to appear in the document.

2. Click the **Insert** menu, and then select **Field** on the menu. The Field dialog box appears (see Figure 7.10).

3. From the **Categories** list box, click **Document Information**.

4. A list of fields appears in the **Field Names** box. These names reference fields in the Document Properties dialog box, many of which are from the Document Summary. Click a field name and then refer to the **Description** at the bottom of the dialog box for an explanation of that field.

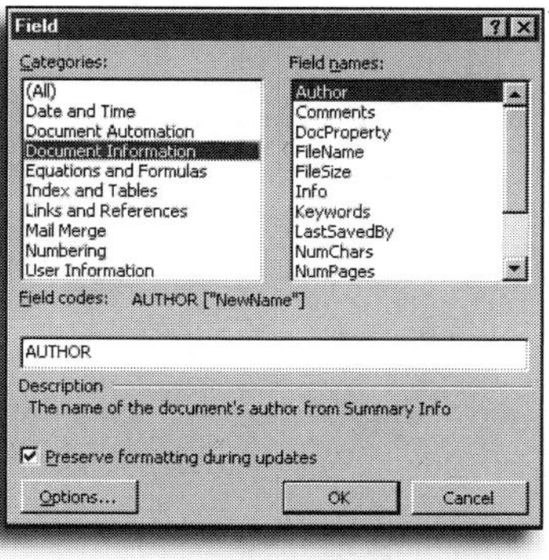

FIGURE 7.10

Choose a field name that matches one of the fields in the Document Summary.

**5.** Click the field name you want to use and choose **OK**. The data appears in your document. Figure 7.11 shows the field codes in a header. (To see field codes in your document, from the **Tools** menu, select **Options**, then click the **View** tab, and click **Field Codes** under **Show**. Choose **OK**.)

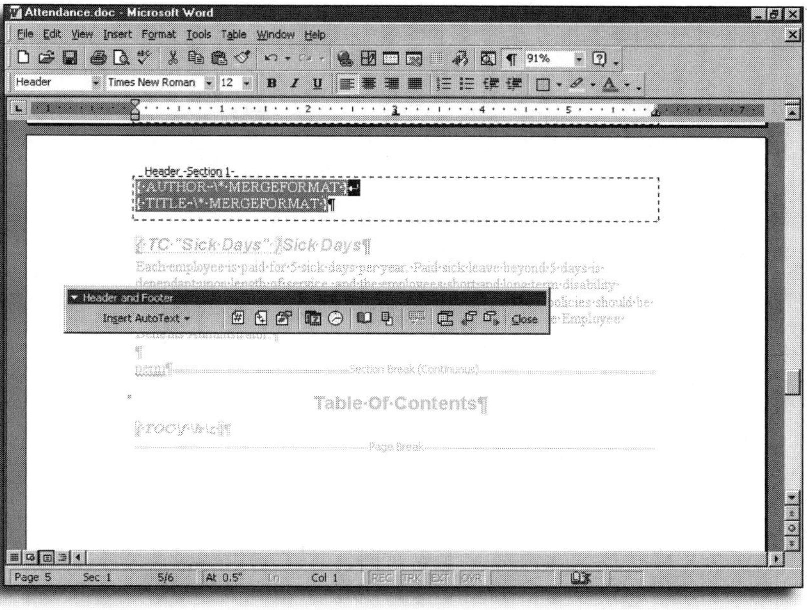

FIGURE 7.11

The field codes in this header pull information from the Document Summary.

**SEE ALSO**
➤ *Learn more about creating headers and footers, page 295*

Finding files can be simplified if you use the field information on the **Summary** tab of the **Document** properties.

### Use Document Summary Information to Find Documents

1. Click the **File** menu and then select **Open** or choose the Open button 🗁 on the Standard toolbar. The Open dialog box appears.

2. In the **Look In** box, display the drive or folder that you want to search for the file.

3. Make sure that **Word Documents** shows in the **Files of Type** box.

4. Click **Tools** and choose **Find**. The Find dialog box opens (see Figure 7.12).

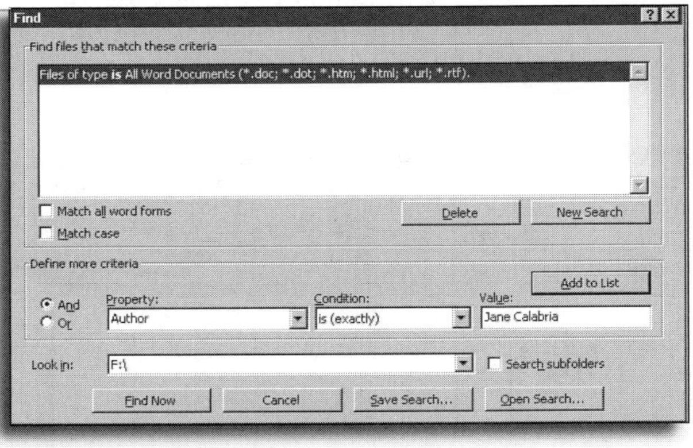

FIGURE 7.12

In the Find dialog box, you specify which Summary field you want to use in your search and for what value you're looking.

5. Under **Define More Criteria**, click **And** or **Or**. When you choose **And** the file found must meet all the criteria; when you use **Or** the file found must meet one criteria or the other but not all.

6. From the **Property** box, select the **Summary** field that contains the information on which you want to base your search, such as **Author**, **Category**, **Keywords**, and so on.

7. From the **Condition** box, select a condition such as **Includes** or **Begins With**. For example, if you choose **Keywords** as the **Property**, **Includes Words** as the **Condition**, and **email** as the **Value**, Word finds all the files

in the Document Summary where the Keywords property contains the text "email."

**8.** In the **Val<u>u</u>e** box, enter the text for which you're searching.

**9.** The **Look <u>I</u>n** box should contain the drive and file path you selected in the Open dialog box. To also search the subdirectories under that, click **Searc<u>h</u> Subfolders**.

**10.** Choose **<u>A</u>dd to List**.

**11.** Choose **<u>F</u>ind Now**.

**12.** The Open dialog box reappears (see Figure 7.13), displaying only the files that met the search criteria. Select the file you want and choose **Open**.

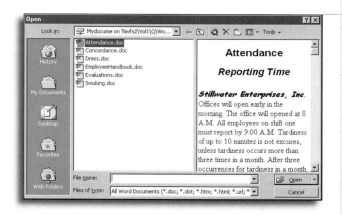

FIGURE 7.13
The result of the search appears in the Open dialog box.

CHAPTER

8

# Protect Your Files and Control File Access

Protect your files from computer viruses

Prevent unauthorized persons from modifying your documents

Use passwords to limit access to your documents

Make documents available to other users by sharing

Create folders to organize and store your documents

Recover files after a crash or power loss

Back up files to prevent their loss

# Avoid Viruses

A computer *virus* is an incomplete piece of programming that can do nothing on its own but, if attached to another program, can take over the other program and carry out its own mission instead of that of the host program. So, when you run the host program, it does something wholly unexpected and usually unwelcome. It may do something benign, like displaying a message on your screen. Or it may do something malicious, like deleting files or reformatting your hard disk.

Part of the programming built into every virus is the ability to spread itself to other programs. When you run a program that is infected with a virus, the virus loads into your computer's memory and waits for opportunities to install copies of itself into other programs on your computer. Then, when you send a newly infected program to someone else, his programs become infected too. It's very easy to pass computer viruses around, without even being aware of it, so you must take extraordinary measures to avoid passing them around.

There are three general categories of viruses:

- *Boot sector viruses*. These infect the program that resides in the boot sector of every hard and floppy disk. Your computer becomes infected when you receive an infected floppy disk, forget to remove it from your disk drive when you turn off your computer, then reboot with it in the drive the next time you turn on your computer. That loads the virus into your computer memory, and from there the virus infects your hard disk and any floppy disks you put into your disk drive.

- *Program file viruses*. These infect executable program files, such as .exe and .com files, and the library (.dll) and overlay (.ovl) files that the executables call into memory from time to time. Your programs become infected when you run them and then the virus infects other programs on your computer.

- *Macro viruses*. These infect specific kinds of data files. Word documents, for example, store programs in the form of Word macros. When you load a document that contains the virus macro or when you create a new document based on a template that contains a macro virus, the macro writes a copy of itself into your Normal template. Because your Normal template is the basis for most of your documents, the virus then gets written into every Word file you load into memory. The next thing you know, you're sharing the file with a coworker and spreading the virus.

How do you avoid viruses? One way is to never download a file from the Internet, open a network file created on someone else's PC, or put floppy disks into your PC that have been in other computers. That's not very practical in today's workplace.

The other way to avoid viruses is to install and use a virus protection program that detects and removes any virus infection from your hard disk or any floppy disks you insert in your drive. You can purchase virus protection software at your local software supplier, probably at less than $100. Most antivirus programs check your programs while your computer is running, scan new programs as you install them, and look for viruses on your floppy disks. The protection program lets you know if a virus is detected. You decide whether to have the antivirus program "cure" the virus or simply remove the file or floppy disk from your system. If the protection program is unable to "cure" the virus, it will alert you so you can take an appropriate action.

Because new viruses are cropping up daily, you need to keep your antivirus program updated. Most programs have downloadable updates via the Internet. When new upgrades of the software are available, upgrade immediately to get the most complete and up-to-date virus protection possible.

Office 2000 has incorporated a virus checking tool into its applications that also lets third-party vendors directly scan Word documents before they are opened. Any antivirus software you buy will therefore supplement Office's general warning tools.

## Protect Templates from Viruses

In working with templates that contain macros, you may see warning messages displayed when you first open the template. This is because macro viruses can affect a document template. The warning message that appears does not necessarily indicate

---

**Concept virus**

If you save a document and Word automatically saves it as a Document Template even though you want to save it as a document, you may have been infected with the Concept virus. The Concept virus is a macro virus and was hidden in some Word 6.0/95 software packages. Microsoft published a repair kit on its Web site, and all the big-name antivirus software packages can detect and remove it, but the virus still gets spread around by unknowing users when they share files.

that the template is infected with a virus, only that it contains macros and, therefore, has the potential for carrying a virus. When the message appears, you have two choices: to use the template with its macros or to use the template without the macros.

Developers of Office 2000 applications may now digitally sign their macros to assure you of their authorship. A digital signature guarantees that the macro originated from the developer who signed it and that the macro has not been altered. If the application turns out to contain a macro virus, you know who is responsible. Word recognizes the digital signatures and won't display a macro warning screen unless the macro is modified. As a user, you have the opportunity to "trust" all documents that are digitally signed by certain authors or developers. These "trusted" documents can be opened without the virus warning. You should therefore confirm that the source (author) is responsible and uses a virus scanner before signing macros.

Word has three levels of security to deter macro virus infections:

- *Low*. If you use this level you must be sure that all your documents, templates, and add-in programs are safe because selecting Low turns off macro virus protection in Word. When you open documents, the macros are automatically enabled.

- *Medium*. At this level, Word will display a warning message if it encounters a macro that is not from a trusted source. You then choose whether to enable the macros or not. If it is possible that the document contains a virus, you should disable the macros.

- *High*. Only macros that have been digitally signed and are from a trusted source are enabled.

The default security setting is High. If High is unsatisfactory, you may change the security setting.

### Setting the Security Level

1. From the **Tools** menu, select **Macro**.

2. Choose **Security** from the submenu.

3. Click the **Security Level** tab, if it's not already selected.

4. Select **High**, **Medium**, or **Low**.

5. Choose **OK**.

When you open a template or load an add-in program that was installed before Word 2000, macros within those files are automatically enabled. However, you can have Word warn you about previously installed templates and add-ins as follows:

### Set Up Warnings for Previously Installed Templates and Add-Ins

1. Open the **Tools** menu and select **Macro**.

2. Choose **Security** from the submenu.

3. Click the **Trusted Sources** tab.

4. Deselect **Trust All Installed Add-Ins and Templates**.

5. Choose **OK**.

If you are using High or Medium security and a file contains signed macros from an unknown author, a dialog box appears with information about the signer's certificate. You then have a choice to trust the signer or not. Trusted signers are added to the list in the Security dialog box on the Trusted Sources tab. At any time, you can remove any of the trusted signers from that list by clicking the **Remove** button.

### SEE ALSO

➤ *Learn how to run macros on page 628*

➤ *Learn more about using templates on page 344*

# Protect Documents

When you create a document that can be accessed by others, you may want to restrict access to that document. Word enables you to create the following document and field protection:

- Require users to enter a password to open or edit a document

- Allow users to open the file in read-only mode

> **Warning**
>
> Word doesn't scan your floppy disks, hard disks, or network drives for macro viruses, so you still need to purchase and install antivirus software.

## Assign Passwords

Use password protection when documents contain sensitive material or you want to limit the number of people who are authorized to edit the document. Only those who know the password may open or edit the document.

### Assign a Password to a Document

1. With the document open, click the **File** menu and select **Save As**. The Save As dialog box appears.

2. Choose **Tools**, **General Options**. The Save dialog box appears (see Figure 8.1).

FIGURE 8.1

You enter passwords in the File Sharing Options section of the Save dialog box.

3. To restrict who may open the document, enter the password you want to assign the document in the **Password to Open** box. Passwords can be as many as 15 characters long and can include letters, numbers, symbols, and spaces. As you enter a password, only asterisks appear in the box. This keeps anyone from reading the password over your shoulder, but it also means you must type carefully to avoid misspellings.

4. People who know the "Open" password can open the document and read it. They can't necessarily make modifications to the document. To restrict who may edit the document, enter a password in the **Password to Modify** box (you may enter both passwords for any document). Only those people possessing this password may modify the document.

**5.** To prevent errors or changes in the original file, click **Read-Only Recommended** to enable that option. When a user opens the file, a recommendation displays a suggestion that they open the file as a read-only document. If that user makes changes, the user must save the file with a different name. The original is thus preserved. You can enable this option even if you don't set passwords for the document.

**6.** If you entered a password in the **Password to Open** box, the Confirm Password dialog box appears when you choose **OK** (see Figure 8.2). Confirm the password by entering it again exactly as before (passwords are case-sensitive, so be sure to capitalize the password the same way as the original). The password appears as asterisks in the text box. Then choose **OK**.

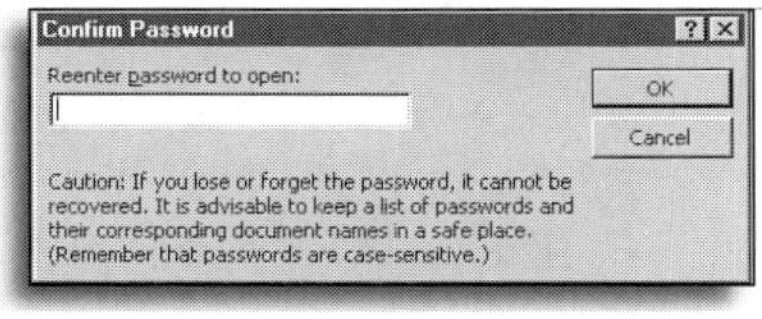

**FIGURE 8.2**
You must confirm the password you entered.

**7.** If you entered a password in the **Password to Modify** box, the Confirm Password dialog box appears when you choose **OK**. Confirm the password by entering it again exactly as before and then choose **OK**.

**8.** Click **Save** to save the file with its password.

When anyone attempts to open the document, a dialog box appears requesting the password (see Figure 8.3). The user must enter the password exactly as you did when you created it. After a user enters the password correctly and chooses **OK**, the document opens.

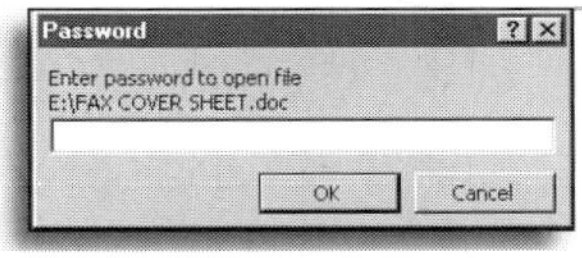

**FIGURE 8.3**
You must enter a password to open a password-protected document.

Users are prompted to enter a password when they try to open the document if you entered a password to modify the document (see Figure 8.4).

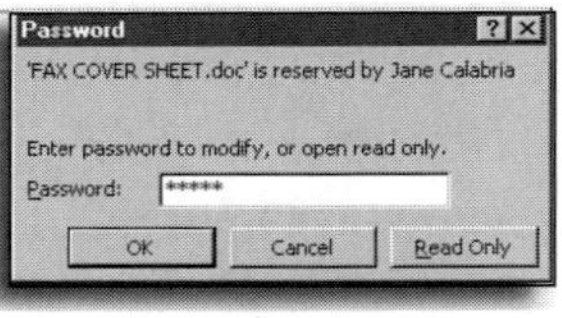

FIGURE 8.4

You must enter a password before you can edit a protected document.

Users who don't know the password can click **OK** and the document opens in read-only mode. Users who enter the correct password can make changes and save the modifications in the original file.

If you selected the **Read-Only Recommended** option when you saved the file, a dialog box appears when a user opens the document, recommending that the document be opened as read-only unless changes to it need to be saved. The user clicks **Yes** to open the file as read-only. After the document has been opened in read-only mode, the user must save it with a new filename to edit it.

**SEE ALSO**

➤ *To learn more about password protect forms, see page 152*

## Share Files

Sharing files is a network concept. On networked Windows computers, users can give each other access to files stored on their local disk drives by "sharing" the folders that the files reside in. Then the other users can "connect" to the shared folders across the network.

Windows NT computers can share their resources by default. You don't normally have to do anything to enable file sharing on them. Windows 9x computers are often set up initially with file sharing capability turned off. You may have to turn it on before you can use it.

If you do turn on file sharing in Windows 9x, you will have to decide whether to use share-level access control or user-level access control. *Share-level* access control is the default. When using it, any folders that you share are effectively shared with everyone on the network. If you want to limit whom has access to the contents of the shared directory, you can protect access with a password.

If you want more control than that over who you share your resources with (and also to eliminate the password hassle), you have to set up user-level access control. With user-level access control you can name the individual network users or groups who can access a folder at the time you share it.

To set up user-level access control you have to have access to a directory of network usernames. You need this access so you can choose who will be allowed to access your shared resource. Later your computer will need it to determine when someone tries to access a shared resource—whether that user is authorized. Windows 9x computers can access two kinds of user directories—Windows NT directories and Novell NetWare directories. To put this another way, if you don't have any Windows NT or Novell NetWare servers on your network, you won't be able to set up user-level access control. Have we lost you? If so, either check with your network administrator or just stick with share-level access control.

### Enable File Sharing on a Windows 9x Computer

1. Make sure you have access to the Windows 9x install files. You may be prompted for their location in step 7 below. Depending on how Windows 9x was installed on your computer in the first place, the install files may be located on your hard disk drive, a CD-ROM disk, or a network file server. If you don't know where the install files are located, ask your network administrator.

2. Close all open programs, and then click **Start** on the Windows Taskbar and select **Settings**. Choose **Control Panel** from the submenu.

3. Double-click the **Network** icon in the Control Panel.

4. Click the **Configuration** tab if it's not already displayed.

5. Choose **File and Print Sharing**.

6. Select **I Want to be Able to Give Others Access to My Files**.

7. Choose **OK** to return to the Network dialog box. If you want to use user-level access control, click the **Access Control** tab. Otherwise skip to step 9.

8. If you clicked the **Access Control** tab, select **User-Level Access Control**. Then enter the name of a domain or computer in the **Obtain List of Users and Groups From** box. Windows may automatically provide the correct name for you.

9. Click **OK** to close the Network dialog box. At this point you may also be prompted to enter the location of the Windows 9x install files. You may also be prompted to restart your computer, which you should do.

SEE ALSO

➤ *Learn more about working within workgroups on page 507*

# Create and Share Folders

Remember that if you want others to be able to read or edit a document, you have to store it somewhere that others will be able to access. Normally your home directory on a local area network is completely private—closed to all users except you. Any documents you plan to share must be stored in publicly accessible directories, normally on file servers.

### Create a Folder

1. Open **My Computer** from the desktop.

2. Open the hard drive or network drive on which you want to place the new folder. (If you want to create a subfolder of another folder, also open the other folder).

3. From the **File** menu, select **New**.

4. Select **Folder** from the submenu.

5. Type the name of the new folder and press Enter.

---

**Create new folders from Save As**

When you have the Save As dialog box open, you can create a new folder, switch to that folder, and then save your file into it all at once. Select the drive (and folder if needed) where you want to put the new folder from the **Save In** drop-down list. Click the **Create New Folder** button. Enter the name of the new folder in the **Name** box in the New Folder dialog box and choose **OK**. Double-click on the folder to open it. Enter a name for your file in the **File Name** box and then choose **Save**.

**Share a Folder**

1. Right-click the folder (new or existing) in the My Computer window.

2. Select **Sharing** from the shortcut menu to open the Folder Properties box (see Figure 8.5).

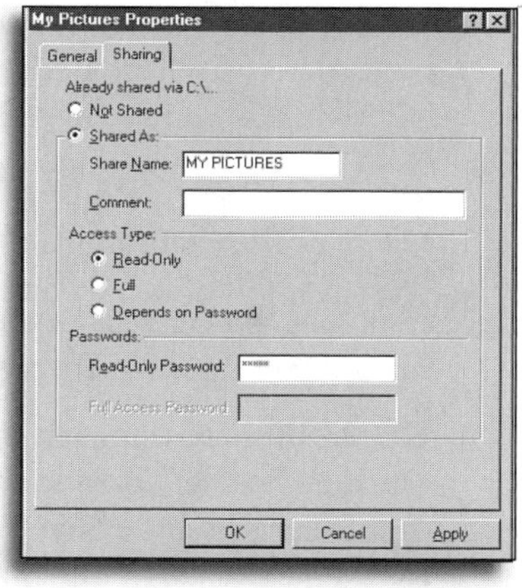

**FIGURE 8.5**

Give the folder a name, choose an access type, and enter a password, if desired.

3. Click the **Sharing** tab if it's not already displayed.

4. Select **Shared As**.

5. If you are using user-level access control, click **Add** to select the names of those whom you want to give permission to access the shared folder.

   If you are using share-level access control, select the access type for the folder that you want to share.

6. Choose **OK**.

# Recover Unsaved Work with AutoRecover

AutoRecover protects you from losing unsaved edits by periodically saving your document for you (every 10 minutes by default). It saves the document in the Windows temporary directory and names it AutoRecovery save of [*filename*] (where [*filename*] is the name of your file). When you close the file or exit Word, Word deletes the AutoRecovery version of your file. But if Word terminates abnormally—it crashes, your system crashes, or the power fails—Word does not delete the AutoRecovery version of your file.

When you terminate abnormally and restart Word, it automatically opens the AutoRecovery version of your file. You can then compare it with the last saved version of your file. If it contains edits that you never had a chance to save, you can use **Save As** to save the AutoRecovery version in place of your last saved version. Alternatively you can close the AutoRecovery version without saving it, and it will cease to exist.

AutoRecover is active by default, but you can turn it off if you want. You might want to turn it off if you have limited memory, free disk space, or a slow processor, because it taxes all these resources. You can also change the default 10-minute save interval and you can tell Word where to save AutoRecovery files.

You do all these things in the Options dialog box (choose **Options** on the **Tools** menu). Activate or deactivate AutoRecover on the **Save** tab, in the **Save AutoRecover Info Every** field. Change the time interval in the **Minutes** field (see Figure 8.6).

FIGURE 8.6

Set up AutoRecover, an automatic creation of backups in this panel of the Options dialog box.

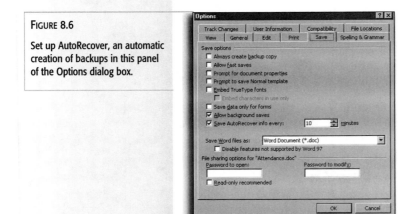

You define a location for AutoRecover files in the **File Locations** tab of the Options dialog box. Select AutoRecover files from the **File Types** list and then choose **Modify**. Select a drive and folder to store your AutoRecover files from the Modify Location dialog box. Choose **OK**.

# Use Automatic Backups

Normally when you save a file, Word just overwrites the currently saved copy of the file. You end up with only one copy of the file, which puts you at high risk of losing it. Word can help you reduce this risk by keeping the previously saved copy of your file as a backup copy whenever you save your file.

The first time you save a document, Word saves it as [*filename*] (where [*filename*] is the name of your file). The second time you save, Word renames the currently saved version of your file to [*filename*].wbk. Then it saves the copy in memory, giving it the name [*filename*].doc. The third time you save, Word deletes the copy named [*filename*].wbk (which was your first saved copy), renames the copy named [*filename*].doc to [*filename*].wbk, and saves the copy in memory to [*filename*].doc. From the second save on, you end up with your two most recent revisions of the file saved on disk.

This is not a fully secure backup scheme by any definition, but it does give you some level of comfort. It also lets you retrieve edits that you may have deleted in your most recent version of your file. The drawback is that it doubles the amount of disk space occupied by your Word data files. If you are short of disk space, don't turn on this feature. You also can't activate Fast Saves if you're using this feature.

**SEE ALSO**

➤ *To learn more about fast saves, see page 135*

To activate automatic backups, open the **Tools** menu, choose **Options**, click the **Save** tab on the Options dialog box, and select **Always Create **B**ackup Copy**.

# Back Up Data Files

To truly preserve your files, you need to back them up to floppy disks, backup tapes, or another drive (such as a network drive) or computer. You do this using the backup features of your operating system or with a special backup program.

If you are working on a network in your office, you may not have to back up any files you store on the network drives. Your system administrator probably has a backup system in place to back up any files stored on network drives. However, any files you store on your own hard disk are probably not being backed up for you, in which case you must back them up yourself.

When you back up files properly, you are then able to restore those files should something catastrophic happen like a hard disk failure. Backups should be performed regularly—the more frequently the better. You don't want to risk losing everything.

PART

# Increase Productivity

# Use Tables to Organize Information

Create, modify, and format tables

Enter, sort, and rotate text

Import, link, and embed worksheets

Perform calculations in tables

# Know When to Use Tables

A *table* organizes information in *columns* and *rows*. You enter table information in *cells*, which are the rectangles made by the intersection of the columns and rows. Each cell is independent of all other cells. You can have almost any number of rows and columns in a table. You also have a great deal of control over the size and formatting of each cell. A table cell can contain text, graphics, and just about anything that a Word document can contain. Use tables to organize information in your documents, even when you want information to appear in columns, but not as if it is in a table. You can print tables without borders, so the end result is columns of information. The advantage of using tables to enter the data instead of tabbed columns is that text will wrap within a table cell and formatting table cells is an easy task.

Tables give you the ability to design an orderly document layout. They are particularly helpful in laying out forms, but a two-row, three-column table can even act as the structure for a three-fold brochure.

For catalogs and price sheets, or even computer manuals, set up tables with two columns and multiple rows. Then place your picture or headline text in one column and your descriptive text in another. This type of structure is often referred to as side-by-side columns or parallel columns.

When should you not use tables to work in columns? When you want text to flow down the first column and then continue at the top of the next column. This style of columns is referred to as newspaper or snaking columns. Use Word's Column command to achieve this, because it works more naturally with text flow.

When should you use tabs instead of a table? When you want to line up numbers in a column by their decimal points, it's a little easier to do with tabs. Tabs are also a better choice when you want to use dot leaders (periods that connect the text). Otherwise, do the text in tables and then remove the borders to look like you typed the text with tabs.

# Insert and Delete Tables

Adding a table to your document is a simple matter, provided you have some basic information in mind about how you want the table to look. First, you need to know the number of columns and rows (although you can add and delete columns and rows you don't need). Second, think about any special structural changes you may need—splitting or merging cells, for example—that may involve adding a row or column initially. Then move your cursor to the spot in your document where you want the table to appear, and begin.

The complexity of your table determines which tool you should use to create it—the Insert Table command for simpler tables or the Draw Table tool for more complex tables.

### Create a Simple Table

**1.** Place your insertion point where you want to insert the table.

**2.** Open the **Table** menu and choose **Insert**.

**3.** Select **Table** from the submenu. The Insert Table dialog box appears (see Figure 9.1).

**4.** In the **Numbers of Columns** and **Number of Rows** text boxes, enter the values for the number of columns and rows you want your table to have. Don't worry about knowing the exact number, you can adjust these later.

**Margins count**

Before you create a table, set your page margins. Word automatically draws the table between the margins and then divides that space equally into the number of columns you specified. If you set your margins after you create the table, you will have to adjust the width of your table to match the margins. You may also have to adjust your column widths, especially if you've set them randomly to fit the table contents.

**Caution: Leave a blank space before you create a table**

It's a good idea to leave a blank space (press Enter) before you create a table on a blank page. If you forget to do this, and at some later point need to type text above and outside of the table, place your cursor in the first cell of the table and press Ctrl+Shift+Enter.

FIGURE 9.1

Enter or select the number of columns and rows you want in your table.

5.  Under **AutoFit Behavior**, select the option to set the initial width of the table and columns:

    *   **Fixed Column Width**. Select this option to specify the exact width of each column in the table. Enter the width (in inches) in the text box. If you choose Auto, Word makes the table stretch from the left to right margin and evenly divides that space into the number of columns you specified.

    *   **AutoFit to Window**. Use this option to make the table as wide as the window allows. The table is then divided into evenly sized columns based on the number of columns you specified.

    *   **AutoFit to Contents**. This option creates the desired number of columns, but the width of the columns changes based on the amount of text you enter in to them.

6.  To apply one of Word's automatic table formats to the table, choose **AutoFormat**, select the desired format, and then choose **OK** (see more on AutoFormat in the "Apply Automatic Formatting" section later in this chapter).

7.  To use the current settings as the model for all new tables created after the current one, select **Set as Default for New Tables**.

8.  Choose **OK**. A blank table appears in your document with your insertion point in the first cell.

A quick way to insert a table is to choose **Insert Table** 🔲 on the Standard toolbar and then drag over the desired number of rows and columns (see Figure 9.2). When you release your mouse button, the table appears in your document at the insertion point.

After you create a table, you can set the overall width of the table (in percentage of page width or in inches), how you want it aligned horizontally on the page (left, right, centered, or indented), and whether you want to wrap text around the outside of the table.

**Use the Table and Borders toolbar**

When working in tables, you'll find the Tables and Borders toolbar helpful. Display the toolbar by opening the **View** menu and selecting **Toolbars**, then selecting **Tables and Borders**.

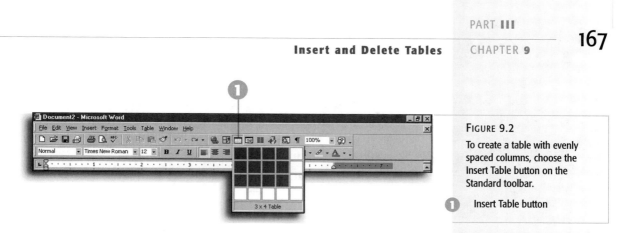

FIGURE 9.2

To create a table with evenly spaced columns, choose the Insert Table button on the Standard toolbar.

1    Insert Table button

### Setting Table Properties

**1.** Place your cursor inside the table.

**2.** Open the **Table** menu and choose **Table Properties**. Alternatively, right-click the table and choose **Table Properties**.

**3.** When the Table Properties dialog box appears, click the **Table** tab (see Figure 9.3).

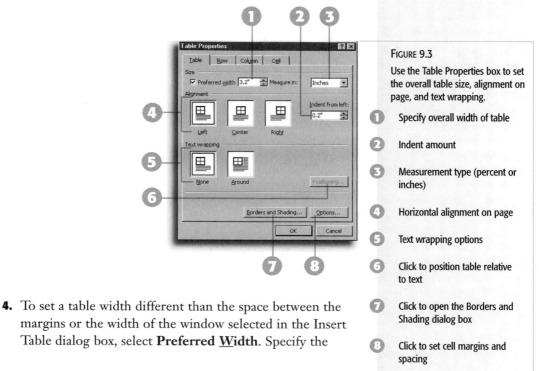

FIGURE 9.3

Use the Table Properties box to set the overall table size, alignment on page, and text wrapping.

1    Specify overall width of table

2    Indent amount

3    Measurement type (percent or inches)

4    Horizontal alignment on page

5    Text wrapping options

6    Click to position table relative to text

7    Click to open the Borders and Shading dialog box

8    Click to set cell margins and spacing

**4.** To set a table width different than the space between the margins or the width of the window selected in the Insert Table dialog box, select **Preferred Width**. Specify the actual width in the text box. Use a percentage if you chose **Percent** from the **Measure In** box or a number of inches if you chose **Inches** as the unit of measure. If you're working on a Web page, using percentages is a better idea (you never know the size of a browser window).

5. For a table that doesn't stretch across the entire page, you need to specify its horizontal location on the page. Click **Left**, **Center**, or **Right**. If you aligned the table on the left but would like the table indented from the left margin, enter the number of inches in the **Indent from Left** box.

6. To have your body text wrap around the table, select **Around** from the **Text Wrapping** options. Choose **Positioning** to specify how you want the table positioned in relation to the paragraph, column, or margin.

7. Choose **Options** to specify cell margins, spacing between cells, whether you want to allow the table to break across pages, and whether you want the table to automatically resize to fit its contents. Make your choices and choose **OK** to return to the Table Properties dialog box.

8. Choose **OK**.

Selecting the table and pressing Delete does not remove the table from your document; it only removes the text from the table. To delete a table, you must have your cursor inside the table and then open the **Table** menu, select **Delete**, and then choose **Table**. A quicker method is to select the table, and cut it to the Clipboard by pressing Ctrl+X, by clicking on the Cut button ⬚, or choosing **Cut** from the **Edit** menu.

## Draw Tables

When you insert a table in your document, it stretches from the left to right margin and evenly divides that space into the number of columns you specified (unless you selected a column width option in the Insert Table dialog box).

Another option for inserting a table in your document is to draw your table. That way you draw the table to the size and shape you want. You can add columns and rows in a variety of configurations.

## Draw a Table

1. Place your insertion point where you want your table to appear in the document.

2. Click the **Table** menu and select **Draw Table**. The Tables and Borders toolbar appears and your mouse pointer becomes a pencil. When you draw a table, Word requires that you be in Print Layout or Web Layout view (if you are in Normal view, the Office Assistant may appear and ask if you want to switch to Print Layout view). Figure 9.4 explains the Tables and Borders toolbar.

   If the Tables and Borders toolbar is already showing, choose **Draw Table** on the toolbar to display the pencil cursor.

3. To set the outside dimensions of the table, move your mouse pointer to the spot where you want the upper-left corner of the table to be, and then drag diagonally. Release the mouse button when the mouse pointer is at the spot where you want the lower-right corner of the table to be. (Actually, you can start at any corner as long as you drag diagonally toward the opposite corner.)

4. Then use the pencil to do the following things: Draw the lines for the column and row borders by dragging from one edge of the table to the other or from one column or row border to another (Word keeps your lines straight). Or draw from any corner of a cell to the diagonally opposite corner to draw diagonal lines through cells. Or create a second table inside any cell of the first table. If you draw a line by mistake, choose **Eraser** from the Tables and Borders toolbar and click the line you drew to remove it.

5. When you've finished drawing the table, disable the pencil cursor, either by clicking the Draw Table icon again to de-select it or by double-clicking in one of the cells to begin entering text.

**SEE ALSO**

➤ *Learn how to change margins on page 290*

*Learn how to change margins on page 290*

### Should you insert or draw your table?

Which method you use to create a table is a personal decision. Most of the time we find ourselves inserting a table. It's faster than drawing and we find that we don't need to be concerned about size and shape. But for complex tables—ones with cells that span multiple columns or rows, with unevenly spaced columns or rows, or with diagonally divided cells—we find that we can more easily set the table up the way we want it if we draw the table. Also, drawing tables is just more fun.

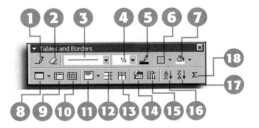

| | | |
|---|---|---|
| ❶ Draw Table | ❿ Split Cells | |
| ❷ Eraser | ⓫ Align | |
| ❸ Line Style | ⓬ Distribute Rows Evenly | |
| ❹ Line Weight | ⓭ Distribute Columns Evenly | |
| ❺ Border Color | ⓮ Table AutoFormat | |
| ❻ Borders | ⓯ Change Text Direction | |
| ❼ Shading Color | ⓰ Sort Ascending | |
| ❽ Insert Table | ⓱ Sort Descending | |
| ❾ Merge Cells | ⓲ AutoSum | |

# Format Tables

Formatting options for tables are extensive. You can apply borders and shading to cells, groups of cells, or the entire table. Text can be rotated and cells can be merged.

Shading and borders give a professional look to tables and assist in the readability of the data contained in the table. Formatting can be applied using Word's automatic formatting options or by manually selecting options.

## Apply Automatic Formatting

The quickest and easiest way to format a table is to use one of Word's predefined table formats.

### AutoFormat a Table

**1.** Place the insertion point anywhere in the table.

**2.** Click the **T**a**ble** menu and select **Table Auto**F**ormat** to open the Table AutoFormat dialog box, as shown in Figure 9.5. Another way to open this dialog box is to choose **Auto**F**ormat** in the **Insert Table** dialog box when you create a table or click the Table AutoFormat button 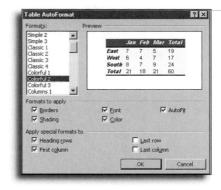 on the Tables and Borders toolbar.

**FIGURE 9.5**
The AutoFormat dialog box offers several preset formats that you can apply to your table.

**3.** A list of available formats appears in the **Forma**t**s** box. When you click on one of the formats, the **Preview** box displays a sample of the format.

**4.** Under **Formats to Apply,** click the check boxes to select or deselect the options you want applied to your table (look at the preview to see how the items you check affect the table format):

- **B**orders turns on or off the border style specified by the format.
- **S**hading turns the shading for that format on or off.
- **F**ont uses the font specified by the format or returns to the default font for the template on which the document is based.
- **C**olor retains or removes the color that the format adds to a table.
- **AutoF**it fits the table and column width to the text in the table, and turning it off spaces the columns evenly over the width of the table (between the left and right margins).

**5.** Under **Apply Special Formats To,** select the options you want to use for specific rows or columns of your table (look at the Preview to see how your selections affect the table format):

- **Heading R**ows adds or removes special formatting (shading, boldface, colored text, and so on) applied to the heading row of your table. A heading row, which is generally the first row of your table, is the row that repeats at the top of each page of your table.
- **First C**olumn adds or removes special formatting applied to the first column of your table, where you may have row titles entered. The table format may add shading or bold text to that column to make it look different from the rest.
- **Last Row** adds or removes special formatting applied to the last row of a table, such as borders or shading.
- **Last Col**umn adds or removes special formatting applied to the last column of the table, such as shading, bold text, or borders.

6. Choose **OK**. The selected formatting is applied to the table.

Automatic formatting of a table is convenient when you need to make a table look good fast.

## Which Table AutoFormat Should You Use?

There are lots of Table AutoFormats to choose from. This, of course, serves primarily to make it hard to choose an AutoFormat. Here are some rules to help you reject inappropriate choices:

- Low resolution printers don't always print shading well, and photocopiers tend to butcher shading. So, if you will be printing or photocopying your table, we recommend you lean toward unshaded, uncolored table formats. If you want to use a shaded or colored format, test it on your printer (and maybe on a photocopier) before you declare it a winner.

- If you will be publishing your table to a Web site, use the Web formats. HTML has very limited table border formatting capabilities and the Web formats pretty much reflect all the possibilities (except for background colors). If you use any other table format, you will find that, when you save your document in HTML format, the table will end up looking like the Web formats anyway. On the other hand, if you want your Web table to have background colors, you can choose a colored format. But the table borders will either disappear entirely or look like the borders in the Web formats.

- If readers will work with your document online in Word format or you will be exporting it to, say, a PowerPoint presentation, use the 3D effects formats or any high-color formats that you like. In this case what you see really is what you get. If you like it, use it.

## Select Table Components

To perform some formatting types to your table, you must select cells, rows, and columns. Table 9.1 provides you with tips on how to select areas of your table.

**To undo table formatting**

You can undo table formatting by clicking the **Undo** button on the Standard toolbar. You might want to save several versions of your document with different table formatting options to compare them before you make a final decision on table formatting.

TABLE 9.1    **Selecting table components**

| To Select | Do This |
|---|---|
| Cell | Click the left edge of the cell between the text and the cell border (when you see a pointer).<br>*Or*<br>Triple-click inside the cell.<br>*Or*<br>Put your insertion point in the cell and open the **Table** menu, choose **Select**, and then select **Cell**. |
| Row | Click to the left of the row (in the margin area) when you see a pointer.<br>*Or*<br>Put your insertion point in the row and open the **Table** menu, select **Select**, and then choose **Row**. |
| Column | With your insertion point in the column, click the column's top gridline or border when you see a down-pointing arrow. Alternatively, hold down the Alt key and click the column.<br>*Or*<br>Open the **Table** menu, choose **Select**, and then select **Column**. |
| Multiple cells, rows, or columns | Drag across the cell, row, or column; or select a single cell, row, or column; hold down the Shift key, and then click another cell, row, or column where you want the selection to end. |
| Text in the next cell | Press Tab |
| Text in the previous cell | Press Shift+Tab |
| Entire table | Click the table and then press Alt+5 on the numeric keypad (Num Lock must be off); or press Alt and double-click the table.<br>*Or*<br>Open the **Table** menu, choose **Select**, and then select **Table** (with your insertion point somewhere in the table). |

If you need to reduce a selection to fewer cells or extend a selection to adjacent cells, hold down the Shift key and press an arrow key repeatedly.

After you select cells, you can apply table formatting or text formatting to the contents of those cells using the standard techniques for changing fonts and paragraph attributes.

**SEE ALSO**

➤ *To learn about changing fonts and font attributes, see page 75*

## Apply Manual Formatting

To customize the appearance of your table, apply formatting such as borders, shading, or fonts to individual cells, rows, or columns of the table. You need to select the cells, columns, rows, or the entire table to indicate to which cells you want to apply formatting. Then choose the formatting options you want to apply to your selection, including font, font size, bold, underline, italic, centering, left or right alignment, text color, and so on.

## Apply Table Borders and Shading

Normally, a new table in Word has a single, thin border around each cell in the table. There is no shading.

### Add Table Borders and Shading

**1.** Select the table cells that you want to modify.

**2.** Click the **Format** menu and select **Borders and Shading**. The Borders and Shading dialog box opens.

**3.** Click the **Borders** tab to work with border options (see Figure 9.6).

> **Use the Tables and Borders toolbar for formatting**
>
> Instead of menus, consider using the icons on the Tables and Borders toolbar as shown in Figure 9.4.

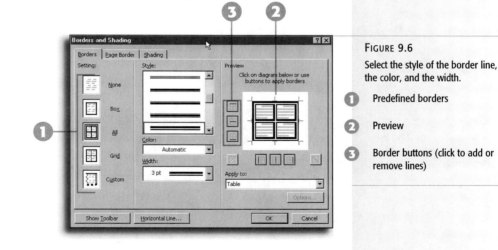

**FIGURE 9.6**

Select the style of the border line, the color, and the width.

**1** Predefined borders

**2** Preview

**3** Border buttons (click to add or remove lines)

**Adjacent borders**

Border formatting can create conflicts when adjacent cells share a border that is formatted differently for each cell. For example, if you format a thin right border in cell 1 and format a heavy left border in cell 2, what happens? Word accepts formatting options in chronological order, so the cell 2 border options win. The common border is a heavy border.

- Under **Setting**, click one of the preset border options: **None** to remove all borders from the selected cells, **Box** to insert a box border around the selected cells, select **All** to insert a box border with shadow formatting around the selection, **Grid** to place a 3D box border around the selection to make the border look like a window frame, or **Custom** to create a border using the options you click in the Preview window. When you choose any of these settings, the current selections in **Style**, **Color**, and **Width** apply to the borders.

- From the **Style** list, select the type of line you want to use for the border, including dotted, dashed, and wavy lines.

- Click the **Color** drop-down list to select a color to apply to the border.

- From the **Width** drop-down list, choose the thickness of the border line, from 1/4-point to 6 points.

- In the Preview box, click on the individual border lines or use the border line buttons to apply or remove borders or change the attributes for a particular border (select the attributes first and then add the border).

- From the **Apply To** drop-down list, select whether to apply the border to **Cell** or **Table**.

4.  Select the **Shading** tab to choose shading options (see Figure 9.7).

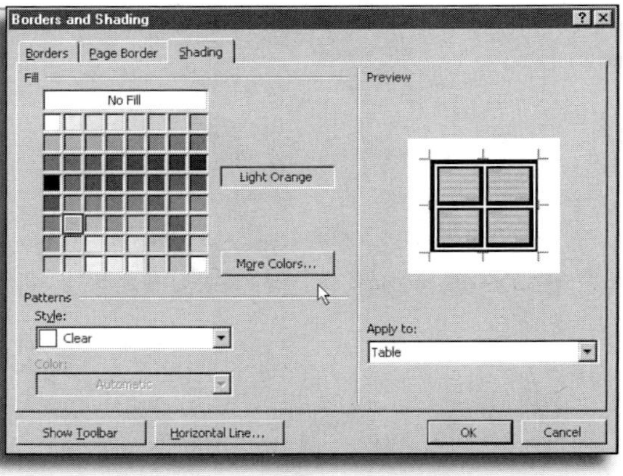

FIGURE 9.7

On the Shading tab, select the background fill color for the selected cells.

- Under **Fill**, select the color or shade of gray you want to fill the selected cells.

- From the **Patterns Style** drop-down list, choose a shading percentage for the color you selected under Fill or a pattern of lines such as **Lt Horizontal** or **Dk Trellis**.

- If you selected a pattern of lines, select the **Color** of the lines from the drop-down list. The Fill color then becomes the background color for the pattern. When using patterns behind text, make the pattern small, the color light, and the text big and bold.

- From the **Apply To** drop-down list select whether to apply the shading options to **Cell** or **Table**.

**5.** Choose **OK**.

To quickly choose shading colors, border line styles, border line colors, and border line widths, use the Tables and Borders toolbar. Open the **View** menu and select **Toolbars**, **Tables and Borders** to display the toolbar, or choose **Tables and Borders** on the Standard toolbar. Select the cells to which you want to add borders and shading, and then click on the appropriate button on the toolbar. Table 9.2 lists the buttons on the toolbar that you can use for borders and shading. Refer to Figure 9.4 to view the full toolbar.

TABLE 9.2    **Tables and borders toolbar buttons**

| Button | Description | Icon On Toolbar |
|---|---|---|
| Line Style | Sets the style of the border lines (dotted, dashed, wavy, double, and so on) | |
| Line Weight | Sets the thickness of the border lines | |
| Border Color | Sets the color of the border lines | |
| Borders | Specifies where the border appears (top, bottom, left, right, box) | |
| Shading Color | Sets the color of the background shading for the selected cells (you cannot specify the percentage) | |

**SEE ALSO**

➤ *Learn more about creating AutoText entries on page 123*

**Where are the cells?**

When you remove the borders from a table, the table could be difficult to edit—you can't always tell where cells start and end. Give yourself a break (you deserve it) by displaying gridlines to see the boundaries of the table and its cells. Unlike borders, gridlines are non-printing. To turn gridlines on or off, open the **Table** menu and choose **Hide Gridlines** or **Show Gridlines**.

**Repeat table formats**

Save table formatting and structure for re-use by selecting the table and saving it as an AutoText entry. Then all you have to do is call for the AutoText entry when you want a similar table.

**Need more rows?**

Pressing the Tab key while you are in the last cell of a table automatically adds a new row to your table.

**Setting tabs within tables**

When you insert a tab (Ctrl+Tab) within a cell of a table, the default tab settings are used. When you set a tab within a cell (click on the ruler) the tab setting applies to that cell only, as Word treats each row like a different paragraph. To set a tab setting for an entire column, select the column first, and then set the tab using the ruler. All types of tabs can be set within a table, such as decimal, right-aligned, and so forth.

**Inserting tabs within tables**

Because Tab moves you to the next cell, you must press Ctrl+Tab to insert a tab in a table cell.

# Enter Data in Tables

Entering and editing text in tables is similar to performing these operations in other areas of your document. Click in the table cell where you want to enter text and type. The text wraps within the cell, and pressing Enter starts a new paragraph within that cell. You use the Delete and Backspace keys to remove unwanted text.

To start a new line within a cell, press Enter. To start a new paragraph within a cell, press Shift+Enter. The difference between pressing Enter and Shift+Enter might not be apparent to you at first. The difference lies in the spacing between lines. If you have not changed the default paragraph spacing, you will see no difference.

To move from cell to cell within the table, click in the cell where you want to place your insertion point or use the arrow keys. For some navigation tips, see Table 9.3.

**TABLE 9.3   Keyboard shortcuts to move around in a table**

| Press This | To Move Here |
| --- | --- |
| Tab | The next cell in the row (if you press Tab when you're in the last cell of the table, Word adds another row to the table). |
| Shift+Tab | The previous cell in a row. |
| Alt+Home | The first cell in the current row. |
| Alt+Page Up | The top cell in the current column. |
| Alt+End | The last cell in the current row. |
| Alt+Page Down | The last cell in the current column. |

SEE ALSO

➤ *For information about changing line and paragraph spacing, see page 209*

➤ *To set tabs using the ruler, see page 206*

# Rotate Text

Because horizontal space may be at a premium, you might want some of your table text to appear in a vertical orientation.

### Rotate Text in a Table

**1.** Select the text you want to rotate.

**2.** Click the **Format** menu and select **Text Direction** or choose Change Text Direction [image] on the Tables and Borders toolbar.

**3.** When the Text Direction - Table Cell dialog box appears (see Figure 9.8), click on the **Orientation** you want to use. The Preview window shows you how the text will look.

**4.** Choose **OK**.

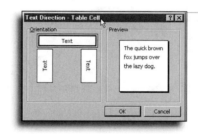

FIGURE 9.8
Select the orientation you want to make your text display vertically.

The selected text changes direction to match the orientation option you chose in the dialog box.

# Sort Table Data

When you sort data in a table, you set the order of the rows in the table based on a value or text in one of the columns. You can indicate that you have headings in your table to prevent them from being melded into the table data, and you can set additional parameters for your sort.

To perform a quick alphabetical sort based on the first word in a cell, place your cursor in the table and click the Sort Ascending

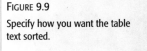 or Sort Descending  button on the Table toolbar. To sort by a single column, select the column and click the ascending or descending icons. The following instructions teach you how to perform more complex sorts.

### Sort Data in a Table

1. Select the columns you want to sort. If you are sorting the entire table, click somewhere within the table to place your insertion point there or select the table.

2. Click the **Table** menu and select **Sort**. The Sort dialog box appears (see Figure 9.9).

**FIGURE 9.9**

Specify how you want the table text sorted.

3. From the **Sort By** drop-down list, select the column on which you want to base the sort. If you select **Header Row** under **My List Has**, the text in the first row replaces the choices **Column 1**, **Column 2**, and so on in the **Sort By** list.

4. From the **Type** drop-down list, select one of the following:
   - Select **Text** to sort the list alphabetically
   - Select **Number** to sort numerically
   - Select **Date** to sort by date or time

5. Click **Ascending** to sort the list in A to Z, 0 to 99 order. Click **Descending** to sort the list in Z to A, 99 to 0 order.

6. When you choose a column for the first (primary) sort, the **Then By** drop-down list is available. This lets you set a secondary sort criteria, so if two items in the first sort are the same, the secondary sort sets the order.

**Do you need a second sorting order?**

Typically, you sort a list of names alphabetically by last name. The second sort order addresses those instances where you have more than one "Smith" or "Jones." For a secondary sort order, select the options for the **Then By** sort the same way you did for the primary sort.

**7.** If your list has a row of column titles, click **Header Row** under **My List Has** to avoid including that row in the sorting.

**8.** Choose **OK**.

Although you rarely sort one column individually, there are occasions when the information in one column is independent of the columns next to it and may need sorting. It is possible to sort a single column without sorting the entire table.

### Sort a Single Column

**1.** Select the column you want to sort.

**2.** Choose the **Table** menu and select **Sort**.

**3.** Choose **Options** to open the Options dialog box (see Figure 9.10).

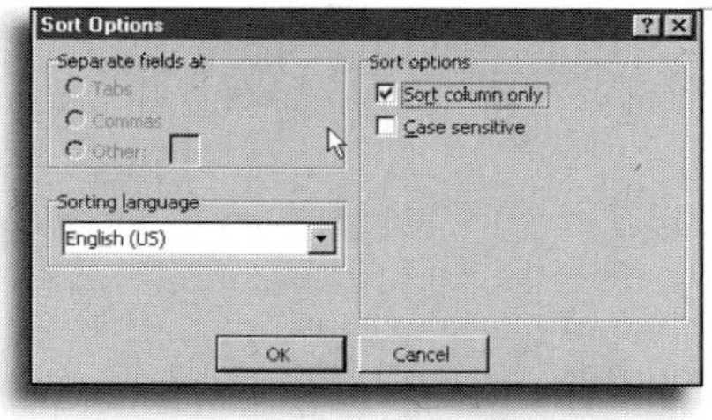

FIGURE 9.10
Select the **Sort Column Only** option.

**4.** Click **Sort Column Only**.

**5.** Choose **OK** to close the Options dialog box.

**6.** Choose **OK** to close the Sort dialog box and apply the sort options to the column.

**SEE ALSO**

➤ *To learn more about sorting of lists, see page 222*

## Convert Text to Tables and Tables to Text

Often a list makes a perfect table. This is particularly true when you create a list and later decide to add a column to the list. You'll find adding data is easier in a table than in a column, or a list created with tabs. You also can convert columns to a table, using the same procedure. When you convert columns to a table, the number of columns you are converting should match the number of columns in the table (see step 2 in the next task).

### Convert a List to a Table

1. Select the text and open the **Table** menu. Choose **Convert**, and then select **Text to Table**.

2. The Convert Text to Table dialog box appears. Indicate the number of columns you want, and how you want the table to fit on the page.

3. Then select the method used to separate the columns:

    - **Paragraphs**. Choose this if you want to break to a new column when Word encounters paragraph marks.

    - **Tabs**. Choose this to break to a new column when Word encounters a tab mark.

    - **Commas**. Choose this to break to a new column when Word encounters a comma. This is useful when you have a list of names separated by commas, such as Jones, Peter.

    - **Other**. Choose this if you have consistently used a character—such as a dash or a colon—and type the character in the text box.

4. To have Word AutoFormat the table, click the **AutoFormat** button and choose a layout. Otherwise, skip to step 5.

5. Click **OK**. Word converts your list to a table.

If you decide that you no longer want a table, convert your table to text in much the same way as "Converting Text to Tables," described previously.

Select the table, and open the **Table** menu, choose **Convert**, and select **Table to Text**. In the Convert Table to Text dialog box, indicate how you want the columns separated—by paragraph marks, tabs, commas, or other marks.

# Modify Tables

The width of columns and the height of rows in Word tables are adjustable. Cells can be split into more cells or merged together in one cell. Tables can be split also, or headers can be added to the top of each column when tables run over one page in length.

## Delete and Insert Rows and Columns

Removing the contents of a cell or cells and leaving a blank cell is an easy matter of selecting the cell(s) and pressing Delete (choose **Undo**  or press Ctrl+Z if you didn't mean to do that).

### Delete a Row or Column

1. Move the insertion point to any cell in the row or column to be deleted, or select the cells to be deleted.

2. Choose the **T**able menu, select **Delete**, and then choose **C**olumns, **R**ows, or C**e**lls. Choosing **Tables**, **C**olumns or **R**ows immediately deletes the table, column, or row in which you have your cursor or that you selected. If you chose C**e**lls, the Delete Cells dialog box appears (see Figure 9.11).

**FIGURE 9.11**

Choose **Delete Entire R**ow or **Delete Entire C**olumn.

3. Click **Delete Entire R**ow or **Delete Entire C**olumn.

4. Choose **OK**. The row or column is deleted.

### Insert Rows or Columns

1. Select the column or row next to where you want to insert new column(s) or row(s). To insert more than one column or row, select the same number of rows or columns as you want to insert.

Quickly delete rows or columns

Select the row or column to be deleted and right-click the selection. Choose **Delete Columns** or **Delete Rows** on the shortcut menu. Or, choose **Cut** on the Standard toolbar.

**Adding a new row**

If you are simply adding (not inserting) rows, press the Enter key just outside of the last row in the table and a new row appears automatically.

**Inserting from the toolbar**

The **Insert Table** button 🔲 on the Tables and Borders toolbar has a down arrow next to it. When you click that down arrow, a menu appears with choices to insert rows, columns, cells, and tables.

   **2.** Choose the **Table** menu, select **Insert**, and choose **Columns to the Left**, **Columns to the Right**, **Rows Above**, or **Rows Below** to insert a new, blank column or row (or the same number of columns or rows as you selected).

You can append rows or columns to your table at any time. To append a row at the bottom of the table, move the insertion point to the last cell in the table and press Tab. To append a column after the last column on the right, click just outside the table's right border, open the **Table** menu, choose **Select**, and then select **Column**. Then choose **Table**, **Insert**, **Columns to the Right**.

Here's how to copy or move an entire column or row from one location in a table to another:

**Copy or Move a Table Column or Row**

   **1.** Select the column or row you want to move or copy.

   **2.** To copy the selected row or column, choose **Copy** 🖹 on the Standard toolbar or press Ctrl+C. To move the selected row or column, choose **Cut** ✂ on the Standard toolbar or press Ctrl+X.

   **3.** Move your insertion point to the new location for the row or column. Your selected row or column will be inserted above or to the right of the location of the insertion point.

   **4.** Choose **Paste** 🖹 on the Standard toolbar or press Ctrl+V.

## Change Column Width

The text you enter in a column of cells may need more or less room than the width of the column. To adjust the spacing, you must change the width of the table column. To quickly change the width of a column with the mouse, use one of these methods:

   ▪ Point at the right border of the column whose width you want to change. The mouse pointer changes to a pair of thin vertical lines with arrowheads pointing left and right. Drag the column border to the desired width (see Figure 9.12).

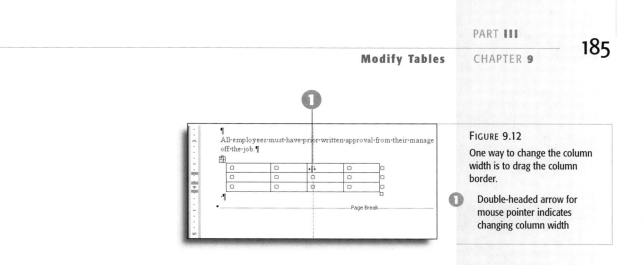

**FIGURE 9.12**

One way to change the column width is to drag the column border.

**1**   Double-headed arrow for mouse pointer indicates changing column width

- With your insertion point in the table, the ruler shows the column separators. Point to the column separator over the right border of the column until the mouse pointer becomes a two-headed arrow (the **Move Table Column** ScreenTip appears). Then drag the separator until the column is the desired width (see Figure 9.13).

**FIGURE 9.13**

Another method for changing the column width is to drag the column separator on the ruler.

**1**   Two-headed arrow mouse pointer and ScreenTip

When you need to be exact in setting the column size, use the Cell Height and Width dialog box.

### Change Cell Height or Width Using the Dialog Box

1. Move the insertion point to any cell in the column you want to change.

2. Open the **Table** menu and select **Table Properties**, or right-click the cell and select **Table Properties**. The Table Properties dialog box appears. Click the **Column** tab (see 9.14).

3. Make sure **Specify Height** is selected.

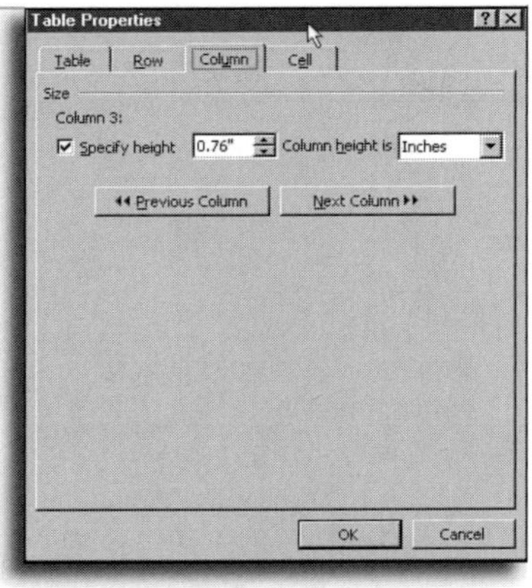

FIGURE 9.14

Enter the column width in inches or as a percentage of the total table width.

4. From the **Column Height Is** drop-down list, select the method of measurement you want to use to specify the column width. Use **Percent of Table Width** if the width of the table can vary based on the size of the window (useful for Web pages). To enter an exact size, choose **Inches**.

5. If your measurement choice for setting the column width was **Percent of Table Width**, enter the percentage in the **Specify Height** text box. Otherwise, enter the number of **Inches** wide you want the column.

6. Choose **Next Column** or **Previous Column** to modify the width of other columns in the table.

7. Choose **OK** when you've finished specifying column widths to apply your changes to the table.

To evenly space two or more adjacent columns over their entire width and make the columns the same width, select the columns and then open the **Table** menu and select **AutoFit**. Choose **Distribute Columns Evenly** from the submenu. Alternatively, click the **Distribute Columns Evenly** button 🔳 on the Tables and Borders toolbar.

To automatically fit a column to the widest entry in that column, place your cursor in one of the cells in that column and choose **AutoFit** from the **Table** menu (or right-click in the cell and select **AutoFit** from the shortcut menu). Then select **AutoFit to Contents**. An even faster method is to double-click the right border of the column. To display the column widths for the entire table, hold the Alt key down as you click one of the borders of the table or the column markers in the ruler. The measurements are displayed on the ruler.

## Change Row Height

Row height in a table is usually based on the font size or the greatest number of lines in any cell in that row. To adjust the row height using the mouse:

- Select the row you want to change. Point at the top or bottom border of the row whose height you want to change. The mouse pointer changes to a pair of thin horizontal lines with arrowheads pointing up and down (see Figure 9.15). Drag the row border to the desired height.

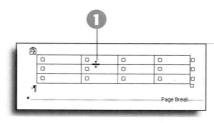

**FIGURE 9.15**

Drag the border of the row to increase or decrease the height of the row.

**1** Double horizontal lines with arrowheads indicate changing row height

- When in Page Layout view, select the row that you want to change. The vertical ruler shows the row separators. Point to the row separator over the border of the row until the mouse pointer becomes a two-headed arrow and the **Adjust Table Row** ScreenTip appears (see Figure 9.16). Then drag the separator until the row is the desired height.

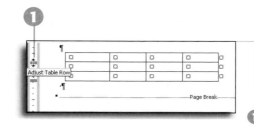

**FIGURE 9.16**

Drag the row separator on the vertical ruler to change the height of the row.

**1** Two-headed arrow and ScreenTip

### Change Row Height Using a Dialog Box

1. Select the row(s) that you want to change.

2. Open the **Table** menu and select **Table Properties** to open the Table Properties dialog box, or right-click a cell in the row and select **Table Properties** from the shortcut menu. Select the **Row** tab (see Figure 9.17).

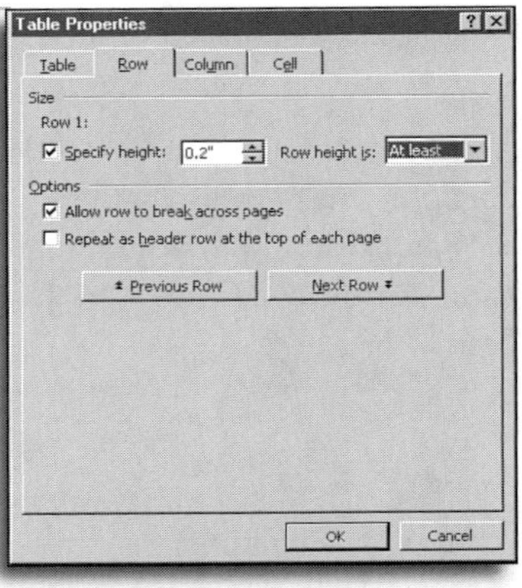

FIGURE 9.17

You may specify the minimum or exact row height in inches.

**Using tables as forms**

If you want to use a table to create a fill-in form that will be printed after it is filled in, be sure to specify fixed row heights for all the rows in the table. Otherwise, the table rows might change size and make the table too big for your page if too much information is entered in a table row. The drawback is that excess text will not be seen or printed. Consider using a fill-in form for this purpose as discussed in Chapter 25, "Design Custom Forms for Use in Word."

3. Make sure that the **Specify Height** option is selected.

4. Enter the height of the row (in inches) in the **Specify Height** text box.

5. From the **Row Height Is** drop-down list, select **At Least** if you want the setting to be the minimum height but allow the height to increase with a larger font or increased amount of text. Select **Exactly** if you want the row height to always remain the same, which means that some of the text entered in the row may not be seen.

6. Choose **Previous Row** or **Next Row** to set the row height for other rows in the table.

7. Choose **OK**.

To evenly space two or more adjacent rows over their entire height and make them the same height, select the rows and then open the **Table** menu, choose **AutoFit**, and select **Distribute**

**Rows Evenly**. Alternatively, right-click the row(s) and select **Distribute Rows Evenly** from the shortcut menu, or click the **Distribute Rows Evenly** button ⊞ on the Tables and Borders toolbar.

SEE ALSO

➤ *To learn about changing font and font size, see page 75*

## Merge and Split Cells

Word tables have the flexibility to enable you to merge several cells into one. The cells must touch each other horizontally or vertically (cells in the same row, cells in the same column, or cells that make a rectangle).

### Merge Cells

**1.** Select the cells you want to merge.

**2.** Click the **Table** menu and select **Merge Cells**, or right-click the selection and choose **Merge Cells** from the shortcut menu, or click the **Merge Cells** button on the Tables and Borders toolbar.

### Split Cells

**1.** Select the cell or cells you want to split (it doesn't have to be a cell that was merged earlier).

**2.** Click the **Table** menu and select **Split Cells**. Alternatively, right-click the cell and choose **Split Cells** from the shortcut menu. You can also click the **Split Cells** button ⊞ on the Tables and Borders toolbar. The Split Cells dialog box appears (see Figure 9.18).

FIGURE 9.18

Enter the number of rows and columns into which you want to split the selected cell(s).

**3.** Enter the **Number of Rows** or **Number of Columns** into which you want to split the cell.

**Use a pencil and eraser**

One easy way to split cells is to use the **Draw Table** pencil 🖉 on the Tables and Borders toolbar. Drag from one side of the cell to another to create new columns or new rows. To merge cells, click the **Eraser** button 🖉 and then click on the unwanted border between the cells.

**Splitting rows**

When an automatic page break falls in the middle of a table, the table is automatically split between the two pages. Sometimes this page break falls in the middle of a row, leaving the beginning of the row on one page and the end on another. It usually makes the row text difficult to read. To prevent a row from being split by an automatic page break, select the row and choose **Table Properties** from the **Table** menu (or right-click the row and choose **Table Properties**). Click the **Row** tab. Then deselect the **Allow Row to Break Across Pages** option.

4. (Optional) If you want to quickly change your entire table to a new configuration of columns and rows, click **Merge Cells Before Split** to place a check mark there. This option merges all the cells in the table into one cell, and then splits the table into the number of rows and columns specified in the Split Cells dialog box.

5. Choose **OK**.

## Split a Table

At times, a table becomes unwieldy, containing so many columns or rows it doesn't fit well on one page, or is difficult to read. When this happens, consider creating a header row of information to make it easier to read your table. When page breaks interfere, split the table into two or more tables.

### Split a Table

1. Place your insertion point in the row that you want to be the first row of the second table.

2. Click the **Table** menu and select **Split Table**. Alternatively, press Ctrl+Shift+Enter.

To join the tables together again, delete the hard return between the tables (or choose **Undo** ↺ on the Standard toolbar or press Ctrl+Z if you just split the table).

## Use Headings

Sometimes your tables are split by a page break. When this happens, the column headings you had on the first page won't appear on the second page unless you instruct word to repeat the headings.

### Create Table Headings

1. Select the rows of your table that you want to use as headings.

2. Choose the **Table** menu and select **Heading Rows Repeat**.

# Create Nested Tables

*Nested tables* are tables within tables. This is a new and very useful tool in Word 2000. As people who spend 50 percent of our computing time in Word, we are excited about this new feature. When would you need a nested table? Well, suppose you used a table to create a Web page, or a printed brochure. Tables are great for these kinds of documents, helping to keep text where you need it, and organizing your document or page into columns. But what happens when you want to add say, pricing information. Wouldn't a nested table be just the tool? We certainly think so! Figure 9.19 displays a nested table in cell A1.

### Nest One Table Inside the Cell of Another Table

1. Put your cursor in the cell where you want to add the nested table.

2. From the **Table** menu, select **Insert** and then **Table**. Alternatively, click the **Insert Table** button 🔲 on the Tables and Buttons toolbar.

3. Enter the **Number of Columns** and the **Number of Rows** you want in the nested table.

4. Choose **OK**.

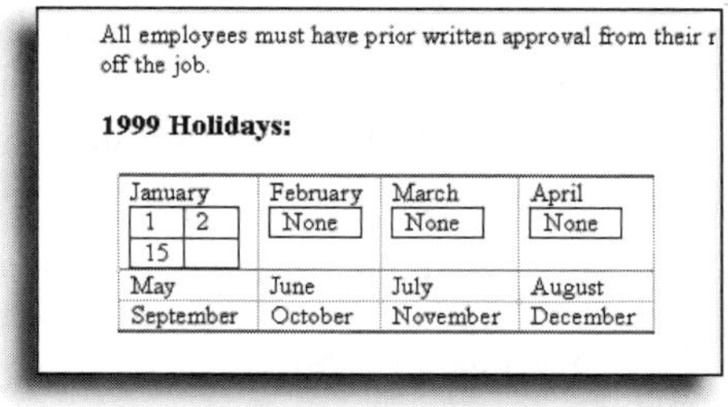

**FIGURE 9.19**
You can place a table inside the cell of another table.

Formatting changes you make for the cell, column, row, or table that contains the nested table will affect the contents of the nested table. However, if you have set different formats for any of the components of the nested table, format changes to the host table will not override them.

# Perform Calculations in a Table

Table calculations resemble some worksheet operations. Word is designed to handle simple calculations in a table. If you find you need to perform many or complicated formulas, you should consider using Excel and importing or embedding a worksheet into your document. For simple calculations, use a Word table.

## Perform Calculations

1. Click in the cell where you want the results of the calculation to appear.

2. Open the **T**a**ble** menu and select **Formula**. The Formula dialog box appears (see Figure 9.20).

3. Word tries to anticipate your needs by entering a formula for you. If you don't want to use that formula, delete it and enter your own formula or choose a function from the **Paste F**u**nction** drop-down list (click on this with the Help question mark to see a button that opens a list of function definitions).

4. To reference the contents of a table cell, type the cell addresses in the parentheses in the formula. Each cell has an address, which is a combination of its column name and its row number. The first column on the left is A, the second is B, and so on. The first row is 1, the second is 2, and so on. Therefore, the address (or cell reference) of the cell in the third row down and second column across is B3. Formulas must begin with an equal sign (=). A formula might be =B3+B6; a function might be =SUM(B3,B6).

5. From the **Number Format** drop-down list, select a format for the numbers (currency, percentage, and so on).

6. Choose **OK** and the result appears in the selected cell.

Keep in mind that the result of the calculation is a field. If you change the data in the referenced cells (changing a number), update the calculation by selecting the field and pressing F9.

**SEE ALSO**

➤ *Learn how to import worksheets on page 407*

# Add Graphics to Tables

Scanned pictures, clip art, or drawings can all be placed within a table (see Figure 9.21). For example, to prepare a price list of your company's products, scan a picture of each product and save it. Then create a table showing the item name, model number, description, and price. In one column, insert the scanned picture of the item. Each row would represent a different product in the price list.

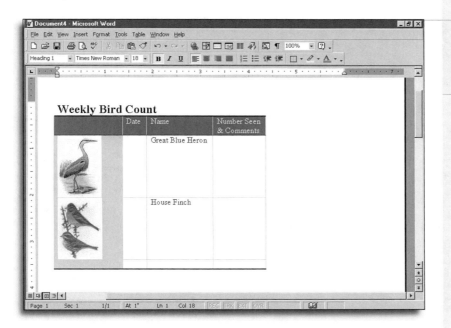

FIGURE 9.21
A table identifying birds to watch in your neighborhood includes pictures of some of the birds.

### Insert a Graphic Into a Table

1. Put your cursor in the cell where you want to place the graphic.

2. Open the **Insert** menu, select **Picture**, and choose one of the following:

   - **Clip Art** opens the Insert ClipArt dialog box. Select one of the pieces of prepared art and click on it. Choose the **Insert Clip** button from the pop-up menu. To close the dialog box, click the Close (X) button.

   - **From File** opens the Insert Picture dialog box, from which you select the location and filename of the picture file you want to use. Then choose **Insert**.

   - **AutoShapes** places the Draw and AutoShapes toolbars on your screen. You use the tools to draw shapes such as stars and arrows or to create an illustration.

   - **WordArt** lets you create shaped text to insert in the table.

   - **From Scanner or Camera** lets you capture and insert pictures from your scanner or digital camera.

3. After the graphic object is inserted in the table (WordArt and AutoShapes float above the text), it's usually too small or too big for the space. Click once on the object to display sizing handles (small black boxes around the edge of the object). Point to one of the handles until your mouse pointer becomes a two-headed arrow and then drag toward the center of the graphic to make it smaller or away from the center to make it bigger (if you use a corner handle when you drag, you won't distort the graphic).

4. To change other properties of the graphic, double-click the graphic to open a formatting dialog box.

# Control Paragraph Spacing, Alignment, and Breaks

Align text horizontally and vertically

Control where words, sentences, paragraphs, lines, and pages break

Use hyphenation and non-breaking spaces

Set and change tab settings

# Know Your Alignment and Text Flow Options

After character-level formatting (covered in Chapter 5, "Change the Appearance of Text"), the next formatting unit in Word is the paragraph. Word treats the paragraph as a single unit for formatting purposes. The kinds of formatting you can apply that affect paragraphs include

- *Horizontal alignment.* The way the paragraph appears within the right and left margins. You can left-align, right-align, center-align, and justify paragraph text.
- *Vertical alignment.* Distribution of paragraphs on a page, inserting only as much space as necessary to evenly distribute the paragraphs on the page. You can align text with the top or bottom of a page, center text, or distribute text equally between the top and bottom margins.
- *Indentation.* The amount of space between the paragraph and the page margin. You can set paragraph indents from the left margin, the right margin, or both.
- *Line and paragraph spacing.* Line spacing is the vertical space between lines. Paragraph spacing is the vertical space before and after paragraphs. By controlling these two types of spacing separately, you can create single-line spacing within paragraphs (line spacing) and double-line spacing between paragraphs (paragraph spacing) without pressing the Enter key twice between paragraphs.
- *Line and page breaks.* Determines where a new page starts or where a new line starts on a page.

# Align Text Horizontally

Horizontal text alignment describes how lines of text align with the left and right margins on the page. The purpose of alignment is to make documents attractive and readable, and you should strive for balance between each of these attributes. The four alignment options in Word are as follows (see Figure 10.1):

- *Left-aligned*. In a left-aligned paragraph, the left ends of lines are even and the right ends are uneven. Standard text paragraphs are generally either left-aligned or justified. The default setting for Word paragraphs is left-aligned. Left-aligned—*ragged right*—paragraphs are considered to be easier to read than other alignment types because the uneven line lengths help you to maintain your place vertically when reading long blocks of text. Left-aligned paragraphing is popular among publishers of material that is not inherently easy to read—reports, technical manuals, and so on.

- *Right-aligned*. In a right-aligned paragraph, the right ends of lines are even and the left ends are uneven. Right-alignment is useful only in rare circumstances, such as when you want to right-align page numbers.

- *Centered*. In a centered paragraph, the lines of the paragraph are centered between the left and right margins. Both ends of lines are uneven. Centered alignment is commonly used for headings and title pages, invitations, or text that you need to emphasize by placing it alone on a line within a paragraph.

- *Justified*. In a justified paragraph, the lines are even on both the right and left, except for the last line. The amount of space between words varies, however. Justified paragraphs appear mostly in printed matter—books, magazines, and newspapers. Justified text can look very attractive on the printed page. Word adjusts the amount of space between words to achieve even line lengths. This variation in word spacing from line to line can become a problem with justified paragraphs. If the spacing variation from line to line is too radical, it can make your work both harder to read (because the spacing problem distracts the reader) and unattractive to look at (with "rivers" of whitespace running down your paragraphs).

Should you decide to use justified paragraphs, you should do a few things to minimize word spacing problems:

- Hyphenate words at line endings. Hyphenation enables Word to minimize the amount of word spacing variation between lines. Word can help you with hyphenation; see the section, "Use Hyphenation to Control Line Breaks," later in this chapter. But watch out for excessive hyphenation that can detract from the readability of your writing.

- Keep text lines relatively long. More words per line translate into less variation in word spacing. If you will be using two or more text columns, consider abandoning justified paragraphs.

- Use a proportional font such as Times New Roman or Arial. Nothing you can do will make monospaced fonts and paragraph justification work well together.

**Alignment versus justification**

Some software programs refer to horizontal paragraph alignment as *justification*. In these programs, text will be *left-justified*, *center-justified*, *right-justified*, or *fully-justified*.

**FIGURE 10.1**

Four types of paragraph alignment are available in Word.

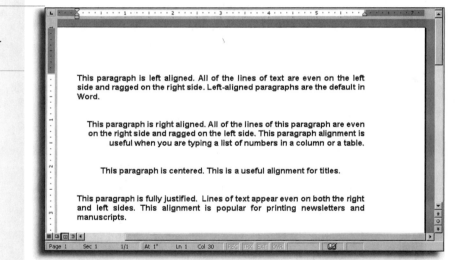

**Aligning Text Horizontally**

1. Position your insertion point in the paragraph. Alternatively, select several paragraphs.

2. Click the appropriate paragraph alignment button as shown in Table 10.1.

When your cursor is in a paragraph you can identify the paragraph's alignment by looking at the alignment buttons; the button for the current alignment setting is depressed.

**TABLE 10.1    Horizontal alignment shortcuts**

| To | Click | Press |
|---|---|---|
| Left-align a paragraph | ▤ | Ctrl+L |
| Center a paragraph | ▤ | Ctrl+E |
| Right-align a paragraph | ▤ | Ctrl+R |
| Justify a paragraph | ▤ | Ctrl+J |

You can also set paragraph alignment from within the Paragraph dialog box.

### Align Paragraphs Using the Paragraph Dialog Box

**1.** Put your cursor in the paragraph or select the paragraph(s) you want to format.

**2.** Open the **Format** menu, and select **Paragraph** to open the Paragraph dialog box, as shown in Figure 10.2. Click the **Indents and Spacing** tab, if it's not already selected.

**Right-click to format paragraphs**

Access the Paragraph dialog box by placing your cursor in a paragraph, right-clicking your mouse, and choosing **Paragraph** from the pop-up menu.

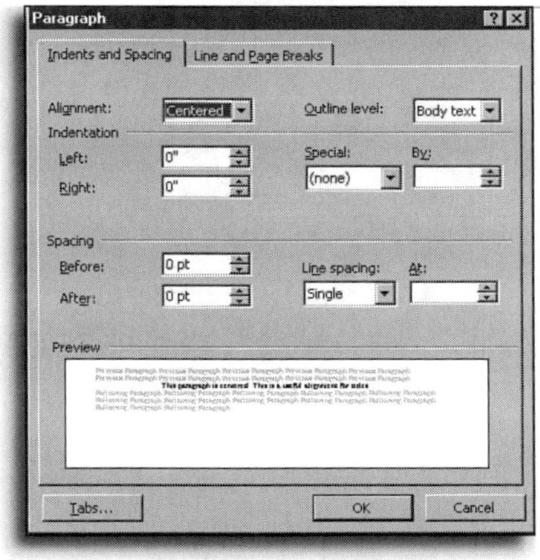

**FIGURE 10.2**
The sample box in the Paragraph dialog box shows how the current indentation settings appear.

**3.** From the **Alignment** drop-down list, select **Left**, **Centered**, **Right**, or **Justified**.

**4.** Click **OK**.

**When you need varying alignment on the same line of text**

You can separate text into tabbed columns and align each column separately. For example, you may need one column decimal-aligned and another left-aligned. The easiest way to do this is through the use of tables. See Chapter 9, "Use Tables to Organize Information," to learn how to create tables.

# Align Text Vertically

Most of the time you won't care about vertical alignment of text. You want text to print from the top of the page down, and that's what Word does. But occasionally you might want to center text on a page vertically. For example, you might want to create a title page in which text is centered both horizontally and vertically. Or you might want to print a short letter and by centering it vertically, it fills the printed page in a more balanced look.

Also, you can justify an entire page vertically. This means that Word distributes the paragraphs on the page evenly, inserting as much space as necessary.

### Center or Justify Text Vertically on a Page

1. Open the **File** menu, and select **Page Setup** to open the Page Setup dialog box.

2. Click the **Layout** tab (see Figure 10.3).

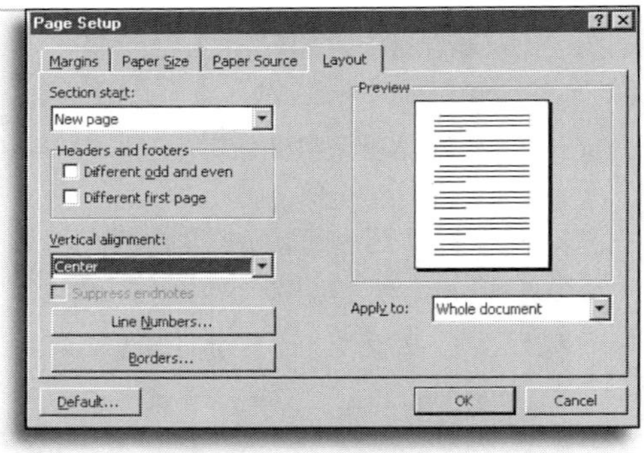

**FIGURE 10.3**

Select how you want your text to align between the top and bottom margins.

3. From the **Vertical Alignment** drop-down list, select **Top** (aligns with top margin), **Center** (centers the text between the top and bottom margins), or **Justified** (distributes paragraphs evenly from top to bottom margin).

4. From the **Apply To** drop-down list, select the portion of the document to which you want to apply this setting—**This Section**, **This Point Forward**, or **Whole Document**. If you have not divided your document into sections, **This Section** does not appear in the list.

5. Click **OK**.

Generally, you would want to apply vertical centering or justification to a single-page document or, if applying it to a page in a multi-page document, you would want to define that page as a separate section of the document. For example, if you want to vertically center or justify the title page of a document, you would first insert a section break between that page and the rest of the document. Then you would apply the vertical alignment to the section consisting of the title page.

**SEE ALSO**

➤ *Learn more about section breaks on page 287*

# Set Indents

In a paragraph that is *not* indented, the lines of text begin at the left margin and end at the right margin. An *indent* is additional whitespace inserted between the margin and the paragraph text. Use paragraph indentation to set paragraphs apart from one another.

You can set paragraph indents from the left margin, the right margin, or both. Word permits you to indent either entire paragraphs, just the first line of a paragraph, or to create a *hanging indent* (the first line is flush with the margin, but the remaining lines are indented). The three methods of setting indentation in Word are by using the ruler, menu commands, or keyboard shortcuts.

## Indent Using the Ruler

Because indentation is a paragraph attribute, you need to select the paragraphs you want to indent prior to choosing indentation preferences. However, if you're only setting the indentation for one paragraph, you can position the insertion point anywhere in the paragraph. After the indentation for a paragraph has been set, that setting carries down to any new paragraphs you create by pressing Enter while in the current paragraph.

To use the ruler to set paragraph indentation, you must be able to view it. Display the ruler by clicking the **View** menu and

**Tabs are useful for indenting first lines**

You can always indent the first line of a paragraph by inserting a tab at the beginning of the paragraph. However, if you use the techniques outlined here, you can automate the indentation of your paragraphs, thus avoiding the necessity of inserting whitespace at the beginning of each paragraph.

**Don't use spaces to indent paragraphs**

Never use the Spacebar to indent paragraphs. This wastes time and keystrokes and makes your document look sloppy. Also, using the Spacebar only works with monospaced fonts; it never works properly with proportional fonts. Use the Tab key or, better yet, use Word's indentation tools described here.

selecting **Ruler** (to turn off the ruler display choose the **View** menu, and then select **Ruler** again). Or, to quickly display the ruler without leaving it permanently on, move your mouse pointer to the top edge of the work area; keep the mouse there for a second or two, and the ruler slides down onto your work area but disappears when you move the mouse pointer away.

The *ruler* has triangles that mark the paragraph indents (see Figure 10.4). By dragging these markers, you change the indent settings for the selected paragraphs. A dotted vertical line shows the new position of the indent as you drag the indent markers. With ScreenTips enabled, you can more easily identify the ruler attribute markers.

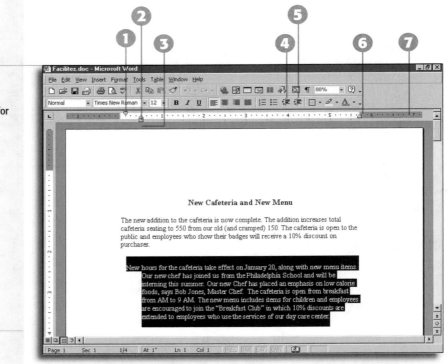

FIGURE 10.4

Drag the appropriate indent marker to set the indentation for the selected paragraphs.

1 First Line Indent marker

2 Hanging Indent marker

3 Left Indent marker

4 Decrease Indent button

5 Increase Indent button

6 Right Indent marker

7 Ruler

To change indentation using the ruler markers:

- Drag the First Line Indent marker to change the left indent of the first line of a paragraph.

- Drag the Hanging Indent marker to change the left indent of all lines of a paragraph except the first one (that is, to create a hanging indent).

- Drag the Left Indent marker to change the left indent of the whole paragraph, including the first line.

- Drag the Right Indent marker to change the right indent of the whole paragraph, including the first line.

**SEE ALSO**

➤ *Learn how to enable ScreenTips on page 650*

## Indent Using Menu Commands

Paragraph indentation also can be set in the Paragraph dialog box.

### Setting Paragraph Indentation

1. Position your cursor in the paragraph or select the paragraphs you want to indent.

2. Open the **Format** menu, and select **Paragraph** to open the Paragraph dialog box. Alternatively, right-click and select **Paragraph**. Click the **Indents and Spacing** tab if it isn't already selected.

3. In the Indentation area of the dialog box, enter the number of inches you want to indent the paragraph in the **Left** or **Right** boxes, or click the up and down arrows in the boxes to increase or decrease the indentation settings.

   To indent the first line of the paragraph, select **First Line** from the **Special** drop-down list. Then enter the number of inches you want to indent the first line in the **By** box, or use the up and down arrows to select the measurement.

   To indent all the lines of the paragraph on the left except the first line of the paragraph, select **Hanging** from the **Special** drop-down list. Then in the **By** box enter the number of inches you want to indent all but the first line, or use the up and down arrows to select the measurement. Unless you specify a Left indent for the entire paragraph, the first line of the paragraph remains flush with the left margin.

4. Click **OK** to apply the settings.

**It's too hard to drag indent markers!**

Click the small box at the left side of the ruler until you see the indent marker you need. Then click the ruler at the measurement where you want that indent placed (click in the gray area of the ruler beneath the inch markings).

## Indent Using Keyboard Shortcuts

To quickly indent paragraphs using only the keyboard, use the shortcuts listed in Table 10.2.

TABLE 10.2    **Indenting shortcuts**

| To | Do This |
|---|---|
| Indent whole paragraph 1/2 inch from the left margin. | Choose Increase Indent or press Ctrl+M. |
| Decrease the left indent of a paragraph by 1/2 inch. | Choose Decrease Indent or press Ctrl+Shift+M. |
| Indent the first line of a paragraph. | Press Tab. |
| Create a hanging indent. | Press Ctrl+T. |
| Remove a hanging indent. | Press Ctrl+Shift+T. |
| Remove all paragraph formatting. | Press Ctrl+Q. |

The easiest way to indent the first line of a paragraph is to use the Tab key. However, this does not create an "inheritable" indent, as the other methods do. That is, if you indent a paragraph using the Tab key, then press Enter to create a new paragraph, the new paragraph inherits the indentation of the original paragraph, all except the first line indent created by inserting a tab character. If you want to create an inheritable first line indent, create it by using a style.

**SEE ALSO**

➤ *Learn how to create and apply paragraph styles on page 241*

# Work with Tabs

Tab stops help you set text at a horizontal position on your page, such as two inches from the left margin. When you press the Tab key, Word moves the insertion point (and any paragraph text to the right of it) to the next tab stop. By default, Word sets tab stops at half-inch intervals across the width of the page. You may find that half-inch tabs do not suit your text layout, but you can change the position of the tab stops. You can also define how the text aligns at each tab stop.

We find that the default tab settings or the use of tables serves us well in everyday use of Word and we rarely have occasion to change tab settings. We do however, change them when we need to, without hesitation. For example, we often change the default tab settings when we use tabs in headers and footers, tables of contents and indexes, or inside table cells.

If you ever find yourself faced with the decision whether to set a tab stop or just hit the tab key several times, we highly recommend that you set the tab stop, especially if the tab setting will do service in multiple paragraphs. If you ever have to go back and reformat those paragraphs, it will be much easier if you don't have to fiddle with multiple tab stops across the page.

The five types of tab stops are as follows (see Figure 10.5):

- Left. The left edge of text lines up at the tab stop (this is the default and standard type of tab stop).
- Center. The text centers on the tab stop.
- Right. The right edge of the text lines up at the tab stop.
- Decimal. The decimal point lines up at the tab stop. This is occasionally useful for aligning columns of numbers.
- Bar. A straight vertical line appears at the tab stop. The text does not realign on this type of tab. Also, you can only set a bar from the Tabs dialog box. The bar is a relic of versions of Word in which you had to set up tables with tabs. You used the bar to set vertical borders between columns in tabbed tables.

**SEE ALSO**

➤ *Learn how to create a table of contents and an index on page 548*

➤ *For more information about creating tables, see page 165*

➤ *To learn more about using tab settings within table cells, see page 178*

➤ *Learn about creating headers and footers on page 295*

## Create Custom Tab Stops

Although Word provides tab stops at every 1/2 inch from the left to right margins on your page, you can move, remove, or add tab stops. You can use the ruler to set tab stops or you can specify them in the Tabs dialog box.

---

**Consider tables instead of tabs**

We frequently use tables instead of changing tab stops. Even if you are creating a list that contains as few as two columns, it's faster to insert a two-column table (with no borders) than setting tab stops and using the Tab key. Most importantly, tables wrap text within a cell, tab settings do not wrap text.

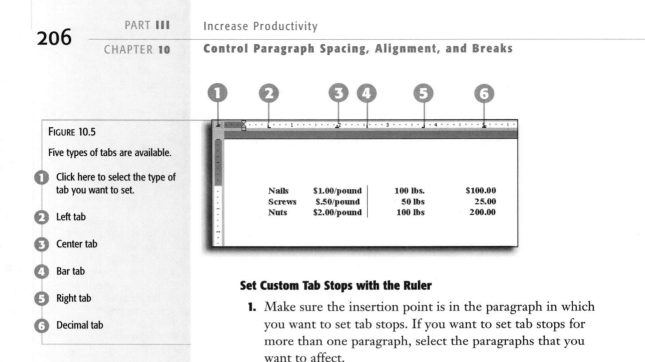

FIGURE 10.5

Five types of tabs are available.

1 Click here to select the type of tab you want to set.

2 Left tab

3 Center tab

4 Bar tab

5 Right tab

6 Decimal tab

### Set Custom Tab Stops with the Ruler

1. Make sure the insertion point is in the paragraph in which you want to set tab stops. If you want to set tab stops for more than one paragraph, select the paragraphs that you want to affect.

2. Put Word in Normal view or Print Layout view, so that you can see the tab/indent symbol on the left end of the ruler (refer to Figure 10.5). Repeatedly click the tab/indent symbol until you see the symbol for the type of tab you want to set. If you aren't sure which type of tab a symbol represents, rest the mouse pointer on the symbol for a moment; a ScreenTip will appear describing the symbol.

3. Point at the location on the ruler where you want to place the tab stop (keep your mouse pointer near the bottom gray border of the ruler).

4. Hold down the left mouse button. A tab symbol of the type you selected in step 3 appears in the ruler, along with a dashed vertical line on your page, showing where the tab stop falls in relation to your text.

5. Drag the mouse left or right until the tab stop is at the correct position and then release the mouse button. If you release the mouse button before you have moved the tab symbol where you want it, point at the tab symbol again and drag it left or right until it appears where you want it.

6. Repeat steps 2 through 5 as necessary until you have set all desired tab stops.

When you set a tab stop manually, all the default tab stops to the left of it disappear. Default tab stops to the right of your right-most manually set tab stop remain in effect.

The ruler method of setting tabs is the most intuitive. However, some people prefer to use the Tabs dialog box to set tabs because it is more precise. Using the dialog box, you can set the exact position of a tab by entering a number in the **Tab Stop Position** field instead of eyeballing the tab setting.

One benefit of this is that you can enter tab stops using any of several measurement systems. You can enter the number using inches (3.55"), centimeters (7cm), millimeters (99mm), picas (9pi) or points (300pt).

### Position Tab Stops Precisely with the Tabs Dialog Box

1. Make sure the insertion point is in the paragraph in which you want to set tab stops. If you want to set tab stops for more than one paragraph, select the paragraphs that you want to affect.

2. Open the **Format** menu, and select **Tabs**, or double-click the ruler. The Tabs dialog box appears (see Figure 10.6).

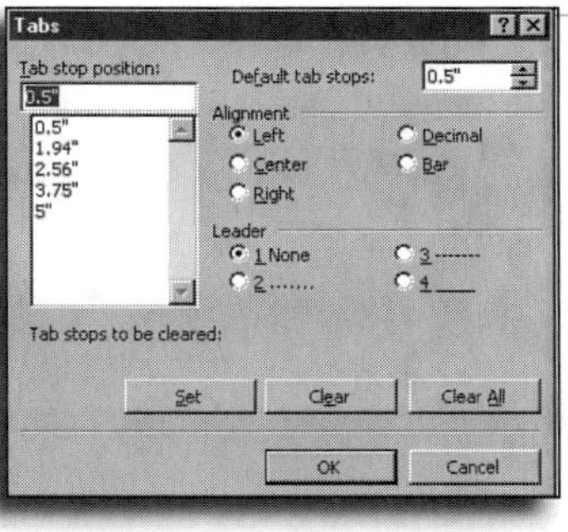

**Removing a tab stop**

If you set a tab stop by mistake and you want to remove it entirely, drag its tab symbol below the ruler. The tab symbol disappears.

**About tab settings and inheritance**

When you press Enter at the end of a paragraph, the new paragraph will inherit the tab settings of the original para-graph. You therefore have to clear the tab settings if you want the new paragraph to return to the default tabs at every 1/2 inch. To do this, either click **Clear All** in the Tabs dialog box (**Format**, **Tabs** in the menu) or simply drag all of the tab stops off the ruler.

**FIGURE 10.6**

In the Tabs dialog box you can set and clear tabs.

3. In the **Tab Stop Position** text box, enter the tab position as a number of inches ("), millimeters (mm), centimeters (cm), picas (pi), or points (pt) from the left margin. (If you enter a plain number, Word assumes your default measurement system.)

4.  Under **Alignment**, click the type of tab stop you want to set—**Left**, **Center**, **Right**, **Decimal**, or **Bar**.

5.  Click **Set**.

6.  Repeat steps 3 through 5 for each tab stop you want to set. When finished, click **OK**.

## Set Tabs with Leaders

*Leaders* are repeated characters that appear to the left of a tab stop. They "lead up" to the tab stop. The most commonly used characters for leaders are periods, but Word also offers dash and underline leaders (see Figure 10.7). The most common use for leaders is in tables of contents and indexes to make it easier for the reader to line up a table entry with its page number on the right side of the page. You can also use leaders in paper-based forms to create underlined spaces for people to complete.

**Setting even-spaced tab stops**

By changing the default tab stop setting to something other than 0.5", you can create a set of evenly spaced tab stops automatically. To do this, enter the spacing you want to use in the **Default Tab Stops** box in the Tabs dialog box.

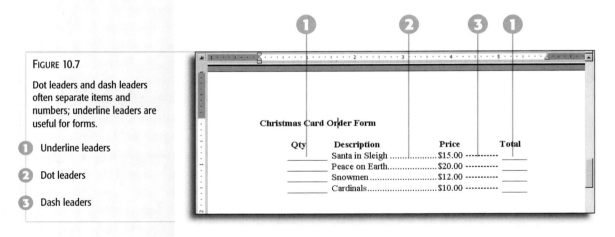

FIGURE 10.7

Dot leaders and dash leaders often separate items and numbers; underline leaders are useful for forms.

1  Underline leaders

2  Dot leaders

3  Dash leaders

### Add Tab Leaders

1.  Make sure the insertion point is in the paragraph in which you want to set tab stops. If you want to set tab stops for more than one paragraph, select the paragraphs that you want to affect.

2. Open the **Format** menu, and select **Tabs** or double-click the ruler.

3. The Tabs dialog box appears (refer to Figure 10.6).

4. Enter a new tab stop position in the **Tab Stop Position** text box, or select one of the existing tab stops listed beneath it.

5. Under **Leader**, select **1 None** to remove leaders, **2** for dot leaders, **3** for dash leaders, or **4** for underline leaders.

6. Click **Set**, and then click **OK**.

## Move and Delete Custom Tab Stops

You can move or delete tab stops with either the ruler and mouse or the Tabs dialog box.

### Moving a Tab Stop with the Mouse

1. Point at the tab symbol on the ruler.

2. Hold down the left mouse button and drag the tab symbol to its new position.

3. Release the mouse button.

To quickly delete a tab stop, point at the tab symbol, hold down the left mouse button, and drag the tab symbol down and off the ruler. The symbol disappears.

You also can use the Tabs dialog box to clear a tab (open the **Format** menu, and select **Tabs**). Select the tab from the list beneath **Tab Stop Position** and then click **Clear**. Click **Clear All** to remove all the tab stops and restore the default tabs. Then click **OK** to close the dialog box.

# Set Line and Paragraph Spacing

The amount of vertical space between lines in a paragraph is the *line spacing*. The amount of space between paragraphs is *paragraph spacing*. By default, Word uses single-spacing for both line and paragraph spacing. This means that the amount of space between lines depends on the design of the font you are using; in general, that means there is just enough space to keep the *descenders* of letters above from touching the *ascenders* of letters below.

**Tips on modifying tab settings**

When you want to modify the tab settings for a paragraph or group of paragraphs, you must click in the paragraph you want to change or select all the paragraphs you want to change. Don't assume that by changing one paragraph with the tab settings that you are affecting the other paragraphs with the same settings.

Most people use single-spacing for their finished documents, but you may want to print a draft with double- or triple-spacing to leave room for an editor to insert comments. If you really want to refine the look of a document, you may want to make fine adjustments to vertical spacing by specifying the point size of the spacing between the lines.

Most people also add one line of space between paragraphs to set the paragraphs apart by pressing the Enter key twice. But you can automatically set spacing between paragraphs so that you need to press the Enter key only once. You can set the amount of space above a paragraph, the amount below, or both. We recommend that, to avoid getting tangled up in spacing problems, you either set the space above or below the paragraph, not both. As regards the choice between adding space above versus space below, that is purely personal. We prefer to add space above but we know people who are perfectly happy adding space below.

Setting paragraph spacing automatically may save you only one keystroke per paragraph, but it provides one other benefit as well. You can set the inter-paragraph spacing at something other than one line if you want. For example, you could set it at one-half or one-quarter of a line. That is, if you are using a 12-point font, you could set the space above each body paragraph at 3 points or 6 points. You still get the whitespace that tells the reader where the paragraph breaks are, but you do it without giving away so much whitespace.

### Change Line or Paragraph Spacing

1. Make sure the insertion point is in the paragraph in which you want to set spacing. If you want to set spacing for more than one paragraph, select the paragraphs that you want to affect.

2. Open the **Format** menu and select **Paragraph**. The Paragraph dialog box opens (see Figure 10.8). Click the **Indents and Spacing** tab if it isn't already selected.

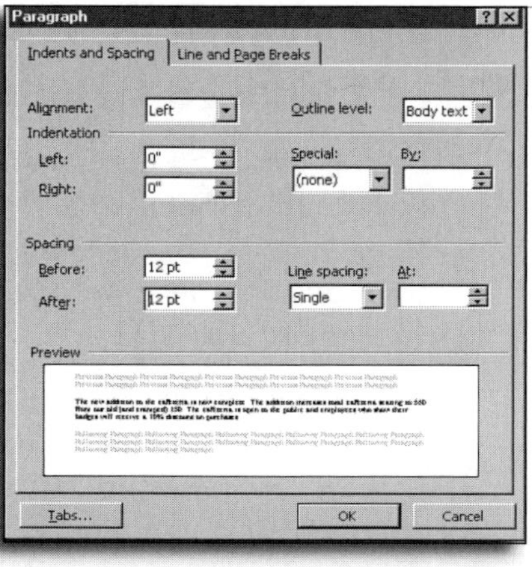

FIGURE 10.8
Select the desired vertical spacing between lines of text from the **Line Spacing** drop-down list.

**3.** To change line spacing, select the desired spacing from the **Line Spacing** drop-down list:

- **Single**, **1.5 lines**, or **Double**. Space between lines is the choice you make here, single, one-and-one-half lines, or double lines.

- **Exactly**. Space between lines is exactly the value, in points, that you enter in the **At** text box. (There are 72 points in an inch.)

- **At Least**. Space between lines is at least the value, in points, you enter in the **At** text box; Word increases the spacing if the line has characters with larger font sizes or graphics that need more vertical space.

- **Multiple**. Changes spacing by the factor you enter in the **At** text box. For example, enter 3 to triple the line spacing.

**4.** To add additional spacing before or after the paragraph, enter the desired amount of space (in points) in the **Before** or **After** text boxes, or click the up and down arrows to increase or decrease paragraph space in half-line increments.

**5.** Click **OK**.

To change line and paragraph spacing, you also can right-click and choose **Paragraph** to open the Paragraph dialog box.

# Control Word, Sentence, Paragraph, Line, and Page Breaks

When you create a document, Word helps you control the flow of text on the printed page. You control where words, sentences, and paragraphs break. Word controls where lines and pages break. In a document organized in columns, Word controls where the columns break.

In a long or complex document, you might want to control organization by breaking the document into sections. Usually you insert section breaks manually, but Word occasionally inserts section breaks for you. For example, when Word creates a table of contents, it separates the table of contents from the rest of the document by inserting a section break.

Although Word controls line and page breaks, you can force line and page breaks whenever you need to. You can also use hyphenation and non-breaking spaces to influence where Word breaks lines. You can use Word's pagination tools to influence where page and column breaks occur.

**SEE ALSO**

➤ *For more on inserting sections, see page 286*

➤ *To learn about creating columns, see page 330*

## Insert Line Breaks

Normally, if you want to force text to appear on the next line, you press Enter, which forces a *paragraph break*. Occasionally, however, you may want to force text to appear on the next line without starting a new paragraph. You want to force a *line break*. You can do this by pressing Shift+Enter.

One example of a line break application is to center a title that is more than one line long. You want to balance the lengths of the lines by choosing where the lines break. If you have defined the paragraph so that it has whitespace below it, pressing Enter to force a paragraph break inserts extra, unwanted space between the lines. But pressing Shift+Enter to force a line break does not introduce extra whitespace.

# Use Hyphenation to Control Line Breaks

Normally during word wrap, Word breaks lines at spaces or hyphens. If you don't want a hyphenated word (say, for example, a hyphenated last name) to be separated by a line break, you can use a *non-breaking hyphen* instead. Press Ctrl+Shift+Hyphen where you would normally type the hyphen, or click the **Insert** menu, and select **Symbol**, select the **Special Characters** tab, click **Nonbreaking Hyphen** in the **Character** box to select it, and choose **Insert**.

On the other hand, you may want to define where a long word should break, to prevent Word from moving the entire word down to the next line and creating a gap in the line above. You could insert a hyphen, which would cause the word to break at the hyphen. The problem with this is if you ever edit the paragraph, the word might no longer fall at the end of the line. But the hyphen still appears. The solution is either to insert an *optional hyphen* or to turn on automatic hyphenation.

You only see an optional hyphen if the word it is in falls at the end of a line where it extends past the right margin. In that circumstance, the line breaks at the hyphen and the hyphen appears, separating the word between lines. But if the word does not appear at the end of a line, the hyphen is invisible.

To insert an optional hyphen, position your insertion point in the word where you want to put the hyphen and then press Ctrl+Hyphen.

Using optional hyphens and non-breaking hyphens enables you to manually control the hyphenation of your text. The other alternative is to have Word hyphenate line endings automatically or have Word prompt you for hyphens where it thinks they are appropriate.

### Turn on Automatic or Prompted Hyphenation

1. Open the **Tools** menu, and select **Language**. Then choose **Hyphenation** from the submenu. The Hyphenation dialog box appears (see Figure 10.9).

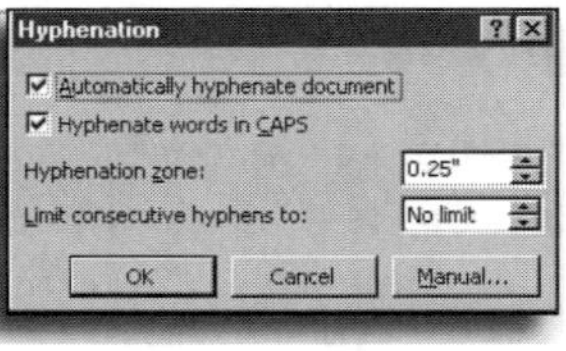

FIGURE 10.9

Set the hyphenation zone and the number of consecutive hyphens you want.

2. Click **Automatically Hyphenate Document** to place a check mark there.

3. (Optional) If you want to hyphenate words that appear in all uppercase letters, click **Hyphenate Words in CAPS** to place a check mark there.

4. Specify the amount of space to leave between the end of the last word in the line and the right margin in the **Hyphenation Zone** box. To reduce the number of hyphens, make the hyphenation zone wider. Make the hyphenation zone narrower to reduce the raggedness of the right margin. In justified paragraphs, a narrower zone causes Word to permit less variation in the amount of space it permits between words on each line.

5. Enter the maximum number of consecutive lines that you want Word to hyphenate in the **Limit Consecutive Hyphens To** box. By default Word allows unlimited consecutive hyphenated lines. But hyphenated line endings make a document harder to read (and uglier), so you may want to use this feature to limit the number of consecutive hyphenated lines.

6. Click **OK** to apply your settings to the document. Choose **Manual** to have Word immediately begin the hyphenation process but stop at each possible hyphen to allow you to accept, reject, or change the hyphen position (see Figure 10.10).

When you choose **OK** or **Manual** in the Hyphenation dialog box, Word immediately begins hyphenating your document. If you choose **Manual** in the Hyphenation dialog box, Word prompts you with a dialog box whenever it thinks a word needs to be hyphenated. Choose **Yes** to accept the hyphen position or **No** to reject hyphenation of the word. If you prefer to hyphenate the word at a position other than that offered by Word (this often happens with technical jargon that doesn't appear in the spelling dictionary), use the arrow keys to move the insertion point to that location, and then choose **Yes**. When the manual hyphenation process is complete, a dialog box appears stating that hyphenation is complete. Click **OK** to return to your document.

If you selected **Automatically Hyphenate Document** in the Hyphenation dialog box, then you later continue entering new text, Word automatically hyphenates line endings each time it wraps text to the next line. It does so even if you closed the Hyphenation dialog box by choosing **Manual**.

On the other hand, if you did not select **Automatically Hyphenate Document** but closed the dialog box by choosing **Manual**, Word only does the prompted hyphenation. When it is finished with that, if you enter new text into the document, Word does not automatically hyphenate line endings as you type.

## Use Non-breaking Spaces to Control Line Breaks

Because Word breaks lines at spaces or hyphens, it may separate words that you want kept on the same line, such as a person's first and last name.

To prevent two words from being separated onto different lines, use a non-breaking space. A *non-breaking space* has the same appearance as any other space in your text, but Word won't treat

**Turning hyphenation off**

If needed, you can turn off automatic hyphenation for individual paragraphs. To do this, place your cursor in a paragraph, open the **Format** menu and select **Paragraph**. Click the **Line and Page Breaks** tab. Select **Don't Hyphenate**. Choose **OK**. To turn hyphenation off for multiple paragraphs, select the paragraphs involved first; then open the **Format** menu and select **Paragraph**. Click the **Line and Page Breaks** tab. Select **Don't Hyphenate**. Choose **OK**.

it as a space when it determines where to wrap a line of text to the next line. The two words on either side of the non-breaking space stay together on the same line.

To use a non-breaking space in your text, position your insertion point where you want to put the non-breaking space and then do one of the following:

- Open the **Insert** menu and select **Symbol**. Select the **Special Characters** tab (see Figure 10.11) and then click **Nonbreaking Space** to select it. Click **Insert** and then click **Close** to exit the dialog box.

- Press Ctrl+Shift+Space.

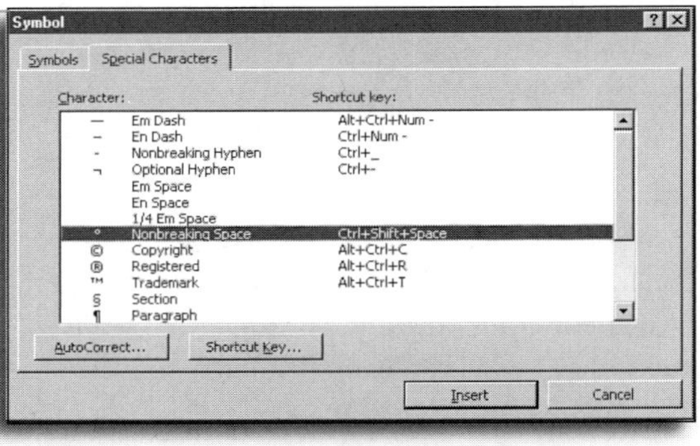

FIGURE 10.11

Use **Special Characters** to insert typesetting characters, such as the non-breaking space.

## Insert Page Breaks

Word automatically creates a new page when the text you are entering reaches the bottom margin of the current page. However, you can also create page breaks in your document.

To insert a page break, place your insertion point where you want to start the new page and then do one of the following:

- Open the **Insert** menu, and select **Break**. Click **Page Break** in the Break dialog box (see Figure 10.12) and click **OK**.

- Press Ctrl+Enter.

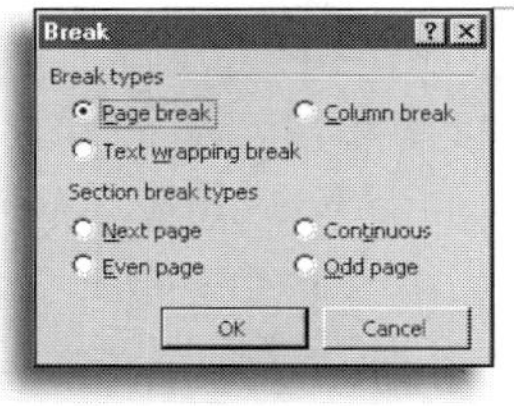

FIGURE 10.12

To start a new page, click **Page Break** and then click **OK**.

In Page Layout view, you can clearly see the end of one page and the beginning of another. In Normal view, automatic page breaks appear as dotted lines that stretch across the page while manual page breaks display as a dotted line with the notation "Page Break" in the middle (see Figure 10.13).

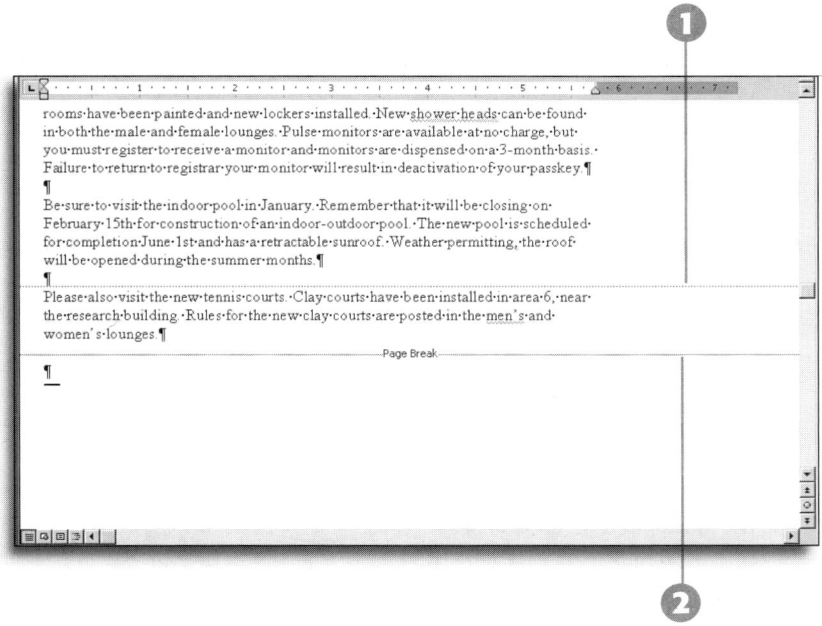

FIGURE 10.13

The page break you insert looks like a dotted line with "Page Break" in the middle when seen in Normal view.

1  Automatic page break

2  Manual page break

To remove a manual page break, place your insertion point on the break line and then press the Delete key. Or, place your insertion point immediately after the page break and press Backspace. Inserting a manual page break, of course, affects the automatic page breaks that follow it, causing them to be repositioned.

# Use Pagination Tools to Control Page and Column Breaks

Word normally inserts page breaks automatically, based on the paper and margin sizes you select, so that text fills each page from margin to margin. You can prevent Word from inserting page breaks in or between certain paragraphs. For example, you might not want page breaks to appear between headings and the body text that follows them. Or you might not want a page break to appear within a list. Finally, you can cause a page break to occur whenever a certain kind of paragraph appears.

# Keep the First and Last Lines with a Paragraph

A document of more than one page or column may contain a paragraph that begins its first line or column on page one and continues the rest of the paragraph on page two. This single line of text at the bottom of the first page or column is called an *orphan*.

When all the lines of the paragraph except the last one are on one page or column, and the last line is on the next page or column, the single line on the next page or column is called a *widow*.

Leaving widows and orphans is considered to be poor page layout. By default, Word prevents widows and orphans from occurring in your text. In the case of an orphan, Word moves the first line of the paragraph to the next page or column. Where a widow occurs, Word moves the previous line in the paragraph to the next page or column to join the widow line, so that two lines of the paragraph appear at the top of the next page or column. Either way leaves a blank line at the bottom of the page or column, so that the bottom margin won't be even with the bottom margin of the other pages or columns in your document.

### Turn Off Automatic Widow and Orphan Control

1. Select the paragraph to control. Then click the **Format** menu and select **Paragraph**, or right-click and then click **Paragraph**, to open the Paragraph dialog box.

2. Select the **Line and Page Breaks** tab (see Figure 10.14).

3. Click **Widow/Orphan Control** under Pagination to deselect the option.

4. Click **OK**.

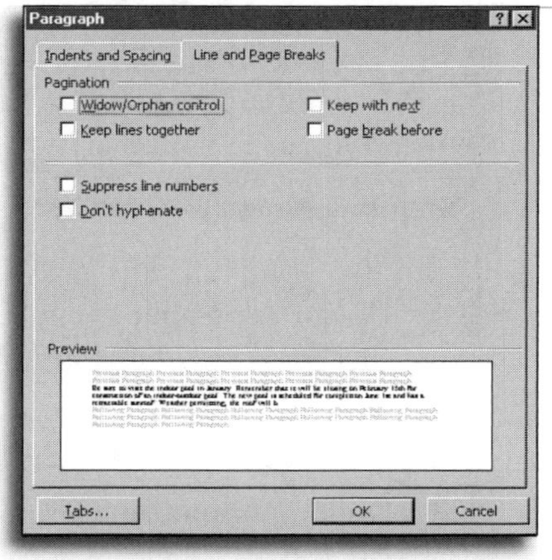

FIGURE 10.14
You can control the flow of text in
your document by selecting one of
the Pagination options.

Widow and orphan control is an alternative to using the tried-
and-true system of editing the text to eliminate the problem,
which is more precise but far more time consuming.

## Prevent a Page Break Within a Paragraph

You can specify that a paragraph not be split by a column or
page break.

### Prevent Page Breaks or Column Breaks Within a Paragraph

1. Select the paragraph or paragraphs you want to keep from
   breaking.

2. Click the **Format** menu and select **Paragraph**, or right-click
   and then click **Paragraph**, to open the Paragraph dialog
   box.

3. Click the **Line and Page Break**s tab (refer to Figure 10.14).

4. Under **Pagination**, click **Keep Lines Together**.

5. Click **OK**.

If you set this for multiple consecutive paragraphs, Word does not insert a page or column break within any of the paragraphs. But it might insert a page or column break between the paragraphs.

# Keep Multiple Paragraphs Together

You may not want a page or column break to separate two paragraphs from each other. For example, you never want a heading to appear at the bottom of a page, without any text following it.

### Keep Two Paragraphs Together

1. Make sure the insertion point is in the first paragraph.
2. Open the **Format** menu and select **Paragraph**, or right-click and then click **Paragraph**, to open the Paragraph dialog box.
3. Click the **Line and Page Breaks** tab (refer to Figure 10.14).
4. Under **Pagination**, click **Keep with Next**.
5. Click **OK**.

# Force Page Breaks at Headings

In a long document with multiple main headings, you might want each main heading to appear at the top of a new page.

### Start a New Page for a New Heading

1. Make sure the insertion point is in the heading paragraph.
2. Open the **Format** menu and select **Paragraph**, or right-click and then click **Paragraph**, to open the Paragraph dialog box.
3. Click the **Line and Page Breaks** tab (refer to Figure 10.14).
4. Under **Pagination**, click **Page Break Before**.
5. Click **OK**.

Typically, you would use this feature as part of the definition of a paragraph style.

### SEE ALSO

➤ *Learn more about paragraph styles on page 241*

# Work with Lists

# Sort Lists

Sorting lists is a convenient tool and it allows you to enter text into a list in any order. Once text is entered, you can sort the list in the order that suits you.

When Microsoft Word sorts text, rules govern the sort order. It helps to understand how Word sorts text:

- You choose whether you want to sort alphabetically, numerically, or by date.

- You have a choice of sorting in ascending order (A to Z or zero to 9) or in descending order (Z to A or 9 to zero).

- Paragraph marks (¶) separate items to be sorted. Tabs separate fields within each item.

- Items beginning with punctuation marks or symbols (such as !, #, $, %, or &) are sorted first, followed by items beginning with numbers and then by items beginning with letters. Dates are treated as three-digit numbers.

- If the sort is by numbers, all other characters are ignored. The numbers can be anywhere in a paragraph.

- If the sort is by date, only the following are accepted as date separators: hyphen (-), forward slash (/), comma (,), and period (.). Only the colon (:) is recognized as a time separator. If the item isn't recognized as a date or time, Word puts the item at the beginning or end of the list (depending on whether the list is sorted in ascending or descending order).

- When more than one item begins with the same character, Word looks to subsequent characters to determine the sort order.

Word sorts lists by the first word in the list, unless you have tabs separating columns of items. In that case Word considers the tabs as field markers (a *field* is a single piece of information, usually associated with databases, which in this case refers to the text in a particular tabbed column). The text in the first column is considered Field 1, the text in the second column is Field 2, and so on. That way it's possible to sort based on the second or

---

**Paragraph marks make a list**

You don't necessarily have to set out text in a "list" format to use Word's sorting feature. Because Word defines list items as text followed by paragraph marks (hard returns), any set of paragraphs can be sorted as a list.

subsequent column items instead of the first word of the line. You can name each field by adding the field names as the first line of your list, as shown in Figure 11.1. By doing this you can sort using the descriptive field names instead of the non-descriptive, generic names "Field1," and so on.

### Sort a List

1.  Select the text you want to sort. Each item in the list should be on a separate line. If each line has multiple items of information, the lines should be separated by tabs. The first line may optionally consist of column headers or field names.

2.  Click the **Table** menu and select **Sort**. The Sort Text dialog box appears (see Figure 11.1).

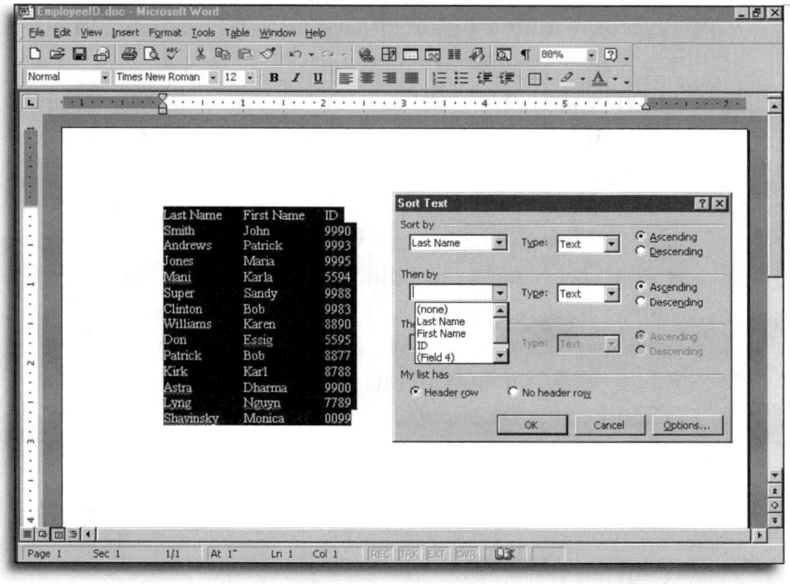

3.  If your list has a line of column titles (field names), select **Header Row** under **My List Has**. This avoids including that line in the sorting and changes the choices in the **Sort By** field from "Field 1," "Field 2," and so on, to the names in the header row.

> **Only one tab per column, please**
>
> If you are setting up a text list in tabbed columns, and you want the columns to line up nicely, set tab stops for each column. Do not insert multiple tab characters between columns to line them up. If you insert more than one tab, Word will interpret them as multiple columns. For example, it you tab twice between columns one and two, Word will assume column two for that row has no data in it and that the data that you intend to be in column two is really in column three.

**FIGURE 11.1**

For a tabbed list, select the field by which you want to sort. If the first line in your list is a field name or column title, it should appear in the Sort By list as shown here. With no header line, the generic names Field 1, Field 2, and so forth, appear in the Sort By list.

**4.** From the **Sort By** drop-down list, select one of the following:

**Field 1** (or the name of the first column) if you want to sort the lines based on the first word on each line, **Field 2** (or the name of the second column) if you want to sort the lines based on the text in the second tabbed column, and so on.

If the items in the list don't have tabbed columns or you don't want to use the tabs as field separators, select **Paragraphs** (especially if the items have more than one line in the paragraph).

**5.** From the **Type** drop-down list, select **Text** to sort the list alphabetically, **Number** to sort numerically, or **Date** to sort by date or time.

**6.** Click **Ascending** to sort the list in A to Z, 0 to 99 order. Click **Descending** to sort the list in Z to A, 99 to 0 order.

**7.** When you choose a field for the first (primary) sort, the **Then By** drop-down list is available. This lets you set a secondary sort criterion so if two items in the first sort are the same, the secondary sort sets their order. For example, you have a list with last name, first name, and phone number for a set of people. You sort alphabetically by last name. However, if you have two Smiths, you would want Ellen Smith to come before John Smith, so you want the secondary sort to be by first name. Select the options for the Then By sort the same way you did for the primary sort.

**8.** Click **OK**.

SEE ALSO
➤ *Learn more about fields and sorting on page 488*
➤ *Learn how to convert tabbed text to tables and how to sort tables on page 179*

## An alternative to sorting tabbed columns

An alternate way to sort lists is to convert the text to a table and then sort the table text. You can convert the text back to tabbed columns after sorting, if you want to.

# Create a Numbered or Bulleted List

Lists help to organize and clarify your writing. Bulleted lists clearly set forth the points you want to make. Numbered lists set forth the order of action or importance. Outline numbered lists allow you to create outlines in a variety of styles. Word makes it easy by automatically applying the proper paragraph formatting to your bulleted and numbered paragraphs. Word indents the paragraphs for you, applies the number or bullet style to each new paragraph as you type, and adjusts the number sequence automatically when you add or subtract items.

### Start a Numbered or Bulleted List As You Are Entering Text

**1.** Position your insertion point where you want the first bulleted or numbered item to appear.

**2.** Choose Bullets  or Numbering from the Formatting toolbar.

**3.** Word automatically inserts the first bullet or number, properly punctuated and tabbed (see Figure 11.2), and sets up the paragraph formatting with a hanging indent (a paragraph where all the lines are indented except the first line). When you press Enter at the end of the paragraph, a new bullet or the next number appears at the beginning of the next paragraph. This happens each time that you press Enter.

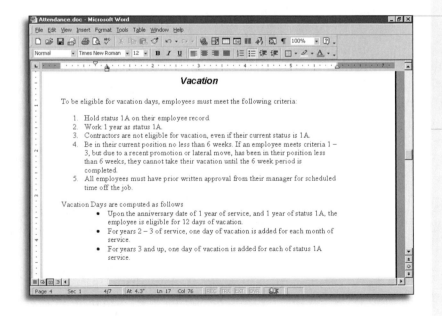

**FIGURE 11.2**

Bulleted lists are generally used for lists of items, while numbered lists work well for steps that must be done in order or paragraphs that must be assigned a value (such as priority).

You can discontinue the bullets or numbering three ways:

- Choose Bullets ⊞ or Numbering ⊞ from the Formatting toolbar. This converts the selected bulleted or numbered paragraph into a standard paragraph.

- Press Enter twice at the end of the last paragraph in the list. The first time you press Enter, a new bulleted/numbered paragraph appears. The second time you press Enter, a new standard paragraph appears and the bullet/number formatting disappears from the blank paragraph above.

- Press Backspace twice. The first Backspace removes the bullet or number and punctuation. The second Backspace causes the paragraph to revert to normal paragraph formatting.

If you are still in the habit of pressing Enter twice to insert whitespace between paragraphs, and you want a blank line between each bulleted/numbered paragraph, you can make Word add the extra carriage return.

Create the first bulleted/numbered paragraph in one of the ways described above. Press Enter twice at the end of the first item paragraph. The second press of the Enter key will kill the bulleting/numbering. Then, for the second item in your list, restart the bulleting/numbering. Thereafter, when you press Enter once, Word automatically inserts two hard returns for you after each bulleted/numbered paragraph. This method only works if Word AutoFormatting is enabled for automatic bulleted/numbered lists.

One last note about using this method: Rather than go to all this trouble, we would recommend that you press Enter only once between paragraphs. Then, if you want whitespace between the paragraphs, use paragraph formatting to add it.

Word AutoFormats lists by default. If Word does not behave as described previously, perhaps list AutoFormatting has been turned off. Turn it on again by opening the **Format** menu, selecting **AutoFormat**, and then choosing **Options** from the dialog box. You also can select the **Tools** menu, and then choose **AutoCorrect**. In the AutoCorrect dialog box that opens, select

**AutoFormat starts numbered lists for you**

Word automatically starts a numbered list if you type a number followed by a period, hyphen, closing parenthesis, or greater than sign, and then type a space or tab and more text.

the **AutoFormat** tab. Make sure a check mark appears in the **Lists** check box in the **Apply** section of the dialog box. You should also click the **AutoFormat as You Type** tab and check both **A̲utomatic Bulleted Lists** and **Automatic N̲umbered Lists** under **Apply as You Type**.

When you need to apply bullets or numbers to existing text, select the paragraphs that will constitute the bulleted or numbered paragraphs, then click the Bullets ▦ or Numbering ▦ icon in the Formatting toolbar. Word automatically reformats the selected paragraphs and bullets them or numbers them in order. If you have two hard returns between paragraphs, you'll discover that Word is clever enough not to bullet or number the blank paragraphs in-between each of your bulleted/numbered paragraphs.

**SEE ALSO**

➤ *To learn about adding spacing between paragraphs without adding extra carriage returns, see page 209*

➤ *To learn more about AutoFormat and controlling AutoFormat options, see page 251*

# Edit a Numbered or Bulleted List

To delete a bulleted or numbered paragraph from a list, select the paragraph and press Delete. Any subsequent numbered paragraphs are automatically renumbered. Word also renumbers the list if you move paragraphs within a numbered list.

If you interrupt the list with paragraphs that don't have bullets or numbering, and then you want to continue the list from where you left off, do one of the following:

- For bulleted lists, click where you want the new paragraph to begin and choose Bullets from the Formatting toolbar.

- For numbered lists, click where you want the new paragraph to begin. Open the **Fo̲rmat** menu and select **Bullets and Numbering** or right-click and select **Bullets and Numbering** to open the Bullets and Numbering dialog box. Select the **Numbered** tab, and then select the numbering style you are using in the list. Select **C̲ontinue Previous List** and then click **OK**.

**AutoFormat starts bulleted lists for you**

When you type an asterisk, one or two hyphens, a greater than sign, or an arrow created by a greater than sign and a hyphen or equal sign, Word starts a bulleted list. Word also turns a symbol or an *inline graphic* (a picture that's treated like a character) followed by two or more spaces into the start of a bulleted list.

To restart the numbering in a list at 1, click **Restart Numbering** in the Bullets and Numbering dialog box.

It is also possible to add items to an existing bulleted or numbered list.

### Add New Items to an Existing Bulleted or Numbered List

1. Position the insertion point at the end of the paragraph after which you want to add the new item.

2. Press Enter. A new paragraph appears with a new bullet or number. Word automatically renumbers any subsequent numbered paragraphs.

3. Type the new text. If you press Enter at the end of the paragraph, a new bulleted or numbered paragraph starts.

4. Repeat steps 1 through 3 as many times as needed.

# Remove Numbers and Bullets

When you no longer need the numberings or bullets but want to retain text, select the paragraphs from which you want to remove the bullets or numbering and click Bullets 📇 or Numbering 📇 on the Formatting toolbar.

# Change Number or Bullet Formatting

When you apply bullets or numbers to your paragraphs, Word applies its *default* formatting. For a bulleted paragraph, this means that Word places a round bullet on the left margin and indents the rest of the paragraph 1/4 inch. For a numbered paragraph, it means that Word places an Arabic number and a period on the left margin and indents the rest of the paragraph 1/4 inch.

### Change the Bullet or Number Style of Existing Lists

1. Select the paragraphs to which you want to apply the bullets or numbering; or, if creating new paragraphs, place the insertion point where you begin typing.

**2.** Click the **Format** menu and select **Bullets and Numbering,** or right-click and select **Bullets and Numbering,** to open the Bullets and Numbering dialog box (see Figure 11.3).

**3.** Click the **Bulleted** tab and click the desired style to change the style of bullets. Select **None** to remove bullets.

Click the **Numbered** tab and select the desired numbering style (see Figure 11.4), or click **None** to remove the numbering from the list.

**4.** Click **OK**.

If none of the number or bullet styles offered by Word meets your needs, you can create your own number styles or select different symbols for your bullet lists.

### Create Custom Numbering Styles

1. Position your insertion point where you want the numbered list to start or select the existing paragraphs to which you want to apply the numbering.

2. Open the **Format** menu and select **Bullets and Numbering** to open the Bullets and Numbering dialog box.

3. Click the **Numbered** tab.

4. Click **Customize**.

5. The Customize Numbered List dialog box appears (see Figure 11.5).

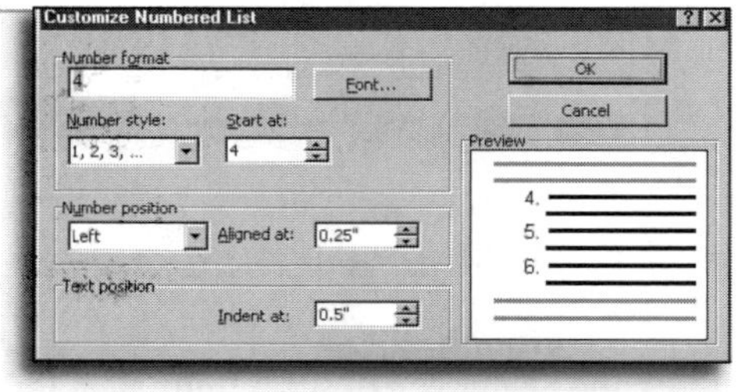

FIGURE 11.5

Set the options to create your own numbering style for your list.

FIGURE 11.5

Set the options to create your own numbering style for your list.

6. Set the options to customize your list:

   For numbered lists, choose **Font** to set the font options for the numbers. Select a **Number Style** from the drop-down list and specify what number or letter to **Start At**. Select the alignment of the paragraph under **Number Position** and set the **Aligned at** position, and then specify the number of inches the paragraph text is indented in the **Indent At** box.

7. Click **OK**.

### Select a Different Symbol for Your Bulleted List

1. Position your insertion point where you want the bulleted list to start or select the existing paragraphs to which you want to apply the bullets.

2. Open the **Format** menu and select **Bullets and Numbering** to open the Bullets and Numbering dialog box.

3. Click the **Bulleted** tab.

4. Choose **Cus_tomize**.

5. The Customize Bulleted List dialog box appears (see Figure 11.6).

**FIGURE 11.6**

Select a bullet style and set font and position options in the Customize Bulleted List dialog box.

6. Set the options to customize your list:

   • Select a **B_ullet Character** from the bullet styles shown.

   • Click **_Font** to change the font options (such as size or bold) for the bullet symbol.

   • Click **B_ullet** to open the Symbol dialog box (see Figure 11.7). Select an appropriate symbol font from the **_Font** box, click the symbol you want to use (hold down your mouse button on a symbol to magnify it), and click **OK**. The symbol replaces whichever **B_ullet Character** is currently selected.

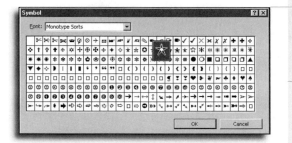

**FIGURE 11.7**

Select a font that has the symbol you need and then click the symbol you want to use.

- Set the position of the bullet relative to the left margin by specifying the number of inches in the **Indent** **At** box under **Bullet Position**.

- Specify the left indentation of the following lines of text in the **Indent At** box under **Text Position**.

**7.** Click **OK**.

# Use Pictures As Bullets

We have become familiar with the picture bullets used on Web pages. It's easy to incorporate them into your own documents or Web pages when you create them in Word.

### Use Pictures As Your Bullets

**1.** Position your insertion point where you want the bulleted list to start or select the existing paragraphs to which you want to apply the bullets.

**2.** Open the **Format** menu and select **Bullets and** **Numbering** to open the Bullets and Numbering dialog box.

**3.** Click the **Bulleted** tab.

**4.** Choose **Picture**. The Picture Bullet dialog box appears (see Figure 11.8).

FIGURE 11.8

Select one of the available bullet clips, click **Import Clips** to get pictures from an outside source, or click **Clips Online** to download more pictures from the Web.

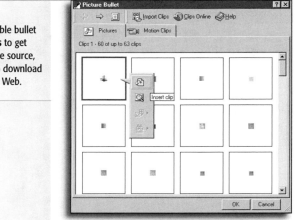

5. Select the bullet picture you want and choose **Insert Clip** from the pop-up menu.

**SEE ALSO**

➤ *For more information about clip art, see page 364*

# Use Outline Numbered Lists

You use an *outline numbered list* when you need two or more levels of numbering or bullets in the same list. A numbered outline is an example of an outline numbered list, but you can also have bullets within a bulleted list.

In an outline numbered list, such as the one shown in Figure 11.9, the numbers or bullets are assigned to paragraphs based on how far they're indented from the left margin. A Level 1 paragraph is on the left margin, a Level 2 paragraph is indented 1/4 inch from the left margin, a Level 3 paragraph is indented 1/2 inch from the left margin, and so on. All the Level 1 paragraphs share the same style bullet or number, all the Level 2 paragraphs share another bullet style, and so on. For example, in the traditional outline style, the Level 1 paragraphs have Roman numerals (I, II, III), the Level 2 paragraphs have capital letters (A, B, C), and the Level 3 paragraphs have Arabic numerals (1, 2, 3).

To create an outline numbered list, set up your list with numbers as described in "Create a Numbered or Bulleted List" earlier in this chapter. For a paragraph that is not Level 1, put your cursor in that paragraph and click the **Increase Indent** button 🔲 on the Standard toolbar or press **Tab**. Each time you indent the paragraph, it goes down one level. To bring a paragraph up one level, click the **Decrease Indent** button 🔲 or press Shift+Tab.

After you type the last paragraph in the list, press Enter, and then choose **Numbering** 🔲 from the Formatting toolbar to end the list. (You also can end the list by pressing Enter twice or pressing Backspace twice.)

**Tab and Enter keys don't work as expected?**

If the Tab and Shift+Tab keys don't change the outline level of your paragraph, and pressing Enter creates a normal paragraph instead of another numbered paragraph, it is because you chose one of the outline numbering formats from the second row of the Bullets and Numbering dialog box. Choose one of the outline numbering formats from the first row and the Tab and Enter keys will work fine. Later, if you want, you can reformat the list to the second row format of your choice.

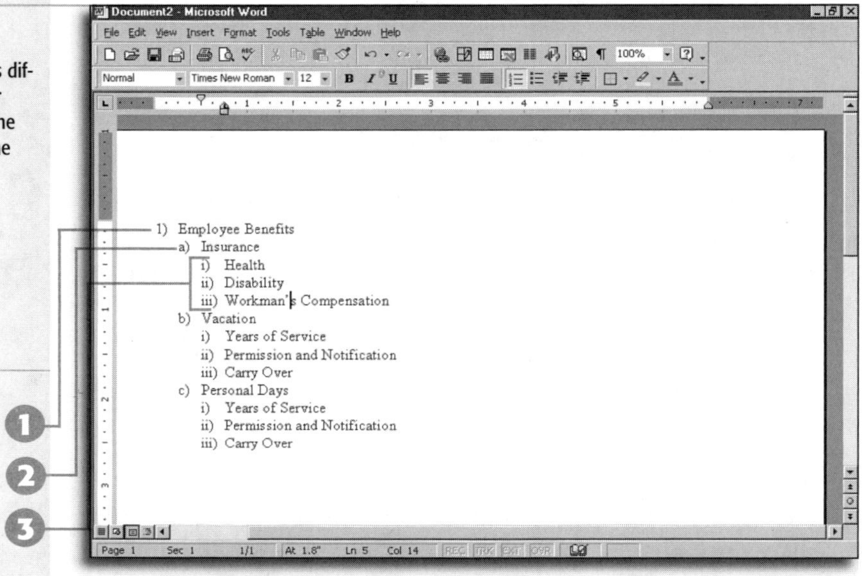

FIGURE 11.9

This outline numbered list has different numbers and letters for each item based on how far the paragraph is indented from the left margin.

**1** Level 1

**2** Level 2

**3** Level 3

The default numbering format that appears may not meet your needs, but you can change it. Exactly how you do that depends on whether you want to reformat an existing outline list or you want to set up formatting for any future outline lists that you plan to create in your document.

### Format an Outline Numbered List

**1.** If you want to reformat a list that you have already created, select it first. If you want to define formatting for a list that you have not created yet, place the insertion point in an empty paragraph.

**2.** Open the **Format** menu and select **Bullets and Numbering** to open the Bullets and Numbering dialog box.

**3.** Click the **Outline Numbered** tab (see Figure 11.10).

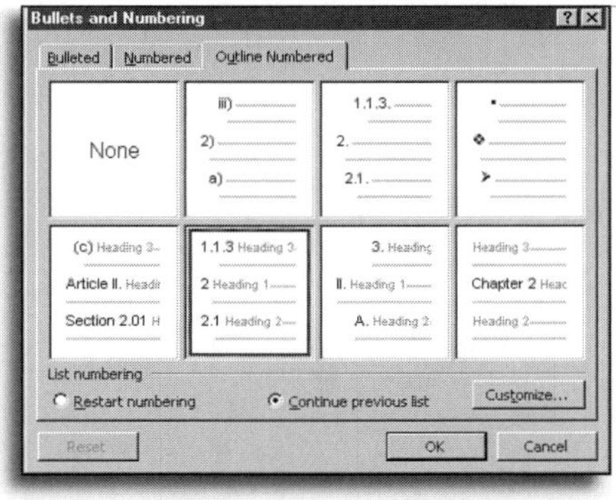

**FIGURE 11.10**
Select the style of outline numbered list you want and then choose OK.

4. Select the style of numbering/lettering or bullets you want. If you are reformatting an existing, selected list, choose any of the formats. If you are setting up formatting for a list not yet created, select one of the formats from the top row only. The second-row formats are not really designed for outline lists but rather are for outlining your whole document. Their outline levels are linked to Word's built-in **Heading n** styles. The Tab and Shift+Tab keys and the Increase Indent ⊞ and Decrease Indent ⊞ buttons do *not* behave as they do with the top row formats or with simple bulleted and numbered lists. Pressing Enter does *not* create a new numbered paragraph, but rather creates a standard paragraph of Normal style, because that is how the **Heading n** styles are programmed to behave.

5. Click **OK**.

If you don't like the available outline numbering styles, you can customize them. Click **Customize** when you're in the **Outline Numbered** tab of the Bullets and Numbering dialog box. In the Customize Outline Numbered List dialog box, you can select, for each outline level, the number format and style, the starting number, the font, the number position and alignment, indent point for any text you want to include, and paragraph styles.

**SEE ALSO**

➤ *Learn more about styles on page 238*

# Format Efficiently Using Styles

Create and assign paragraph styles

Modify styles

Use automatic formatting

# Use Styles for Consistency and Efficiency

Styles make formatting documents easier. Styles eliminate the tedium of repeating the same formatting tasks over and over. A *style* is a set of formatting commands saved under a single name; each time you want to apply those same commands to another text selection you only have to call up that name.

For instance, when you format a heading so that it is 24-point Times New Roman bold, centered, and colored blue, each time you create a new heading that you want formatted in the same way, you must reformat. Alternatively, you can save the formatting as a style and select the style name from the Style list on the Formatting toolbar to apply that same formatting to the text.

Using styles is not only faster but also ensures a consistent look throughout your document. You are assured that all paragraphs with a given style assigned to them are formatted identically.

When you need to change the formatting of all your headings, you can change the style definition and the new formatting is applied to all the text assigned that style. You don't have to work through the document changing one paragraph at a time with the attendant risk that you will miss a paragraph or make a mistake.

Because Word lets you base one style on another, you can create families of styles. For example, you may have three different heading styles for different types of headings. *Main Head* is the main heading style. *Subhead 1* is for lower level headings and is based on the Main Head style. *Subhead 2* is for the lowest level headings and is based on the Subhead 1 style. After the document is written, you may decide to change the font of headings from Times New Roman to Arial. You make that change to Main Head. Because Subhead 1 is based on Main Head, and Subhead 2 is based on Subhead 1, the new font affects them as well. So you have changed the font of every heading paragraph in the document with a single change.

There are two types of styles in Word:

- Paragraph styles. These affect entire paragraphs. Every paragraph has a style; the default style is called Normal.

- Character styles. These affect portions of text that are not necessarily paragraphs and affect only the character formatting of the selected text. Word doesn't have a default character style name, although the default font is Times New Roman, 12 point. Also, there is a style called Default Paragraph Font that converts any text to the character formatting of the underlying paragraph style.

This chapter concentrates on paragraph styles.

**SEE ALSO**

➤ *To learn more about character styles, see page 92*

# Stylize Quickly Using Themes

An easy way to make a well-designed document is to use a theme. A *theme* provides a "look" for your document by using a set of unified design elements and color schemes. When applied to a document, the theme customizes the body and heading styles, background color or graphic, bullets, horizontal lines, hyperlink colors, and table border color.

Word provides a variety of themes when you install it, but it doesn't automatically install all of the themes that come with it. If you want to see what other themes are available on the Microsoft Office 2000 CD-ROM, you can choose an uninstalled theme in the Themes dialog box, and then choose Install. Or you can run the Microsoft Office 2000 setup program, where you can see which themes are available and which have been installed, and you can install or uninstall any of the themes listed.

You can also download themes from the Web by choosing **Office on the** **W**eb from the **Help** menu. If you have FrontPage 4.0 or later installed, you can also use the themes from FrontPage.

### Apply a Theme to a New Document

**1.** Open the **File** menu and choose **New**.

**2.** In the New dialog box, click the **Web Pages** tab.

3. Double-click **Web Page Wizard**.

4. Follow the instructions in the wizard.

Although themes seem geared to Web pages, you can also use them for print documents.

### Apply a Theme to an Existing Document

1. Open the document.

2. Select **Theme** from the **Format** menu. The Theme dialog box appears (see Figure 12.1).

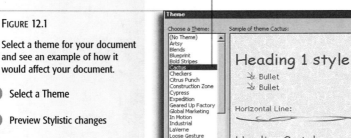

FIGURE 12.1

Select a theme for your document and see an example of how it would affect your document.

1 Select a Theme

2 Preview Stylistic changes

3 Click to set the current theme as your document default

3. From the **Choose a Theme** list, select the theme you want. The **Sample of Theme [Selected Theme]** window shows examples of the changes that theme will make to the document background, styles, horizontal lines, bullets, and hyperlinks.

4. Select the options you want:

   • **Vivid Colors**. Select this option to have the theme colors appear brighter and more vibrant.

   • **Active Graphics**. Select this option to have 3D bullets instead of 2D (flat) bullets.

- **B**ackground Image. Select this option to see a background graphic in your document. Deselect it to remove the graphic background.

**5.** (Optional) To make the current theme settings the default for new documents, choose **Set Default** and select **Yes** (see Figure 12.2).

**6.** Choose **OK**.

To change to a different theme, open the Theme dialog box and select a different theme.

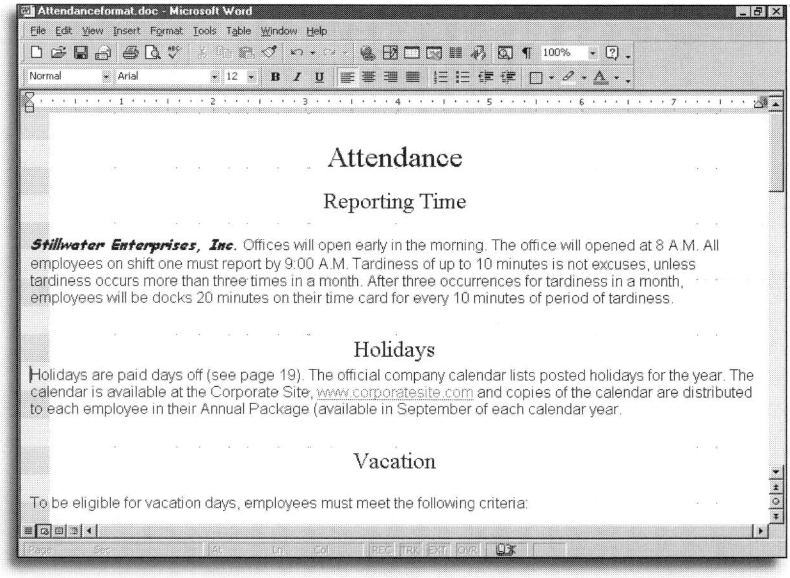

FIGURE 12.2

This document uses the Checkers theme. When you select a theme, Word displays your document in Web Layout view.

# Assign Paragraph Styles

Paragraph styles can include both character and paragraph formatting definitions—font, size, color, font styles (bold, italic, underline), font effects (subscript, superscript, small caps, strikethrough, and so on), as well as shaded backgrounds and borders, indents, alignment, line and paragraph spacing, and so on.

**Picture bullets**

If you want to insert picture bullets to document text after a theme has been applied, select the paragraphs to which you want to add the bullets and then click **Bullets** ▦.

**Apply Paragraph Styles**

1. To apply a style to existing text, select the paragraph or paragraphs to which you want to assign the style (or place your insertion point in the paragraph to affect only that paragraph). If you want to apply a style when entering new text, place your insertion point where you want the newly styled text to appear.

2. Choose a style from the **Style** list on the Formatting toolbar. When you click the down arrow next to the Style box, you see each style name displayed in the style's font. The symbols to the right of the style name indicate whether the style is a paragraph or a character style and show the font size and paragraph alignment of the style (see Figure 12.3).

3. Click the name of the style you want to apply to the selected paragraph(s).

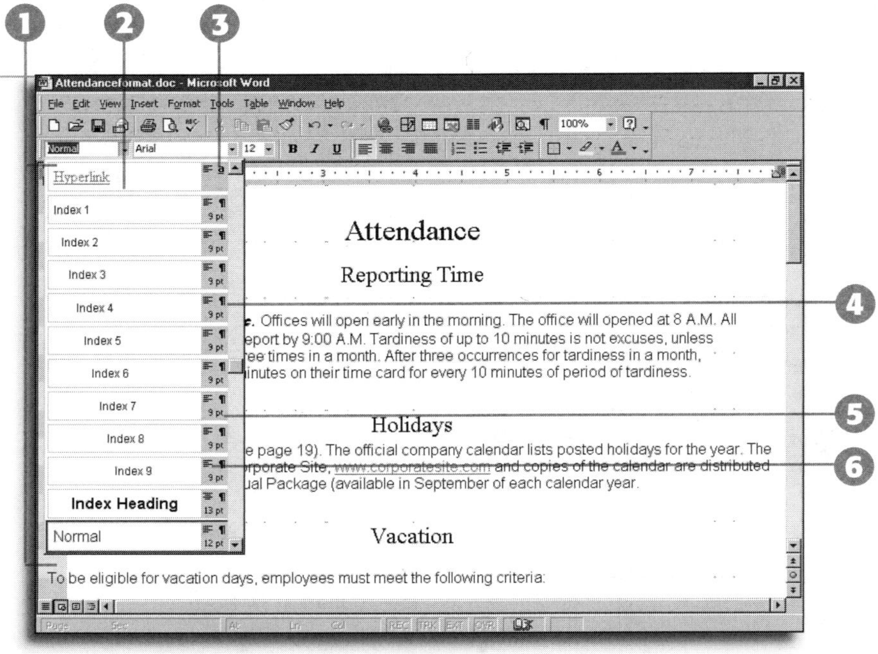

**Styles are applied to entire paragraphs**

You don't have to select the entire paragraph to apply a paragraph style. Select a part of a paragraph, or place your cursor in the paragraph before you select the style, and the style will be applied to the entire paragraph. This is true for paragraph styles only, not character styles.

FIGURE 12.3

Paragraph styles display a paragraph mark next to them; character styles show an underlined letter "a" next to them.

1 Style list

2 Style name

3 Character style

4 Paragraph style

5 Font size

6 Alignment symbol

# View Style Names

Word displays the name of the paragraph style of selected text (or text where your insertion point is located) in the Style list on the Formatting toolbar.

### View Formatting Applied to Text

1. From the **Help** menu, select **What's This?**, or press Shift+F1 to activate What's This? Help. The mouse pointer looks like a question mark.

2. Click in the text. A balloon appears with information about character and paragraph formatting (see Figure 12.4).

**Faster navigation**

If you apply heading styles in your document, you can navigate quickly through your document using the **Document Map**. This is an outline listing of the document's headings, in a separate pane to the left of your document window. To turn it on, click the **View** menu and select **Document Map**. Move your insertion point to a part of the document by clicking the heading for it in the Document Map.

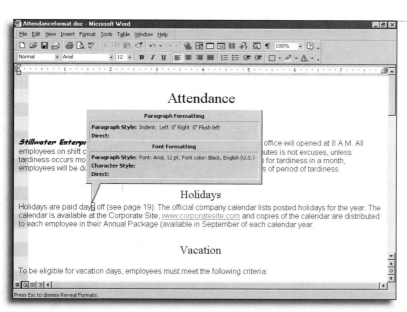

**FIGURE 12.4**
Click in the text with the What's This? mouse pointer to see the applied character and paragraph formatting.

3. Repeat step 2 as needed for other text.

4. Press Esc to turn off the What's This? pointer.

### View the Names of Paragraph Styles Next to the Document Window

1. Switch to Normal view (click the **View** menu, and select **Normal** or choose **Normal View** 📄 from the View buttons at the bottom left of your screen).

2. Click the **Tools** menu, and then select **Options**.

3. When the Options dialog box appears, click the **View** tab (see Figure 12.5).

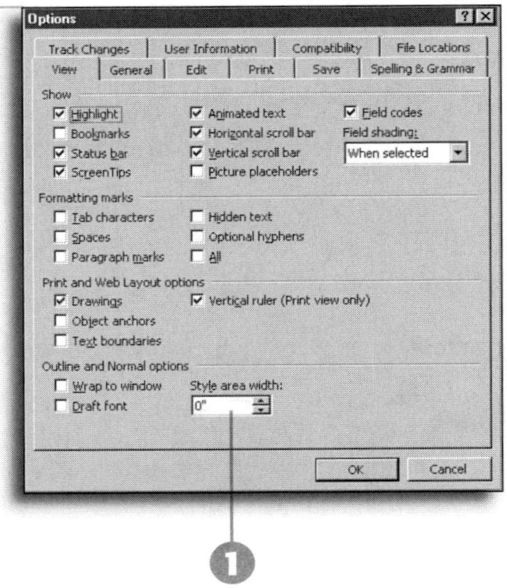

FIGURE 12.5

Increase the **Style Area Width** to create the style area pane next to your document window.

1 Style area width

4. In the **Window** section, change the **Style Area Width** to a positive number (such as 1 inch).

5. Click **OK**. A style area pane appears on the left side of the document, and the style names of the paragraphs in your document show in that pane (see Figure 12.6).

The style area pane only appears when you are in Normal view.

If you want to resize the style area, drag the border left or right.

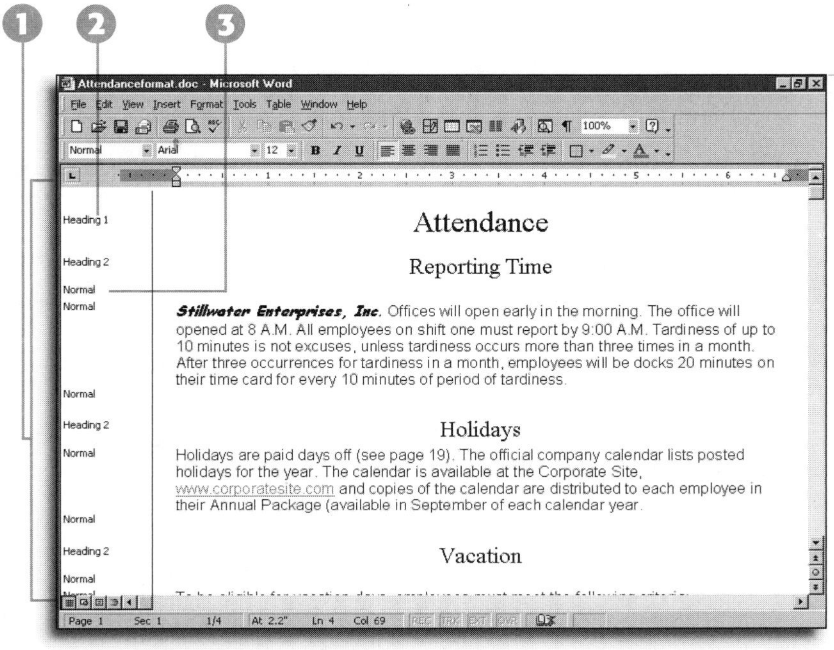

FIGURE 12.6
The style area pane shows the styles of the paragraphs to the right. You only see the style pane when you are in Normal view.

1 Style Area pane

2 Paragraph with Heading 1 style

3 Style name

# Use Word's Default Styles

Word provides a set of predefined styles, some of which it automatically applies to your text as you write. Other styles you must apply manually. If your document doesn't have any special or unusual formatting, you can use just the predefined styles. If you don't like the way they are formatted, you can either reformat the text directly or redefine the styles to your liking.

The predefined styles include a default paragraph style called *Normal*, a set of heading paragraph styles called Heading 1 through Heading 9, and styles for special types of text, such as headers, footers, and footnotes. When you create a new document using the default *template* (normal.dot), you can see some of these styles in the style list. Others only appear in the style list after you create a paragraph of the type that the style governs.

**Word templates**

All Word documents are based on templates, which are separate Word files to which Word assigns the extension .dot. Besides the default template, normal.dot, that Word assigns to all new, blank documents that you create, Word also provides a series of special templates. If you want to create a letter, a memo, or a report, you can use templates that Word provides just for those types of documents. Those templates include additional styles for the special types of paragraphs included in those types of documents.

To see what I mean, try this exercise. Create a new document using the New icon 🗋 on the Standard toolbar. Unless you have made changes to the program, Word automatically bases the new document on the default template (normal.dot). Now open the style list (click the arrow next to the word *Normal* in the Formatting toolbar). You will see five styles listed: Normal, Headline 1, Headline 2, Headline 3, and Default Paragraph Font. The first four are paragraph styles, the last a character style. If you see additional styles, changes have been made to your normal.dot template.

Normal is the default paragraph style that Word automatically applies to all paragraphs in the body of your document. Enter some text in your document. As you create a few paragraphs notice that the word "Normal" always appears in the Style box on the toolbar. Your document might look like the one in Figure 12.7.

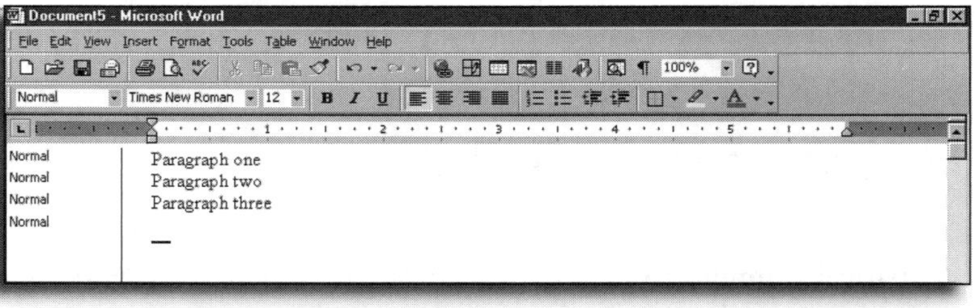

**FIGURE 12.7**

Create this document to test Word's predefined styles. Switch to Normal view to see the style pane.

Now move the insertion point into one of your paragraphs and choose Heading 1 in the style list. You'll see the word *Heading 1* appear in the style box.

Assign the styles *Heading 2* and *Heading 3* to the same paragraph. Notice that each time you assign a new style, the formatting of that paragraph changes to reflect the definition of the new style.

Click the **View** menu, and select **Header and Footer**. (This is what you do to create a header or footer.) Notice that the word Header appears in the style box. Open the style list again. Notice that now two new styles, Header and Footer, appear in the list. Word added the two new styles and assigned them to the header and footer paragraphs that you haven't even typed yet.

If you add a footnote, a table of contents, or any number of other predefined constructs to your document, you will notice that Word automatically adds one or more predefined styles to the text you added. And each new style is preformatted for you. If you don't like the formatting that Word assigned to your Heading 1 paragraph, you can reformat the paragraph directly, or you can redefine the style and Word then automatically reformats your paragraph (and all others based on the style) in accordance with your redefinition of the style.

**SEE ALSO**

➤  *Learn more about Word templates on page 343*

➤  *To create headers and footers, see page 319*

# Create and Apply a New Style

If the predefined formats don't meet your needs, you can create your own styles. The two methods to create styles are by using current formatting as an example or by specifying options in the Style dialog box.

### Create a New Style from Existing Formatted Text

1. Select a paragraph to which you want to apply the new style.

2. Apply the formatting to the paragraph that you want included in the new style definition. You can include both paragraph and character attributes such as font, bold, italic, and so forth.

3. With the insertion point anywhere in the paragraph, click in the **Style** box on the Formatting toolbar (or press Ctrl+Shift+S) to highlight the current style name.

4. Type the new style name and press Enter.

You can't create character styles using the method outlined previously—only paragraph styles. To create a character style you have to use the Style dialog box. This is also an alternative method for creating paragraph styles.

**The current style overwrote my new formatting!**

Don't enter the name of an existing style when you create your new style. If you do, that style's formatting is applied to the paragraph and the formatting changes you made are lost. If this happens, you can recover the formatting by choosing the **Edit** menu and selecting **Undo**, or by clicking **Undo** ↶ . Then repeat steps 3 and 4 with a new name.

### Creating Styles Using the Dialog Box

1. Open the **Format** menu and select **Style** to open the Style dialog box (see Figure 12.8).

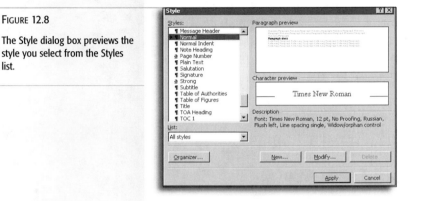

FIGURE 12.8

The Style dialog box previews the style you select from the Styles list.

2. Click **New**. The New Style dialog box appears (see Figure 12.9).

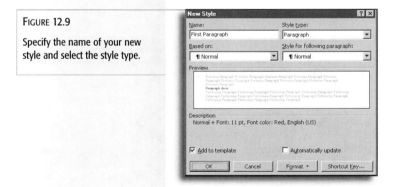

FIGURE 12.9

Specify the name of your new style and select the style type.

3. In the **Name** text box, enter the name for the new style.
4. From the **Style Type** drop-down list, select **Paragraph**.
5. If you want to base the new style on an existing style, select the base style you want to use from the **Based On** drop-down list. The new style is identical to the *base* style, except for changes you make in the definition of the *new* style.

Changes you make to the *base* style also affect the *new* style, as long as the change to the base style does not conflict with a defined attribute of the new style.

6. If paragraphs of this style will always be followed by a paragraph of another specific style—for example, a heading paragraph always followed by a body text paragraph—choose the following style in the **Style for Following Paragraph** drop-down list.

7. If you want the new style to be part of the template on which the current document is based, select **Add to Template** to place a check mark there. If you don't check this option, you can only use the new style in the current document.

8. Click **Automatically Update** if you want any manual formatting changes you make to any paragraph assigned this style to automatically be added to the style definition. This causes all manual changes to a paragraph's formatting to appear immediately in all paragraphs of the same style. This does not apply to the Normal paragraph style.

9. Choose **Format** and select **Font** or **Border** to specify the font or border and shading of the new style. The appropriate dialog box opens for you to select formatting options. Click **OK** to return to the New Style dialog box. Notice that the Preview box shows how the style will look, and the Description area defines the style in words.

   Choose **Format** and select **Paragraph** to set the style's alignment, indents, and line and paragraph spacing, **Tabs** to set the new style's tab stops, or **Numbering** to specify a numbering or bullet style.

10. Click **OK** to return to the Style dialog box.

11. Choose **Apply** to assign the new style to the current text or paragraph. Choose **Close** to save the new style definition without assigning it to any text.

**SEE ALSO**

➤ *Learn more about Word templates on page 343*

➤ *Learn more about character styles on page 92*

---

**Updating styles automatically**

If the idea of having a change in one paragraph automatically appear in other paragraphs makes you nervous, don't choose **Automatically Update** in the New Style or Modify Style dialog box. Instead, when you make a manual change to a paragraph's formatting, if you then want to apply that change to all paragraphs having the same style, re-apply the style to the paragraph. A dialog box appears giving you the choice of updating the style with the manual change you just made or removing the manual changes by re-applying the style formatting. If you choose to update the style, all paragraphs having that style assigned are also updated.

# Modify Styles

Whether you defined the style or it's one of Word's predefined styles, you can change the style's formatting settings. Be aware, however, that when you modify the style, all text in the document that has that same style also changes.

### Modify a Style

1. Open the **Fo̲rmat** menu and select **S̲tyle** to open the Style dialog box (see Figure 12.10).

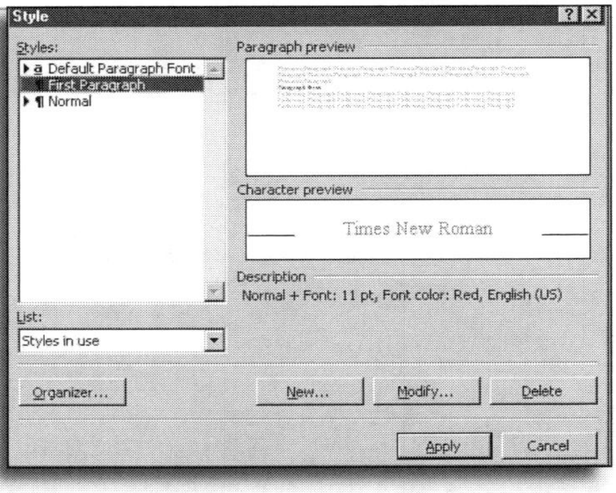

FIGURE 12.10

Choose the style you want to change from the **Styles** list and click **Modify**.

2. Select the style you want to modify from the **Styles** list. If the style you want to change isn't displayed, select which styles you want displayed from the drop-down **L̲ist**:

    • **All Styles** displays all styles available to the current document, whether or not they're currently assigned to text in the document. Available To means all styles defined in the document or in a template attached to the document or in a global template.

    • **Styles in Use** shows all styles that have been assigned to text in the current document.

    • **User Defined Styles** shows any user-defined styles in the current document.

3. Choose **M̲odify**. The Modify Style dialog box appears, which looks the same as the New Style dialog box (refer to Figure 12.9). Specify the style's new format settings.

**4.** Click **OK** to return to the Style dialog box.

**5.** Choose **Close** to exit the dialog box.

A quick way to modify a style is to make your formatting changes to a paragraph assigned that style. Select the paragraph, open the Style list in the toolbar, and reselect the currently assigned style. The Modify Style dialog box appears (see Figure 12.11). Select **Update the Style to Reflect Recent Changes**. Choose **OK**.

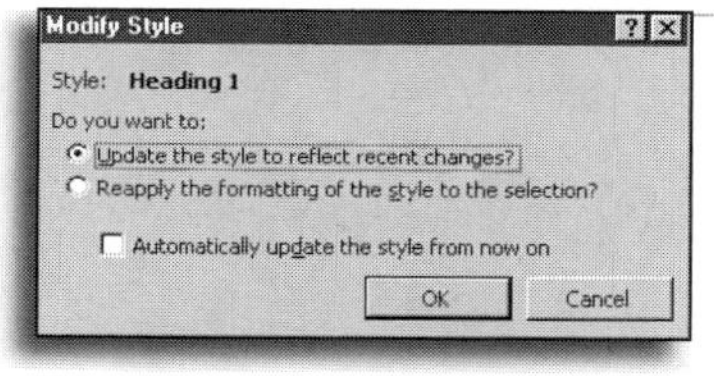

The one thing you can't do in the Modify Style dialog box

You can make any change you want to an existing style, except one. You can't change a character style into a paragraph style or vice versa.

**FIGURE 12.11**

Choose to update the style so that your formatting changes become part of the style definition.

# Apply Automatic Formatting

Microsoft has automated a lot of small, tedious chores that we had to do manually in older word processing programs. Many of these are formatting chores, and Word collects them under the term AutoFormat. You can control what formatting chores Word performs automatically in the AutoFormat panels of the AutoCorrect dialog box. The benefit of using AutoFormat is that you can concentrate more on the content of your document and less on the details of formatting.

AutoFormat works two different ways—as you type or on command:

- **AutoFormat as You Type**. Automatically formats headings, bulleted and numbered lists, borders, numbers, symbols, and so on, as you type.

- **AutoFormat on Command**. Automatically formats selected text or the entire document in one pass.

You don't have to do anything to activate AutoFormat. By default, **AutoFormat as You Type** is enabled—you just enter text and Word formats it as you go. You can change the default to **AutoFormat on Command**, which allows you to manually run AutoFormat. This is similar to the way in which you can spell check a document—as you type, or manually, using the menu commands or toolbar icons.

### AutoFormat Text

1. To AutoFormat a block of text, select it. To AutoFormat the entire document, make sure that no text is selected.

2. From the **Format** menu, select **AutoFormat** to open the AutoFormat dialog box (see Figure 12.12).

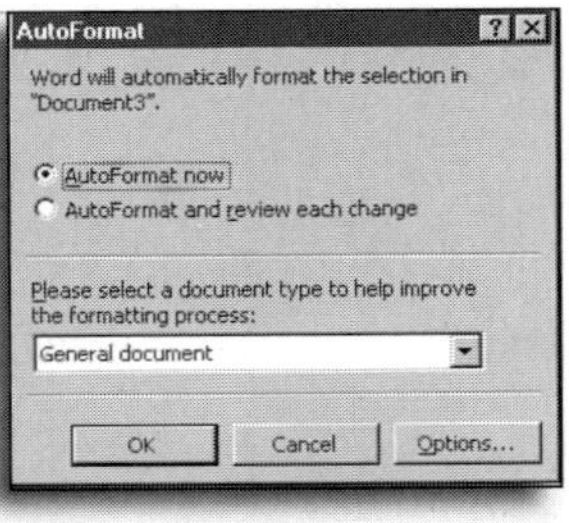

FIGURE 12.12

When you click OK, Word AutoFormats your entire document in one pass.

3. Click **AutoFormat Now** if you want Word to format the document without prompting you to review the changes.

   Click **AutoFormat and Review Each Change** if you want the opportunity to accept or reject each change proposed by Word.

4. Choose the type of document you have created in the drop-down list labeled **Please Select a Document Type to Help Improve the Formatting Process**. This helps Word to AutoFormat the document properly.

5. If you want to limit the types of formatting Word does, choose the **Options** button to display the AutoFormat panel of the AutoCorrect dialog box. Make your selections and then click **OK** to return to the AutoFormat dialog box. The AutoFormat options are described more fully later in this chapter.

6. Click **OK** to begin the AutoFormat process.

If you choose **AutoFormat Now**, Word formats the document, and that's that. If you choose **AutoFormat and Review Each**

**Change**, Word formats the document and then presents a new AutoFormat dialog box (see Figure 12.13). This version of the document looks very different from the first version.

FIGURE 12.13
Accept or reject formatting changes, or use the **Style Gallery** to apply further formatting to the document.

In the new AutoFormat dialog box, you can do the following:

- Accept or reject all Word's formatting changes without further review.

- Review each change that Word made and accept or reject each change individually.

- Use the Style Gallery to apply a new template to the document and, in so doing, completely change the look of the document.

If you choose to review each change, all changes that Word made are displayed in your document as *revision marks* and the Review AutoFormat Changes dialog box appears (see Figure 12.14). You can scroll manually through your document and highlight any changed text, or you can use the two **Find** buttons in the dialog box to have Word search for and highlight changes for you.

When a change is selected, you can click the **Reject** button. This deletes the change and restores the original formatting. If you then change your mind, you can click the Undo button [↩]. When you are finished reviewing, click **Cancel**. Then, in the AutoFormat dialog box, click **Accept All** to accept the changes that you did not manually reject in the Review AutoFormat Changes dialog box.

**SEE ALSO**

➤ *For more information about using revision marks, see page 508*

## Change Templates with the Style Gallery

AutoFormat assigns styles to every paragraph in your document. This is good because, once a document is completely styled, you can make wholesale formatting changes quickly and easily. You can edit the styles or, better yet, you can switch to other templates that use styles with the same names.

The Style Gallery streamlines the formatting process for you. It enables you to try out different templates on your document, to preview how your document looks in a given template, and then to switch to that template if you like it.

If you choose Style Gallery in the Theme dialog box (**Format**, **Theme**), the Style Gallery dialog box appears, looking similar to that in Figure 12.15, but with your document displayed, not the one pictured.

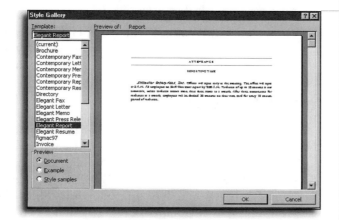

FIGURE 12.15

The Style Gallery lets you see what your document would look like using different templates.

In the list on the left-hand side of the screen you can choose from the available templates. In the list, **(current)** is the template currently attached to your document. As you choose each template in the list, you can see, in the picture at the right, how your document looks as formatted by the chosen template. By clicking the **Example** and **Style Samples** choices in the **Preview** section, you can also see sample documents and examples of the styles in the template to get a further idea of what each template offers.

When you choose another template and click **OK**, Word replaces your current template with the one you chose and applies the new formatting of the template to your document.

## Work Better with AutoFormat

AutoFormat changes the formatting in your document based on a set of rules that it follows. That is, it looks for specific patterns of characters and makes corresponding format changes. For example, it changes some hyphens to em dashes, others to en dashes, and leaves yet others alone, depending on the context of each hyphen.

If you know the character patterns AutoFormat looks for, you can help it along by entering text in those patterns. For example, you can follow a word with two hyphens, then another word (no spaces around the hyphens), knowing that AutoFormat will convert the hyphens to an em dash. Therefore, you may find it useful to review Appendix A, "Changes Made by AutoFormat," which lists the things AutoFormat can do for you.

## Control AutoFormat Options

All AutoFormat options are turned on by default when you install Microsoft Word. You can, however, disable selected AutoFormat options or turn off AutoFormat entirely by disabling all AutoFormat options. You can set options for AutoFormat As You Type separately from options for AutoFormat On Command.

### Set AutoFormat Options

1. From the **Tools** menu, select **AutoCorrect** to open the AutoCorrect dialog box.

2. Choose the **AutoFormat as You Type** tab to display those options. Choose the **AutoFormat** tab to display the **AutoFormat on Command** options.

3. Select and deselect the options you want. If you are not sure what effect an option will have, click the **Help** icon and then choose the option.

4. When you have selected all the options that you want, click **OK** to set them.

You can also set AutoFormat options during an AutoFormat by choosing the **Options** button in the AutoFormat dialog box (see Figure 12.13 earlier in this chapter).

# CHAPTER

# 13

# Print with Ease and Efficiency

Edit, print, and change document margins while in Print Preview mode

Use printing options effectively

Print multiple copies or pages, portions of text, documents properties, envelopes, and labels

Print to a fax program or send a document using an email program

Change print defaults

# Know Your Print Options

A document printed from Word takes its printing preferences from two areas in the Word program: the Print dialog box and the Page Setup dialog box.

The Print dialog box contains information about the print job, such as which printer to use, what to print (documents, document properties, and so forth) and how many copies to print (see Figure 13.1).

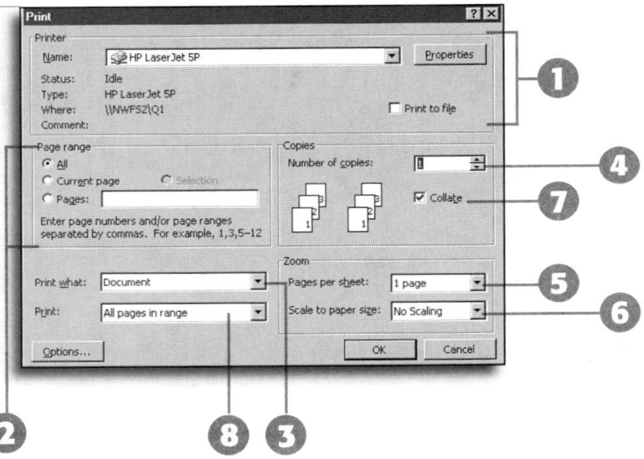

FIGURE 13.1

Choose the **File** menu and select **Print**, or press Ctrl+P, to view the Print dialog box and change print job settings.

**1** Select printer

**2** Select page range

**3** Select what to print

**4** Indicate number of copies

**5** Specify number of pages to print per sheet

**6** Choose what paper size to scale to

**7** Select collate to put multiple pages in order

**8** Specify even or odd pages, or all pages in range

The Page Setup dialog box contains the document paper size and orientation, as well as the paper source. Here, you indicate if you are going to manually feed a paper source, such as an envelope or special pre-printed form (see Figure 13.2), and which paper tray the printer should use.

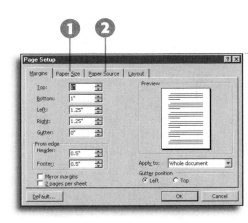

FIGURE 13.2

Choose the **File** menu and select **Page Setup** to indicate paper source and size.

1 Indicate paper size

2 Indicate paper source

One-page documents sent to a local printer usually require little or no intervention on your part. It's possible that you will not need to access the Print or Page Setup dialog box if your printing needs are small, infrequent, or your documents are simple in layout and small in size.

It's very simple to print a single copy of the entire document on the default Windows printer using the default print options. The default print options, set in the Print dialog box, drive what happens when you click the Print button on the Standard toolbar 🖨. Using the Print button, you can quickly print a single copy of the document and bypass the Print dialog box.

**SEE ALSO**

➤ *To learn more about sections, see page 286*

**Printing several documents at once**

From the **File** menu, choose **Open**. In the Open dialog box, specify the folder where the documents are stored that you want to print. Select the documents you want to print (for adjacent files on the list, click the first file and then hold down Shift and click the last file you want on the list; hold down Ctrl and click on nonadjacent files). Click **Tools** and select **Print**.

# Enable Background Printing

*Background printing* enables you to continue working in Word while your print job is being sent to the printer. If you have not enabled background printing, when you print a document, the Print dialog box appears on your screen and stays on your screen as long as it takes for the print job to be sent to the printer (see Figure 13.3). Background printing comes with a small cost, however. Background printing needs more memory than printing without background capabilities and print jobs can take longer.

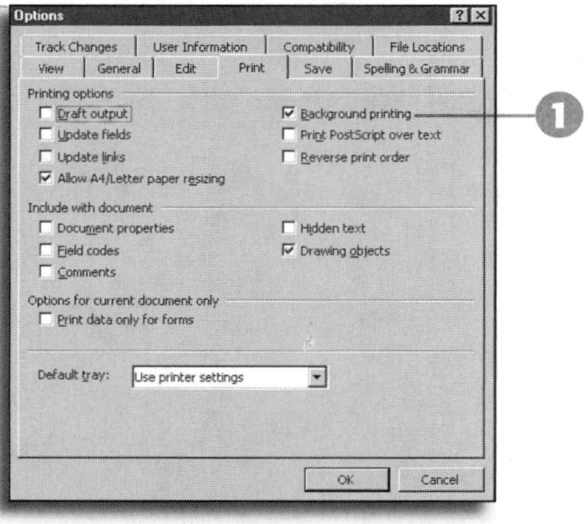

FIGURE 13.3

Enabling Background printing in the Options dialog box **Print** tab prevents the pesky Print dialog box from appearing and allows you to continue to work in Word during the printing process.

**❶** Disable/enable background printing here

**Another route to background printing**

What happens when you've already opened the Print dialog box and suddenly remember that you need to enable background printing? Don't panic—choose **Options**. Then select **Background Printing** and choose **OK**.

To enable/disable background printing, open the **Tools** menu and choose **Options**. On the **Print** tab of the Options dialog box, click the **Background Printing** box to place a check mark and enable it; click again to remove the check mark and disable it. When background printing is enabled, the status bar indicates the page numbers of documents being printed—while they are printing—as you continue to work in Word.

If system memory or printing speed is a concern to you, disable background printing. Open the **Tools** menu, select **Options** and then click the **Print** tab. Remove the check mark in the box under **Printing Options**.

# Modify Documents While in Print Preview Mode

Word's Print Preview feature lets you view your document on the screen exactly as it will be printed. While Print Layout view also displays your document in its final form, Print Preview offers some additional features that you may find useful.

For example, you can change margins while in Preview mode, view multiple pages at one time, zoom, and edit text.

To preview an open document, click the **Print Preview** button on the Standard toolbar. Figure 13.4 displays a document in Print Preview mode.

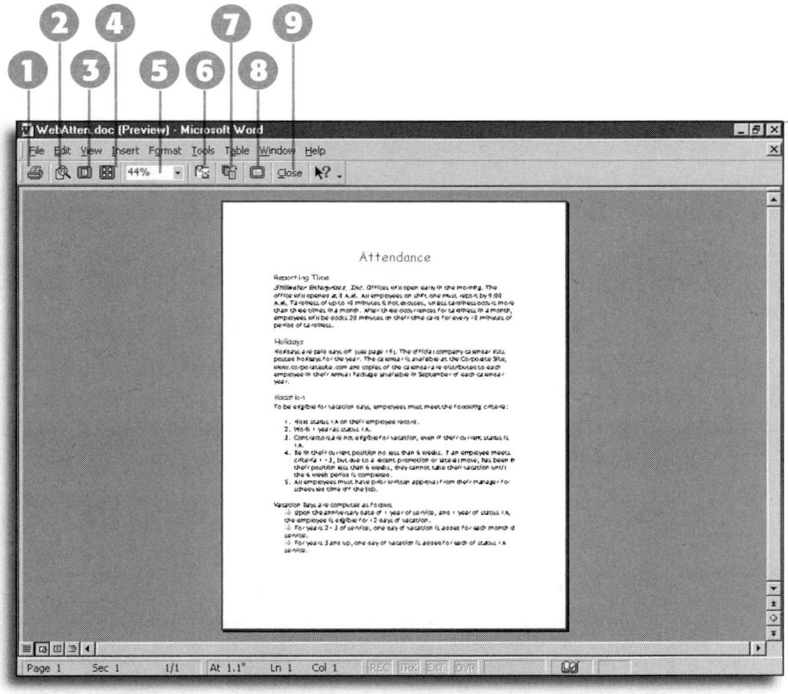

FIGURE 13.4

View multiple pages and vertical and horizontal rulers while in Preview mode.

1 Print

2 Magnifier

3 One Page

4 Multiple Pages

5 Zoom

6 View Ruler

7 Shrink to Fit

8 Full Screen

9 Close Preview

To navigate, edit, or print while in Print Preview mode:

- Press Page Up or Page Down, or use the scrollbar to scroll through pages.
- To view multiple pages, click the **Multiple Pages** button and then drag over the page icons to preview more than one page at a time (see Figure 13.5).

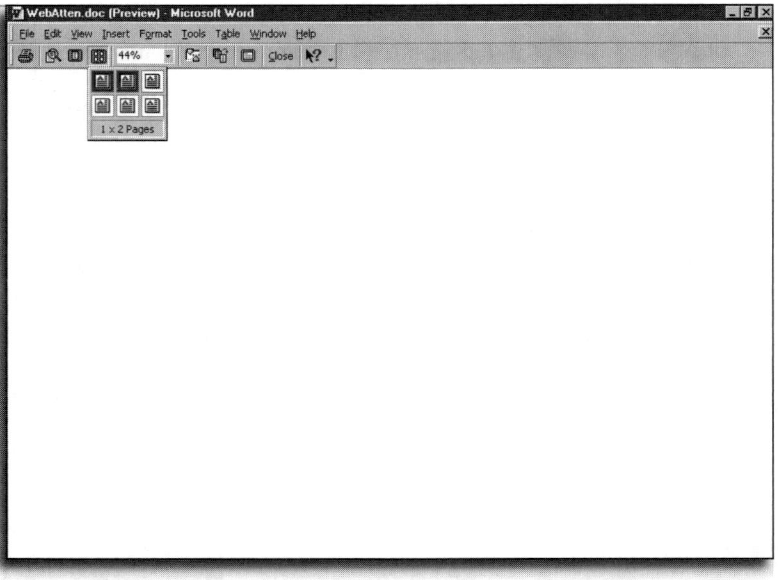

FIGURE **13.5**

Select the number of pages and layout for viewing from the Multiple Pages drop-down menu.

- To view only one page, click the **One Page** button.
- To select zoom magnification preferences, use the **Zoom** drop-down list (refer to Figure 13.4).
- To view the document full screen—without the Word program framing your document (see Figure 13.6)—click the **Full Screen** button. To exit Full Screen view, press the Esc key. Alternatively, click **Close Full Screen** on the Full Screen floating toolbar that appears when you enter Full Screen view.
- The mouse pointer looks like a magnifying glass in Print Preview. Click with the magnifying glass in the document to enlarge that part of the document. Click again in the document to return to the previous magnification.
- To edit text, click the **Magnifier** button on the Print Preview toolbar and click in the text to edit it.
- To print the entire document, click the **Print** button.

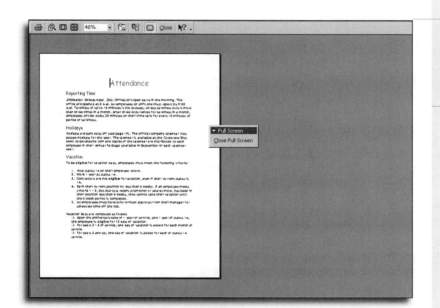

FIGURE 13.6
Navigate through document pages while in Full Screen view using the Page Up and Page Down keys on your keyboard.

- To print with options, open the **File** menu and choose **Print**. The Print dialog box appears. Select your print options in the dialog box.

- Click **Close** or press Esc to close the Print Preview window and return to your document.

## Change Margins

Although you can set margins in the Page Setup dialog box, you can't get a full document view of how those margin settings affect your document. Changing the margins in Print Preview does give you that view. Keep in mind that setting margins while in Print Preview is a visual approach to margins; you don't have the opportunity to indicate that you want margins at say, 2.1.

### Change the Margins

1. Start in Print Preview Mode. If the ruler isn't visible, click **View Ruler** 📇. Horizontal and vertical rulers appear (see Figure 13.7).

2. The white area on the ruler represents the document space between the current margins, the gray area represents the document space outside of the current margins. Between these two areas is a lighter gray line that marks the margin itself. Point at that margin line and the mouse pointer becomes a two-headed arrow and a ScreenTip indicates the name of that margin (such as "Left Margin").

3. Drag the gray line in one of the directions indicated by the arrows. As you drag, a dashed line extends across the document to show where the margin is.

4. Release the mouse button when the margin line is in the desired location. If it's not in the correct location, either drag the margin again or press Ctrl+Z to undo it.

**Watch what you're dragging**

When dragging the left margin marker, it's very easy to point to the wrong spot and accidentally drag one of the indent markers. If this happens, you changed the indent settings but not the margin. Make sure the ScreenTip says "Left Margin" before you begin dragging.

**FIGURE 13.7**

Drag the lighter gray line at the edge of the white area to change the margin.

**1** ScreenTip shows you are pointing at the margin line

**1**

**SEE ALSO**

➤ *To learn how to set indents using the ruler, see page 201*

➤ *To learn about setting margins with the Page Setup dialog box, see page 290*

## Adjust Pages to Fit Paper Sizes

Trying to squeeze a document to fit on one page can be difficult, but Print Preview can help. To fit your document on one page, click the **Shrink to Fit** button 🔳. Word adjusts formatting, such as font size, to reduce the page count to one page, when possible. This is most useful when you have a small amount of text that spills onto the document's last page.

If you save your document after using the **Shrink to Fit** option, the document is saved with new formatting, including the change in font size that was necessary to fit the document on a single page. After you save, there is no quick way to restore the original font size.

What if your document normally prints on legal size paper (that's the size paper you picked in the Page Setup dialog box), but you need to print out a copy on letter size. You could reduce it on a copy machine, or you could use Word's *print zoom* feature.

### Reduce or Enlarge Your Text to Print on One Page

**1.** Choose **Print** from the **File** menu to open the Print dialog box (refer to Figure 13.1).

**2.** From the **Pages per Sheet** list box, select **1 Page**.

**3.** Select the size paper you are going to print on from the **Scale to Paper Size** list box.

**4.** Choose **OK** to print the document.

Print zoom also makes it possible to print more than one page of a multiple page document (up to 16 pages per sheet) on one sheet of paper. Under **Zoom** in the Print dialog box, changes **Pages per Sheet** to **2 pages** (or 4, 6, 8, or 16). The **Scale to Paper Size** option should be **No Scaling**. Choose **OK** to print. Word decreases the font size and size of any graphics, and then groups the pages on the sheet.

### SEE ALSO
➤ *To learn more about themes, see page 239*

➤ *To learn more about watermarks, see page 383*

# Select a Printer and Paper Source

To change printers, choose a printer from the drop-down list of the Print dialog box (see Figure 13.8). Printers that are currently installed on your system are listed in the drop-down list.

Depending on your printer, printing envelopes can require that you change the paper source on the printer. In most cases, however, when you print envelopes, Word changes the paper source to manual feed. The paper source determines which tray the printer pulls from when printing the document. You might also need to change the paper source when you are printing to preprinted forms. For example, companies with shared printers often load their preprinted company letterhead in one tray, while another tray contains plain, blank paper. One of those two trays

---

**A4/Letter paper adjustments**

The standard size of paper in the United States is letter (8.5 x 11 inches). Other countries use A4 (210 x 297mm) as their standard paper size. It's longer and narrower than letter size. For international businesses, this is a problem. Word automatically adjusts documents formatted for one of these papers to print correctly on the other size by changing the font size. To have Word do this automatically, choose **Options** from the **Tools** menu. Click the **Print** tab. Under **Printing options**, select **Allow A4/Letter Paper Resizing**.

**Adding themes**

A theme changes the overall appearance of your document by customizing the body and heading styles, the background colors or graphics, bullets, horizontal lines, hyperlink colors, and table border colors. When you view the document in Print Preview, you won't see the background. You'll only see the flat (2D) version of the theme formatting. That's also what you see when you print the document, even on a color printer. The backgrounds aren't designed for printed documents, nor are some of the theme graphics. They are meant for Web pages. If you want a picture in the background of a printed document, use a watermark.

is the default tray and it might not always be the paper you need. And, depending on the printer model you are using, you can tell Word to print from one paper tray for the first page of a document and a different tray for the balance of the document.

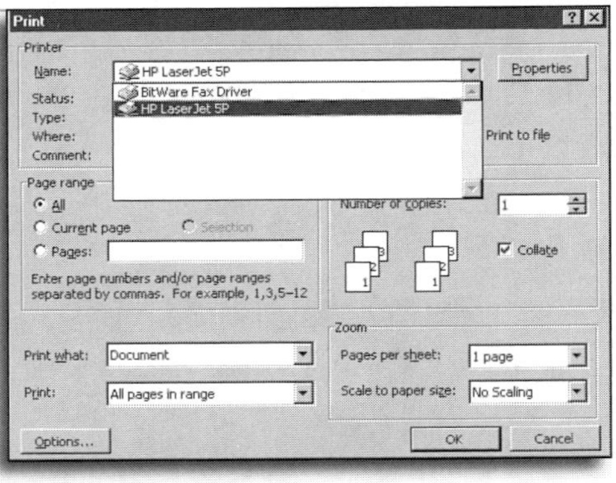

FIGURE 13.8

Select print destinations from the drop-down list in the Print dialog box. Print destinations may include not only actual printers but also software programs. These might include such programs as WinFax, which would fax your file, and Adobe's Acrobat PDFWriter, which would turn your document into a PDF file readable by Adobe Acrobat.

### To Change the Default Paper Source

1. Open the **File** menu and choose **Print**.
2. Click the **Options** button on the Print dialog box.
3. Select the default paper source from the **Default Tray** drop-down list.
4. Choose **OK** to return to the Print dialog box.

### To Change the Paper Source for the Current Document

1. Open the **File** menu and choose **Page Setup**.
2. Click the **Paper Source** tab and select the paper source from the drop-down list.
3. For a different first page, specify a tray in the **First Page** box and then a tray in the **Other Pages** box.
4. Choose **OK**.

## Print Multiple Copies

When you print multiple copies of a document, it is helpful to *collate* those copies. In this way, sets of your document print in the order that you need them—so that you can staple or bind your copies.

### Print Multiple Copies

1. Open the **File** menu and choose **Print** or press Ctrl+P. The Print dialog box appears.

2. In the **Number of Copies** box, enter the desired number of copies or click the up or down arrow to set the number you want.

3. Verify that the **Collate** option is selected to have the copies collated.

4. Click **OK**.

## Print Specified Pages or Portions of Text

Most of the time you will want to print the entire document, but you can print just part of a document, ranging from a single sentence to multiple pages.

If you want to print a selection of text, you must first select the text. To print a single page within a multiple page document, position your cursor on that page before you select an option from the Print dialog box.

Open the **File** menu and choose **Print**. Select one of the following options in the **Page Range** section in the Print dialog box:

- To print selected text, choose **Selection**.
- To print the page on which your cursor is currently positioned, choose **Current Page**.
- To print specified pages, choose **Pages** and enter the page numbers in the text box. For example, entering 1–3 prints pages 1 through 3, and entering 2,4 prints pages 2 and 4. You can also enter a combination, such as 1–3,5,7,12.
- To print a section, type s followed by the section number (as in s1).
- To print a range of sections, type s followed by the section number, and separate the section range with a dash (as in S2–S4). To print noncontiguous sections, separate sections with a comma (s1, s5). To print sections that contain pages that span the sections, type p3s1-p5s4.

---

**Print two-sided pages**

To print two-sided output to a standard one-sided printer, select odd or even pages in the **Print** drop-down list of the Print dialog box. Print the odd-numbered pages, flip the printed pages over and place them back in the paper tray, and print the even-numbered pages. Select **All Pages in-Range** to return to printing all pages. Check your printer's manual to ensure that you flip or turn the pages over correctly for printing, and allow the pages to cool before you reinsert them into the printer so they don't curl and cause a paper jam.

SEE ALSO

➤ *Learn how to create mail merge documents on page 485*

# Print Document Properties or Document Information

You can make document information print by default

To print document information each time you print a document, or to print field codes, hidden text, and other nonprinting characters, open the **Tools** menu and select **Options**. On the **Print** tab indicate which items you want under the **Include with Document** section.

Document property information is printable and you can print property information for a current document or for several documents at once. In addition, you can print styles, comments, AutoText, and key assignments.

To print document information, select the item to print in the **Print What?** drop-down list of the Print dialog box. Figure 13.9 displays a document properties printed page.

FIGURE 13.9

When you select an item other than **Document** in the **Print What?** box, the print job goes directly to the printer. You cannot Print Preview document information.

| Filename: | EAGLELTR.DOC |
|---|---|
| Directory: | F:\Q\UWord |
| Template: | C:\Program Files\Office97\Templates\eagle.dot |
| Title: | 17 December, 1998 |
| Subject: | |
| Author: | Jane Calabria |
| Keywords: | |
| Comments: | |
| Creation Date: | 12/19/97 1:37 PM |
| Change Number: | 2 |
| Last Saved On: | 12/25/97 11:27 PM |
| Last Saved By: | Jane Calabria |
| Total Editing Time: | 23 Minutes |
| Last Printed On: | 12/23/97 9:42 PM |
| As of Last Complete Printing | |
|     Number of Pages: | 2 (approx.) |
|     Number of Words: | 223 (approx.) |
|     Number of Characters: | 1,272 (approx.) |

SEE ALSO

➤ *Learn how to add revision marks and comments to documents on page 513*

➤ *To add summary information to documents, see page 140*

Instant address

Word automatically picks up an address from your letter and inserts the address on your envelope—but not if your address is more than five lines of text. If you have a long address, highlight the entire address. Then select the **Tools** menu, and choose **Envelopes and Labels**. Word inserts the highlighted address.

# Print Envelopes

Word can send envelope information to your printer and depending on your printer, you can select the envelope size you need.

### Print Envelopes

**1.** Open the **Tools** menu and choose **Envelopes and Labels**.

**2.** Click the **Envelopes** tab (see Figure 13.10).

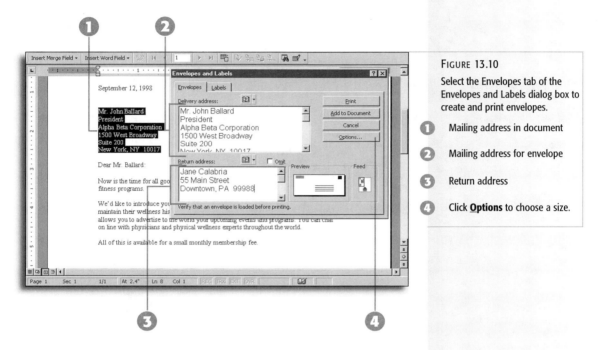

FIGURE 13.10

Select the Envelopes tab of the Envelopes and Labels dialog box to create and print envelopes.

**1** Mailing address in document

**2** Mailing address for envelope

**3** Return address

**4** Click **Options** to choose a size.

**3.** Enter the mailing address information on the **Delivery Address** area (the address appears automatically if you have a letter open that has an inside address). To format the address, select the address text, right-click it, and then click **Font** on the shortcut menu.

**4.** If the return address is not automatically supplied from your User Information or you need to put a different return address on the envelope, enter the address in the **Return Address** area. Select **Omit** if you have pre-printed envelopes and don't need a return address printed.

---

**Help the post office help you**

Postal regulations suggest envelopes and mailing labels be printed in all caps with no punctuation.

---

**Default return address**

To create a return address that will automatically appear each time you create an envelope, open the **Tools** menu and select **Options**. Click the **User Information** tab. Type the return address in the **Mailing Address** box. Choose **OK**.

5. To select an envelope size, the type of paper feed, whether to add a barcode, and other options, click the **Options** tab (see Figure 13.11). After you have selected the options you want, click **OK**.

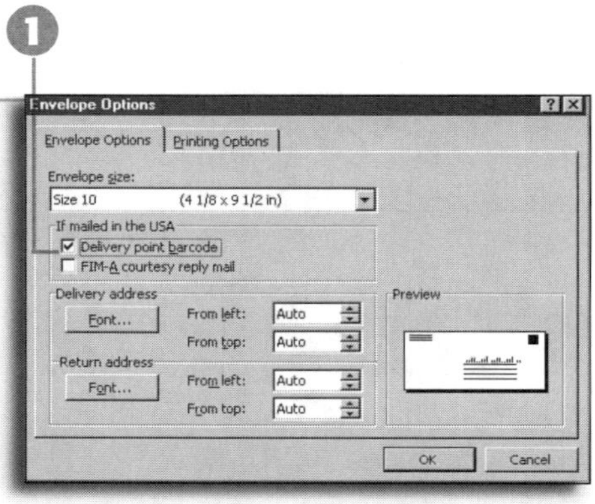

FIGURE 13.11

In the Envelope Options dialog box, select the size envelope you want to print and then click OK.

1  Barcode option

6. To print the envelope, insert the envelope in the printer as shown in the **Feed** box, and then click **Print**.

To add the envelope as a separate section at the beginning of the document, click **Add to Document**. This is particularly useful if you print this document often and need to send it to the same address each time. Then, every time you update the file and print it, the envelope is also printed. Also, you can click on that page and print it, making as many copies as you need. To change an existing envelope that's already a section in a document, click **Change Document**. You can print the envelope when you print the document.

Many companies prefer to have their logo appear with the return address, which is why they buy pre-printed stationery. Using AutoText, you can automatically include your graphic logo on all the envelopes you print.

**Avoid paper jams and sealed envelopes**

To avoid gummed-up envelopes as they come out of your laser printer, purchase envelopes designed for laser printers. The glue on laser printer envelopes is designed to "take the heat" as it passes through the printer. And to avoid creased envelopes and paper jams, use your printer's straight paper path—don't let the envelopes curl as they go through the printer. Using the straight paper path helps reduce jams, creases, folds, and even reduces the likelihood of heating up the envelope glue.

**Barcodes**

Don't forget to add barcodes. One of the options found in the Envelopes dialog box is the printing of a barcode. According to the United States Post Office, using bar-codes helps to speed your mail.

### Add a Graphic Logo to Your Return Address

1. Open a blank document.

2. Insert the graphic logo in the document (you must have the logo saved as a file or be able to scan it in from Word) by choosing **Picture** from the **Insert** menu and then selecting **From File**. Locate the file and double-click on it.

3. Select the logo in your document by clicking on it once.

4. Open the **Insert** menu, choose **AutoText**, and then select **New**.

5. In the **Please Name Your AutoText Entry** box, type `EnvelopeExtra1`.

6. Choose **OK**.

7. Close the document without saving it.

The next time you print an envelope, Word will automatically insert the logo as long as it is stored as the AutoText entry EnvelopeExtra1.

**SEE ALSO**

> *To learn how to print multiple envelopes to different addresses, see page 500*

> *To learn more about inserting graphics, see page 363*

> *To learn more about AutoText, see page 123*

# Print Labels

You can print return address mailing labels or individual shipping labels (if your printer can accommodate them). Use labels when you are mailing to many recipients: it will save you from running to the printer to hand feed or stack envelopes and it is a faster method than printing envelopes individually. If you want to print labels with a different address on each label, you should use a mail merge document.

### Print Labels

1. From the **Tools** menu, select **Envelopes and Labels**.

2. Select the **Labels** tab (see Figure 13.12).

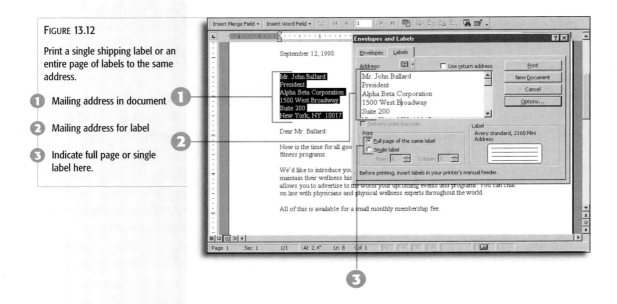

FIGURE 13.12

Print a single shipping label or an entire page of labels to the same address.

**1** Mailing address in document

**2** Mailing address for label

**3** Indicate full page or single label here.

**3.** Enter the address information, and then select the options you want. To format the address, select the address text, right-click it, and then click **Font** on the shortcut menu.

**4.** Under **Print**, select **Full Page of Same Label** if you want a sheet of the same addresses or **Single Label** if you only want one label to print. Specify the **Row** and **Column** if you are printing on a page of labels.

**5.** To select the label size you'll be printing, click **Options** (see Figure 13.13).

FIGURE 13.13

Choose the type of printer, select from the list of available label sizes, and then click OK.

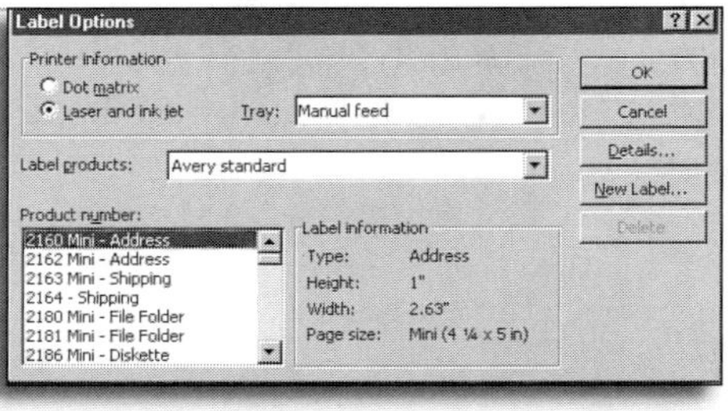

**6.** To print the label(s), insert the label or sheet of labels in the printer and then click **Print**.

**SEE ALSO**

➤ *To print sheets of labels that contain different names and address, see page 498*

# Print Booklets

Booklets are tricky to create. Several steps are involved, including a little bit of planning. To print a booklet you must do the following:

- Format your text and pages for smaller sheets of paper than normal and lay out with two pages per sheet.

- Print on both sides of each sheet of paper, rearranging the order pages print so that when all the sheets are bound together, the pages appear in the correct order. This is the hard part, and Word does not provide any help.

- Bind the sheets of paper together down the center line of each page, between the pages. You may have to buy a new stapler to do this, because the standard office stapler cannot reach that far across a sheet of paper.

Begin by laying out your text to print two pages side-by-side on each sheet of paper and changing the margins.

### Lay Out a Booklet

**1.** From the **File** menu, select **Page Setup**. The Page Setup dialog box appears (see Figure 13.14).

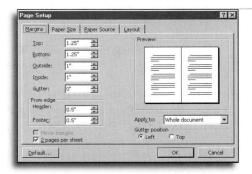

**FIGURE 13.14**

Select **2 pages per sheet** to set up the document as a booklet.

**A word about margins in a booklet**

If you are printing a small booklet, you probably want smaller margins than normal, perhaps 3/4 inch or less on every side. You might, on the other hand, want to increase the **Gutter margin** from its normal setting of zero. The gutter margin is an extra inside margin that you can add to compensate for the paper lost to the binding process. The size of the gutter margin depends on how many sheets of paper you will bind together. A small booklet (not more than, say, 32 pages, which would be eight sheets of paper bound together) may not need any extra gutter margin.

2. On the **Margins** tab, select **2 pages per sheet**. Adjust the margins as needed. Notice that, instead of left and right margins, you are now working with inside and outside margins.

3. Click the **Paper Size** tab. Select the appropriate paper size from the **Paper Size** list box. Change the **Orientation** to **Landscape**.

4. Choose **OK**.

Each page in your document will be half a sheet when printed. Unless you are printing to oversize paper, this means that each page will be about half the size of the pages you are accustomed to working with. So you will have to format and lay things out differently than normal. You might want to use smaller than usual fonts, say, 8- or 9-point for body text, headers, and footers. Maybe 10- or 12-point for titles and subtitles. But test this on your printer. Small font sizes may not print well if you are using a low-resolution printer (300dpi or less).

You might want to use smaller graphics, tables, and headlines as well. You may have to forgo wrapping text around larger pictures.

When you print your booklet, you have to print the pages out of order so that, when you bind the pages together, they will appear in the correct order. This is the tricky part. Also, you don't want every other page of the booklet to be blank, so you have to print on both sides of each sheet of paper.

Finally, if the total number of pages in your document is not a multiple of four, you need to append enough blank pages to the end of your document to make it a multiple of four pages in length. This makes it easier to calculate the order of printing of pages.

Here is the procedure for printing:

**Print a Booklet**

1. Insert enough extra pages at the end of your document so the total number of pages is a multiple of four (4, 8, 12, 16, and so on). For example, a 9-page document needs three blank pages (for a total of 12, divisible by four), a 10-page document needs two blank pages and an 11-page document

needs one blank page. If you don't insert the blank pages, the formula in step 2 won't work. If you want the blank pages at the end of the book to be truly blank (no headers or footers printed) force a section break between your last real pages and the blank pages, then remove page numbers, headers, and footers from the section of blank pages.

**2.** Divide the total number of pages in your document by two. This is the center or "anchor" page of your booklet. ("Anchor" page is our definition, not a term used by Microsoft.) This will be an even number and is the left anchor page. The next consecutive number is your anchor right page. For example, if 20/2=10, pages 10 and 11 are your left and right anchor page numbers. Remember the anchor page numbers.

**3.** Print the first side of each sheet of paper as follows:

Open the Print dialog box and enter the page numbers to print on the first pass. Here is the order in which to enter the page numbers:

Last even page, first odd page, next-to-last even page (counting backward), next odd page (counting forward), and so forth. Stop at the page numbers that precede your anchor pages. In our example of a 20-page booklet, the pattern looks like this:

20, 1, 18, 3, 16, 5, 14, 7, 12, 9

In this example, the anchor pages are 10 and 11, so we stopped at 12 and 9.

Click **OK**. The pages will print with the higher page number of each pair on the left side of the page, the lower number on the right.

**4.** Print the other side of all of your pages as follows:

Put the stack of printed pages back in your printer, blank side toward the print head, without shuffling them.

Open the Print dialog box and enter the page numbers to print on the second pass. Here is the order in which to enter the page numbers:

Left anchor page, right anchor page, next lower even page (counting backward), next higher odd page (counting forward), and so on until you run out of pages. In our example, the pattern looks like this:

10, 11, 8, 13, 6, 15, 4, 17, 2, 19

If your printer reverses the order of printing, choose to print in reverse order (**Options**, **Reverse Print Order**).

Click **OK** to print. This time the pages will print with the lower page number of each pair on the left side of the page, and the higher number on the right.

The formula above may look complicated, but it really is not. You count even pages backward from the last page to the first:

20, 18, 16, 14, 12, 10, 8, 6, 4, 2

You count odd pages forward from page one:

1, 3, 5, 7, 9, 11, 13, 15, 17, 19

You merge the lists and then divide the merged list in half:

20, 1, 18, 3, 16, 5, 14, 7, 12, 9

10, 11, 8, 13, 6, 15, 4, 17, 2, 19

If you have a duplex printer (that automatically prints pages two-sided), we suggest that you not use the duplex printing feature when printing your booklet. Do it like the rest of us—print one side, turn the stack over, print the other side. But if you really must print the whole document in one run, you can merge the last two lists, pair-wise and in reverse order, to end up with this:

20, 1, 2, 19, 18, 3, 4, 17, 16, 5, 6, 15, 14, 7, 8, 13, 12, 9, 10, 11.

If all these numbers make your head spin, and you just can't see how to apply them to your 47-page booklet, you can make the whole process more concrete by creating a mock-up of your booklet. To do this, staple together enough sheets of paper to accommodate all the pages in your document. (Divide by four the number of pages in your document. If the result includes a fraction, round up to the next whole number. The result is the number of sheets you will need.) Fold the sheets in half along the staple line. Number the pages by hand, assigning page one to the cover. Unfold. Unstaple. Don't shuffle the pages. The page numbers are now arranged in print order.

# Cancel Print Jobs

After a job has been sent to the printer, you can cancel a print job from Word without having to switch to the Printer control box in Windows.

To cancel a print job with background printing turned off, press Esc or click the **Cancel** button.

To cancel a print job while background printing is enabled, double-click the printer icon located on the status bar. This icon only appears if you have background printing enabled, and during the print job.

**You may have to act quickly to cancel print jobs**

When printing a single page document, using background printing, the printer icon may disappear from the status bar before you have a chance to double-click it. In that case, the job is probably already printing and you cannot stop it.

# Print to a Fax Program

If your system has been set up for faxing (you must have a fax/modem and fax software), you can fax a document directly to one or more recipients using your computer as a fax machine.

Faxing a document can be handled in two ways: Depending on how your fax system is installed, you may find the fax program (such as Microsoft Fax or WinFax) listed as a printer in the Print dialog box. If this is the case, the quickest way to send a fax is to print the document with the fax program selected as the printer. As a result, your document does not print to the printer, but starts the fax program, prompts you to fill in the address and phone number and so forth, and faxes the document when you are ready. During this process, most fax software also asks you if you want to send a cover sheet and you can include a cover sheet with the information you specify.

You may have a fax program that does not show in the list of your printers. In that case, you can send a fax using the **Send To** command in Word.

### Use the Send To Command to Send a Fax

1. Open the **File** menu and choose **Send To, Fax Recipient**.
2. Select Microsoft Fax (or your installed fax program) as the destination printer in the Print dialog box, and click **OK**.

**Caution: Do not let Word create a cover sheet for other fax programs**

If you are using a program other than Microsoft Fax and choose **Send to Fax Recipient** from the menu, Word prompts you for a cover sheet during the faxing process. At the end of the Fax Wizard, Word starts your fax program. Do not create the cover sheet during the Wizard or Word creates a new document consisting of the cover sheet only and that is the document your fax program attempts to send. If you need a cover sheet, wait until Word starts your fax program, at which point you can send a cover sheet from within your fax program.

The Fax Wizard starts. The wizard is a step-by-step program that takes you through the process of preparing the fax, choosing a cover page, and selecting recipients. After each step, click **Next** to continue the process. Click **Back** to go back to the previous step. After the final step, click **Finish**.

**3.** If you requested a cover sheet, Word displays it. You can make any additions or changes to the cover sheet at this time.

**4.** Click the **Send Fax Now** button to send the fax.

Word also provides a fax cover sheet template wizard. To create a cover sheet, open the document you want to fax and perform the following steps.

**Create a Fax Cover Sheet**

**1.** Open the **File** menu and choose **New**.

**2.** When the New dialog box appears, select the **Letters & Faxes** tab.

**3.** Word offers three fax templates: Contemporary Fax, Elegant Fax, and Professional Fax. Although you may choose any of these, using the Fax Wizard may be more helpful for your first fax because it not only creates the fax cover sheet but helps send the fax too. The following steps take you through creating your fax using the Fax Wizard, so select that icon and click **OK**.

**4.** After the Fax Wizard introductory screen appears, click **Next** to continue (when using a wizard, Next continues to the next step, **Back** takes you back to the previous step, **Finish** ends the task, and **Cancel** exits the wizard without completing the task).

**5.** The Fax Wizard asks you to specify the document you want to send. Select from one of the following choices:

- Select **The Following Document** if you plan to send a document that's already prepared. Then, choose the name of the document from the drop-down list (the document must be open). Then select **With a Cover Sheet** or **Without a Cover Sheet**. Click **Next**.

- Select **Just a Cover Sheet with a Note** if you only plan to put a note on the cover sheet and don't want to send an accompanying document.

6. The Fax Wizard asks what program you plan to use to send the fax: **Microsoft Fax** or **A Different Program Which Is Installed On This System**. If you select **A Different Program**, you must then choose the program from the drop-down list in **Which of the Following is your Fax Program?** If you don't have a fax program or a modem installed on your system, you must select **I Want to Print My Document So I Can Send It From a Separate Fax Machine**.

7. Click **Next**. The Fax Wizard asks you to enter the names of the recipients (see Figure 13.15) of your fax. If you are working with Microsoft Outlook or Microsoft Schedule+ and maintain a personal address book in one of those programs, you can click the **Address Book** button and select a recipient's name. If not, enter the recipients' names and fax numbers (including area code) in the **Name** and **Fax Number** boxes (notice that you can address the same fax to different people at different fax numbers). After you've used the Fax Wizard you'll be able to pick the names of previous recipients from the drop-down list the next time you use the wizard.

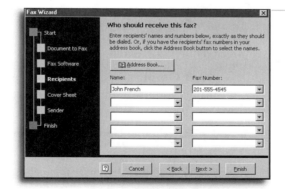

**FIGURE 13.15**

Enter the names and fax numbers of the people to whom you are sending the fax.

8. Click **N**ext. Select the style of fax cover sheet you want to use (if you chose to use a fax cover sheet): **Professional**, **C**ontemporary, or **E**legant. Click **N**ext.

9. Enter the information about the sender of the fax on this screen by filling in the **N**ame, **C**ompany (if there is one), **M**ailing Address, **P**hone, and **Fax** boxes, if Word has not filled these in for you. Click **N**ext.

10. Click **F**inish. The fax cover sheet document appears on your screen. Enter any additional information you need on the cover sheet, replacing any of the **Click Here and Type** fields by clicking on them and typing over the field text with your own information. To place a check mark in any of the check boxes, double-click the box. Add any message you want to send on the fax cover sheet in the Comments area.

11. When your fax cover sheet is ready, click **Send Fax Now.**

If you do not have a fax program or modem and choose to print the cover sheet for faxing on a separate machine, the **Send Fax Now** button doesn't appear; just print the cover sheet as you would any other document.

## Change Print Defaults

You can set document print defaults by clicking the **Options** button in the Print dialog box. Figure 13.16 lists these various printing options.

These default settings apply for all new documents. Some of the most commonly used options include the following:

- **Draft Output**. Produces draft output that prints faster but may lack some graphics and formatting (depending on your specific printer).

- **Update Fields**. Updates the contents of all document fields before printing.

- **Reverse Print Order**. Prints pages in last-to-first order. This setting produces collated output on printers that have face-up output.

---

**Fax cover sheet templates**

If you choose to use the Professional, Elegant, or Contemporary Fax templates, your document opens with the boilerplate text and you must replace any sample text or **Click Here** fields with your own information. Then you print the document so that you can send the fax on a separate fax machine or choose the **File** menu, and select **Send To**. From the submenu choose **Fax Recipient** if you have a fax program and modem installed on your system.

- **Background Printing**. Permits you to continue working on the document while printing is in progress. This setting uses additional memory and usually results in slower printing.

- **Document Properties**. Prints the document's properties in addition to its contents.

- **Comments**. Includes document comments in the printout.

After setting the desired printing option defaults, click **OK** to return to the Print dialog box.

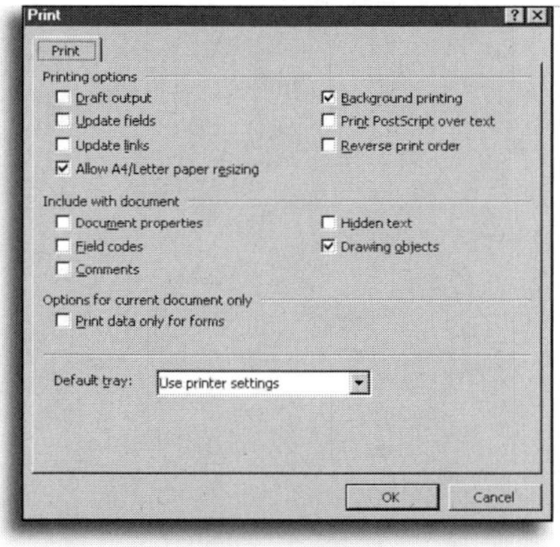

FIGURE 13.16
Click the **Options** button in the Print dialog box to see all the printing options.

PART

*IV*

# Create Professional Documents

CHAPTER

*14*

# Lay Out Pages and Sections

Configure page setup, margins, paper size, and orientation

Create headers, footers, and sections

Add page numbering

Apply page borders

# Know Your Page and Section Formatting Options

Page formatting in Word refers to the overall look of the printed page or Web page. It includes such things as the page margins, the paper size and orientation, column formatting, headers, footers, and page numbering. In a simple document, when you set these parameters, they affect the whole document. For most documents, that is good enough. However, if you need to set up different pages or parts of pages differently from each other, Word permits you to divide a document into *sections* and then set page formatting differently for each section.

**SEE ALSO**

➤ *To learn more about creating and working with Web pages, see page 603*

# Create and Remove Sections

If your document needs more than one section, you can create new sections by inserting section breaks. You can insert breaks manually or Word may insert them for you. Section breaks mark the division between two sections, and like the paragraph marker, a section break marker stores the page formats of the preceding section. There are three kinds of section breaks:

- *Continuous.* A continuous section break forces a paragraph break so that the new section begins immediately following the preceding section, typically on the same page as the previous section, so you can have two types of formatting on the same page. This type of section break is useful in documents such as newsletters, in which the titles of the articles may stretch across the page but the text of the articles is formatted in two columns.

- *Next Page.* A next page section break forces a page break, so that the new section begins at the top of the next page. This type of section break is useful for setting major breaks in a document such as the start of a new chapter. If you need to restart the page numbering for each chapter, a next page section is a logical choice.

- *Odd Page or Even Page.* When you use an even page or odd page section break, the section break forces either one or two page breaks, so that the new section begins on the next even- or odd-numbered page. Use this type of section break in a bound document, where a major break in the document, such as a new chapter, should always begin on an even or an odd page.

As you can see in Figure 14.1, Word marks the location of section breaks by displaying a double horizontal line with the label "Section Break" followed by the type of break. You can see section break markers in Normal view but they aren't displayed in the Web Layout or Print Layout views (unless you make your hidden characters visible by clicking **Show/Hide** [¶] on the Standard toolbar), Print Preview mode, or on the printed document or Web page.

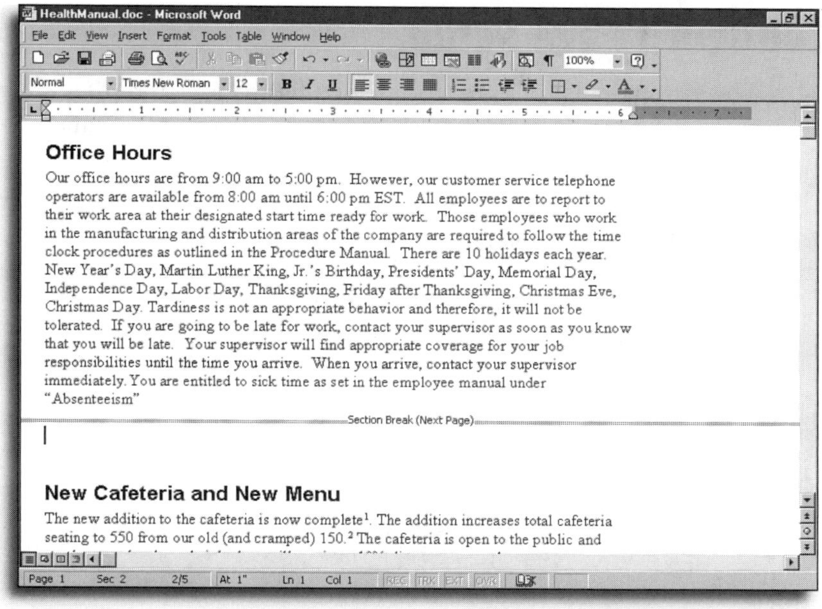

FIGURE **14.1**
Section breaks as they appear in Normal view.

### Insert a Manual Section Break

1. Position your insertion point where you want the new section to begin.

2. From the **Insert** menu, select **Break** to open the Break dialog box (see Figure 14.2).

FIGURE 14.2

Select the type of section break you want to insert.

3. Under **Section Breaks**, click the type of section break you want to insert: **Next Page**, **Continuous**, **Even Page**, or **Odd Page**.

4. Click **OK**.

To remove a section break, position the insertion point right after the break marker and press Backspace. Or position the insertion point on the break marker and press Delete.

**Deleting section breaks can delete formatting**

When you delete a section break, text in the section before the break assumes the page formatting that was set for the section that follows the break.

# Configure Page Setup

The starting point of page layout is setting the page setup options. Use setup options to change your document's orientation, margins, or paper size. Configure page setup in the Page Setup dialog box.

### Change Page Setup Options

1. Click the **File** menu and select **Page Setup**.

2. The Page Setup dialog box appears (see Figure 14.3). Select the tab that contains the options you want to set:

FIGURE 14.3

Select the tab that contains the options you want to set, such as the **Paper Source** tab.

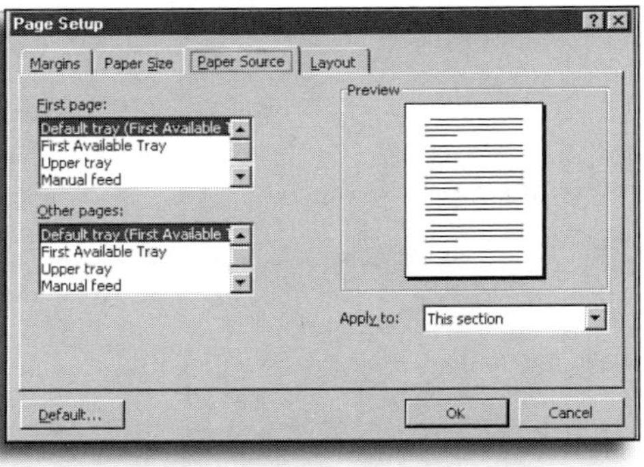

- **Margins**. Set the top, bottom, left, and right margins for your pages. See the "Set Margins" section later in this chapter for more details.

- **Paper Size**. Specify the paper size you're using and whether the page will print in portrait or landscape orientation. See the "Control Paper Size and Orientation" section for more details.

- **Paper Source**. If you have a printer with more than one tray, specify which tray your first page paper is in and which tray contains the paper for your other pages.

- **Layout**. Select the types of headers and footers you need for your document (see "Create Alternating Headers and Footers" later in this chapter), what type of vertical alignment you want to use on your pages, or turn on line numbering (useful where you need to reference different lines in a document).

3.  From the **Apply To** drop-down list, select the portion of the document to which you want to apply your settings: **This Section**, **This Point Forward**, **Whole Document**, or **Selected Sections**. These options appear frequently when you're setting page formats.

    - **Whole document**. Word applies your changes to the entire document.

    - **This Point Forward**. If you choose this, Word will insert a next page section break at the insertion point when you choose **OK** and apply your changes to all sections below the new section break.

    - **This Section**. This option only appears if the document has more than one section. Word applies your changes to the current section only.

    - **Selected Sections**. This only appears if text is selected that straddles more than one section. Word applies your changes to the selected sections.

4.  To save the settings as the new default settings for the current document, as well as all new documents based on the

same template, choose **Default**. When a dialog box appears asking if you want the change to become the default for all new documents using this template, choose **Yes**. Choose **No** to make the settings the default for only the current document.

5. Click **OK** to accept your changes and close the dialog box.

**SEE ALSO**

➤ *For more information on the vertical alignment of text, see page 196*

## Set Margins

The distance from the edge of the paper to the beginning of your text area is the *margin*. Each page has four margins: left, right, top, and bottom. Change margin settings when the default settings are not suitable for your document layout or printing preferences. Changing the margin settings affects the entire document, unless you have created sections and you specify that the margins apply only to specific sections.

There are two methods for changing margins: the dialog box method and the ruler method. The ruler method is available in two views: Print Layout view and Print Preview, and it works the same way in both places.

The advantage of using the dialog box method is that you can set all four margins at once and you don't have to change to the Print Layout view. However, you do need to enter precise margin values.

### Set Page Margins Using the Dialog Box

1. Click the **File** menu, and select **Page Setup**, or when you're in Print Layout view double-click in the gray area to the left of the ruler.

2. When the Page Setup dialog box appears, select the **Margins** tab (see Figure 14.4).

---

**What section is this?**

Word numbers the sections in your document. To find out which section your cursor is in, check the status bar at the bottom of your screen. Following the page number is the section number (such as "Sec 3").

**Our preferences for setting margins**

We find the ruler provides the fastest way to set margins. We reserve using the Page Setup dialog box for large documents that have special margin needs, such as a larger inside margin for bound documents.

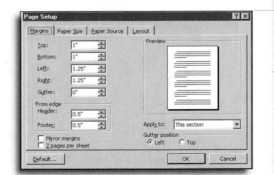

3. Enter the desired margin size (you don't need to enter the inch mark) in the **Top**, **Bottom**, **Left**, and **Right** text boxes, or click the up and down arrows to set the desired value. The **Preview** shows you the effect of your margin settings.

4. For documents that will be bound with spiral binding or in a three-ring binder, you may need to leave extra space to allow for the part of the page that will be hidden in the binding, which is called the *gutter*. To do this, enter the desired width of this binding area in the **Gutter** text box. Normally, Word adds this gutter on the left side of the page (although you can select **Top** as the **Gutter Position**). However, if you plan to print on both sides of the paper, you should choose **Mirror Margins** to place a check mark there. With *mirror margins* selected, the gutter space appears on the left side of odd-numbered pages and the right side of even-numbered pages (notice that your left and right margins become *inside* and *outside* margins) so the gutter is always on the inside part of the pages.

5. In the **From Edge** area, enter the distance the **Header** and **Footer** appear from the top and bottom edge of the paper.

6. From the **Apply To** drop-down list, select where the new margins will apply: **Whole Document**, **This Point Forward**, **This Section**, or **Selected Sections**.

---

**Two pages on a sheet**

When you create a newsletter, brochure, or booklet, you should consider printing two of your document pages on a single sheet of paper (in the Page Setup dialog box select **2 pages per Sheet**). Many newsletters are printed with two letter-sized pages on 11 × 17 inch paper. Booklets and brochures often have two pages printed on one sheet of 8.5 × 11 inch (letter size) or 8.5 × 14 inch (legal size) paper. The paper orientation is landscape for printing. If you choose this option, you should check your margins for necessary adjustments.

**Default margins**

Word sets the default margins as 1 inch at the top and bottom and 1.25 inch at the right and left. The header and footer settings are .5 inch from the edge. If these settings don't match your needs for most of your documents, change them in the dialog box and click **Default**.

**7.** If you want to save the settings as the new default settings for this document or all new documents based on the current template, choose **Default**. When a dialog box appears asking if you want the change to become the default for all new documents using this template, choose **Yes**. Choose **No** to make the settings the default for only the current document.

**8.** Click **OK** to close the dialog box and apply the margins to your document.

**SEE ALSO**

➤ *Learn about views on page 53*

➤ *Learn about Print Preview mode on page 260*

The second method for setting page margins uses the mouse and the ruler. This method enables you to work visually instead of doing arithmetic in your head because you can immediately see how your changes affect your document.

To display the ruler, choose the **View** menu, and select **Ruler** or position the mouse pointer near the top edge of the work area and hold it there. If you use the second method, the ruler stays visible until you move your mouse pointer away from the top of the document window.

**See your entire page**

You don't have to switch to Print Preview to see the entire page from Print Layout view. Select **Page Width** or **Whole Page** from the **Zoom** drop-down list on the Standard toolbar.

You must be working in Print Layout view or Print Preview mode if you want to use the ruler to set margins (in Web Layout view you're not really concerned with margins). You'll probably find it easier to work in Print Layout view because the ruler is usually larger in this view, therefore easier to work with. But in Print Preview you can see the entire page on the screen, so you can really get a view of the results of any changes you make.

**Warning! Be careful not to use indent markers**

The indent markers on the rulers do not change the margins of your document, only the indentation for your current or selected paragraphs. To change margins using the ruler, change to Print Layout view first, and use the margin markers as described here.

In both of these views you can see both the horizontal ruler at the top of the page and a vertical ruler on the left edge of the page. To switch to Print Layout view, click the **View** menu, and select **Page Layout** or choose the **Page Layout View** button in the bottom-left corner of the screen. To switch to Print Preview mode, choose the **File** menu, and select **Print Preview** or click the **Print Preview** button .

On each ruler, the white area of the ruler displays the typing area between the margins. The dark gray areas on either side of the typing area display the margins, as shown in Figure 14.5. A light gray line between the white and dark gray areas is the margin marker (don't confuse these with the triangular indent markers). You might not be able to see the margin marker on the left, but it is there. If you want to see the left margin marker, you can drag the left indent markers to the left a little bit, then back to their original position.

### Change a Margin Using the Ruler

1.  Point at the margin marker on the horizontal ruler, at the left or right end of the white bar, or at the top or bottom margin markers on the vertical ruler.

2.  When the mouse pointer changes to a two-headed arrow (the help tip displays Left Margin, Right Margin, Top Margin, or Bottom Margin), click and drag the margin to a new position.

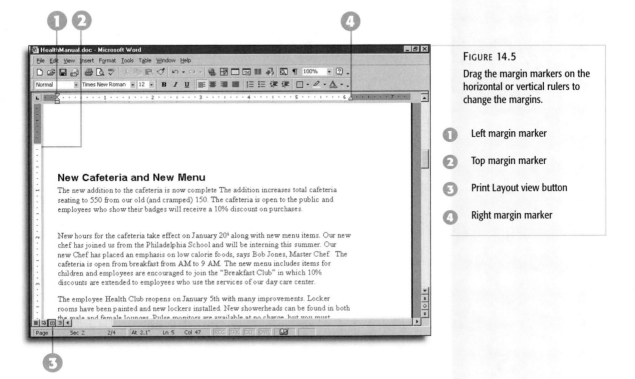

FIGURE 14.5

Drag the margin markers on the horizontal or vertical rulers to change the margins.

1. Left margin marker

2. Top margin marker

3. Print Layout view button

4. Right margin marker

**Quickly display ruler settings**

To view ruler settings such as margins, indents, and tabs, point to the ruler element whose setting you want to see, then hold down both the Alt key and the mouse button. The settings appear on the ruler and remain until you release the Alt key.

# Control Paper Size and Orientation

The default paper size is set at 8 1/2×11 inches and in *portrait orientation* (the shorter edge of the paper is the top). To specify a different paper size, select from several standard paper and envelope sizes or define a custom paper size. You can also print in *landscape orientation*, so the long edge of the paper is the top.

## Specify Paper Size and Orientation

1. Click the **File** menu and select **Page Setup** on the menu. The Page Setup dialog box opens.

2. Select the **Paper Size** tab to display the paper size and orientation options (see Figure 14.6).

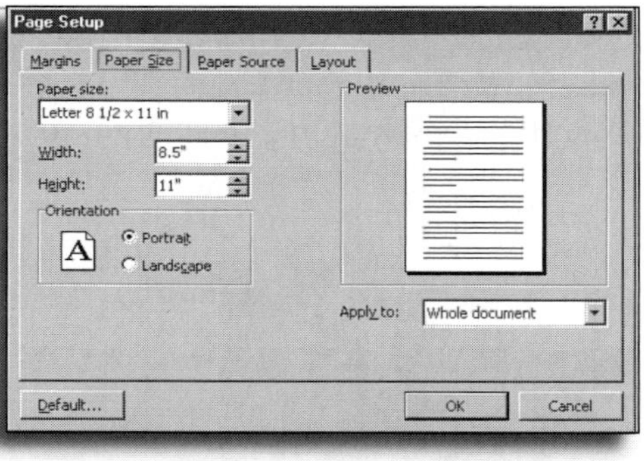

FIGURE 14.6

Choose your paper size and orientation in the Page Setup dialog box.

3. From the **Paper Size** drop-down list, select a predefined paper size. If the paper size you need isn't listed, select **Custom Size** and enter the appropriate values in the **Width** and **Height** boxes.

4. Under Orientation, select **Portrait** or **Landscape**. See the tiny page sample next to these options if you're not sure which is which; it changes to show you the orientation you selected.

5. From the **Apply To** drop-down list, select the portion of the document to which you want your settings to apply: **Whole Document**, **This Point Forward**, or **This Section**.

6. To save the settings as the new default settings for the current document, as well as all new documents based on the

same template, choose **Default**. When a dialog box appears asking if you want the change to become the default for all new documents using this template, choose **Yes**. Choose **No** to make the settings the default for only the current document.

**7.** Click **OK**.

SEE ALSO

➤ *To learn more about printing booklets, see page 273*

# Add Headers and Footers

Text that repeats at the top of every page is a *header*; text that repeats at the bottom of every page is a *footer*. Use headers and footers to help readers know which document they've picked up, what page they're on, or what chapter they're currently reading.

Normally, the header and footer text appears 1/2 inch from the edge of the page. You change this in the Page Setup dialog box, as described in the "Set Margins" section of this chapter, in the **From Edge** section of the **Margins** tab. The body text starts and ends at the top and bottom margins unless you have several lines in the header or footer, or you change the **From Edge** values to be greater than the margin. In those circumstances, the margins adjust so the body text starts after the header and ends just before the footer.

Headers and footers can vary within a document. Choices include:

- The same header and footer on every page
- A different header and footer for the first page only
- Different headers and footers for odd numbered pages than those on even numbered pages
- Different headers and footers for each section of the document

A complex document with multiple sections—for example, a technical manual—might combine all the possible variations. That is, each section might have its own set of headers and footers of all three kinds—first page, odd pages, and even pages.

**Add a Header or Footer to Your Document**

1. Click the <u>View</u> menu and select <u>Header and Footer</u>. The document appears in Print Layout view with the header area indicated by a nonprinting dashed-line box (see Figure 14.7). Regular document text is gray, and the Header and Footer toolbar is displayed.

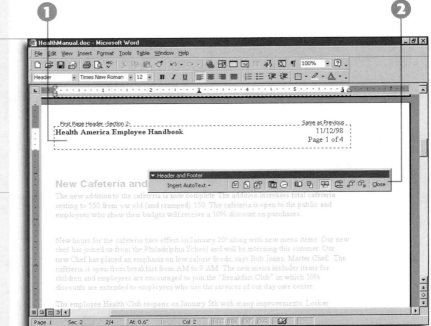

FIGURE 14.7

The header or footer appears in a dashed-line box, and the document text is grayed and inaccessible while viewing the header or footer.

1 Header box

2 Header and Footer toolbar

2. Type the header or footer text. Edit and format the text as you would anywhere else in the document. Both the header and the footer have two tabs set to help you align your text: a center tab at the center of the page and a right tab at the right margin.

3. Use the toolbar buttons, described in Table 14.1, to add page numbers, total page numbers, date, time, and so on.

4. Choose **Close** on the Header and Footer toolbar to return to the document.

TABLE 14.1    **Header and Footer toolbar buttons**

| Action | Button |
|---|---|
| Inserts an AutoText entry AutoText drop-down list | Insert |
| Inserts a page number code | |
| Inserts the total number of pages in the document | |
| Opens the Page Number Format dialog box | |
| Inserts a date code for the current date | |
| Inserts a time code for the current time | |
| Opens the Page Setup dialog box | |
| Displays or hides the document text | |
| Makes the header or footer the same type of header or footer (first page, odd pages, or even pages) as the one in the previous section or breaks that link when you deselect it | |
| Switches between the header and the footer on the same page | |
| Shows the previous header or footer | |
| Shows the next header or footer | |
| Close the Header and Footer toolbar and return to document editing | Close |

**SEE ALSO**

➤ *Learn more about AutoText on page 123*

➤ *Find out more about inserting date and time fields on page 531*

# Create Alternating Headers and Footers

Normally, the same header and footer appear on every page of your document. However, if you plan to print on both sides of the paper and bind the document, you may find it more visually pleasing to have the page numbers on the outside corners of the pages, which means the left side of even-numbered pages and the right side of odd-numbered pages.

**Not just for page numbers**

Alternating headers and footers give you quite a few page lay-out opportunities besides changing the placement of your page numbers. For example, you may have the company logo appear in the even page header and the company name in the odd page header. Then, when you open the document, you'll see the logo across from the company name. Or, you might want the author's name on the even pages and the document title on the odd pages.

#### Set Up Different Odd and Even Page Headers or Footers

1. Click the **View** menu and select **Header and Footer** and then choose **Page Setup** on the Header and Footer toolbar. Or, click the **File** menu and select **Page Setup**. The Page Setup dialog box opens (see Figure 14.8).

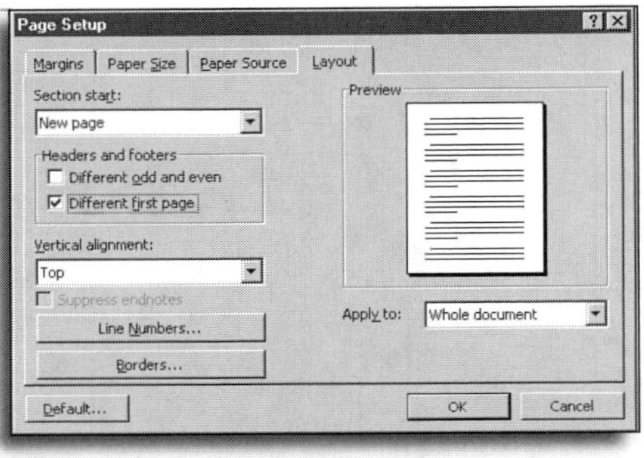

FIGURE 14.8

The Headers and Footers options enable you to have different headers and footers on odd or even pages, or a different header and footer for just the first page.

2. Click the **Layout** tab if it's not already selected.
3. Click **Different Odd and Even** to place a check mark there.
4. Click **OK** to close the Page Setup dialog box.

Using the instructions from the "Add Headers and Footers" section earlier in this chapter, you need to create a header and footer on an even page. Then click **Show Next** 🔳 on the Header and Footer toolbar to see the header or footer for an odd-numbered page. Create the header and footer that you want to appear on all the odd-numbered pages. Choose **Close** to return to your document.

## Edit Headers and Footers

Editing headers and footers is similar to making changes in the main body of your document. Adding, removing, and formatting text follows the same procedures.

#### Edit a Header or Footer

1. Click the **View** menu, and select **Headers and Footers**. The header on the current page appears in edit mode, outlined by a dashed box. The Header and Footer toolbar also appears.

If you need to modify the footer, click **Switch Between Header and Footer** 🔁 from the Header and Footer toolbar.

2. Click in the Header or Footer box and then edit or format the text as you would in any other portion of your document.

3. When your modifications are complete, choose **Close** on the Header and Footer toolbar to return to normal editing of your document.

While you were in Headers and Footers view, the body text of your document was grayed out and not editable. When you close Headers and Footers view and return to Print Layout view you can see your headers and footers grayed out and not editable.

**SEE ALSO**

➤ To set tabs for different alignments on the same line, see page 204

➤ To use tables as an alternative solution to placing different text alignments on the same line, see page 171

➤ Learn more about styles on page 237

➤ To add watermarks to your document by using graphics in your header or footer, see page 383

You should keep a couple of cautions in mind when you want to edit different types of headers and footers within the same document:

■ Edit the correct header or footer. When you have alternating headers and footers, different first page headers and footers, or different headers and footers for different sections of your document it's very easy to edit the wrong one. Before you start editing, position your insertion point on a page that uses the type of header or footer you want to modify. Then follow the steps for editing. Also check the text at the top of the header or footer box to verify which one you're editing.

■ Make sure **Same as Previous** is not on. This is important if your document has multiple sections. If **Same as Previous** is active, the current header or footer inherits its contents from the header or footer of the same type (first page, odd

---

**A handy shortcut**

When you are in Print Layout view, you can toggle quickly between editing body text and editing headers and footers by double-clicking on the grayed-out text. Double-clicking a header or footer puts you in header/footer edit mode. Double-clicking body text closes header/footer edit mode.

**Left-, center-, and right-aligned text on one line**

Word automatically assigns the built-in styles Header and Footer to header and footer paragraphs. The special characteristic of both of these styles is that they have a center-aligned tab at the center of the page and a right-aligned tab at the right margin. This lets you enter left-aligned text, then press Tab to enter centered text, then press Tab again to enter right-aligned text, all on one line.

pages, or even pages) in the previous section of the document. You could accidentally change the header or footer in another section without meaning to. To avoid this, look for the words "Same as Previous" in the top border of the header or footer that indicate this feature is active. To turn off **Same as Previous**, click the **Same as Previous** icon 🖳 in the Headers and Footers toolbar.

## Create a First Page Header or Footer

The first page of a document, such as a multipage letter or a report, may need a different header or footer than the remainder of the document. For example, the first page of a letter might look much the same as any letter but the subsequent pages might have a header that identifies the recipient, the date of the letter, and the page number.

### Make a Different Header or Footer for the First Page

1. Click the **File** menu and select **Page Setup** or choose **Page Setup** from the Header and Footer toolbar. The Page Setup dialog box opens (refer to Figure 14.8).
2. Click the **Layout** tab.
3. Click **Different First Page** to place a check mark there.
4. Choose **OK** to close the Page Setup dialog box.

When you create the header and footer for the first page (see the instructions for adding headers and footers in "Add Headers and Footers" earlier in this chapter), the header box is marked "First Page Header" and the footer box is "First Page Footer." If you want nothing to appear on the first page, don't enter any text in the box. When you choose **Show Next** on the Header and Footer toolbar, the header and footer boxes on the next page are labeled "Header" and "Footer." Enter the text in these boxes that you want to appear on all later pages.

For information on formatting the page numbers in your headers and footers, or starting the page numbering with a different number (making the page after the title page start at page 1), refer to the "Add Page Numbering" section of this chapter.

# Add Page Numbering

Printed documents longer than one page should have page numbers. You can set up page numbering in two ways. Either insert a page number code while editing headers and footers, or insert page numbers from the **Insert** menu. Both methods insert a page number code in your document's header or footer, but there are two differences. If you insert the page number code manually while editing a header or footer, you can embed the number in other text. This enables you, for example, to have your page number look something like this: Page x of y. If you use the **Insert** menu method to have Word insert the page number code for you, the page number will stand alone. However, when you use this method, Word puts the page number code inside a frame, then inserts the frame into your header or footer. A *frame* is a box which you can move anywhere on the page. You can put borders around a frame, put shading inside a frame, insert graphics into a frame, and edit the text inside a frame separately from other text in your document. By inserting your page numbers this way, you can achieve special effects, such as having the page number appear in a shaded, bordered box set outside the normal page margins of your document.

To add a page number code while editing a header or footer, follow the "Add Headers and Footers" instructions earlier in this chapter. When the header or footer box appears in the edit mode, position your insertion point where you want the page number to appear and then click **Insert Page Number** on the Header and Footer toolbar. If you want to note the total number of pages in the document (such as Page 1 of 12), add the appropriate text and then click **Insert Number of Pages** where you want the total to appear.

### Add Page Numbering

1. Click the **Insert** menu and select **Page Numbers** to open the Page Numbers dialog box (see Figure 14.9)

2. From the **Position** drop-down list, select the position on the page where you want your page numbers to appear: **Top of Page (Header)** or **Bottom of Page (Footer)**.

**Why have two ways to insert page numbers?**

Including the page number in your header or footer allows for the inclusion of other text with the page number, such as "Introduction/page 1." Inserting the page number with the **Insert** menu puts the number in a movable frame that you may position and format separately from other text. Also, it's the method to use when you want page numbering but aren't going to use headers and footers.

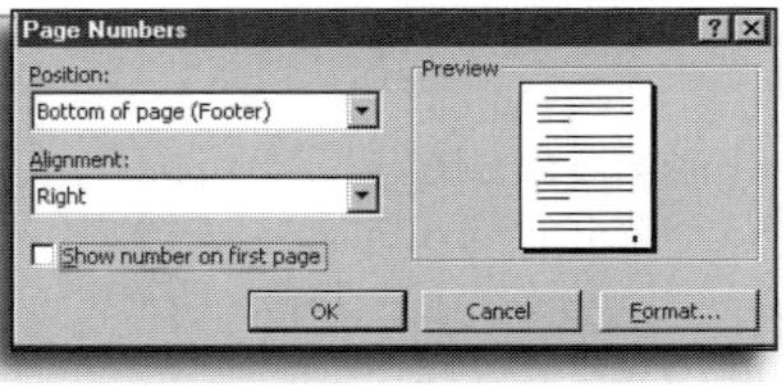

FIGURE 14.9

Deselect **Show Number on First Page** if you don't want a page number to appear on the first page.

**3.** From the **Alignment** drop-down list, select **Left**, **Center**, or **Right** to specify the horizontal position of the page number in relation to the right and left margins. If you're printing on both sides of the paper (and have set up mirror margins) and you want the page numbers positioned near the binding, select **Inside**; to put them away from the binding select **Outside**. This creates the page numbers that alternate position on even or odd pages without creating alternating odd/even headers or footers as described earlier in this chapter.

**4.** If you want the page number to appear on the first page, click **Show Number on First Page** to place a check mark there. Deselecting this option creates a separate header or footer for the first page, as discussed earlier in this chapter.

**5.** Click **OK**. A number appears in the position you specified on the page.

When you insert a page number, Word automatically switches you to Print Layout view so you can scroll to the portion of the page where the page number appears to check its appearance.

**Page numbers are grayed out!**

The Page Numbers option is grayed out on the **Insert** menu when you're in Web Layout or Outline view. No page numbers exist for Web documents because they are just one big page. To add page numbers, switch to Normal or Print Layout view. You can only see the page numbers in Print Layout view.

## Format Page Numbering

You can define the style of page numbering used in your document or in a section of your document, combine the page number with a chapter number, or set the starting number for your page numbering. Word automatically inserts the correct codes and formatting for you.

### Format Page Numbers

**1.** Click the **Insert** menu and select **Page Numbers** to open the Page Numbers dialog box (refer to Figure 14.9).

**2.** Choose **Format** to open the Page Number Format dialog
box (see Figure 14.10).

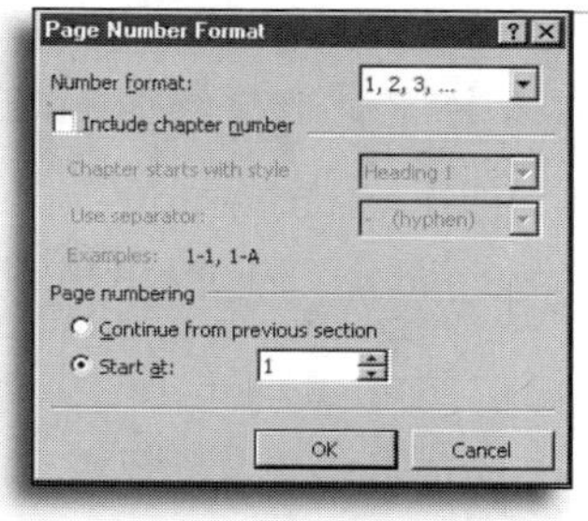

FIGURE 14.10
Enter 1 as the starting page number for the section that starts on
the page after the title page.

**3.** Select the style of numbering you want to use from the
**Number Format** drop-down list: Arabic (1, 2, 3), lowercase
letters (a, b, c), uppercase letters (A, B, C), lowercase Roman
numerals (i, ii, iii), or uppercase Roman numerals (I, II, III).

**4.** (Optional) To have Word insert a combined chapter and
page number so that the page numbers might look like "I-1"
or "A:1," there are a couple of steps you must take before
you format the page numbering. You must use a consistent
paragraph style for your chapter titles (such as Heading 1).
Do not apply the chapter title style to any other paragraphs
in your document. The chapter titles also have to be numbered (click the **Format** menu, and then **Bullets and
Numbering**). Select the **Outline Numbered** tab, and then
choose a multilevel list type that is linked to the Heading
styles (from the bottom row of options). Then, in the Page
Number Format dialog box, click **Include Chapter
Number** to place a check mark there. Select the name of
the chapter title style you are using from the **Chapter
Starts with Style** box. From the **Use Separator** drop-down
list, select a number separator to appear between the chapter
number and the page number—hyphen (I-1), period (1.1),
colon (A:1), em dash (II—1), en dash (A–1).

**5.** Click **OK** to return to the Page Numbers dialog box.

**6.** Click **OK** to accept your formatting changes, or **Close** to
close the dialog box without accepting your changes.

**SEE ALSO**

➤ *Learn more about styles and how to apply them on page 247*

➤ *For more information on multilevel numbering, see page 233*

# Modify Page Numbering for Different Sections

If you have different sections in your document, you can set up page numbering differently in each section. For example, you might want to number your table of contents in lowercase Roman numerals, but start the first chapter as page 1 using Arabic numerals.

### Start New Page Numbers for Another Section

1. Set up the page numbering for the first section (your table of contents) using the instructions in the "Format Page Numbers" section earlier in this chapter.

2. Move your insertion point to the next section.

3. Click the <u>I</u>nsert menu and select **Page N<u>u</u>mbers** and set the position and alignment for your page numbers. Then choose **<u>F</u>ormat** to open the Page Number Format dialog box (refer to Figure 14.10).

4. Follow the instructions under Format Page Numbers to set the format of page numbering you want to use or to include chapter numbers in the page numbering.

5. Under Page Numbering, click **Start <u>A</u>t** and type a starting page number in the text box.

6. Choose **OK** to return to the Page Numbers dialog box.

7. Click **OK** to accept your formatting changes.

Repeat these steps for each section in which you want to have different page numbering.

Alternatively, you can format page numbers from the Header and Footer view. Just click the **Format Page Numbers** button in the Header and Footer toolbar to reveal the Format Page Numbers dialog box, then follow the numbered instructions that appeared earlier in this section.

## Create an Unnumbered Title Page

One problem you may have when you don't show the page number on the first page is that on the next page the number is "2." After a title page you want the number to be "1." The solution is to insert a next page section break after the title page and number the pages differently in each section.

### Create an Unnumbered Title Page

1. Place your insertion point after the text on your title page and then click the **Insert** menu and select **Break**.

2. From the Break dialog box, click **Next Page** under **Section Breaks** and then click **OK**.

3. Don't assign page numbers to the title page section, but insert them in the second section. Follow the instructions under the "Modify Page Numbering" section, entering 1 as your page number in the **Start** **At** box.

Other formatting differences between the first page and the rest of the document or section, such as margins or vertical centering, can also be accomplished using a section for the first page and another section for the remainder of the document. Refer to "Create and Remove Sections" earlier in this chapter.

# Create Page Borders

Use page borders when you want to dress up a document for presentation, such as a title page, an announcement, or an invitation. Borders can be a single line outline, have a shadow, be three-dimensional, be decorative, or combine thick and thin lines.

Word offers several predefined border settings:

- **None** removes all borders from the page.
- **Box** inserts a box border around the page.
- **Shadow** inserts a box border around the page and applies a preset shadow formatting to the border.

- **3-D** inserts a box border around the page and applies preset 3D border formatting.

- **Custom** lets you create a border using the options you click in the Preview window.

### Add a Border to a Page

**1.** Click the **Format** menu and select **Borders and Shading**. The Borders and Shading dialog box appears (see Figure 14.11).

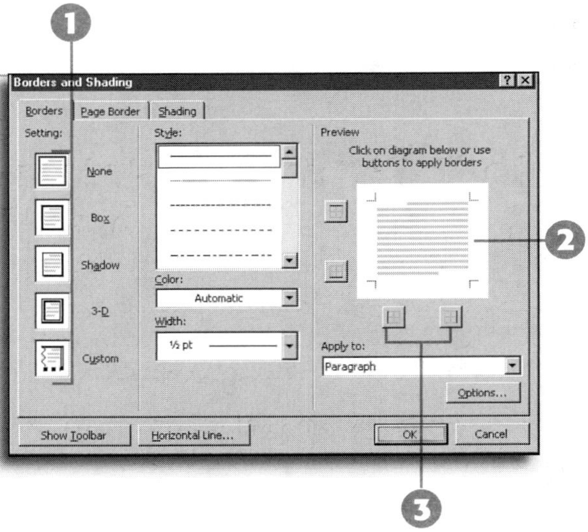

FIGURE 14.11

Select a predefined border under Setting or create your own by specifying style, color, width, art, or position.

1. Predefined borders

2. Preview

3. Buttons to apply borders

**2.** Select the **Page Border** tab.

**3.** Specify the options you want:

- Under Setting, select one of the preset border options listed earlier in this section. When you choose any of these settings, the current selections in **Style**, **Color**, and **Width** apply to the borders.

- From the **Style** list, select the type of line you want to use for the border, including dotted, dashed, and wavy lines.

- Click the **Color** drop-down list to select a color to apply to the border.

- From the **Width** drop-down list, choose the thickness of the border line from 1/4-point to 6 points (more for decorative borders).

- From the **Art** drop-down list select a graphical border design.

- From the **Apply To** drop-down list, select the portion of the document on which you want the border to appear (the options are described in the "Configure Page Setup" section). Note that these options also include **This Section—First Page Only** and **This Section—All Except First Page**.

4. Choose **Options** to open the Border and Shading Options dialog box (see Figure 14.12). This dialog box is where you specify the exact position of the border on the page in relation to the edge of the page or the text. The default setting is 24 points, about 1/3 inch from the edge of the paper. Choose **OK** to return to the Borders and Shading dialog box.

**Using preview to make custom borders**

The Preview box shows you how your borders will look but also lets you define different borders on different sides of the page or have no borders on designated sides of the page. Choose the **Custom** setting and then select the border attributes. In the Preview box, click on the individual border lines or use the border line buttons to apply or remove borders. Change the attributes and then use the Preview box again to apply a different line style on another side (this doesn't work with art borders).

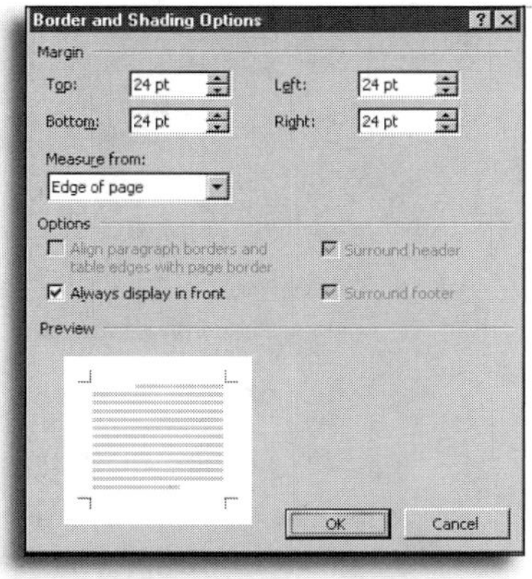

**FIGURE 14.12**

Specify the location of the border on the page by entering values in the Margin boxes and designating where the measurements start in the **Measure From** box.

5. Click **OK** to apply your border to the page or pages you specified (see Figure 14.13).

FIGURE 14.13

A page border makes a handsome title page.

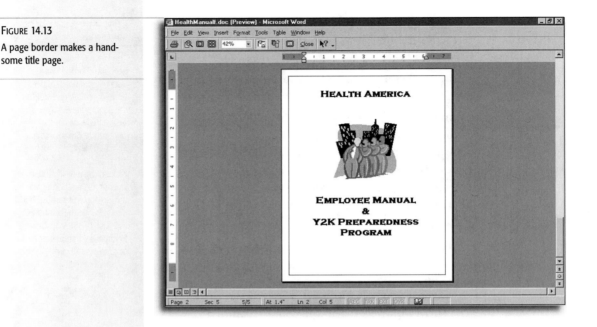

### Modify an Existing Border

1. Click the **Format** menu and select **Borders and Shading**.

2. In the Borders and Shading dialog box, select the **Page Border** tab (refer to Figure 14.11).

3. Select the options you want using the instructions from the previous section. To change only one side of a border, click **Custom** under **Setting**. Specify the new border attributes. Then, under Preview, click the border you want to change.

4. Click **OK** to apply your modifications to the page border.

Page borders add distinction to certificates and awards and make title pages stand out. You want to be conservative, however, in your use of boxes. If you have a page border, you should think twice about also adding lines between columns, boxes around graphics, and borders on paragraphs. Too many lines detract from your page content.

**SEE ALSO**

➤ *Learn about text borders on page 89*

# Organize Documents with Outlines, Footnotes, and Endnotes

Generate outlines

Create footnotes and endnotes

# Generate Outlines

The purpose of an outline is to organize a document by setting forth its basic parts in a logical order. The outline becomes the framework on which you build your document.

Word's Outline view lets you reduce a large document down to its headings for easier viewing and organization of the document. When a document is in Outline view, you can reorganize it quickly and easily by rearranging the order of the headings, demoting headings to lower levels, and promoting headings to higher levels. All text (including lower-level headings) nested beneath a heading go with it when you move, demote, or promote the heading.

**Outline view versus outline numbering**

Don't confuse Word's Outline view with paragraph outline numbering (which is discussed in Chapter 11, "Work with Lists"). Paragraph outline numbering refers to the assignment of numbers to paragraphs in a multi-level fashion, and Word also helps you to do that. Outline view works with paragraph heading styles to help you organize an entire document.

To view a document in Outline view, click the Outline View icon at the bottom of the screen or click the **View** menu and select **Outline**. When you switch to Outline view, the Outlining toolbar appears on your screen and a heading symbol appears in front of each paragraph of your document. If a paragraph has a heading style attached to it, it is a heading paragraph and its heading symbol is a plus or minus sign. It is a plus sign if the heading has subheadings or body text below it. It is a minus sign if the heading has no subheadings or body text below it. If a paragraph does not have a heading style attached, Outline view treats it as a body text paragraph (even though you might intend it to be a heading) and its "heading" symbol is a small square (see Figure 15.1).

To see your document headings in the hierarchical form shown in Figure 15.1, either promote your heading paragraphs to outline headings in Outline view or apply Word's predefined heading styles (Heading 1 through Heading 9) to your headings. Both methods accomplish the same thing, which is the assignment of Word's predefined heading styles to your heading paragraphs. You may change the format of these styles to suit your document, but don't change the names or their hierarchical relationship. Heading 1 is a major heading, Heading 2 is a subheading under Heading 1, Heading 3 is a subheading under Heading 2, and so on.

You can hide the *subordinate text* in Outline view (the body text under the heading) and show only the main headings. You may also show only the first line of every paragraph, as we did in Figure 15.1. When the subordinate text is hidden, the outline is *collapsed*. A line under the heading represents the subordinate text, and a plus sign appears in front of the heading indicating that there is subordinate text. When you show the subordinate text again, the outline is *expanded*. Keep in mind that selecting a heading (by clicking its heading symbol) also selects the subordinate text under it, whether collapsed or not. Therefore, if you move, copy, or delete the heading, you'll also be moving, copying, or deleting its subordinate text.

Table 15.1 describes how to collapse and expand headings.

**Don't want to use Word heading styles?**

The Outline view automatically works with Word's heading styles (Heading 1, Heading 2, and so on). If you've assigned other names to your paragraph styles but want to use them in Outline view without converting them to Word's heading styles, you need to assign Outline levels to those styles. Open the **Format** menu and choose **Style**. Select the style from the **Styles** list and then choose **Modify**. Click **Format** and choose **Paragraph**. Click the **Indents and Spacing** tab. Choose an **Outline** level (**Body Text** or **Level 1** through **Level 9**). Choose **OK** twice and then **Apply**. You can also apply outline levels to individual paragraphs using the Paragraph dialog box.

TABLE 15.1    **Collapsing and expanding headings**

| To | Do This |
|---|---|
| Collapse all text below a specific level of heading. | Choose the number button on the Outlining toolbar for the lowest heading you want to display. For example, choose Show Heading 4 [4] to show heading levels 1 through 4. |
| Collapse or display all subheadings and body text under a heading. | Double-click the plus sign next to the heading. |
| Collapse or expand text under a heading, one level at a time. | Click the heading text, and then choose Collapse [−] or Expand [+] on the Outlining toolbar. |
| Collapse or expand all body text in the document. | Choose Show All Headings [All] on the Outlining toolbar. |
| Display the first line only of body text. | Choose Show First Line Only [≡] on the Outlining toolbar. An ellipsis (...) after the first line indicates that additional lines of text are collapsed. |

**SEE ALSO**

➤ *For more information on creating, applying, and modifying styles, see page 247*

# Create Outlines from Scratch

The best way to start writing a long document is to organize it with an outline. When you create the outline in Outline view, you're also creating the document by creating its headings.

### Create and Organize a Document with an Outline

1. Start a new document.

2. Switch to Outline view by choosing Outline View from the view buttons at the bottom left of the screen [⊞], or by clicking the **View** menu and selecting **Outline**.

3. Type each heading you want to include in the document, pressing Enter after each one. Word automatically applies the Heading 1 style to each heading.

4. To change the heading level (and also its style), drag the plus or minus sign that precedes the heading. Drag the sign to the right to *demote* the heading to a lower level or drag it to the left to *promote* the heading to a higher level.

Alternatively, place the text cursor anywhere in a heading paragraph and then choose the Demote icon ⬜ or the Promote icon ⬜ on the Outlining toolbar. To demote a heading to *body text*, click on the Demote to Body Text icon ⬜ in the Outlining toolbar.

5. To change the order of the headings in the document, drag the plus or minus symbol in front of the heading up or down to the desired location. Or put the text cursor is anywhere in the heading paragraph, then choose Move Up ⬜ or Move Down ⬜ on the Outlining toolbar.

6. When you have the headings in the desired order and at their proper levels, switch to the Print Layout view or the Normal view (click the appropriate view button at the bottom of the screen) to add the body text, graphics, tables, charts, and so on.

**SEE ALSO**

➤ *Learn how to create a PowerPoint presentation from a Word outline on page 413*

## Use Outline View to Rearrange Existing Text

If you created a document without using outlining and later you want to use Word's Outline view to review or reorganize it, you can do so at any time by switching to Outline view. If you assigned any of Word's predefined heading styles (Heading 1 through Heading 9) to any paragraphs, they automatically show up as the corresponding outline levels. If you assigned custom styles to which outline levels had been assigned (in the Paragraph dialog box), or if you assigned outline levels directly to any paragraphs (again in the Paragraph dialog box), those paragraphs will also appear as the corresponding outline levels. All other paragraphs—even your heading paragraphs—appear in Outline view as body text paragraphs. But you can promote any body text paragraph to any level of heading that you want, and you can demote a heading to body text.

Do any of the following:

- *Demote the Heading Level.* Drag the plus or minus symbol preceding the heading to the right. A vertical line appears as

---

**Moving headings with subordinate text**

Moving headings up and down in the outline is easy. But if the headings have subordinate text and you want the subordinate text to move with the heading, you need to select the subordinate text. Do this one of two ways: Click on the plus sign in front of the heading before you move the heading or collapse the heading so the subordinate text will automatically stay with it during the move.

you drag, showing the heading level. When the line is at the level you want, release the mouse button. Or place the insertion point in the heading and then choose Demote 🠞 on the Outlining toolbar. To demote the heading to body text, choose Demote to Body Text 🠞 on the Outlining toolbar.

- *Promote the Heading Level.* Collapse the heading. Drag the plus or minus symbol preceding the heading to the left. A vertical line appears as you drag (see Figure 15.2), showing the heading level. When the line is at the level you want, release the mouse button. Or place the insertion point in the heading and then choose Promote 🠜 on the Outlining toolbar.

**FIGURE 15.2**

A vertical line indicates the heading level when you drag a heading to the left or right.

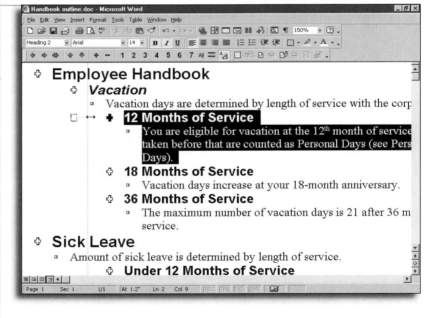

- *Promote Body Text to a Heading.* Drag the small square icon next to a body text paragraph to the left to promote that paragraph to a heading and assign the corresponding heading style to it. Alternatively, place a text cursor anywhere in the paragraph, and then choose Promote 🠜 in the Outlining toolbar.

- *Demote a Heading to Body Text*. Select a heading paragraph, and then click the Demote to Body Text icon ⇨ in the Outlining toolbar. The heading paragraph becomes a body text paragraph as Word assigns the Normal style to it. The plus or minus symbol that preceded it becomes a small square symbol.

- *Move Text*. Unless you are moving body text paragraphs, you might want to make it easier to see what you are doing by collapsing all headings first (choose ▬ on the Outlining toolbar). Then drag the plus or minus symbol in front of the heading up or down in the document. As you drag, you'll see a horizontal line (see Figure 15.3). When that horizontal line stops at the location where you want to put the text, release the mouse button. Or place the insertion point in the heading and then choose Move Up ⬆ or Move Down ⬇ on the Outlining toolbar to move the heading up or down one line at a time. Each time you click one of these icons the selected heading moves above the one above it or below the one below it.

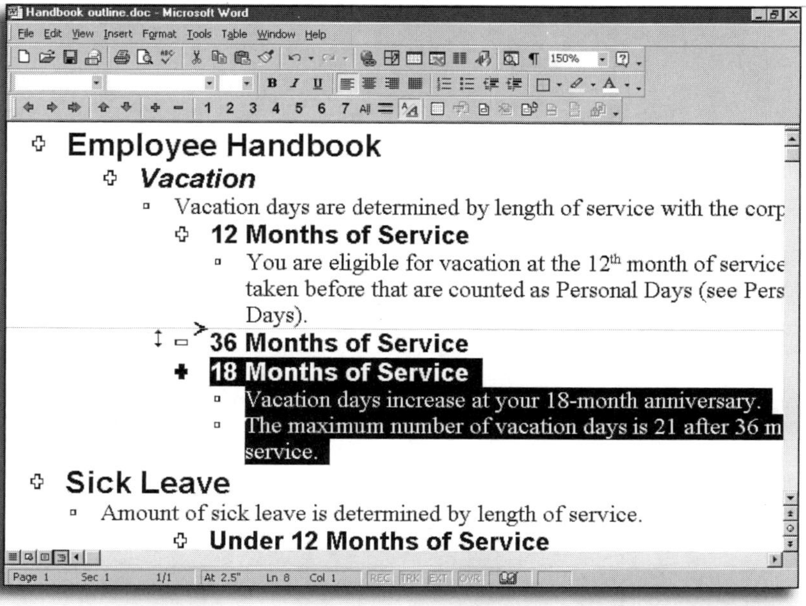

FIGURE 15.3
When you drag headings up or down the document to move them, a horizontal line indicates where the heading will appear after you release the mouse button.

- *Cut, Copy, or Paste Text.* Collapse the heading. Click the plus or minus symbol to select the heading and its subordinate text. Cut or copy the selected heading. The cut or copy also takes the heading's subordinates—all subheadings and body text that are nested beneath it. Move the insertion point to the location where you want the text to appear, then paste. The heading (and all its subordinates) appears at the new insertion point.

- *Delete Text.* Collapse the heading. Click the plus or minus symbol to select the heading and its subordinate text. Press the Delete key to delete the heading *and* its subordinate text.

Whether you're moving or deleting entire sections of a document (in which sections might span multiple pages and include graphics, charts, and the kitchen sink) or just rearranging paragraphs, Outline view provides the easiest way to do it. Outline view lets you do the operations on the heading symbols. When you click a symbol, Word automatically selects the heading and all its subordinate headings and text for you, instead of requiring you to manually select the text, as you would have to do in other views.

## Use Keyboard Shortcuts in Outline View

Use keystrokes instead of the mouse in Outline view to organize a document by moving, promoting, and demoting headings. Using keystrokes, you don't have to waste time moving your hand back and forth between the keyboard and mouse.

Most outline manipulation keystrokes use the Alt and Shift keys and the arrow keys. So you can use the arrow keys to move the insertion point into a paragraph, then use Alt+Shift and the same arrow keys to move the paragraph in the outline hierarchy. You never have to take your hands off the keyboard, and you can work very fast. Try it! Table 15.2 shows the outline keystrokes.

TABLE 15.2 **Keystrokes to manipulate text in Outline view**

| To | Press These Keys |
| --- | --- |
| Promote text to a higher-level heading | Alt+Shift+Left arrow |
| Demote text to a lower-level heading | Alt+Shift+Right arrow |
| Demote a heading to body text | Alt+Shift+Keypad 5 (if Num Lock is off) or Ctrl+Shift+N |
| Move selected headings up | Alt+Shift+Up arrow |
| Move selected headings down | Alt+Shift+Down arrow |
| Expand text under selected heading | Alt+Shift+Plus sign |
| Collapse text under selected heading | Alt+Shift+Minus sign |
| Expand or collapse all text | Alt+Shift+Alphabetical Keyboard Asterisk or Alt+Shift+A |
| Show only the first line of body text | Alt+Shift+L |
| Show only headings down to heading level $n$ | Alt+Shift+$n$ (where $n$ is a number from 1 to 9 on the top row of the alphabetical keyboard) |

Notice in the last entry of Table 15.2 that to display only outline headings down to level $n$, you press Alt+Shift+a number key $n$ on the top row of the alphabetical keyboard, *not* on the numeric keypad. Also notice that, for most of the arrow keys and the Plus and Minus keys, you can use the ones on the numeric keypad only if Num Lock is turned off, but that the Numeric Keypad Asterisk never works and the Numeric Keypad Slash always works. Go figure!

# Add Footnotes and Endnotes

Writers use *footnotes* and *endnotes* to provide references to *source documents* for the document text, to provide more detailed explanations or definitions that might otherwise distract the reader if left in the main body of the document, or to make comments on the text. Footnotes appear at the bottom of the page with the text they reference. Endnotes appear at the end of a chapter, section, or document.

The two parts to each footnote or endnote are the reference mark—a number, character, or combination of characters appearing in the body of the document—and the note text. You may automatically number the marks or create your own custom marks. If you use the automatic numbering, Word renumbers the note reference marks if you add, delete, or move notes.

The note text can be any length and format, and you can format the line that separates the notes from the body of the document.

To view the note text, rest the mouse pointer on the note reference mark. The note text appears in a pop-up box above the mark (see Figure 15.4). Double-click the note reference mark to display the note text in a note pane at the bottom of the screen. If you are using Print Layout view, footnotes display at the bottom of the page, endnotes at the end of the document.

**Which to use—footnote numbers or footnote symbols?**

Should you use footnote numbers or symbols? The general rule is: Use numbers if you have a large number of footnotes or if you intend to use endnotes; use symbols (asterisks, and so on) if you have just an occasional footnote, no more than one every few pages.

**FIGURE 15.4**

Point to the reference mark to see the note text appear in a pop-up box above the number.

**1** Reference number

**2** Note text

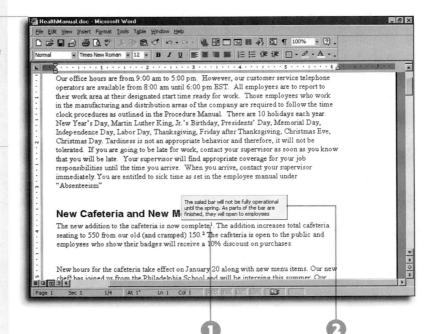

### Add a Footnote or Endnote

1. Place the insertion point where you want the note reference mark to appear.

2. Choose the **Insert** menu and select **Footnote**. The Footnote and Endnote dialog box appears (see Figure 15.5).

3. Select **Footnote** or **Endnote**.

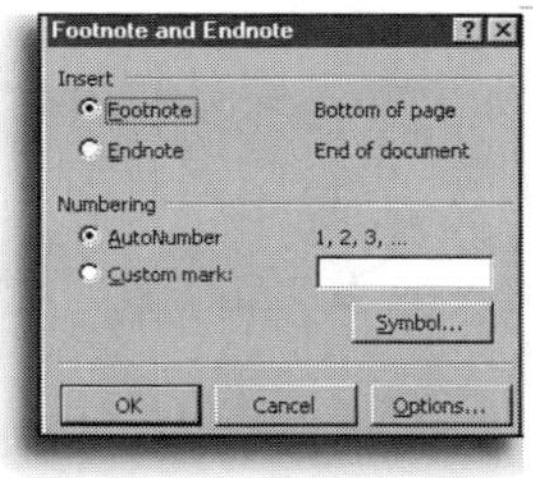

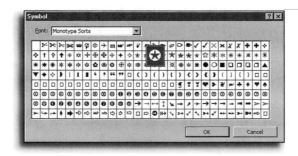

**FIGURE 15.5**

Choose **Footnote** or **Endnote** and then select a numbering option.

4. Under **Numbering**, select **AutoNumber** or **Custom Mark**. If you choose **Custom Mark**, insert the symbol or symbols for the reference mark or choose **Symbol** to open the Symbol dialog box (see Figure 15.6), where you can choose one or more symbols. Choose a font, click the symbol you want to use, and then click **OK**.

**FIGURE 15.6**

Select the font that contains the type of symbol you need, click a symbol, and then click **OK**.

5. (Optional) Choose **Options** to open the Note Options dialog box (see Figure 15.7). Click the **All Footnotes** or **All Endnotes** tab, depending on the type of notes you're creating. The following options are available:

   From the **Place At** drop-down list, select where you want to place the note on the page or in the document.

If you chose **AutoNumber** in step 4, select the numbering system you want to use from the **Number Format** drop-down list. In the **Start At** box, enter or select the number you want to start the note numbering with. Click **Continuous**, **Restart Each Section**, or **Restart Each Page** to specify that you want the numbering to be continuous or to have it start over at each section break or page break in your document.

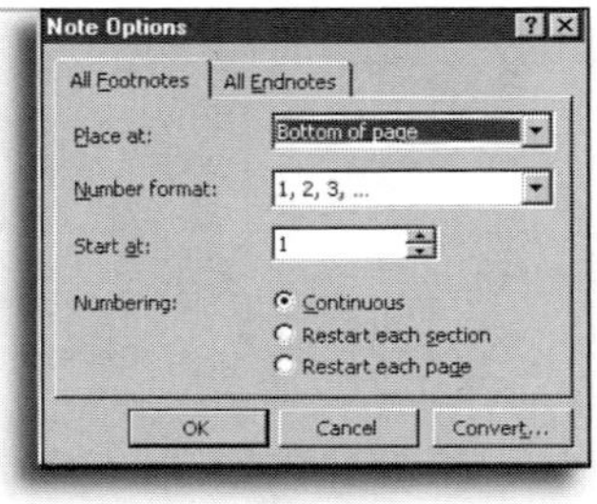

FIGURE 15.7

Set options for where the note will appear and how the numbering will be done.

6. Choose **OK** to close the Note Options dialog box, if you opened it in step 5. Choose **OK** again to close the Footnote and Endnote dialog box.

7. Type the note text in the footnote pane (see Figure 15.8). Apply formatting as desired or, better yet, reformat the Footnote text style (which automatically appears in the **Style** list when you insert your first footnote).

8. Choose **Close** to close the footnote pane or click in the document to continue typing.

## Edit Footnotes and Endnotes

After your footnotes or endnotes are in place, you might need to change the note text, move the reference marks, change the number format, convert the footnotes to endnotes or vice versa, and so on. Follow these instructions to revise your footnotes and endnotes:

- To change note text in Normal view, double-click the note reference mark to open the footnote pane. Edit the text in the footnote pane as you would the document text. Choose **Close** to close the footnote pane or click in the document text to continue typing. In Print Layout view you can edit note text directly, since footnote text appears at the bottom of the page and endnote text appears at the end of the section or document.

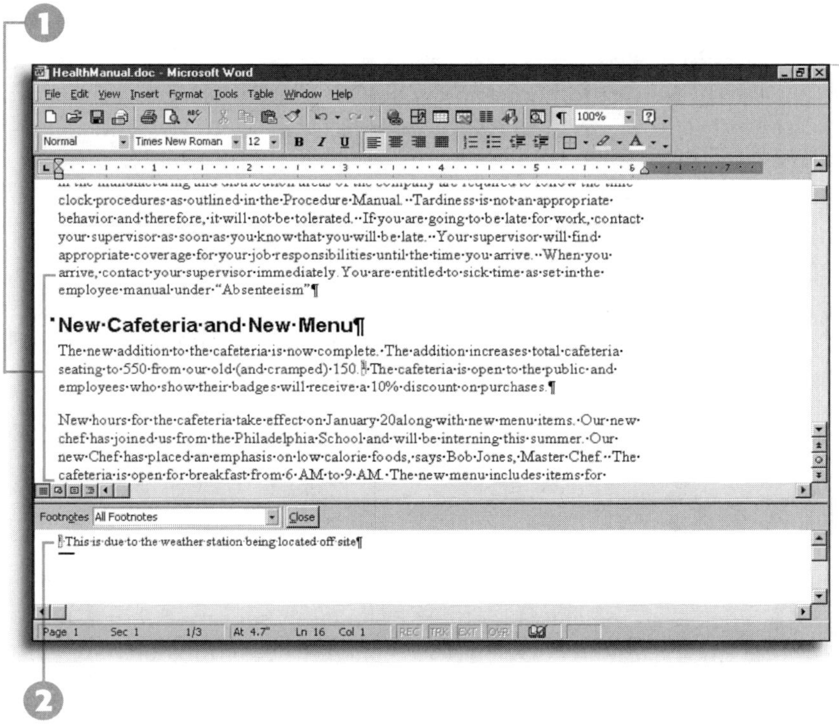

FIGURE 15.8
Enter the footnote or endnote text in the footnote pane.

1 Document text

2 Footnote pane

- To format the note text or reference mark, you can format the note directly or format the styles Word assigns to them. When you create footnotes or endnotes in a document, Word automatically assigns two predefined styles to the note and reference mark. The note text receives the paragraph style called Footnote Text, which inherits the formatting of the Normal style but is reduced in size. The reference mark receives the character style called Footnote Reference, which includes the superscript font attribute.
- To move the reference mark, select the mark and drag it to its new location. Or cut it and paste it to its new location. If you move text that has a note reference associated with it, make sure you move the note reference mark too. Word renumbers the reference, if necessary.

■ To change the number format of the notes, choose the **Insert** menu and select **Foot<u>n</u>ote** to open the Footnote and Endnote dialog box. Choose **<u>O</u>ptions** and specify the numbering system you want to use (refer to Figure 15.7). Choose **OK** to close the dialog box and then choose **OK** to return to the document.

■ To convert footnotes to endnotes, or vice versa, choose the **<u>I</u>nsert** menu and select **Foot<u>n</u>ote** to open the Footnote and Endnote dialog box. Choose **<u>O</u>ptions** and then choose **Convert**. In the Convert Notes dialog box (see Figure 15.9), click the conversion option you want—**Convert All <u>F</u>ootnotes to Endnotes, Convert All <u>E</u>ndnotes to Footnotes,** or **<u>S</u>wap Footnotes and Endnotes**—and choose **OK**. Choose **OK** to close the Note Options dialog box and then **Close** to return to the document.

FIGURE 15.9

Select the conversion option you want.

To delete an individual footnote or endnote, select the note reference mark and press Delete. Don't merely delete the note text; the reference remains in the body of your document and a blank line appears in your footnotes.

### Delete All Automatically Numbered Footnotes or Endnotes

1. Click the **<u>E</u>dit** menu and select **R<u>e</u>place**.

2. When the Find and Replace dialog box appears (see Figure 15.10), click the **Rep<u>l</u>ace** tab if it's not already selected.

3. Choose **<u>M</u>ore** to see more options.

4. Click in the **Fi<u>n</u>d What** box and then choose **Special**. From the pop-up menu, select **<u>E</u>ndnote Mark** or **<u>F</u>ootnote Mark**.

5. Leave the **Replace Wi<u>t</u>h** box empty. Choose **Replace <u>A</u>ll**.

6. Choose **Close** to close the dialog box.

Unfortunately, you can't remove all custom note reference marks at one time. You must delete them one at a time.

---

**Go to or browse footnotes**

You can jump directly to any footnote or endnote reference in your document with Go To (F5, Ctrl+G, or from the **Edit** menu, select **Go To**). You can browse your footnote/endnote references with the Browse buttons below the scrollbar on the right.

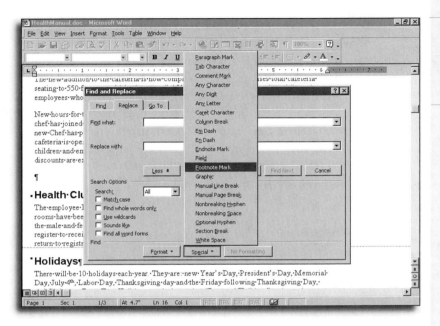

FIGURE 15.10

With the insertion point in the **Find What** box, click **Special** and choose **Endnote Mark** or **Footnote Mark**.

## Edit Note Separators

Footnotes are separated from the body of the page by a short line called a *footnote separator*. If a footnote continues on the next page, the continued portion of the footnote is separated from the body of the page by a longer line called a *footnote continuation separator*. You can also define a *footnote continuation notice*—text that appears below the footnote and notifies the reader that the footnote continues on the next page. Endnotes have the same features, only they are called the endnote separator, endnote continuation separator, and endnote continuation notice.

### Change Any Footnote Separator Item

1. Go to Normal view, if you are not already there, by choosing the **View** menu and selecting **Normal**.

2. Open the Footnotes or Endnotes pane by choosing the **View** menu and selecting **Footnotes**. The View Footnotes dialog box appears (see Figure 15.11).

3. In the **Footnotes** or **Endnotes** drop-down list, choose the item you want to change (see Figure 15.11). If you are in the Footnotes pane, you can choose the **Footnote Separator**, **Footnote Continuation Separator**, and **Footnote Continuation Notice**. If you are in the Endnotes pane, you can choose the **Endnote Separator**, **Endnote Continuation Separator**, and **Endnote Continuation Notice**. If you have both footnotes *and* endnotes in your document, switch between the **Footnote** pane and the **Endnote** pane by returning to the View Footnotes dialog box from the View menu.

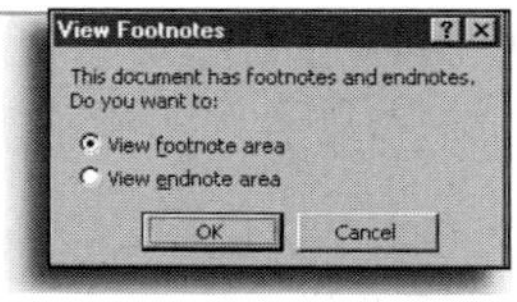

**FIGURE 15.11**

If your document has both footnotes and endnotes, choose which to view in the View Footnotes dialog box.

4. Make any changes you want to the item you have chosen. You can edit the separators, remove them, or add text, graphics, or borders to them. Same with the continuation notices.

5. Choose **Close** when you are finished. To see the results of your changes, switch to Print Layout view.

If later you want to restore a separator to its original format, you can go back into the **Footnotes** or **Endnotes** pane, choose the item you want to restore, and choose **Reset**.

# CHAPTER
# 16

# Apply Columns

Create columns

Edit columns

Use newspaper columns

# Know Your Column Options

An attractive way to lay out a large document or a promotional publication is to use columns. Columns break the page into two or more vertical segments so that the lines of text are shorter and easier to read. This type of layout is also more flexible for placing graphics, tables, and graphs in combination with text. That's why you see columns used frequently for brochures, pamphlets, and newsletters. There are several ways to create documents with columns; one quick method is to base your document on a Word template that uses columns, such as the Directory.dot template shown in Figure 16.1. When you use this template, simply type or paste your text into it. But often you create a document and then you decide to reformat it into columns. That's what you learn in this lesson—how to apply columns without the use of a preformatted template.

FIGURE 16.1

One quick way to create a good looking document in column format is to base it on a Word template formatted with columns, such as the Directory.dot template. Here, a new document based on this template is ready for you to insert (type or paste) your own text.

The two types of columns in Word are

- Side-by-side columns. These are useful for video scripts, three-fold brochures, résumés, invoices, or phone lists. Set them up using Word's table feature. With the table borders eliminated, the document doesn't resemble an ordinary table. Or, use linked text boxes that are set next to each other.

- Newspaper columns. These are used in newsletters, where text flows from one column to the next. When the text reaches the bottom of the first column, it continues at the top of the column to its right.

**SEE ALSO**

➤ *Learn more about using tables to create side-by-side columns and grids on page 164*

➤ *To learn more about creating and linking text boxes, see page 424*

➤ *Learn more about replacing template boilerplate text on page 353*

# Use Newspaper Columns

When you specify columns using the Column command in Word, Word defaults to *Newspaper* column formatting. This type of column gets its name because the text flows like the text in a newspaper. Newspaper columns divide the area between the left and right margin on a page into vertical segments. You specify the number of columns and the column width, as well as the space between columns.

Text in newspaper columns flows down the page until it reaches the bottom margin, and then it continues at the top of the next column, and so on. When the text fills the last column on the right of the page and reaches the bottom margin, a new page begins.

Newspaper columns are not the only column types in Word. Side-by-side (or parallel) columns are used to present information in a tabbed-like format—where columns have headers and the text in the columns, though related to the text in other columns, does not flow like one continuous "article" or story. Text flows down the first column until it reaches the end of the row or you deliberately stop it. Then it starts again at the top of the next column, and so forth. However, when it gets to the point where you want the last column on the page to end, you start the text again in the first column, below the first column text you entered earlier.

**No "Web" newspaper columns**

Newspaper columns do not work on Web pages without adding HTML code. We suggest that the easiest way to create a column look for Web pages is to format your text using tables, not columns.

How do you know what type of column to use? It isn't always obvious:

- Side-by-side columns work well in documents that need an item in the first column with a related item in the second. For example, a catalog of new products displays the picture in one column and the description in the column next to it. A translated story appears in English in one column and German in the column next to it. A video script has one column that describes the action, with the narration in the column next to it, and a description of the scenery in the third column. These three examples all work well with tables.

- Use newspaper columns when you need flowing text that will wrap around objects and automatically continue at the top of the next column. That's why newsletters use newspaper columns. Brochures, technical manuals, and other long documents use newspaper columns because columns make it easier to read a lot of text. However, that doesn't mean that you can't create a technical manual that uses side-by-side columns.

## Use text boxes instead?

Text boxes can be set at any size and the text in them can be formatted differently than surrounding text. That makes them ideal for smaller articles in newsletters that you want to separate from the columnar text. Word's text boxes can also be linked, so the text in a text box on page 1 of a newsletter can continue in another text box on page 4 of the newsletter. Text boxes are ideal for sidebar stories, as you can also add shading and borders to the text box to set it apart from the normal flow of text.

# Create Columns

A column definition applies to the entire document, unless that document has sections. In that case, each section may be formatted with different column settings. If you select text before defining columns, the column definition applies to the selected text only. Word inserts continuous section breaks before and after the selection.

To see the columns on your page, you must be in Print Layout view. Open the **View** menu and select **Page Layout** or click the Page Layout View icon ▣ at the bottom-left corner of your screen. In Normal view you see only one column, even if you have three or four columns defined, and text wraps within the space defined as the width of the column it is in, which usually makes the text crowd over to the left side of the screen.

Word has five preset column layouts:

- One. One column of text stretches from the left to right margins on the page. This is the default column setting.

- Two. The page is divided into two columns of equal width.

- Three. The page is divided into three columns of equal width.

- Left. The page is divided into two unequal width columns with the wider column on the right, and the left column one half the size of the right column.

- Right. The page is divided into two unequal width columns with the wider column on the left, and the right column one half the size of the left column.

### Define Document or Section Columns with Preset Column Types

**1.** Unless you specify otherwise, Word formats the entire document in columns. To apply columns to only a portion of the document, select the paragraphs involved. Word inserts section breaks before or after the text, as needed. To apply columns from the position of your insertion point to the end of the document, move the insertion point to the location where you want columns to begin.

**2.** Open the **Format** menu and select **Columns** to open the Column dialog box  (see Figure 16.2).

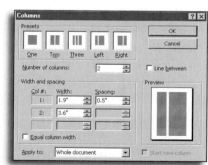

**3.** Under **Presets**, click the format you want: **One**, **Two**, **Three**, **Left**, or **Right**.

---

**You have to have at least one**

Although we speak of adding columns to a document, there is always at least one column in a document—Word won't let you set zero columns.

---

**FIGURE 16.2**

The Columns dialog box gives you a choice of five preset column definitions. To create unequal columns, remove the check from the **Equal Column Width** box.

4. From the **Apply To** drop-down list, select one of the following options:

- **Whole Document**. Applies column definition to entire document. This is available only if the document has not been divided into sections.

- **This Section**. Applies the column definition to the current section (where your cursor is). Available only if you have divided the document into sections.

- **This Point Forward**. Word inserts a section break at the current cursor location and applies the new column setting to the section after the break.

- **Selected Text**. Appears as an option when you have text selected before opening the Columns dialog box. Word creates section breaks before and after the selection.

5. To display a vertical line between your columns, click **Line Between** to place a check mark there.

6. Choose **OK**.

A quick method for applying columns, provided you want columns of equal widths, is to use the **Columns** button 🔲 on the Standard toolbar (see Figure 16.3). Choose **Columns** and then drag over the desired number of columns (only four show initially but keep dragging to the right if you need five or six). When you release the mouse button, your document or section formats in the number of columns you specified.

FIGURE 16.3

Choose **Columns** and then drag to the right until the number of columns you want are highlighted.

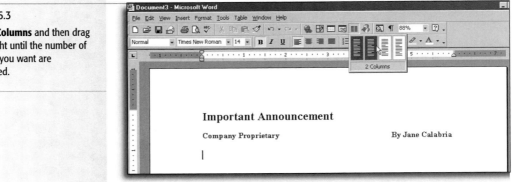

# Enter and Edit Text in Columns

Although it's usually easier to apply column settings to existing text, there's no reason why you can't first define the columns and then enter the text. Entering, editing, and formatting text in columns is no different than working in a document with only one column, except that your text will wrap at the column margin instead of the page margin. Cutting, copying, pasting, deleting, and inserting text is the same, except that it affects how the text flows from one column to another rather than from one page to another.

Figure 16.4 shows a technical document as it was originally submitted in plain text. Although it's in Courier font, which is easy to read, the document is long. Figure 16.5 shows the same technical document formatted into two columns and text formatted as headings for easier reading. Note how the same text flows between columns and adjusts after headings are added.

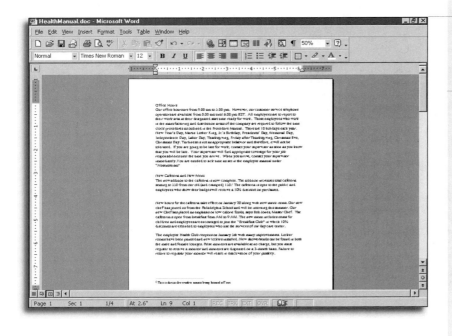

**FIGURE 16.4**

A document that doesn't have columns can appear long and uninteresting.

FIGURE 16.5

A document that is formatted into columns is easier to read and more appealing. Text adjusts by flowing to the next column. Be sure to format headings for interest.

1. Left margin of left column

2. Right margin of left column

3. Space between columns

4. Left margin and indent markers for right column

5. Right margin of right column

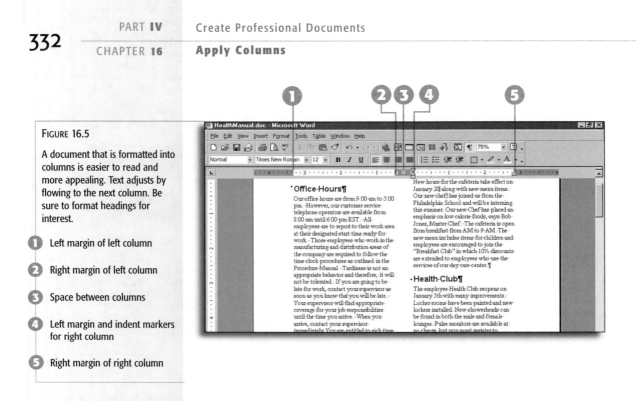

When you enter text and it reaches the bottom margin, the text wraps to the top of the next column (or to the top of the next page, if it's the last column on the page). You can change the text flow, ending the first column and starting in the next column by inserting a break.

### Insert a Manual Column Break

1. Position your insertion point where you want the column break to occur.

2. Open the **Insert** menu and select **Break** to open the Break dialog box (see Figure 16.6).

3. Click **Column Break** and click **OK**.

Like a manual page break, the column will always break at that point you have placed it in the text. The column break can be deleted by clicking it or clicking just before it and pressing Delete; or click just after it and press Backspace.

To move between columns of text, click in the column where you want to place your cursor.

**The quickest way to insert a column break**

The quickest way to insert a column break is by pressing Ctrl+Shift+Enter.

**FIGURE 16.6**
Click **Column Break** to break the column and continue the remainder of the text in the next column.

## Revise Column Structure

Even if you selected a preset column definition, you can still change the number of columns, the width of the columns, and the spacing between columns.

### Change Number, Width, or Spacing of Columns

**1.** Move the cursor to the columns you want to modify.

**2.** Open the **Format** menu and select **Columns** to open the Columns dialog box (refer to Figure 16.7). The options in the dialog box reflect the current settings for the columns where your cursor is located.

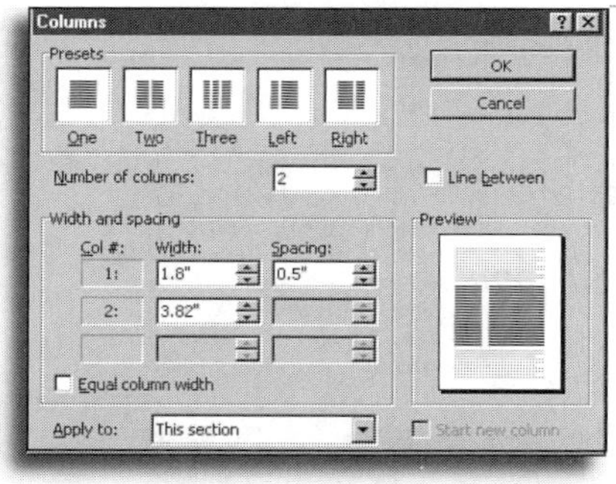

**FIGURE 16.7**
One way to change the column widths is to modify the settings in the Columns dialog box.

**3.** To apply a different predefined column format, click the desired format in the **Presets** area of the dialog box.

**4.** To change the width of or spacing between columns, change the values in the **Width** and **Spacing** boxes for the column you want to change (deselect the **Equal Column Width** option if you want to make the column widths different sizes). The **Preview** box shows you how the settings affect your document.

**5.** Choose **OK**.

The column width and spacing can also be changed using the mouse and the ruler. As you can see in Figure 16.8, a column marker appears on the ruler to show the separation between the columns. Point to the middle of the column marker and then drag left or right to change the width of the columns (if you set equal columns, all the columns change). Drag the left or right side of the column marker to change the spacing between the columns.

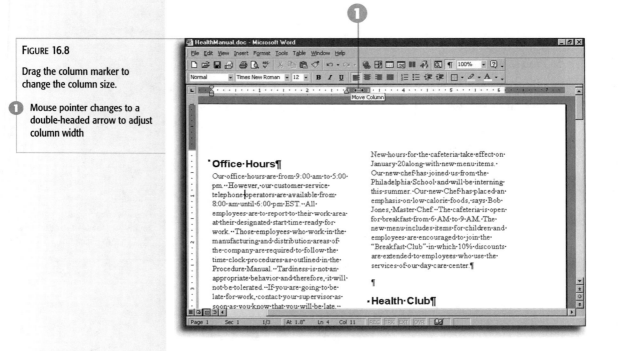

**FIGURE 16.8**

Drag the column marker to change the column size.

**1** Mouse pointer changes to a double-headed arrow to adjust column width

For complex documents such as newsletters, sections help you define articles. One article can be formatted in two columns and another in three columns (see Figure 16.9).

### Defining Different Column Settings for a New Section

1. Position your insertion point at the beginning of the text where you want the new column format to start.

2. Open the **Format** menu and choose **Columns**.

3. When the Columns dialog box appears, choose the options you want for the columns.

4. In the **Apply To** box select **This Point Forward**. If you click the **Start New Column** box, a page break is inserted and your new format options appear on a new page. If you leave the box blank, your formatting options change the columns, but keep them on the same page.

5. Click **OK**.

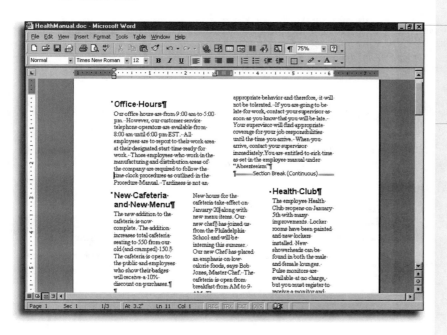

FIGURE 16.9
When you switch column formats, Word adds a section break. In this document, one section has a two-column format and the other has a three-column format.

When you get to the end of the article and you want to switch back to the original column settings or an entirely different set, follow the preceding procedure again.

**SEE ALSO**

➤ *Learn more about section breaks on page 286*

# Delete and Move Columns

When you want to delete (or remove) the column settings from your document or a section of the document, convert the column text back to one column of text.

### Converting Multiple Columns to One Column

1. Select the text that you want to change from multiple columns to a single column (place your insertion point in the document or section).
2. Open the **Format** menu and select **Columns** to open the Columns dialog box (refer to Figure 16.7).
3. Under **Presets**, click the **One** option.
4. Click **OK**.

A quick way to convert text in columns back to single-column text is to select the text (or click in the document or section). Then choose the Columns icon on the Standard toolbar and drag to the left to select a single column.

Newspaper columns don't work like columns in tables or worksheets, so you can't select the entire column and then move it elsewhere—cut and paste the text instead. When you remove the text from one column, the text below moves up to fill the gap. Then when you paste the text in another column, the text moves down to make room for the text you pasted.

# Balance Column Length

Balancing column length becomes important when the last page of your document doesn't have a full page of text but your text is formatted into columns. The columns are not of equal length, and one or more columns on the page may be empty. When you balance the column length, Word puts text in each of the columns on the page and makes the columns of equal length.

For example, in Figure 16.10 you see a document where the columns on the final page only partially fill the page.

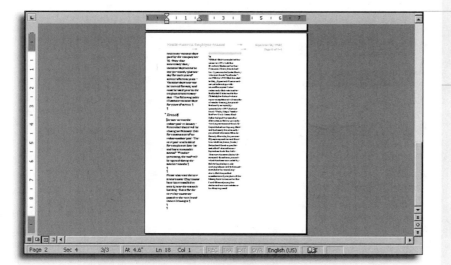

The person who created this document needs to put a mailing label at the bottom of the page and would like to have the text columns distributed across the top of the page and all of equal length. To do this, the columns need to be balanced. Figure 16.11 shows the result of balancing the columns.

### Balance Column Length

1. Create your columns, if your text is not already set up in columns.

2. Switch to Normal Layout view (open the **View** menu and select **Normal**).

3. Click at the end of the rightmost column of the columns you want to balance.

4. Open the **Insert** menu and select **Break** on the menu. The Break dialog box appears (see Figure 16.12).

5. Select **Continuous** under **Section Breaks**.

6. Click **OK**. Word inserts a continuous section break.

FIGURE **16.11**

Each of the three columns contains text, and the column lengths are even.

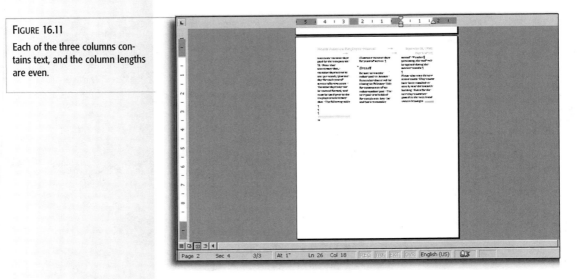

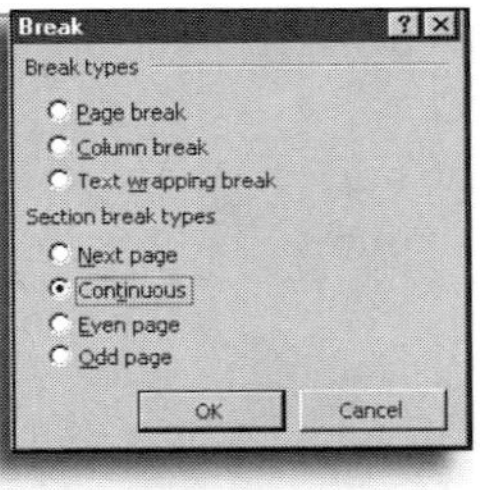

FIGURE **16.12**

Select a continuous section break to balance your columns.

## Keep Text Together in Columns

If you're not worried about balanced columns, but you would like to ensure that specific text does not get split from one column to the next, keep the text together by forcing the start of a new column. Figure 16.13 shows an example of text that has been separated awkwardly by the column break in the document.

### Forcing Text to Start at the Top of a Column

1. Switch to Print Layout view (open the **View** menu and select **Print Layout** or choose Print Layout View 🔲 in the lower-left corner of your screen).

2. Click where you want the new column to start.

3. Open the **Insert** menu and select **Break** (refer to Figure 16.12).

4. Select **Column Break**.

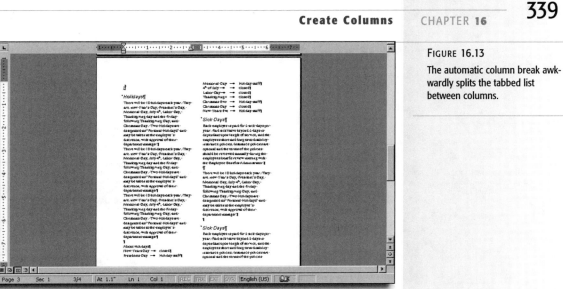

FIGURE 16.13
The automatic column break awkwardly splits the tabbed list between columns.

5. Click **OK**. The text after your cursor moves to the top of the next column.

Figure 16.14 shows the result of adding a column break before the tabbed text. It moves the text to the top of the next column.

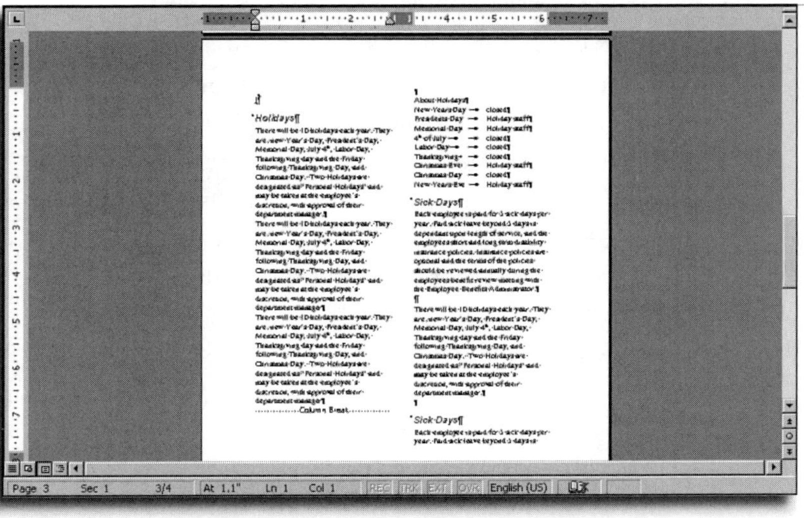

FIGURE 16.14
Inserting a column break forced the tabbed text to the next column.

This technique is also useful for putting headings and headlines at the top of a column. Insert a column break just before the heading or headline text.

# Add a Heading That Spans Columns

When you're creating a document such as a newsletter, making a title run across more than one column can effectively define an article (see Figure 16.15).

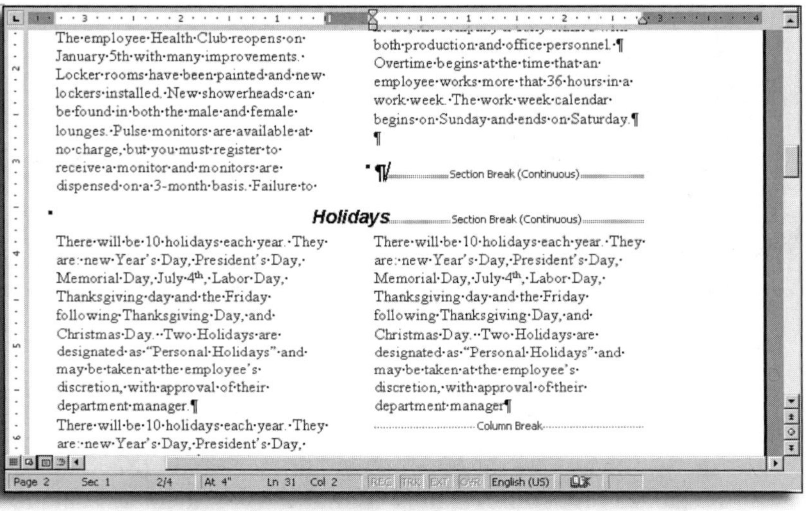

FIGURE 16.15

Use section breaks to make the heading span all the columns.

### Create a Title or Heading Spanning More Than One Column

1. Format your text in columns, if it isn't already.

2. Switch to Print Layout view (open the **View** menu and select **Print Layout** or choose Print Layout View 🔲).

3. Select the heading text.

4. Choose Columns 🔳 on the Standard toolbar and then drag to the left to select a single column. Word creates a continuous section break before and after the heading, with single-column formatting for that section.

5. Center your heading on the page.

# CHAPTER 17

# Create, Modify, and Apply Templates

# Know Your Templates

*Templates* are one of the fundamental features of Microsoft Word. They are the basis of all Word documents. If you choose the correct template when you create a new document, the template can do much of the work of styles and page layout for you. You definitely want to understand the significance of templates and how to use them to your advantage.

Every time you create a document, you are using a template. Even when you open the **File** menu, choose **New**, and then select **Blank Document**, your new document uses the template called "NORMAL."

Templates are Word files that usually have the extension .dot, as opposed to the .doc extension that Word assigns to regular (nontemplate) documents. (Templates may, however, have any extension—including .doc.) The contents and settings of a template are available to any document based on it, and can include the following:

- Boilerplate text and graphics
- Page layout characteristics
- Paragraph and character styles
- AutoText entries
- Customized toolbars, menus, and shortcut keys
- Programming, including wizards, WordBasic macros, and *projects*—programs written in Visual Basic for Applications

SEE ALSO

➤ *Learn how to create a custom letterhead template on page 471*

# Settings and Features Found in the Default Template

Word's default template is called *normal.dot* and all documents are based on it. Optionally, you may attach any other template to a Word document. If you do, the document is based on both that template and normal.dot.

Word creates a new document based on normal.dot if you do any of the following:

- Start up Word in any way that does not open an existing document.
- Create a new document by clicking New 🗋 on the Standard toolbar.
- Open the **File** menu and choose **New**, then choose **Blank Document** (which is how the normal.dot template is identified in the New dialog box).

You can change the initial settings of new documents by changing the settings of normal.dot. If normal.dot ever becomes corrupted, or if you want to quickly return it to its original settings, you can simply delete it or move it out of the folders in which Word looks for templates.

When Word fails to find normal.dot, it creates a new normal.dot file that has the settings of the original, default normal.dot file.

# Locate Existing Templates

You can store a template anywhere you want. However, when you open the **File** menu and choose **New**, Word looks for templates in the following locations:

- The User Templates location, as set in the Options dialog box, or the Workgroup Templates path if no template files appear in the User Templates location.
- The Word program folder.

For Word 2000, the default User Templates location is C:\Program Files\Microsoft Office\Templates. However, templates may be located in several other places as well. On a computer using user profiles (all Windows NT computers and some Windows 9x computers), there may be a templates folder in each user's profile folder tree. A computer that has been upgraded to

Word 2000 from earlier versions may have templates in other directories as well because earlier versions of Word stored templates in a variety of places. Computers connected to a network may have access to Workgroup templates located on a file server. If you are running Microsoft Office, all Office applications look to the same locations for their templates so that you may see templates in these folders for Excel, Access, FrontPage, and PowerPoint.

The Word or Office setup program places normal.dot in the Templates folder and the specialized templates in subfolders. When you open the New dialog box, this is not apparent. The Blank Document template (called normal.dot) and the Web Page template are both located under the **General** tab. The other tabs in the dialog box act as categories, and the other templates on your system are displayed under the most appropriate category (see Figure 17.1).

FIGURE 17.1

The tabs in the New dialog box act as categories for the different templates on your system.

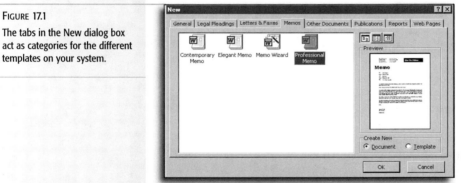

Although you may see other templates stored in the Templates folder on your computer, you may not see all of them displayed in the New dialog box. Word's New dialog box only displays templates (*.dot), documents (*.doc), or wizards (*.wiz).

**SEE ALSO**

➤ *For more information on file management and creating subdirectories, see page 127*

➤ *To learn more about possible virus contamination in templates, see page 149*

# Obtain New and Updated Templates

Word comes with numerous templates in addition to normal.dot. You should base your documents on named templates whenever possible because they generally make the job of creating attractive, functional documents much easier than starting with a blank document.

The other templates help you create nicely formatted letters, memos, reports, fax cover sheets, résumés, newsletters, Web pages—almost any kind of standard document. They include features specific to the kind of document you would create with them.

For example, Word comes with four templates for creating interoffice memos. The first three each set up memos for you, with all the *boilerplate* text (To:, From:, Date:, Subject:, second page headers and footers, and so on.) in place, and labels to show you where to insert your own content. Each template includes page formatting, styles, and graphical elements that lend a special look to your memo—professional, contemporary, or elegant. All you have to do after choosing one of these templates is enter your text (see Figure 17.2).

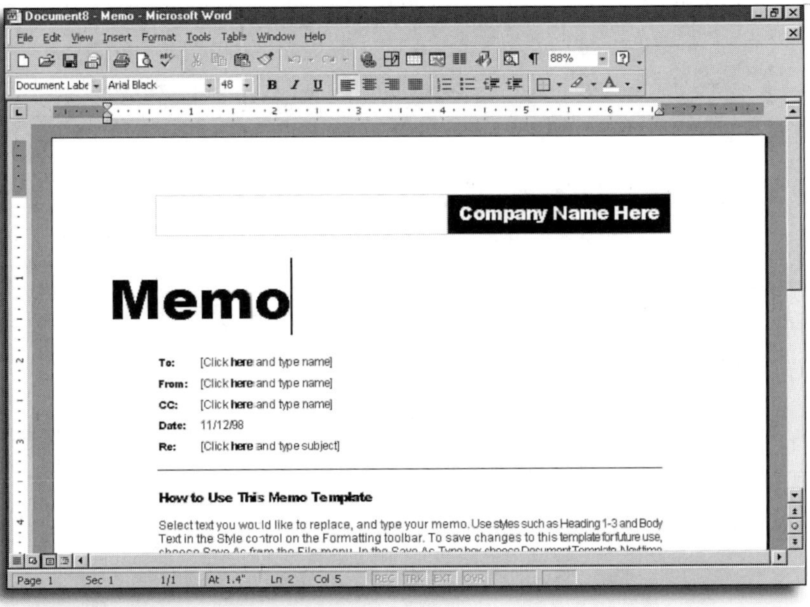

**FIGURE 17.2**

This document is based on the Professional Memo template and is ready for you to replace the sample text with your own.

The fourth memo template is really a wizard—the Memo Wizard. It prompts you for all sorts of variables, such as which of the three memo templates you want to use, what boilerplate text will be included, who the recipients will be, and what text will appear in headers and footers (see Figure 17.3).

FIGURE 17.3

On the left side, the opening screen of the Memo Wizard displays a map of all the steps the wizard takes you through.

After you have made your choices and the memo appears onscreen, the wizard remains in memory and, in the guise of the Office Assistant offering you a menu of choices, lets you change your original choices. You can keep tweaking the memo until it looks just right. Each time you use the Memo Wizard to create another memo, it remembers the choices you made for the previous memo, so that you don't have to re-choose every option every time, but just the ones that you want to change (see Figure 17.4).

You can get lots of templates in addition to those that are installed with Word. If you didn't install all the templates during the initial installation of Word, you can get more from the Word or Office CD by re-running Setup. The Microsoft Office CD includes even more templates.

### Install Templates from the Word or Office CD

1. Choose **Add or Remove Features**, click on the plus sign (+) before **Microsoft Word for Windows**, and then on the plus sign before **Wizards and Templates**.

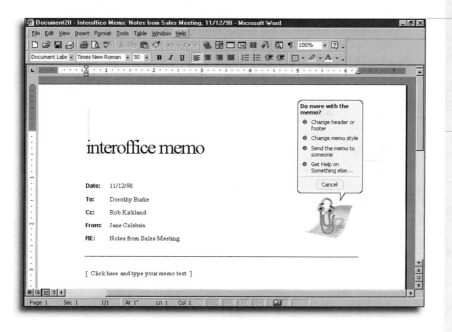

**2.** Click on the category of templates you want and select **Run from My Computer**, **Run from CD** (which means you have to have the CD in the CD-ROM drive to run that group of templates or wizards), or **Installed After First Use** (Word prompts you to insert the CD when you try to run the Wizard or template).

**3.** Choose **Update Now**.

If you have access to the World Wide Web, you can download even more templates from Microsoft's Web site. Do it from within Word by opening the **Help** menu and choosing **Office on the Web**.

# Attach a Template to a Document

You can attach a template to a document either when you create a new document or later. You can also make global templates available to a document.

If you attach a template to a document when you are creating a new document, the boilerplate text and graphics stored in the template become part of the document. If you attach a template to an existing document the boilerplate text and graphics do not become part of the document, but the page formatting, styles, AutoText entries, and special menus and toolbars become available to the document.

**SEE ALSO**

➤ *For more information on wizards, see page 462*

➤ *Learn how to apply styles on page 241*

➤ *Learn how to apply automatic formatting on page 251*

➤ *To use AutoText efficiently, see page 123*

➤ *To customize toolbars and menus, see page 640*

# Choose a Template for a New Document

### Create a New Document Using a Template Other Than normal.dot

1.  Open the **File** menu and choose **New** to open the New dialog box (see Figure 17.5).

FIGURE 17.5

The Preview window shows an example of the type of document you can create with the selected template.

2.  Select the tab containing the template you want to use. Then select the icon for the template on which you want to base your document. (If the template you want to use does not appear in any tab, choose Cancel; then move the template you want to use into the Templates folder or a subfolder; then start over at step 1.)

3. In the **Create New** section, select the **Document** option. (It may already be selected.)

4. Click **OK**.

5. Replace any sample text on the template with your text and add any additional text necessary to finish the document. Use the provided styles to format your text.

## Attach a Template to an Existing Document

The template you used to start a new document may not have all the formatting features you need. For example, you start with a blank document to create a new brochure and then realize there is a brochure template you could use. You need to apply that template to the partially completed document in order to add the page layout and style characteristics to your brochure.

### Attach a Different Template to an Existing Document

1. Open the document to which you want to attach the template.

2. Open the **Tools** menu and choose **Templates and Add-Ins**. This opens the Templates and Add-ins dialog box (see Figure 17.6).

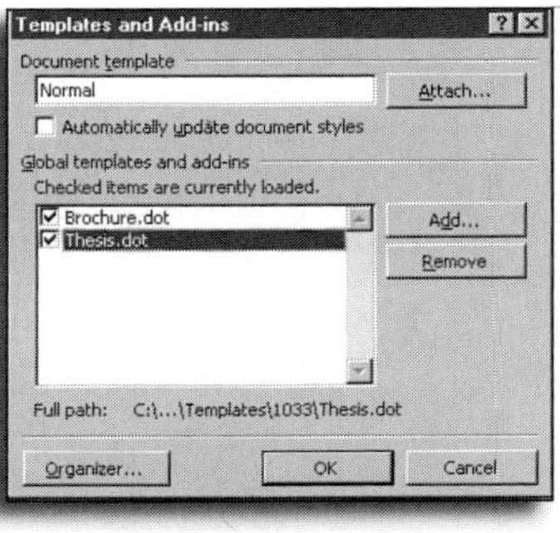

FIGURE 17.6
Attach a different template to your document to use that template's styles.

3. Click the **Attach** button. The Attach Template dialog box opens. Select the template you want to attach, and then click **Open**. The filename and path (location) of the template appears in the **Document Template** field.

**Using a wizard**

Some of the files in the Template folders are actually wizards. When you choose a wizard instead of a template, the wizard prompts you for information in a series of steps, then uses one of the templates and the information you provide to build your document for you.

**4.** To have style formatting from the new template automatically override style formatting already used in the document, select the **Automatically Update Document Styles** option.

**5.** Click **OK**. The settings of the new template are now available to your document. If you selected **Automatically Update Document Styles** in step 4, style formatting in your document may automatically change to reflect the formatting of styles in the new template.

## Use Global Templates

You can make the settings of one or more templates available to a document without actually attaching the templates to the document. Instead, you can declare them *global templates*. A global template resides in RAM throughout a Word session and makes its settings available to all documents opened during that session. If you copy a global template into the Startup folder, it then loads into RAM at computer startup and is automatically available to all Word documents during all Word sessions.

To set up a template as global, you have to add it to the list of global templates. To use a global template with a particular document, you have to open the document in Word while the global template is in memory.

### Add a Template to the List of Global Templates

**1.** Open the **Tools** menu and choose **Templates and Add-Ins**. This opens the Templates and Add-ins dialog box (refer to Figure 17.6).

**2.** In the **Global Templates and Add-Ins** section, choose **Add**. The Add Template dialog box appears.

**3.** Choose the template that you want to make global, then click **OK**. The template appears in the list of global templates.

To make a global template available to documents during the current Word session, load it into memory. Open the Templates and Add-ins dialog box, add a check mark to the check box next to the global template, and click **OK**.

To make a global template available to documents during all future Word sessions, move the global template to the Microsoft Office Startup folder (C:\Program Files\Microsoft Office\Office). With the template in the Windows Startup folder, each time you restart the computer, the template loads into memory at system startup. When the global template is stored in the Office Startup folder, it starts when you start Office.

To make a global template temporarily unavailable to documents, remove it from RAM. To do that, open the Templates and Add-ins dialog box, remove the check mark from the check box next to the global template, and choose **OK**.

To make a global template permanently unavailable to documents, remove it from RAM, then remove it from the list of templates by selecting it in the list in the Templates and Add-ins dialog box and choosing the **Remove** button.

# Modify and Create Templates

The ready-made templates don't always meet your needs completely. Perhaps you would like to modify one slightly (or radically) to conform it to company standards or to your personal preferences. It's a simple matter either to modify an existing template or to create a new one.

You can create a new template in any number of ways. You can create it from scratch, just as you would create a new, blank document. You could turn a suitable document into a template. You could open another template, make changes in it, then save your changes as a new template.

Having created a new template, you can add features to it from other documents or templates and you can rename those features. Alternatively, you can modify an existing template by opening and editing it, by copying features into it from other templates or documents, or by renaming its features.

# Create a New Template

You can create a new template based on an existing template, and the new template will contain all the elements of the base template plus any text or formatting you add.

### Create a New Template

1. Open the **File** menu and choose **New** to open the New dialog box.

2. Select the template on which you want to base your new template. If you want the new template to start out blank, base it on the **Blank Document** template on the **General** tab.

3. Under **Create New**, select the **Template** option.

4. Click **OK**. A new document-editing screen appears based on the template you selected. Its default name (in the title bar) is Template*n*, where *n* is a number.

5. Enter the boilerplate text and other items that you want to be part of the new template. Make changes to any existing text or formatting. Apply new formatting to the text as desired. Create any new styles you might need. Define AutoText. Create custom toolbars, menus, and keystrokes.

6. Open the **File** menu and select **Save As** to open the Save As dialog box or click the Save button 🖫 on the Standard toolbar.

7. Select the folder in which you want to store the template. If you want the template to be available when you create new documents, be sure to select a folder where Word looks for templates (by default, that's C:\Program Files\Microsoft Office\Templates and its subfolders).

8. Enter your filename in the **File Name** text box. Be sure to use a different name from the template you selected in step 2, or the new template will replace the original one.

9. Click **Save**. The template is now available for use the next time you start a new document. Be sure to close the new template file before using it.

# Create a Template from a Document

Sometimes you will find it useful to create a template based on an existing Word document. If you have applied a considerable amount of formatting and styles in a document, creating a template from the document saves you from having to re-create the formatting by creating a new template. This is especially useful for documents whose formatting you intend to use again and again.

### Create a Template from a Document

1. Open the document on which you want to base the new template.

2. Make desired changes in the document. This would include removing nonboiler-plate content. It might also include adding placeholder text telling the user what to replace it with.

3. Save the document as a template by opening the **File** menu and choosing **Save As** to open the Save As dialog box.

4. Select **Document Template** from the **Save as Type** drop-down list. The **Save In** box usually changes to display the Templates folder.

5. Open the folder where you want the template saved. Because Word organizes its templates by category, storing your template in the correct folder makes it easier to find when you want to use it.

6. Type a descriptive name for the template in the **File Name** text box.

7. Choose **Save**.

# Modify an Existing Template

When you modify a template, changes that you make are not reflected in existing documents that were created based on the template. Only new documents are affected. Rather than modifying a template, it's often better to create a new template based on it. This way the original template is still available should you change your mind.

---

**Create a custom letterhead**

Create a template to use as your custom letterhead. Include a date and time field and add graphics, logos, or watermarks. Make the template available for use by all in your company by distributing the template or placing it on a shared network drive. For help in creating your letterhead template, see the "Create a Letterhead Template" section in Chapter 22, "Create Office Documents Quickly and Efficiently."

**Modify a Template**

1.  Open the **File** menu and choose **Open** to open the Open dialog box (see Figure 17.7).

2.  In the **Files of Type** drop-down list choose **Document Templates (*.dot)**.

3.  Navigate to the folder containing the template you want to modify. Select the template you want to change. Choose **Open**. (If you choose **Open as Copy** from the **Open** drop-down list, you will leave the original template intact.)

4.  Make the desired modifications and additions to the template's text and styles.

5.  Save and close the template when you are finished modifying it.

**Recycle old templates**

You can use old templates from earlier versions of Word (Word for Windows 95/Word 6.0, Word 97) to create new documents in Word.

# Update Documents with Template Changes

After you modify a template, you can force the style formatting in existing documents to update to the new formatting of the template.

**Automatically Update Template Changes to Documents**

1.  Open the **Tools** menu and choose **Templates and Add-Ins** (see Figure 17.8).

2. Select the **Automatically Update Document Styles** option. Click **OK**.

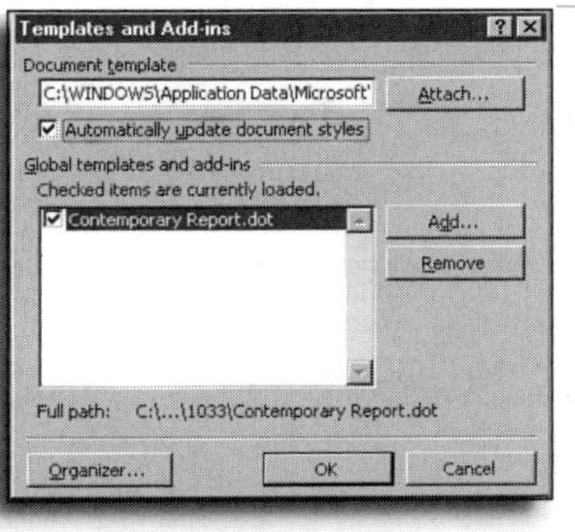

FIGURE 17.8

Be sure to check **Automatically Update Document Styles** when you want template changes reflected in your document.

3. The paragraph and character styles in your document automatically update to reflect the styles in its attached template.

4. If you don't want other documents to be updated automatically the next time you open them, go back into the Templates and Add-ins dialog box and turn off the **Automatically Update Document Styles** option after you have updated the document you wanted to update.

# Use the Organizer

When you create or modify a template, you might want to copy settings from other templates, rather than re-create the settings from scratch. After you have copied a setting into a template, you might want to rename it to conform to the naming convention you have adopted in the new template. If you copy a setting by mistake, you will want to delete it from the target.

You can use the Organizer to do all these things. The Organizer lets you easily copy settings to or from templates or documents, or rename or delete settings in templates or documents.

## Copy Template Settings

You can copy styles, macros, and custom toolbars to either templates or documents. You can copy AutoText entries only to other templates. You can't copy page layout settings or customized menus or shortcut keys with the Organizer.

**Use the Template Organizer**

1. Open the **T**ools menu and choose **Templates and Add-Ins**.

2. In the Templates and Add-ins dialog box, choose **Organizer**. The Organizer dialog box opens (see Figure 17.9).

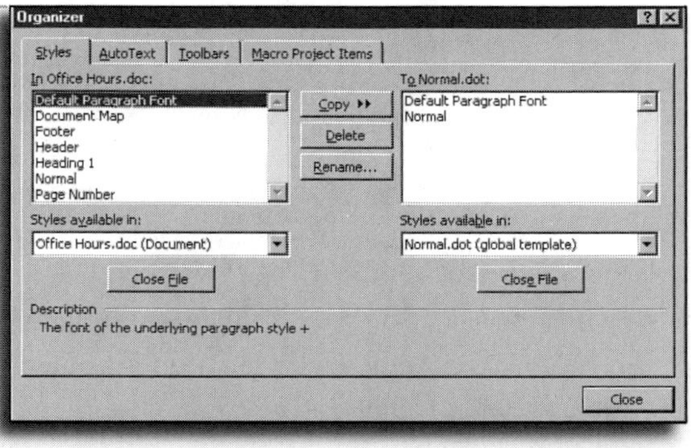

FIGURE 17.9

FIGURE 17.9

The Organizer shows the settings of two templates or documents, side by side. You can copy settings from the left to the right.

3. Click the **Styles** tab. If the source template does not appear in the left window (labeled **In OfficeHours.doc** in Figure 17.9), choose **Close File** then **Open File**. If the target template does not appear in the right window (labeled **To Normal.dot** in Figure 17.9), choose **Close File** then **Open File**. (Each of these is really just one button whose label changes when you choose it.)

4. When you choose **Open File** (for the source template) or **Open File** (for the target template) the Open dialog box appears. Select the template or document that you want, then choose **Open**. The settings of the chosen document then appear in the **In [** *filename* **]** window (for the source template) or the **To [** *filename* **]** window (for the target template).

5. Choose the tab for the type of setting you want to copy—**S**tyles, **A**utoText, **T**oolbars, **M**acro Project Items.

6. In the left window, select one or more features you want to copy. (You can use the Shift and Control keys to select multiple items.) Then choose **C**opy. The selected items appear in the right window. (You also can copy items from the right to the left. When you select an item in the right window, the copy button changes to indicate that it copies from right to left.)

7. If you copy an item by mistake, select it in the right window and choose **D**elete. If you want to rename an item after you have moved it, select it in the right window and choose **Rename**. (You can also delete or rename items in the left window.)

8. Repeat steps 5 and 6 for each tab. Choose **Close** when you are finished.

## Rename Templates

Occasionally you need to rename a template to add a more descriptive name or make it follow a newly devised file naming scheme.

### Rename a Template

1. In either the Open or Save As dialog box, select **Document Template** from the **Files of T**ype or **Save as T**ype dropdown list.

2. Select the template file and choose **Rena**me from the **Tool**s menu. Alternatively, right-click the filename and choose **Rena**me from the shortcut menu.

**3.** A box appears around the name and the filename is highlighted (see Figure 17.10). Type the new name for the template with the .dot file extension and then press Enter.

**4.** Close the dialog box.

Any pre-existing documents based on a renamed or deleted template will lose access to the template. But any of the template-based styles used in the document will still be available, having been incorporated into the document when you used them.

## Delete Templates

Removing a template from your system can be accomplished without leaving Word.

### Delete a Template

**1.** In either the Open or Save As dialog box, select **Document Template** from the **Files of Type** or **Save as Type** drop-down list.

**2.** Select the template file and choose **Delete** from the **Tools** menu. Alternatively, right-click the filename and choose **Delete** from the shortcut menu.

**3.** A dialog box appears asking for confirmation of the deletion. Choose **Yes**.

A notice that you can't delete the template may appear if you have the template open or a document open that has that template attached. Close the open document or template and try again. If that fails, try deleting it using My Computer or Windows Explorer.  You may need to close Word before you try to delete the template using My Computer or Windows Explorer.

PART

V

# Incorporate Data and Objects from Other Sources

CHAPTER

18

# Insert Graphics and Special Characters

Insert graphics and clip art

Crop, resize, move, and delete graphics

Wrap text around graphics

Use special characters and symbols

Create a watermark

# Insert Clip Art

Word comes with a library of *clip art*, which is comprised of drawings and pictures you use to add visual appeal and interest to your documents (check your software agreement on the clip art to see if there are any limitations in using the art in items you sell). Adding clip art to documents is easy and it can be the added element that draws attention to your document versus someone else's in a competitive market.

### Add Word Clip Art to a Document

1. Place your insertion point where you want to put the clip art picture or drawing in your document.

2. Open the **Insert** menu and choose **Picture**; then choose **Clip Art** from the submenu to open the Insert ClipArt dialog box (see Figure 18.1).

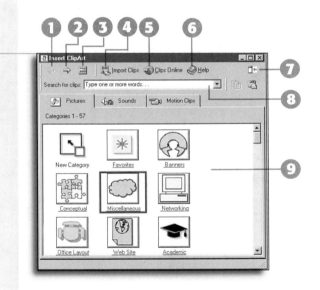

FIGURE 18.1

Choose a clip art category and then select a picture to insert in your document.

1 Back

2 Forward

3 All Categories

4 Import Clips

5 Clips Online

6 Help

7 Change to small window

8 Enter search keyword here

9 Clip Categories

**3.** The **Pictures** tab is displayed, showing a set of clip art categories.

**4.** Click a category picture to display the clips in that category. When you point to one of the clips, the graphic format and categories for that clip appear as a pop-up.

**5.** Click once on the clip to see a menu, (see Figure 18.2).

**6.** Choose **Insert Clip** to insert the clip in your document.

**7.** Close the dialog box window.

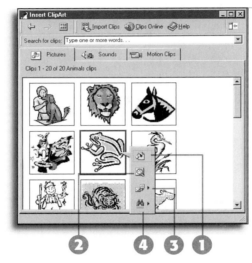

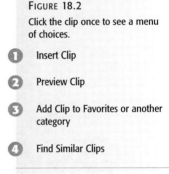

FIGURE 18.2
Click the clip once to see a menu of choices.

**1** Insert Clip

**2** Preview Clip

**3** Add Clip to Favorites or another category

**4** Find Similar Clips

The Insert ClipArt dialog box provides you with assistance if you have difficulty finding the piece of art you need. Type a keyword (such as lion) in the **Search for Clips** text box and press Enter to display all the possible clips that meet that description, such as the picture of a lion in the Animals category.

Use the Import Clips 📇 or Clips Online 🖼 buttons to find additional clip art on your system or from the Web.

Table 18.1 describes the icons that appear in the Insert ClipArt dialog box and how they help you find the clip you need.

TABLE 18.1  **Icons in Insert ClipArt dialog box**

| Icon | Description |
| --- | --- |
| | Takes you back to the previous set of pictures you viewed. |
| | Takes you forward to the next set of pictures you will view. |
| | Displays all the categories. |
| | Click to browse your system or network drives for clip art not included in the clip gallery. |
| | Click to connect to the Microsoft Web site for more clips. |
| | Opens Help screen for clip art. |
| | Shrinks the window to one-third its current size. |
| | Expands the window to its full size again. |
| | Inserts the clip in the document at your cursor position. |
| | Opens a preview window to give you a magnified view of the clip. |
| | Opens a dialog box from which you select a category for the selected clip art. If it's a frequently used clip, select **Favorites** to add it to that category. |
| | Opens a dialog box from which you can link to best matching clips or other clips that match the keywords assigned to that file. |
| | Copies clip art to insert into the document (in lieu of using menu) or copies it to place it in a different category. |
| | Pastes the copied clip art onto a different tabbed page or category. |

Use the Copy and Paste icons on the Insert ClipArt dialog box to organize clips. In this way, you can add clips to different categories. To delete a clip from the Gallery, right-click it and select **Delete** from the pop-up menu. To add a keyword to a clip, right-click it and select the **Keywords** tab in the clip Properties box. Select **New Keyword** and add your new keyword.

**No ClipArt Gallery?**

Although the ClipArt Gallery normally installs as part of Office, not all the clip art is loaded. To load the complete Gallery, you must insert the setup disk into your disk drive and run a Custom setup, which allows you to specify items you need.

# Add a Graphics Image

A *graphic* is a drawing or picture that is created by a graphics application or scanned (or photographed with a digital camera) and stored on disk. Graphics files are created by a variety of applications, including Windows Paint, Microsoft PowerPoint, CorelDRAW!, and AutoCAD, and can be incorporated into Word documents (see Figure 18.3).

**Need help with ClipArt?**

Click the **Help** icon on the Insert ClipArt dialog box. The help screen that opens relates exclusively to the ClipArt Gallery. Here, you can learn more about organizing and customizing your ClipArt Gallery and how to troubleshoot clip problems.

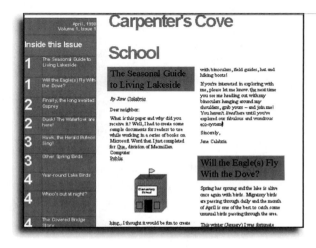

**FIGURE 18.3**
This document uses a graphic that was drawn in Microsoft PowerPoint.

Whether you create a graphic yourself, using a drawing or graphics program, or you scan an image from a drawing, painting, or photograph, the picture can be inserted into Word provided you saved it in a graphics format that is acceptable to Word. Be careful scanning photographs or pictures from published materials, such as books or magazines, as these items usually are copyrighted. You or your company can be sued for using them without permission.

### Add a Graphic to a Document

1. Place your insertion point where you want the graphic to appear.

2. Open the **Insert** menu and choose **Picture**. From the submenu select **From File** to open the Insert Picture dialog box (see Figure 18.4).

FIGURE 18.4

Select the graphics file and click **Insert**.

**Graphics file formats**

The file format of a graphics file can tell you a lot about a file. TIFF and JPEG files probably originated as scanned images—JPEG as photographs. PCX, BMP, and GIF files probably originated in Paint-style programs. All of these are bitmap formats. They don't resize as well as vector formats such as WMF, EPS, and CGM, which originated in Draw-style programs. GIF and JPEG are the two standard file formats used when putting pictures on Web pages—GIF for computer-generated graphics, JPEG for photographs.

3. If necessary, select the folder where the graphic is stored from the **Look In** drop-down list.

4. The **Files of Type** drop-down list is automatically set to display **All Pictures**, but you can select the specific type of graphics file you want to appear in the list.

5. Select the name of the file you want to use from the listed files, enter the name in the **File Name** text box, or highlight the file as shown in Figure 8.4. Click the down arrow next to **Views** on the toolbar and then select **Preview** to see a preview of the selected file.

6. Click any of the following options from the **Insert** drop-down list, if appropriate (see Figure 8.4):

    - **Insert**. Inserts the picture at your cursor position in the document.

    - **Link to File**. By default, Word embeds pictures in the document, which adds to the size of the file. Choose this option to reduce the size of the file by linking to it. One benefit of linking is that the graphic in the document updates immediately if any changes are made to the original file.

    - **Insert and Link**. Inserts the picture into the document and links to the source file so the picture is immediately updated if the original graphic is changed.

**7.** Choose **Insert** to add the graphics image to your document.

The graphic appears near your insertion point, or as near as Word can place it. You may have to move it and size it to fit your layout. The instructions to help you do that are in the sections "Crop and Resize Graphics" and "Delete, Move, and Copy Graphics" later in this chapter.

**SEE ALSO**

➤ *To learn more about linking and embedding, see page 393*

## Crop and Resize Graphics

Before you can crop and resize a graphic, you must select it using one of these methods:

- To select a single graphic, click on it. Sizing handles (small hollow boxes) appear around the graphic to indicate that it's selected (see Figure 18.5).

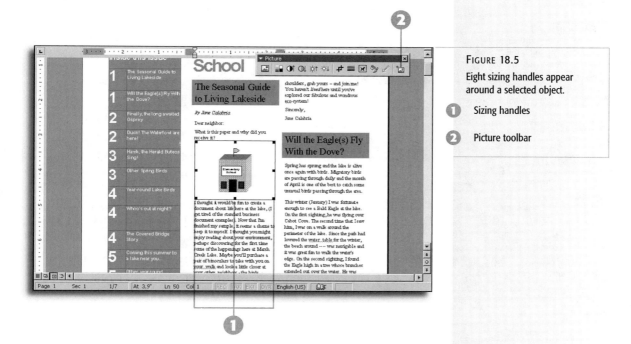

FIGURE 18.5
Eight sizing handles appear around a selected object.

1 Sizing handles

2 Picture toolbar

- To select more than one graphic, click the first item you want to select, hold down the Shift key, and then click on each additional item you want to select.

- If you accidentally select an item that you didn't want, hold down Shift and click on the item to remove the sizing handles and deselect it.

- To deselect an item, click in a blank area away from the graphic.

Make the selected graphic larger or smaller by dragging one of the sizing handles. When you point at the handle, the mouse pointer becomes a two-headed arrow showing the direction in which you may drag (see Figure 18.6). Drag toward or away from the center of the graphic until the image is the size you need.

FIGURE 18.6

The mouse pointer becomes a two-headed arrow when you point at a sizing handle.

**1** Two-headed arrow for resizing

**Maintain aspect ratio**

When you size the graphic you can make it too thin or too wide, too short or too tall. To keep the image in proportion (the height to width ratio, or *aspect ratio*, remains the same), use a corner handle when sizing the image and drag toward or away from the center of the graphic. If you do distort the image, use the Reset feature to get back to the original shape and size.

Your image may have more background than you need. You can trim (crop) the excess from a selected graphic.

**Crop a Graphic**

**1.** Select the graphic and choose Crop [icon] on the Picture toolbar.

**2.** Position the mouse pointer over the handle on the side you want to crop and drag toward the center of the image until the portion of the picture you wanted to trim disappears.

**3.** Release the mouse button.

This displays the portion of the graphic that you want to show. Cropping doesn't eliminate the rest of the graphic; it's still stored in your document file. You can drag the cropping handles back out to see part of the original picture. Although using the mouse immediately shows you the result of your cropping and sizing, it isn't precise. When you need to enter exact measurements to get the correct size or trim, you should use the options in the Format Picture dialog box.

### Size a Picture Using the Format Picture Dialog Box

1. Select the graphic and open the **Format** menu and select **Picture**, choose Format Picture 🖾 on the Picture toolbar, or right-click the graphic and select **Format Picture** from the pop-up menu.

2. When the Format Picture dialog box appears, select the **Size** tab (see Figure 18.7).

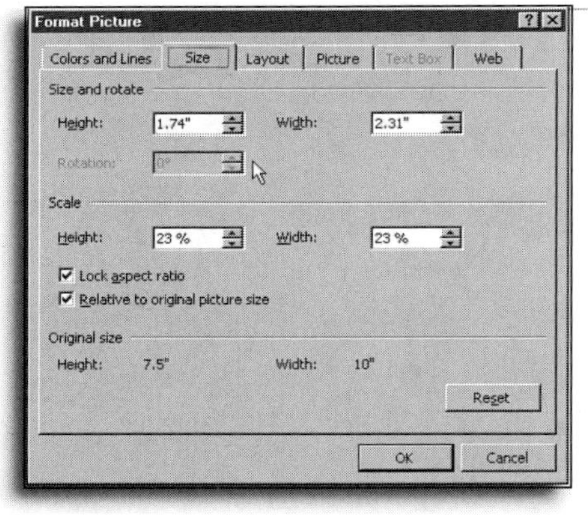

**FIGURE 18.7**
Enter the dimensions or the scale percentage to size your image.

3. To keep the image in proportion (maintain the ratio between the width and height), click **Lock Aspect Ratio** to place a check mark there.

4. Under **Size**, change the **Height** or **Width** measurement (the other dimension automatically adjusts when you press Tab to keep the graphic in proportion if you locked the aspect ratio). Or, to use percentages instead of exact dimensions, change the **Height** or **Width** percentage in the Scale area.

5. Choose **OK** to apply your modifications to the image.

**Crop a Picture Using the Format Picture Dialog Box**

1. Select the image and open the **Format** menu and choose **Picture**, choose Format Picture 🖼 on the Picture toolbar, or right-click the graphic and select **Format Picture** from the pop-up menu.

2. When the Format Picture dialog box appears, select the **Picture** tab (see Figure 18.8).

3. Enter the exact measurement (in inches) of the amount you want to crop from the **Left**, **Right**, **Top**, or **Bottom** of the picture.

4. Choose **OK** to apply your modifications to the image.

Although using the dialog box to crop your pictures is a more accurate method, you have to know exactly how much you want to trim to get the desired effect. Using the Cropping tool gives you more immediate visual feedback. Try combining the methods—first cropping with the tool and then refining with the dialog box options—for the best results.

**Crop close**

Unless the background is vitally important to a picture, crop as close to the central element or focus of the picture as possible. For example, a portrait of a person should not show a lot of whitespace around the head but should be cropped closely to and concentrate on the face.

# Delete, Move, and Copy Graphics

Deleting a graphic is a simple matter of selecting the graphic and then pressing the Delete key.

To move a graphic, point to the middle of the graphic until your mouse pointer becomes a four-headed arrow (see Figure 18.9), hold down your mouse button, and drag the outline of the graphic to the new location. Then release the mouse button and the graphic appears at the new location.

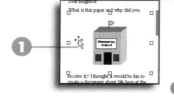

**FIGURE 18.9**

When your mouse pointer becomes a four-headed arrow, you can drag the selected graphic to its new location.

① Four-headed mouse pointer for moving graphics

### Position a Graphic Using the Format Picture Dialog Box

1. Select the picture and open the **Fo̱rmat** menu and choose **P̱icture**, choose Format Picture 🖼 on the Picture toolbar, or right-click the graphic and select **Format P̱icture** from the pop-up menu.

2. When the Format Picture dialog box appears, select the **Layout** tab.

3. Select a Wrapping style other than **I̱n Line with Text**. Choose **A̱dvanced**.

4. Click the **Picture Position** tab (see Figure 18.10).

**FIGURE 18.10**

When positioning of a graphic becomes critical to your document, use the advanced layout options.

**5.** To set the horizontal position of the graphic on the page, there are three options:

- **Alignment**. This positions your picture to the Left, Right or Center **Relative To** a Column, Margin, Page, or Character. It is particularly useful in documents like newsletters, where you have columns of text.

- **Book Layout**. Use this when you have facing pages and you need to position the picture **Inside** or **Outside Of** the Margin or Page.

- **Absolute Position**. This selection sets the exact position of the upper-left corner of the picture in inches **To the Left Of** the Column, Margin, Page, or Character.

**6.** To set the vertical position of the graphic on the page, specify one of the following:

- **Alignment**. Position the picture at the Top, Bottom, Center, Inside, or Outside **Relative To** the Margin, Page, or Line.

- **Absolute Position**. Sets the exact position of the upper-left corner of the picture in inches **Below** the Margin, Page, Paragraph, or Line.

**7.** Click the **Move Object with Text** option to have the graphic move with the text where your insertion point was at the time that you inserted the graphic in your document. As you add or delete text before the paragraph, the graphic moves up and down the page the same number of lines as the paragraph unless it's close to the bottom or top of the page.

**8.** Click **Lock Anchor** to anchor the graphic to the same page where that text is (even though the paragraph moves, the graphic remains where you placed it on the page until the text moves to another page and it jumps to the same page as the text). Deselecting both these options lets you move the graphic freely around the page.

**The anchor**

When you choose the **Move Object with Text** option, you see a small anchor when you select the picture. The anchor marks the paragraph text to which the picture is anchored. When this text moves within the document, the picture moves with it. You can drag the anchor to another paragraph and thus anchor the picture to that text.

**9.** Select the **Allow O̲verlap** option to be able to overlap the graphic and another paragraph.

**10.** Choose **OK** to have your modifications apply to the graphic.

To move the graphic to another page or another document, select it, choose Cut on the Standard toolbar, position your insertion point where you want the graphic to appear, and then choose Paste on the Standard toolbar. To copy a graphic, select it, choose Copy on the Standard toolbar, position your insertion point where you want the copy to appear, and then choose Paste on the Standard toolbar.

## Wrap Text Around Graphics

A graphic causes a break in your text (this doesn't apply to inline graphics). The text immediately after the graphic doesn't start until the next line after the picture, leaving whitespace to the left or right of the graphic. This is called a top-and-bottom text wrap and is Word's default setting for wrapping text around a picture. However, you may want your text to wrap around the image, as in Figure 18.11.

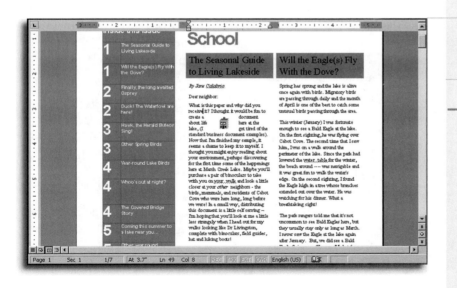

**FIGURE 18.11**
The text wraps around this graphic.

### What are inline graphics?

Inline graphics act like characters in a line of text. The small icon pictures that appear throughout this book in the middle of paragraphs are inline graphics. This wrapping choice is also useful for inserting graphic representations of letters at the beginning of important paragraphs, almost like an illuminated manuscript of the Middle Ages. Although most graphics inserted into text are inline graphics by default, you can choose **In Line with Text** from the text wrapping options to make the selected picture an inline graphic.

**Set Text Wrap Options**

1. Select the image.

2. Open the **F**o**rmat** menu and select **P**i**cture**, choose Format Picture on the Picture toolbar , or right-click the graphic and select **Format P**i**cture** from the pop-up menu.

3. When the Format Picture dialog box appears, select the **Layout** tab (see Figure 18.12).

**Adjusting the wrap**

The text wrapping options are also available when you click **Text Wrapping** on the Picture toolbar. There is one more option available that isn't in the dialog box. Choose **Edit Wrap Points** to see a dotted-line outline showing the text wrap boundary (this choice automatically changes the wrap type to **Tight**). Move the points on the boundary line to eliminate awkward breaks in words or lines that make reading difficult. Choose **Edit Wrap Points** again when you finish adjusting the boundary to turn off the display.

4. Under **Wrapping Style**, select a style of text wrap—**In Line with Text**, **Square**, **T**i**ght**, **Behind Text**, or **In F**r**ont of Text**—depending on how close you want the text to wrap around the picture.

5. Choose **Advanced** to set text wrapping specifics in the Advanced Layout dialog box (see Figure 18.13).

6. Select the **Text Wrapping** tab. Under **Wrap Text**, select the sides on which you want the text to wrap—**Both Sides**, **Left Only**, **Right Only**, or **Largest Only**.

7. To set the distance between the edge of the picture and the beginning of the text wrapping around it, enter the distance in the **Top**, **Bottom**, **Left**, and **Right** boxes under **Distance from Text**.

8. Choose **OK** to close the Advanced Layout dialog box.

9. Choose **OK** to close the Format Picture dialog box.

**9.** Select the **Allow O̲verlap** option to be able to overlap the graphic and another paragraph.

**10.** Choose **OK** to have your modifications apply to the graphic.

To move the graphic to another page or another document, select it, choose Cut 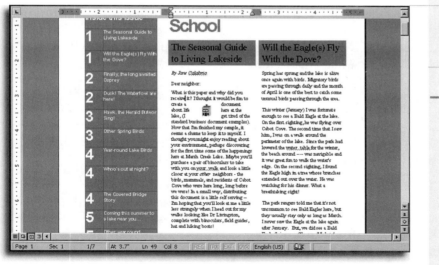 on the Standard toolbar, position your insertion point where you want the graphic to appear, and then choose Paste on the Standard toolbar. To copy a graphic, select it, choose Copy on the Standard toolbar, position your insertion point where you want the copy to appear, and then choose Paste on the Standard toolbar.

## Wrap Text Around Graphics

A graphic causes a break in your text (this doesn't apply to inline graphics). The text immediately after the graphic doesn't start until the next line after the picture, leaving whitespace to the left or right of the graphic. This is called a top-and-bottom text wrap and is Word's default setting for wrapping text around a picture. However, you may want your text to wrap around the image, as in Figure 18.11.

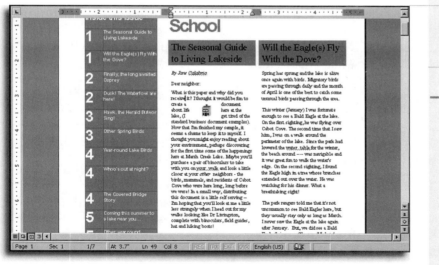

**FIGURE 18.11**
The text wraps around this graphic.

### What are inline graphics?

Inline graphics act like characters in a line of text. The small icon pictures that appear throughout this book in the middle of paragraphs are inline graphics. This wrapping choice is also useful for inserting graphic representations of letters at the beginning of important paragraphs, almost like an illuminated manuscript of the Middle Ages. Although most graphics inserted into text are inline graphics by default, you can choose **In Line with Text** from the text wrapping options to make the selected picture an inline graphic.

### Set Text Wrap Options

**1.** Select the image.

**2.** Open the **F̲ormat** menu and select **Pi̲cture**, choose Format Picture on the Picture toolbar 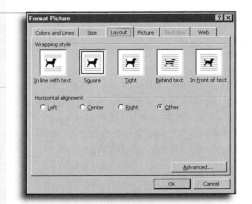, or right-click the graphic and select **Format P̲icture** from the pop-up menu.

**3.** When the Format Picture dialog box appears, select the **Layout** tab (see Figure 18.12).

FIGURE 18.12

Select the options for how you want the text to wrap around your picture.

**4.** Under **Wrapping Style**, select a style of text wrap—**I̲n Line with Text**, **S̲quare**, **T̲ight**, **B̲ehind Text**, or **In F̲ront of Text**—depending on how close you want the text to wrap around the picture.

**5.** Choose **A̲dvanced** to set text wrapping specifics in the Advanced Layout dialog box (see Figure 18.13).

**6.** Select the **Text Wrapping** tab. Under **Wrap Text**, select the sides on which you want the text to wrap—**Both S̲ides**, **L̲eft Only**, **R̲ight Only**, or **La̲rgest Only**.

**7.** To set the distance between the edge of the picture and the beginning of the text wrapping around it, enter the distance in the **Top̲**, **Bottom̲**, **Left̲**, and **Right̲** boxes under **Distance from Text**.

**8.** Choose **OK** to close the Advanced Layout dialog box.

**9.** Choose **OK** to close the Format Picture dialog box.

---

**Adjusting the wrap**

The text wrapping options are also available when you click **Text Wrapping** on the Picture toolbar. There is one more option available that isn't in the dialog box. Choose **Edit Wrap Points** to see a dotted-line outline showing the text wrap boundary (this choice automatically changes the wrap type to **Tight**). Move the points on the boundary line to eliminate awkward breaks in words or lines that make reading difficult. Choose **Edit Wrap Points** again when you finish adjusting the boundary to turn off the display.

PART **V**

**Work Faster with Placeholders**     CHAPTER **18**    377

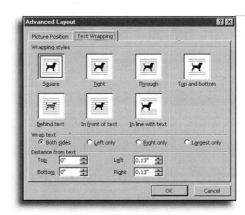

**FIGURE 18.13**
The Advanced Layout dialog box offers the additional text wrapping options of **Through** and **Top and Bottom**.

# Work Faster with Placeholders

Although it's nice to see graphics as you work, displaying them can slow down screen scrolling and use system resources, such as RAM. One way to speed up the screen refresh so scrolling is faster is to replace the graphics with empty rectangles called *placeholders*. These placeholders mark where the graphics will appear in the printed document. The graphics aren't eliminated from the document; they're just temporarily hidden.

To display placeholders instead of the graphics, open the **Tools** menu and select **Options**. Then on the **View** tab, click **Picture Placeholders** to place a check mark there before you choose **OK** (see Figure 18.14).

Word inserts *field codes* in the document where linked graphics appear. Linked graphics are created when you select a graphics file (not clip art) and choose to link. To do this, choose **Insert**, **Picture**, **From File** and in the Insert Picture dialog box, choose the **Link to File** option from the Insert drop-down menu when you insert the graphic. The screen shows this field code instead of the picture when field codes are displayed (see Figure 18.15). To display field codes, choose **Options** from the **Tools** menu, click the **View** tab, and then select **Field Codes**.

**WordArt as inline objects**

You can insert WordArt as an inline or floating object. For some very cool effects, try using WordArt objects as bullets and banners!

FIGURE 18.14

Display your graphics as place-holders from this dialog box.

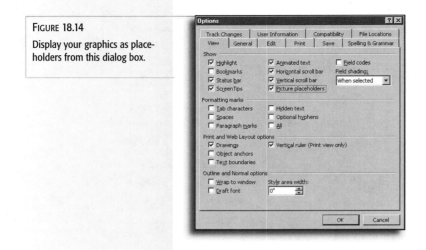

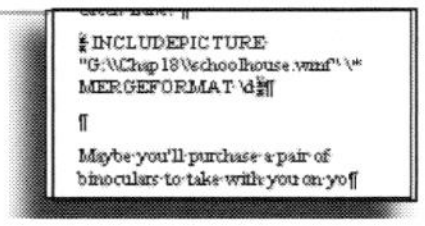

FIGURE 18.15

A picture field code tells the file-name and location of the picture file.

Although the field code shows in your document onscreen, the picture still prints properly. The picture also appears when you preview the file.

**SEE ALSO**

➤ *To learn other ways that Word uses fields and field codes, including displaying field codes, see page 531*

# About Special Characters and Symbols

Symbols are characters that do not appear on your computer keyboard, such as letters with accents used in words from languages other than English, stars, bullets, happy faces, the copyright symbol, the registration mark, long (em) dashes, and Greek letters used in mathematical expressions. Even though these characters aren't on your keyboard, Word can still insert them into your documents.

What's the difference between special characters and symbols? Special characters also don't appear on your computer keyboard, and some items appear as both symbols and special characters. Special characters are more the type of characters needed by typesetters, such as the copyright symbol (©), ellipses (…), em spaces (a wider than normal space), and em dashes (—). Table 18.2 gives an example of or describes what the special characters are.

**TABLE 18.2   Special characters**

| Name | Description |
| --- | --- |
| Em dash | — a typographer's long dash (use instead of two hyphens) |
| En dash | – a typographer's dash (as opposed to a hyphen) |
| Nonbreaking hyphen | Keeps a hyphenated word from being split between two lines |
| Optional hyphen | Marks where a word should be hyphenated if it appears at the end of a line (it doesn't appear until the word needs to be broken at the end of a line) |
| Em space | A larger than normal space |
| En space | A larger than normal space, but not as large as an em space |
| Nonbreaking space | A space between words that prevents the words from being split between two lines |
| Copyright | © |
| Registered | ® |
| Trademark | ™ |
| Section | ß |
| Paragraph | ¶ |
| Ellipsis | … (use instead of three periods) |
| Single opening quote | ' |
| Single closing quote | ' |
| Double opening quote | " |
| Double closing quote | " |

## Insert a Symbol

The symbols you have available to insert in your text depend on the fonts you have installed on your computer. Some fonts are specifically for symbols, such as Wingdings and Monotype Sorts. Other fonts, such as Arial and Times New Roman, have a few symbols as part of the font character set.

### Insert a Symbol

1. Place your insertion point where you want the symbol to appear.

2. Open the **Insert** menu and choose **Symbol** to open the Symbol dialog box (see Figure 18.16). Click the **Symbols** tab if it's not already on top.

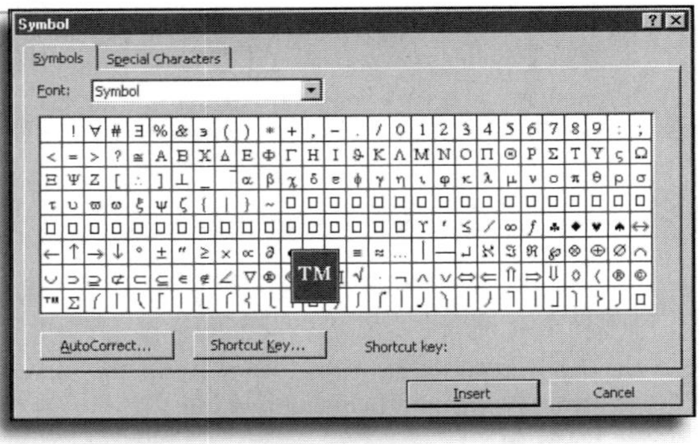

FIGURE 18.16

Select the symbol you want to insert and choose **Insert**.

**Not enough fonts and symbols?**

You can purchase font software as well as graphics software that includes fonts not found in a standard Windows install. For the most part, these software programs install their fonts in Windows, adding the fonts to your lists of available fonts and symbols. Most software packages also enable you to select which fonts to install, and we recommend that you install only the fonts you think you will use. Fonts can take up large amounts of disk storage space.

3. From the **Font** drop-down list, select the symbol set you want to use. Choose **(normal text)** to see the list for the current font, which includes letters with diacritical marks, currency symbols, the paragraph symbol, the registered mark, the trademark symbol, the copyright symbol, and so on. There are a number of symbol fonts, such as Symbol, Wingdings, Zapf Dingbats, or Monotype Sorts, that have Greek letters, mathematical symbols, arrows, pointing hands, snowflakes, bullets, and more.

4. Look through the grid of symbols for the one you want. Click a symbol square to see an enlarged view of the symbol.

5. To insert the selected symbol in your document, choose **Insert** or double-click the symbol.

6. Choose **Close** to close the dialog box after you insert one or more symbols. Choose **Cancel** to close the dialog box without inserting a symbol.

Although some symbols are available in normal text (such as the copyright, registration mark, em dash), you may also use symbols from the Wingdings font to enhance your documents. Wingdings is shipped with Windows. If you have added other fonts, you may have more symbol fonts to choose from— Bookshelf, Common Bullets, Marlett, Monotype Sorts, Zapf Dingbats, and so on.

**SEE ALSO**

➤ *To create AutoCorrect entries, see page 118*

**AutoCorrect**

Choose **AutoCorrect** to add a symbol or special character to the AutoCorrect list.

# Insert a Special Character

Although some items (such as the copyright symbol) appear on both the **Symbols** tab and the **Special Characters** tab, it's easier to access them in Special Characters where you don't have to search through the grid to find them. If you have deleted the AutoCorrect entries for the copyright © and registered trademark symbols ®, you can still insert them as special characters or symbols.

**Insert a Special Character**

1. Put your insertion point where you want the special character to appear.

2. Open the **Insert** menu and choose **Symbol**.

3. When the Symbol dialog box appears, click the **Special Characters** tab (see Figure 18.17).

4. Select the special character you want from the list and then choose **Insert**, or double-click the character to insert it in your text.

5. Choose **Close** to close the dialog box after you insert a character. Choose **Cancel** to close the dialog box without inserting a character.

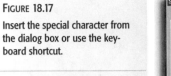

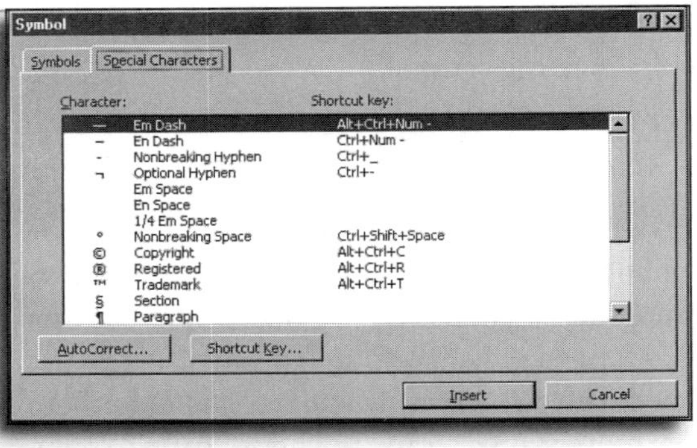

FIGURE **18.17**

Insert the special character from the dialog box or use the keyboard shortcut.

## Assign Shortcut Keystrokes to Symbols

To quickly insert symbols or special characters that you use frequently, use the keyboard shortcut keys assigned to them (refer to Figure 18.16). For those symbols or special characters that don't already have keyboard shortcuts, you need to assign keys.

### Assign Shortcut Keystrokes to Symbols

1. Open the **Insert** menu and choose **Symbol**. Click the symbol to which you want to assign the shortcut keys (refer to Figure 18.16).

2. Choose **Shortcut Key**. The Customize Keyboard dialog box appears (see Figure 18.18).

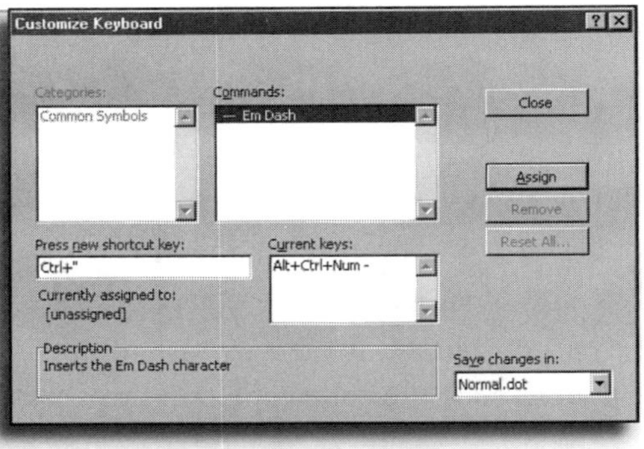

FIGURE **18.18**

Displaying assigned shortcut keys.

3. Click in the **Press <u>N</u>ew Shortcut Key** text box.

4. Press the shortcut key combination you want to assign (the shortcut keys are a combination of Shift, Ctrl, and/or Alt, and a letter or number key, such as Alt+Ctrl+C that produces the copyright symbol). Its description appears in the **Press New Shortcut Key** text box. Underneath the text box Word displays **Currently Assigned To** and the symbol or operation to which the shortcut key combination is assigned. If it has already been assigned, clear the **Press New Shortcut Key** text box and try another combination. If Word displays [unassigned] then choose **<u>A</u>ssign** to assign your combination to the symbol.

5. Choose **Close** to return to the Symbols dialog box, and then choose **Close** to return to your document.

**SEE ALSO**

➤ *To create more keyboard shortcuts, see page 649*

# Apply a Watermark

A *watermark* is text or graphics that appear on the top of or behind document text. Watermarks are often found on preprinted letterheads. You use watermarks with printed documents; Web pages use *backgrounds*.

With Word, you can create your own watermarks, such as a logo that appears behind the text of your letter, or the word DRAFT to indicate that a document is not in it's final form (see Figure 18.19). Another example of the use of watermarks is for proprietary documents where the word CONFIDENTIAL appears behind the text of each page.

When you create a watermark for your document, you must start it in a header or footer if you want it to appear on every page. This doesn't confine it to the top or bottom of the page, but simply gives it an anchor; then it prints wherever you place it on the page.

**Single-page watermarks**

If you only want a watermark to appear on a single page, you don't have to put it in a header or footer. Just insert a picture, text box, or WordArt on the page. After you size and position it, apply the watermark coloring and send it behind the document text.

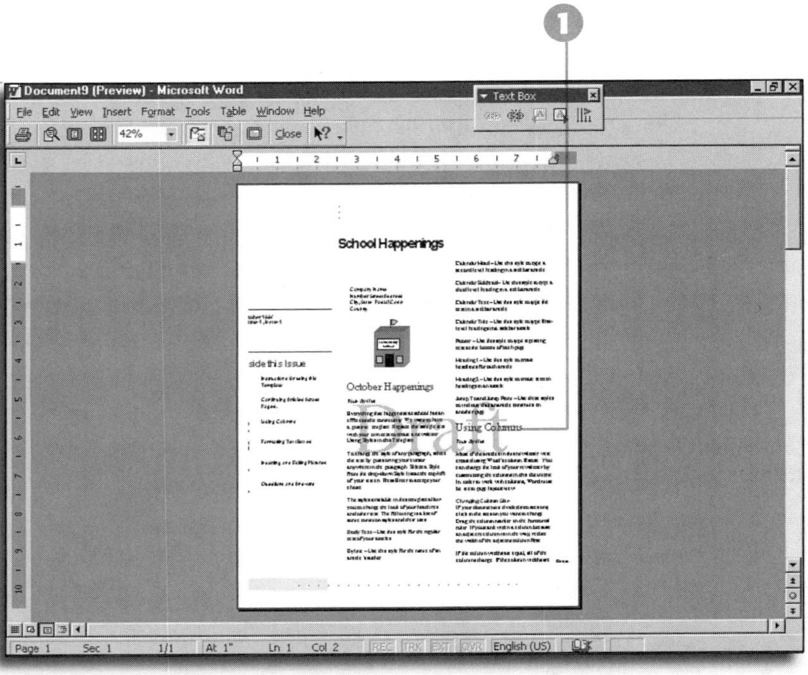

FIGURE 18.19

The watermark DRAFT indicates that this newsletter is a work in progress.

**1** Watermark

### Watermark Creation Is a Two Step Process

1. Insert the graphic, object, or text.

2. Format the graphic, object, or text as a watermark, or with light fill colors so that it appears faded like a watermark.

The details of these two steps are explained in the following two sections.

## Insert Objects to Be Used As Watermarks

To insert the watermark, complete the following steps.

### Create a Watermark

1. Open the **View** menu and choose **Header and Footer**.

2. Choose **Show/Hide Document Text** 🖻 on the Header and Footer toolbar to hide the document text.

3. To insert a graphic in your header or footer, go to the **Insert** menu and select **Picture**. From the submenu select **Clip Art**

or **From File**. Select the piece of clip art or the graphic file you want to insert, and then choose **Insert** or **Insert**.

To insert text (such as DRAFT) click the **Insert** menu and select **Text Box**. Then drag the rectangle shape in the approximate position where you want the text to appear on your page. Type the watermark text in the box. Format the text with a light shade so it doesn't obscure your document text.

To insert WordArt as a watermark (see Figure 18.20), insert the WordArt while you are in Header/Footer view. Position the WordArt where you want it on the page. Then, change the WordArt fill and line color to a light shade.

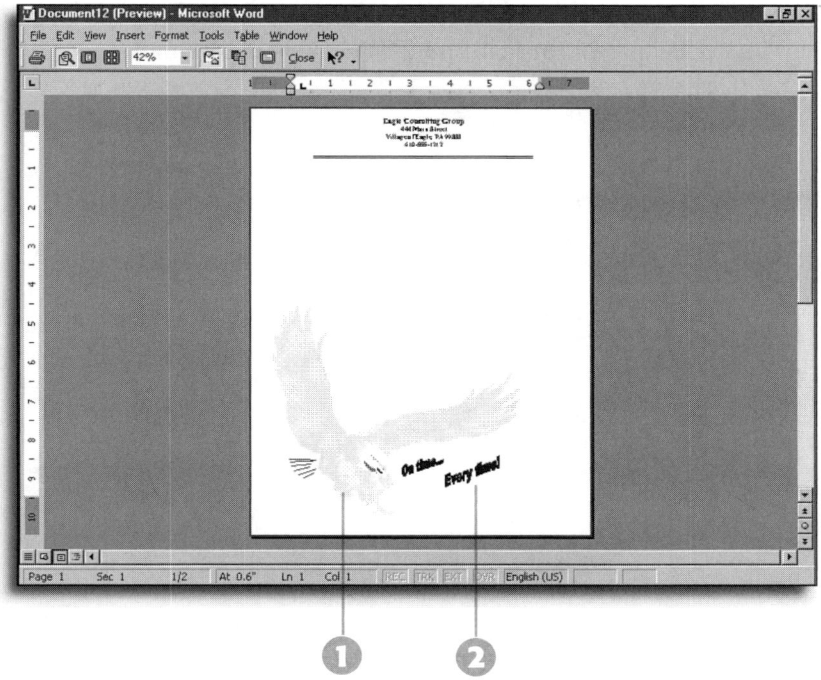

FIGURE 18.20
After you insert the graphic into the header or footer, you can size it, position it, and format it for use as a watermark.

1. Graphic as a watermark—resized and repositioned

2. WordArt object as a watermark

**SEE ALSO**

➤ *To learn more about working with headers and footers, see page 295*

➤ *To insert, size, and reposition pictures and graphics, see page 367*

➤ *To insert, format, and reposition WordArt, see page 440*

## Format Objects As Watermarks

### Format an Object As a Watermark

1. Open the **Format** menu and choose **Picture** or **Object** from the submenu. Alternatively, choose the Format Picture icon 🖼 on the Picture toolbar. The **Format** menu is context-sensitive; it may read **Object**, **Picture**, **WordArt**, and so forth, depending on the item you have inserted and selected.

2. Select the **Picture** tab. Under **Image Control**, select **Watermark** from the **Color** drop-down list to format the picture with settings that work well for watermarks (see Figure 18.21).

3. To control how the document text wraps around the picture, select the **Layout** tab and then click on the **Behind Text** option.

4. Choose **OK**.

**FIGURE** 18.21

Use the Watermark color setting to use Word's preset options for your watermark.

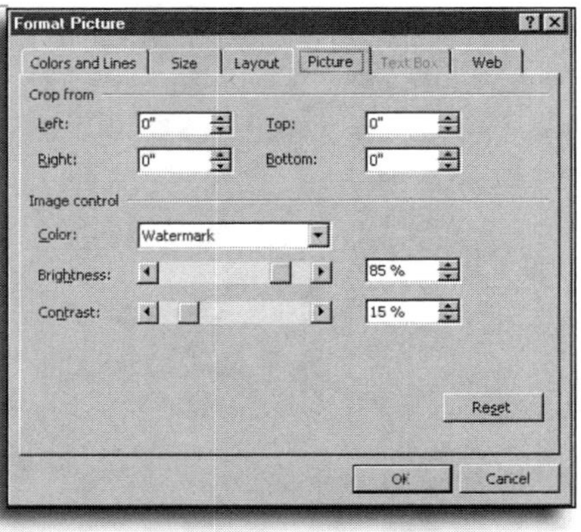

Before you print a large document that has a watermark, print a page or two to make sure that the watermark doesn't obscure the text. It may look fine in Print Preview, but some printers may darken the watermark or may not be able to print the watermark and text in the same spot. You can make adjustments after you see the print sample.

Some graphics files just won't translate well to watermarks and appear too dark on a printed page. Should you have this problem, try one of the following methods to lighten the graphic:

- Lighten the text in a text box by choosing a text color such as light gray. Select the text and choose Font Color **A** on the Formatting toolbar to pick a color.

- Lighten a WordArt object by choosing the **Format** menu and selecting **WordArt**. Then select a lighter fill color on the **Colors and Lines** tab.

- Lighten drawing objects by choosing the **Format** menu and selecting **AutoShape**. Then choose a lighter fill color from the **Colors and Lines** tab.

- Click the **Format** menu and select **Picture** or choose the **Format** menu and select **Object** for imported graphics. Then change the fill color on the **Color and Lines** tab. On the **Picture** tab select **Watermark** from the **Color** drop-down list. For scanned pictures you can adjust the brightness or contrast, but you may have to edit the picture in an image editing program.

### Format a Text Box

1. Select the text box. Open the **Format** menu and choose **Font**. Select the options to format the text as you want it (you should change the **Color** to a lighter shade) and choose **OK**.

2. To rotate the text within the box, choose the **Format** menu and select **Text Direction** and select the rotation option you want (see Figure 18.22).

3. Use options on the Drawing toolbar to format the borders and background color of the text box.

4. Open the **Format** menu and choose **Text Box**. Select the **Layout** tab and choose **Behind Text**. Choose **OK**.

5. Choose **Close** on the Header and Footer toolbar.

FIGURE 18.22

Select the text direction to rotate your text within the text box.

**1** Select the desired direction for the text box.

**2** Text Box toolbar

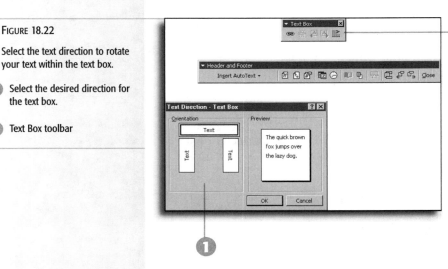

**I can't see the watermark!**

You must switch to Print Layout view or open Print Preview to see the watermark as it will appear when printed.

**Letterhead**

Watermarks can be used in templates to make a letterhead.

To remove a watermark from your document, you must delete it from the header or footer.

**Remove a Watermark**

1. Open the **View** menu and choose **Header and Footer**.

2. Switch to the header or footer box that contains the watermark.

3. Select the watermark text box or graphic and press the Delete key.

4. Choose **Close** on the Header and Footer toolbar.

SEE ALSO

➤ *For more information on formatting drawings and AutoShapes, see page 426*

➤ *Learn more about text boxes, see page 424*

➤ *To learn how to create a letterhead template, see page 471*

# Insert a Picture from a Scanner or Digital Camera

A picture that you have scanned and saved can be retrieved the same as any graphic—by selecting **Picture** on the **Insert** menu and then choosing **From File**. However, if you have a scanner connected to your computer and you have Microsoft Photo Editor installed, you can scan and capture scanned images into your document without first saving them in an intermediate file format.

The same goes for pictures from your digital camera. You can upload pictures to your computer, save them in an intermediate file format, then import the resulting files. Or you can capture them directly via Microsoft Photo Editor.

One slight catch: your scanner or camera must be TWAIN-compliant. TWAIN is a standard interface between scanners and software. Virtually all scanners and digital cameras have TWAIN drivers, so this is not much of a barrier. (TWAIN is also what we call a "cute" acronym; it stands for "*t*echnology *w*ithout *a*n *i*nteresting *n*ame." Oy vay!)

### Insert a Picture from a Scanner or Digital Camera

1. Position your cursor where you want the picture to appear in your document.

2. Open the **Insert** menu and choose **Picture**. Select **From Scanner or Camera** from the submenu.

3. If you have more than one scanner or camera available, choose the one you want to use under **Device**.

4. Choose **Web Quality** or **Print Quality**. Web quality is lower resolution than print quality.

5. If you are scanning and using your scanner's default settings, choose **Insert**. If you are uploading from a camera or you want to change your scanner's settings, choose **Custom Insert**, then follow the instructions that came with your device.

6. The image appears in your document. Use the tools on the Picture toolbar to make any changes there that you need—cropping, special effects, brightness, contrast, color, and so on. Adjust the position and size of the photo as you would any other graphic in Word.

---

**Installing Microsoft Photo Editor**

To install Microsoft Photo Editor, insert the Office CD in your CD-ROM drive and run Setup. Choose **Add or Remove Features**. Under Office Tools, select **Microsoft Photo Editor** and choose **Run from My Computer**. Choose **Update Now**.

# CHAPTER
# *19*

# Integrate Word Data with Other Programs

# Know Your Data Integration Options

Word works well with all Microsoft Office applications as well as non-Microsoft applications, such as Lotus 1-2-3. Word is capable of recognizing and converting to and from a wide variety of foreign file formats. In addition, like most Windows-based programs, Word supports *Object Linking and Embedding* (*OLE*), a standard set of tools for integrating data from diverse programs. As a result, you can work with data from other programs in a variety of ways. For example:

- You can use Access data files as data sources in mail merges in Word.
- You can link Excel ranges to reports you create in Word.
- You can open either Access or Excel files or Excel graphs directly in Word, which converts them to text, and formats them as tables.

Several ways to integrate Word documents with data from other programs are

- Copy and paste
- Insert a file into a Word document
- Link and embed
- Import and export
- Create hyperlinks

This chapter discusses pasting, file insertion, linking, embedding, and importation/exportation of files. We define each method, discuss the differences between them, and suggest when to use each to integrate Word data with data created in other applications.

**SEE ALSO**

➤ *To learn how to create hyperlinks, see page 596*

# Know When to Paste, Insert, Link, or Embed

When you want to include the contents of an entire file, typically you insert the file. When you want to include parts of a file in your Word document, typically, you paste, link, or embed. When you insert files into your Word document, once the file is selected, there are no additional dialog boxes in which you must answer questions. The insert just happens. The exception to that rule is when you insert a spreadsheet file, in which case you must tell Word which sheets you want to insert (you can insert all sheets of the file).

To further help you decide which method to use when working with external files, choose to Link to external data if any of the following conditions are true:

- Updates to the original data object need to appear automatically in your Word document.

- The data being linked to will be maintained and updated in the original file to which you are linking.

- You will always be able to maintain the link to the original file. For example, if you plan to distribute your Word document to others who will need the linked data updated, they must also have access to the original file, and that access must be in the same file path.

Embed external data if any of the following conditions are true:

- You want to be able to manipulate your copy of the embedded data independently of the original object.

- There is a likelihood that you will not be able to maintain the link between your Word document and the object to which it is linked.

Insert a file or paste data if the other program does not support OLE.

# Copy and Paste from Other Applications

Copy and paste are standard Windows skills. You have undoubtedly been cutting/copying and pasting within Word and between applications for as long as you've been working with Windows.

However, when you paste information from the Clipboard into a Word document, Word may handle the information in different ways, depending on where the information originated:

- If the data came from a Word document, Word simply pastes it in, retaining its original format.

- If the data is textual in nature and came from a program for which Word has a conversion program, Word converts the information to Word text format.

- If the data came from a database program such as Access or a spreadsheet program such as Excel, Word converts the information to Word text, and formats it as a table so as to retain the original column and row format of the data.

- If the data in the Clipboard is in a format that Word cannot convert or is not textual in nature (for example graphics or sound), but Word can associate the data with an *OLE object application*, Word embeds the data as an object. See "Link and Embed Objects" later in this chapter.

- If Word cannot convert the data in the Clipboard and cannot associate the file with an OLE object application, Word pastes the data as is, which may mean the data is unrecognizable and you have to use the **Undo** command ⟲ (or Ctrl+Z) to remove the pasted data.

Instead of using the **Paste** command and relying on Word to decide what format to use on the pasted data, you can use the **Paste Special** command (on the **Edit** menu) to control the format of the pasted data.

### Paste Objects Using Paste Special

1. Copy your object to the Windows Clipboard.

2. Position your cursor in the receiving document at the position you want to paste the object. Open the **Edit** menu and choose **Paste Special**.)

**3.** The Paste Special dialog box appears (see Figure 19.1).

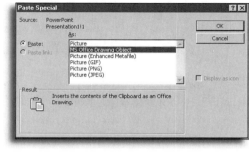

FIGURE 19.1

In the Paste Special dialog box you can choose the format of the pasted data.

**4.** Click **Paste** to embed the Clipboard contents in your document. No link is made to the source file, so the data does not change when the source file is modified.

Click **Paste Link** to insert the Clipboard contents and create a link to the source file (save the source file before you link it in Word). The object in Word updates when the source file is modified.

**5.** Select the formatting options for your object in the **As** box. The options change depending on the type of object you're inserting. When you select an option, a description appears under **Result**. For example, if you select Formatted Text (RTF) for an Excel worksheet, Word inserts the Clipboard contents as text, but with font and table formatting. Selecting Microsoft Excel Worksheet Object lets you edit the inserted object using Microsoft Excel tools if you are embedding the object, or inserts it as a picture if you linked the file.

**6.** Check **Display as Icon** to have the object appear as an icon in your document. You have to double-click the icon to open or edit the object.

**7.** Choose **OK**.

**SEE ALSO**

➤ *To learn more about cut, copy, and paste, see page 63*

➤ *To learn about using the Office Clipboard to collect and paste multiple items, see page 68*

# Link and Embed Objects

Word users can either link to data created in another program or embed data created in another program. The data linked to or embedded retains its identity with the program in which it was originally created.

Contrast this to pasted or inserted data. When you insert a file (and if possible when you paste data), the inserted data is converted to Word format, just as if you had entered it manually into your document. But embedded or linked data does not become Word data. Rather, it is a "foreign object" which is "contained" by the Word file. That is why OLE is called *object* linking and embedding. The source application is called the *object* application and the destination application is called the *container* application.

You cannot edit linked or embedded data with Word. Rather, you have to edit it with the program in which it was created. If you try to edit the linked or embedded data, Word will try to open the program in which the data was created. If the program isn't available, you can't edit the data.

If the source program supports OLE2, you can edit the data *in-place*, that is, within a window that appears around the data object right in your Word document (see Figure 19.2); Word's menus and toolbars are replaced temporarily by those of the source program. (Clicking in the Word document outside the data object causes Word's menus and toolbars to reappear and the other application's frame around the object to disappear.) If the source program supports OLE1 or DDE (Dynamic Data Exchange, the predecessor to OLE), the data object appears in its own program's window when you try to edit it.

## Link to an Existing Object

When you link to data created in another program, for example to cells in an Excel spreadsheet, the data appears in your Word document but actually continues to be stored in the Excel data file. All that is stored in your Word file is a pointer to the location of the Excel file.

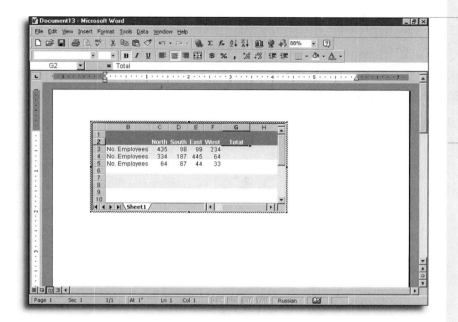

FIGURE 19.2
When you double-click the embedded spreadsheet range, it appears in an Excel window inside your Word document, and the Excel menu and toolbars replace the Word menu and toolbars.

Linking to data has its benefits. First, if someone updates the data in the spreadsheet file, the update appears automatically in your Word document. If you have access to the program in which the data was created, you can update the original data by simply double-clicking the linked data object in your document. This causes the original file to be opened in the program, and when you save your changes you are saving them to the original file. Second, because your file only contains a pointer to the original object, your file does not get appreciably bigger. The drawback to linking is that you may not be able to update the data in your file if the source file is moved to another location or deleted.

### Link an Entire File to Your Document

1. Position your insertion point in the document where you want the linked object to appear.

2. Open the **Insert** menu and choose **Object**.

3. When the Object dialog box appears, click the **Create from File** tab (see Figure 19.3).

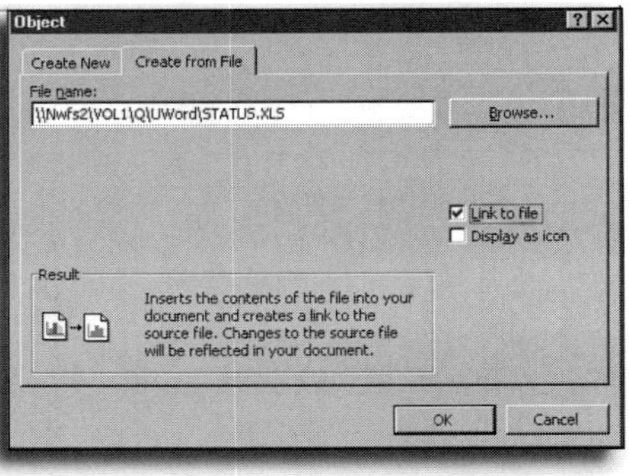

FIGURE 19.3

To link to an existing file, open the Object dialog box and check **Link to File** after you enter the filename.

4. Type the filename you want to insert in the **File Name** box, or choose **Browse** to select the file from a list.

5. Click **Link to File** to place a check mark there.

6. (Optional) If you want to display the linked object as an icon (useful for online documents), click **Display as Icon** to place a check mark there. An icon appears in your document text, and you must double-click it to open or edit the object. When you print the document, the icon is printed.

7. Click **OK**. Figure 19.4 shows a linked object, which is a slide from a Microsoft PowerPoint presentation.

You may not be able to insert some graphics files as linked objects. These must be added by opening the **Insert** menu and selecting **Picture**.

### Link to Part of a File

1. Open the file that contains the data that you will link to in Word. If you just created the file and haven't saved it yet, save it now. You cannot link to data that has not been saved to disk.

2. Select the data, open the **Edit** menu, and choose **Copy** to place a copy in the Clipboard.

3. Position your insertion point in the Word document where you want the linked object to appear. Then open the **Edit** menu and choose **Paste Special** to open the Paste Special dialog box.

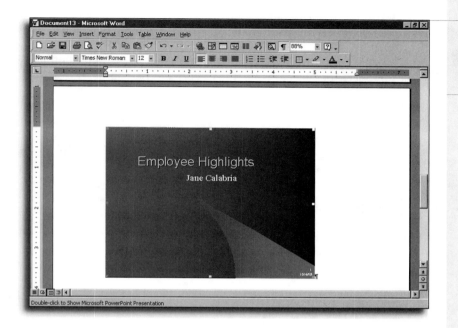

FIGURE 19.4
This illustration is a linked object; the source is a PowerPoint presentation file.

**4.** In the dialog box, choose **Paste Link** and a data format.

**5.** (Optional) If you want to display the linked object as an icon (useful for online documents), click **Display as Icon** to place a check mark there.

**6.** Choose **OK**.

To make changes to a linked object, you must open the source file in the application where it was created and modify it there. To do this, you may either open it in the standard way or you may double-click the object in your Word document. If you open the source file by double-clicking the object in Word, the originating application opens in a separate window with the source file in Edit mode. Click outside this window to return to Word without closing the source application. The modifications appear in the object in Word, even if you haven't saved the file in the source application. When you do close the source application window, you'll be prompted to save the source file.

If your Word document is open when you make changes to the source file, the object in your document is updated immediately. If not, the next time you open your document, the data will be

**Drag-and-drop linking**

You can also set up an object link by holding down the Ctrl and Shift keys while dragging the object to be linked from the source file to the target Word file.

updated automatically. If you don't want the automatic updating, open the **Tools** menu and choose **Options**, select the **General** tab, and deselect the **Update Automatic Links at Open** option. To update the object manually, select it and press F9.

Word does have an option to automatically update linked files when you print the document. To enable this option, open the **Tools** menu and choose **Options**. Then click the **Print** tab on the Options dialog box (see Figure 19.5). Click **Update Links** to put a check mark in the box, and then choose **OK**.

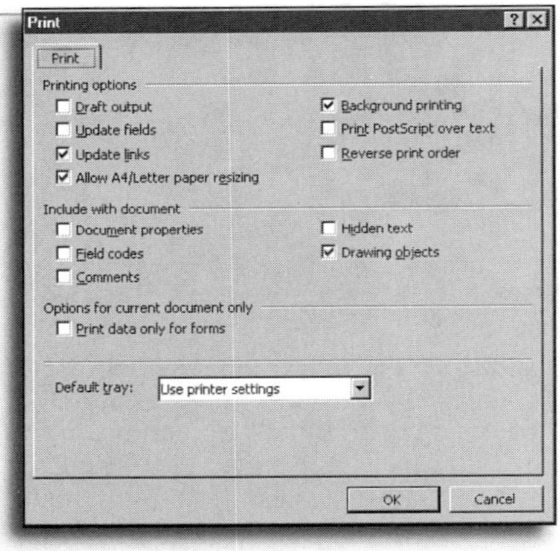

FIGURE 19.5
To have your linked files update automatically when you print, select **Update Links**.

If you would rather update the linked object manually, open the **Edit** menu and choose **Links** (see Figure 19.6). Select the object you want to update manually (hold down Ctrl and click on each object to select more than one). Click **Manual** and then choose **OK**.

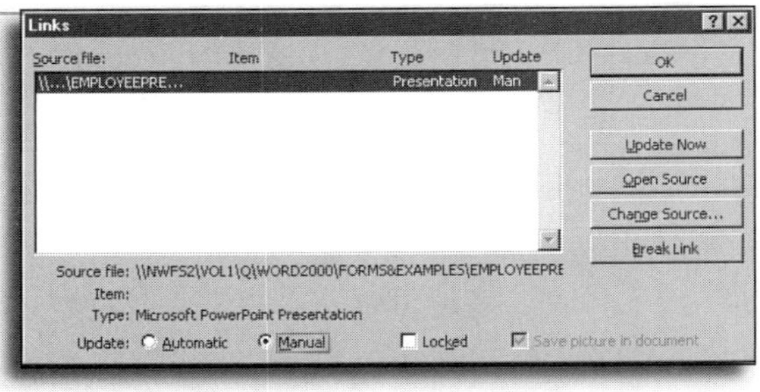

FIGURE 19.6
To switch to manual updating of your links, click **Manual**.

To manually update the linked object, open the **Edit** menu and choose **Links**. Select the object you want to update manually and choose **Update Now**. Choose **OK** to close the dialog box. Alternatively, select the object in your document and then press F9. You are not prompted by Word to update the link if you turned off automatic linking, so you have to be careful to update the object in Word every time you modify the source file.

To prevent a linked object from being updated, open the Links dialog box and click **Locked** to place a check mark there. Choose **OK**.

**SEE ALSO**

➤ *For more information on inserting pictures, see page 367*

## Embed an Existing Object

When you embed data in a Word document, you insert a *copy* of the original data object, and Word does not maintain a link to the original. If someone changes the original copy of the data, that change is not reflected in the copy embedded in your document. If you have the program with which the embedded data object was originally created, you can double-click the data object to open it in that program and edit it. But you are editing your copy only, not the original data.

Embedding data has its benefits. First, you can change the embedded data without affecting the original. Second, you don't have to maintain any link to the original data file.

You can see the embedded data in your Word file whether or not you have access to the program that created it. But you must have access to the program that created the data if you want to edit it.

### Embed an Entire File in a Word Document

1. Position your insertion point in the document where you want the embedded object to appear.
2. Open the **Insert** menu and choose **Object**.
3. When the Object dialog box appears, click the **Create from File** tab (see Figure 19.7).

---

**Caution: Don't move linked files**

Word cannot update a linked object if the source file is moved or renamed. If you move or rename a linked object's source, open the Links dialog box, select the linked object, and choose **Change Source**. Enter the name of the file to which you want to reconnect in the **File Name** box and choose **Open** to return to the Links dialog box. Then choose **OK**.

FIGURE 19.7

To embed an existing file, open the Object dialog box and deselect **Link to File** after you enter the filename.

4. Type the name of file you want to insert in the **File Name** box, or choose **Browse** to select the file from a list.

5. Deselect **Link to File**.

6. (Optional) If you want to display the object as an icon (useful for online documents), click **Display as Icon** to place a check mark there.

7. Choose **OK**. Figure 19.8 shows an embedded object, which is a Microsoft Excel workbook. The entire file is contained within the Word document, so when you double-click the object to edit it, you can change the worksheet being displayed.

FIGURE 19.8

When you double-click an embedded Excel workbook, you can display different worksheets in that file by clicking the sheet tabs.

① Excel Sheet tabs

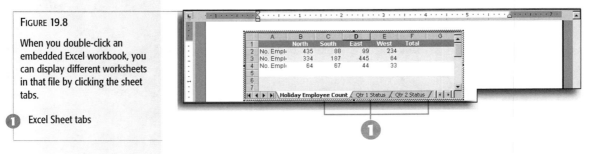

### Embed Part of a File in a Word Document

1. Open the file that contains the data that you want to link to in Word. Select the data and copy it into the Clipboard.

2. Position your insertion point in the Word document where you want the linked object to appear. Open the **Edit** menu and choose **Paste Special** to open the Paste Special dialog box.

3. In the dialog box, choose a data format.

4. (Optional) If you want to display the linked object as an icon (useful for online documents), click **Display as Icon** to place a check mark there.

6. Choose **OK**.

You update the embedded object by double-clicking it and making the changes directly from Word. Many of the toolbar and menu selections from the source program are available when you are editing an embedded object. However, any changes made to the source file aren't reflected in the embedded object, and modifications you make to the embedded object from Word do not appear in the source file.

## Create and Embed a New Object

It's also possible to embed a blank embedded object, such as a blank Excel worksheet, into a Word document. You might want to do this if you intend to create the embedded object on the spot. For example, you may want to embed sales figures that are not yet part of an Excel worksheet. You might prefer to enter the sales figures into a worksheet rather than directly into your Word document, because then you can use Excel's features to calculate the totals and format the numbers.

In another example, you might want to create an expense report form in Word. You might want to embed an Excel expense worksheet in the form where users would enter their numeric expense data, so that the form would total up the data automatically. If such an Excel worksheet did not exist yet, you could embed a blank Excel worksheet object in your form and create the expense worksheet on the spot. The interesting aspect of this is that the Excel worksheet object would exist *only* in your Word document; there would be no copy of it in any Excel file.

### Embed a New, Blank Object into a Word Document

1. Place your insertion point in the document where you want the object to appear.

2. Open the **Insert** menu and choose **Object**.

**Drag-and-drop embedding**

You can also embed an object by dragging the object to be linked from the source file to the target Word file. Because you must select the object before dragging, you don't have to embed the entire object when you use drag-and-drop. The **Display as Icon** option is not applied when using this method.

**3.** When the Insert dialog box appears, click the **Create New** tab (see Figure 19.9).

FIGURE 19.9

Select the type of object you want to insert in your document and choose **OK**.

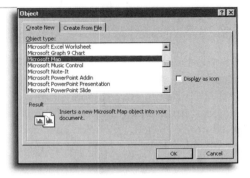

**4.** From the **Object Type** box, select the type of object you want to create.

**5.** (Optional) If you want to display the object as an icon (useful for online documents), click **Display as Icon** to place a check mark there.

**6.** Choose **OK**. A blank embedded object appears in your document (see Figure 19.10). Double-click the object to enter data.

FIGURE 19.10

When editing an embedded object, such as with Microsoft Map, you have access to the tools and menu commands from the source program.

**Embedding a blank Excel worksheet does not embed the Excel program!**

Users who double-click an embedded blank Excel worksheet must have Excel installed on their PC in order to open the worksheet, even though it is blank. This is true of any source application for any embedded object.

To enter data into an embedded object, double-click it. When you finish adding data to the embedded object, click outside the border around the object to return to document editing.

# Work with External Files

Linking and embedding aren't the only ways to bring data or text in from files created by applications other than Word. You can insert an entire file into Word. You also have the option of exporting Word files to other applications.

## Insert Files into Word Documents

Inserting is a good alternative if you need to put an entire file into a Word document. That way you don't need to open the file to get at its contents. Open the **Insert** menu and choose **File** to open the Insert File dialog box, which is a standard file browser dialog box. Locate and select the file you want to insert and choose **OK**.

If the file you insert is not a Word file and is textual in nature (as opposed to graphics or sound), Word uses its file conversion filters to convert the contents to Word format. For a file that is not textual, you should not try to insert it as a file but rather as a picture or an object. (To insert a picture choose the **Insert** menu and select **Picture**. To insert an object, choose the **Insert** menu and select **Object**.)

If Word cannot convert the file, consider re-running the Office or Word Setup program to see if you can install a *filter* for the file type in question. Alternatively, just open the program and copy the contents to the Clipboard, then paste it into your document.

SEE ALSO

➤ *To insert pictures into Word documents, see page 367*

## Import and Export Files to and from Word

You can easily import files into Word or export files from Word. Importing and exporting converts files to and from Word format. When you import a file, Word automatically converts it to Word format if it can. To export a file, you save it in Word by choosing the **File** menu and selecting **Save As**, but choose another file format in the **Save as Type** field before you choose

**Save**. Word then automatically converts the file to the chosen file format.

When you open a non-Word data file in Word, it detects the file format of the file, converts the file to Word format, and then opens it. All you have to do differently from opening a Word file is choose **All Files (\*.\*)** in the **Files of Type** field of the Open dialog box, then choose the foreign file. Alternatively, if you know the filename, just type it in and choose **Open**.

Occasionally Word might not be able to convert the type of file you want to open. If not, consider re-running the Office or Word Setup program to see if you can install a *filter* for the file type in question. Or you could just open the program in which the file was created and try saving it in a file format that Word can recognize. (To save go to the **File** menu and select **Save As**.) Then try opening the file again in Word.

The following list displays file formats that Word can open to or save to (see Table 19.1). This is not a complete list of file formats, but rather those that are most popular.

**For a complete list of Word file conversion formats**

Search the Help Index for "file" and open the document called "File Format Converters Supplied with Microsoft Word." If you need a converter not supplied with Word, contact the source application manufacturer or search the Microsoft Web site at www.microsoft.com.

**TABLE 19.1   File formats recognized by Word**

| Program or File Format | Versions | Open | Save |
|---|---|---|---|
| HTML (Web pages) | Up to 2.0 | X | X |
| WordPerfect for DOS | 5.x and 6.0 | X | not 6.0 |
| WordPerfect for Windows | 5.x and 6.x | X | not 6.x |
| Excel | 2.x through 97 | X | |
| Word for Windows | 2.x | X | X |
| Word for Windows | 6.0/95 | X | In binary format |
| Word for Windows | 97 (no conversion necessary) | | |
| Word for Macintosh | 4.x and 5.x | X | X |
| Works for Windows | 3.0 | X | X |
| Works for Windows 95 | 4.0 | X | X |
| Lotus 1-2-3 | 2.x, 3.x, 4.0 | X | |

Word can also open and save text-only files or rich-text format (RTF) files.

**SEE ALSO**
➤ *Open and save documents on page 128*
➤ *To save documents as HTML documents, see page 591*

# Integrate Excel Data

Word processing and spreadsheet programs are two of the most frequently used PC applications. Microsoft Office includes both Word and Excel and these two programs work closely together to enable you to exchange and import data.

## Import Excel Worksheets into a Table

There are several ways to insert Microsoft Excel worksheet data into a document. One way is to insert the worksheet as a linked object or embedded object. Another is to copy and paste a worksheet from Excel into Word.

### Import Excel Data As a Table

1. Open the Word document into which you want to insert the worksheet and the Microsoft Excel workbook that contains the data you want.

2. Switch to Excel and select the entire worksheet or a range of cells.

3. Open the **Edit** menu and choose **Copy**. Alternatively, click the Copy icon 🖻 on the Standard toolbar.

4. Switch to the Word document and position your insertion point where you want the Excel data to appear.

5. Open the **Edit** menu and choose **Paste Cells**.

The worksheet appears as a table in your document. You edit it as a table and format it as a table. However, any formulas or calculations (such as sums) that were part of the worksheet are not available in Word. It has been converted to text.

To be able to modify figures and have automatic calculations occur, you should either link or embed the worksheet data. A *linked* worksheet appears in your document, but its data is stored in the original Microsoft Excel workbook. Word automatically updates the worksheet in your document when changes are made to the Excel worksheet. If you want to edit the worksheet data when you are in Word, select the object, click the **Edit** menu, and select **Links**, select the name of the workbook, and choose **Open Source** to open Microsoft Excel with the workbook open.

### Insert a Linked Excel Worksheet

1. Open the Word document into which you want to insert the worksheet and the Microsoft Excel workbook that contains the data you want.

2. Switch to Excel and select the entire worksheet or a range of cells. If you have not yet saved the worksheet, save it now. You cannot link to an unsaved worksheet.

3. Open the **Edit** menu and choose **Copy**. Alternatively, click the Copy icon 📇 on the Standard toolbar.

4. Switch to the Word document and position your insertion point where you want the Excel data to appear.

5. Open the **Edit** menu and choose **Paste Special**. The Paste Special dialog box appears (see Figure 19.11).

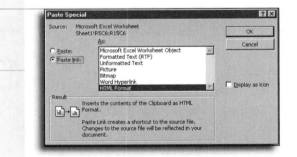

FIGURE 19.11

Choose **Paste Link** from the Paste Special dialog box.

6. Select **Paste Link**.

7. From the **As** box, select **Microsoft Excel Worksheet Object**.

8. Choose **OK**. The worksheet appears in the document and looks like a table.

When the Excel workbook is modified, Word updates your table automatically.

An *embedded* worksheet is an actual worksheet stored in your Word document. When you want to edit an embedded object, you double-click it. The toolbars and commands from Microsoft Excel temporarily replace the Word toolbars and commands so you can make your changes and return to your Word document. Or, right-click the object and select **Worksheet Object**, **Open** from the shortcut menu, which opens the source file in Microsoft Excel where you can edit the data.

### Embed an Excel Worksheet in a Word Document

1. Open the Word document where you want to embed the Excel worksheet.

2. Open the Microsoft Excel workbook that contains the data that you want to use to create an embedded object.

3. Select the entire Excel worksheet or a range of cells.

4. Still in Excel, open the **Edit** menu and choose **Copy**. Alternatively, click the Copy icon ![copy icon] on the Standard tool-bar.

5. Switch to your Word document and position your insertion point where you want the worksheet to appear.

6. Open the **Edit** menu and choose **Paste Special** to open the Paste Special dialog box (see Figure 19.12).

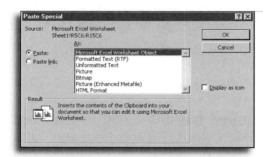

7. Select **Paste**.

8. In the **As** box, select **Microsoft Excel Worksheet Object**.

9. Choose **OK**.

Although the object appears as a table when you click off it, you cannot format it as a table. Any formatting and editing must be

**Where did all my data go?**

If the embedded worksheet looks blank after you entered data and saved your file, do one thing before you panic: Double-click the embedded object and check the bottom left of the worksheet area. You'll see some sheet tabs there. Excel allows you to have multiple worksheets, so make sure the correct sheet tab is selected. The other sheets may be blank.

**FIGURE 19.12**

Select **Paste** when you want to embed the worksheet.

**Quickly embed an entire worksheet**

An entire worksheet object can be quickly embedded. Open the **Insert** menu and select **Object**. Click the **Create from File** tab. In the **File Name** box, enter the name of the workbook from which you want to create the embedded object (choose **Browse** to select the filename). Deselect the **Link to File** option. Choose **OK**.

done using Excel's tools. Double-click the object to edit it. When you double-click it, an Excel window opens and Excel's tools are available for editing and formatting (see Figure 19.13). When you are ready to return to your document, click outside the border around the worksheet.

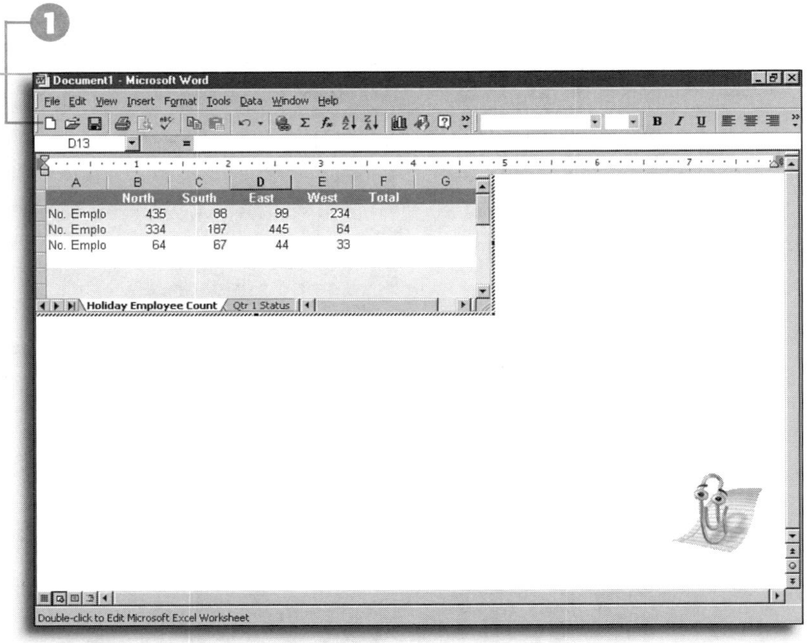

FIGURE 19.13

When you double-click an embedded Excel worksheet, the toolbars from Excel appear on your screen.

**1** Excel Toolbar appears here

**SEE ALSO**

➤ *To create Word tables, see page 165*

➤ *Master cut, copy, and paste on page 63*

## Embed a Blank Excel Worksheet

Although you can embed an existing worksheet, you can also start from scratch by embedding a new, blank worksheet in your document.

Starting with a blank embedded worksheet gives you the functionality of Microsoft Excel without having to create the worksheet in Excel, and then embed it in Word.

### Embed a New, Blank Excel Worksheet into a Word Document

  **1.** Position your insertion point in your Word document where you want to insert the object for a worksheet.

  **2.** Open the **Insert** menu and choose **Object**. Select the **Create New** tab (see Figure 19.14).

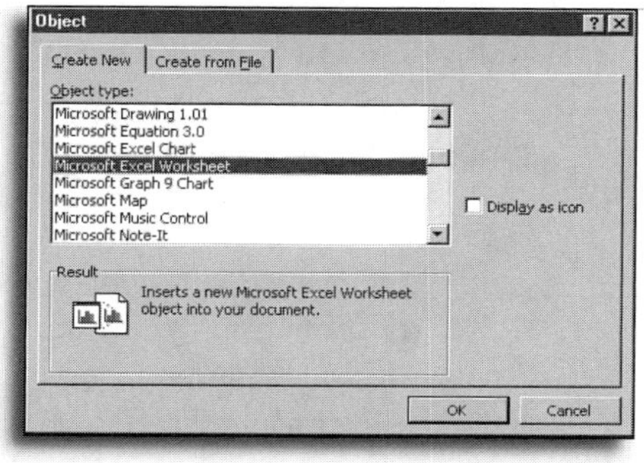

FIGURE 19.14

Select **Microsoft Excel Worksheet** to insert a worksheet object in your document.

  **3.** From the **Object Type** list, select **Microsoft Excel Worksheet**.

  **4.** Choose **OK** and begin creating the worksheet (choose **Microsoft Excel Help** from the **Help** menu for assistance if you're not familiar with Excel).

Another method for embedding a blank worksheet is to choose Insert Microsoft Excel Worksheet on the Standard toolbar. As with the Insert Table button, a drop-down area appears where you drag across the boxes to select the number of rows and columns you want in the worksheet. After you release the mouse button, the object is inserted at your insertion point. From that point it behaves as any other embedded worksheet.

## Import Excel Charts

Excel creates charts and graphs based on the data in a worksheet. Save yourself the effort of re-creating the chart in Word (using Microsoft Graph) by importing that chart into your Word document as an illustration for a report or proposal.

### Import an Excel Chart

1. Place your cursor at the position in your document where you want the chart to appear.

2. Open the Excel workbook that contains the chart, either as a separate sheet or part of a worksheet.

3. Select the chart by clicking on it.

4. From the **Edit** menu, select **Copy**. Alternatively, click the Copy button 🖺 on the Standard toolbar.

5. Open the Word document.

6. Do one of the following:

   • Open the **Edit** menu and select **Paste**, or click the Paste button 🖺 on the Standard toolbar. This embeds the chart in the document. Double-click the chart to edit it using Excel's menu and toolbar commands. Any changes to the embedded chart will not affect the original chart.

   • Open the **Edit** menu and select **Paste Special**. When the Paste Special dialog box appears (see Figure 19.15), select **Microsoft Excel Chart Object** from the **As** list. Select **Paste** and then choose **OK**. When you want to edit the chart, double-click it and use the Microsoft Excel features to make changes to the chart. Any modifications will not change the source chart.

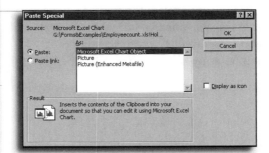

FIGURE 19.15

Select **Microsoft Excel Chart Object** to insert a chart in your document.

   • Open the **Edit** menu and select **Paste Special**. When the Paste Special dialog box appears (see Figure 19.15), select **Microsoft Excel Chart Object** from the **As** list. Select **Paste Link** and then choose **OK**. This choice inserts the chart into your document as a picture. You must edit the chart in the original Excel worksheet. Any changes to the original will be reflected in the chart in the document.

As with Excel worksheets, you can embed a new chart into your document that you create there but which has no links and does not affect any Excel worksheets.

### Embed a New, Blank Excel Chart into a Word Document

1. Position your insertion point in your Word document where you want to insert the object for a chart.

2. Open the **Insert** menu and choose **Object**. Select the **Create New** tab.

3. From the **Object Type** list, select **Microsoft Excel Chart**.

4. Choose **OK**. A sample chart appears on the **Chart** Sheet; edit the chart data on the **Sheet1** tab (choose **Microsoft Excel Help** from the **Help** menu for assistance if you're not familiar with Excel).

# Integrate PowerPoint Data

PowerPoint and Word information are interchangeable in many ways. You can, of course copy and paste text and graphics between the two programs. You can also

- Create a PowerPoint presentation from a Word outline
- Link a PowerPoint slide(s) or presentation into a Word document
- Embed a PowerPoint slide(s) or presentation into a Word document

## Create a Presentation from a Word Outline

With Microsoft PowerPoint installed on your computer, you can create a PowerPoint presentation from a Word document if you use heading styles in your Word document. When PowerPoint reads the Word document, it converts heading styles to outline levels in your presentation. For example, a Word Heading 1 style becomes the title of a new slide in PowerPoint. Heading 2 styles become the first level of text, and so forth. A good way to be sure that you have the appropriate heading styles where needed is to view the document in Outline view.

Figure 19.16 shows a Word document in Outline view that contains heading styles. Figure 19.17 shows the resulting PowerPoint slides created from the Word document.

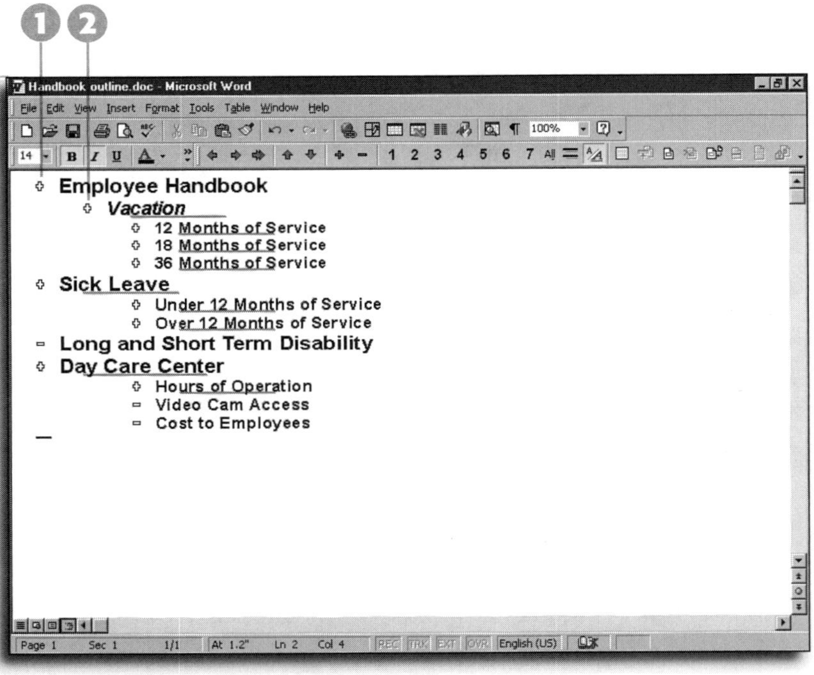

FIGURE 19.16

PowerPoint slides can be created from Word documents using heading styles.

**1** Heading 1 paragraph will become a slide title

**2** Heading 2 text becomes the slide bullet text

### Create a PowerPoint Presentation from a Word Document

1. Open the document in Word. Check to ensure your heading styles are correctly formatted.

2. Open the **File** menu and choose **Send To**, then select **Microsoft PowerPoint**.

3. The Microsoft PowerPoint program opens, displaying your Word document in outline form.

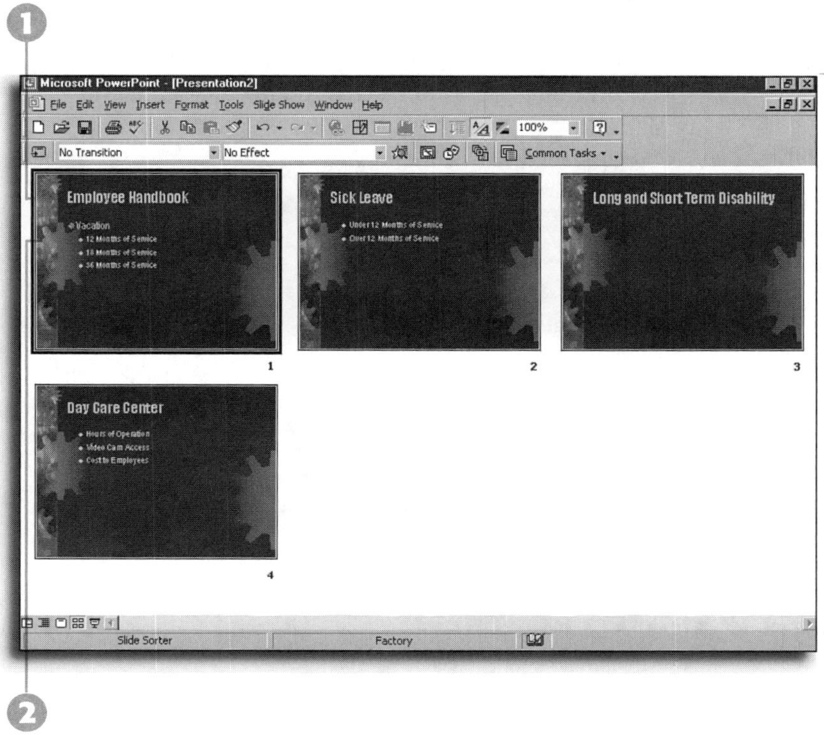

FIGURE 19.17

In the PowerPoint slide sorter you see the resulting slides, where the titles are the Heading 1 paragraphs from the Word document.

1 Slide title is the same as Heading 1 paragraph

2 Bullet text is the same as Heading 2 text

**SEE ALSO**

➤ *Learn how to work with heading styles on page 241*

➤ *Create Word outlines on page 310*

# Embed PowerPoint Slides

A single slide, several slides, or an entire PowerPoint presentation can be embedded into a Word document. When you embed multiple slides or an entire presentation, the first slide is displayed in the document. To view the other slides, double-click the first slide and the PowerPoint slideshow begins. Embedding part or all of a presentation file is useful when you're preparing an online document that others may share and use even if they don't have PowerPoint. It's also helpful if you have slides such as organization charts or graphs that you'd like to change from your Word document without changing the original presentation.

**Others must have PowerPoint to run the slideshow**

When you embed a PowerPoint presentation, others will be able to view a single slide; but if they don't have PowerPoint installed, they cannot see the slideshow when they double-click. You should consider packing the PowerPoint viewer with the presentation and emailing them to non-PowerPoint users so that they can view the slideshow even if they can't edit the file.

**Embed a PowerPoint Object into a Word Document**

1. Open the document in Word and the presentation in PowerPoint that you want to embed into the Word document.

2. Switch to PowerPoint Slide Sorter view.

3. Select and copy the slide or slides, or the entire presentation.

4. Switch to the Word document. Position your cursor where you want to insert the objects.

5. Open the **Edit** menu and choose **Paste Special**. If you are embedding a single slide, choose **Microsoft PowerPoint Slide Object** in the **As** box. If you are embedding multiple slides or the entire presentation, click **Microsoft PowerPoint Presentation Object** in the **As** box.

6. Select **Paste** and then choose **OK**.

## Link to PowerPoint Slides

To link PowerPoint slides to your Word document, save the PowerPoint presentation. Open both the Word document and the PowerPoint presentation you want to link.

**Link a PowerPoint Slide to a Word Document**

1. With both programs and files open, switch to PowerPoint Slide Sorter view.

2. Select and copy the slide(s) you want to link.

3. Switch to Word and open the **Edit** menu and select **Paste Special**.

4. Choose **Paste link**.

5. In the **As** box, click **Microsoft PowerPoint Slide Object**.

6. Choose **OK**.

**Link a PowerPoint Presentation to a Word Document**

1. Open Word and the document in which you want to place the link.

2. Open the **Insert** menu and choose **Object**.

3. Click the **Create from File** tab. In the **File Name** box, type the name of the PowerPoint file.

4. Click the **Link to File** check box.

5. Click **OK**.

Like an embedded object, Word displays the first slide in the document. Double-click the slide to view the entire slideshow.

# Integrate Access Data

To insert data from Microsoft Access into your Word document, you need to insert the contents of a table or a query. Use a query to filter, sort, and select specific fields so you get exactly the data you need to view in Word.

## Import a Database

### Insert the Contents of an Access Table or Query into a Document

1. Place your cursor at the location in the document where you want to insert the Access table or query contents.

2. Display the Database toolbar (right-click any toolbar and select **Database**) and then choose Insert Database 🖳.

3. Click **Get Data**.

4. To use Microsoft Access or Word to retrieve, filter, and sort the data, skip to step 5.

   To use Microsoft Query to retrieve, filter, and sort the data, click **MS Query**. Then construct your query. Skip to step 9.

5. From the **Files of Type** drop-down list, select **MS Access Databases**.

6. Enter the name of the Microsoft Access database you want in the **File Name** box or select the file. Then click **Open**.

7. Depending on whether you are working from a table or a query, click the **Tables** or **Queries** tab. Select the table or query you want and choose **OK**. The Database dialog box notes the name of the chosen file and table/query (see Figure 19.18).

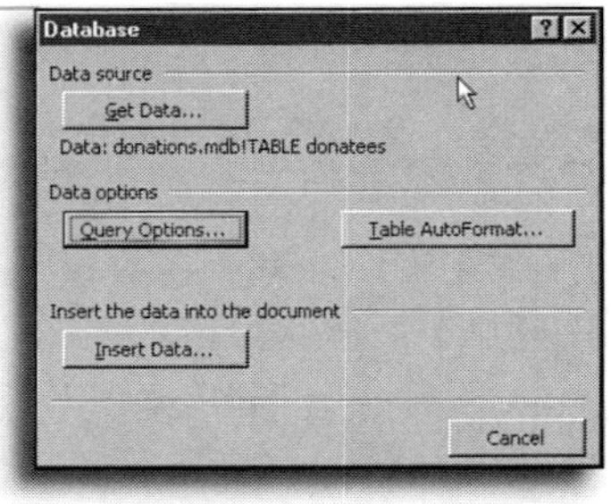

FIGURE 19.18

The name of the database file and the table or query selected appears under **Get Data**.

8. (Optional) Click **Query Options** if you want to choose a subset of the records or fields or both to include in the Word table.

9. Click **Table AutoFormat** to customize the Word table formatting. Select the appropriate options and then choose **OK**.

10. Choose **Insert Data**. The Insert Data dialog box appears (see Figure 19.19).

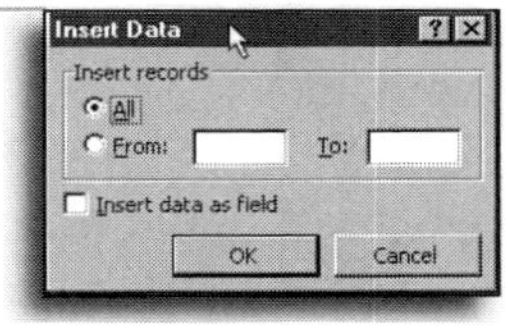

FIGURE 19.19

Enter the range of records you want to include in the document, unless you select **All**.

11. Under **Insert Records**, select the records to include in the Word table.

12. To be able to update the data in the Word table when the source data changes, select **Insert Data as Field**.

13. Choose **OK** to close the Insert Data dialog box.

14. The data appears in the document as a table. After you save the document, you can use it as the data source for a mail merging.

# Export a Database

### Export Access Data to a Word Document

1. Starting in Microsoft Access, open the database you want. Then open a database object—query, table, form, or report.

2. To export only part of the data, select the rows or columns you want.

3. Open the **File** menu and select **Export**.

4. From the **Save as Type** drop-down list, select a file format for the exported data (such as **Microsoft Word Merge**).

5. Enter a name for the new document in the **File Name** box.

6. Choose **Save**.

# Add Drawings and WordArt

Create drawings in Word documents

Edit and modify drawings

Add 3D and other special effects to drawing objects

Insert a WordArt object

# Know What You Need to Draw

In addition to inserting graphics and clip art to your Word document, Word provides tools to create your own drawings. Use these tools when you want to draw lines, boxes, flowcharts, and organization charts. By using Word tools, you don't need to switch to a graphics or drawing program and you can draw exactly the item you need.

Even if you aren't a whiz at drawing, Word's drawing tools allow you to combine basic shapes to create simple drawings. Plan out what you want to draw and visualize the basic shapes that make up the whole. Then use the drawing tools to create the final product.

For more complex drawings, you are probably better off using a more powerful drawing package such as CorelDRAW, Adobe Illustrator, or MacroMedia Freehand. Then import the drawing into your Word document. If you don't have one of these more powerful programs, then rely on clip art. Check the Microsoft Web site (www.microsoft.com) for additional pieces, if the Clip gallery doesn't have what you need.

**SEE ALSO**

➤ *To learn how to import pictures made by drawing programs, see page 367*

➤ *To learn how to insert clip art into your document, see page 364*

# Create a Drawing

Using Word drawing tools you can create simple shapes, lines, boxes, text boxes, ovals, and circles. To these shapes you can add text, shadows, and 3D effects. You can also rotate, flip, and resize objects (see Figure 20.1).

When you choose Drawing 🔳 on the Standard toolbar to display the Drawing toolbar, Word automatically switches to the Print Layout view. Print Layout or Web Layout view is necessary to work with drawn objects.

To create drawing objects—lines, arrows, rectangles, ovals, text boxes, 3D shapes—select the object or tool on the Drawing toolbar. Table 20.1 lists and briefly describes the buttons on the Drawing toolbar.

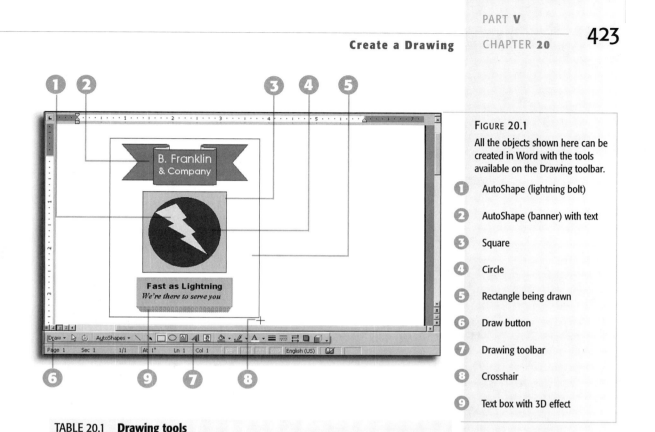

**FIGURE 20.1**

All the objects shown here can be created in Word with the tools available on the Drawing toolbar.

1. AutoShape (lightning bolt)
2. AutoShape (banner) with text
3. Square
4. Circle
5. Rectangle being drawn
6. Draw button
7. Drawing toolbar
8. Crosshair
9. Text box with 3D effect

**TABLE 20.1**   **Drawing tools**

| Button | Name | Description |
| --- | --- | --- |
| | Draw | Displays a menu of drawing commands |
| | Select Objects | Selects drawing objects |
| | Free Rotate | Rotates objects to any angle |
| | AutoShapes | Displays a pop-up menu of different shapes |
| | Line | Draws straight lines |
| | Arrow | Draws arrows |
| | Rectangle | Draws rectangles and squares |
| | Oval | Draws ovals and circles |
| | Text Box | Creates a box to place text anywhere on the page without putting it inside another shape |

*continues…*

**TABLE 20.1  Continued**

| Button | Name | Description |
|---|---|---|
| | Insert WordArt | Lets you create a WordArt object in your document |
| | Insert Clip Art | Lets you select a piece of clip art to insert in your document |
| | Fill Color | Applies fill colors or attributes to selected objects |
| | Line Color | Applies color or patterns to selected lines or outlines |
| | Font Color | Applies color to selected text |
| | Line Style | Applies a line thickness or style to a selected line or outline |
| | Dash Style | Applies a dashed line style to a selected line or outline |
| | Arrow Style | Applies an arrow style or direction to a selected line or arrow |
| | Shadow | Applies a shadow to a selected object |
| | 3D | Applies a three-dimensional (3D) setting to a selected object |

Each Word drawing object has attributes, many of which can be changed. For example, you can change the thickness or position of a line, or the color of a box. The procedures for changing object attributes are found throughout this chapter.

**SEE ALSO**

➤ *Learn to insert graphics and clip art on page 363*

## Draw Lines and Boxes

To draw a line or arrow, choose Line ▨ or Arrow ▨ on the Drawing toolbar, and position the mouse pointer (crosshair) where you want the line or arrow to start. Hold down the mouse button and drag to the end of the line or arrow, and then release the mouse button. Hold down the Shift key as you drag to make a straight horizontal or vertical line or arrow.

To draw a rectangle, choose Rectangle ▨ on the Drawing toolbar, position the mouse pointer (crosshair) where you want one corner of the rectangle to be, hold down the mouse button and drag diagonally to the opposite corner, and then release the mouse button.

To draw an oval, choose Oval ⬭ on the Drawing toolbar, position the mouse pointer (crosshair) where you would imagine one corner of a rectangle surrounding the oval to be, hold down the mouse button and drag diagonally to the opposite corner, and then release the mouse button.

### Add a Text Box

**1.** Choose Text Box ▣ on the Drawing toolbar.

**2.** Position the mouse pointer (crosshair) where you want one corner of the box to be, hold down the mouse button and drag diagonally to the opposite corner, and then release the mouse button.

**3.** After the box is drawn, enter your text by clicking inside of the text box and typing. Your text wraps within the margins of the box.

**4.** (Optional) Format the text using the formatting tools or menu commands.

Figure 20.1 displays some of these different objects drawn on a page.

**SEE ALSO**

➤ To format text, see page 74

## Select Shapes from a Menu

Word contains too many objects you can draw to display them on the Drawing toolbar. Additional shapes not displayed on the Drawing toolbar such as block arrows, flowchart items, stars, banners, hearts, smiley faces, and callouts can be found when you choose **A̲utoShapes** on the Drawing toolbar.

### Insert AutoShapes

**1.** Open the **A̲utoShapes** drop-down menu on the Drawing toolbar. Select the category of shape you want on the Drawing toolbar and click the shape. The following list describes the techniques for drawing items found on the **L̲ines** category.

---

**Draw the perfect circle or square**

Hold down the Shift key as you draw an oval or rectangle, and when you release the mouse button you will have the perfect circle or square. Hold down Ctrl as you draw an oval or rectangle from the center out. Hold down both Ctrl and Shift to draw a square or circle from the center out.

- For lines, arrows, and double arrows (arrowheads at both ends), click at the beginning of where you want the line to begin and drag to the point you want the line to end. Release the mouse button.

- For curves, click in your document to begin the curve, and click at each point you want the curve to bend. End the curve by double-clicking.

- For freeforms, click in your document to begin the freeform, and click at each corner to create a series of straight lines joined at sharp angles. Alternately, click to begin the freeform and drag to draw in any direction. Double-click to end the freeform.

- For scribbles, click in your document and drag in any direction you want to draw. Double-click to end the scribble.

2. For shapes not in the Lines category, position the mouse pointer (crosshair) where you want one corner of the box to be, hold down the mouse button and drag diagonally to the opposite corner, and then release the mouse button.

3. (Optional) To keep the AutoShape proportional, hold down the Shift key as you drag your mouse. To alter the perspective of a scribble, hold down the Ctrl key as you drag your mouse.

## Modify a Drawing

Before you modify, move, or size lines and objects, you must be able to select the lines or objects. A selected line or object displays *sizing handles* (small hollow boxes) at the line endpoints or on each side and corner of an object (see Figure 20.2).

To select a drawn object, do the following:

- To select a single line or object, click it.

- To select more than one line or object, click the first item you want to select, hold down the Shift key, and then click each additional item you want to select.

**Use the tear-out menu**

To make AutoShape selections quickly, float the AutoShapes menu by "tearing it out" of the Drawing toolbar. To do this, click the AutoShapes drop-down menu on the toolbar, grab the gray bar at the top of the AutoShapes drop-down menu, and drag it to your work area.

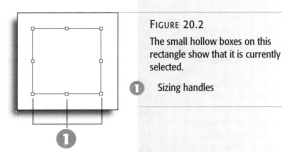

FIGURE 20.2

The small hollow boxes on this rectangle show that it is currently selected.

❶ Sizing handles

- To select a group of adjacent objects, choose Select Objects ▣ on the Drawing toolbar and drag a rectangle (selection box) around the items you want to select. When you release the mouse button, all items totally within the rectangle will have sizing handles and the selection box will disappear.

- If you want the selected objects to always act together as if they were one object, choose **Dr̲aw** on the Drawing toolbar and click **G̲roup** from the pop-up menu.

- If you accidentally select an item that you didn't want, hold down Shift and click the item to remove the sizing handles and deselect it.

**SEE ALSO**
➤ *To resize clip art and imported graphics, see page 369*

## Change the Size of Lines and Objects

It's not easy to draw an item the exact size you want it, but changing the size after you draw it isn't difficult.

### Change Line and Object Size

**1.** Select the item.

**2.** Point to one of the sizing handles and drag it in the appropriate direction (see Figure 20.3):

- Drag the handles at either end of a line or arrow in any direction to shorten or lengthen the line or change the position of the endpoint. To keep the line straight as you drag, hold down the Shift key.

- Drag the center top and bottom handles of an object toward or away from the center of the object to make it shorter or taller.

**Don't overlook the power of grouping objects**

Grouping objects can save you from formatting or moving objects individually. To group objects, select the objects and choose **Dr̲aw**, and then **G̲roup** from the Drawing toolbar. Once grouped, selected objects appear "as one" when you select them again. For more information on grouping items, see "Order, Align, Group, and Layer Objects" later in this chapter.

**FIGURE 20.3**

When you point to a sizing handle the mouse pointer changes to a two-headed arrow showing in which direction you can drag the handle.

**1** Two-headed arrow mouse pointer

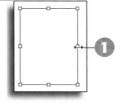

- Drag the center left and right handles of an object toward or away from the center of the object to make it narrower or wider.

- Drag the corner handles diagonally away or toward the center of the object to make it bigger or smaller. Dragging the corner handles in other directions changes the overall dimensions of the object. To keep the dimensions in the same proportions as the original, hold down the Shift key as you drag.

- AutoShapes have an additional handle (a small yellow diamond, shown in Figure 20.4). When you drag this handle it adjusts the shape.

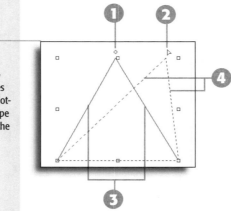

**FIGURE 20.4**

When you drag the yellow diamond on the triangle it changes the angle of the triangle. The dotted outline shows how the shape will appear when you release the mouse button.

**1** Yellow diamond

**2** Mouse pointer

**3** Original shape

**4** New shape

**3.** As you drag, you'll see a dotted line outline of the shape or line showing you how the item will look when you release the mouse button.

**4.** When the item is the size you want, release the mouse button.

If you add text to a shape, as explained in "Add Text to Shapes" later in this chapter, you may have to size the object again to accommodate the text.

To set the exact size of an item (height, width, length) in inches, double-click the item to open the Format AutoShape dialog box. Alternatively, right-click the object and click **Format Aut̲oShape** on the pop-up menu. Then select the **Size** tab, enter the dimensions you want in the **H̲eight** and **Wi̲dth** boxes, and then choose **OK** (see Figure 20.5). To keep the height and width in the same proportions when you size the item, check **Lock A̲spect Ratio** before you change the dimensions.

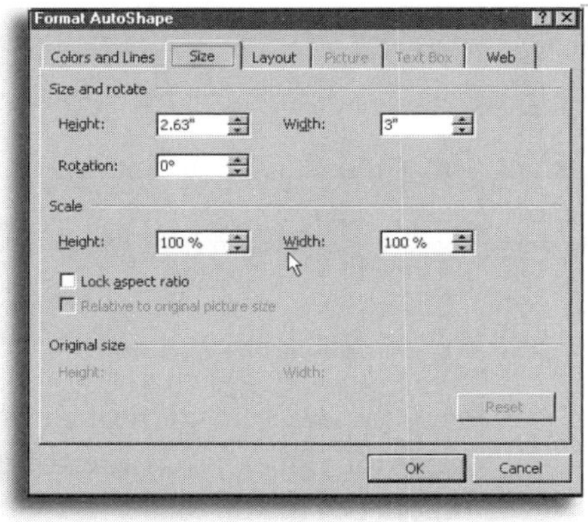

**FIGURE 20.5**
Enter the exact dimensions you want to apply to the object.

## Move Lines and Objects

### Move Lines and Objects within a Page

**1.** Select the line, arrow, or object.

**2.** Point in the middle of the line, arrow, or object (or on the outline of the object if it has no fill). Be sure to avoid the sizing handles. The mouse pointer becomes a four-headed arrow (see Figure 20.6).

**3.** Hold down the mouse button and drag the dotted-line duplicate of the item to its new location.

**4.** Release the mouse button when you have the dotted-line duplicate in the position where you want the item to go. The item appears in that spot.

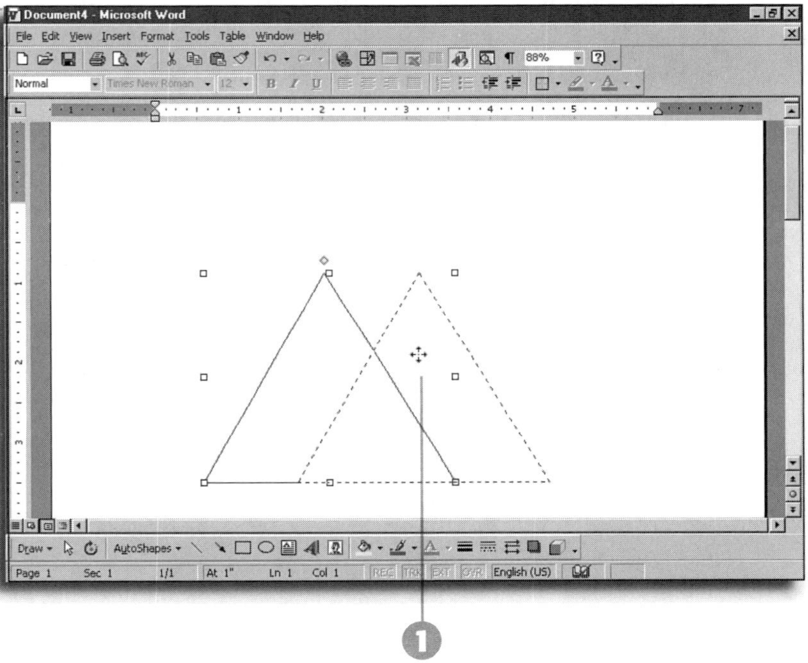

FIGURE 20.6

The mouse pointer becomes a four-headed arrow, which indicates you're ready to move the item.

❶ Four-headed arrow mouse pointer

❶

To set the exact position of an item on a page, specify the position of the upper-left corner of the object in the Format AutoShapes dialog box.

### Set the Exact Position of the Object on the Page

**1.** Double-click the object to open the Format AutoShape dialog box. Alternatively, right-click the object and click **Format Aut_o_Shape** on the pop-up menu.

**2.** When the Format AutoShape dialog box appears, select the **Layout** tab. Choose **_A_dvanced**.

**3.** Click the **Picture Position** tab (see Figure 20.7).

**4.** To set the horizontal position of the graphic on the page, there are three options:

- **Alignment**. This positions your object to the Left, Right, or Center **Relative To** a Column, Margin, Page, or Character. It is particularly useful in documents like newsletters, where you have columns of text.

- **Book Layout**. Use this when you have facing pages and you need to position the object Inside or Outside **Of** the Margin or Page.

- **Absolute Position**. This selection sets the exact position of the upper-left corner of the object in inches **To the Left Of** the Column, Margin, Page, or Character.

**5.** To set the vertical position of the object on the page, specify one of the following:

- **Alignment**. Positions the object at the Top, Bottom, Center, Inside, or Outside **Relative To** the Margin, Page, or Line.

- **Absolute Position**. Sets the exact position of the upper-left corner of the object in inches **Below** the Margin, Page, Paragraph, or Line.

**6.** Choose **OK** twice.

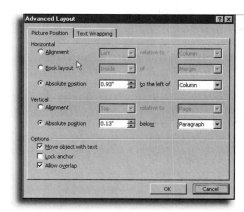

**FIGURE 20.7**
Enter the vertical and horizontal distances to precisely position the object on the page.

Dragging a line, arrow, or object to another page is not always practical, (although you can do it while viewing multiple pages at one time) so if you must move an item to another page, use the **Cut** and **Paste** commands. Right-click the object and choose **Cut** on the pop-up menu. Right-click to position your insertion point on the page where you want to put the item, and then choose **Paste** from the pop-up menu.

## Modify Line Attributes

Lines have characteristics such as thickness, style, dash, arrowheads, and color. Some of these attributes may also be applied to the outlines of rectangles, ovals, and shapes.

To apply a line attribute to a selected line, arrow, or shape outline, do one of the following:

- Choose Line Style 🔳 on the Drawing toolbar to select line thickness or style (double, thin-thick, thick-thin, and so on). Click **More Lines** on the **Line Style** palette to open the Format AutoShape dialog box (see Figure 20.8) to the **Colors and Lines** tab, which offers a greater selection of line style options:

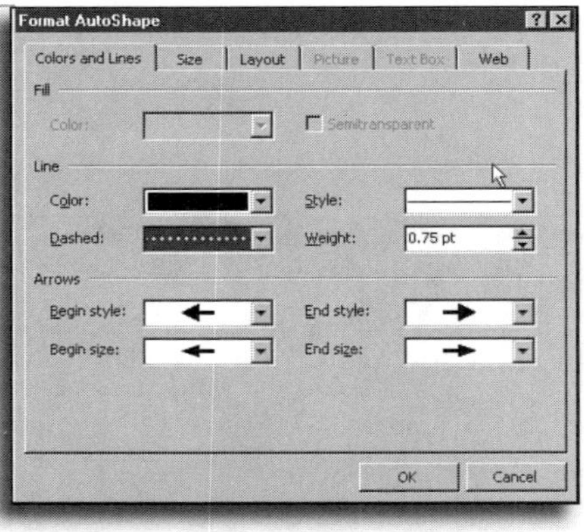

FIGURE 20.8

Double-click the object or right-click it and choose **Format AutoShape** to open the Format AutoShape dialog box.

- Choose Dash Style 🔳 on the Drawing toolbar to select a dashed or dotted line style.
- Choose Arrow Style 🔳 on the Drawing toolbar (not applicable to object outlines) to set the style and direction of arrowheads. Click **More Arrows** on the Arrow Style palette

to open the Format AutoShape dialog box, which offers a greater selection of arrowhead options (refer to Figure 20.8).

- Choose Line Color [icon] on the Drawing toolbar to apply the current color to the line, arrow, or outline. Click the down arrow next to the button to see a greater selection of colors. Click **No Line** to remove a shape's outline (if you choose this option with a line or arrow, the item becomes invisible, but it is still there). Click **Patterned Lines** to add dot, crosshatch, diagonal line, and other patterns to the line. Choose **More Line Colors** to see a greater selection of colors.

- Double-click the line, arrow, or outline to open the Format AutoShape dialog box (see Figure 20.8) that offers all the line attribute options and allows you to set the line thickness in 1/4-point increments. You can also open the Format AutoShape dialog box by right-clicking the line, arrow, or outline and then selecting **Format AutoShape** from the shortcut menu, or by opening the **Format** menu and selecting **AutoShape**.

## Modify Fill Attributes

Ovals, rectangles, and shapes have fill attributes. The available types of fills include the following:

- **No Fill**.  Leaves the item empty so you can see any text or objects behind it.

- **Solid Color**.  Fills the item with one color.

- **Pattern**.  Fills the item with a pattern (dots, crosshatch, diagonal lines, horizontal lines, vertical lines, and so on) in two colors—one for the pattern (Foreground) and one for the Background behind the pattern.

- **Gradient**.  The fill varies from light to dark shades of the same color (One-Color), from one color to another color (Two-Color), or in a preset pattern of many colors (Preset). You then pick the Shading Style to specify in what direction the gradient should display.

**Removing a line or outline**

Removing the line around an object, which is really the *outline*, is different from removing a line. When you remove the outline, you leave only the fill color of the item (a nice way to get a shaded shape). You select the item and choose **No Line** from the Line Color [icon] options. Applying **No Line** as the color of a line, however, does not remove the item from your page—only the color from the line. If you accidentally click the part of the page where the line is, you'll see the handles that show it's still there. To remove a line, you must delete it. Select the line and press the Delete key.

- **Texture**. Fills the item with texture graphics such as green marble or granite.

- **Pictures**. Fills the item with repeated copies of a picture you have on file (such as a logo or the Windows wallpaper graphics).

### Apply Fill Attributes to a Selected Object

**1.** Choose **Fill Color** 🖾 on the Drawing toolbar to apply the current fill color.

**2.** Click the down arrow next to the **Fill Color** to choose from a palette of colors. Click **No Fill** if you don't want the item to have a fill. Choose **More Fill Colors** if you want to see a larger selection of colors or you want the color to be semi-transparent, so you can see items or text behind it but still have a fill color in your item.

**3.** To choose a fill other than solid color, click the arrow next to the **Fill Color**, and then select **Fill Effects**. This opens the Fill Effects dialog box (see Figure 20.9).

In the Fill Effects dialog box, you can see how your choices will look before you click **OK**. In the lower-right corner of the dialog box is a **Sample** box that previews the fill you've chosen.

FIGURE 20.9

Select the tab for the type of fill you want to use and then select a fill or specify how you want the fill to appear.

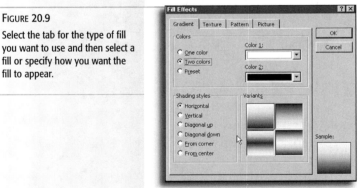

## Rotate, Flip, and Add Shadows

Many drawing objects can be rotated, flipped, or enhanced with shadows. Select the item you want to enhance and apply any of these effects:

- Free Rotate.  To rotate a selected object, choose Free Rotate
  [icon] on the Drawing toolbar, position the mouse pointer over
  one of the four rotating handles at the corners of the object,
  and drag in a circular motion until the object is at the
  desired angle.

- Rotate 90°.  To rotate a selected object 90° clockwise or
  counterclockwise, choose **Dr̲aw** on the Drawing toolbar,
  click **Rotate or Fli̲p** on the pop-up menu, and then select
  **Rotate R̲ight** or **Rotate L̲eft**.

- Flip.   To flip an object horizontally (so it looks like its mirror image) or vertically (so it's upside down), choose **Dr̲aw**
  on the Drawing toolbar, click **Rotate or Fli̲p** on the pop-up
  menu, and then select **Flip H̲orizontal** or **Flip V̲ertical**.

- Shadow.   Apply a shadow to a selected object by choosing
  **Shadow** on the Drawing toolbar and selecting the style of
  shadow you want from the pop-up palette. To adjust the
  position of the shadow, choose **S̲hadow Settings** from the
  pop-up palette to make the Shadow Settings toolbar appear
  and use the nudge buttons on the toolbar to move the
  shadow. Click the down arrow next to the **Shadow Color**
  button on that toolbar to pick a color for the shadow.

Shadow On/Off [icon] adds or removes the shadow from the item.

Nudge Shadow Up [icon] moves the shadow up (in relation to the
item) by small increments.

Nudge Shadow Down [icon] moves the shadow down by small
increments.

Nudge Shadow Left [icon] moves the shadow to the left by small
increments.

Nudge Shadow Right [icon] moves the shadow to the right by
small increments.

Shadow Color [icon] lets you change the color of the shadow by
picking one from the selection provided (choose More Colors to
see a larger selection), or allows you to make the shadow color
semitransparent.

# Order, Align, Group, and Layer Objects

As you add objects to your drawing, they appear on top of the ones you drew first and sometimes they cover up the objects you want to appear on top. For example, you may draw a circle and then draw a bigger circle around it, but you won't be able to see the small circle because it's covered up—send the bigger circle to the back. To address this problem, change the order of an object in the stack.

### Change Object Order

1. Select the object you want to reposition.

2. Choose **Dra̲w** on the Drawing toolbar.

3. From the Draw menu, click **O̲rder**.

4. Pick an ordering command from the submenu:

   - **Bring to Fron̲t** puts the item on top of the stack.

   - **Send to Bac̲k** puts the item at the bottom of the stack.

   - **Bring F̲orward** brings the item up one layer in the stack.

   - **Send B̲ackward** sends the item down one layer in the stack.

   - **Bring in F̲ront of Text** puts the item in front of the document text.

   - **Send Be̲hind Text** puts the item behind the document text.

To line up two or more selected objects or space them evenly apart, choose **Dra̲w** on the Drawing toolbar, click **A̲lign or Distribute** on the pop-up menu, and then select one of the alignment or distribution options such as **Align C̲enter**, **Align T̲op**, **Distribute H̲orizontally**, and so on.

Items can be grouped, or viewed by Word as a single item. This is particularly useful if your drawing is made up of many components and you want to move those components. By grouping them first, you can then select and move one item, instead of many. You can have as many groups in your drawing as you like and you can ungroup items at any time. To create a group, hold down the Shift key while you select the items to be grouped and from the **Draw** menu, select **Group**. To break the grouping back into individual components, select the item and choose **Ungroup** from the Draw menu. To create a group from the same items again without having to select each item, select one of the items and choose **Regroup** from the **Draw** menu.

## Add Text to Shapes

Instead of creating text boxes for diagrams, you can add text in any of the Word drawing shapes (except arrows, lines and freeforms). To add text, right-click the object and then click **Add Text** on the pop-up menu. An insertion point appears in the shape; enter your text.

If the object already has text and you want to change it, right-click the object and choose **Edit Text** from the pop-up menu.

Once the text is inside the shape, you can select the text and format it.

## Edit Curves, Freeforms, and Scribbles

Creating the exact curve, freeform, or scribble you want, at the time you draw it, is difficult. It's likely you will have to edit these shapes to refine them.

### Edit Curves, Freeforms, or Scribbles

1. Select the curve, freeform, or scribble you want to modify.
2. On the Drawing toolbar, choose **Draw**.
3. From the menu that pops up, click **Edit Points**. A small black dot appears at each point the line bends or changes angles (see Figure 20.10). These black dots are *points*.

**Ungrouping clip art**

Some of the pictures in the Clip Art Gallery can be ungrouped, which allows you to remove unwanted parts of the picture or select and change colors of specific items (like the hair or clothing colors). After you insert the picture, select it and then click **Draw**. If the **Ungroup** command is available, then you can do it. Be careful—you may delete too much or have difficulty regrouping the pieces back into one picture (you'll find out quickly if you move the pieces and find one left behind).

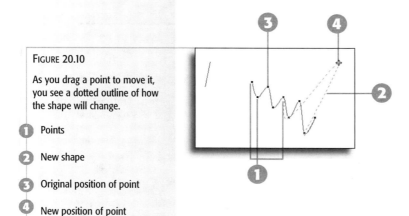

FIGURE 20.10

As you drag a point to move it, you see a dotted outline of how the shape will change.

**1** Points

**2** New shape

**3** Original position of point

**4** New position of point

**4.** To move the point, place your mouse pointer over it, hold down the left mouse button, and drag the point to another location.

To delete a point, place your mouse pointer over it, hold down Ctrl, and click.

To add a point, place your mouse over the curve, freeform, or scribble where you want the new point to appear, hold down Ctrl, and then click.

**5.** When you are finished editing points, click somewhere off the curve, freeform, or scribble.

# Use 3D Shapes and Effects

To give your lines and shapes a three-dimensional look, add 3D effects to them.

### Create a 3D Object

**1.** Draw or select the item you want to make three-dimensional.

**2.** Choose the **3-D** button ▥ on the Drawing toolbar.

**3.** Select the 3D style you want from the pop-up palette (see Figure 20.11).

When you want to adjust the 3D effect, choose 3-D  on the Drawing toolbar and select **3-D Settings** to display the 3D Settings toolbar (see Figure 20.11). Use the buttons on this toolbar to tilt the object, change the depth of the 3D effect, change the direction of the 3D effect, change the location of the light source, select a material finish, and choose a color for the 3D portion of the object. Table 20.2 describes the 3D Settings toolbar buttons.

TABLE 20.2   **3D Settings toolbar buttons**

| Button | Name | Description |
| --- | --- | --- |
| | 3D On/Off | Turns the 3D effect on or off. |
| | Tilt Down | Makes the top of the object look like it's tilting toward the viewer. |
| | Tilt Up | Makes the top of the object look like it's tilting away from the viewer. |
| | Tilt Left | Makes the left side of the object look like it's going away from the viewer as the right side comes closer. |
| | Tilt Right | Makes the right side of the object look like it's going away from the viewer as the left side comes closer. |
| | Depth | Makes the object look thicker. You select the depth (in number of points) from a list or enter a custom depth. |
| | Direction | Lets you select the direction you want the 3D effect to extend from the samples. Perspective makes the 3D effect extend toward a single point, while Parallel extends all sides of the 3D effect parallel to one another. |

*continues…*

TABLE 20.2    **Continued**

| Button | Name | Description |
|---|---|---|
| | Lighting | Sets which direction the light is coming from and where the shadows fall. Select **Bright**, **Normal**, or **Dim** for the brightness of the light. |
| | Surface | Lets you choose one of four surface options: **Wireframe** to see only the outlines of the object and the 3D effect without the surfaces being filled in, **Matte** to make the surfaces look unreflective or dull, **Plastic** to make the surfaces look like plastic, or **Metal** to make the surfaces look like polished metal. |
| | 3D Color | Lets you apply a color to the 3D effect (use **Fill Color** to color the object itself). Select from the colors displayed or click **More 3-D** colors to see a greater selection. |

**Apply 3D to several objects at one time**

To add the same 3D effects to several objects at one time, select the objects by holding down the Shift key while you click them, then click the 3D effect.

# Insert a WordArt Object

*WordArt* is a program packaged with Microsoft Word. WordArt allows you to add interest to your text with preset shapes. With WordArt objects, your text can be curved, twisted, and rotated.

Access WordArt while in Word by choosing **Insert WordArt** on the Drawing toolbar or by opening the **Insert** menu and selecting **Picture**, and then **WordArt**. The WordArt window appears at your insertion point.

### Insert a WordArt Object

1. Select the WordArt effect you want from the WordArt Gallery dialog box (see Figure 20.12). Choose **OK**.

2. When the Edit WordArt Text dialog box appears (see Figure 20.13), replace the "Your Text Here" in the **Text** box with your own text.

3. Choose a **Font** from the drop-down list and choose a **Size**. If you want bold or italic type, click the appropriate buttons.

4. The WordArt object appears in your document, with sizing handles around it to show it's still selected. Word also displays the WordArt toolbar (see Figure 20.14).

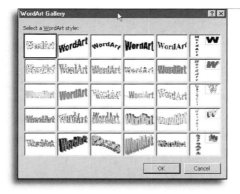

FIGURE 20.12
Select the WordArt effect you want to use.

FIGURE 20.13
Enter your text in the Edit WordArt Text dialog box.

FIGURE 20.14
The WordArt toolbar has the tools you need to modify the WordArt object.

Deselect the WordArt by clicking somewhere else in your document. The WordArt object can then be moved and sized like other graphics objects.

## Format WordArt Objects

Changing the appearance of the WordArt can be as simple as selecting a new look from the WordArt Gallery to making the individual changes manually until the new look suits you. Use the tools on the WordArt toolbar to help you set colors, rotation, letter heights, alignment, and character spacing. Open the Format WordArt dialog box to make more specific modifications. See Table 20.3 for a list of the WordArt toolbar buttons and what they do.

TABLE 20.3   **WordArt toolbar buttons**

| Button | Name | Description |
|---|---|---|
| | Insert WordArt | Inserts a new WordArt object in your document at the cursor position. |
| | Edit Text | Opens the Edit WordArt Text dialog box so you can change the text of your WordArt. |
| | WordArt Gallery | Opens the WordArt Gallery of predefined effects. |
| | Format WordArt | Opens the Format WordArt dialog box where you select fill colors, position, size, and text wrapping options. |
| | WordArt Shape | Displays a palette of preset shapes to apply to the WordArt object. |
| | Free Rotate | Enables the Free Rotate tool (drag a corner of the object to set it at a new angle). |
| | Text Wrapping | Displays choices for how you want the text to wrap around the WordArt object. |
| | WordArt Same Letter Heights | Changes the height of the lowercase letters to match that of the uppercase letters. |
| | WordArt Vertical Text | Gives the text a vertical orientation. |
| | WordArt Alignment | Offers a set of alignment options to align the WordArt text within the boundaries of the object. |
| | WordArt Character Spacing | Changes the spacing between the letters of the WordArt text (selections range from Very Tight to Very Loose). |

To edit the text of the WordArt object, double-click in the middle of the WordArt and the WordArt box appears, allowing you to change the text entry.

To modify the appearance of a WordArt object (change the shape, rotation, and so forth), click the object once to display the WordArt toolbar and use the toolbar to select appearance changes. Additionally, you can

- Use the sizing handles to change the height and width of the graphic.
- Use the yellow diamond handles to adjust the shape of the WordArt.
- Use the buttons on the WordArt toolbar to modify the WordArt (see Table 20.3).

# Add Impact with Charts

Create, embed, import, and link charts

Modify and edit charts

# Create a Chart

Charts and graphs, such as pie charts or column graphs, are valuable tools in illustrating data. Often, reports such as a business annual report contain charts illustrating data such as sales and profits. Word doesn't create charts, but uses a program called Microsoft Graph, which is packaged with Office and installed by default. There are several ways to include charts in a Word document:

- Create a chart while working in Word, using Microsoft Graph.

- Paste a chart from another application into a Word document.

- Import data or a chart from other programs (such as Microsoft Excel or Lotus 1-2-3) into a Microsoft Graph chart.

- Paste a chart or insert a chart file from another application into your Word document but link it back to the original file and application so the chart in your document updates when changes are made to the original.

- Embed a chart object from another application (such as a Microsoft Excel Chart) into your document.

**SEE ALSO**
➤ *Learn more about importing files on page 393*
➤ *Understand pasting and linking files on page 396*
➤ *To embed objects, see page 403*

## Create a Chart with Microsoft Graph

The following steps show you how to insert a chart using Microsoft Graph into your Word document.

### Create a Chart with Microsoft Graph

1. Place your insertion point where you want the chart to appear.

2. Open the **Insert** menu and select **Object**.

3. When the Object dialog box appears, click the **Create New** tab (see Figure 21.1).

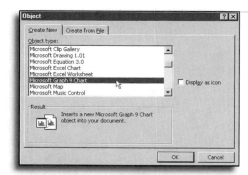

**FIGURE 21.1**

Select **Microsoft Graph 9 Chart** from the Object dialog box and click **OK**.

**4.** From the **Object Type** box, select **Microsoft Graph 9 Chart**.

**5.** Choose **OK**.

**6.** A column chart and a *Datasheet* window appear (see Figure 21.2). The Datasheet contains sample data that you replace to create your own graph. The chart is transformed automatically as you add your data and select formatting options, until it becomes the chart you want.

**7.** To replace the sample data, click in the cell in the Datasheet where you want to put new data and then type your own data there. Press Enter to accept the data and move down one row; press Tab to move one cell to the right and Shift+Tab to move one cell to the left (the arrow keys also help you navigate in the Datasheet). Choose **View Datasheet** on the Standard toolbar to close the Datasheet.

**SEE ALSO**

➤ *Learn how to work "in-place" on embedded objects on page 401*

### Understanding the Datasheet

Each number or *value* in the Datasheet is plotted as a data point on the chart, represented as points on a line, the top of columns, the end of bars, dots in a scatter chart, points in an area, or pie slice percentages. The data that appears in the rows of the Datasheet are called Series or *Series data*. Each row represents a line, a set of bars or columns of the same color, or an area on a chart. The words at the beginning of each row are the Legend labels. The *Legend* is the area on a chart that has a small symbol or color next to a label, so you can tell what series the lines or bars on the chart represent. The titles at the top of each column (the first row of the Datasheet) are the Categories. They appear on the chart as the labels for the *Category axis*, which is also called the X-axis.

FIGURE 21.2

The Datasheet contains the data that generates the graph. Note that the toolbars and menus change to include buttons and commands you'll need to work with charts.

**1** Chart

**2** View Datasheet button

**3** Chart Type button

**4** Datasheet

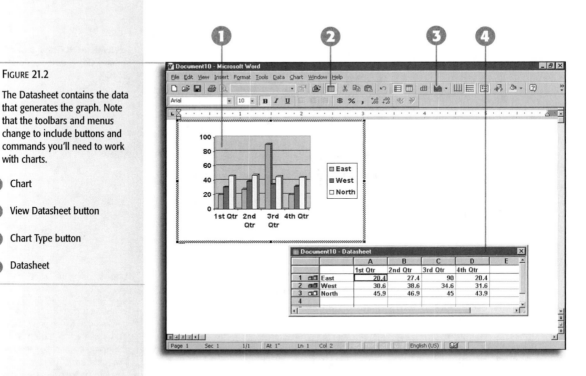

### Editing embedded objects

When you edit embedded objects, such as a Microsoft Graph Chart, the object appears in a box. Outside the box, you can still see your document. As long as you work in the box, the toolbars and menu commands change to those used in the application in which the object is created. When you click outside the box, the document becomes active and the tools and menus return to the Word toolbars and menu commands.

**8.** Click the down arrow next to the Chart Type button ![chart type icon] on the Standard toolbar to select a chart from the types shown. Then click the picture of the type of chart you want to create.

**9.** Click outside the border around the graph to return to the Word document (double-click on the chart to return to the Microsoft Graph 9 program).

The sample data that appears in the Datasheet when you start a new chart is always the same. It serves as an aid that helps you enter the data in the right places. Be sure to delete any of the sample data that remains after you've entered your own information.

# Create a Chart from a Table

Data that exists in a table (such as sales and profit data) can act as the data for your chart. If you have the data you need for a chart in a Word table, there's no need to enter the data again in the Datasheet. Instead, start the chart with the following steps.

### Create a Chart from a Table

1. Create the table in Word. Put text labels in the cells in the top row and in the left column. Put numbers in the other cells.

2. Select all the cells in the table (click in the table to put your insertion point there and then open the **Table** menu, choose **Selec̲t**, and then select **Ta̲ble** from the submenu), unless your table includes a row or column of totals. In that case, select all the cells except those total rows or columns.

3. Open the **I̲nsert** menu and select **O̲bject** and then select the **C̲reate New** tab in the Object dialog box.

4. Select **Microsoft Graph 9 Chart** from the **O̲bject Type** box.

5. Choose **OK**. The data from your table appears in the Datasheet.

6. Choose Chart Type ▨ on the Standard toolbar and then select a chart type.

7. Click outside the graph area to return to your Word document.

This is a quick method of entering data without having to type it in the Datasheet. It eliminates the step of replacing or deleting the sample text and your readers will see the original data in the document in the form of a table.

**SEE ALSO**

➤ *Learn how to create tables on page 165*

# Modify a Chart

Once a Microsoft Graph 9 chart is embedded in your document, double-click the middle of the chart to activate Microsoft Graph 9 and modify the chart.

**What type of chart?**

The Chart Type dialog box lists 14 types of charts. Which one should you use? Use pie charts to show the parts of a whole or percentages. Use column charts to compare values over time. Use line charts to show trends over time. Use XY charts to show demographic statistics or groupings of data. Use an area chart to show and compare trends. Access the Chart type dialog box from the Chart pull-down menu.

To help you in modifying the chart, tips pop up when you point to the various components of the chart. This helps you in identifying the item you want to change (see Figure 21.3).

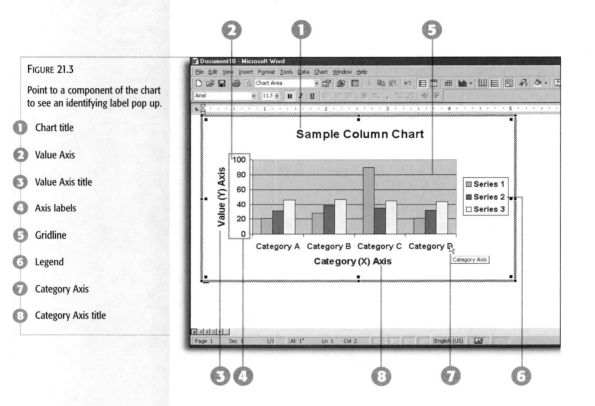

FIGURE 21.3

Point to a component of the chart to see an identifying label pop up.

1 Chart title

2 Value Axis

3 Value Axis title

4 Axis labels

5 Gridline

6 Legend

7 Category Axis

8 Category Axis title

You can modify the chart when you're in Microsoft Graph 9 in a number of ways, from changing the data to altering its appearance. The following list gives you some suggestions on how you can modify your chart:

- To edit the data, open the Datasheet by choosing View Datasheet on the Standard toolbar. Replace data by clicking in the cell and typing the new value or label. Press Enter or move the insertion point to the next cell to accept the change.

- To change the chart type, open the **Chart** menu and select **Chart Type** to open the Chart Type dialog box (see Figure 21.4). From the **Chart Type** list, select the type of chart you want. Then make a selection from the **Chart Sub-Type** options and choose **OK**.

FIGURE 21.4

When you select a chart type, a set of chart sub-types appears.

**Be careful how you click**

When you are trying to double-click on an item, be careful not to pause too long between clicks, and definitely don't click to select the item and then double-click it to change its attributes. A single click on an item selects all the items in a series (click on a red bar and all the red bars are selected). If you pause and then click on that item again, only that item is selected. The options you choose apply only to that one item. Watch the selection handles around the items that indicate if they're selected; if the series is already selected, click somewhere off the items first and then double-click one of the items in the series to open the dialog box.

- To change the color of bars, lines, or areas, double-click on the item to open the Format Data Series dialog box, as shown in Figure 21.5. For pie chart slices, click once on the pie and then double-click the slice you want to change to open the Format Data Point dialog box. Set the line style and color or the area color or pattern (click **Fill Effects**) by clicking on the appropriate options. Then choose **OK** to apply them to the chart.

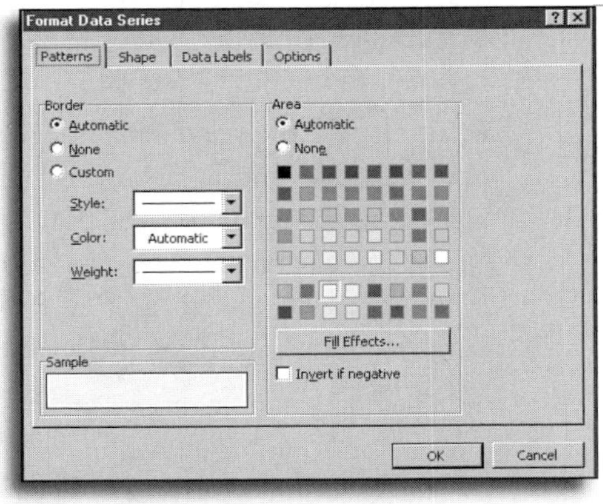

FIGURE 21.5

Select the line color, style, or thickness for line charts, or the area color for other charts.

- To change the number format (how the numbers appear) of the chart values, double-click the numbers on the *value axis* (Y-axis) to open the Format Axis dialog box and then select the **Number** tab (see Figure 21.6). Choose a number format (such as currency or percentage) from the **Category** box. The options vary with each category, so you may have to specify number of decimal places, symbols, appearance of negative numbers, use of a thousand separator, date and time formats, and so on. Choose **OK**.

- To set the interval between the numbers or specify the minimum or maximum values, double-click the numbers on the value axis (Y-axis) to open the Format Axis dialog box and then select the **Scale** tab (see Figure 21.7). Change the **Major Unit** number to specify the interval between numbers, which also sets the spacing between the *gridlines* (lines that act as a reference to help you evaluate data in relation to the axes). Enter values in the **Minimum** and **Maximum** boxes to change those values. Choose **OK**.

- To change the appearance or position of the legend, double-click the legend to open the Format Legend dialog box. On the **Patterns** tab, set the border style around the legend and the background color. On the **Font** tab, set the font of the legend text. On the **Placement** tab (see Figure 21.8), select the position for the legend in relation to the graph. Choose **OK**.

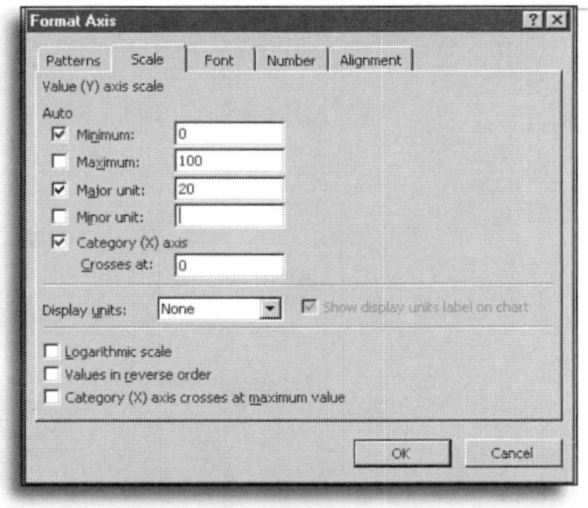

**FIGURE** 21.7

Specify the interval between numbers on the value axis by changing the **Major Unit** value.

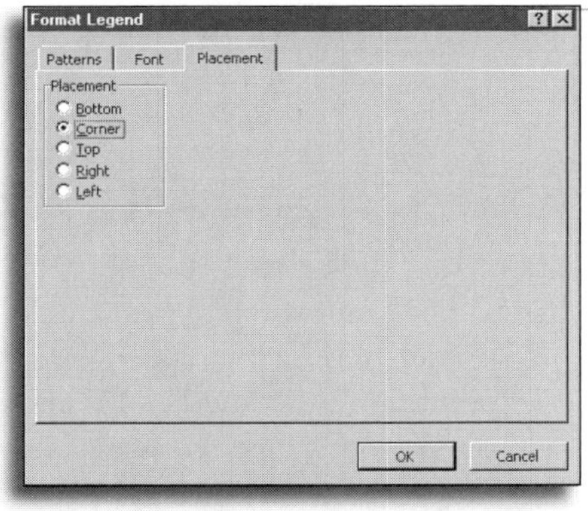

**FIGURE** 21.8

Select the position where the legend appears in relation to the graph.

■ To add titles to the value and category axes, click open the **Chart** menu and select **Chart Options** on the menu to open the Chart Options dialog box (see Figure 21.9). Select the **Titles** tab and enter the title text in the **Category (X) Axis** or **Value (Y) Axis** box. Click in the **Chart Title** box and enter a title for the entire chart. Click **OK**.

FIGURE 21.9

Enter the titles you want to appear next to the axes or for the chart as a whole.

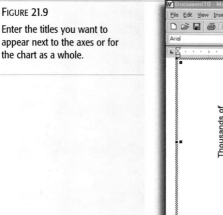

FIGURE 21.9

Enter the titles you want to appear next to the axes or for the chart as a whole.

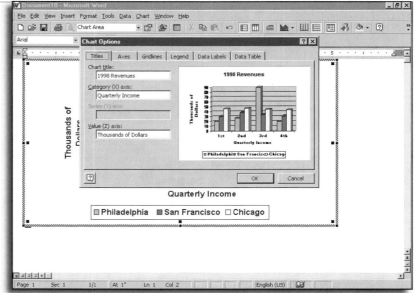

When you complete your modifications, click outside the graph border to return to your Word document. Move the graph by pointing in the middle of it and dragging it to a new position on the page. Change the size of the chart by selecting it and then dragging one of the handles (small hollow boxes surrounding the chart) toward or away from the center of the graph. After you click outside the graph, it acts like any graphic inserted into a word document.

**SEE ALSO**

➤  *To learn more about sizing and moving graphics, see page 367*

# Import Data into a Chart

Although you have the capability to enter data directly in the Datasheet to generate your chart, you don't want to enter figures that you already have stored in a file in another application. Microsoft Graph can import that data for you and then generate the chart, as long as the originating file is a delimited text file (separated by tab characters, commas, or spaces) or a spreadsheet file.

Microsoft Graph can import files that have the following file formats: .txt or .csv (delimited text files), .wks or .wk1 (Lotus 1-2-3 files), .xls (Microsoft Excel worksheet or workbook), .xlw (Microsoft Excel 4.0 workbook), .xlc (Microsoft Excel 4.0 or earlier chart), or .slk (SYLK, or symbolic link, files). If you have data in another type of file, check your application and see if it can save the file in one of the listed formats.

The imported data cannot have more than 4,000 rows or 4,000 columns. Microsoft Graph won't display more than 255 data series—and you wouldn't want it to.

### Import a File

1. Create a new graph.

2. When the Datasheet appears, click in the cell where you want the upper-left corner cell of your imported data to appear.

3. Open the **Edit** menu and select **Import File**, or click the Import File 🖼 on the toolbar. The Import File dialog box appears (see Figure 21.10).

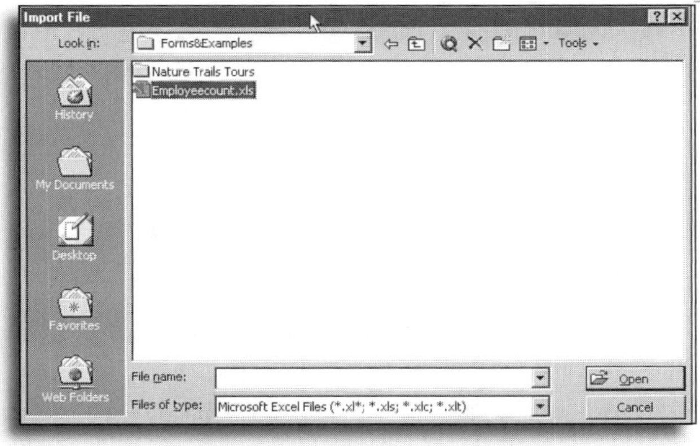

**FIGURE 21.10**
Select the file you want to import.

4. From the **Look In** drop-down list, select the drive and folder where the file you're importing is stored.

5. From the **Files of Type** drop-down list, select the file format of that file.

**Bring only the data you need**

When you're selecting the data to import, don't include blank rows, columns, or any columns or rows that have totals in them. If you do accidentally import a file with rows or columns you don't want included in the chart data, double-click the column or row header. The data turns gray. If necessary, delete rows or columns.

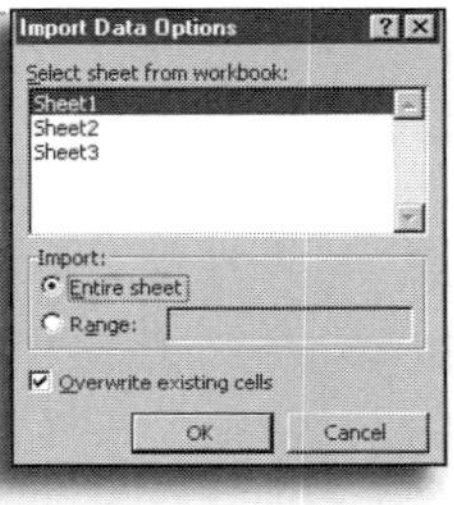

**6.** Select the file you want and choose **Open** or double-click the filename. If the file isn't listed, enter the name in the **File Name** box.

**7.** If the file you selected is a text file, the Text Import Wizard opens. Following the steps in the wizard, you specify how the imported data is currently organized and how you want it arranged in the Datasheet.

If the file you're importing is a spreadsheet, a dialog box appears (see Figure 21.11). Specify which sheet you want to use in the dialog box (if it's a Microsoft Excel worksheet). Specify whether you want to import the entire worksheet or a range (enter the range reference or the range name), and if you want to **Overwrite Existing Cells** to replace all the current data in the Datasheet. Choose **OK**.

FIGURE 21.11

When you import spreadsheet data it's useful to indicate which sheets you want to import (as shown), or to name the range in the **Range:** field.

Instead of using the **Import** command, it may be easier for you to copy the data and then paste it into the Datasheet. This gives you more control over which cells you copy.

**Copy Data into a Datasheet**

**1.** Open the program and document or worksheet where the data is stored.

**2.** Select the data.

**3.** Open the **Edit** menu and select **Copy**.

**4.** Switch to your Word document and double-click the Microsoft Graph chart.

**5.** Open the Datasheet if it's not already onscreen (choose View Datasheet on the Standard toolbar).

**6.** Click in the cell where you want the upper-left corner of the copied data to appear.

**7.** Open the **Edit** menu and select **Paste**.

To have the chart update automatically when the original data is modified, open the **Edit** menu and select **Paste Link** when you paste it into the Datasheet.

**SEE ALSO**
➤ *If you want more information on linking, see page 396*

## Paste a Chart

Charts created in other applications can be pasted into Word. By pasting charts, you can use the features many chart and graphing programs contain that are not a part of Microsoft Graph 9.

### Paste a Chart into a Word Document

**1.** Open the program and document or worksheet where the chart is stored.

**2.** Select the chart.

**3.** Open the **Edit** menu and select **Copy**.

**4.** Switch to your Word document and position your insertion point where you want the chart to appear.

**5.** Open the **Edit** menu and select **Paste** menu. The chart is inserted and can be moved or sized using the same method as you use for graphics.

If you want the chart to update automatically when the original data is modified, open the **Edit** menu and select **Paste Special**. When the Paste Special dialog box appears, click **Paste Link** and then choose **OK**.

**SEE ALSO**
➤ *To learn how to import Excel charts, see page 411*

## Embed a Chart

Another alternative for placing an existing chart in your document is to embed it.

**Embed a Chart**

1. Place your insertion point where you want the chart to appear in your document.

2. Open the **Insert** menu and select **Object**.

3. When the Object dialog box appears, select the **Create from File** tab.

4. Enter the name of the file in the **File Name** box or choose **Browse** to select the file.

5. Remove the check mark from **Link to File**. When you do this, Word embeds the file in the document.

6. Choose **OK**.

After the chart appears in your document, you can size and move it as you would any graphic. If you embedded the file, double-click in the middle of the chart to see the toolbars and menu commands of the source application so that you can modify the chart.

# Use Word at Work— Real World Solutions

# CHAPTER
# 22

# Create Office Documents Quickly and Efficiently

Create and send a fax using the Fax Wizard

Create a résumé with the Résumé Wizard

Create a newsletter with the Newsletter Wizard

Create a letterhead template

Create business cards

Create a memo

**How to use this chapter**

This chapter is designed as a refresher and provides step-by-step instructions for creating some popular specialized and customized documents in Word. Use this chapter when you need to create these documents quickly and you don't need the background and supporting information. The steps to create these types of documents are covered here.

# Choose Appropriate Formatting Options for Documents

You are about to create a document. Do you start with a blank document, or do you use one of the templates provided by Word? If you use a template, you'll save steps because a lot of the formatting is done for you. Don't be put off if there's not a specific template for the type of document you want to create. Find a template that has most of the types of formatting you need, and use that.

For example, suppose you want to prepare a product information sheet about a new product. The Brochure template sounds like that's the type of document you want, but it might not work for you—it's in landscape orientation and is set up to fold in three sections. However, you do need something with three columns. Why not use the Newsletter Wizard? You only need to use the first two pages for your product sheet, but you'll get column formatting, graphics placement, and title formatting. If that's what you need in your document, use the newsletter format to start you on your way.

What we are advising is that you shouldn't choose or overlook a template based on its name. Investigate the elements that are contained in Word templates—don't let Microsoft's naming labels get in your way. And speaking of labels—have you thought of using the Envelopes and Labels feature to create business cards? See the "Create Business Cards" section later in this chapter to do just that.

**Missing wizards?**

If you don't see the wizards mentioned here, more templates and wizards are available on the CD you used to install Word. Run the Setup program and choose **Add or Remove Features**. Under Microsoft Word for Windows, select **Wizards and Templates**, and then choose the templates you want to install. You can also download additional templates and wizards from the Microsoft Web site by opening the **Help** menu and choosing **Office on the Web**.

# Create and Send a Fax with the Fax Wizard

The Fax Wizard helps you send an electronic fax, merge several names to a fax, or print a cover sheet to send using a fax machine.

### Run the Fax Wizard

1. Open the document you want to fax (unless you're only sending a cover sheet with a note). Click the **File** menu and select **New**.

2. When the New dialog box opens select the **Letters & Faxes** tab.

3. Click the Fax Wizard icon to select it and then choose **OK**.

4. The Fax Wizard dialog box appears (see Figure 22.1). The left side of the dialog box has a progress chart.

FIGURE 22.1

Like the Fax Wizard, most Word Wizards have a progress chart on the left to show you where you are in the process of creating your document.

5. Choose **Next**. The Fax Wizard asks `Which document do you want to send?` The name of the document that is currently open automatically appears in the drop-down list box under **The Following Document** (see Figure 22.2).

6. To send the current document, click **The Following Document** and leave the name of the current document in the box.

   To send a short message, you can include the message on the cover sheet and send it alone. To do this, click **Just a Cover Sheet with a Note**.

7. If you are sending a document with your cover sheet, click **With a Cover Sheet** to send a cover sheet with the document you chose or **Click without a Cover Sheet** to send the document by itself.

8. Choose **Next**. The Fax Wizard asks you to identify the fax software you are going to use to send the fax. **Microsoft Fax** is one of the choices. If you have another fax program, click

Navigating wizards

Most wizards have four buttons you need to understand. **Next** accepts the information on the current screen and continues the process on the next screen of the wizard. **Back** takes you back to the previous screen of the wizard. **Cancel** stops the process and closes the wizard without saving your changes. **Finish** completes the process, accepts all your settings, closes the dialog box, and creates the document. There is also a Help button, in the form of a question mark (?), that you can click to get help about the screen you are currently viewing.

A **D**ifferent Fax Program Which is Installed on this System. Then select the name of your fax program from the drop-down list below **Which of the Following is Your Fax Program?** If you don't see your fax program listed, choose **O**ther and select the name of your fax software.

If you don't have fax software loaded on your system, click **I Want to P**rint **My Document so I Can Send it from a Separate Fax Machine**.

FIGURE 22.2

Select the document you want to fax (with or without cover sheet) or choose to only send a cover sheet.

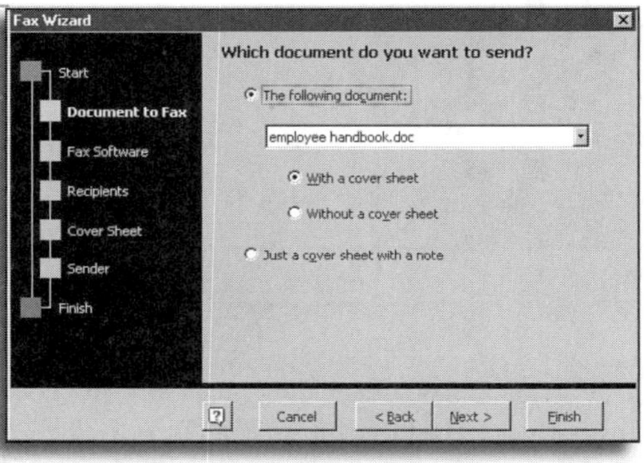

9. Choose **N**ext. The Fax Wizard asks you for the names of the recipients of your fax. If you have used the Fax Wizard before, the names of recent recipients appear in the drop-down boxes and you can click a name to select it as a recipient. Or, you can click in a box and enter a name and then the corresponding fax telephone number (exactly as they should be dialed, including numbers your system requires to reach an outside line). If you use Microsoft Outlook, choose **Address Book** and select a name from your address book.

10. Choose **N**ext. If you chose to create a cover sheet, the Fax Wizard lets you select one of the three styles of cover sheets it has available—**P**rofessional, **C**ontemporary, or **E**legant. Click the style you want to use.

11. Choose **N**ext. This screen asks who the fax is from. The Fax Wizard automatically pulls information from Word's User Information (click the **T**ools menu, select **O**ptions, and select the **User Information** tab to see what data is stored

about you, and make any necessary changes). Enter or replace the information in the **Name**, **Company**, **Mailing Address**, **Phone**, and **Fax** fields. Or, click **Address Book** and select information from your Outlook Address Book.

If you elected not to use a cover sheet, you won't see this screen.

12. Choose **Next**. The final screen of the wizard reminds you to add any prefixes to the phone numbers that you need to access an outside line.

13. Choose **Finish**. The fax cover sheet document opens. Several **Click Here and Type** fields appear (see Figure 22.3). Click once on a field to select it and then enter the required information. Delete any fields that you don't want to appear on your fax cover sheet, and modify any other text as necessary.

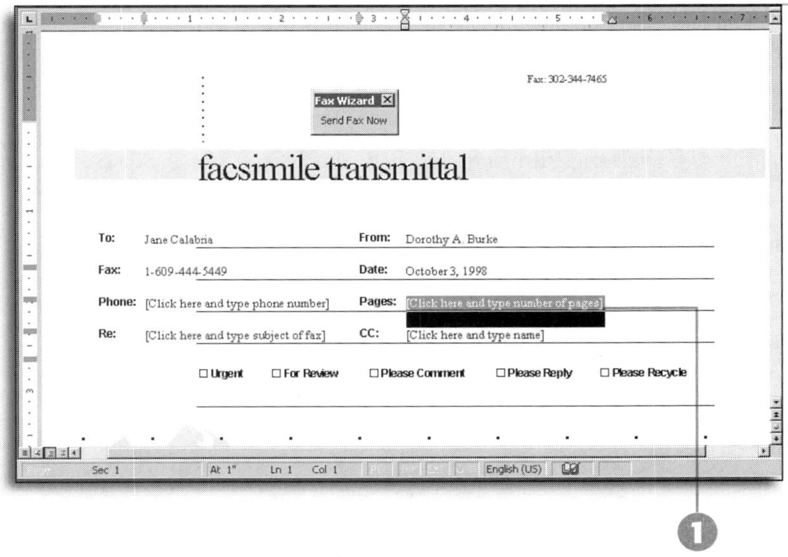

FIGURE 22.3

Click on a **Click Here and Type...** field and then type the appropriate information.

**1** Highlighted "Click here and type" field

14. Choose **Send Fax Now** on the Fax Wizard toolbar to send the fax.

If you chose to send only a cover sheet with a note, click the field where it says **Click Here and Type Any Comments** and type your note. Then choose **Send Fax Now**.

If you are printing the fax so you can send it on a separate fax machine, you won't see the Fax Wizard toolbar. For a fax addressed to a single recipient, just print the document. For a fax addressed to multiple recipients, choose Merge to Printer on the Mail Merge toolbar.

**SEE ALSO**

➤ *To use the Print command to fax a document, see page 277*

# Create a Résumé with the Résumé Wizard

Whether you're job hunting or you need a professional-looking employment biography to accompany business documents, the Résumé Wizard helps you prepare a neat, professional, and organized document.

### Create a Résumé Using the Résumé Wizard

1. Click the **File** menu and select **New**.

2. When the New dialog box appears, select the **Other Documents** tab.

3. Click the **Résumé Wizard** icon to select it and then choose **OK**. The Résumé Wizard dialog box appears.

4. Choose **Next**. The wizard offers you three styles of résumés—**Professional**, **Contemporary**, or **Elegant**. A preview of each style appears beneath the option. Click the style you want to use.

5. Choose **Next**. The Résumé Wizard lets you select the type of résumé you're preparing. Use **Entry-Level Résumé** if you're entering the job market or have limited experience, **Chronological Résumé** to list your experiences in chronological order, **Functional Résumé** to show your administrative-level experience in several areas, or **Professional Résumé** to highlight your education and accreditation.

**6.** Choose **Next**. On this screen enter your contact information in the **Name**, **Address**, **Phone**, **Fax**, and **Email** fields. Be sure to include area codes with the phone numbers.

**7.** Choose **Next**. The Résumé Wizard lists a series of headings that can appear on the résumé style you chose. Click the ones you want included on your résumé to check those boxes and remove the check marks from the headings you don't want to use.

**8.** Choose **Next**. Another set of heading choices appears. These can be included, but you probably won't use them unless they're relevant to the objective of the résumé. Click to check the headings you want to use.

**9.** Choose **Next**. The résumé headings you selected are listed on this screen. If you want to add another heading, type the heading in the text box and then choose **Add**. To set the order of appearance in your résumé, select a heading by clicking on it and then choose **Move Up** or **Move Down** to move the heading up or down in the list. To remove a heading from the list, select it and then choose **Remove**.

**10.** Choose **Next**. You've filled in all the information needed for the résumé, so choose **Finish**.

When the résumé document opens, it displays a series of fields marked in gray and enclosed by brackets ([ ]). Click those fields and enter the necessary information to complete the résumé document. Then you save and print the résumé as you would any document.

The Office Assistant may appear (see Figure 22.4), offering help options you might need in finishing your résumé:

- **Add a Cover Letter**. When you select this option, a sample letter appears that you can modify and save.

- **Change Visual Style of the Résumé**. This option returns you to the screen where you may choose a professional, contemporary, or elegant style to set the appearance of the résumé.

- **Shrink to Fit**. Choose this option if you need to squeeze your résumé on one page. Be aware that sometimes this option doesn't work because you have too much text to fit on one page.

- **Send Résumé to Someone**. When you select this option, Word asks if you want to **Email** or **Fax** the résumé. Click the appropriate choice and then choose **OK**. If you selected **Email**, Word sets up a mail message and attaches the résumé to it. If you chose to send the résumé by fax, the Fax Wizard opens (see the instructions on using the Fax Wizard earlier in this chapter).

Click one of those topics to get more help on your résumé, or **Get Help on Something Else** if you need help with something that's not related to a résumé or this Wizard, or click **Cancel** to close the Office Assistant.

FIGURE 22.4

The Office Assistant offers a list of helpful topics related to sending or improving the appearance of your résumé.

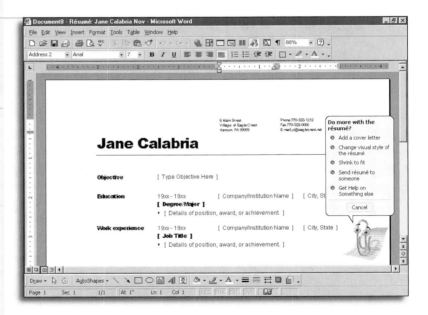

**SEE ALSO**

➤ *To email a document, see page 570*

➤ *Learn more about Word fields on page 531*

# Create a Newsletter with the Newsletter Wizard

Newsletter layout can be a daunting task. Word's Newsletter Wizard provides easy and attractive layout of your document. Run the wizard first, and write the articles (or paste the text) into the newsletter after you have finished with the wizard.

### Create a Newsletter with the Newsletter Wizard

1. Open the **File** menu and choose **New**.

2. When the New dialog box appears, select the **Publications** tab.

3. Click the **Newsletter Wizard** icon to select it and then choose **OK**.

4. The Newsletter Wizard dialog box appears. Choose **Next**. The Newsletter Wizard offers three general layout styles: **Professional**, **Contemporary**, or **Elegant**. Click one of the options to select it. Then click **Black and White** or **Color** to choose how the newsletter will appear.

5. Choose **Next**. Type the name of your newsletter in the text box. Click **Date** if you want to include the date by the title, and then enter the date in the text box. If you want volume and issue numbers, click **Volume and Issue** and enter the text in the box.

6. Choose **Next**. If you want to leave room on the back of the newsletter for a mailing label, click **Yes**; otherwise, click **No**.

7. Choose **Next**. The wizard is done collecting information. Choose **Finish**.

The newsletter appears, but the articles are instructions for using the newsletter template (see Figure 22.5). One of your first steps should be to print the sample newsletter so that you can read and refer to the articles. The articles include information on the styles used in the newsletter and to what paragraphs you should apply them, about column formatting, text boxes, and linking text boxes to continue articles on another page, and inserting and editing pictures. There are also suggestions for customizing the template by adding footers, symbols to mark the end of articles, and page borders.

FIGURE 22.5

The newsletter document created by the wizard contains instructions for creating your own newsletter.

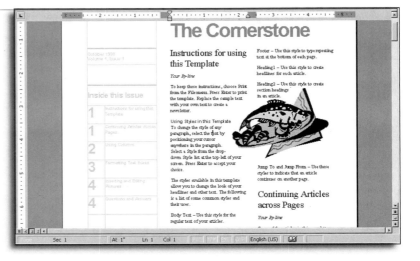

**Linked text boxes**

Linked text boxes are a way to begin an article on one page and then finish it on another page, which is not necessarily the next page. Create the text boxes you want to use for the article, select the first box and then click it using the right mouse button. On the pop-up menu, click **Create Text Box Link**. Then click the text box where you want the remainder of the text to flow.

Next you need to replace the sample articles with your own text. The pictures in the newsletter are from Word's clip art gallery, and you'll probably have to replace those too.

The Office Assistant appears with some help options to guide you through completing your newsletter:

- **Add or Remove a Picture**. When you click this option, the Office Assistant provides simple instructions for replacing a picture. To delete a picture, click it to select it and then press Delete. To add a picture, click the **Insert** menu and select **Picture**, and then select **From File**.

- **Regenerate the Table of Contents**. Click this option and Word regenerates the table of contents for you.

- **Cancel**. Choose **Cancel** to close the Office Assistant.

You don't have to go through this entire process to create the next issue of your newsletter if you save your document as a template. Open the **File** menu and select **Save As**. From the **Save as Type** drop-down list, select **Document Template**. Then click **Save**.

**SEE ALSO**
➤ *For information on inserting pictures, see page 364*
➤ *For information on working with styles, see page 237*
➤ *To learn how to regenerate a table of contents, see page 548*
➤ *For information on creating templates from documents, see page 254*

# Create a Letterhead Template

Two ways that you can create custom letterhead in Word are

- Edit a Word letterhead template, adding your own headers and footers, logo, graphics, and so forth.

- Custom-design a letterhead template from scratch.

Here, we discuss the custom design of a letterhead template from scratch, using some advanced features. The benefit to the design-from-scratch approach is that you will spend most of your time building and creating. If you redesign an existing Word letterhead template, you may find yourself spending more time undoing and deleting design elements before you build. After you create a custom letterhead, you can share the letterhead template by distributing it to others or by placing it on a shared network drive.

The following steps outline the method for quickly creating a template file. Many types of Word skills are used in creating letterhead templates and you will need to draw upon such skills as adding headers and footers, working with graphics, and creating fields, to build your template.

### Create a New Letterhead Template

1. Click the **File** menu and choose **New** to open the New dialog box.

2. Click the **General** tab, if it's not already selected.

3. Select the **Blank Document** icon.

4. Under **Create New**, click **Template**.

5. Choose **OK**.

6. Enter any text or fields that you want to be part of the new template, create headers and footers, add page numbering, insert graphics or watermarks, create any styles that you want to use, and apply formatting to the text.

7. Click the **File** menu and choose **Save,** or choose Save 🖫 on the Standard toolbar. When the Save As dialog box appears, select the folder to store your template and name and save the template.

---

**Custom templates: Page 2**

Custom templates typically consist of one page. What happens when your business letter is two pages long? You don't want to use your first page letterhead for the second page of your letter. Anticipate that users will have second pages and select **Different First Page** on the **Layout** tab of the Page Setup dialog box when you first begin your template design. This will result in blank second pages when users insert a page break. To format your second page with headers, footers, or logos, enter a page break at the end of your Template page 1 and then set up the headers, footers, and logos on page 2.

**Template folder structure**

Word comes with several template folders such as General, Letters & Faxes, and Web pages. When you open the **File** menu and choose **New**, folders are represented by tabbed pages in the dialog box. If you save templates in the Templates folder, you will see them on the **General** tab. If you save templates in a subfolder of Templates, you will see them in the corresponding tab and a new tab will appear when you create a subfolder.

The template is now available for use the next time you start a new document. Be sure to close the new template file before using it.

**SEE ALSO**

➤ *To modify existing Word templates, see page 353*

➤ *To create online forms using templates, see page 528*

➤ *For more information on creating headers or footers, see page 295*

➤ *For more information on adding page numbers to a document, see page 288*

➤ *Learn how to create fields on page 531*

## Insert Graphics

Typically, a letterhead contains a company logo, a graphic, or even a picture of a person (such as a real estate agent, insurance agent, or consultant).

### Inserting a Logo or Other Graphic on the First Page of Your Template

**1.** Position your insertion point on the first page of the template. Don't worry if you don't want the graphic at exactly that position on the page, because you can move it later.

**2.** Open the **Insert** menu and choose **Picture**; then choose **From File**. The Insert Picture dialog box opens (see Figure 25.6).

**3.** From the **Look In** drop-down list, select the drive and folder where the graphic is stored.

**4.** From the **Files of Type** drop-down list, select the graphic format of the file (choose **All Pictures** if you aren't certain of the format).

**5.** Select the file from the list or type the name of the graphic file in the **File Name** box.

**6.** Choose **Insert**.

**7.** Size and move the graphic as needed.

**FIGURE 22.6**
Select the file you want to insert as a picture in your template.

**SEE ALSO**

➤ *To learn more about inserting graphics into documents, see page 367*

➤ *For more information on sizing and cropping graphics, see page 369*

➤ *For more information on moving graphics, see page 372*

➤ *To apply a watermark, see page 383*

# Insert Time and Date Fields

Saving time is one purpose behind using a template. You want to add any elements to your letterhead template that would be repeated in all the letters written by you or your company.

One element that is common to all letters is the date. To save the user of the template time, you should add a Date and Time field to your template that automatically inserts the current date in the letter being created.

### Inserting a Date and Time Field in Your Template

1. Place your insertion point where you want the Date and Time field to appear.

2. Open the **Insert** menu and choose **Field**. The Field dialog box opens (see Figure 22.7).

3. Select **Date and Time** from the **Categories** list.

4. From the **Field Names** list, select the field that produces the date that you want added to your template.

   • **CreateDate** inserts the date the document was created.

   • **Date** enters today's date, so the date changes whenever you open the document.

- **PrintDate** inserts the date the document was last printed.
- **SaveDate** inserts the date the document was last saved.
- **Time** inserts the current time.

5. Choose **Options** to set the date and time format you want to use from the **Date-Time** formats, select the date and time formatting you want applied to the date. Choose **Add to Field** and then choose **OK** to return to the Field dialog box.

6. To keep the character formatting you apply to the resulting date whenever Word updates the field, click **Preserve Formatting During Updates** to enable that option.

7. Choose **OK**.

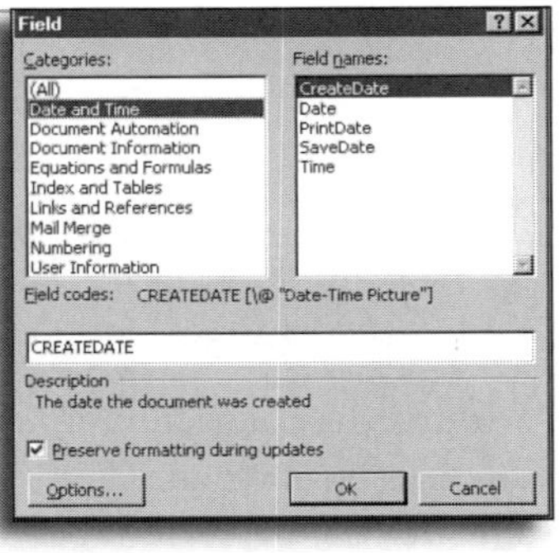

FIGURE 22.7

Choose the type of Date and Time field that best suits your needs and then click **Options** to see different date and time formats.

The current date appears in your document, but the gray shading behind it indicates that the date is a field and not plain text.

## Create a Letter Using the Custom Template

After you create your template follow these steps to create a letter.

### Create a Letter

1. Click the **File** menu and choose **New**. When the New dialog box opens, select the template you have created.

2. Be sure **Document** is selected under **Create New**.

3. Choose **OK**. The template opens with the fixed elements you created in place, such as the headers and footers, page numbers, graphics, watermarks, and boilerplate text.

4. Enter the text for the letter and save the file.

# Create a Memo with Memo Wizard

Memorandums, or memos, are basic business documents. Memos should be easy to read, concise, and meaningful. Word's Memo Wizard helps you set up and format your memo document.

### Run the Memo Wizard

1. Open the **File** menu and choose **New**.

2. Click the **Memos** tab of the New dialog box.

3. Select the **Memo Wizard** icon and choose **OK**.

4. When the Memo Wizard dialog box opens, click **Next** to continue.

5. Select the style of memo you want to create—**Professional**, **Contemporary**, or **Elegant**—and then click **Next**.

6. If you want to include a title at the top of your memo document, click **Yes** and then enter the title text in the text box. If not, click **No**. Then click **Next**.

7. Indicate which items you want to include in the header of your memo document: **Date**, **From**, **Subject**, or **Priority**. In the text boxes next to these options, enter the **Date**, **From**, and **Subject** text you want to appear in the header. Click **Next**.

8. Specify who should receive your memo by checking **To** or **Cc** and then entering the names of the recipients in the appropriate boxes. Or, click in the appropriate text box and then choose **Address Book** to select people listed in your Address Book.

9. If you have a large distribution list, you may want to have the list of recipients appear on a separate cover page. In that case, click **Yes**. Otherwise, click **No**. Click **Next**.

10. Select the closing items you want at the end of the memo—**Writer's Initials**, **Typist's Initials**, **Enclosures**, or **Attachments**. In the appropriate text boxes, enter the initials or the number of enclosures. Click **Next**.

11. For memos that have more than one page, select the items you want to appear in the header and footer for subsequent pages: **Date**, **Topic**, **Page Number** for the header or **Date**, **Confidential**, **Page Number** for the footer. If you chose to include a topic, enter the text for the topic. Click **Next**.

12. Click **Finish**. The Office Assistant appears and offers you the opportunity to change the header or footer, change the memo style, or send the memo to someone else via email or fax (starts the Fax Wizard). Close the Office Assistant if you don't need help, or click the item with which you need assistance.

13. Click the **Click Here and Type Your Memo Text** field and begin typing the body of your memo. The field is indicated by the square brackets surrounding the click here text. Click any other editable fields in your memo, such as **Priority**, and make the appropriate adjustments.

14. Save your memo and print it.

**SEE ALSO**
> *For information on creating templates from documents, see page 355*

---

**Save time by reusing your memo**

Do you like the way your memo looks? Rather than going through this entire process the next time you write a memo, you should save your document as a template. Open the **File** menu and select **Save As**. From the **Save as Type** drop-down list, select **Document Template**. Then click **Save**. To save a blank résumé, delete specific information, leaving the boilerplate information before you save the document as a template.

# Create Business Cards

Business cards can be expensive to a small or upstart business. Often you can print business cards inexpensively by purchasing business card stock and creating the cards in Word. Some stationery manufacturers supply business card templates for use in Word. We recommend that you use these templates if available.

Otherwise, you can create your own template and print it on perforated business card stock available from your office supply store or paper product catalog. All you have to do is get your card text and artwork to fit properly in the business card spaces.

### Create Business Cards

1. Open the **Tools** menu and choose **Envelopes and Labels**.

2. Click the **Labels** tab on the Envelopes and Labels dialog box.

3. Choose **Options**.

4. Under Printer Information, select **Laser and Ink Jet** as the type of printer you have (dot matrix printers aren't recommended for creating business cards).

5. From the **Label Products** drop-down list, select **Avery Standard** or **Avery A4 and A5 sizes**.

6. From the **Product Number** list, select one of the business card options. If the business card stock you chose is an Avery product, look for the same number that appears on the box. Otherwise, click each of the business card options and then check the Label information area until you see dimensions that match the size of one card (such as 3.5 inches wide by 2 inches high).

**7.** Choose **OK**.

**8.** In the **Address** area, enter the text you want to appear on a single business card. Or, leave this area blank if you want to format the text after you create the business card document. It's often easier to add the text in the document to make one business card that suits you, and then copy the text to each of the other cards on the page.

**9.** Select **Full Page of the Same Label** under Print.

**10.** Choose **New Document**.

**11.** From the **Table** menu, select **Show Gridlines** to see the outline of each business card.

**12.** Format and align the text.

**13.** To add graphics to the business cards, insert the picture or object. Size the graphic to fit on the business card. Copy the graphic to each card on the page.

**14.** Print a test page and see if your cards fit on the business card template. Adjust any spacing if needed.

**15.** Save and print your document (see Figure 22.8).

**SEE ALSO**

➤ *To learn more about inserting, sizing, and formatting graphics, see page 367*

➤ *For more information on tables, see page 165*

➤ *For more information on creating labels, see page 271*

**Keep business cards from curling**

Use the straight paper path on your laser printer when you print business cards (envelopes, too). This will keep the cards from becoming curled, or bowed as they come out of the printer.

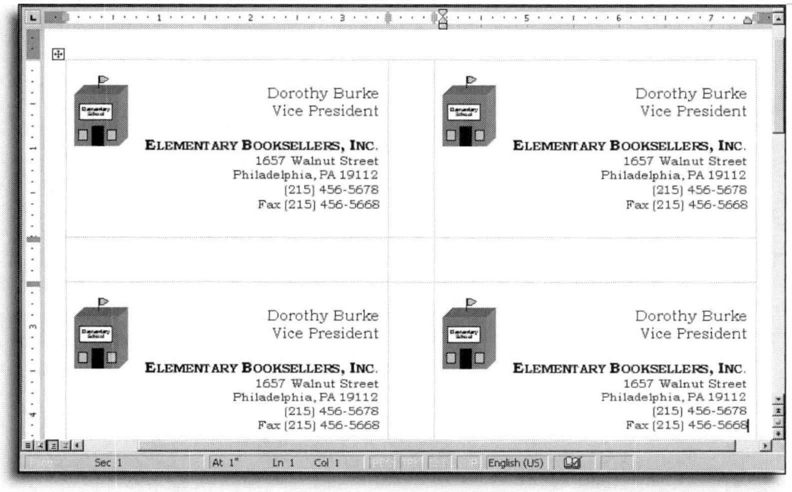

**FIGURE 22.8**
Using the Label feature, it's possible to create business cards in Word.

# Create Mail Merges, Catalogs, and Lists

Create mailing lists and generate personalized form letters

Create databases and product catalogs or lists from those databases

Import or merge data from other database programs

Print envelopes or mailing labels from a database

# Know Your Mail Merges, Catalogs, and List Options

A mail merge is an operation that takes the information from a *database* (such as a mailing list) and merges it with a document to create a set of form letters, envelopes, or labels.

A database is a collection of information that can be sorted, extracted, and queried. An example of a database is an address book that stores a person's first name, last name, street address, city, state, and zip code. Each unique piece of information, such as the last name, is a *field* and the complete set of information for each person is a *record*. These terms are standard database terms and their use and description apply to Word as well as other programs in which you can create databases. Many databases are created and stored in table format. In a table, columns represent the database fields and rows represent the database records.

Word provides several methods of working with database information. You can

- Create and maintain a database in Word and use it to generate letters, documents, envelopes, faxes, or labels.
- Retrieve data from existing databases created in other programs.
- Update or add new data to databases created in other programs.

Documents used for mail merge purposes are called *main documents* and databases are referred to as the *data_source*.

Word has somewhat limited capabilities when it comes to databases, although those capabilities will probably serve you well for most of your mail merge needs. However, when databases are extremely large (thousands of records), database information changes frequently (needs daily updating) or needs to be accessible to many people for the purposes of entering, sorting, or retrieving data, use a bona fide database program such as Microsoft Access for your data source.

Word can provide direct access to other database programs that support *Open Database Connectivity* (*ODBC*). An industry standard, ODBC enables database and other programs to share information. For example, Word can create envelopes based on data stored in Microsoft Access or Lotus Approach. In this chapter, we discuss the most commonly used, basic communications with external databases; through importing and merging.

Although mailing lists and mass mailings are the most frequent use of the merge feature in Word, it's also possible to combine database information with repetitive text to create lists and catalogs. For example, to create a membership directory for an organization, you combine a mailing list database with text labels such as "Member's Name" and "Member's Address" to produce a list. For each member in the list, the name of the member is retrieved from the database and displayed next to the "Member Name" text. Instead of having each member listed on a separate page, each page of the listing shows as many members as can fit on the page. A catalog is created in the same way, with product data drawn from the database and combined with standard text from the main document.

# Create a Mail Merge

A Word mail merge involves three pieces:

- Data Source.  The data source (database) contains the individualized information that "personalizes" each version of the final merged document. Frequently this is a list of names and addresses, but it doesn't have to be limited to mailing information. It can also contain information such as an employee date of hire.

- Main Document.  This document holds the static text that remains the same in each merge. It also contains a set of field codes that tell Word where to put the information from the data source.

- Merged Document.  The result of the merge operation, this document can be a set of labels, envelopes, or form letters. Each, label, envelope, or page is a combination of the data from one record in the data source and the common text in the main document.

Word organizes the process of merging the main document with the data source and helps you through the merge in a step-by-step manner using the Mail Merge Helper (see Figure 23.1).

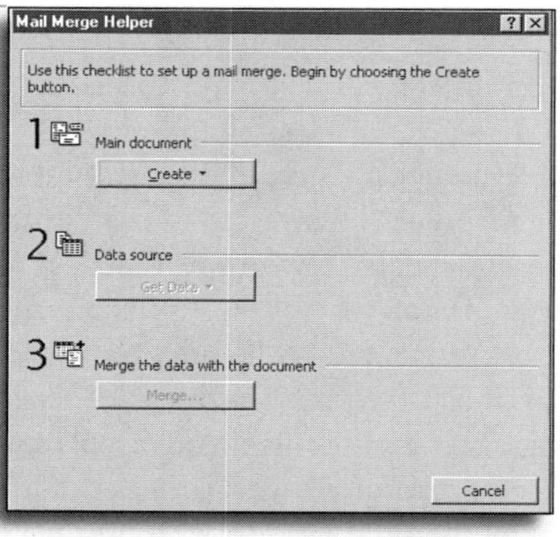

FIGURE 23.1

Follow the three steps of the Mail Merge Helper to perform your mail merge.

# Merge Documents Using Variable Data

The mail merge process is complex. The following steps outline the overall process. For the specifics on creating and maintaining a database, see the "Create a Database" section later in this chapter. For more about creating the main document, see the "Prepare a Main Document" section later in this chapter.

### Begin a Mail Merge

1. Click the **Tools** menu and select **Mail Merge** to open the Mail Merge Helper dialog box.

2. Under step 1, Main Document, choose **Create**.

3. On the menu that appears, click the type of main document you want to create—**Form Letters**, **Mailing Labels**, **Envelopes**, or **Catalog**.

4. After you make the selection, a dialog box appears. Choose **Active Window** to turn the document you currently have open into your main document for the mail merge. Choose **New Main Document** to open a new document to create the main document.

**5.** Under step 2, Data Source, choose **G**et Data.

**6.** A new menu appears. You need to identify your data source through this menu. Choose from the following:

- Select **C**reate Data Source to start a completely new data source document. If you make this selection, turn to page 490, "Create a Database", later in this chapter for instructions on creating a new database.

- Select **O**pen Data Source to use an existing data source document (you then specify the filename and location).

- Select Use **A**ddress Book to use an electronic mail address book or contact list from Microsoft Outlook 97 or Schedule+ 95, or the Personal Address Book.

**7.** Under Main Document, choose **E**dit. Select the main document you want to edit (such as "Form Letter: Document1"). Insert the text, graphics, and merge fields you need for the main document (see the sections later in this chapter on creating form letters, labels, and envelopes). Save and name the file.

**8.** Return to the Mail Merge Helper. Under step 3, Merge the Data with the Document, choose **Me**rge. The Merge dialog box appears (see Figure 23.2). From the **Me**rge To dropdown list, specify how you want to output the merge:

- **New Document**. Creates a document that has each of the merged form letters, labels, or envelopes in it. If you don't have a large number of records, this selection gives you the opportunity to view the result of your merge or edit each one before you print it.

- **Printer**. Sends the merged document directly to the printer.

- **Electronic Mail**. Sends each document to the recipient via electronic mail. Your system must include a MAPI-compatible (Messaging Application Programming Interface) electronic mail program such as Microsoft Schedule+ or Microsoft Exchange. There must be a

---

**Returning to the Mail Merge Helper**

At any stage in the mail merge process, you return to the Mail Merge Helper dialog box by opening the **Tools** menu and selecting **Mail Merge** or by choosing Mail Merge Helper on the Mail Merge toolbar, if it is displayed.

field in the data source containing the email address. Choose **Setup** to specify that field, enter a subject line for the email memo, and select whether to send the merged document as an attachment. Choose **OK** to return to the Merge dialog box.

- **Electronic Fax**. Sends each document to the recipient via electronic fax (your system must include a MAPI-compatible electronic fax program). There must be a field in the data source containing the fax address. Choose **Setup** to specify that field and enter a subject line for the fax memo. Choose **OK** to return to the Merge dialog box.

9. Under **Records to Be Merged**, click **All** or **From**. If you select **From**, enter the record numbers in the **From** and **To** boxes that specify the range of records you want to merge. If you only want to merge specific records or records of a certain type, choose **Query Options** and set conditions on the merge.

10. Under **When Merging Records**, click **Don't Print Blank Lines when Data Fields Are Empty**. This prevents blank lines from appearing in your letters, labels, and envelopes as a result of blank fields (which is the default for merging). For example, a Suite or Address2 field might be blank if there is no suite number or building name for an addressee.

11. Choose **Merge**.

Depending on the **Merge To** option you select, Word will begin printing the merged documents, sending email messages or faxes, or displaying the merged documents on your screen.

After you create the main document, the Mail Merge toolbar appears. Table 23.1 describes the tools on this toolbar.

**Create a data source without starting a mail merge**

If you want to create a data source, such as a mailing list, before you begin a mail merge, it's still easiest to go through the mail merge process. Follow the steps described here, but leave the main document blank and delete it when you are finished. Alternatively, create a data source in a table, merging it later. Remember to make the field names the first row of the table.

**FIGURE 23.2**
Set the options for your merge output.

TABLE 23.1    **Tools on the Mail Merge Toolbar**

| Button | Name | Click To |
|---|---|---|
| | Insert Merge Field drop-down list | Select from a list of database fields that you want to add to your main document. |
| | Insert Word Field drop-down list | Select from a list of non-database fields that you can add to your document (such as Fill-In, which prompts the user for text to insert in the document, or Merge Record #, which inserts the number of the current merge record). |
|  | Show Fields/Values | See how the database information will look in the final merged document. |
| | First Record | Goes to the first record in the data source file. |
| | Previous Record | Displays information from the previous data record. |
| | Go to Record | Enter the number of the record you want to see, and then press Enter to go to that record. |
| | Next Record | Displays information from the next data record. |
| | Last Record | Goes to the last record in the data source file. |
| | Mail Merge Helper | Opens the Mail Merge Helper dialog box. |

*continues…*

TABLE 23.1   **Continued**

| Button | Name | Click To |
|---|---|---|
| | Check for Errors | Reports errors in the main document or data source that may cause merging problems. |
| | Merge to New Document | Starts the mail merge and creates a new document that contains the results of the merge. |
| | Merge to Printer | Starts the mail merge and automatically prints the resulting document. |
| | Mail Merge | Opens the Mail Merge dialog box so you can set options for the mail merge. |
| | Find Record | Searches for specified data records. |
| | Edit Data Source | Opens the Data Form dialog box so that you can view, modify, add, or delete records. |

**SEE ALSO**

➤ *Learn how to query on page 501*

# Create a Database

Word keeps Data Source files in table form. Each column of the table represents a field; each row represents a record (see Figure 23.3). The first row of the table (called the header row) shows the field names used in the data source.

### Create a Data Source File

1. Select **Create Data Source from the Mail Merge Helper**. The Create Data Source dialog box opens (see Figure 23.4). Word provides a list of suggested field names for your data source, and they are listed in the **Field Names in Header Row** box. Do one of the following to customize the list:

**Creating a useful data source**

The key to creating a useful data source is to create a separate field for each piece of data on which you may need to sort or use alone. For example, a data source that contains a single field name in which you enter a first and last name would make it impossible to create a letter that starts "Dear Tom". A single name field would result in "Dear Tom Jones."

**FIGURE 23.3**
Word data source files are stored in tables. The table columns represent fields and rows represent records.

**1** Database toolbar

| FirstName | LastName | JobTitle | Company | Address1 | Address2 | City | State | PostalCode | Country | HomePhone |
|---|---|---|---|---|---|---|---|---|---|---|
| Barbara | Shea | | Well Center | 55 Main Street | | Phoenixville | PA | 99884 | | |
| Jill | Jones | President | Loose Weight and Keep it Off | 98B4 Summerset Lane | | Landenberg | PA | 19350 | | |
| Joe | Smith | Manager | Smiths Fitness Center | 232 Penn Green Road | | Orlando | FL | 99888 | | |
| Mary | Auburn | President | Free Weights | 6300 Eagleview Lane | | Eagle | MN | 88998 | | |
| Helen | Purvin | President | Fitness for Fifties | 240 Long Lane | | Scranton | PA | 99999 | | |
| Ed | Woloszyn | Vice President | Fitness for Men | 5999 B Harcourt Lane | | East Scranton | PA | 18504 | | |
| Bradley | McCumming | President | Power Up | 2 SweetWater Lane | | Bloomsburg | KY | 99880 | | |
| Harma | Kirkland | Manager | Kids Are Fit | 99 Pumpkin Lane | | Levittown | PA | 19056 | | |
| Elizabeth | Star | Fitness Coordinator | Wellness Center | 98 Old Stream Parkway | | New Haven | CT | 99888 | | |

**FIGURE 23.4**
Customize the field names for your data source file in the Create Data Source dialog box.

> **Create Data Source**     ? ×
>
> A mail merge data source is composed of rows of data. The first row is called the header row. Each of the columns in the header row begins with a field name.
>
> Word provides commonly used field names in the list below. You can add or remove field names to customize the header row.
>
> Field name:          Field names in header row:
>
> [                ]          Title
>                            FirstName
>    Add Field Name >>       LastName
>                            JobTitle           Move
>                            Company
>    Remove Field Name       Address1
>                            Address2
>
>    MS Query...             OK          Cancel

- To remove a field name from the list, select the name and choose **Remove Field Name**.

- To add a new field name, enter the field name in the **Field Name** box and then choose **Add Field Name**. If the **Add Field Name** button is grayed out, the field name you entered isn't legal. The field name must start with a letter, followed by letters, numbers, or underscore (_) characters. Spaces aren't allowed, and the name can't be more than 40 characters long.

**Required fields**

You choose the field names and order in which your data source should appear. Word doesn't require you use a certain number of fields. However, field names must be unique (such as fname for first name and lname for last name) and if you plan to distribute the merged output via electronic mail or fax you must include a field that has the email address or fax address.

- To change the order of the field names, select a field name and click the up or down **Move** button next to the **Field Names in Header Row** box to move the field up or down in the list. Although the order doesn't matter to the merging process, it does help to have a logical order for data entry.

2. Choose **OK**. The Save As dialog box appears. Type a name for the data source file in the **File Name** box, and specify where you want the file stored from the **Save In** drop-down list. Choose **Save**.

3. A dialog box appears telling you that you have not added any records to the data source file. To begin adding records, choose **Edit Data Source**.

4. The Data Form dialog box opens (see Figure 23.5). The field names are listed on the left side of the dialog box in the order you set. A text box follows each field name. Enter the information for the first record in the data source by filling out the text boxes. Press Enter or Tab to move to the next box down; press Shift+Tab to move to the previous box. The up and down arrow keys also help you move from box to box.

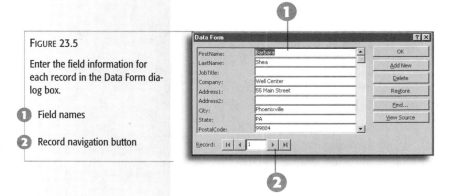

FIGURE 23.5

Enter the field information for each record in the Data Form dialog box.

**1** Field names

**2** Record navigation button

5. When you finish entering the data for one record and press Enter after completing the last field, a new record automati-

cally opens. Use the record navigation buttons at the bottom of the dialog box to move from record to record ◄ ► or to the beginning ◄◄ or end ►► of all the records.

6. If you don't complete all the fields in a record and you want to start a new record, choose **Add New** to add a new, blank record to the end of the data source. Then type the field information into that record.

   To delete an entire record, display the record you want to remove from the file and then choose **Delete**.

   To undo any changes you made to the displayed record, choose **Restore**.

7. When you've finished adding records, choose **OK** to return to the main document.

## Add and Delete Records

Forgot a field or record? Need to add or remove a record? Editing the data source can be done from the data form or from the table in the data source file.

### Modify the Database from the Data Form

1. Click the **Tools** menu and select **Mail Merge** to open the Mail Merge Helper.

2. Under **Data Source,** choose **Edit** and select the name of your data source file. Or, choose Edit Data Source 📝 on the Mail Merge toolbar. The Data Form dialog box appears (see Figure 23.6).

3. Do one of the following:

   • To start a new record, choose **Add New** to add a new, blank record to the end of the data source. Then type the field information into that record.

   • To delete an entire record, display the record you want to remove from the file and then choose **Delete**.

   • To undo any changes you made to the displayed record, choose **Restore**.

4. Click **OK**.

---

**Merging an Access database**

When selecting the data source for the merge, specify the file-name and location of the Access database and click **Open**. If the data you want to use is in a table in the database, click the **Tables** tab of the Microsoft Access dialog box, select the table, and choose **OK**. If it's in a query, click the **Queries** tab, select the Query, and choose **OK**. The remainder of the merge process is exactly as when you create a data source in Word.

### Modify the Database from the Data Source

1. Click the **Tools** menu and select **Mail Merge** to open the Mail Merge Helper.

2. Under **Data Source** choose **Edit** and select the name of your data source file. Or, choose Edit Data Source 🖉 on the Mail Merge toolbar. When the Data Form dialog box appears, choose **View** Source from the data form.

3. Do one of the following:

   • To add a new record, choose Add New Record 🖩 on the Database toolbar. Word appends a new row at the bottom of the table. Enter the information for each field for that record. Save the file to save the information you added.

   • To delete a record, click in the row where the record appears and then choose Delete Record 🖩 on the Database toolbar.

   • To add, remove, or rename the fields in the data source, choose Manage Fields 🖫 on the Database toolbar to open the Manage Fields dialog box (see Figure 23.7). To add a field, type the name of the new field in the **Field Name** box and choose **Add**. To remove a field, select the name from the **Field Names in Header Row** list and choose **Remove**. To rename a field, select the name from the **Field Names in Header Row** list and choose **Rename**. Choose **OK**.

4. Save and close the file.

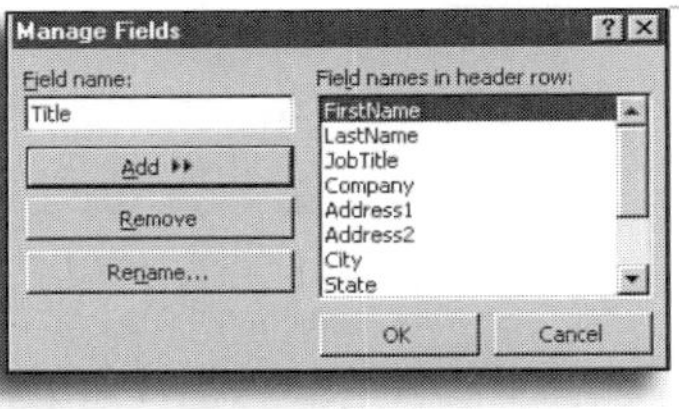

FIGURE 23.7
Add, remove, or rename fields in
the Manage Fields dialog box.

If you're no longer in the main document where you can easily
access the Data Source file through the Mail Merge Helper,
open the file by clicking the **File** menu and selecting **Open** or
choosing Open on the Standard toolbar 📂. Edit the data as you
would any table in a Word document (add a column to add a
field; add a row to add a record) and then save the file.

**SEE ALSO**

➤ *Learn more about navigating through tables on page 178*

## Sort Records

In a mail merge, the main documents are generated in the order
in which you entered your records. You may want to sort records
so your output is generated in a certain order, such as zip code
order or alphabetical order.

### Sort Mail Merge Records

1.  Click the **Tools** menu and select **Mail Merge** to open the
    Mail Merge Helper, or choose Mail Merge Helper 📧 on
    the Mail Merge toolbar.

2.  Under step 3, Merge the Data with the Document, choose
    **Query Options**.

3.  Select the **Sort Records** tab (see Figure 23.8).

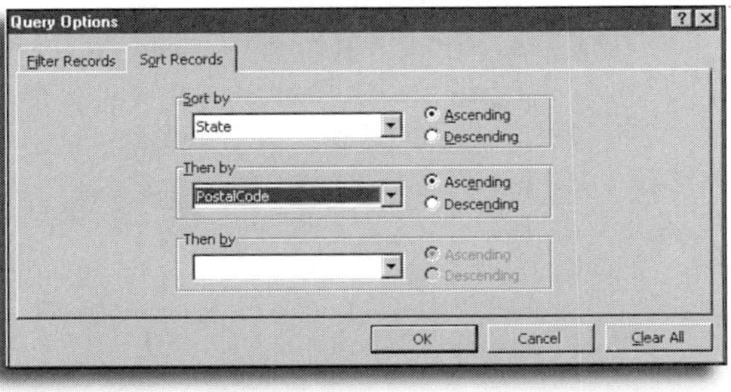

FIGURE 23.8
Select the field in the data source
that you want to sort by and then
choose the order.

4. From the **Sort By** drop-down list, choose the field you want to use to sort the records.

5. Click **A̲scending** if you want the records sorted by that field in an A–Z, 1–99 order. Choose **Descending** to sort the files in Z–A, 99–1 order.

6. Steps 4 and 5 set up the primary sort. If you want to set up a secondary sort, select a field from the **T̲hen By** drop-down list and click **Asce̲nding** or **Desce̲nding**. A secondary sort is useful when you have a mailing list sorted by the last name. If there is more than one person with the same last name, the secondary sort by first name will list those people in order of their first names.

7. If necessary, the sort can be refined further. Select a field from the **Then B̲y** drop-down list, and then click **Ascendi̲ng** or **Descending**.

8. Choose **OK** to close the Query Options dialog box and continue with the merge.

This method assumes that you have already initiated the mail merge process, specified a main document, and created or opened a data source file. If you're not in the middle of a mail merge and you want to sort a data source file, open that file and sort the data table in the document using table sorting methods.

**SEE ALSO**

➤ *Learn more about sorting tables on page 179*

➤ *To find and replace text, see page 110*

## Finding records

To locate specific records in a large table, use the Find Record button 🔳 on the Database toolbar. In the **Fi̲nd What** box, type the text you want to locate and indicate the name of the field to search in the **In Fiel̲d** box.

# Prepare a Main Document

Main documents in a mail merge can be form letters, mailing labels, envelopes, catalogs, or lists. Several different types of main documents can use the same data source, so you can make form letters, envelopes, and mailing labels from the same mailing list file.

# Write a Form Letter

A form letter consists of text and graphics that you want to appear on each recipient's letter, plus a series of merge fields in which the information relating to that recipient appears. The information in the merge fields is what "personalizes" the form letter.

After you've created your data source file, you're ready to prepare your form letter. When you close the Data Form, Word returns you to the main document; or click the **File** menu and select **Open** and then select the main document file to open it.

The Mail Merge toolbar appears on your screen, but the document is blank. Enter any text or graphics you want to appear on each recipient's letter. When you want to insert a piece of information from your data source, choose **Insert Merge Field** on the Mail Merge toolbar and select the field name you want. A field code appears in the document (see Figure 23.9). It acts as a placeholder for the data from each record in the data source.

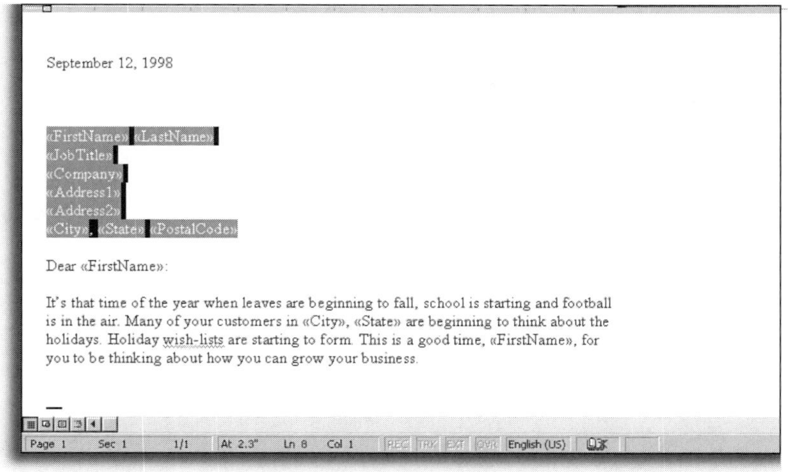

FIGURE **23.9**
The field codes appear in the form letter with double-angle brackets around them.

Remember to add any required punctuation, so the information flows with the rest of the document text. To be sure that the data displays properly, choose Show Fields/Values 🔲 on the Mail Merge toolbar to see the information from your first record displayed.

**Formatting fields**

To apply character formatting to fields, select the field(s) and use the formatting toolbar or the **Font** or **Format** menu to choose formatting options.

When you've completed the document, save it. Then, choose Mail Merge Helper 🖳 on the Mail Merge toolbar to continue with the mail merging process. Alternatively, choose Mail Merge 🔲 to specify mail merging options, choose Merge to New Document 🔲 to activate the merge and create a new document that combines the main document text with the records in the data source, or choose Merge to Printer 🔲 to print the mail merge documents.

## Create Mailing Labels

To create mailing labels from the data source, begin following the mail merge process steps from "Merge Documents Using Variable Data," making sure to select Mailing Labels as the type of Main Document you want to create. Then complete the following steps.

### Create Mail Merge Labels

1. Click the **Tools** menu and select **Mail Merge** to open the Mail Merge Helper dialog box.

2. Under step 1, Main Document, choose **Create**.

3. On the menu that appears, click **Mailing Labels**.

4. After you make the selection a dialog box appears. Choose **Active Window** to turn the document you currently have open into your main document for the mail merge. Choose **New Main Document** to open a new document to create the main document.

5. Under step 2, Data Source, choose **Get Data**.

6. On the menu that appears, select **Create Data Source** to start a completely new data source document, select **Open Data Source** to use an existing data source document, or select **Use Address Book** to use an electronic mail address book or contact list from Microsoft Outlook or Schedule+.

7. If you are using an existing data source file, the Label Options dialog box appears (see Figure 23.10).

---

**Not just for mailing labels**

You should also choose the mailing label option when you want to create business cards, postcards, file folder labels, name badges, disk labels, audio cassette labels, video face and spine labels, tent cards, note cards, ID cards, rotary file cards, CD labels, and divider and portfolio labels. Printable sheets are already made up for these items, and you can choose them from the list of available products. With the appropriate information in your database, this makes a quick way to prepare many items at one time.

If you created a new data source file, Word returns you to the blank main document. Open the **Tools** menu and select **Mail Merge** or choose Mail Merge Helper 🖳 on the Mail Merge toolbar to open the Mail Merge Helper dialog box. Click **Setup** to open the Label Options dialog box.

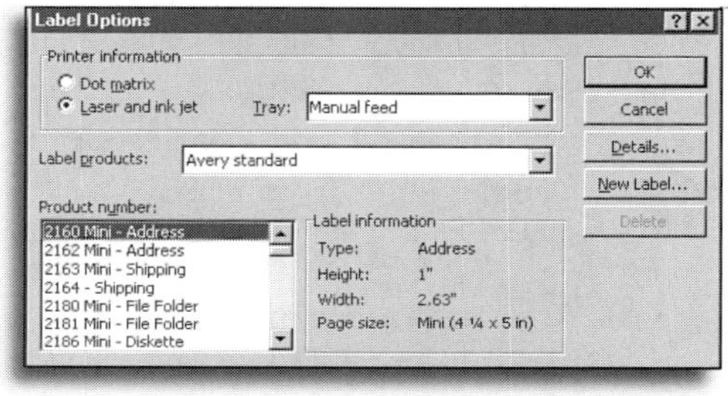

**FIGURE 23.10**

Select the manufacturer and product number of the labels you plan to use.

8. Under **Printer Information**, select the type of printer you'll be using—**Dot Matrix** or **Laser and Ink Jet**. From the **Tray** drop-down list, select the tray or bin where you put the labels for printing.

9. From the **Label Products** drop-down list, select the brand or type of labels you use. The **Product Number** listings differ depending on your selection. Choose the **Product Number** you use, or the nearest in size. If the size label you want to use isn't listed, choose **New Label** and fill in the dimensions.

10. Choose **OK**. The Create Labels dialog box opens (see Figure 23.11) .

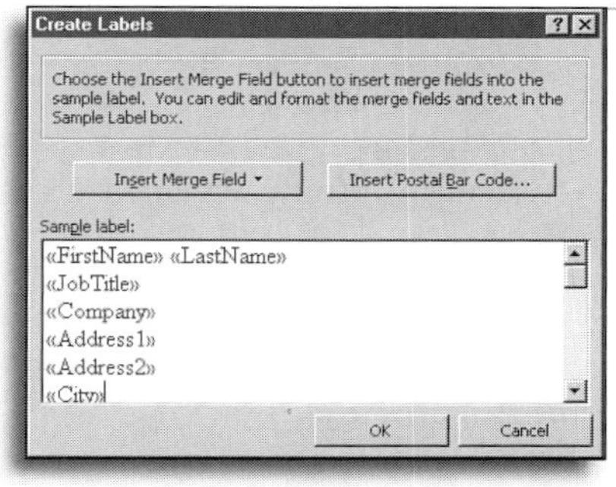

**FIGURE 23.11**

Add the merge fields to organize the data on the labels.

11. Choose **Insert Merge Field** and select the merge field code you want to insert in the label. Repeat this for each merge field you want to use. Remember to add the correct spacing and punctuation so the label prints correctly.

12. If your label has room and you want to speed your mail through the United States Postal System, choose **Insert Postal Bar Code** button to print the delivery bar code on the label. To use this feature, do not customize or rename the **address1** and **Postalcode** fields in your database. These are the fields from which Word will create the bar code.

13. Choose **OK** to return to the Mail Merge Helper.

14. Choose **Merge** and select the appropriate output options to print the labels or create a new document.

**SEE ALSO**

➤ *For additional information on printing labels, see page 271*

## Create Merge Envelopes

Printed envelopes can appear much more "personal" than those with labels. Whether you print to envelopes or create mailing labels is a personal preference, but your decision may be affected by the printer you are using. For example, most laser printers found in the home and small business are not designed for high volume printing.

When you print envelopes, you should use the straight paper path on your printer, and many printers don't stack documents well when they are ejected from the straight paper path. If you're printing a large quantity of envelopes, your envelopes could end up on the floor!

Printing labels takes less "wear and tear" on your printer, as you can print multiple labels on one page, but as we said, labels aren't as personal as printed envelopes.

So, if you have a small quantity of envelopes to print, we recommend you print directly to the envelope. If you have a large quantity to print, consider labels or consult your printer manual

**U.S. Post Office bulk mail requirements**

For bulk mailing, refer to the requirements of the U.S. Post Office regarding proper addressing (all uppercase, no punctuation). Create your label form with those requirements in mind and keep the caps lock on when you enter data into your database. If you don't want all caps in your database, once your labels are ready to print, select the entire document and format the font for All Caps.

or manufacturer to find the most efficient way to print large quantities of envelopes. You may be able to purchase a special envelope feeder for your printer.

### Create Mail Merge Envelopes

1. Click the **T**ools menu and select **Mail Me**rge to open the Mail Merge Helper dialog box.

2. Under step 1, Main Document, choose **C**reate.

3. On the menu that appears, click **Envelopes**.

4. A dialog box appears. Choose **A**ctive **Window** to turn the document you currently have open into your main document for the mail merge. Choose **N**ew **Main Document** to open a new document to create the main document.

5. Under step 2, Data Source, choose **G**et **Data**.

6. On the menu that appears, select **C**reate **Data Source** to start a completely new data source document, select **O**pen **Data Source** to use an existing data source document, or select **Use A**ddress **Book** to use an electronic mail address book or contact list from Microsoft Outlook or Schedule+.

7. Depending on your choice in the previous step, you need to do one of the following:

   • If you created a new data source, click Mail Merge Helper 🖼 on the Mail Merge toolbar to return to the Mail Merge Helper dialog box. Then choose **S**etup under **Main Document**.

   • If you opened an existing data source file from the Mail Merge Helper, a dialog box appears saying that you need to set up the main document. Choose **S**et **Up Main Document**.

8. The Envelope Options dialog box appears (see Figure 23.12). Select the **Envelope S**ize you want to print from the drop-down list.

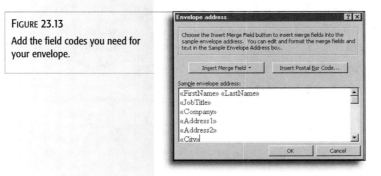

FIGURE 23.12

Select the size of envelope you want to print and how you want the return and delivery address to look.

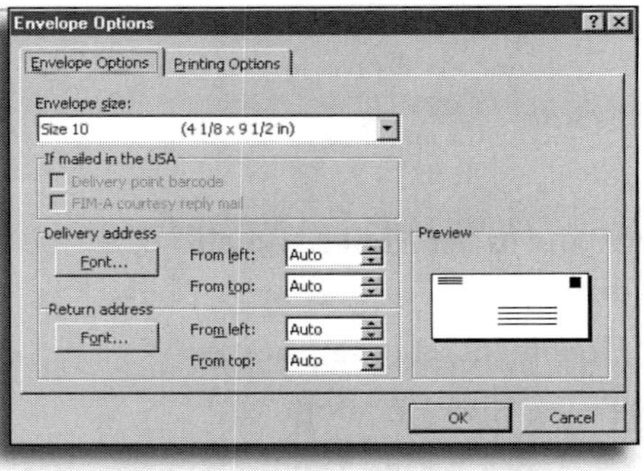

**9.** To set the appearance of your envelope, choose **Font** under **Delivery Address** or **Font** under **Return Address** and make your font choices for the address. To position the addresses on the envelope, set the distance **From Left** and **From Top** of the envelope for the delivery address and **From Left** and **From Top** for the return address.

**10.** Choose **OK** and the Envelope address dialog box appears (see Figure 23.13). Choose **Insert Merge Field** and select the merge field code you want to insert in the envelope. Repeat for each merge field you need to insert. Remember to add the correct spacing and punctuation so the address prints correctly.

FIGURE 23.13

Add the field codes you need for your envelope.

**11.** To speed your mail through the U.S. Postal System, choose **Insert Postal Bar Code** to print the delivery bar code on the envelope.

**12.** Choose **OK** to return to the Mail Merge Helper.

**13.** Choose **Merge** and select the appropriate output options to print the envelopes or create a new document.

SEE ALSO

➤ *For additional information on printing envelopes, see page 268*

# Select Data

Your data source file may be a generalized file, such as a large mailing list, but you only want to send a particular form letter to a select group of members of the list. In the case of a mailing list, you may need to select addressees in one city or state.

To set up the conditions of a selective merge, you need to use the Query Options feature of the mail merge process.

### Filter Records Prior to a Merge

**1.** Access Query Options from the Mail Merge Helper prior to doing the merge by choosing the **Query Options**, or if you have clicked **Merge** and opened the Merge dialog box you choose **Query Options** there. The Query Options dialog box opens (see Figure 23.14).

**2.** Select the **Filter Records** tab if you plan to set conditions to select only certain records for your merge.

**3.** In the **Field** box, select the field you want to use to set the conditions of your merge. For example, if you only want to send your form letter to people in a particular city, choose the **City** field.

**4.** From the **Comparison** box, select the type of comparison you want to make (**Equal To**, **Not Equal To**, **Greater Than**, **Less Than**, **Is Blank**, and so on).

**To change label or envelop size**

If you change printers or need to change the size or modify envelopes, open the envelope main document and open the **Tools** menu and select **Envelopes and Labels**. In the Envelopes and Labels dialog box, make your changes. To change labels, open the **Tools** menu, choose **Mail Merge** and create a new mailing labels main document.

**Filter criteria**

The information entered in the **Field**, **Comparison**, and **Compare To** boxes is called the *filter criteria* because they filter out any records that don't meet that criteria.

5. In the **Compare To** box, enter the exact value to which you want to compare the field information. In the **City** example, you would enter the name of the city.

6. If you want to evaluate more than one condition, fill out the boxes in the second row. In the first box of the line, select **And** to select records that match *all* the filter criteria or select **Or** to select records that match *any* of the filter criteria.

7. If you want to sort the records, click the **S͟ort Records** tab and follow the instructions under the "Sort Records" section earlier in this chapter.

8. Choose **OK** to close the Query Options dialog box and continue with the merge.

The merged documents include only those records that meet the conditions of your query.

# Create Catalogs and Lists

Using Word's mail merge feature and its capability to pull unique pieces of information from a data source (database) file, it's possible to create a catalog, membership directory, parts list, or similar document. The method is similar to merging a form letter with a mailing list. The resulting document, however, is quite different. With catalogs, directories, and lists, data is stored in a source document, but the merged information is combined into a single document.

### Create a Catalog or List

1. Start a new document.

2. Click the **T͟ools** menu and select **Mail Me͟rge** to open the Mail Merge Helper dialog box.

3. Under step 1, Main Document, choose **C͟reate**.

4. On the menu that appears, click **C͟atalog**. With a catalog main document, all the merged data is placed in one resulting merged document and the text you add to the main document is repeated for each set of data.

**5.** After you make the selection, a dialog box appears asking whether you want to use the active document window when you create the document or a new document window. Choose **Active Window** to turn the document you currently have open into your main document for the merge.

**6.** Under step 2, Data Source, choose **Get Data**.

**7.** On the menu that appears, click **Create Data Source**. Set up the fields you want to use. Choose **OK**.

**8.** The Save As dialog box appears. From the **Save In** drop-down list, select the drive and folder where you want to store the data source file. Enter the name of the data source in the **File Name** box. Choose **Save**.

**9.** When the dialog box appears asking if you want to add data records or edit the main document, choose **Edit Data Source** to enter the data to create the data source.

**10.** In the **Data Form**, enter the specific information for each record that you want to add to the database (see Figure 23.15). Choose **Add New** to add a new record. When you've added all the records, choose **OK**.

FIGURE **23.15**
This database for a price list uses only four fields.

**11.** In the main document, insert the text and graphics you want repeated with each data record. With your insertion point where you want the data from the data source to appear, choose **Insert Merge Field** on the Mail Merge toolbar and click the field name that you want to insert from the menu that appears. Repeat this for each field you want to display for all the records in your data source (see Figure 23.16).

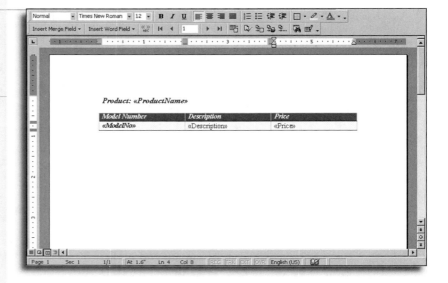

FIGURE 23.16

The main document contains the boilerplate text, formatting, and fields needed to create the final document.

**12.** Return to the Mail Merge Helper by choosing Mail Merge Helper 🗐 on the Mail Merge toolbar. Under step 3, **Merge the Data with the Document**, choose **Merge**. In the Merge dialog box, select **New Document** from the **Merge To** drop-down list.

**13.** Under **Records to be Merged**, select **All** or **From**. If you chose **From**, enter the range of record numbers in the **From** and **To** boxes that you want to merge. If you only want to merge specific records or records of a certain type, choose **Query Options** and set conditions on the merge.

**14.** Under **When Merging Records**, click **Don't Print Blank Lines when Data Fields Are Empty** if you don't want any blank lines in your catalog, directory, or list because there was no entry in a particular field.

**15.** Choose **Merge**.

**16.** After the catalog or list document appears (as shown in Figure 23.17), add headers, footers, or any additional text you need for the overall document. Then print the document as you would any other Word document.

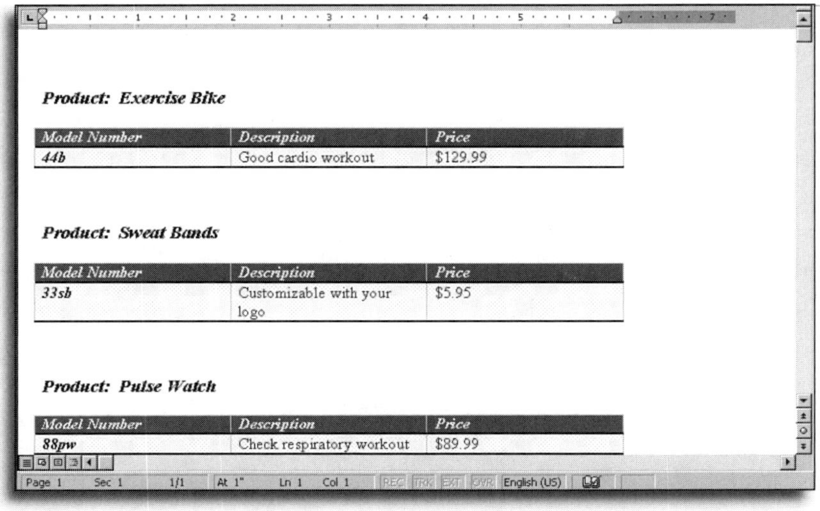

**Product:** *Exercise Bike*

| Model Number | Description | Price |
|---|---|---|
| *44b* | Good cardio workout | $129.99 |

**Product:** *Sweat Bands*

| Model Number | Description | Price |
|---|---|---|
| *33sb* | Customizable with your logo | $5.95 |

**Product:** *Pulse Watch*

| Model Number | Description | Price |
|---|---|---|
| *88pw* | Check respiratory workout | $89.99 |

Page 1   Sec 1   1/1   At 1"   Ln 1   Col 1   REC TRK EXT OVR English (US)

**FIGURE 23.17**
The resulting price list has an entry for each record in the database.

# Manage Workgroup Documents

Track document changes through revision marks

Insert comments into documents, which are not part of the document printed text

Route documents (through email) to various recipients

Create multiple versions of a document

# Know When to Track, Route, and Version Documents

A *workgroup* is a number of people who combine their talents on a specific project or event. The members of a workgroup might belong to a single department, they might represent technical talents from many departments, or they might be a group of administrators whose only shared workgroup interests are the use of standard forms or letters. But most often, workgroups are project-oriented.

Word provides a variety of tools in support of workgroups. Revision marks let multiple editors see which editor made what changes. Comments let multiple reviewers work on a document. Routing permits you to send documents to a group of people, one after another, for their review. Revision marks allow many people to edit a document and track (by color) who edited what. Highlights work just like highlighter pens, allowing you to use color to bring important points to the attention of the reader. Versioning allows you to keep different versions of the same document, so that you can determine which version suits you best.

Consider using these tools when you are sharing documents, when you are working as part of a group, when you want to track your own revisions to your own document, or when you want to retain interim versions of a document as you prepare for the final version.

Sometimes workgroup projects involve working together online, or collaborating online as Microsoft refers to it. You can learn more about online collaboration in Chapter 27, "Use Word As an Email Editor and Collaboration Tool."

## Track Documents

Word provides two tools for helping several people compose and edit documents together—revision marks and comments. For either of these tools to work properly in a workgroup, it is important to know *who* made *which* revisions or comments.

Word tracks this information by pulling information from the **User Information** tab of the Options dialog box.

**SEE ALSO**

➤ *To set user information, see page 650*

## Track Document Changes

Word can track edits to documents with *revision marks*. When you enable tracking of edits, all added text appears (by default) underlined and in a different color from the original text. All deleted text remains in the document but appears (by default) crossed out with strikethroughs. If more than one person edits the document, each person's modifications appear in a different color. Word can provide different colors for up to eight authors or reviewers. To track edits in this way, you have to turn on revision marks.

### Turn on Revision Marks

**1.** Open the document that you want to edit.

**2.** Open the **Tools** menu and select **Track Changes**, **Highlight Changes** to open the Highlight Changes dialog box (see Figure 24.1). Click **Track Changes While Editing** to enable that feature. If you want to see the revisions when you view the document, click **Highlight Changes on Screen** to place a check mark in the box. To see the revisions in the printed document, click **Highlight Changes in Printed Document** to place a check mark in the box. Choose **OK**.

> **Caution: Fill in your Word user information**
>
> If you don't configure your User information in Word, revisions you make will identify you as "enduser," "unknown," or "Preferred User." Others will not be able to identify who you are when reviewing your changes.

> **Not all changes are marked as revisions to a document**
>
> Some formatting changes (including font styles and paragraph formatting) are not tracked and marked as revisions when tracking is turned on. For example, if tracking is activated, and you bold some text, the text appears as bold in the document, with no tracking references. We know of no reliable method for tracking formatting changes in Word.

> **Turn on revisions quickly**
>
> To quickly turn on document tracking, double-click TRK on the status bar. This puts the document in Revision mode, and changes you make to the document will display as revision marks.

> **FIGURE 24.1**
> In the Highlight Changes dialog box, indicate if you want the text highlighted on the screen or in the printed document.

Or, choose Track Changes [icon] on the Reviewing toolbar (see Figure 24.2). To display the Reviewing toolbar, open the **View** menu and select **Toolbars**, **Reviewing**, or right-click a toolbar and click **Reviewing** on the pop-up menu. When changes are being tracked, **TRK** appears on the Status bar, as shown in Figure 24.2. When changes are not being tracked, TRK is dimmed. Table 24.1 lists the tools available on the Reviewing toolbar.

FIGURE 24.2

Use the Reviewing toolbar to quickly insert or review comments; highlight text; and track, accept, or reject changes.

1. Review toolbar

2. Revision

3. Reviewer pop-up

4. TRK

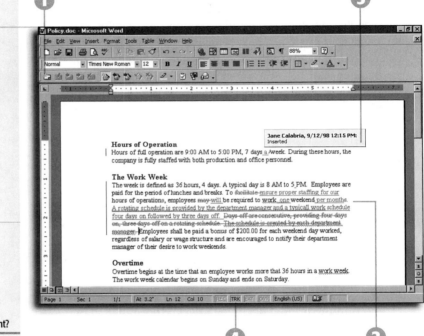

**Onscreen or printed document?**

It's most efficient to choose both Highlight Changes on Screen and Highlight Changes in Printed Document when you choose to highlight changes in a document. Even if you're not planning to print the document, if you choose to display changes onscreen only, and you do print the document, you may suffer from a temporary panic attack when you see that the changes are missing from the printed copy.

**3.** Make modifications as you would in any Word document. Any additions you make appear in color and are underlined. Deletions are in color, underlined, and have strikethrough applied. A vertical line appears in the left margin wherever a change appears in the document. Note that you won't be able to change the revision formatting (for example, you won't be able to remove the underlining).

**4.** Save the document.

TABLE 24.1 **Reviewing toolbar**

| Button | Tool | Description |
|---|---|---|
| | Insert Comment | Inserts a comment into the document at the insertion point. |
| | Edit Comment | Displays all comments in the Comments pane for editing or viewing. |
| | Previous Comment | Goes to previous comment in document and displays comment text in pop-up. |
| | Next Comment | Goes to next comment in document and displays comment text in pop-up. |
| | Delete Comment | Deletes the selected comment from the document. |
| | Track Changes | Marks revisions in the document and tracks them by the name of the modifier. |
| | Previous Change | Locates and selects the previous tracked revision. |
| | Next Change | Locates and selects the next tracked revision. |
| | Accept Change | Accepts the selected revision and removes the highlighting. |
| | Reject Change | Rejects the selected revision and removes the highlighting. |
| | Highlight | Highlights text when you choose this button and then select the text. |
| | Create Microsoft Outlook Task | Opens Microsoft Outlook (if you have the program) and allows you to enter a task there. |
| | Save Version | Saves a version of the document. |
| | Send to Mail Recipient (as Attachment) | Sends the current file as an attachment to a mail message. |

To change the color or formatting that Word uses to mark your revisions, open the **Tools** menu and select **Options** and then click the **Track Changes** tab (see Figure 24.3). For any of the following categories, choose a different type of formatting with **Mark** or **Color**:

■ **Inserted text**

■ **Deleted text**

■ **Changed formatting**

■ **Changed lines** (lines that appear by the margin to indicate changed text or formatting within the paragraph)

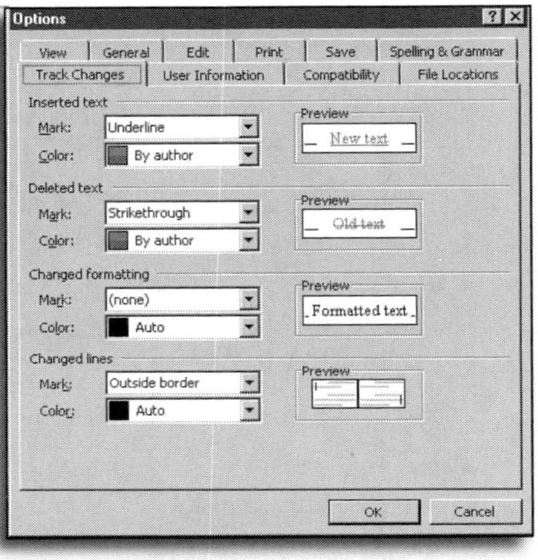

FIGURE 24.3

Make changes to the formatting settings in the **Mark** boxes or select different colors for different events.

When the document author or the final editor receives the document with the changes from all the editors, that person determines whether to accept or reject the changes by doing one of the following:

■ Select the revised text. Open the **Tools** menu and select **Track Changes**, and then **Accept or Reject Changes** to open the Accept or Reject Changes dialog box (see Figure 24.4). This dialog box stays on the screen while you edit the document or scroll to find changes, until you choose **Close**. Under **View**, click the option that displays the revisions in the manner easiest for you to use: **Changes with Highlighting** shows both changes and revision marks, **Changes without Highlighting** shows the changes but doesn't display the revision marks, **Original** doesn't display changes or revision marks. Choose **Accept** to accept the selected change, **Accept All** to accept all the changes in the document, **Reject** to reject the selected change, or **Reject**

**All** to reject all the changes in the document. Choose ←
**F<u>i</u>nd** or → **F<u>i</u>nd** to move to the previous or next revision.

- Select the modification and then **choose Accept Change** or Reject Change on the Reviewing toolbar.

- Choose Previous Change or Next Change on the Reviewing toolbar to move from one revision to another. Then choose Accept Change or Reject Change .

FIGURE 24.4

The Accept or Reject Changes dialog box also tells you who made the revision and when.

When you accept changes, any inserted revisions become part of the document, deletions are removed from the document, formatting changes are applied permanently to the appropriate text, and the revision marks disappear. When you reject changes, inserted modifications are removed, deletions are restored to the document, formatting changes are removed, and revision marks disappear.

The only way to prevent unauthorized persons from changing the document or from removing marked revisions is to protect the document *and* give it a password. Open the **<u>T</u>ools** menu and select **<u>P</u>rotect Document**. Select **<u>T</u>racked Changes** and then type a password in the **<u>P</u>assword** box. Click **OK**. Only those users who possess the password can unprotect the document and remove the tracking changes.

**SEE ALSO**

➤ *For more on protecting documents, see page 151*

## Insert Comments

Reviewers may want to add a comment to the author or pose a question without changing the document text. (Or the author may want to insert comments for the reviewers.) To add a comment, choose Insert Comment on the Reviewing toolbar or open the **<u>I</u>nsert** menu and select **<u>C</u>omment**. Type your comment in the comment window at the bottom of the screen (see Figure 24.5).

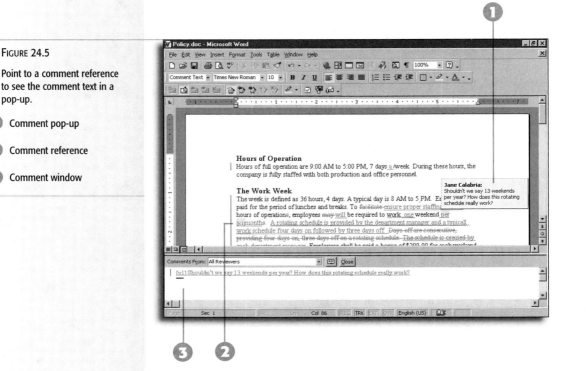

---

**Adding a comment to the text**

To make a comment part of the
document text, choose Edit
Comment  on the Reviewing
toolbar. Select the comment text in
the **Comment** pane, choose Copy
on the Standard toolbar or
press Ctrl+C. Click in the document
where you want the comment text
to appear, then choose Paste
on the Standard toolbar or press
Ctrl+V.

A comment reference mark appears next to the text on which
you're commenting. When reading a document with comment
marks, point to the comment reference mark. The comment
pops up above the text.

After entering the comment in the comment window, choose
**Close** to close the window. Choose Edit Comment on
the Reviewing toolbar to open the comment window again or
double-click the comment reference mark. (If you can't see the
comment reference mark, click the Show/Hide icon ¶ on the
Standard toolbar, or leave the comment window open as you
work through the document. Edit and review comments in the
comment window.

# Route Documents

If you're using your email program to mail documents to members of your workgroup, consider routing them instead. When you *route documents*, you can use the same distribution list as you would when you email—the difference here is how Word handles the mail. With routing, you list the mail recipients at the time you mail the document, but the document arrives in the first recipient's mailbox only. After that person is done with his revisions, the document is routed to the next person on the list, and so forth, ultimately being returned to the original sender.

This, of course, only works when you are email-enabled and Word is configured properly with your email program. You must have an email system using Microsoft Exchange, Lotus cc:Mail, or another mail system compatible with MAPI (Messaging Application Programming Interface) or VIM (Vendor Independent Messaging).

## Create a Routing Slip

To route a document, you must first prepare a routing slip.

### Create a Routing Slip

1. Open the document you plan to route.
2. Open the **File** menu and select **Send To, Routing Recipient** to open the Routing Slip dialog box (see Figure 24.6).

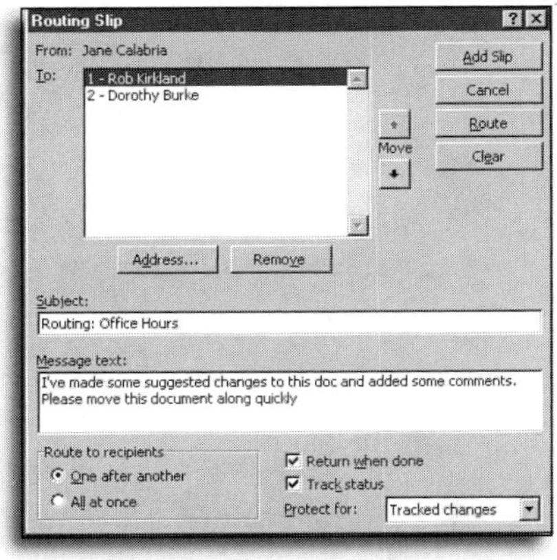

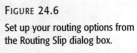

**FIGURE 24.6**
Set up your routing options from the Routing Slip dialog box.

If you haven't set up Microsoft Exchange on your system, a wizard appears to help you specify your Exchange Server, the mail software you'll be using, the name and location of your mailbox file, any passwords you need to open your mail software, and the location of your address book. After you finish the wizard, the Routing Slip dialog box appears.

**3.** Choose **A̲ddress** to select the recipients of the document (see Figure 24.7).

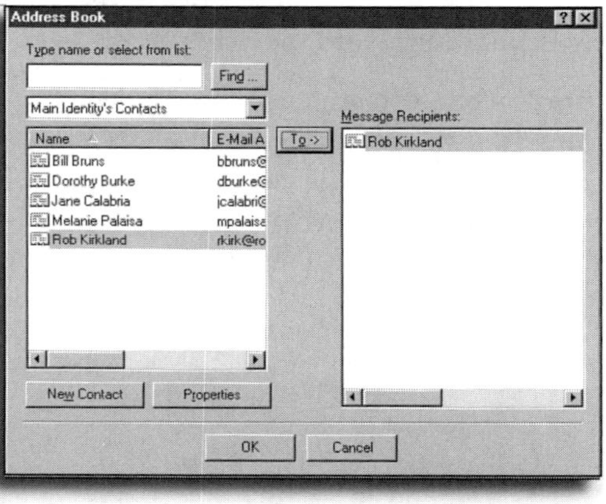

FIGURE 24.7

Enter the names of the recipients or select them from the list of names in your Address Book.

**Be sure to include a message when routing**

Although Word includes a text message in your routed document that instructs the recipient to continue, the message does not contain a list of all recipients. The first person in the routing list sees that the message is from the sender. However, the second person sees that the message is from the first person, not the original sender. Consider putting a message or list of recipients in the routing slip as a courtesy.

**4.** Select the database, distribution list, or address book that contains the names you want to use for routing in the **S̲how Names from The** drop-down list.

**5.** In the **Type Name or Select from List** box, enter the recipient's name or select the recipients from the list of people in your address book (hold down Ctrl while clicking on names to select more than one name).

**6.** Choose **T̲o** and then choose **OK**. The names you selected or entered appear in the **T̲o** box. After you have entered names, the **OK** button (see Figure 24.6) changes to **A̲dd Slip**.

**7.** To set the order of names in the routing list, click on a person's name and then click the up or down **Move** arrow to move the name up or down the list.

**8.** Word automatically enters a subject for the message in the **S̲ubject** box, based on the opening lines of the document. Edit or replace the subject text.

9. In the **M**essage text box, enter the message you want to accompany the document.

10. Under **Route to Recipients**, click **O**ne after Another to have the document routed to the first person on the list and then to the second and then to the third, and so on. If you click the **All at Once** option, everyone on the routing list will receive the message at the same time. The recipients won't have the opportunity to read the comments and revisions of others before passing the document on to the next person, which may result in duplication of effort.

11. Click **Return when Done** to enable that option. This makes sure that the document is routed back to you after everyone on the list is finished with it.

12. Click **Track Status** to place a check mark there. When you enable this option you will receive a message whenever someone forwards the document on to the next person on the routing list.

13. From the **Protect For** drop-down list, select one of the following options:

   • **Comments** lets reviewers insert comments but not change the contents of the document.

   • **Tracked Changes** turns on revision marking to track all changes the reviewer makes in the document.

   • **Forms** routes a form that you want recipients to complete without modifying the form itself.

   • **(None)** doesn't track the reviewers' changes, so you can't highlight or merge them.

14. Choose **Route** to route the document.

   Choose **Add Slip** to close the dialog box without routing the document. When you're ready to route the document, open the document, choose the **File** menu and select **Send To**, and then select **Next Routing Recipient**.

**SEE ALSO**

➤ *For more information about emailing Word documents, see page 570*

➤ *To learn more about collaborating online, see page 576*

---

**Avoid selecting distribution groups**

Word treats a group as one person and sends the document to everyone in the group at once, instead of routing it to each one in turn. Instead of selecting a group, specify the names of the individuals in the group to preserve the sequential ordering necessary to routing.

**Caution! Protecting for tracked changes protects the original file**

When you protect the routed document for tracked changes, any changes you make to the original after the file has been sent are entered into the document as revisions. You cannot turn off revisions or accept your own changes until the original document is routed back to you. Even if you save the document with a different name, changes you make are treated as revisions.

## Edit the Routed Document

When you receive an email message with a routed document attached, open the attachment as per the instructions in your email software (in most cases, you double-click on the attachment icon). Figure 24.8 shows a Word-routed document received by a Lotus Notes Mail User. When the user double-clicks the attachment, Word starts.

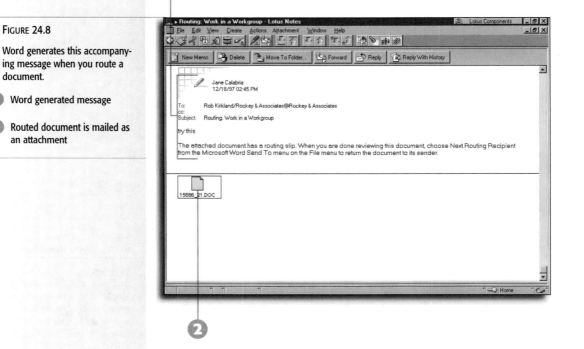

FIGURE 24.8

Word generates this accompanying message when you route a document.

**1** Word generated message

**2** Routed document is mailed as an attachment

After you double-click an attachment and make your revisions or comments, you're ready to send the document along to the next person on the routing list. Remember that you are now working in Word (regardless of the email program you used when you received this attachment). Open the **File** menu and then select **Send To**. From the submenu select **Next Routing Recipient**.

If you want to route the document to someone who isn't on the original routing list, open the **File** menu and select, **Send To**. From the submenu select **Other Routing Recipient**.

When document routing is completed and returned to the originator, Word creates a message indicating that the routing process is complete. Figure 24.9 shows the routed document returned to the originator in Microsoft Outlook.

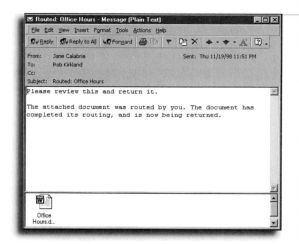

**FIGURE 24.9**
Word indicates that the routing process is complete and presents an opportunity to merge the routed document with the original.

Double-clicking the document icon starts Word and opens the file. A message appears (see Figure 24.10) asking if you want to merge the document changes with the original file. Your choices are

- **OK**. Word merges the routed document with the original document (you must indicate the filename during this process). The original document now contains revisions and you can accept or reject the changes.
- **Cancel**. Ends merging and routing processes.

**FIGURE 24.10**
When you open a routed document at the end of its travels, Word prompts you to merge the document with the original file.

Indicate how you want to treat the returned message and the routing process is complete.

# Highlight Document Text

Just as you use a highlighter pen on printed text, Word has a highlighter for you to use to emphasize text in your printed document as well as onscreen. When you share the document with others, they can easily spot the important points in the document.

To highlight text in your document, click the Highlight button [icon] on the Reviewing or Formatting toolbar and then select the text you want to emphasize. Or, select the text first, and choose **Highlight**.

If you want to change the color of the highlighting, click the down arrow next to the Highlight button [icon] and then click on one of the colors.

This type of highlighting is done manually and is different from the automatic highlighting Word uses to track revisions in a document (see "Track Document Changes" earlier in this chapter).

# Create Multiple Versions of a Document

Another option for working with documents that you want reviewed by several people is to have Word save the current version of the document automatically each time you or another person closes the document after modifying it. All the versions are stored in a single document, but only the most current version displays. The date and time the version was saved is automatically recorded, as is the name of the person making the revisions.

You can view any one of the previous versions in a separate window by opening that version from the Versions dialog box.

**Prepare a Document for Versioning**

**1.** Open the document to be reviewed. Make sure you set it up to track changes if you want to see the revisions made by the reviewers (refer to "Track Document Changes" earlier in this chapter).

**2.** Open the **File** menu and select **Versions** to open the Versions dialog box (see Figure 24.11).

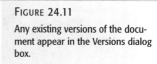

FIGURE 24.11
Any existing versions of the document appear in the Versions dialog box.

**3.** Choose **Save Now** to store the current state of the document as a separate version and open the Save Version dialog box (see Figure 24.12). In the **Comments on Version** box, enter any information that will help identify the purpose or special characteristics of that version. Then click **OK**. To read the full text comments for each version of a document, open the **File** menu and choose **Versions**. Select the version, and choose **View Comments**.

FIGURE 24.12
Enter comments that provide information on the types of revisions made in that version.

**Quickly save a version**

When you want to quickly save a version of the document, choose the Save Versions icon on the Reviewing toolbar. It opens the Save Version dialog box where you enter a comment and click **OK**.

4. Click **Automatically Save a Version on Close** to save a new version whenever the file is closed.

5. Choose **Close** to close the dialog box.

6. Send the document to the reviewers.

If you want to view a specific version of the document, open the **File** menu and select **Versions** to open the Versions dialog box. Click the version you want to see from the list of **Existing Versions** and then choose **Open**. Word opens the version as a second document window (see Figure 24.13).

FIGURE 24.13

Word shows the two versions of the same document in separate windows.

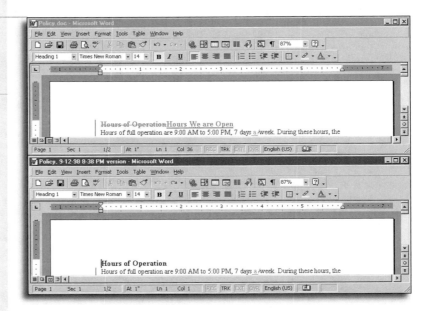

Word can compare two versions of the document to see how they differ, but they must be separate files.

**Save a Version of a Document**

1. Open the **File** menu and select **Versions** to open the Versions dialog box.

2. In the **Existing Versions** box, select the version you want to save as a separate file.

3. Choose **Open** to open the version in its own document window.

**4.** Open the **File** menu and select **Save As**.

**5.** Enter a name for the file in the **File Name** box.

**6.** Choose **Save**.

### Compare File Versions

**1.** With one version open, open the **Tools** menu and select, **Track Changes**, then choose **Compare Documents**.

**2.** The Select File to Compare With Current Document dialog box opens (see Figure 24.14).

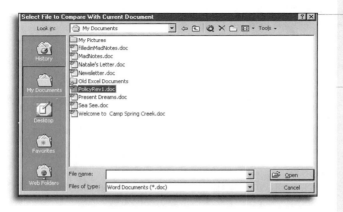

**3.** Click the name of the file to which you want to compare the current document or enter its name in the **File Name** box.

**4.** Choose **Open**.

Any modifications in the other file appear as revisions in the current document.

One problem with using different versions or allowing several reviewers to each work on a copy of the same document is gathering all the comments and modifications into one document. Additionally, one reviewer can make inaccurate or incorrect changes to the document, and if the person who compiles the final version isn't careful, he could accept revisions that make the final document incorrect. Use caution and read the document when accepting revisions.

### Merge File Versions

1. Open the document (usually the original) in which you want all the changes and comments to appear.

2. Open the **Tools** menu and select **Merge Documents**. The Select File to Merge Into Current Document dialog box opens (see Figure 24.15).

FIGURE 24.15

Select the name of the file that has the changes you want to merge with the current document.

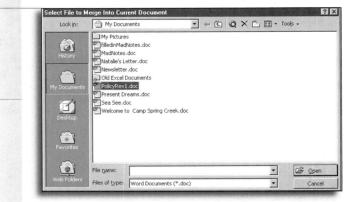

3. Select the document that has changes that you want to merge with the current file.

4. Choose **Open**.

5. Repeat steps 2 to 4 for each document you want to merge with the current document.

6. Review all the comments and accept or reject the changes.

7. Save the document.

# Design Custom Forms for Use in Word

Create user and hard copy forms

Edit, modify, and fill in forms

**Feedback on your Web site**

It's useful to have feedback from the viewers of your Web pages to know how they liked your Web site and what information is useful for visitors to your site. Use Word to create the form to collect this information.

# Types of Forms

Forms are useful documents for gathering and displaying information. There are three types of forms you can create in Word:

- Web forms
- User forms
- Hard copy (printed) forms

Creating user and hard copy forms is covered in this chapter. Web forms are defined here but creating Web forms is covered extensively and described further in Chapter 29, "Create Other Web Documents and Forms."

## Web Forms

Web forms collect data from people in your own organization via your company intranet or from people who view your Web site on the World Wide Web. These forms are designed to be viewed and completed in a Web browser and submitted to a database on an HTTP server. These are the forms we call *online* forms. Examples of these types of forms are Web site registration forms, customer inquiry forms, feedback forms, and so forth.

Forms created for the Web may require additional support files and server support, so you should consult your Web administrator as the first step in planning your form. The Web administrator will be able to tell you what types of items you can use or what types of information you can collect and in what format you need to put them.

In planning the layout of Web forms you should also be aware of the types of formatting that won't convert well for reading on the Web. You learn more about creating Web forms in Chapter 29.

## User Forms

*User* or *onscreen forms* are filled in while working in Word. These forms are usually distributed and collected via email or a shared folder on a network. Microsoft has historically referred to these forms as "online" forms, but we reserve the word "online" for Web documents. Examples of these types of forms are customer information forms for use by a sales department, order forms, and so forth.

## Hard Copy Forms

*Hard copy forms* are intended to print first and then be filled in on the printed copy. Examples of hard copy forms are fax cover sheets, employee application forms, and purchase requisitions.

All forms consist of *boilerplate* information, (information that cannot be changed by users), also known as static text, and *fields* in which users fill information. In the case of hard copy forms, check boxes or blank lines take the place of fields.

**SEE ALSO**

➢ *For more information on building forms for use on browsers, see page 608*

# Plan Your Form

The first consideration you should make when designing a form is how users will provide the information on the form. Will they write information on a paper form, such as a form you create for sending faxes? Or, will they fill in the form onscreen, saving the information they provide? Of the forms users fill out on the computer, or onscreen, some can be opened in Word as new documents, filled out, and then saved. Forms can also be distributed via email, and the filled in forms are then sent back as replies.

Designing hard copy and user forms is easy and doesn't have the design restrictions you'll find in designing forms for the Web. Keeping forms simple is always a good idea. They should be easy to read and easy to fill in.

Whether the forms will be printed and then completed or filled out onscreen, there are design considerations you should make when planning your forms:

**Control layout with tables and frames**

When preparing forms, it's important to control text placement on the form. Tables do that easily, but to ensure that table cells remain the same size for all users, specify the height of the rows and columns in the Table Properties dialog box. Deselect **Allow Row to Break Across Pages** in the same dialog box. Text outside of a table should be put in frames or text boxes to control text placement on your form.

- Put the most important information at the top of the form.

- Only ask for information that you intend to use. The shorter the form, the better response you will get from those who need to fill in the form.

- Leave sufficient white (blank) space to make the form easier to read and fill in.

- Align text and controls for ease of completion. For example, it's easier for the user if the check boxes are always in the same position.

- Don't crowd the text or make it too small to read.

- Shade areas to indicate required or important fields to complete, but avoid shading on forms intended for faxing, as shading doesn't fax well.

- Make any text in a shaded area bold, so it can be distinguished from the background.

- Use color to mark areas of your form, especially onscreen. However, limit yourself to one or two colors and keep the bulk of the text black. Too many colors are hard on the eyes. Avoid light colored text if you are going to print the form or fax it.

- When distributing forms via email, always include a short message and add clear instructions on how to return the completed form.

**SEE ALSO**
➤ *Learn more about tables on page 183*

# Create a User Form

Create user forms when you need to register people, take customer orders, gather customer information, perform surveys and evaluations, and so forth.

The user form is based on a template. After it's created, users fill in the form by opening a new document based on that template. The resulting form is saved as a document and the unaltered template can be used again to create new documents.

Remember to use tables in your form, as they help you organize the layout of form elements. The Forms toolbar has both the

Draw Table and Insert Table buttons to help you create tables where you need them. The steps to creating a form follow. If you are familiar with forms and fields, you'll find the following instructions to creating a form a good guide to getting up and running quickly. If you are creating a form for the first time, review the following instructions and find more detailed information on each of the steps in form design later in this chapter.

### Create a User Form

1. Open the **File** menu and select **New**. When the New dialog box appears, select the **General** tab if it's not already selected. Click the **Blank Document** icon.

2. Under **Create New**, select **Template** and choose **OK**.

3. Add the boilerplate text or graphics you want in your form (refer to the "Insert Text" section of this chapter for more information on adding boilerplate text).

4. If it isn't visible, turn on the Forms toolbar (see Figure 25.1) by opening the **View** menu and selecting **Toolbars**, **Forms**.

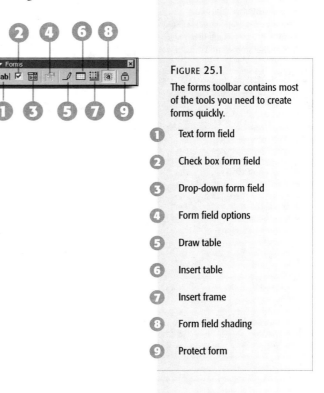

FIGURE 25.1

The forms toolbar contains most of the tools you need to create forms quickly.

1.  Text form field

2.  Check box form field

3.  Drop-down form field

4.  Form field options

5.  Draw table

6.  Insert table

7.  Insert frame

8.  Form field shading

9.  Protect form

5. To add the fields you want the user to fill in, click in the document where you want the field to appear, and then insert the appropriate form field from the Forms toolbar (see the "Insert Fields" section later in this chapter for instructions on adding fields to your form).

6. After the form is complete, (see Figure 25.2 for an example) choose Protect Form 🔒 on the Forms toolbar. When you protect the form, the users can only enter information in the form fields. They can't change any other part of the form. This also helps the user move from field to field quickly in the form (for more information, see "Protect Forms" later in this chapter).

7. Save and close the template.

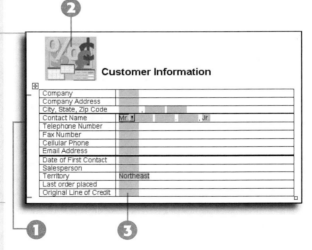

**FIGURE 25.2**

Here, a customer information form includes graphics and tables. Forms can also include drawings, special characters, and WordArt.

1 Static text

2 Graphic

3 Form fields

**SEE ALSO**

➤ *Learn more about templates on page 343*

➤ *To create tables, see page 165*

➤ *To add graphics to documents, see page 363*

## Insert Text

When you're building a form, it's generally easiest to enter the static, or boilerplate, information first. This includes the form title, instructional or explanatory text, labels for fields, and so on.

The Forms toolbar (refer to Figure 25.1) contains tools to help you create tables or isolate text from other text in the form:

- Draw Table lets you draw a table wherever you want it on the page.

- Insert Table inserts a table at your insertion point.

- Insert Rows appears on the Forms toolbar if you have a row selected in a table, and replaces the Insert Table button. Choose Insert Rows to insert a row before the selected row.

- Insert Frame creates a box (called a *frame*). Choose Insert Frame on the Forms toolbar and then drag a rectangle to specify the position, size, and shape of the frame.

**SEE ALSO**

➤ *Learn more about inserting, drawing, and formatting tables on page 163*

➤ *Create frames and wrap text on page 375*

➤ *Learn how to customize your toolbars and add an Insert Frame button on page 640*

## Insert Fields

Fields are placeholders for *variables* (information that may change in a document). Word has many different types of fields for different purposes. For example, when you insert page numbers, Word inserts a page number field in the document. Word adds a date field to your document when you click the **Insert** menu and select **Date and Time**. You learn more about date and time fields later in this chapter and more about page numbers later in this section.

You can't see the field codes in a document unless you click the **Tools** menu and select **Options**, then select the **View** tab, and click **Field Codes** under **Show** to enable the option. The field codes in a document appear between braces (curly brackets {}), as shown in Figure 25.3.

Forms have three special types of fields:

- Text form field **ab**. A fill-in field in which users insert text.
- Check box form field **☑**. Puts a check box next to an option.
- Drop-down form field **▤**. A drop-down list box, from which users may select from one of several options.

**Warning! Boilerplate text can be changed**

Unless you protect your form (see "Protect Forms" later in this chapter), users can change the boilerplate text and alter your template.

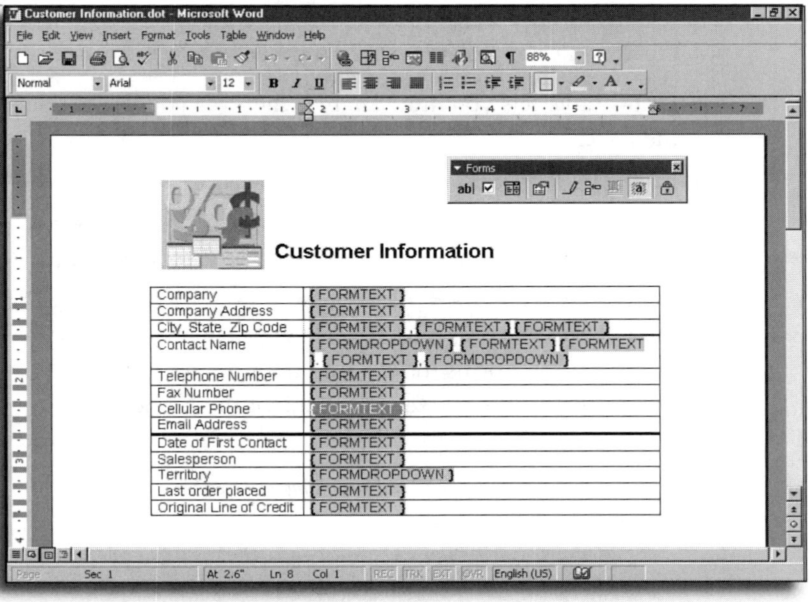

FIGURE 25.3

The field codes in this form appear with gray shaded backgrounds. Document protection must be disabled to view field codes.

To insert a field in your form, click where you want the field to appear and then click the appropriate button on the Forms toolbar.

You need to define the field options to determine how the field will work in your form. Each type of field has its own options. To set the options, double-click the field or choose Form Field Options [icon] on the Forms toolbar to open the Field Options dialog box for that particular type of field. Specify the options and then choose **OK**. You won't be able to see the full functionality of the form fields until you protect the document (see "Protect Forms," later in this chapter).

In designing a Text Form field, you specify the type of text the user can enter in the field—regular text, numbers, date, time, calculation, and so on. You can enter the default text that appears in the field, set the maximum length of the field, or specify the format for the text, date, time, or numbers. Figure 25.4 shows the Text Form Field Options dialog box. Choose **OK** to accept your settings and close the dialog box.

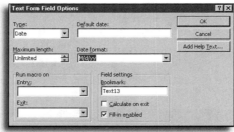

**FIGURE 25.4**

The options in the Text Form Field Options box are set for the "Date of First Contact" field on the form.

For a Check Box Form field, you specify the size of the check box and decide whether the box should be checked automatically when the user opens the document (the user can change that) by clicking **Not Checked** or **Checked** under Default Value. Choose **OK** to accept your settings and close the dialog box. Figure 25.5 shows the Check Box Form Field Options dialog box.

**Formatting fields**

To apply character formatting to fields, select the field(s) and use the formatting toolbar or the **Font** or **Format** menu to choose formatting options.

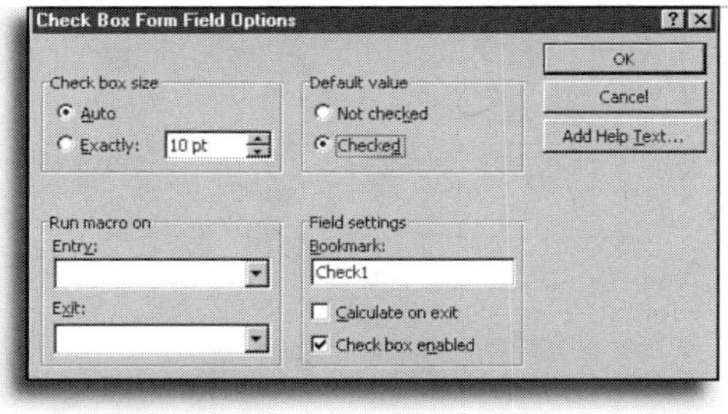

**FIGURE 25.5**

Set the size of the box and choose whether or not it should be checked by default.

The Drop-Down Form Field options let you add the list of options from which the user chooses, as shown in Figure 25.6. Enter an item for the list in the **Drop-Down Item** box and then click **Add** to add it to the list. Use the **Move** arrows to set the order of the items in the list. The first item in the list will be the default option in the drop-down box. Choose **OK** to accept your settings and close the dialog box.

When you select the options for the field, choose **Add Help Text** to enter information that guides the user in filling out the form (see Figure 25.7). On the **Status Bar** tab, click in the **Type Your Own** box and enter the text to appear on the status bar when the user clicks on the field. Alternatively, click **AutoText Entry** and select the AutoText entry that acts as the help message (you must create the appropriate AutoText entry before opening this dialog box). On the **Help Key (F1)** tab, enter the text that appears when the user presses F1 for help on a field or select the appropriate AutoText entry. Choose **OK** to return to the Field Options dialog box.

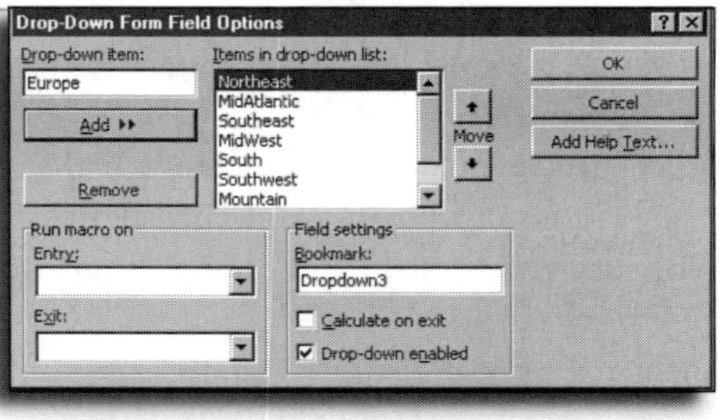

FIGURE 25.6

Create the list of items that appear when the user clicks on the field in the form.

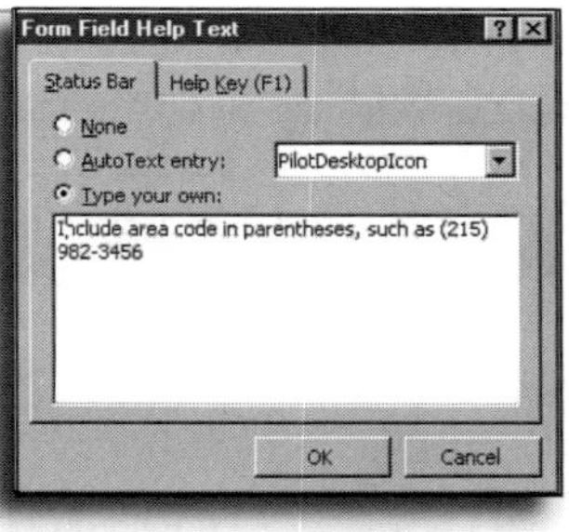

FIGURE 25.7

Enter instructions that you want the users to see on the Status bar when they click the field.

To trigger a macro when users enter text in a field, or exit from a field, specify the macro name in the **Run Macro On** area of the Field Options dialog box, in either the **Entry** or **Exit** box (depending on when you want to activate the macro).

To help the users of the form locate fields, turn the field shading on by choosing Form Field Shading 🗚 on the Forms toolbar. Normally, the form field shading is on, in which case choosing Form Field Shading would turn the shading off.

**SEE ALSO**
➤ *To learn how to create macros, see page 621*
➤ *To learn more about AutoText, see page 123*

# Create a Printed Form

Some forms need to be printed before they can be filled in by others. These types of forms include fax cover sheets (our example here). Even with fax modems on every PC in the company, there is often a need to fax information from hard copy (such as a magazine article). Most companies maintain fax machines for this purpose and keeping a stack of fax cover sheets in the fax room to save others from having to run back to their PCs to create a cover sheet in Word. Other printed forms used in the office include phone message pads and supply requisitions.

### Create a Printed Form

1. Create a new form.

2. Add any text or graphics you want on the form (see Figure 25.8).

3. To insert check boxes, use Word's field feature (these are the fields you use when you create a user form). Click in the document where you want to place the check box. Then choose Check Box Form Field ☑ on the Forms toolbar.

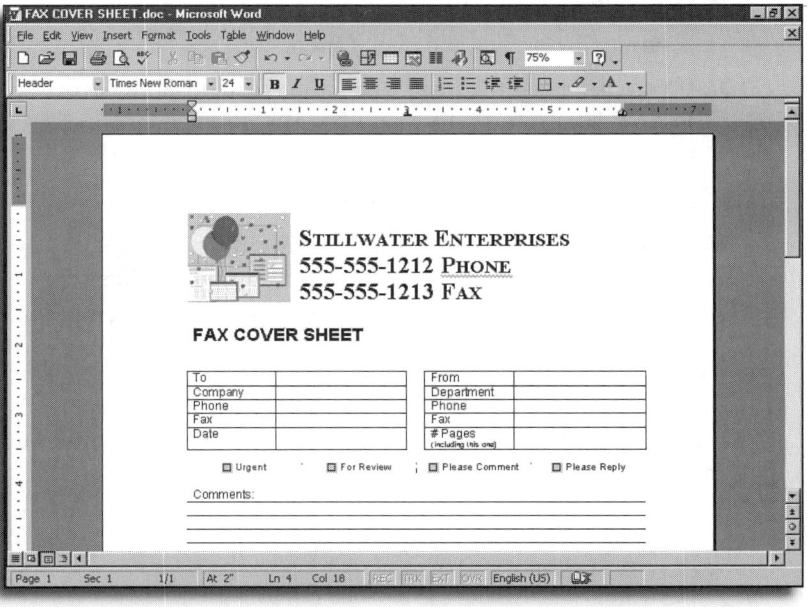

**Good form design begins on paper**

One sheet of paper and a few minutes of time are all you need to plan a form. Unless design is not a consideration, save time later by taking a moment to plan and lay out your form elements on paper before you create the form in Word.

**FIGURE 25.8**
Consider using tables in your form to help you organize the text and fields as shown here on a fax cover form.

**4.** Save and print the form.

You now have a form you can duplicate so others can fill it in.

**SEE ALSO**

➤ *To learn how to insert a table, see page 165*

# Edit and Modify a Form

Modifying printed forms is easy—open the document, edit it, and save your changes.

Modifying user forms is a little more complicated. You must open and modify the template, removing any protection assigned to the template.

### Modify a User Form

1. Click the **File** menu and select **Open**. The Open dialog box appears. From the **Files of Type** box, select **Document Templates (*.dot)**.

2. In the **Look In** box, specify the drive and folder where the form template is stored (such as \Program Files\Microsoft Office\Templates\Other Documents). Select the template from the list of files and click **Open**.

3. If you protected the form when you created it (see "Protect Forms" later in this chapter), click the **Tools** menu and select **Unprotect Document.**

4. Make your changes to the form template.

5. Protect the form again before you save it by choosing Protect Form 🔒 on the Forms toolbar or by clicking the **Tools** menu and selecting **Protect Document**, **Forms**, and choosing **OK**.

6. Save and close the template.

You must close the form template before you can use it to fill out a form onscreen.

# Protect Forms

It's a good idea to restrict users to designated areas (sections) of a form so they can't change your boilerplate (static) text, graphics, headers or footers, page numbering, fields, and so on.

### Protect a Form

1. With your form document open, open the **Tools** menu and select **Protect Document**. The Protect Document dialog box appears (see Figure 25.9).

FIGURE 25.9

Choose **Forms** to restrict users to entering data in fields on the form.

2. Click **Forms**. This prevents changes to the form, except in form fields where the user is expected to enter data or in unprotected sections. If the document is divided into sections, specify which sections are to be protected by choosing **Sections** and selecting the sections you want to protect.

3. Enter a password in the **Password (Optional)** box so only authorized users can remove the protection and change the form; otherwise any knowledgeable user can unprotect the document.

4. Choose **OK**.

### SEE ALSO

➤ Learn how to create sections on page 286

When users open a protected form, they may only enter information in unprotected fields and sections. For onscreen forms, this simplifies data entry in addition to keeping unauthorized people from changing your form.

# Fill in a User Form

After the form template has been created, the form is ready for users to populate.

### Fill in a User Form

1. Open the **File** menu and select **New**. In the New dialog box, select the appropriate tab and then click the icon for the form template you want to use. Select **Document** under **Create New** and choose **OK**.

2. Enter information in the form fields (see Figure 25.10). For check boxes, click to check the box or press **X** when the box is highlighted. For drop-down fields, click the down arrow next to the field to see the list of available items and then click the item you want. If you're unsure what to enter, check the Status bar or press F1 to see any help text on how to fill in the field.

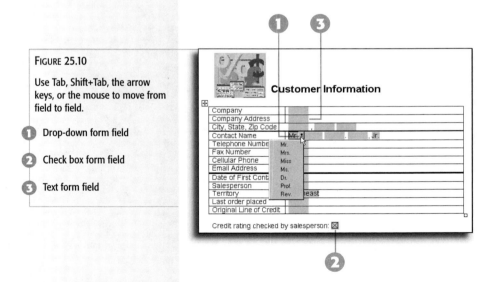

FIGURE 25.10

Use Tab, Shift+Tab, the arrow keys, or the mouse to move from field to field.

1. Drop-down form field

2. Check box form field

3. Text form field

3. Press Tab and Shift+Tab to move forward or backward through the fields. The arrow keys also help you navigate through the form.

4. When you have completed the form, save it.

After the file is saved, you can print it, fax it, or email it. If you're on a network with shared access to files, others can open the file and view it.

CHAPTER

26

# Work with Long Documents

Create and modify a master document to manage and bind several files into one

Generate a table of contents

Create an index

Insert, display, and delete bookmarks

Navigating a long document

When working with long documents, you'll find Word's **Go To** command very useful. Open the **Edit** menu and select **Go To** (alternatively, press F5). The Find and Replace dialog box appears. Click the **Go To** tab and indicate the page, section, bookmark, and so forth, that you want to go to. For more information on using the Find and Replace dialog box, see Chapter 6, "Use Proofing Tools."

# Know When to Use Master Documents

Working with long documents is cumbersome, particularly when several files created by several users need to be combined into one seamless report. For example, documents and reports such as annual reports, corporate policies, or employee handbooks are often the combined efforts of a team of people representing several departments. Each of these people create a separate file for their contribution to the report from which a final product is generated. When the files are bound into one large report, the need for page numbers, headers and footers, a table of contents, an index, and consistent formatting becomes apparent (and often a headache) to the individual responsible for the final, printed version.

Word's solution to this problem is the *master document*, which acts as a binder for a set of separate files called *subdocuments*. The master document helps manage all the subdocuments that are its components. A master document can be managed by one person, or managed as a cooperative effort of many.

A master document contains links to separate files, which can be opened and edited while working in the master document, or individually outside of the master document. The master document manages the "big picture," keeping a total page count and viewing all files as the sum of the whole. This enables you to create and work in a smaller, single file versus working in many files or in one very large file.

**SEE ALSO**
➤ To learn how linking works, see page 393

# Create a New Master Document

The master document serves as a skeleton on which you hang the various parts (subdocuments) of the entire document. Therefore, you need to start by creating that skeleton. This means starting with an outline. The main headings of your outline become the titles of your subdocuments. When you save the master document, Word assigns filenames to the subdocuments based on their titles.

**Create a New Master Document**

1. Start a new document.

2. Click the **View** menu and select **Outline** to switch to the Outline view, or click the Outline View button 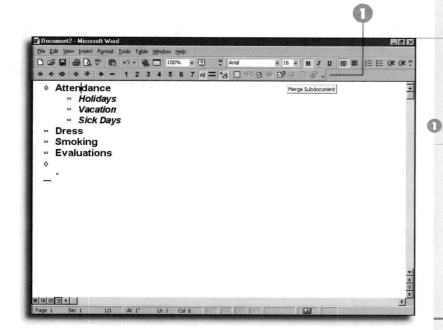. In Figure 26.1 you see the headings that are the beginning of an employee handbook.

**FIGURE 26.1**

The seven headings in this document will become the titles of seven subdocuments in the master document.

1 Outlining toolbar

3. Create an outline for the master document to serve as the skeleton of the master document. Use Word's built-in heading styles (Heading 1, Heading 2, and so on) or use Promote ⬅ and Demote ➡ on the Outlining toolbar to set the outline levels. (Demote indents the heading to the right and Promote moves the heading to the left while in outline view.)

4. Select all of the text in your document. Be certain that your text is formatted with heading styles or in outline level as Word will divide your document into subdocuments based on your styles. For example, each Heading 1 style will become a new subdocument.

**Pluses and minuses**

In front of each heading in your outline you see a plus or a minus. The plus means the topic has additional headings or text contained within it. If you do not see those headings beneath a main topic, place your cursor inside the heading text and click the Expand button on the Outlining toolbar ⊞. Click the Collapse button ⊟ if you only want to see the main heading. Headings with a minus sign indicate that there is no other text beneath that heading. Change the outline level of a heading by dragging the plus or minus to the left or right.

5. Choose Create Subdocument 📄 on the Outlining toolbar (see Figure 26.2). Each subdocument becomes its own section within the master document. To view a subdocument icon for each subdocument, click the Master Document View button 🔲 on the Outlining toolbar.

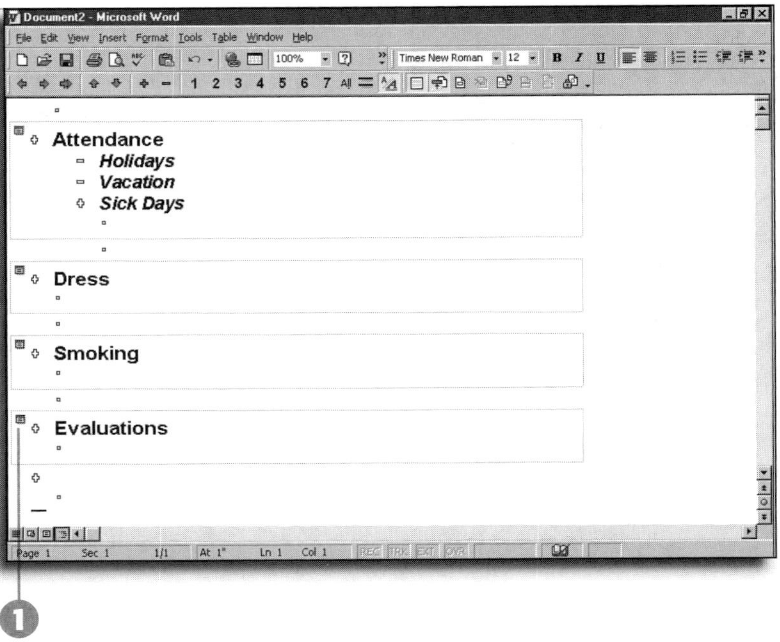

FIGURE 26.2

In Master Document view, subdocuments are displayed with boxes around their contents. If you switch to Outline view, subdocuments are surrounded by section breaks.

① Subdocument icon

6. Save the master document by clicking the **File** menu and selecting **Save As** on the menu. When the Save As dialog box appears, select a location for the master document from the **Save In** drop-down list. Enter a name for the document in the **File Name** box. Choose **Save**. Word assigns a filename for each subdocument based on the first characters in the heading for the subdocument. For example, in the employee handbook example illustrated in Figure 26.2, Word also saved four documents (Attendance.doc, Dress.doc, Smoking.doc, and Evaluations.doc) as illustrated in Figure 26.3 when the master document was saved as Employee Handbook.doc.

FIGURE 26.3
Filenames for subdocuments are created by Word using the text found at the beginning of the subdocument. In this example, each subdocument was defined by the style Heading 1, and the Heading 1 text becomes the filename.

By default, subdocuments are collapsed (you only see the document names, as in Figure 26.4) when you open a master document. Choose Expand Subdocuments on the Master Document toolbar to see all the text in a subdocument. The same button becomes the Collapse Subdocuments button when the subdocuments are expanded.

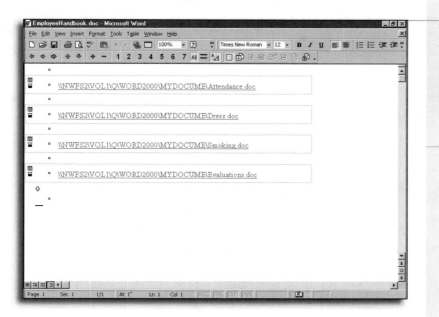

FIGURE 26.4
When you open a saved master document, the subdocuments are collapsed and you see only the document names and their paths. The names are hyperlinks—double-click the filename to open a subdocument.

To edit text or print a subdocument from within the master document, you need to expand the subdocument first.

After all the subdocument text in the master document is complete, add your headers and footers, table of contents, and an index from the master document.

**SEE ALSO**

➤ *To learn more about creating outlines and using the Outlining toolbar, see page 310*

➤ *For more information on using Styles, see page 237*

# Create a Master Document from an Existing Document

What do you do when you've already started the document and realized that you should have created it as a master document? Convert the document into a master document by following these steps.

### Convert a Document to a Master Document

**1.** Open the document you want to convert to a master document.

**2.** Click the **View** menu and select **Outline** to open the Outline view.

**3.** Apply Word's built-in heading styles or specify outline levels to set up the outline of the master document.

**4.** Select the headings and text you want to divide into subdocuments. Remember to format the first heading you select with the heading style or outline level that you want to use to designate the beginning of each subdocument.

**5.** Choose Create Subdocument ⬚ on the Outlining toolbar.

**6.** Save the master document by clicking the **File** menu and selecting **Save As**. Enter a filename and location for the master document. Choose **Save**. Word assigns a filename for each subdocument based on the first characters in the heading for the subdocument.

After you've converted your document into a master document, you can insert or create subdocuments to add to it.

# Edit and Modify Master Documents

Editing the text of a master document can be handled two ways: directly in the master document or from the subdocument files.

When you want to modify the text contained in a subdocument, you can open that file directly. For example, to change the employee handbook, you open Attendance.doc and make your changes there. Because the subdocument in the master document is only a pointer to this file, any modifications to Attendance.doc automatically appear in the master document after Attendance.doc is saved.

This capability to open the subdocuments as separate files is what makes it possible for several authors to work on the same master document simultaneously.

If you have the master document open and you would like to work directly in the subdocument file, double-click the subdocument icon at the top of that subdocument and the subdocument file opens. If the subdocuments are collapsed, the names of the subdocuments become hyperlinks to the subdocument files—click the name of the file and the file opens. When you save the subdocument file, the modifications appear in the master document.

**SEE ALSO**

➤ *Learn more about hyperlinks on page 589*

## Add an Existing Document to the Master Document

To insert an existing document into the master document, follow these steps.

**Insert a Subdocument**

1. Open the master document in the Outline view.

2. Place your insertion point where you want to insert the existing document. This should be in a blank line between existing subdocuments.

3. Choose Insert Subdocument 📑 on the Master Document toolbar.

---

**Hyperlinks**

Hyperlinks are specially marked text that jumps you to a specific address on the Web, to a specific file on your hard disk or network drive, or to a specific location in a document (such as a bookmark). In long documents, combining hyperlinks with bookmarks can help anyone reading the document online in navigating the document. You can create your own hyperlinks from text in your document by highlighting the text and then clicking Insert Hyperlink 🖼 on the Standard toolbar.

**Table of contents framed**

The table of contents is not just for printed documents. It's a useful page to include in your Web site and Word 2000 makes it possible to add a table of contents to your Web site as a frame (section of a browser screen you see separate from the Web page you are viewing). To learn more about preparing a table of contents in a frame for your Web site, see "Incorporate Frames" in Chapter 29, "Create Other Web Documents and Forms."

**4.** In the Insert Subdocument dialog box, select or enter the filename of the document you want to add. Choose **Open**.

## Remove a Subdocument from the Master Document

At some point you may decide that one of the subdocuments in your master document does not need to be set up as a separate document. Its text can be incorporated into the master document. You usually do this when there is not sufficient text in the subdocument to warrant a separate file.

### Remove a Subdocument

**1.** Open the master document.

**2.** Select the subdocument you want to remove (click the sub-document icon).

**3.** Choose Remove Subdocument 🖺 on the Master Document toolbar. Any text from that subdocument is incorporated into the master document.

If you mean to totally remove the subdocument and its contents instead of removing the separate subdocument and making its text part of the master document, you must *delete* the document and its text.

# Create a Table of Contents

A *table of contents* lists all the main topics in your document and notes on which page number each topic starts.

Word helps you generate a table of contents for your document automatically. The easiest method for doing this is to assign one of Word's built-in heading styles (Heading 1 through Heading 9) to the headings you want to include in the table of contents. If you don't want to use Word's heading styles, you must assign a table of contents level to the styles you're using or mark text for inclusion in the table of contents. If you've assigned outline levels to your document headings, you set up your table of contents using those levels, much as you do using the Word headings.

**Create a Table of Contents Using Word's Built-In Heading Styles**

1. Apply the built-in heading styles Heading 1 through Heading 9 to the headings in your document that you want to include in the table of contents.

2. Place the insertion point in the document where you want the table of contents to appear. You may want to add a section or page break before your document text so the table of contents is on a separate page. You may also want to add a title for your page, such as "Table of Contents."

3. Click the **Insert** menu and select **Index and Tables**. The Index and Tables dialog box appears (see Figure 26.5).

**Don't include the table of contents title**

When you're assigning styles to your headings, be careful not to assign a style to the heading of your table of contents. Otherwise, when you generate your table of contents, "Table of Contents" will be one of the entries.

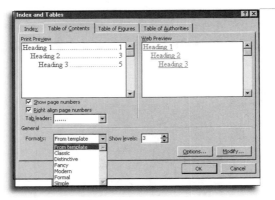

**FIGURE 26.5**

Select the format you want to use for your table of contents.

4. Select the **Table of Contents** tab if it's not already displayed.

5. From the **Formats** drop-down list, select the format that you want to apply to the table of contents. As you click a format, a sample appears in the **Print Preview** window and in the **Web Preview** window (which shows you how the Table of Contents appears in a browser).

6. If you want the page numbers to appear for each topic, click **Show Page Numbers** to enable that option. Click **Right Align Page Numbers** if you want the page numbers lined up on the right margin.

7. In the **Show Levels** box, enter the number of heading levels you want to appear in the table of contents, or use the up and down arrows to select the number.

**8.** From the **Ta<u>b</u> Leader** drop-down list, select the repeat character (leader) you want to appear between the heading and the page number (dots, dashes, or underscores). Select **None** if you don't want any leaders.

**9.** (Optional) If you want to change the format, choose **<u>M</u>odify** (only available if you selected **From Template** as the format) to open the Style dialog box (see Figure 26.6). From the **<u>S</u>tyles** box, select the heading level you want to change in the table of contents and then choose **<u>M</u>odify** to open the Modify Style dialog box. Choose **<u>F</u>ormat** to select the type of format you want to specify and then select the formatting options you desire. Choose **OK** to return to the Style dialog box, and then choose **<u>A</u>pply**.

**FIGURE 26.6**

Select the table of contents style and level you want to change and then choose **Modify**.

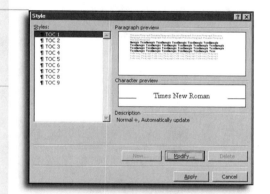

**All page numbers equal to one?**

If you are following along step by step with our instructions, you are generating a table of contents from an outline with no text in each of the subdocuments. This results in a table of contents which shows every page as 1. Once you add text to each of your subdocuments, consequently adding pages, when you update your TOC, the page numbers will change accordingly.

**10.** Choose **OK**. Word generates the table of contents for your document.

**SEE ALSO**

➤ *To learn more about applying styles to document text, see page 247*

## Generate a Table Using Styles

If you don't want to use Word's built-in heading styles and would prefer to assign table of contents levels to the styles currently in the document, complete the following steps.

### Create a Table of Contents Using Styles

**1.** Place the insertion point where you want the table of contents to appear.

2. Click the **Insert** menu and select **Index and Tables**. The Index and Tables dialog box appears (refer to Figure 26.5).

3. Select the **Table of Contents** tab if it's not already selected.

4. Choose **Options** to open the Table of Contents Options dialog box (see Figure 26.7). Click **Styles** to enable that option. Enter a number from 1 to 9 in the **TOC Level** boxes across from the styles you want to assign to the table of contents. Choose **OK**.

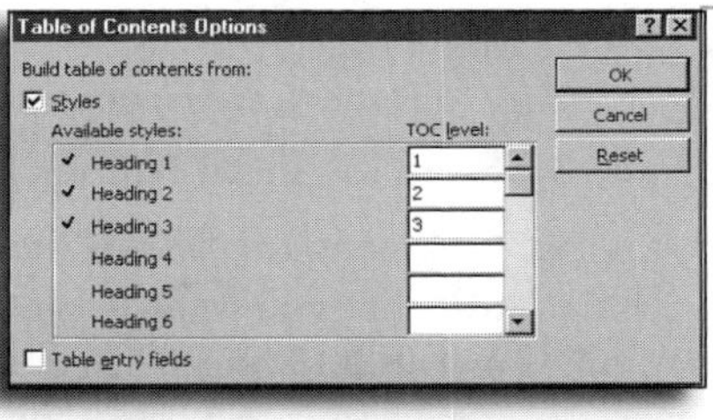

**FIGURE 26.7**

Put a table of contents level number next to each heading style you want to use to generate the table of contents.

5. Follow steps 5 through 10 in the "Create a Table of Contents" section in this chapter.

## Mark Text for Table of Contents

Using styles is not the only method to indicate which text should appear in the table of contents. Table of contents entries can be marked by field codes, marking each entry as you type. Use this method if you have items you want to include in the table of contents, but those items do not have styles associated with them. You can use this method in combination with creating tables of contents using styles.

### Mark Entries for a Table of Contents

1. Place your insertion point immediately before the text you want to include in the contents.

2. Click the **Insert** menu and select **Field**. The Field dialog box appears (see Figure 26.8).

**If a table already exists**

When you insert a table of contents, Word will ask you if you want to replace the current table of contents if one already exists. Click **Yes** to replace the current one; **No** to add a second one.

**Listing figures, maps, pictures, and graphs**

To list illustrations in your table of contents, mark the illustrations or their captions as table entries. When the table of contents is generated, entries will also appear for those items.

FIGURE 26.8

Select the **Index and Tables** category and then the **TC** field name. Then enter the remainder of the code in the **Field Codes** box.

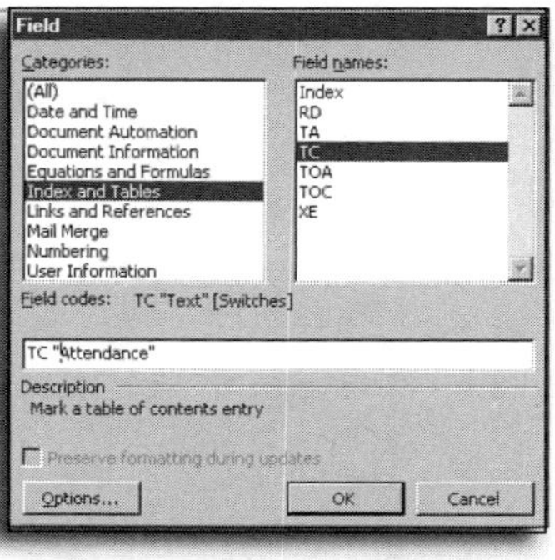

**3.** From the **Categories** list, select **Index and Tables**.

**4.** From the **Field Names** list, select **TC**.

**5.** Following the **TC** in the **Field Codes** box, enter the text that you want to appear in the table of contents. The text should be enclosed in double quotes.

**6.** Choose **OK**. A field code is inserted in the document text but is hidden. Choose **Show/Hide** ¶ on the Standard toolbar to see the code (see Figure 26.9).

FIGURE 26.9

A code is inserted that marks the text for the table of contents.

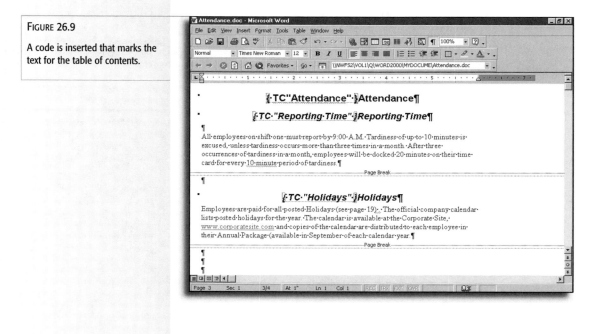

Perform the following steps to generate a table of contents from your marked entries.

**Generate a Table of Contents from Marked Entries**

**1.** Place the insertion point where you want the table of contents to appear.

**2.** Click the **Insert** menu and select **Index and Tables**. The Index and Tables dialog box appears.

**3.** Select the **Table of Contents** tab if it's not already selected.

**4.** Choose **Options** to open the Table of Contents Options dialog box (see Figure 26.10). Click **Table Entry Fields**. Choose **OK** to return to the Index and Tables dialog box.

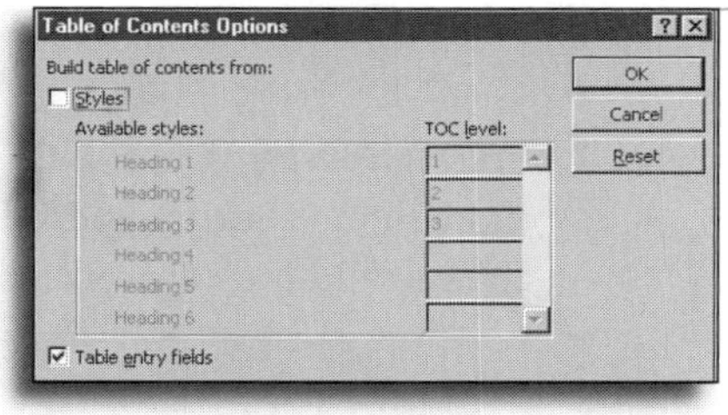

**FIGURE 26.10**

Enable the Table Entry Fields option to generate a table of contents based on fields.

**5.** Choose **OK** to generate the table of contents.

## Update and Delete a Table of Contents

The table of contents does not automatically change when you make changes to the heading text in your document or you add or delete text. Although it's possible to edit the text within the table of contents, any changes won't match your document text. You need to *refresh* the table of contents.

**Update a Table of Contents**

**1.** Select the table of contents.

**2.** Press F9, or right-click the table of contents and click **Update Field** from the shortcut menu. The Update Table of Contents dialog box appears (see Figure 26.11).

---

**Use the table of contents to navigate a document**

The TOC generated by Word 2000 uses hyperlinks. When you click on an item in the TOC, Word jumps you to that point in that document. That's the good news. The bad news is, if you're accustomed to working in previous versions of Word, you know that clicking anywhere within a TOC is necessary in order to update the TOC. With Word 2000, you cannot click "inside" a TOC, you must select the entire TOC before you update it.

FIGURE 26.11

Choose to update only the page numbers or the entire text.

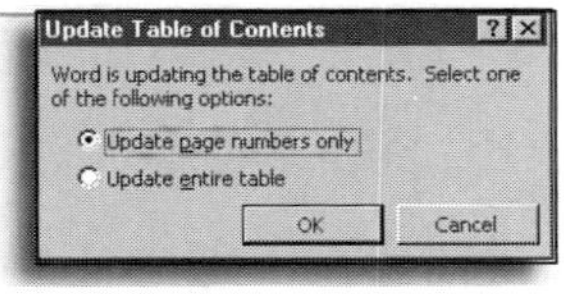

3. Click **Update <u>P</u>age Numbers Only** if you've only moved text around or added or deleted body text. Click **Update Entire Table** if you've added or deleted headings, marked new TOC entries using fields, or if you've changed the style of any headings.

4. Choose **OK**.

Perform the following steps to remove a table of contents.

**Remove a Table of Contents**

1. Select the table of contents.

2. Press Shift+F9 if you don't see a field code (or click the right-mouse button and select <u>T</u>**oggle Field Codes**). The code would look something like:

   `{ TOC \o "1-3" }`

3. Select the field code, including the brackets {}, and press the Delete key.

If you're not familiar with field codes or if your table of contents is short, try this: Select the text of the entire table of contents (the text appears white in a gray field) and then press the Delete key.

# Create an Index

An *index* is a listing that usually appears at the end of the book. The listing is a set of topics covered in the document along with the pages on which the topics are mentioned. The topics are generally listed in alphabetical order.

Start an index by indicating which words, phrases, or symbols you want to include in the index for your document by "marking" them. Then you choose an index design and generate the finished index. To make the index, Word collects all the index entries, sorts them alphabetically, references their page numbers, finds and removes duplicate entries from the same page, and displays the index.

# Mark Text for Index

To create a topic and page reference in your index, you must mark the words or phrases you want to appear in the index. Doing this provides Word a way to know what and where indexed references appear in your document.

### Mark Index Entries

1. Select the text that you want for the index entry.

2. Click the **Insert** menu and select **Index and Tables** to open the Index and Tables dialog box.

3. Select the **Index** tab (see Figure 26.12).

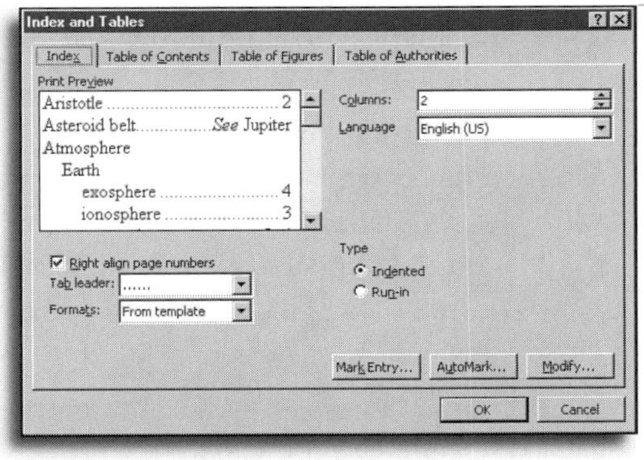

**FIGURE 26.12**
Select the style of index you want for your document.

4. Choose **Mark Entry**. The Mark Index Entry dialog box appears (see Figure 26.13).

5. The selected text appears in the **Main Entry** box. Edit that text or enter new text if the selected text is not exactly what you want to display in the index.

6. Under Options, select **Current Page** as the page number you want cited in the index. If you want to add formatting to the page numbers as they appear in the index, click **Bold** or **Italic** under **Page Number Format**.

**Quick index marking**

A quick way to open the Mark Index Entry dialog box is to select the text you want to mark for the index and press Alt+Shift+X.

7. Choose **Mark** to mark the entry. Choose **Mark All** to mark the first occurrence in each paragraph of your document that exactly matches the text and case of the entry.

8. The dialog box remains open so you may make additional index entries. To make another entry, click in the document to make it active, then select the text in the document or click immediately after it, click back in the Mark Index Entry dialog box to make it active, and repeat steps 5 through 7.

9. Repeat step 7 for each index entry you want to make in this session. Choose **Close** to close the Mark Index Entry dialog box.

Word marks each index entry by inserting a field immediately after the entry text in your document (see Figure 26.14). If the field isn't visible, choose **Show/Hide** ¶ on the Standard toolbar.

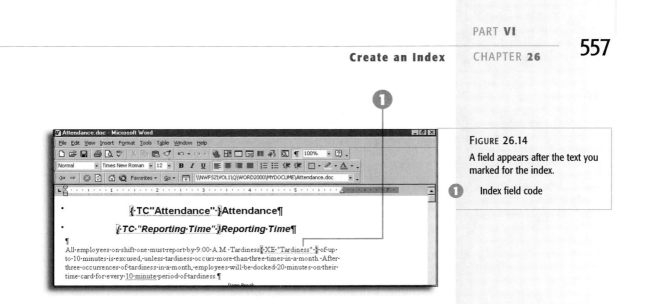

FIGURE 26.14
A field appears after the text you marked for the index.

1   Index field code

## Use a Concordance File

An alternative to marking each index entry in your document is to use a concordance file. A *concordance file* is an index file with two columns—the first column lists the text in the document that you want to index, and the second column lists the index entries to generate from the text in the first column. You use the concordance file to automatically search your document and mark all the matching entries for the index. With a large document, this can save you considerable time in building an index.

### Create a Concordance File

1. Start a new file.

2. Create a two-column table.

3. Enter the words or phrases that you want to mark as index entries in the first column of the table. Because Word will search your document for all the occurrences of this text, you must enter it exactly as it appears in the document. To be sure, make a separate row for all forms of the text you want to search (such as search, searching, searched, searches). Press Tab to move to the second column.

4. Type the text for the main index entry as it will appear in the index. To create a subentry, follow the main entry text with a colon (:) and then the subentry text. Press Tab to go to the next row.

**5.** Repeat steps 3 and 4 until you've entered all the reference information (see Figure 26.15).

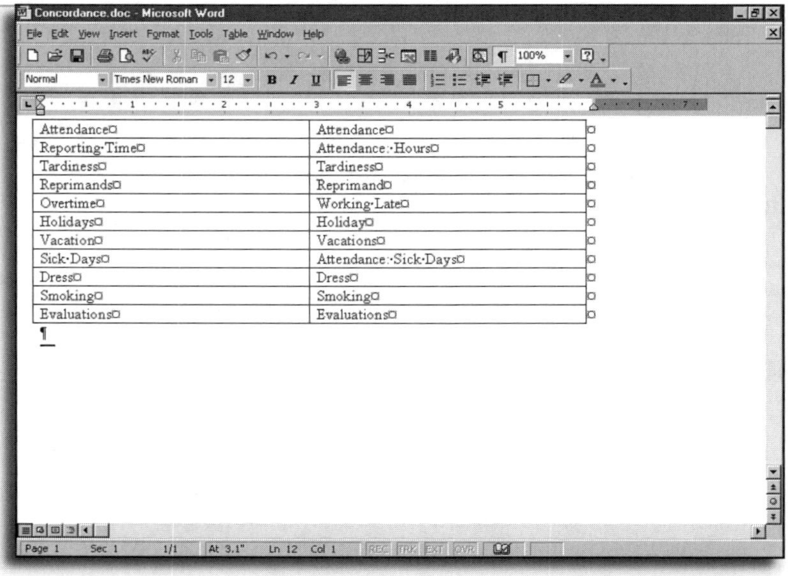

FIGURE 26.15

A concordance file consists of a two-column table with text to be indexed in the left column and index entries in the right column.

FIGURE 26.15

A concordance file consists of a two-column table with text to be indexed in the left column and index entries in the right column.

**6.** Save the concordance file.

To be sure you get the correct entries and to avoid typing each one, use the copy and paste commands. Open both the concordance file and the document you're indexing at the same time. Click the **Window** menu and select **Arrange All** to see both documents. Copy the text from the document and paste it into the first column of the concordance file.

After you have a concordance file, perform the following steps to use it to automatically mark your index entries.

### Mark Index Entries Using a Concordance Files

**1.** With the document you want to index open, click the **Insert** menu and select **Index and Tables**.

**2.** Select the **Index** tab.

**3.** Choose **AutoMark**. The Open Index AutoMark File dialog box appears.

4. Select the file you want to use as the concordance file or enter the name in the **File Name** box.

5. Choose **Open**. Word searches the document text for each text entry you made in the first column of the concordance file. For each exact match found, Word inserts an index entry field with the text from the second column of the concordance file as the index entry text.

# Add Index Cross-References

Terms that are synonyms or that may be fully referenced under another topic generally have a "See topic" or "See also topic" reference in an index. These are index cross-references.

### Create a Cross-Reference for an Index Entry

1. Select the text for which you want to create an index entry.

2. Press Alt+Shift+X to open the Mark Index Entry dialog box (see Figure 26.16).

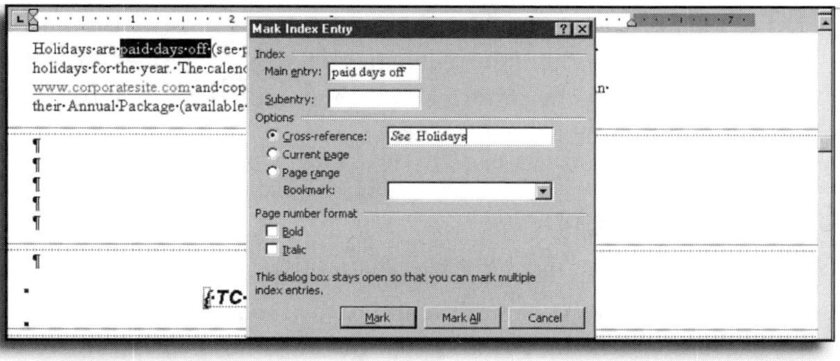

FIGURE 26.16
Enter the cross-reference text and then choose **Mark**.

3. Under **Options**, click **Cross-Reference**.

4. Enter the text you want to use as a cross-reference after the word "See."

5. Choose **Mark**.

6. Choose **Close** to close the dialog box.

## Modify or Delete Index Entries

Word marks each index entry by inserting a field immediately after the entry text in your document. If the field isn't visible, choose **Show/Hide** 🔳 on the Standard toolbar. The field is similar to the entry for the phrase "Attendance" you see in Figure 26.17 as:

```
{ XE "Attendance" }
```

·Attendance{ ·XE·"Attendance"·}·¶

· 　*Reporting·Time*{ ·XE·"Attendance:Reporting·Time"·}·¶
All·employees·must·report·by·9:00·a.m. ··Tardiness{·XE·"Tardiness"·}·of·up·to·5·minutes· will·be·excused·,·unless·it·occurs·more·than·three·times·a·month. ·Time·missed·over·the·5· minute·grace·period·will·be·docked·from·the·employee's·pay. ·Repeated·tardiness·(up·to· one·hour·per·week)·will·cause·a·reprimand. ·Three·reprimands·may·be·cause·for·employee· termination.¶

If you want to delete an index entry, select the field that follows the index text in your document (including the brackets ({})), and then press the Delete key.

To change the text or formatting of an index entry, you must also work with the index entry field. Click inside the quotation marks and edit the text, or select the text inside the quotes and then make your formatting choices.

## Generate an Index

After you have all the index entries marked in your document, you're ready to generate the index. You may want to insert a section or page break at the end of the document where you want the index to start so it begins on a new page.

### Generate an Index

1. Put your insertion point at the location in your document where you want the index to appear.
2. Click the **Insert** menu and select **Index and Tables**. When the Index and Tables dialog box appears, select the **Index** tab (see Figure 26.18).

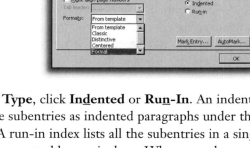

FIGURE 26.18
Select the type and format of the index and then click OK.

3. Under **Type**, click **Indented** or **Run-In**. An indented index lists the subentries as indented paragraphs under the main topic. A run-in index lists all the subentries in a single paragraph, separated by semicolons. When you choose a type, a sample appears in the **Print Preview** window.

4. To choose from the predefined index formats available in Word, select one from the **Formats** list. When you do, the **Print Preview** changes to show you an example of that format.

5. Because the index can be lengthy but the lines are short, you may want to set it up to run in columns. Enter the number of columns you want in the **Columns** box.

6. Page numbers in an index generally follow immediately after the topics. If you would rather have your numbers appear on the right side of the line, click **Right Align Page Numbers**. Choose a character from the **Tab Leader** drop-down list, if you want to join the entry text with the page number by a tab leader.

7. Choose **OK** to generate the index.

## Update and Delete an Index

After your index is in place, you might need to update it to reflect additions or deletions in your text or new index entries. To update the index, select the index text and then press F9.

To remove the entire index from your document, perform the steps that follow.

### Remove an Index

1. Click in the index.

2. Select the index field code including the brackets ({ }) (press Shift+F9 if you can't see the code).

3. Press the Delete key.

If you're not familiar with field codes and your index isn't lengthy, try this instead: Select the text of the entire index (the text is white in a gray field) and then press the Delete key.

# Incorporate Cross-References

A *cross-reference* refers you to another part of the document or to another document where there is more information on the topic being discussed. Word enables you to create different types of cross-references—numbered items, headings, bookmarks, footnotes and endnotes, equations, figures, listings, and tables.

### Create a Cross-Reference

1. Enter the beginning text for the cross-reference such as For more information on this topic, see.

2. Click the **Insert** menu and select **Cross-Reference**. The Cross-reference dialog box appears (see Figure 26.19).

3. From the **Reference Type** drop-down list, select the type of item to which you want to refer—numbered items, headings (must be Word styles Heading 1, Heading 2, and so on), bookmarks, footnotes and endnotes, equations, figures, listings, or tables.

4. From the **Insert Reference To** drop-down list, select the type of reference you want inserted in the document.

5. In the **For Which Heading** box, click the item to which you want to refer. If no items appear, you may need to select a different type of reference.

6. If you're preparing a document that will be used online, click **Insert as Hyperlink**. The reader will then be able to click the cross-reference and jump to the place to which you referred.

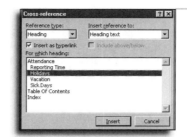

FIGURE 26.19
Select the type of cross-reference
you want.

**7.** Choose **Insert**.

**8.** The reference is inserted but the dialog box remains open to allow you to create additional cross-references. To close the dialog box, choose **Close**.

**SEE ALSO**

➤ *Learn more about hyperlinks on page 589*

## Modify or Delete a Cross-Reference

### Modify a Cross-Reference

**1.** Select the cross-reference in the document. Do not include the introductory text, such as "For more information, see."

**2.** Click the **Insert** menu and select **Cross-Reference**.

**3.** From the **Insert Reference To** box, select the new item to which you want to refer.

**4.** In the **For Which Heading** box click the item to which you want to refer.

**5.** Choose **Insert** and then choose **Close**.

To delete a cross-reference, select the entire cross-reference in the document including the introductory text. Then press the Delete key.

# Use Bookmarks

A *bookmark* is a location in your document or a selection of text that you name for reference purposes. After you place a book-mark, you can return to the same location again and again by selecting the bookmark when you use Word's Go To feature (press Ctrl+G or F5). Bookmarks are especially useful when you're modifying or editing a large document. Create a bookmark when you close the document so on opening it again, you can find where you left off. Bookmarks are also useful as reference points for cross-references, index entries, and macros.

### Add a Bookmark

1. Place your insertion point where you want to insert the bookmark.

2. Click the **Insert** menu and select **Bookmark** to open the Bookmark dialog box (see Figure 26.20).

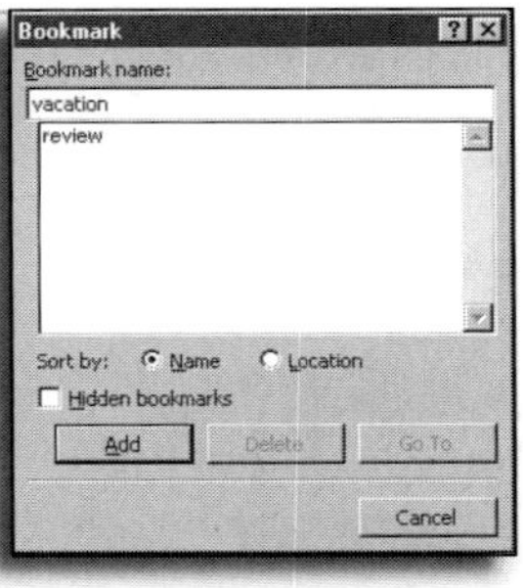

**FIGURE 26.20**

Type the name of the bookmark and click **Add**.

3. Type a name for the bookmark in the **Bookmark Name** box (don't enter any spaces in the name) or select one from the list. If you select the name of an existing bookmark, it will move the bookmark location to the current position of your insertion point.

4. Choose **Add**.

## Displaying Bookmarks

Bookmarks are not normally visible in your document. They appear in square brackets ([]). To see the bookmarks in your document, complete the following steps.

### Display Bookmarks

1. Click the **Tools** menu and select **Options**.

2. Select the **View** tab.

**3.** Under **Show**, click **Bookmarks**.

**4.** Choose **OK**.

# Deleting a Bookmark

### Delete a Bookmark

**1.** Click the **Insert** menu and select **Bookmark**.

**2.** Select the name of the bookmark you want to remove.

**3.** Choose **Delete**.

**4.** Choose **Close**.

PART

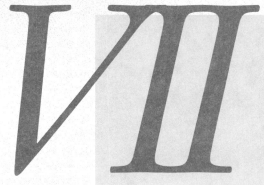

# Use Word with the Internet

# Use Word As an Email Editor and Collaboration Tool

Learn to send email and file attachments from within Word

Use Web folders to share files with others

Take part in an online discussion in a Word document

Collaborate online using NetMeeting

# Attach Word Documents to Email Messages

Word provides you with a set of online collaboration tools that make it easy for you to communicate and share Word documents with other Word and Office users. You can send email messages with attached Word documents, save files to online Web Folders, hold online discussions, and even launch online, real-time meetings. All these online features can be accessed from within the Word window and often make use of a "helper" application such as an email client (like Microsoft Outlook) or Microsoft NetMeeting, which will actually handle the sending of an email message or provide the venue for an online meeting.

Emailing a Word document directly from Word is really a case of computer "slight of hand" and Word actually calls on your default email package (such as Outlook or Outlook Express) to attach the current document to an email message. You supply the recipient's email address and the email (with your document as an attachment) is sent via your Internet service provider (again using your modem) or over your corporate network using your email server.

## Understand Your Email Client

One requirement for sending Word documents as email message attachments is that you have an *email client*—a software package that allows you to send and receive email from your desktop—configured on your computer.

Typical email clients include Microsoft Outlook Express, which is a component of Internet Explorer (an integral part of Windows 98) and Microsoft Outlook 2000, which is one of the applications found in Microsoft Office (see Figure 27.1). To set up either of these email clients or any of the number of other email clients available requires that you have an Internet email account or a corporate email account.

**Use Word as your Outlook email editor**

If you use Microsoft Outlook as your email client, you can specify that Word be used as your default email editor. This allows you to take advantage of all of Word's special features as you create and edit your email messages. To specify Word as your email editor in Outlook, open Outlook and select the **Tools** menu; then select **Options**. On the Options dialog box, click the **Mail Format** tab. Click the **Use Microsoft Word to Edit Email Messages** check box. Click **OK** to close the Options dialog box. Word is now enabled as the editor for all your Outlook mail messages.

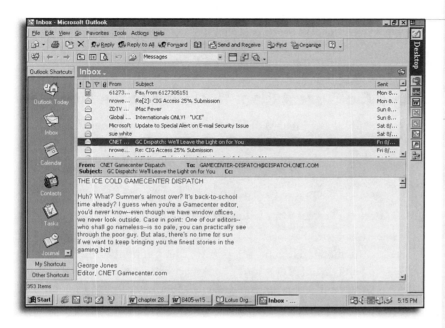

An Internet email account is typically provided by an Internet service provider when you sign up for your Internet connection to use via your modem. This type of account allows you to send messages to and receive messages from an Internet mail server maintained by your service provider. All your outgoing messages start their journey over the Internet to the intended recipient at your provider's mail server. Messages received from others over the Internet reside on the mail server until you download them to the email client on your computer.

Corporate email is usually intended for sending and receiving messages at your place of work and is controlled by a mail server at the company. Corporate email can be totally reserved for in-house communication, or also give you the ability to send and receive Internet email via your company's mail server.

The type of message you are sending (Internet email or corporate email) is not really an issue as far as Word is concerned. When you invoke the mail attachment feature in Word, your current document is attached to a new email message and then sent to the appropriate destination (either an Internet mail server or a corporate mail server). The Word file attachment can then be opened by the recipient of the message.

## Attach the Current Word Document to the Message

Actually attaching a Word document to an email message is very straightforward. You can either create a new document from scratch that you want to send as the attachment or open a file that you've already created. Just make sure that the document is open in the current Word window.

### Attach the Current Word Document to an Email

**1.** Once you have the document open that you want to use as the file attachment, select **File**, then point at **Send To**. Select **Mail Recipient (As Attachment)** from the submenu that appears. Your email client will open a new message window (see Figure 27.2).

FIGURE 27.2

A new message window will open and the attached Word document will appear as an icon in the message.

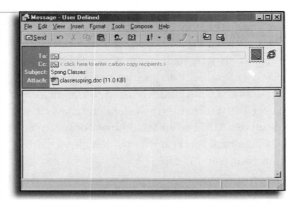

**2.** Depending on your email client, the Word document attachment will appear either as an icon in the header area of the email message (below the Subject line) or in the body text area of the message. Address the message by filling in the recipient address (the To box). Most email clients allow you to click an Address Book button and select the recipient from a list.

**3.** Edit the Subject line if you want (the Subject line in the email will consist of the text on the first line of the document that you've attached to the email message).

**4.** When you are ready to send the email message, click **Send**.

When the recipient of the message reads the email message in his email client, he will be able to open the document by double-clicking on the icon. This will start Microsoft Word and will open the document in the Word window. He can save the document to a new location using **Save As** or print the document.

## Route Attached Word Documents

You can also send a document to a group of people as an email attachment; for instance, let's say you have a document that needs to be edited by several coworkers. This is called *routing*. The great thing about routing is that you build a routing list (a list that includes all the recipients in the order you want them to examine the document) and then send the document as an email message.

The email and the attached document are sent to the first recipient on the list. After that particular person reviews the document, she can send it on to the next person listed on the routing list.

To create a routing list for the current document, select **File**, and then point at **Send To**. Select **Routing Recipient** from the submenu that appears. The Routing Slip dialog box will appear as shown in Figure 27.3.

In the Routing Slip dialog box, build a list of recipients in the To box using the **Address** button (it opens your email address book). Once you've created the list, add any message text you want to include (in the Message text box) and then click **Route**.

The message and attached Word document will be sent to the first recipient on the list via your email client. A message window will not appear during the process, however, so don't be alarmed.

**Caution: Attachment success varies with email client**

If you use a typical (and fairly feature-rich) email client such as Outlook, Outlook Express, Lotus cc:Mail, or Eudora, you probably won't have any trouble attaching files to your email messages or opening attached files that have been sent to you via email. Some email client software does not have the ability to correctly encode or decode attachments so you may end up with mixed results.

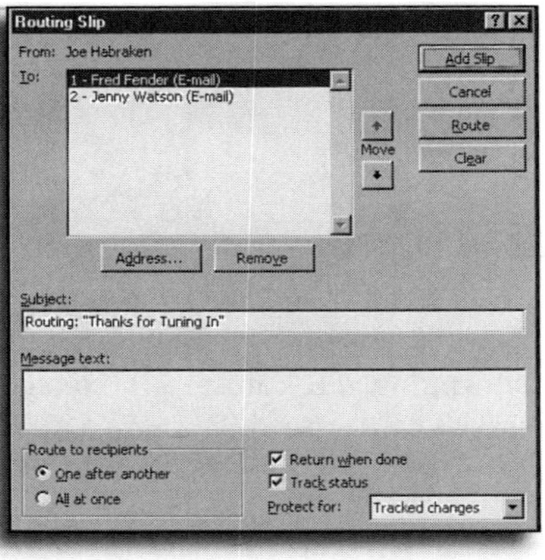

FIGURE 27.3

Documents can be attached to email messages and then routed to a list of recipients by creating a routing slip.

When the recipient (the first person on the Routing list) completes her work on the document in Word, all she has to do is select **File**, point at **Send To**, then select **Other Routing Recipient** from the submenu that appears. In the Routing Slip dialog box that appears, she would then select the next recipient on the list and click **Route** to continue the process.

## Share Word Documents with Web Folders

Attaching Word documents to email messages is just one way you can share files with other users on the Internet. If you have access to a Web site that supports special Microsoft Office extensions, you can save a file to the Web site as if you were saving the file to a folder on your own computer, or to a shared folder on a corporate network.

If you've ever worked on a corporate network, you know that files can be shared by a number of users by saving the files to "communal folders" (folders that can be accessed by a number of users on the network). *Web folders* are the World Wide Web equivalent of these shared corporate folders and you can create them and save files to them. The great thing about Web folders is that any user with access to the World Wide Web and the Web site that contains your Web folder can open the files that you store there and save files of their own to the same folder.

The creation of Web folders does require that you have access to a Web site that supports the use of Web folders. You may have to tell your corporate Webmaster or the creator of the Web site that you want to use as the site for your Web folders, if their particular site supports Web folders.

After you have access to a Web site that supports Web folders, all you have to do is create a new Web folder and then save the appropriate documents to it. If you access the Web using a dial-up connection via your modem, make sure that you connect to the Internet before you attempt to create the Web folder.

**Create a Web Folder on a Web Site and Save a Word Document to It**

  **1.** In the Word application window, create or open the document you want to save to a Web folder.

  **2.** For a new document choose **File**, **Save**; for a document previously saved Select **File**, **Save As**. The Save As dialog box will appear.

  **3.** In the Save As dialog box, click the Web Folders icon on the left side of the dialog box.

  **4.** *Web Folders* will appear in the Save In box. To create a new Web folder, click the **Create New Folder** button at the top of the Save As dialog box. The Add a Web Folder dialog box will appear (see Figure 27.4).

**You can't create Web folders on any Web site**

For you to be able to create Web folders on a particular Web site, the site must support the creation and use of Web folders. A Webmaster at your company will typically set up a site that supports Web folder creation. If you plan on creating your own site on the Web, you may want to use a Web site creation tool, like Microsoft FrontPage, that makes it easy to create Web sites. You will also have to make sure that the site supports Web folders and certain Office extensions. You may want to discuss the creation of such a site with your Internet service provider, especially if they are supplying the space on their Web server for your Web site.

FIGURE 27.4

You can share Word documents with other users by creating a Web folder on a Web site.

 Create new folder

5.  Type a name in the location box (use the format `http://servername/etc./`). Then click **Next**.

6.  The next screen in the Web creation process will ask you to specify a name for the new Web folder (see Figure 27.5). After typing a name for the Web folder, click **Finish** to complete the Web folder creation process.

7.  The Web folder will be created and appear in the Save In box of the Save As dialog box. Click **Save** to save your file to the Web folder.

The Web folder (and your file) will now be available to anyone who has access to the Web site. To save to the Web folder in the future, all you have to do is click the Web Folders icon in the Save As box and then double-click to open the appropriate Web folder. You can also open files in the Web folder when you need them. Just use the **Open** command on the **File** menu and specify the appropriate Web folder.

In some cases you may need a username and password to access a Web site that is used for the sharing of files in Web folders. Speak to your network administrator or the creator of the Web site to get a username and password, if needed.

# Create Online Discussions in Word

Another extremely useful feature for collaborating with coworkers and other Word users is the Web Discussions tool. This feature is new to Word 2000 (and other Office 2000 applications such as Microsoft Excel) and provides you with a way to post discussion messages directly in a Word document. Other users that have access to the Word document can then read the discussion posts and respond to them.

This feature is similar in concept to Internet Usenet groups that provide a venue for the posting and reading of messages concerned with a variety of topics. The great thing about the Word Web Discussions is that they pertain to the document that you must use in collaboration with a particular group of people such as a project team.

While this feature sounds particularly intriguing when you consider collaboration with other users, it does require access to a Web Discussion site on the World Wide Web that supports the Microsoft Office Discussion extensions. Even though the actual discussion posts appear in the Word document, you must be online and connected to the Web Discussion site to take advantage of the Web Discussion feature.

### Post Messages in a Word Document with the Web Discussion Tool

1. Open the Word document you want to place the Discussion posts in. Make sure to connect to the Internet via your modem (your ISP dial-up connection) or corporate Network, if necessary.

2. Select **T**ools, **O**nline Collaboration, and then select **W**eb Discussions. If this if the first time you have used the Web Discussion feature, you will be asked to provide the address of the Discussion server. Enter the name of the Discussion server (in the format servername.com) and then click **OK**.

3. The Web Discussion toolbar will appear above the Word status bar as shown in Figure 27.6. To insert a discussion icon in the document click the Insert in the Document button.

**Taking advantage of the Web Discussion feature**

The Web Discussion feature requires access to a Web Discussion site that you connect to when you are using the Discussion feature in Word. A common platform for Web Discussion servers is Microsoft Internet Information Server, which runs in conjunction with Microsoft NT Server. The creation of a Web Discussion site is beyond the scope of this book, but if you work at a corporation where a Web site is available and you collaborate with other Word users on projects, you may want to discuss the addition of the appropriate Office extensions to the company Web Server with your Webmaster or Network Administrator.

FIGURE 27.6

Once you've connected to the Discussion server, the Web Discussion toolbar will appear at the bottom of the current document window.

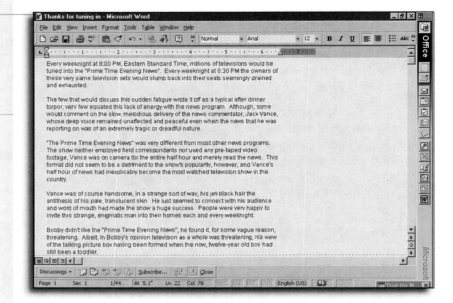

4. A Discussion Text dialog box will appear as shown in Figure 27.7. Enter the discussion subject and the subject text. Then click **OK**.

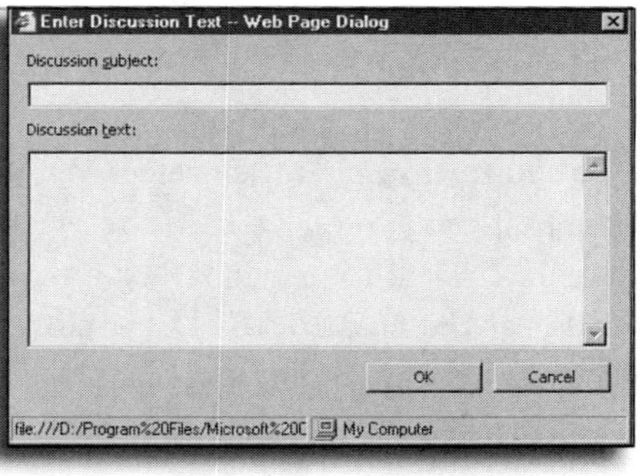

FIGURE 27.7

Enter the subject and text for your new discussion item.

5. The Discussion post will appear in a window at the bottom of the Word window. Use the scrollbar in the discussion window to read the post text.

6. Once you have completed reading the post, you can reply to the post by clicking the message icon at the end of the text (see Figure 27.8). A drop-down menu will appear. Click **Reply**.

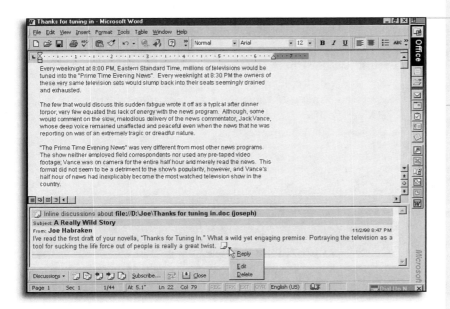

FIGURE 27.8

You can reply to any of the messages that appear in the Discussion panes at the bottom of the Word window.

**7.** Enter your reply text in the dialog box that appears. The subject box will already contain re: and the title of the post you are replying to. When you have finished entering the reply text, click **OK** to post the message.

When you have finished reading and replying to posts in the document, you can click **Close** on the Discussion toolbar to turn off the Discussion feature. The great thing about this feature is that if you forward this document to another user (using a feature such as the Routing feature) he can use the Discussion feature to view the posts that have been placed in the document. This provides a platform for thoughts, comments, and advice related to the particular Word document.

**SEE ALSO**
➤ *For details on routing documents to a list of editors or collaborators, see page 575*

# Collaborate with Others Using NetMeeting

You can hold face-to-face, real-time meetings while you are working in Word by taking advantage of Microsoft NetMeeting. NetMeeting provides audio and video communication over the

**Installing Microsoft NetMeeting**

NetMeeting is typically installed when you install Windows 98 on your computer (along with Internet Explorer). If NetMeeting does not run when you invoke the **Meet Now** command on the Word Collaboration menu, you may have to install NetMeeting. You can click the **Start** button, and then select **Update Windows** from the Start menu (you may have to connect to the Internet via your modem before using this command). Follow the prompts on the Microsoft Windows 98 Update page to download and install NetMeeting. Once you have the NetMeeting installation file on your computer, you can double-click it to install the software and then use it when collaborating from Microsoft Word.

Internet. This allows you to conduct "live" meetings without leaving your office.

Even if you don't have video or audio capabilities on your computer, NetMeeting provides a Chat window that can be used by users to communicate using their keyboards to type messages. NetMeeting also allows you to meet with multiple participants during one NetMeeting session.

NetMeeting connects users by providing several directory servers that give you a list of NetMeeting users currently logged on to the Internet. You connect to a particular user by double-clicking on her name on the server list.

**Start a NetMeeting Online Conference**

1. Select **Tools**, **Online Collaboration**, and then select **Meet Now**. A list of the NetMeeting users currently online on your default directory server will appear in the Word window in the Place a Call dialog box (see Figure 27.9).

FIGURE 27.9

Select the person you want to meet with in the Place a Call dialog box.

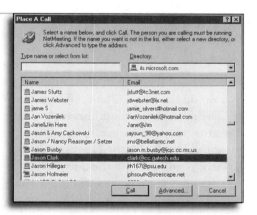

**Previous NetMeeting contacts appear in the SpeedDial list**

If you made calls using NetMeeting before, the contacts that you met with will be listed in your NetMeeting SpeedDial list. When you start an online meeting from within Word, it's assumed that you want to meet with a previous contact and so your SpeedDial list will appear in the Place a Call dialog box. To switch the list to users currently logged on to one of the NetMeeting servers, click the drop-down box on the right of the Place a Call dialog box and select the appropriate server.

2. Select the person you want to meet with using NetMeeting and then click **Call**. The Microsoft NetMeeting window will open on the Windows desktop.

As soon as a connection is made with the selected person, the NetMeeting Current Call window will appear. This window is where the Meeting will take place (see Figure 27.10). You can take advantage of audio and video communication if you and the other participant in the meeting have the appropriate hardware.

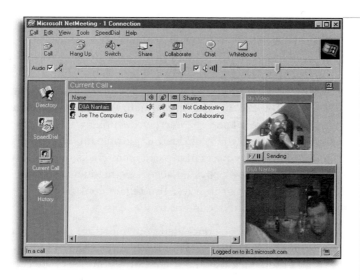

**FIGURE 27.10**
The online meeting is held in the Current Call window.

You can also communicate using a Chat window that allows you to enter text via the keyboard. To use the Chat feature (see Figure 27.10), click the **Chat** button on the NetMeeting toolbar.

You can also share ideas and make your point using the NetMeeting Whiteboard. This feature allows you to draw diagrams, doodle, or otherwise illustrate your discussion points. The whiteboard is shared by all users in the meeting. To open the whiteboard window (see Figure 27.11), click the **Whiteboard** button on the NetMeeting toolbar. A tool palette is provided on the left side of the whiteboard and can be used to draw a variety of shapes on the board itself.

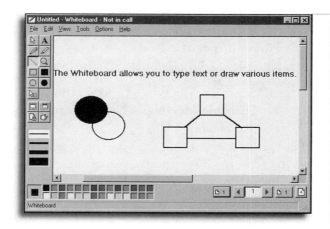

**FIGURE 27.11**
The whiteboard can really help you make your point during the online meeting.

Online collaboration is also a strong suit of NetMeeting and you can actually share your Word documents during the NetMeeting conference. With Word open on the desktop (because you launched NetMeeting from Word, Word should be open), click the Share button on the NetMeeting toolbar. Switch back to Word by clicking the appropriate button on the Windows taskbar. Word and the current document will appear on the screens of all the NetMeeting participants of the current conference. When a particular participant clicks on the Word document, they are provided access to the document and actually have editing capabilities. You regain control of the document by clicking in the document window.

When you have concluded your meeting, notify the other meeting attendees that you are ready to exit the online conference and then click the Hang Up button on the NetMeeting toolbar. You can then exit the NetMeeting application by clicking the Close (X) button in the upper-right corner of the NetMeeting window.

# Schedule a NetMeeting in Word

Because NetMeeting requires that all the participants be online at a particular time (and on a particular NetMeeting server), you can actually send invitations out to participants notifying them of the date and time (and the actual place—a particular directory server) of the meeting. Word supplies you with the command that will actually start the Contacts feature of Microsoft Outlook and open a new Meeting dialog box. You use the window to set the meeting parameters such as time and date and you also build a list of participants.

### Scheduling a NetMeeting Conference

1.  Select **Tools**, **Online Collaboration**, and then select **Schedule Meeting**. A New Meeting dialog box will appear (see Figure 27.12).

**Outlook must be installed to use the Word Schedule Meeting command**

Several Word features rely on other applications that are part of the Microsoft Office suite. NetMeeting had to be installed for you to conduct online meetings, for example. To use the Schedule Meeting command in Word, you must have Microsoft Outlook installed on your computer. It is the Outlook Contact feature that actually supplies the Meeting dialog box that you use to schedule the new meeting.

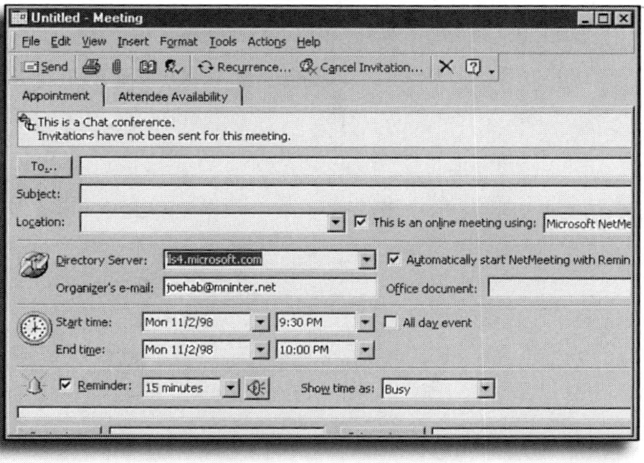

FIGURE 27.12
The New Meeting dialog box allows you to set the time, date, and server for the online meeting, and send invitations to the various participants.

**2.** To insert the participants for the meeting, click in the To text box and enter the names of the people you want to attend the meeting. You can also click the To button to select the attendees from your Outlook address book or Contact list.

**3.** In the **Subject** text box, enter a subject for the meeting.

**4.** In the **Location** text box, enter a location for the meeting.

**5.** Use the **Start Time** and **End Time** drop-down arrows to set the date and appropriate start and end times for the meeting.

**6.** When you have filled in the details for the meeting, click the **Send** button.

The Meeting dialog box will close. Invitations will be sent via email to each of the participants (based on the email addresses that you had entered for each participant in your Outlook address book or Contact list). You have now notified each of the potential meeting participants and they can reply to your invitation as to their availability. Scheduling the meeting in this way assures you that the various participants will be online when this NetMeeting is launched from Word.

**SEE ALSO**

➤ *For details on routing documents to a list of editors or collaborators, see page 575*

# Generate Simple Documents to Be Viewed in Browsers

Understand basic Internet and intranet terms

Use Word to browse HTML documents, Word documents, or Web pages

Create your own HTML documents from Word

Add links from your document to other locations, pages, or Web sites

# Know Your Web, Internet, and Intranet Basics

The *Internet* is a worldwide conglomeration of computer networks. The Internet isn't owned and operated by any one company. It is one network of computers that can talk to one another, and then in turn talk to another network of computers, and so on.

The *World Wide Web* (or just Web) is a component of the Internet. It's a collection of documents accessible through the Internet. These documents contain a special technology called *hypertext*. When you click your mouse on hypertext, you'll be taken to a new document or *Web page*, maybe even to a Web page on a different computer (or *Web site*). Web pages are read through programs called Web *browsers*, such as Internet Explorer or Netscape Navigator. The Web uses a type of address called a *uniform resource locator (URL)* (such as `http://www.microsoft.com/office`) to identify specific documents and locations.

*HyperText Markup Language (HTML)* dictates how Web pages look and work. HTML is a collection of instructions, or *tags*, that tell a browser program how to display a document—when the text is bold, italic, and so on. A Web page has a series of tag entries such as `<B>` to turn on bold and `</B>` to turn off bold. Unfortunately, using these tags is complicated. Fortunately, Word saves you the pain of learning HTML by converting your documents to Web pages for you.

An *intranet* is your company's computer network working with software that serves HTML documents to Web browsers. Your company's *network server* handles all the data traffic of sending and receiving files. A *Web server* program on that computer tells the computer how to deal with requests and transmissions so any computer can communicate on an intranet, no matter what type of computer it is or what operating system it's running.

The individual workstations in the company have browser programs that receive the output from the Web server and translate the HTML code in the Web documents into a visible layout.

## Evaluate Web Tools

Microsoft Word 2000 gives you the tools you need to create various types of Web pages. There are other programs that are also capable of creating Web pages, such as Microsoft FrontPage. You should consider using Word to create your pages under the following conditions:

- You'll be working with other Web authors who frequently use Word.
- You need word processing features such as AutoText and AutoCorrect.
- You have customized features of Word—such as AutoText entries, custom dictionaries, and AutoCorrect entries—that you need to use as you create your Web pages.

There are times, however, when you should consider using another application such as FrontPage to create your Web pages:

- You are working with a large team.
- You, or your team, are managing a Web server.
- You need user authentication for Web page authors.
- You need to use *WebBots* to insert *scripts* and form elements.

Among the tools that Word contains for creating Web pages is the ability to create *hyperlinks*, which allow viewers of the Web pages to jump to other Web sites or files by clicking the hyperlink text or picture. See "Create Hyperlinks" later in this chapter for more information.

Word also compresses pictures or graphics inserted in documents automatically and natively stores JPEG images. Word converts all raster formats (bitmaps such as GIF and JPEG) to PNG (Portable Network Graphics), a new compressed graphic format. When you use a PNG graphic in a document it takes less time to save the document, uses less disk space, and takes less time to download in a Web browser than conventional graphic formats.

The Web toolbar lets you quickly open, search, and browse through any document or jump from one document or site to another. You can go backward or forward among documents you've already opened and add documents you find on the Web to a Favorites folder so you can return to them easily at any time.

## Consider Word and HTML Formatting Conversions

There are some differences between the way Word formats documents and how HTML translates them for the browser software. Here are some of the things you need to know about how your formatting will change, and also some features that won't work with Web pages:

- Whitespace automatically appears in between paragraphs. Press Shift+Enter to create paragraphs without whitespace between them.

- Text columns aren't supported. Use table columns instead.

- Tab settings aren't maintained. Use table columns instead of tabs. To shift the first line of text to the right, use spaces.

- Indents are not supported by HTML.

- Text alignment is in relation to the width of the screen or the cell in a table. HTML doesn't support full justification.

- Bold, italic, underline, strikethrough, superscript, and subscript formats appear on Web pages, but emboss, text animation, all caps, small caps, outline, double strikethrough, outline, shadow, and engrave do not.

- Settings for line spacing, margins, character spacing, kerning, text flow, and spacing before and after paragraphs are lost when the document is converted to HTML.

- Font sizes are limited to major sizes in HTML, so your setting may convert to the closest size. Also, you should keep in mind that people who view your Web pages might not have the same set of fonts you do. The browser converts an unknown font to its default font.

- Use font colors to liven up your page. They are supported in HTML.

- Highlighting is not available for Web pages.

- Graphs, organization charts, and other embedded objects display as graphic images and can't be updated from a Web page (save a copy of the page as a document before you convert it to a Web page).

- Drawing objects such as AutoShapes, text effects, text boxes, and shadows have to be inserted as objects from the Insert menu (they aren't available from the Drawing toolbar).

- Headers and footers, footnotes and endnotes, and cross-references aren't available.

- Page borders can't be used, but you can add backgrounds or themes.

- Page numbering isn't available.

- Web pages don't have margins. You must use tables to control page layout.

# Browse HTML Files

Word can open documents on your company's intranet or Internet sites, if you have a connection to the Internet. You must have a Web browser program, such as Internet Explorer or Netscape Navigator, installed on your computer. Word can open Web documents stored in HTML on your computer or network, as well as regular Word documents.

To preview your HTML pages in a Web browser program that you have installed on your computer, click the **File** menu and select **Web Page Preview** to open your browser program offline and view your page.

Use Word to browse when you want to preview the Web documents you are creating, view related documents, or test links. Having browser capabilities in Word saves you time.

### Open a Web Page or Word Document and Work with Browser-Like Tools

**1.** Display the Web toolbar by clicking the **View** menu and selecting **Toolbars**, and then selecting **Web** from the submenu.

2. Type the URL for the Web page or the filename and path in the **Address** box on the Web toolbar, such as `http://microsoft.com` or `http://www.dba.com/homepage.html` or `\\Server1\files\document.doc`.

3. Press Enter.

To open files or documents you've opened before, try one of these methods:

- The **Address** box maintains a list of recently visited Web sites and documents you opened. To revisit a site or open a document you recently visited, click the down arrow next to the **Address** box and select the site or document you want.

- If you opened the file or visited the Web page in this Word session, Word maintains a history of where you have been. This list also contains the names of Web pages and files you viewed by following hyperlinks. Hyperlinks are the graphics or colored or underlined text you point to that jumps you to another location on the page, another page, or another Web site. To view a previously opened document, choose **Back** ⬅ on the Web toolbar. To go to the next document in the history list, choose **Forward** ➡ on the Web toolbar.

- Make it easy to return to files or Web pages you visit frequently by adding them to your Favorites folder. Choose **Favorites** on the Web toolbar and click **Add to Favorites** to add the currently open document or Web page to the Favorites folder. To view one of the items you added to the Favorites folder, choose **Favorites** and choose **Open Favorites**. Then select the file and choose **Open**.

Being able to browse through files from Word gives you the opportunity to see how your own HTML documents look, as well as search out other documents to which you want to link.

# Modify Existing Word Documents for Online Use

Existing documents can be saved in HTML format for use as Web pages. You may have to first modify the documents to remove any formatting that isn't supported by HTML or switch over to formatting that is (such as changing text columns to tables). Then you save the document in HTML format.

### Saving a File in HTML Format

1. With your document open, click **File**, and then select **Save as Web Page** on the menu.

2. When the Save As dialog box opens (see Figure 28.1), enter the name you want to give the file in the **File Name** box.

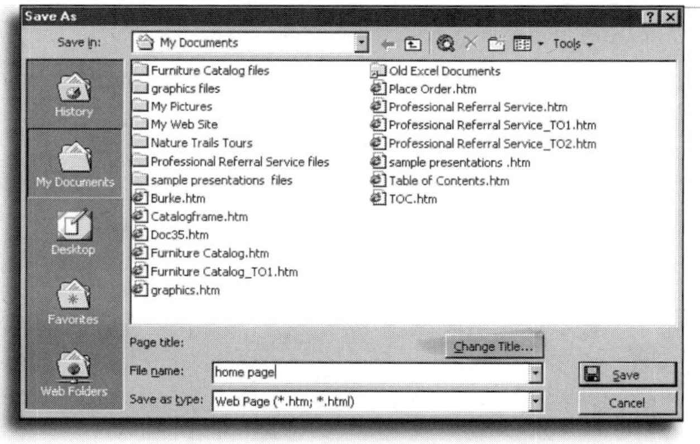

**FIGURE 28.1**

Web pages are automatically saved with the .htm file extension.

3. From the **Save In** box, select the drive and folder where you want to store the file.

4. Choose **Change Title** to enter a title to be displayed in the title bar of the Web browser. Click **OK**.

5. Choose **Save**.

If you included graphics in your document, they will be saved as separate \*.gif files in the same folder as your document. The files do not have the same name as the original picture file, but might be called Image001.gif or Photo001.gif. Be sure to include these files when you copy your HTML to a disk or another network disk.

# Create a Web Document with the Page Wizard

A great way to start creating a Web page is to use the Web Page Wizard, which is available when you click the **File** menu, choose **New** and select the **Web Pages** tab in the New dialog box. The Web Page Wizard is geared more toward creating Web sites than individual pages. There are several Web page templates also listed on the Web Pages tab—Column with Contents, Frequently Asked Questions, Left-Aligned Column, Personal Web Page, Right-Aligned Column, Simple Layout, and Table of Contents—that provide you with the means to create the Web pages you need. You can also use the Blank Web Page template on the General tab to start your Web page.

### Use the Web Page Wizard to Create Web Pages

1. Open the **File** menu and choose **New**.

2. When the New dialog box opens, click the **Web Pages** tab.

3. Click the **Web Page Wizard** icon and choose **OK**.

4. When the first screen of the Web Page Wizard appears, click **Next** to start creating a Web site.

5. In the **Web site title** box, enter the name you want to give your Web site. Then, in the **Web site location** box, enter the filename you want to give your Web site and the path where you want to save it (click **Browse** to select a location and/or name). Choose **Next**.

6. Many browsers support *frames*, which divide the screen into separate panes that have different content. This screen (see Figure 28.2) offers you three choices for setting up your Web site, with or without frames. Select one and then click **Next**.

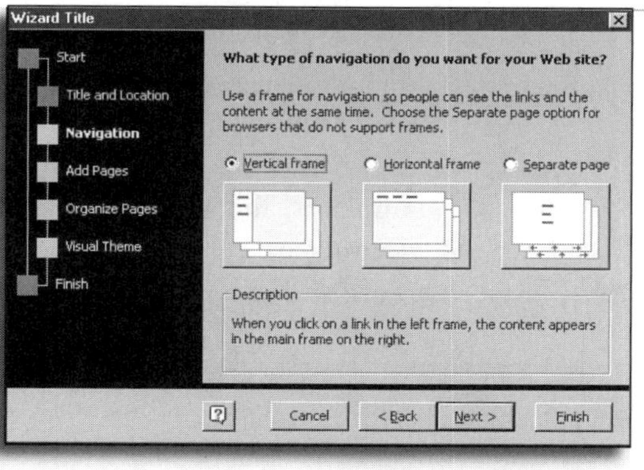


FIGURE 28.2
Select the frame arrangement that works best for your Web site.

- **Vertical Frame**. Click a link in the left frame to see the contents in the right frame.
- **Horizontal Frame**. Click a link in the top frame to see the contents in the bottom frame.
- **Separate Page**. Useful for browsers that don't support frames, the hyperlinks appear on their own page. Clicking on the link opens another page in its place. There are forward and backward navigation links on each page.

7. On this screen (see Figure 28.3) you add the pages you'll need for your Web site. Two blank pages and the Personal Web Page are already listed, but these can be removed if necessary. Choose any of the following to start building your Web site and then click **Next** to continue.

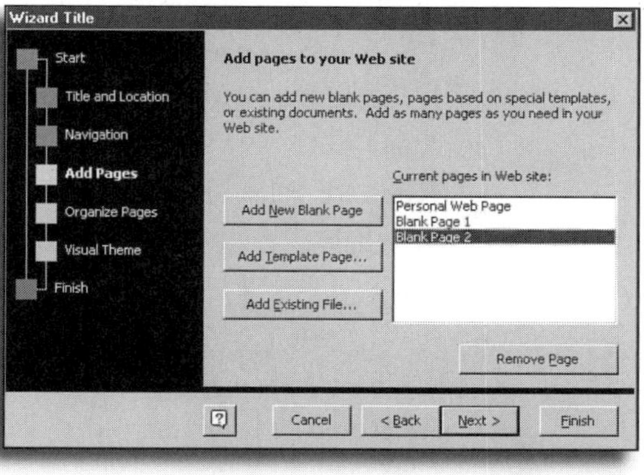


FIGURE 28.3
Add blank pages, new blank pages, or new pages based on the Web page templates to create your Web site.

- **Add _N_ew Blank Page**. Adds a blank Web page to your site.

- **Add _T_emplate Page**. Adds a new page based on a Web page template. A dialog box opens that lists the templates, and a sample page appears in the background (see Figure 28.4). Select the template you want to use and choose **OK**.

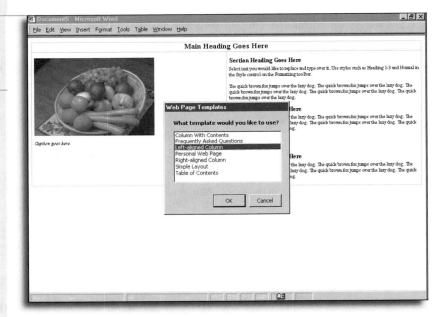

- **Add _E_xisting File**. Opens the Open dialog box so you can select the existing file to add to your Web site. Choose the appropriate drive and folder where the file is located from the **Look _I_n** drop-down list, select the file, and choose **_O_pen**.

- **Remove _P_age**. Removes the selected page from the Web site.

8. Now that you have a list of potential or existing pages, you set the order they'll appear. Select a page and then choose **Move _U_p** or **Move _D_own** to move it up or down in the list. Choose **_R_ename** to give a more descriptive name to the

selected page. When you have the list in the order you want to view the pages, choose **Next**.

9.  Adding a visual theme makes your site more attractive and cohesive. Select **Add a Visual Theme** and then click **Browse Themes** to select the theme for your Web site (see Figure 28.5). Select **No Visual Theme** if you want a white background. Click **Next** to go to the next screen.

**FIGURE 28.5**
A preview of the selected theme appears at the right. Choose OK to use the theme for your Web site.

10. Choose **Finish**. The first page appears on your screen, ready for you to replace or enter text (see Figure 28.6).

If you've already started a document without using a Web page template or the Web Page Wizard, you can still convert it by saving it as a Web page.

To save a Word document as a Web page, choose **File**, **Save as Web Page**.

If your company has a Web site, the manager of that Web site can add your document to the Web server and link it to other documents from your company. If not, store the file on your file server and others in the company can access it by entering its name and location in the address field of their Web browsers or in **Address** box on the Web toolbar.

FIGURE 28.6

This home page was designed using the Web Page Wizard.

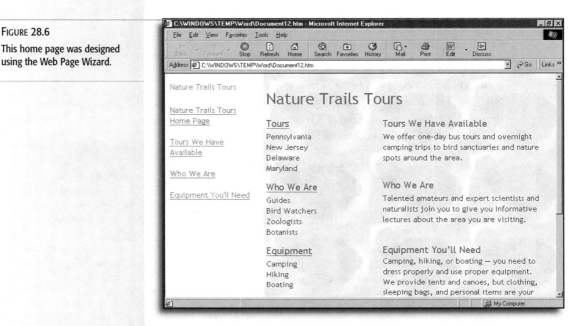

**Previewing your Web page**

If you have a Web browser such as Netscape Navigator or Internet Explorer, it's easy to preview your Web page as you're working on it. Choose **Web Page Preview** on the **File** menu. To switch back to Word, choose the Word icon on the Windows taskbar or close the browser.

**SEE ALSO**

➤ *To learn more about using templates, see page 343*

➤ *For more information about themes, see page 239*

# Create Hyperlinks

On Web pages you see colored and underlined text or graphics that you click to go to another location on the current page, another Web page, an HTML page on the World Wide Web, or an HTML page on an intranet. The colored and underlined text or the graphic is called a hyperlink.

When the hyperlink consists of text, it's called a *hypertext link*. Hypertext links identify Web documents by their URL (uniform resource locator), such as http://www.microsoft.com.

On a Web page (see Figure 28.7) you identify a hypertext link by the following:

- The link text is a different color than the regular text and/or is underlined.

- When you point at the text with your mouse, the mouse pointer changes to a pointing hand.

- When you click a hypertext link, your Web browser automatically searches for and then displays the Web page to which the link points.

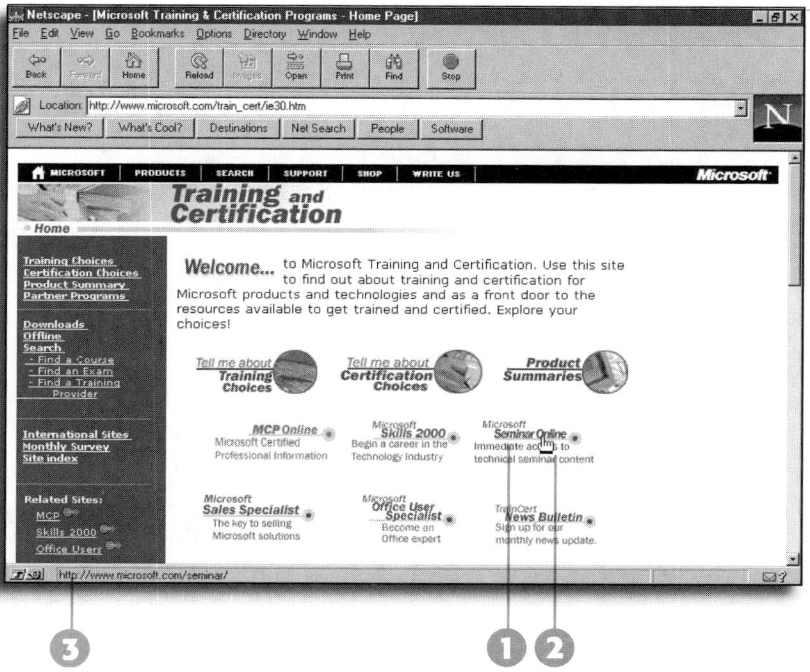

**FIGURE 28.7**

The mouse pointer changes to a pointing hand when it encounters a hypertext link.

**1** Hypertext link

**2** Mouse pointer

**3** The file referenced by the hypertext link

## Set AutoFormat to Create Hyperlinks

One way to have the text in your document marked as a hypertext link is to have Word automatically detect the text as you type and create the hypertext link in your document for you.

### Set AutoFormat to Create Hyperlinks

1. Open the **Tools** menu and choose **AutoCorrect** on the menu.

2. When the AutoCorrect dialog box appears, select the **AutoFormat as You Type** tab (see Figure 28.8).

FIGURE 28.8

To have Word identify and automatically create hypertext links for you, check **Internet and Network Paths with Hyperlinks**.

3. Under **Replace as You Type**, click **Internet and Network Paths with Hyperlinks** to enable that option.

4. Choose **OK**.

After activating this feature, URLs (such as `http://www.microsoft.com`) automatically convert to hypertext links as you enter them in your document. This can be disconcerting, however, if you are writing about URLs in a document (such as providing a reference list of useful Web sites) and Word automatically changes them to hypertext links.

**SEE ALSO**

➤ *For more information on AutoCorrect, see page 118*

➤ *To learn more about AutoFormat, see page 251*

## Manually Insert a Hyperlink

If you've elected not to have Word automatically create hyperlinks for you, you need to insert your links manually as you enter text.

### Manually Insert a Hyperlink

1. Save your document.

2. Position your insertion point where you want to place the hyperlink if you want the URL address or path to appear in the document. If you want to turn existing text into a hyperlink, select the text.

**3.** Open the **Insert** menu and select **Hyperlink** or choose **Insert Hyperlink** 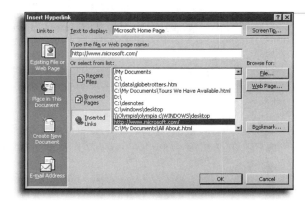 on the Standard toolbar. The Insert Hyperlink dialog box appears (see Figure 28.9).

FIGURE **28.9**
Enter the name and path (or URL) of the document or Web page you want to open, or select one from the list.

**4.** Select an appropriate **Link To** icon:

- **Existing File or Web Page**. In the **Type the File or Web Page Name** text box, enter the filename and path or the URL for the document or Web page to which you want to link or select one from the list. Choose **Recent Files** to see a list of recently opened files, **Browsed Pages** to show the pages you most recently browsed, or **Inserted Links** to display links you recently inserted in documents. To help limit the list, choose **File** to browse for the file in the Link to File dialog box. Choose **Web Page** to look only at Web pages and not at all files.

- **Place in This Document**. Use this to insert a hyperlink to another location within the same document. Links can be made to the top of the document, headings, or bookmarks.

- **Create New Document**. Enter the filename and path of the new document in the **Name of New Document** box. A name and path are automatically entered for you, so you either replace that or click **Change** and select a new path and filename. Then, under **When to Edit**, select whether you want to edit the new document now or later.

* **E-Mail Address**. Enter an address in the **E-Mail Address** box or select one from the **Recently Used E-mail Addresses** list. Enter a subject for the mail received from the hyperlink in the **Subject** box.

5. In the **Text to Display** box, enter the text you want to show as the hyperlink text.

6. Choose **ScreenTip** to enter ScreenTip text that appears in some browsers when the reader points to the hyperlink.

7. Choose **OK**.

This manual method of inserting hyperlinks gives you more control over where you place your hyperlinks and how they appear.

## Edit a Web Document

Word edits existing Web pages without converting the HTML format back to a Word document.

### Edit an HTML Document

1. Open the **File** menu and choose **Open** or click **Open** on the Standard toolbar. Select **Web Pages** from **Files of Type**. Choose the location and then the file you want, and click **Open**.

2. Use Word's regular editing commands to make changes to the document.

3. Click the **File** menu and select **Save** or choose **Save** on the Standard toolbar. The document is automatically saved in HTML format.

You can now store the file on your company's file server for browsing by your coworkers as part of an intranet, or give the file to your Web site manager for loading on the Web server.

# Create Other Web Documents and Forms

Create Web pages from scratch

Add frames

Add data from other applications to your Web pages

Create and use online forms

Create an online catalog

# Design a Web Document from Scratch

Word can save any document as HTML format for use on the Web. You create the document, edit and format the text, and add graphics as you would with a document you intended to print (see Figure 29.1). When you save the file, Word adds the HTML codes required to produce the same or a similar appearance. However, HTML is somewhat limited in dealing with some layout and formatting commands, so your Web page may not look exactly like your document when you created it.

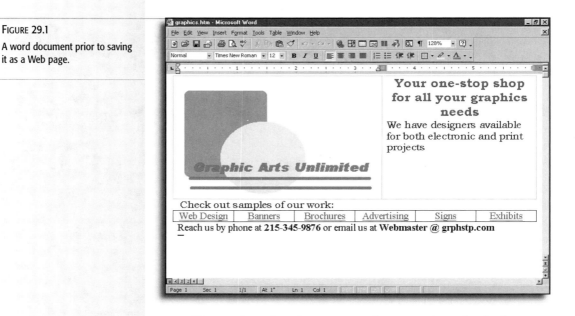

You need to view the page on a browser to see the final output, as shown in Figure 29.2. How much of your formatting is seen on the Web depends on the Web browser you are using and which version of the browser software you have. You may be able to see more of your formatting in Web Page Preview (see Figure 29.3) because it uses a different browser than the one you use for regular Web browsing. You should check your page with both, or have a friend with another browser check it to see that you don't lose too much from the intended look for your page.

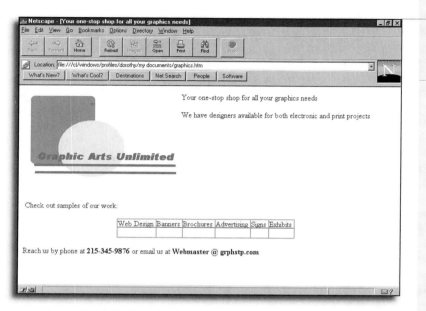

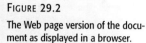

**FIGURE 29.2**
The Web page version of the document as displayed in a browser.

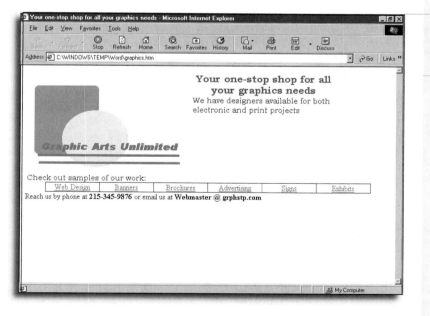

**FIGURE 29.3**
The page as viewed in Web Page Preview.

**Web pages versus Web site**

Word does not publish a Web site for you. It creates all the Web pages (HTML documents) that you need to build a Web site. After you turn the pages over to the Web site or network administrator, that person adds the pages to your Web site server for publication over the Internet or adds them to the network server that publishes them as part of your company's intranet.

The best way to create a Web page from scratch is to draw a sketch first of what you want to appear on the page. This will help you decide which Word features you can use to achieve your design. For example, if you need to organize your text into columns, don't use tabs because they are not supported on the Web; you need to consider doing the page using tables. Once you have a plan, start with the blank Web page template.

### Create a Web Page from Scratch

1. Open the **File** menu and select **New**.
2. Click the **General** tab if it's not already displayed.
3. Select the **Web Page** icon and choose **OK**.
4. Add your text and format it, keeping in mind that some colors, sizes, and fonts aren't supported by Web browsers.
5. Add any graphics.
6. From the **File** menu, choose **Save**.

To test your design, choose **Web Page Preview** from the **File** menu. To test your design with another browser, open the browser software and enter the full path and filename of the Web page in the Address box.

#### SEE ALSO

➤ *To learn more about saving a document as a Web page, see page 591*

➤ *For more information on the differences in formatting for the Web versus print, see page 588*

# Incorporate Frames

*Frames* organize the information seen in the Web browser by dividing the screen into sections. Each section, or frame, can display a separate Web page. A group of frames is called a *frames page*. You open the frames page to display the frames in the browser.

You use frames to create a header for a Web site that doesn't have to be re-opened each time you need to reference it. A frequent use of frames is to display a table of contents for the site.

You create Web pages and then use the Frames toolbar to add frames to the Web page. After you add frames to a frames page, you set the Web pages that appear in each frame.

**Create a Frames Page**

1. Create a Web page from scratch, from a template, or from the Web Page Wizard.

2. Open the **F**_o_**rmat** menu and select **F**_r_**ames**. Then select **N**_e_**w Frames Page**. The Frames toolbar appears. Click one of the new frames buttons:

    • **New Frame L**_e_**ft** ▯. Adds a new frame to the left of the one where your cursor is.

    • **New Frame R**_i_**ght** ▯. Adds a new frame to the right of the one where your cursor is.

    • **New Fra**_m_**e Above** ▯. Adds a new frame above the one where your cursor is.

    • **New Frame B**_e_**low** ▯. Adds a new frame below the one where your cursor is.

3. For additional frames, click in the frame adjacent to where you want the new frame. Then click the appropriate button on the Frames toolbar for the position of the frame. Repeat for each frame you want to add.

4. To set the size of the frame, point to the frame border until the pointer becomes a two-headed arrow and then drag the border to the desired position. For an exact measurement, open the **F**_o_**rmat** menu, select **F**_r_**ames**, and then choose **Frame** _**P**_**roperties**. Then click the **F**_r_**ame** tab and set the _**W**_**idth** and _**H**_**eight**.

5. To hide the frame borders of a selected frame (click in the frame to select it), open the **F**_o_**rmat** menu, choose **F**_r_**ames**, and then select **Frame** _**P**_**roperties**. Click the _**B**_**orders** tab (see Figure 29.4) and then select **N**_o_ **Borders** to turn the border display off or **Sho**_w_ **All Frame Borders** to turn the display on.

**Don't overlook the Web Page Wizard**

The Web Page Wizard has a couple of page designs that include simple frames. You can start your frames page using the Wizard and customize it using the instructions here.

**Header or footer frames**

A header or footer frame remains the same throughout your Web site, even though the contents of other frames change. You must add the header or footer frame first, before you start adding other frames. Open the **Format** menu, select **Frames**, and choose **New Frames Page**. Then click New Frame Above ▯ or New Frame Below ▯ on the Frames toolbar. Drag the border until the frame is the size you want.

**Frame properties**

The quick way to open the Frame Properties dialog box is to click Frame Properties ▯ on the Frames toolbar.

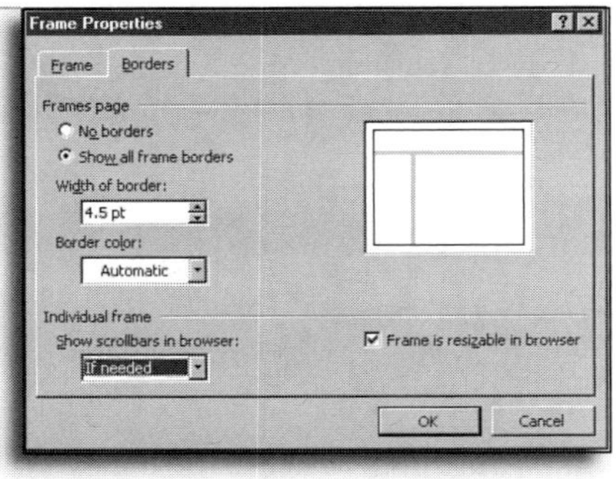

**FIGURE 29.4**

Use the Frame Properties dialog box to display borders, set the border size and color, display scrollbars in the browser, or allow sizing of frames in the browser.

**6.** For viewing from a browser, you can set whether the frames can be resized by selecting or deselecting **Frame Is Resizable in Browser** from the **Borders** tab of the Frame Properties dialog box. You can also turn off the scrollbars for the frame when viewed from a browser by selecting **Never** from the **Show Scroll Bars in Browser** list.

**7.** You specify the initial Web page that a frame displays. Open the **Format** menu, select **Frames**, choose **Frames Properties**, and then click the **Frame** tab (see Figure 29.5). Type the path of the Web document, Web site, or other document in the **Initial Page** box (or click **Browse** to select the filename and location).

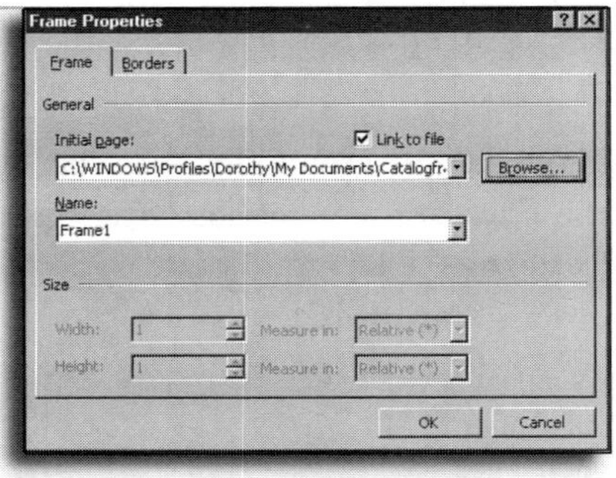

**FIGURE 29.5**

Enter or select the initial page you want displayed in the frame where your cursor is.

**8.** Assign a name to the frame in the **Name** box. Choose **OK**.

**9.** Repeat steps 6 and 7 for each frame.

**10.** Save the frames page (see Figure 29.6).

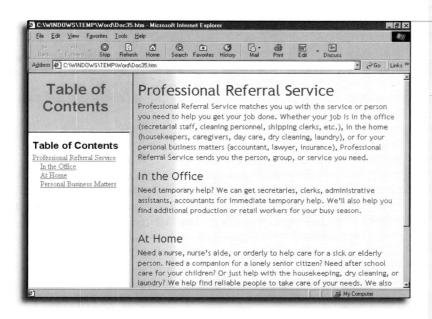

FIGURE 29.6

A frames page that includes a table of contents frame shown in Web Page Preview.

**SEE ALSO**

➤ *For more information on generating a table of contents, see page 548*

# Create Web Pages Using Data from Other Applications

For the same reasons you add data from other applications to your documents, you want to be able to add data to your Web pages. The methods for adding objects to Web pages are the same as for documents. What differs is how these objects appear when viewed with a Web browser.

## Add an Excel Chart

You add an Excel chart to your Web page in the same manner as you would to a document. However, when you save the page in HTML format, a graphics image is created. You can't update the data. Therefore, embedding or linking the chart has little more effect than simply pasting it into the Web page.

---

**Table of contents**

You can set up one of your frames as the table of contents for your Web site. Use Word's built-in heading styles on your Web page to make it easier to generate the table of contents. From the **Format** menu, select **Frames**, and then choose **Table of Contents in Frame**. The Table of Contents frame displays headings in the Web page as hyperlinks.

If you think you'll need to update the chart later, save a backup of your file as a Word document that will update automatically if linked to the data source. Save a copy of that as a Web page with the same name as the original to view an updated version of the chart in a browser.

**SEE ALSO**

➤ *To learn more about inserting Excel charts in Word documents, see page 411*

## Add a PowerPoint Slide

Like the Excel chart, a PowerPoint slide added to a Web page becomes a graphic only—whether it's embedded or linked. If you placed the entire presentation in the Word Web page, it will not display the slide show when you double-click it on a browser, as it will in a Word document.

If you have access to PowerPoint, it would be better to create a Web presentation there and then include those pages in your Web site. Or, even better, have your graphic link to a Power-Point Web presentation. That way you have the flexibility of PowerPoint, its animation features, and its additional drawing tools and techniques, readily available to you.

**SEE ALSO**

➤ *For more information about placing PowerPoint slides and presentations in Word documents, see page 413*

# Build an Online Form

**Server support**

Online forms require additional support files and server support, so you should work with your network or Web administrator when you plan the form.

It's nice to build Web pages and Web sites to provide information to a wider audience, either via the Internet or your company intranet. There are times, however, when you want to get some input (or feedback) from the people who visit your Web pages.

Word provides form tools that you can use to create online forms. They are similar to the Form tools used in Word documents, but the Web form tools are meant to be used with browser software. The form elements—check boxes, option buttons, list boxes, and so on—are called *controls*.

### Add a Form to a Web Page

**1.** Click where you want to insert the control in your page.

**2.** Click the control you want to use on the Web Tools toolbar (to see the Web Tools toolbar, open the **View** menu and select **Toolbars**. Then choose **Web Tools**). Refer to Table 29.1 for a list of form controls you can use on a Web page.

**3.** Then click Properties on the Web Tools toolbar. Select either the **Alphabetic** or **Categorized** tab. Enter properties for the form control (see Figure 29.7). Be sure to include an HTML Name, which identifies the field name when the information is sent to the server.

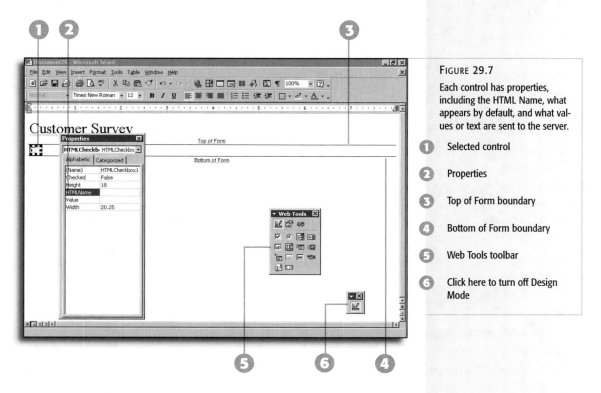

FIGURE 29.7

Each control has properties, including the HTML Name, what appears by default, and what values or text are sent to the server.

1 Selected control

2 Properties

3 Top of Form boundary

4 Bottom of Form boundary

5 Web Tools toolbar

6 Click here to turn off Design Mode

**4.** Repeat the above steps as needed for each control you want to insert. Be sure to include a Submit or Image Submit button on the form so the users can submit the form after they fill it in.

**5.** When you have finished adding text and form controls, click Exit Design Mode on the Web Tools toolbar.

**Form boundaries**

When you insert a form control, a Top of Form boundary appears above the control and a Bottom of Form boundary appears below the control. Other controls for the same form should appear between those boundaries. The boundaries only appear in Design mode and don't show in the Web browser.

**TABLE 29.1   Form controls for Web pages**

| Control | Description | Properties |
|---------|-------------|------------|
| ▢ | Check Box. Use a check box for groups of items where you can select more than one option. | Checked. Appearance by default is True if checked, False if not. Value. The text sent to the Web server if the box is checked. |
| ◉ | Option Button. Use for a group of items from which you can select only one. | Checked. Appearance by default is True if selected, False if not. Value. The text sent to the Web server if the option is selected. |
| ▤ | Drop-down Box. Displays a list of choices. | DisplayValues. Type the items you want to include in the list, separated by semicolons. Do not type spaces between items. MultiSelect. If False, you can select only one item. If True, you can select more than one. Selected. If True, the first item on the list is selected by default. Value. The text sent to the Web server for each item on the list. Values are separated by semicolons. |
| ▤ | List Box. Displays available choices in list format; has scrollbar if choices don't fit box. | DisplayValues. Type the items you want to include in the list, separated by semicolons. Do not type spaces between items. MultiSelect. If False, you can select only one item. If True, you can select more than one. Selected. If True, the first item on the list is selected by default. Value. The text sent to the Web server for each item on the list. Values are separated by semicolons. |
| abl | Text Box. Allows the user to enter one line of text. | MaxLength. Set the maximum number of characters the user can enter (0 is the default, which doesn't restrict the length). Value. The default text to display in the text box, if any. |

| Control | Description | Properties |
|---|---|---|
| | Text Area. Allows the user to enter multiple lines of text. | Columns. The width of the area in number of columns. Rows. The height of the area in number of rows. Value. The default text to display, if any. WordWrap. Choose **Virtual** or **Physical** to have the words wrap in the box. Choose **Off** to not wrap text. WordWrap isn't supported by all browsers. |
| | Submit. Submits the data the user fills in. | Action. Enter the location of the file that opens when the user clicks **Submit**—either "mailto" followed by an Internet mail address or a URL. Caption. The text that appears on the button. Encoding. Stores the MIME (Multipurpose Internet Mail Extensions) type used to encode the submitted form. Method. The method used to submit the form—POST or GET. |
| | Submit with Image. Displays a graphic that the user clicks to submit the data. When the Picture dialog box appears, you must select a picture to use with the button. | Action. Enter the location of the file that opens when the user clicks **Submit**—either "mailto" followed by an Internet mail address or a URL. Encoding. Stores the MIME (Multipurpose Internet Mail Extensions) type used to encode the submitted form. Method. The method used to submit the form—POST or GET. Source. The name of the image source file. |

*continues...*

**ActiveX controls**

You can also insert ActiveX controls in Web forms that are similar to the controls on the Web Tools toolbar, but can offer options to users or run macros that automate a task. When you insert an ActiveX control you write a macro that is stored with the control itself. The macro is written in Visual Basic for Applications and it customizes the behavior of the control. The controls are available on the Control Toolbox toolbar.

**TABLE 29.1    Continued**

| Control | Description | Properties |
| --- | --- | --- |
| | Reset. Resets the form controls to their default settings and removes any data the user has entered in the form. | Caption. The text that appears on the button. |
| | Hidden. Invisible to the user, this control passes information to the server when the user submits the form. | Value. The default text that is sent to the server. |
| | Password. Inserts a box that displays asterisks (*) when the user types to mask what the user is entering. | MaxLength. The number of characters the user can enter. Default is 0, but that doesn't restrict the length. Value (Optional). Default text, displayed as asterisks, for this field. |

## Edit an Online Form

Editing an online form is no different than editing any other document in Word. You open the file and begin making changes.

To add more controls or change the properties of the existing controls, right-click any toolbar and select **Web Tools**. Then choose Design Mode 🖳 to turn on the Design mode. After you've made the appropriate changes, click Design Mode again to turn off the Design mode. Then save the file.

## Fill in an Online Form

When you open an online form in your browser, you recognize the controls placed there and fill them in accordingly (see Figure 29.8):

- Check box. Click on the checkbox to place a check mark there. You may select as many of these options as apply.

- Option button. Click only one option.

- Drop-down box. Click the arrow next to the box to view a list of selections. Click on the option you want.

- List box. Use the scrollbar to move up and down the list. Select more than one option by holding down the Ctrl button as you click on each one.

- Text box. Enter a line of text.

- Text area. Enter several lines of text. Usually text wraps in the box.

- Submit. Click the **Submit** button to submit your data.

- Submit Image. Click the image to submit your data.

- Reset. Click to return all values to the defaults and erase any entries you made.

- Password. Enter a password. All you will see are asterisks (*) as you type.

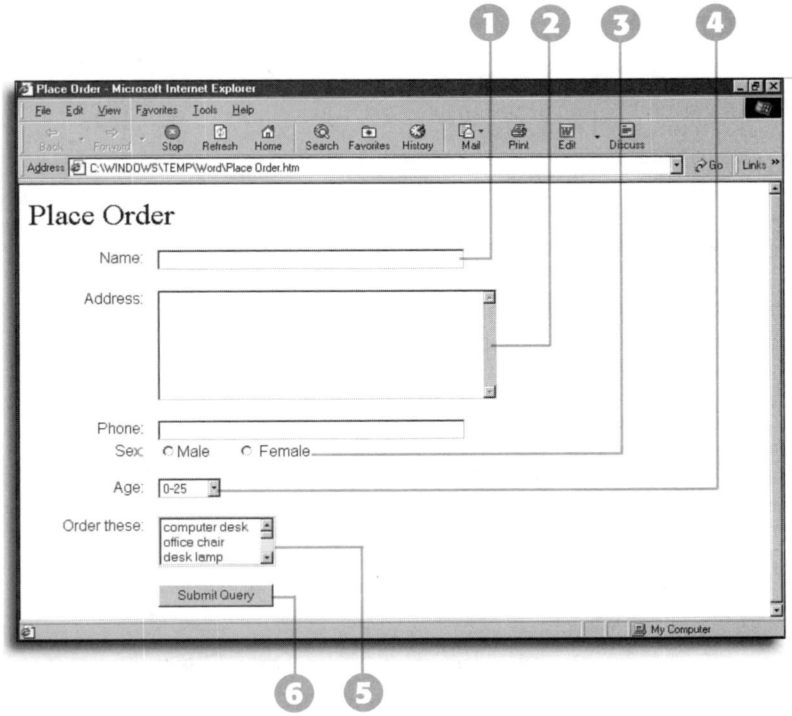

FIGURE 29.8
An order form that uses controls to collect information.

1 Text box
2 Text area
3 Option buttons
4 Drop-down box
5 List box
6 Submit button

# Create an Online Catalog

Just because you're working on Web pages and frames doesn't mean you should forget your lessons about creating documents.

To create the furniture catalog page you see in Figure 29.9, we used mail merging and converted the resulting document to a Web page. Then we created a frame page, with a table of contents frame, to display the catalog online.

FIGURE 29.9

This catalog page started with a mail merge document.

### Create an Online Catalog

1. Start a new document by clicking New [icon] on the Standard toolbar.

2. From the **Tools** menu, select **Mail Merge**.

3. Under **Main Document**, choose **Create** (see Figure 29.10). Select **Catalog**. Choose to use the **Active Window** to create the catalog form.

4. Select **Catalog** as the type of merge document you want to create.

5. Under **Data source**, choose **Get Data**. Select **Create Data Source**. Remove all the current field names in the Create Data Source dialog box (see Figure 29.11) and enter the ones you need by entering the **Field Name** and then clicking **Add Field Name**. Choose **OK** when you've entered all your fields. Enter a **File Name** and click **Save**.

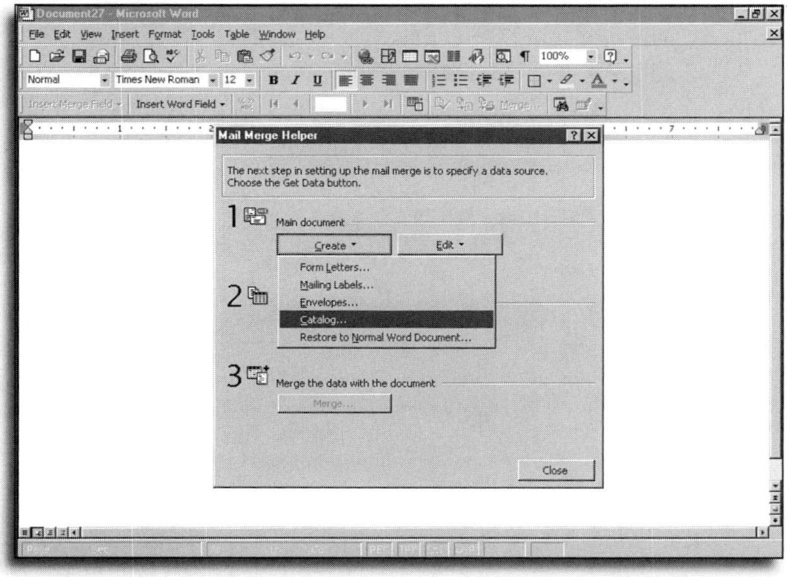

FIGURE 29.10
In the Mail Merge Helper dialog box you can choose to create and edit a data source.

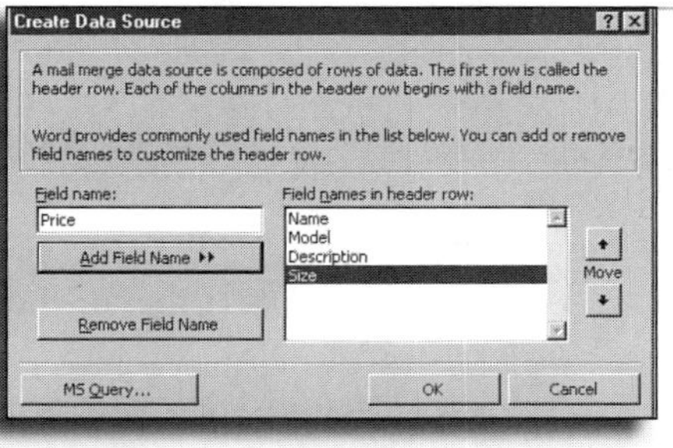

FIGURE 29.11
Add the fields you need for the data you want to display in the catalog.

**6.** In the Data Form (see Figure 29.12), enter the data you need for the catalog. After you complete the data for each item, click **Add New** until all the items have been entered. Then choose **OK**.

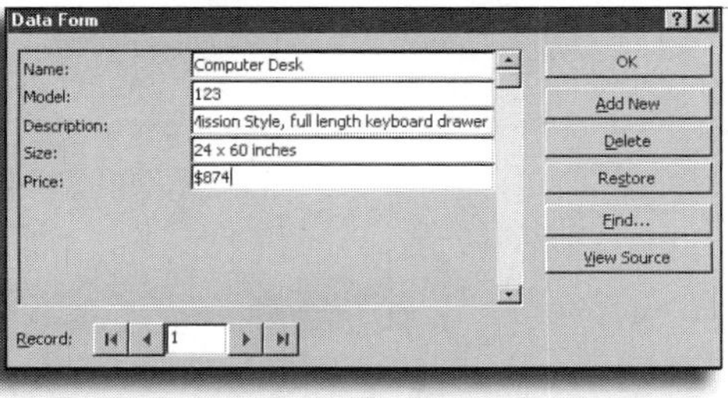

FIGURE 29.12
Enter your product information in the Data Form; click **Add New** to start another item.

**7.** Place your standard text in the main form. Click **Insert Merge Field** on the Mail Merge toolbar when you want to add one of the fields from the data source (see Figure 29.13). Apply Word's built-in heading styles to the product names. When the form is complete, save it.

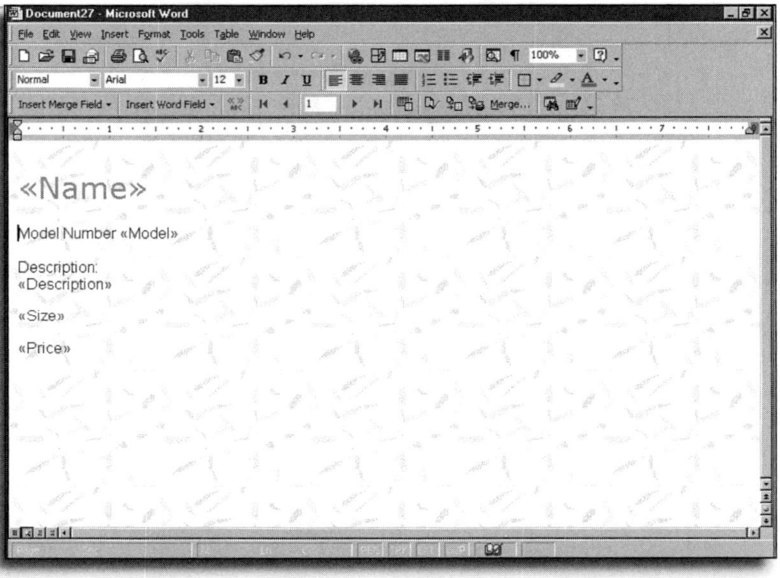

FIGURE 29.13

Write and format the text as a normal document, choosing Insert Merge Field where you want to add data. Then select the field you want to place in the document (the fields appear between angle brackets like << and >>).

**8.** From the **Tools** menu, choose **Mail Merge**. Click **Merge**.

**9.** In the Merge dialog box, select **New document** from the **Merge To** drop-down list (see Figure 29.14). Choose **Merge**.

FIGURE 29.14

Select New Document from the **Merge To** list so you can convert it to a Web page afterwards. It also gives you the opportunity to correct any merging mistakes before you publish your catalog.

**10.** Apply a theme to the merged document (**Format**, **Theme**) or format it yourself, and save it as a Web page. Close the file.

**11.** Start a new document. From the **Format** menu, select **Frames**, and choose **New Frames Page**. Choose the frame layout you want from the Frames toolbar.

**12.** In one frame, select the new catalog document as the initial Web page (click Frame Properties ⊞ ), as shown in Figure 29.15. You may even want to start with a header frame to act as a page banner, as we did in Figure 29.9.

**13.** Save the document as a Web page (**File**, **Save as Web Page**).

**14.** Click in the frame where you want the table of contents to appear and then choose Table of Contents in Frame ▤ on the Frames toolbar. The headings from the catalog document show as hyperlinks in the table of contents.

**15.** Save the Frames page.

PART

# Automate, Customize, and Fine-Tune

# Write Simple Macros

Record, test, and run macros

Edit macros

Write a macro to create templates

**Macro viruses**

Macros can be carriers for computer viruses. When you open a document that has a macro virus, your computer becomes infected. The macro virus is stored in your Normal template and infects every document you create based on that template. Other users who open those documents become infected also. Word can't protect you from macro viruses, although it issues a warning every time you open a document with macros and gives you the opportunity to open it without macros. To avoid spreading viruses through your own macros and documents, use an up-to-date antivirus software to keep your system clean.

# When to Use Macros

Repetitive tasks involving several steps are prime candidates for macros. A *macro* is a set of commands and instructions that is recorded and played back when you command it to run. By creating a macro to perform the steps of a repetitive task, you save yourself time and avoid possible errors.

What could you do with a macro? You could make a macro to perform routine editing or formatting, to combine several commands so you can access them with one keyboard shortcut, to use an option without having to go through one or more dialog boxes, or to automate a complicated set of tasks.

Word has two methods for creating macros—the *macro recorder* or the *Visual Basic Editor*. The recorder acts almost like a tape recorder, noting each command and set of instructions you use in doing a task so it can play back those commands and instructions the next time you ask for them. Word records these commands and instructions for a macro in Visual Basic for Applications programming language. Using the Visual Basic Editor, you modify the instructions or create more flexible and powerful macros.

Because you have to be able to access the macro after you create it, Word allows you to assign the macro to a toolbar, a menu command, or shortcut keys.

The macro is stored, by default, in the Normal template for use in every Word document. However, you may want to store specific macros in the templates where they would be most useful.

**SEE ALSO**

➤ *To learn more about macro viruses and templates, see page 148*

# Record a Macro

Recording macros is similar to making a tape recording of all the steps you perform to do a particular task. However, the macro recorder has some limitations. You can't use the mouse to move the insertion point because the macro recorder doesn't record mouse movements. Instead of using the mouse to select, copy, or move items by clicking or dragging, you must use the keyboard. However, any mouse movements that activate menus, buttons, and commands are recorded.

Here are some tips to keep in mind when working with macros:

- Always plan the steps you want to include in the macro before you start recording. You might even want to run through the task once to be sure what commands you use; write them down if it's a complicated task. Although you can correct a mistake as you're recording, the error and the correction will become part of the macro. You'll have to go back later and edit the macro to remove any unnecessary steps.

- Think ahead to avoid unnecessary steps in the macro. A different order or different method might be cleaner and faster, or prevent having to set up conditions or open an additional dialog box. For example, using the **Find** command is a great way to position your insertion point at a particular phrase but the Find dialog box retains its last entries. If the last setting was to search up or down, the macro may stop when it reaches the beginning or end of the document. Instead, you should include in the macro a step to change the Search setting to All.

- If the macro will be used in many types of documents, don't include anything that is specific to the document you have open when you create the macro.

- Whenever you create a macro it's a good idea to assign it to a toolbar button, a menu, or a shortcut key so you don't have to open the Macro dialog box every time you want to use the macro.

### Record a Macro

**1.** Open the **Tools** menu and choose **Macro**, then select **Record New Macro** from the submenu. The Record Macro dialog box appears (see Figure 30.1).

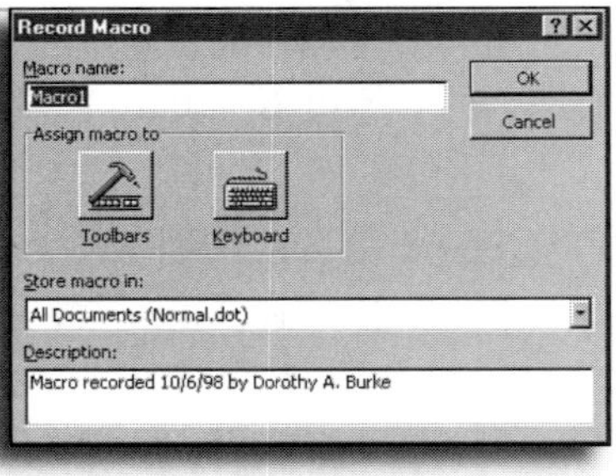

FIGURE 30.1

Enter a name for the new macro and then choose whether you'll assign it to a toolbar or keyboard shortcut.

2. In the **Macro Name** box, type a name for the macro you're about to record. The name must begin with a letter and can contain as many as 80 letters and numbers, but it can't include spaces or symbols. If the **OK** button is grayed out (unavailable), the macro name isn't valid. Be careful not to give the macro the same name as an existing, supplied macro in Word because the new macro actions will replace the existing actions for the supplied macro.

3. From the **Store Macro In** drop-down list, select the template or document in which you want to store the macro. **All Documents (Normal.dot)** is the default setting.

4. Type a description for the macro in the **Description** box. Word automatically enters the date the macro was recorded and who recorded it.

5. To assign the macro to a toolbar or menu, choose **Toolbars** (see the "Assign a Macro to a Toolbar" steps for full instructions). To create a keyboard shortcut to activate the macro, click **Keyboard** (see the "Assign a Keyboard Shortcut to a Macro" steps for instructions).

   After you've assigned a macro to a toolbar or menu and you want to create a keyboard shortcut, choose **Keyboard** in the Customize dialog box to open the Customize Keyboard dialog box. Then choose **Close** to return to the Customize dialog box.

6. If you aren't assigning the macro to a toolbar, menu, or keyboard shortcut—or after you have assigned the macro to a toolbar or keyboard shortcut—choose **OK** to begin recording the macro.

**Supplied macros**

The templates Macros9.dot, Convert9.wiz, and Support9.dot contain macros you can copy into your documents or global template for your own use, such as Save Reminder Install that installs a macro that periodically reminds you to save your work. These macros are located in the Microsoft Office\Office\Macros. If they are not available, you may need to install them by running the Office or Word Setup program.

**7.** The Stop Recording toolbar appears, and your mouse pointer changes to resemble a tape cassette with a pointer. Perform the steps, choose the commands, and enter the instructions to perform the task for which you're creating the macro. The macro recorder records them as you do them (see Figure 30.2).

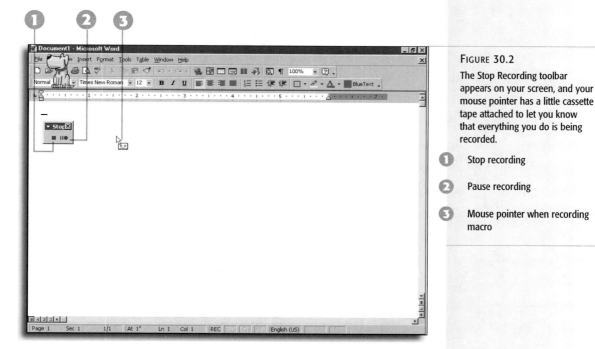

**FIGURE 30.2**

The Stop Recording toolbar appears on your screen, and your mouse pointer has a little cassette tape attached to let you know that everything you do is being recorded.

① Stop recording

② Pause recording

③ Mouse pointer when recording macro

**8.** You can pause the macro recorder and then resume recording where you stopped. To pause the recorder, choose Pause Recording on the Stop Recording toolbar. Choose that same button again to resume recording. The pause is not recorded as part of the macro.

**9.** When the task is finished and you want to stop recording, choose Stop Recording on the Stop Recording toolbar.

### Assign a Macro to a Toolbar

1. When you click the **Toolbars** button while creating a macro (see the preceding procedure), the Customize dialog box appears (see Figure 30.3).

2. Select the name of the macro you're recording from the **Commands** box.

3. Drag the macro name to the toolbar or menu to which you want to assign it. As you drag it onto the toolbar, a thick black vertical line appears indicating where the button will appear when you release the mouse button; when you drag it to a menu, a black horizontal line indicates where the command will appear when you release the mouse button.

4. If you assigned the macro to a toolbar, choose **Modify Selection** in the Customize dialog box to display a menu with options that allow you to change the button name (click **Name**, edit the name, and then press **Enter**). To pick a button image (click **Change Button Image** to pick a picture from the submenu or click **Edit Button Image** and draw a symbol).

5. Choose **Close** to close the Customize dialog box and begin recording the macro.

### Assign a Keyboard Shortcut to a Macro

1. When you click the **Keyboard** button while creating a macro (see step 5 of the recording macros procedure), the Customize Keyboard dialog box appears (see Figure 30.4).

2. Select the name of the macro you're recording from the **Commands** box.

3. Type the key sequence you want to use as the keyboard shortcut in the **Press New Shortcut Key** box. If the text below the box says the key combination is [unassigned], choose **Assign**; if the key combination is assigned to another task, delete it and try another combination.

4. Choose **Close** to begin recording the macro.

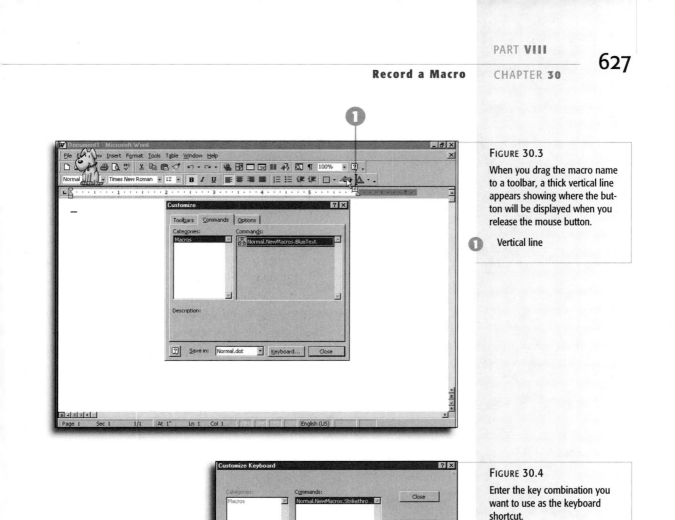

FIGURE 30.3
When you drag the macro name to a toolbar, a thick vertical line appears showing where the button will be displayed when you release the mouse button.

1 Vertical line

FIGURE 30.4
Enter the key combination you want to use as the keyboard shortcut.

**SEE ALSO**

➤ *To customize toolbars, see page 640*
➤ *Learn to create keyboard shortcuts on page 649*

# Test a Macro

After you finish creating your macro, test it out a few times. Vary the circumstances to make sure it works in all conditions. If you have problems, edit the macro to fix it.

Here are some tips when testing your macro:

- Work with files or text that will not be permanently injured if your macro doesn't work correctly. Or, make a copy of the file you want the macro to work with and give the file another name so the original file is protected.

- If you assigned the macro to more than one method—keyboard shortcut, toolbar, or menu—test all the methods to make sure it works equally well in all situations.

- Open a new file (one that uses the same template where you stored the macro) and test the macro there.

- Make sure your macro works when you change the situation. For example, if your macro applies a font attribute, make sure it works when you are using another font. It may always change your font to the one you were using when you recorded the macro.

- If your macro doesn't work properly, note what it isn't doing the way you want it to.

# Run a Macro

To run a macro after you've created it, do one of the following:

- Click the button you added to the toolbar.

- Choose the menu and command you added to the menu.

- Press the key combination you created as the keyboard shortcut.

- Click the **Tools** menu and select **Macro**, then select **Macros** from the submenu. The Macros dialog box appears (see Figure 30.5). Select the name of the macro you want to use and then choose **Run**.

- Press Alt+F8 and the Macros dialog box appears. Select the name of the macro you want to use and then choose **Run**.

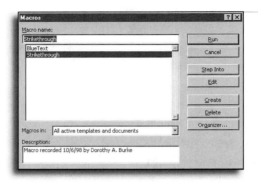

FIGURE 30.5
Select the name of the macro and choose **Run**.

# Edit a Macro

If you need to change or remove a step in your macro, you have two choices: either record the macro again from the start or open the Visual Basic Editor and modify the macro.

**Edit a Macro**

1. Open the **Tools** menu and select **Macro**, then select **Macros** from the submenu. The Macros dialog box appears (refer to Figure 30.5).

2. From the **Macro Name** box, select the name of the macro you want to edit.

3. Choose **Edit**. The Microsoft Visual Basic window opens (see Figure 30.6).

4. Make the necessary changes in the **Code** window (some suggestions follow these steps). You can scroll through all your macros in this window, so be sure you are in the correct macro before making changes.

5. Click the **File** menu and select **Close and Return to Microsoft Word** after you complete your modifications.

6. Test your macro to see that your changes worked.

FIGURE 30.6

The macro being edited is designed to add the strikethrough font attributed to text that is already selected.

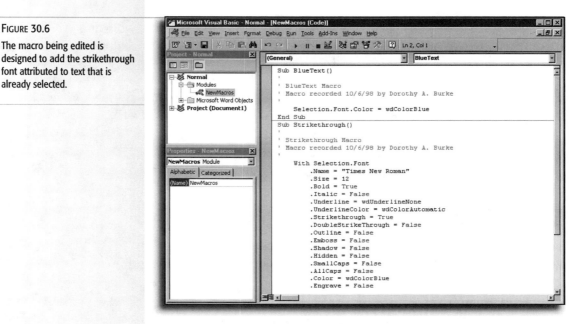

After the Microsoft Visual Basic window is open, the individual lines of code involved in the macro appear in the **Code** window on the right of the screen. Although it's helpful to have a knowledge of the Visual Basic programming language and how it works (especially if you want to add steps and conditional statements), there are some simple things you can do to the macro code to correct or adjust the steps you recorded.

One adjustment you can make to increase the speed and efficiency of your macro is to remove unnecessary lines of code. For example, when you record a macro that selects an option from a dialog box, the macro recorder records all the settings in the dialog box. You should remove the unnecessary ones from the recorded macro by deleting those lines of code.

The following lines of code are for a recorded macro that adds the strikethrough font attribute to selected text:

```
1 Sub Strikethrough()

2 '

3 ' Strikethrough Macro

4 ' Macro recorded 10/6/98 by Dorothy Burke
```

```
5 '
6 With Selection.Font
7 .Name = "Courier"
8 .Size = 12
9 .Bold = True
10 .Italic = False
11 .Underline = wdUnderlineNone
12 .StrikeThrough = True
13 .DoubleStrikeThrough = False
14 .Outline = False
15 .Emboss = False
16 .Shadow = False
17 .Hidden = False
18 .SmallCaps = False
19 .AllCaps = False
20 .ColorIndex = wdBlack
21 .Engrave = False
22 .Superscript = False
23 .Subscript = False
24 .Spacing = 0
25 .Scaling = 100
26 .Position = 0
27 .Kerning = 0
28 .Animation = wdAnimationNone
29 End With
30 End Sub
```

Several lines of code that are unnecessary to the macro can be deleted. The macro could be as simple as:

```
1 Sub Strikethrough()
2 '
3 ' Strikethrough Macro
4 ' Macro recorded 10/6/98 by Dorothy Burke
5 '
6     With Selection.Font
7         .StrikeThrough = True
8 End With
9 End Sub
```

For more information on using Visual Basic with Word macros, open the **Tools** menu, choose **Macro**, and then select **Visual Basic Editor**. When the Visual Basic Editor window opens,

open the **Help** menu and choose **Microsoft Visual Basic Help**
**Contents** and **Index**. Select the **Contents** tab and then select
the **Microsoft Word Visual Basic Reference** topic. (This reference may not have been installed when you installed Word, so
you may not have a copy on your computer. You will have to
install it from the Word setup CD or disks.) You can learn more
about macros in Que's *Special Edition Using Microsoft Word 2000*.

# Copy, Rename, and Delete a Macro

Deleting a macro can be done from the Macros dialog box; however, you will still have to remove the menu commands and toolbar buttons you assigned to the macro—they remain but they
won't work without the macro.

**Delete a Macro**

1. Open the **Tools** menu and choose **Macro**, then select
   **Macros** from the submenu to open the Macros dialog box
   (refer to Figure 30.5).

2. From the **Macro Name** box, select the name of the macro
   you want to delete.

3. Choose **Delete**.

4. When Word asks for a confirmation that you want to delete
   that macro, choose **Yes**.

5. Choose **Close** to close the Macros dialog box.

6. To remove the toolbar buttons and menu commands you
   assigned to the macro, open the **View** menu and choose
   **Toolbars**, and then select **Customize** from the submenu.
   When the Customize dialog box appears, drag the button
   for the macro from the toolbar on the screen or the macro
   menu command from the menu.

7. Choose **Close**.

Copying a macro to another document or template, renaming a
macro, or deleting a macro can all be done from the Organizer.
You reach the Organizer through the Macros dialog box by completing the steps that follow.

### Copy, Rename, or Delete a Macro

1. Open the **Tools** menu and choose **Macro**, and then select **Macros** to open the Macros dialog box.

2. Choose **Organizer**.

3. The Organizer dialog box appears with the **Macro Project Items** tab selected (see Figure 30.7).

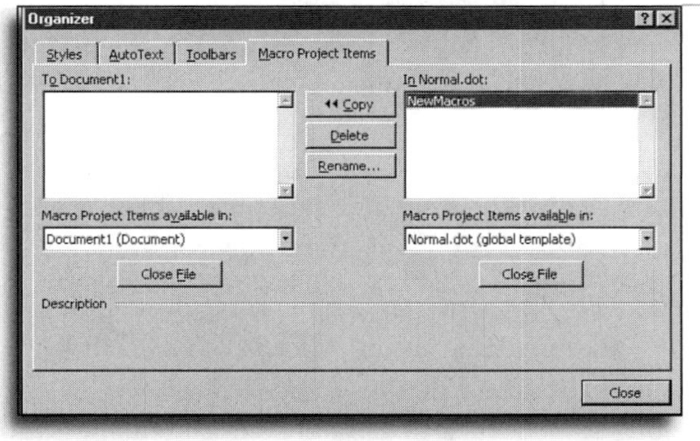

FIGURE 30.7
Use the Organizer to copy, delete, or rename macros.

4. On the right is the **In Normal.dot** box that displays the macros in the Normal document template. On the left is the **To Document**x box that displays the macros used in the document you have open. From either list, select the macro you want to copy, rename, or delete.

   If the macro is in another template that's attached to the current document, select that template from the **Macro Project Items Available In** drop-down list on the right.

   If the document you want isn't listed, choose **Close File** and then choose **Open File**. Select the file you want to use and then click **Open**. The file's macros will appear in that box.

5. Click the appropriate button for the action you want to perform:

   - **Copy** copies the macro from one box to the other, thus copying it from the Normal template to the current document or vice versa, depending on where the macro was stored.

- **D**elete deletes the selected macro (to delete more than one macro, hold down the Ctrl key and click each one you want to delete before choosing **D**elete).

- **R**ename opens the Rename dialog box. Enter the **New name** for the macro and choose **OK**.

**6.** Choose **Close**.

Word supplies a set of useful macros for you. The Macros9.dot template contains macros that you may find useful in your daily work or as samples to review and modify. The macros include one to back up your AutoCorrect entries so you can copy them to another computer, another to add the Symbol dialog box to the find and replace function. There is also one to insert footnotes in the Chicago Manual of Style format.

To use the macros, click the **F**ile menu and select **O**pen, and then change to the Microsoft Office\Office\Macros folder. From the **Files of T**ype drop-down list, select **All Files**. Then double-click the Macros9.dot filename. Run the macros you want and then copy any you need to other documents using the Organizer.

**SEE ALSO**

➢ *Learn more about customizing toolbars and menus on page 640*

# Create a Template Containing Macros

Although macros can be attached to a document, they are powerful tools when combined with templates. They can automate the task of completing documents created with a template and are particularly useful when working with online forms.

When you create a template for an online form, you insert fields on that form. Any macro in the form template can run automatically when the insertion point enters or exits a form field.

### Create a Template Containing Macros

**1.** Create the macros that you want to include in your new template. Create or open the form template that you want to automate.

2. If protection has been applied to the form, choose Protect Form [icon] on the Forms toolbar or click the **Tools** menu and select **Unprotect Document**.

3. Create the macros you want to use in the template and store them in the template.

4. Add the form fields you need in the template.

5. For each form field to which you want to attach a macro, double-click the form field to see the Field Options dialog box (this box differs slightly depending on the type of field you're working on).

6. Under **Run Macro On** (see Figure 30.8), select the macro you want to use with that field from the **Entry** drop-down list (if you want the macro to run when the insertion point enters the field) or from the **Exit** drop-down list (if you want the macro to run when the insertion point exits the field).

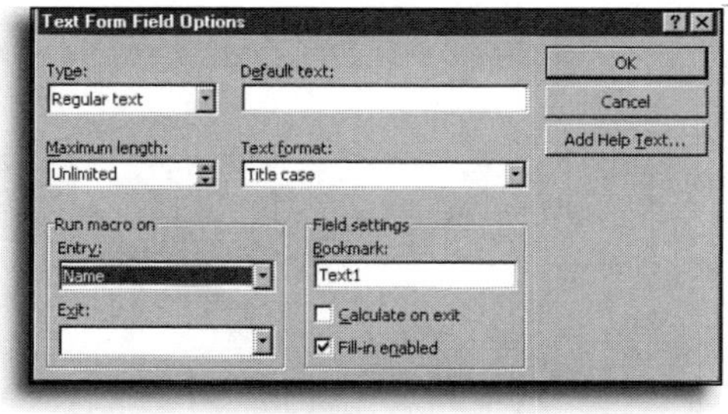

**FIGURE 30.8**
The Name macro automatically enters the username when the user clicks in the text form field.

7. Choose **OK**.

Test the template to see that your macros work properly when you use the template to create new documents.

CHAPTER

*31*

# Customize and Fine-Tune Word

Arrange your toolbars onscreen and customize the buttons to suit the way you work

Add or delete commands on the menu and the shortcut menus

Create additional keyboard shortcuts to speed repetitive tasks

Set up your program and document defaults to tailor Word to your work habits and needs

Make the Office Assistant work and look the way you want

# Position Toolbars

Microsoft Word has a variety of toolbars available for your use. Some you display by clicking the **View** menu, choosing **Toolbars**, and then selecting the toolbar from a submenu (see Figure 31.1). Alternatively, right-click any toolbar to select from the same list.

FIGURE 31.1

When you click the **View** menu and select **Toolbars**, a submenu of toolbars you can display appears.

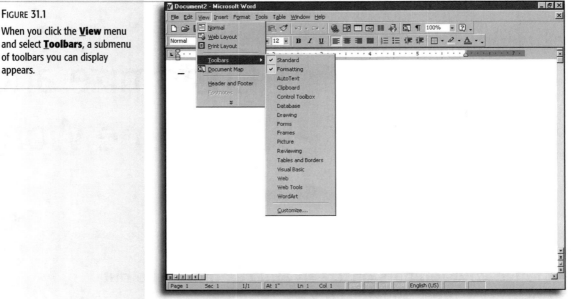

Other toolbars, such as the Mail Merge toolbar or the Stop Recording toolbar, appear automatically when you begin specific tasks.

The Standard toolbar has two buttons that display other toolbars: Tables and Borders ▦ and Drawing ▨. If any of these toolbars already shows on the screen, choosing that same button will close the toolbar.

Toolbars in Word can be docked or floating. A *docked* toolbar is one that is attached to one side of the program window. A *floating* toolbar is not attached and can be moved to any part of the document window.

Docked toolbars have a *move handle* at the top or left side (see Figure 31.2). To change the position of a docked toolbar, drag the toolbar by its move handle. When you drag it to any edge of the program window, the toolbar attaches itself to that side and becomes a docked toolbar once again.

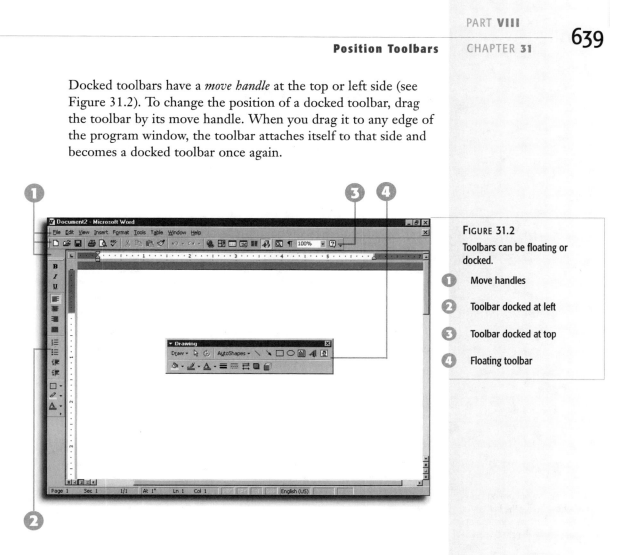

FIGURE **31.2**

Toolbars can be floating or docked.

1. Move handles
2. Toolbar docked at left
3. Toolbar docked at top
4. Floating toolbar

If you drag a toolbar out into the document window, the toolbar becomes a floating toolbar. You move a floating toolbar by dragging the title bar. Click the Close (X) button to close the toolbar. Drag any edge of a floating toolbar to change the size and shape of the toolbar. To dock a floating toolbar, drag it against the side of the program window to which you want to attach it or double-click the title bar to return it to its former docked position.

# Customize Toolbars

Word's toolbars provide shortcuts to commands and dialog boxes, and there are many tools available to you with these toolbars. You still have the capability, however, to add more tools, remove unnecessary tools, or create your own tools or toolbars.

## Add or Remove Buttons

At the end of each docked toolbar is an arrow button (on a floating toolbar, it's the small arrow at the left of the title bar). When you click that button, the **Add or Remove Buttons** appears (see Figure 31.3). Click the down arrow next to that selection to see a submenu of all the buttons on the toolbar plus some related tools you may want to add to the toolbar. The buttons that already appeared on the toolbar have check marks in front of them. To add a button to the toolbar, click on the button to put a check mark in front of it. To remove a button, click to remove the check mark. Click **Reset Toolbar** to return the toolbar back to its default settings.

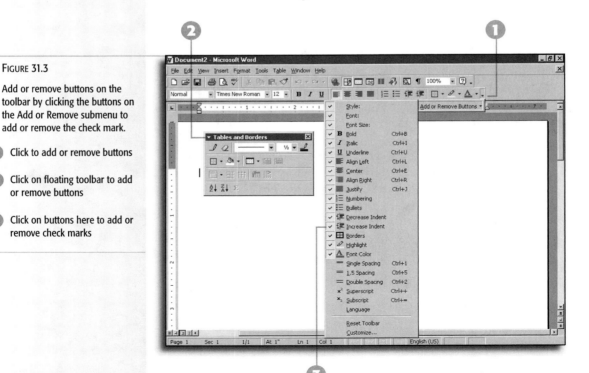

FIGURE 31.3

Add or remove buttons on the toolbar by clicking the buttons on the Add or Remove submenu to add or remove the check mark.

1. Click to add or remove buttons

2. Click on floating toolbar to add or remove buttons

3. Click on buttons here to add or remove check marks

The Add or Remove Buttons submenu only displays some of the tools that are available to add to your toolbar. The Customize dialog box offers a larger range of tools.

### Add or Remove Toolbar Buttons

1. Display the toolbar to which you will add or remove buttons, if it's not already showing on your screen.

2. Click the **View** menu, select **Toolbars**, and then choose **Customize** from the submenu; or right-click a toolbar and click **Customize** on the shortcut menu; or click the Add or Remove Buttons button on the toolbar and choose **Customize**.

3. When the Customize dialog box appears, click the **Commands** tab (see Figure 31.4).

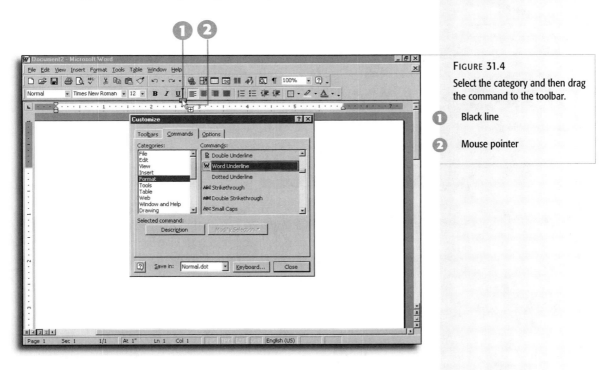

FIGURE 31.4

Select the category and then drag the command to the toolbar.

1 Black line

2 Mouse pointer

4. From the **Categories** list, select the menu title for the command you're adding as a tool or choose **All Commands**, **Macros**, **Fonts**, or the name of one of the specialized toolbars for additional commands. If you're creating a new tool,

you must create a macro first that will perform the commands you want to occur when you choose that tool.

5. From the **Commands** list, click the command you want to use. Drag the command from the Commands list to the toolbar. As you bring the mouse pointer over the toolbar, a thick black vertical or horizontal line appears on the toolbar. That line moves to follow your mouse pointer as you continue to drag along the toolbar. When you release the mouse button, the new button appears at the position of that line. If you accidentally drop the button in the wrong position, drag it to the correct location (you can do this as long as the Customize dialog box is open). If you want to group buttons, click **Modify Selection** and choose **Begin a Group** to add a gray vertical line before the button.

6. Choose **Close** to close the dialog box.

To remove a button from a toolbar, open the Customize dialog box as described in steps 1 and 2. Click the button you want to remove and then drag it off the toolbar. Make sure you don't release the mouse button while your mouse pointer is over another toolbar.

**SEE ALSO**

➤ *Learn more about creating tools based on macros on page 622*

## Create a New Toolbar

If you have a set of favorite tools you'd like to see together, create a toolbar that contains them all. That will save you steps in opening and closing several different toolbars.

### Create a New Toolbar

1. Click the **View** menu and select **Toolbars**, and then choose **Customize** from the submenu; or right-click a toolbar and click **Customize** on the shortcut menu; click the Add or Remove Buttons button on a toolbar and choose **Customize**.

2. When the Customize dialog box appears, click the **Toolbars** tab (see Figure 31.5).

---

**Add built-in menus**

Want to add a menu to a toolbar? Display the toolbar to which you want to add the menu. When the Customize dialog box is open, select the **Commands** tab. Click **Built-In Menus** in the **Categories** box. Drag the menu you want from the **Commands** box to the toolbar.

**3.** Choose **New** to open the New Toolbar dialog box (see Figure 31.6).

**4.** In the **Toolbar Name** text box, type the name of your new toolbar.

**5.** From the **Make Toolbar Available To** drop-down list, select the template or file in which you want to store the toolbar. Storing it in Normal.dot will make it available to most of your documents.

**6.** Choose **OK** to return to the Customize dialog box.

**7.** A small floating toolbar appears on the title bar with the name you selected. Following the instructions under "Add or Remove Buttons" earlier in this chapter, add the tools you want to appear on that toolbar.

**8.** When the toolbar is complete, choose **Close** to close the dialog box. Move your toolbar to position or dock it.

To delete a toolbar from Word, open the Customize dialog box, select the **Toolbars** tab, click the toolbar name in the **Toolbars** list, and then choose **Delete**. When Word asks if you're sure you want to delete it, choose **OK**.

## Set Toolbar Options

Word enables you to choose larger icons for your toolbars, turn the ScreenTips on or off, or add the keyboard shortcut keys to the ScreenTips. ScreenTips are the little yellow tags that tell you what the button is when you point at a toolbar button.

### Set Toolbar Options

1. Open the **View** menu and choose **Toolbars**, then select **Customize** from the submenu; or right-click a toolbar and click **Customize** on the shortcut menu; or click the Add or Remove Buttons button on the toolbar and choose **Customize**.

2. When the Customize dialog box appears, click the **Options** tab (see Figure 31.7).

FIGURE 31.7

Check the toolbar options you want to use.

3. Select the option to enable it:

   - **Standard and Formatting Toolbars Share One Row** docks both of these toolbars on a single row.

   - **Large Icons** enlarges the toolbar buttons to make them easier to see.

   - **List Font Names in Their Font** displays font choices in their own font in the Formatting toolbar.

   - **Show ScreenTips on Toolbars** turns the ScreenTips on (click to remove the check mark if you want to turn the ScreenTips off). You can also turn on ScreenTips by clicking the **Tools** menu and selecting **Options**, choosing the **View** tab, and then enabling **ScreenTips under Show**.

- **Show S̲hortcut Keys in ScreenTips** adds the keyboard shortcut combinations to the ScreenTips. For example, when you point to Italic on the Formatting toolbar, "Ctrl+I" displays after "Italic" in the ScreenTip.

**4.** Choose **Close** to close the dialog box.

# Customize Menus

Ever wish you could just click a command in the menu, instead of having to open dialog boxes and choose options to get the result you want? The solution is to add the command to the menu. You can also customize the shortcut menus that appear when you right-click.

## Add Menu Commands

### Add a Menu Command

**1.** Open the T̲ools menu and choose **C̲ustomize** to open the Customize dialog box (see Figure 31.8).

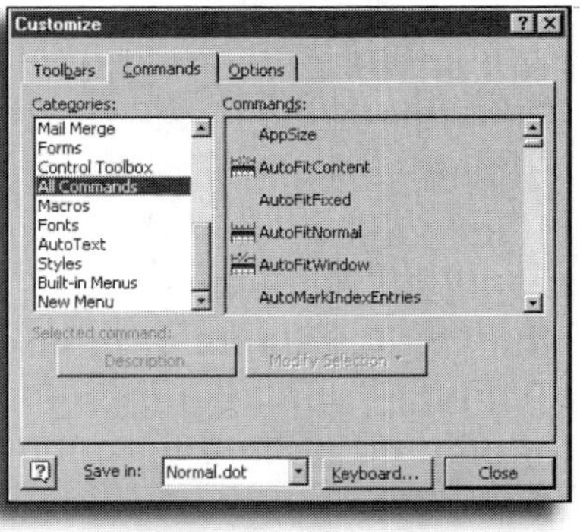

**FIGURE 31.8**

Select the **All Commands, Macros, Fonts, AutoText,** or **Styles** category when adding menu commands.

**2.** Select the **C̲ommands** tab.

**3.** From the **Categories** box, select a command category:

- **All Commands** to select from all available commands.

- **Macros** to add a menu command that runs a macro (you must create the macro first).

- **Fonts** to add a command that applies a particular font.
- **AutoText** to add a command that inserts an AutoText entry (create the AutoText entry first).
- **Styles** to add a menu command to apply a style.

**4.** Select the command you want to add from the **Commands** list. Then drag it to the appropriate menu. As you move your mouse pointer over the menu, a thick horizontal line appears. When you release the mouse button, the new command appears at the location of the horizontal line (see Figure 31.9).

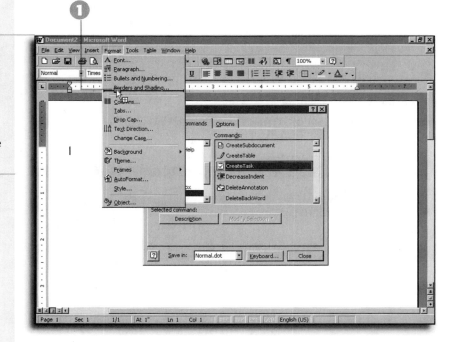

FIGURE 31.9

Drag the command to the menu and release the mouse button when the dark line is where you want the command to appear.

**1** Line indicates where the new command will be added to the menu.

**5.** (Optional) If you want to change the name of the command, choose **Modify Selection**. In the **Name** box on the pop-up menu, click the name to edit it. Press Enter when your modifications are complete.

6. (Optional) The commands on the menus are grouped to keep similar commands together. Thin horizontal lines separate these groups on the menu. To create a group that includes your new command, choose **Modify Selection** and then click **Begin a _G_roup** on the pop-up menu. To move other commands into that same group, click and drag them below the thin horizontal line.

7. Choose **Close** to close the dialog box.

If you need to delete a menu command, open the Customize dialog box. Click the menu command you want to delete and then drag it off the menu.

To create a new menu on the menu bar, open the Customize dialog box and select the **_C_ommands** tab. Select **New Menu** from the **Cate_g_ories** list. Drag **New Menu** from the **Comman_d_s** list to the menu bar. Choose **_M_odify Selection** and click in the **_N_ame** box to modify the menu name. Press Enter to accept the new menu name. Then add commands to the new menu.

## Change Shortcut Menus

In addition to adding commands to the menu on the menu bar, Word allows you to modify the shortcut menus that appear when you right-click an item.

### Modify Shortcut Menus

1. Open the **_T_ools** menu and select **_C_ustomize** on the menu.

2. When the Customize dialog box appears, click the **Tool_b_ars** tab.

3. Click **Shortcut Menus** on the **Tool_b_ars** list to check the box. The Shortcut Menus toolbar appears (see Figure 31.10).

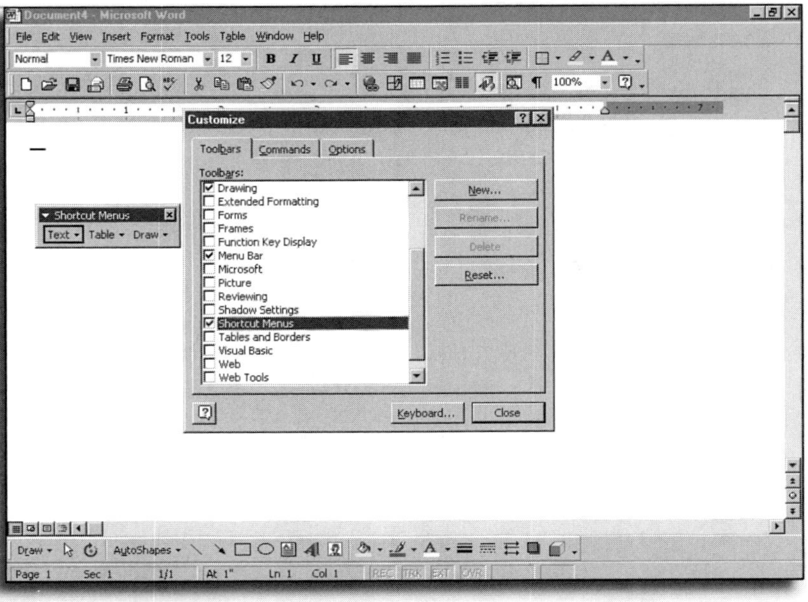

FIGURE 31.10

Check the Shortcut Menus toolbar to make it visible so you can customize it.

4. Click one of the categories on the Shortcut Menus toolbar. Then click the shortcut menu you want to modify.

5. To add a command, select the **Commands** tab and then select a category for the command from the Categories list. Drag the command from the **Commands** box to the appropriate location on the shortcut menu. Using the position of the horizontal line as a guide, release the mouse button when the mouse pointer is in the correct location.

To delete a command, click the shortcut menu that contains the command you want to delete. Drag that command off the menu.

6. Choose **Close** to close the Customize dialog box.

The Shortcut Menus toolbar only remains visible while you are modifying the shortcut menus.

# Make Your Own Keyboard Shortcuts

Word has keyboard shortcuts for many of the menu commands. By using these key combinations, you save time (if you're a touch typist) by not having to move your hands from the keyboard while you're typing. Learning the key combinations requires memorization—you either sit down and memorize the key combinations or you learn them by repetition. These shortcut keys appear next to the command on the menu, so you see them each time you use the command on the menu. For a full list of keyboard shortcuts, check the **Help** index for **Keys**, **Shortcut** and then select the type of shortcuts you need. For commands that you use frequently but that don't have keyboard shortcuts, you may want to create your own.

### Create Keyboard Shortcuts

1. Open the **Tools** menu and choose **Customize**.

2. When the Customize dialog box opens, choose **Keyboard**. The Customize Keyboard dialog box appears (see Figure 31.11).

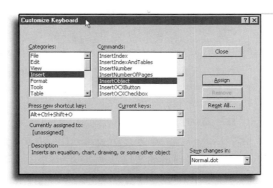

FIGURE 31.11
Enter your new keyboard combination in the **Press New Shortcut Key** box.

3. Click the **Save Changes In** drop-down list and select the template or document in which you want to save the keyboard shortcut. Saving them in Normal.dot makes them available to all documents.

**4.** From the **C**ategories box, select the category that contains the command for which you are creating the shortcut.

**5.** From the **Co**mmands box, select the item for which you are creating the shortcut. If there is a shortcut already assigned to that command, it will appear in the **C**urrent **Keys** box.

**6.** Click in the **Press N**ew **Shortcut Key** box and press the keyboard shortcut key combination you want to assign to the selected command. For example, press Ctrl+Shift+S.

If the combination you enter is already assigned to a command, that command will appear below **Currently Assigned To** (for example, Ctrl+Shift+S is currently assigned to Style). In that case you need to delete the key combination and try another one, unless you want to replace the old assignment with your new command.

When the combination you enter is not already assigned to a command, [unassigned] appears below **Currently Assigned To**. Choose **A**ssign to assign that combination to the selected command. The key combination moves to the **C**urrent **Keys** box.

**7.** Choose **Close** to close the Customize Keyboard dialog box.

**8.** Choose **Close** to close the Customize dialog box. In the future you can use your newly created shortcut instead of the menu commands to do the task you selected.

Shortcut keys are also assigned to macros, styles, or symbols.

**SEE ALSO**

➤ *To learn more about assigning keyboard shortcuts to macros, see page 622*

➤ *To learn more about styles, see page 237*

➤ *For more information about symbols, see page 382*

# Set Program Options and Defaults

Default settings specify what options are in effect when you start a document or set up how a particular operation works *unless* you change the settings. In other words, default settings are how things work normally. If you don't like the default settings used by Word for fonts, margins, file locations, styles, and so on, Word lets you change the defaults. After you make the modifications, your new settings become the default for documents created from that moment on.

## Set View Preferences

To control what normally appears on your screen, and how your program window looks, you need to set the View options. Some of the View options displayed in the dialog box depend on the current view (Normal, Print Layout, Outline, Web Layout), so you should switch to the view for which you want to set the defaults. Then click **Tools** on the menu and select **Options** to open the Options dialog box. Click the **View** tab. Table 31.1 describes the View options.

TABLE 31.1 **View options**

| Action | Option |
|---|---|
| Display drawings created with drawing tools. Deselect this option to hide the drawings and speed up the screen refresh (drawings will still print normally). | **Drawings** |
| Display object anchors (show that an object is attached to the paragraph next to the anchor symbol) if **Show/Hide** button on the Standard toolbar is clicked or **All** is checked under **Nonprinting Characters** in the Options dialog box. | **Object Anchors** |
| Display dotted lines around page margins, text columns, and objects that are helpful when working with the document layout. | **Text Boundaries** |
| Speed up screen display in documents with a great amount of formatting by displaying all character formatting as bold and underlined, and graphics as empty boxes. | **Draft Font** |
| Increase the refresh speed on your screen so you can scroll faster through a document that has lots of graphics; displays boxes in the place of each graphic in the document. | **Picture Placeholders** |

*continues...*

TABLE 31.1    **Continued**

| Action | Option |
|---|---|
| Display animated text onscreen; deselect this to see how the printed text will look. | **Animated Text** |
| Display ScreenTips when you point to a button on a toolbar. See "Set Toolbar Options" earlier in this chapter for more information. | **ScreenTips** |
| Display highlight shading applied by the Highlight tool on the Formatting toolbar. | **Highlight** |
| Make any bookmarks in your document appear with square brackets ([]) around them. | **Bookmarks** |
| Display field codes in curly brackets ({}) instead of displaying the results of fields (for example, {USERNAME\* Caps\ *MERGEFORMAT} appears in place of your name as the Word user). | **Field Codes** |
| Easily identify fields by shading them. Choose **Always** or **When Selected** from the drop-down list. | **Field Shading** |
| Display symbols or characters to indicate where you inserted **Tab Characters**, **Spaces**, **Paragraph Marks**, **Optional Hyphens**, or **Hidden Text** in your documents. Click **All** to display all these marks. | **Formatting Marks** |
| Display the status bar at the bottom of your program window. | **Status Bar** |
| Display the vertical ruler at the left of the document window. | **Vertical Ruler** |
| Display a horizontal scrollbar at the bottom of your document window. | **Horizontal Scroll Bar** |
| Display a vertical scrollbar on the right side of the document window. | **Vertical Scroll Bar** |
| Wrap text to the width of the document window. Deselect to wrap text as it will print. | **Wrap to Window** |
| Display the style area, where the style names appear across from the paragraphs. Enter a measurement to display the style area; enter 0 to remove the style area from the screen. | **Style Area Width** |

# Set General Options

For generalized defaults that control the operation of Word and help WordPerfect users adjust to Word, you need to set General options. Click the **Tools** menu and select **Options** to open the Options dialog box. Then click the **General** tab. Table 31.2 describes the General options.

### TABLE 31.2    **General options**

| Action | Option |
|---|---|
| Automatically adjust the page numbering and automatic page breaks in your document as you work. Deselect this option to speed up document editing and scrolling but select it again before your final save. | **Background Repagination** |
| Display or demonstrate the Word equivalent of WordPerfect for DOS keystrokes. | **Help for WordPerfect Users** |
| Switch the functions of Page Up, Page Down, Home, End, and Esc to the WordPerfect for DOS equivalent. | **Navigation Keys for WordPerfect Users** |
| Change the background color of the document window to blue and the text to white, as it appears on the WordPerfect for DOS screen. | **Blue Background, White Text** |
| Be alerted by a sound when certain events or actions occur in Word. | **Provide Feedback with Sound** |
| See special animated cursors and mouse pointers during some Word operations (saving, printing, repagination, AutoFormatting, find and replace) to help identify the operations. | **Provide Feedback with Animation** |
| Allow you to select or verify the file format converter to convert a file to a Word document when it's opened (otherwise, Word does it for you automatically). | **Confirm Conversion at Open** |

*continues…*

**TABLE 31.2    Continued**

| Action | Option |
|---|---|
| Automatically update any linked objects, pictures, or data in a document when it is opened. | Update Automatic Links at Open |
| Send the current document as an attachment when you choose the **File** menu, select **Send To** and then choose **Mail Recipient** from the submenu. Deselect this option to include the text of the document in the mail message. | Mail As Attachment |
| Display your most recently used files at the bottom of the **File** menu. | Recently Used File List |
| Specify the number of files displayed in the **Most Recently Used File** list. Enter or select a number to change this. | Entries |
| Select the unit of measurement for the horizontal ruler and for measurements you enter in dialog boxes. | Measurement Units |
| Change the default unit of measure to pixels in dialog boxes. | Show Pixels for HTML Features |

Choose **Web Options** to disable features not supported by specific browsers, specify Word as the default editor for Web pages created in Office or for all other Web pages, and set file-name and location options. Web options also involve the output format and target monitors for displaying graphics in browsers. You can also set the default font character set.

Choose **E-Mail Options** to create an email signature and set the default theme and font for new mail messages and replies.

## Change Editing Options

The default settings for text selection, copying and cutting, pasting, and moving text are part of the Edit options. To change these options, click the **Tools** menu and select **Options** to open the Options dialog box. Then click the **Edit** tab. Table 31.3 describes the Edit options.

## TABLE 31.3  **Edit options**

| Action | Option |
| --- | --- |
| Delete and replace selected text as soon as you start typing new text. When this option is deselected, Word inserts the new text immediately before the selected text. | **Typing Replaces Selection** |
| Move selected text when you drag it (hold down Ctrl to copy it) and insert it at the cursor position when you release the mouse button. | **Drag-and-Drop Text Editing** |
| Select the entire word and the space after it when you select part of the word. | **When Selecting, Automatically Select Entire Word** |
| Insert the contents of the Clipboard at the insertion point when you press the Insert key. | **Use the INS Key for Paste** |
| Replace existing text as you type, one character at a time (double-click OVR on the status bar to turn it off and on after you enable this option). | **Overtype Mode** |
| Add or delete spaces before or after text you paste from the Clipboard or delete (either by cutting it or by using the Delete key). | **Use Smart Cut and Paste** |
| Increase or decrease left indent when you press Tab or Backspace. | **Tabs and Backspace Set Left Indent** |
| Be able to capitalize French words that begin with accented letters, such as Étude. | **Allow Accented Uppercase in French** |
| Specify which application to use when editing photos. You select from applications that are installed on your computer. | **Picture Editor** |
| Be able to double-click anywhere on a page and begin typing. | **Enable Click and Type** |
| Set the paragraph style to use when no other is specified. | **Default Paragraph Style** |

**SEE ALSO**
➤ *To learn more about how to select and edit text, see page 60*

# Set Print Options

Printing options such as reverse order, draft output, background printing, and items to include with the document when printing, can be reached in two ways. The first is by clicking the **Options** button in the Print dialog box. The second is by opening the Options dialog box and selecting the **Print** tab.

**SEE ALSO**
➤ *To learn more about printing options, see page 258*

# Choose How and Where to Save Files

You want to save files quickly and frequently and avoid loss of data. The Save options set up how your files are saved, and the File Location options determine where they are saved. Click the **Tools** menu and select **Options** to open the Options dialog box. Then click the **Save** tab. Table 31.4 describes the Save options.

**TABLE 31.4   Save options**

| Action | Option |
| --- | --- |
| Save the previous version of a document with a .bak extension each time you save a document. When you save the file again, the new backup copy replaces the previous one. The backup file is stored in the same folder as the current version. | **Always Create Backup Copy** |
| Save only the changes and append them to the document file, which cuts down the time it takes to save files. However, the size of the saved file may increase significantly if you made several modifications because the file keeps all the changes. Deselect this option before your final save to decrease the size of the final file. This option is grayed out when you choose **Always Create Backup Copy**. | **Allow Fast Saves** |

| Action | Option |
|---|---|
| Open the Document Properties box when you initially save the file to allow you to enter information such as title, subject, author, keywords, and comments. | **Prompt for Document Properties** |
| Prompt you each time you save a document to save any changes to the default settings in the Normal template. If you deselect this option, Word automatically saves the Normal template without asking. | **Prompt to Save Normal Template** |
| Store any TrueType fonts you used as part of the document, so others who open the document can view the formatting even though they don't have the same font set as you do. This increases the size of the document file. | **Embed TrueType Fonts** |
| Embed only the font used in the document instead of all those available in the font set. This minimizes the increase in size caused when you selected **Embed TrueType Fonts**. | **Embed Characters in Use Only** |
| Saves only the data entered in an online form, instead of the entire document, and stores it as a single, tab-delimited record for use in a database. The file is saved intext-only format. | **Save Data Only for Forms** |
| Continue working while Word saves files. | **Allow Background Saves** |
| Create a document recovery file in case you lose power or your system hangs. When you start Word up afterward, Word displays the AutoRecover file, which may contain information that you entered since your last save. Don't think AutoRecover is the same as Save—you must still save your file when you've finished. | **Save AutoRecover Info Every_** |

*continues...*

TABLE 31.4    **Continued**

| Action | Option |
|---|---|
| Set the time interval at which AutoRecover runs (enter a number between 1 and 120). | **Minutes** |
| Set the file format Word uses by default each time it saves a file. | **Save Word Files As** |
| Excludes any features of Word 2000 that were not also included in Word 97. | **Disable Features Not Supported by Word 97** |
| Specify the password needed for a person to open the file. | **Password to Open** |
| Specify the password needed for a person to be able to edit the document and save the file with the modifications. | **Password to Modify** |
| Display a recommendation when someone tries to open the file. The recommendation is that the file be opened in read-only mode, so the document has to be saved with a different name before modifications can be saved. This preserves the original copy. | **Read-Only Recommended** |

The default location for storing Word document files is the **My Documents** folder. Of course, at any time you can save to any of your folders, but you can also change the default file locations.

The File Location options also set the default locations for your clip art files, templates, workgroup templates, user options, AutoRecover files (you should specify a location for these files), tools, and startup files. If some of these files are kept on network drives, you should designate the proper path.

### Change the Default File Locations

1. Open the **Tools** menu and choose **Options** to open the Options dialog box.

2. Click the **File Locations** tab (see Figure 31.12).

**3.** Select **Documents** from the **File Types** box.

**4.** Choose **Modify**.

**5.** In the Modify Location dialog box, select the drive and folder where you normally want your documents stored from the **Look In** drop-down list or enter the path in the **Folder Name** box.

**6.** Choose **OK** to return to the Options dialog box.

**7.** Choose **OK** to close the Options dialog box.

SEE ALSO
➤ *To learn more about saving files and using passwords, see page 151*

## Specify Spelling and Grammar Preferences

Do those green, wavy lines that mark a grammar error annoy you? Turning this option off is only one of the spelling and grammar preferences. To set the options to make spelling and grammar checking work the way you want them to, click the **Tools** menu and select **Options** to open the Options dialog box. Then click the **Spelling & Grammar** tab. Table 31.5 describes the spelling and grammar options.

TABLE 31.5  **Spelling and Grammar options**

| Action | Option |
| --- | --- |
| Mark spelling errors with a red wavy underline as you type. | **Check Spelling As You Type** |
| Hide the red wavy line under potential spelling errors. | **Hide Spelling Errors in This Document** |
| Display a list of suggested spellings for possible errors whenever you spell check the document. | **Always Suggest Corrections** |
| Check spelling against the Main Dictionary but ignore any custom spelling dictionaries. | **Suggest from Main Dictionary Only** |
| Skip words in uppercase during a spell check. | **Ignore Words in UPPERCASE** |
| Skip words that contain numbers during a spell check. | **Ignore Words with Numbers** |
| Skip any Internet or file addresses during a spell check. | **Ignore Internet and File Addresses** |
| Specify the spelling dictionaries in use, other than the Main Dictionary. | **Custom Dictionary** |
| Select, edit, add, or delete custom dictionaries. | **Dictionaries** |
| Automatically check for and mark possible grammatical errors as you type, marking them with a green wavy underline. | **Check Grammar As You Type** |
| Hide the green wavy line under possible grammatical errors. | **Hide Grammatical Errors in This Document** |
| Check spelling as you check the grammar. Deselect this option to check the spelling only. | **Check Grammar with Spelling** |
| Display the Readability Statistics dialog box after checking the grammar. For most standard documents, you want a Flesch Reading Ease score of 60 to 70 or a Flesch-Kincaid Grade Level score of 7.0 to 8.0. | **Show Readability Statistics** |

| Action | Option |
|---|---|
| Set the level which you want the grammar checker to use in finding grammatical errors—**Casual**, **Standard**, **Formal**, **Technical**, or **Custom**. To set your own style, choose **Custom** and then click **Settings** to select the items the checker should look for. | **Writing Style** |
| Run the spelling and grammar checker on the current document. | **Recheck Document** |

SEE ALSO

➤ *For more information about using the spell checker, see page 96*

➤ *To learn more about running the grammar checker, see page 105*

## Add User Information

User information identifies you for tracking changes, making comments, adding return addresses to envelopes, and so on. The original entries result from the data you enter when you install Word. If you didn't install Word yourself, the data may be incorrect, and in any case it may be incomplete. You want the information to be entered as it would for letters and other formal documents.

To add your complete information, click the **Tools** menu and select **Options** to open the Options dialog box. Then click the **User Information** tab. Enter your personal information and choose **OK** to close the dialog box.

## Modify Page Setup Defaults

Each template controls the default formatting for the documents created based on that particular template. As you learn to change the defaults for page setup, styles, and fonts, you should note that you are given the opportunity to modify not only the document, but also to add the change to the template on which the document is based. Adding that change to the template makes it the default for all future documents based on that template.

You don't have to open a template to make default formatting changes. For example, to change the default margins, paper size, and alternating headers and footers, you open the Page Setup dialog box while in your current document and set the changes there.

### Change Default Page Setup Options

1. On the **File** menu, select **Page Setup**.

2. When the Page Setup dialog box opens, change the settings that you want to use as your defaults.

3. Choose **Default**.

4. As shown in Figure 31.13, Word asks for confirmation that you want to change the default settings for page setup and tells you that the change will affect all new documents based on the current template. Choose **Yes**.

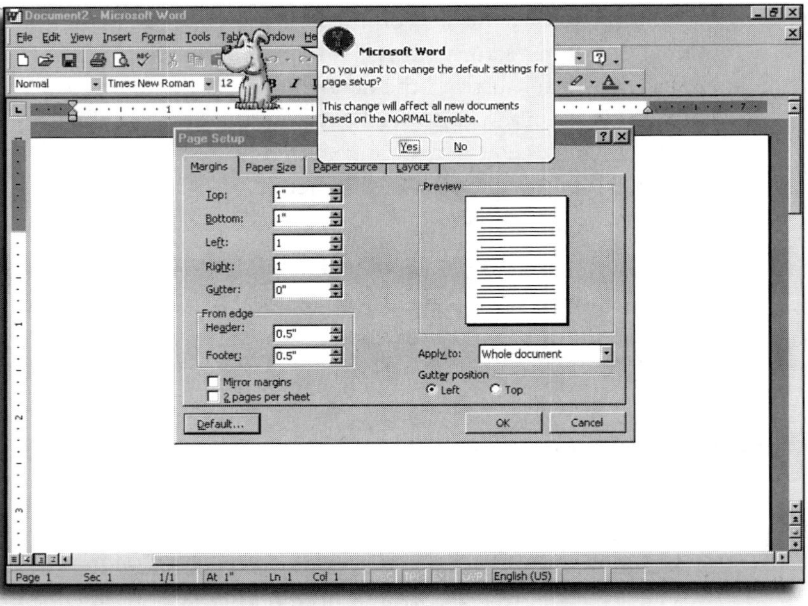

FIGURE 31.13

Click **Yes** to add your formatting changes to the template.

As you're saving your document, be sure to update the template when prompted so your changes are incorporated into the template.

SEE ALSO

➤ *To learn how to set margins, see page 290*

➤ *For information on setting paper size and orientation, see page 294*

➤ *To learn more about modifying templates, see page 353*

## Set Default Fonts

Are you getting tired of Times New Roman? That's the default font in Word, and the default font size is 12 points. Times New Roman is one of the fonts that ships with Windows, so in choosing that font Microsoft could be sure that most people would have it. However, if you have more fonts installed on your computer and would prefer to use something other than Times New Roman, you could change your default font.

### Change the Default Font

1. Open the **Format** menu and choose **Font** to open the Font dialog box (see Figure 31.14).

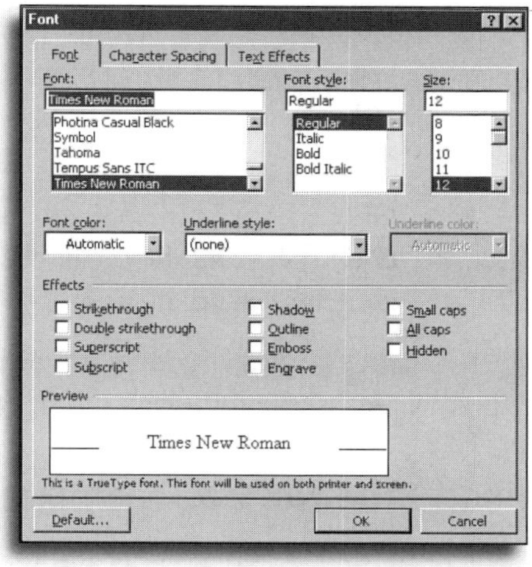

FIGURE 31.14

Click **Default** to make the current font settings into your default font.

2. Select the font, font style, size, and so forth that you want for your default font.

3. Choose **Default**.

4. Word asks for a confirmation that you want to save the settings as your default font and add them to the template. Click **Yes**.

**SEE ALSO**
➤ *To learn more about setting font options, see page* 74

## Set Default Styles

Styles are stored in the document where you create them or in the template on which the document is based. As you are modifying the Heading 1 through Heading 9 styles or the Normal styles, which are usually generated by the template, you have the option to add your alterations to the template so they are available for new documents.

### Set Default Styles

1. Open the **Format** menu and choose **Style** to open the Style dialog box.
2. Select the style you want to modify from the **Styles** list.
3. Choose **Modify**.
4. In the Modify Style dialog box, click **Add to Template**.
5. Choose **Format** and then select the formatting options you want to apply to the style.
6. When you return to the Modify Style dialog box, choose **OK** to return to the Style dialog box.
7. Choose **Apply** to apply and save your changes and then close the dialog box. Choose **Close** to save your changes and close the dialog box.

As you save the document, Word may prompt you to save changes to the template. Click **Yes** to save the style changes.

## Modify the Normal Template

Because most documents and templates are based on the Normal.dot template, modifying that template changes many of the defaults in effect when you start new documents. For example, to change the Heading 1 through Heading 9 and Normal styles or the tabs, edit the Normal template.

**Modify Normal.dot**

1. Open the **File** menu and choose **Open**.

2. When the Open dialog box appears, select **Document Templates (*.dot)** from the **Files of Type** drop-down list.

3. Locate the template folders (usually in the \Program Files\Microsoft Office\Templates folder).

4. Select **Normal.dot** from the list of files.

5. Click **Open**.

6. Make your formatting changes and then save the template.

Any changes you make to the page setup, styles, tabs, and so forth will change any new documents you create based on the Normal template.

**SEE ALSO**

➤ For more information on modifying templates, see page 353

# Customize Office Assistant

The Office Assistant can use system resources. Depending on your system configuration, you may find that it slows down your computer. If you don't experience problems with the Office Assistant, set options for exactly how much help you require from the Office Assistant in the Office Assistant dialog box.

To customize the Office Assistant, click the Assistant and click the **Options** button. The Office Assistant dialog box appears. Click the **Options** tab to set options. Table 31.6 highlights some important Office Assistant Options.

TABLE 31.6    **Office Assistant options**

| Option | Description |
| --- | --- |
| Respond to F1 Key | Activates the Office Assistant when you press the F1 key. Clearing this option and pressing F1 opens the Word Help Topics window. |
| Move When in the Way | Moves the Assistant when dialog boxes are present on your screen. Minimizes the Assistant if it is not used for a five minute period. |
| Guess Help Topics | Shows Help topics before you ask for them based on the task you are performing. |
| Display Alerts | Shows up to alert you to a potential problem. |
| Make Sounds | Turns on Office Assistant sounds. |
| Using Features More Effectively | Shows tips on features as you work with them. |
| Using the Mouse More Effectively | Shows tips on using the mouse more effectively. |
| Keyboard Shortcuts | Displays shortcut keys you can use while you work. |
| Only Show High Priority Tips | Displays only the very important tips. |
| Show the Tip of the Day at Startup | Shows a Tip each time an Office program starts. |

Options that you set for the Office Assistant effect how the Assistant works and appears in all Office programs (such as Excel, PowerPoint, and so forth).

To choose a different Office Assistant character, click the **Gallery** tab of the Office Assistant dialog box. Click the **Back** or **Next** button until you find the Assistant you want. Figure 31.15 shows the Genius Assistant.

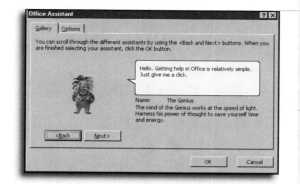

**FIGURE 31.15**

If you have Internet access, you can visit the Microsoft home page (www.Microsoft.com) to download additional Office Assistants to add to your Gallery.

# PART

# IX

# Appendixes

# Changes Made by AutoFormat

| When You Type | AutoFormat Does This |
| --- | --- |
| A number followed by a period, hyphen, closing parenthesis, or greater than sign, and then a space or tab, followed by text. | Turns it into a numbered list. |
| An asterisk, one or two hyphens, a greater than sign, or an arrow created with a greater than sign and a hyphen or equal sign, followed by a space or tab, and then text. | Turns it into a bulleted list. |
| A symbol (inserted by using the **Insert** menu's **Symbol** command) followed by two or more spaces and then text. | Turns it into a bulleted list where the symbol is the bullet. |
| An inline graphic (within 1.5 times the height of the text) followed by two or more spaces and then text. | Turns it into a bulleted list where the inline graphic is the bullet. |
| Three or more hyphens or underscores. Available only on the **AutoFormat As You Type** tab. | Creates a single thin line border above the paragraph. |
| Three or more equal signs. Available only on the **AutoFormat As You Type** tab. | Creates a double-line border above the paragraph. |
| Three or more number signs. Available only on the **AutoFormat As You Type** tab. | Creates a decorative line border above the paragraph. |
| Three or more tildes. Available only on the **AutoFormat As You Type** tab. | Creates a single wavy line border above the paragraph. |
| Three or more asterisks. Available only on the **AutoFormat As You Type** tab. | Creates a dotted line border above |

| | the paragraph. |
|---|---|
| A salutation, such as "Dear Mr. Smith:". | Offers to start the Letter Wizard. |
| Straight quotation marks (" and '). | Turns them into typesetter quotes (curly) such as "" and ''. |
| Fractions, such as 1/2 or 1/4. | Changes them to 1/2 or 1/4. |
| Ordinal numbers such as 1st or 2nd. | Changes them to 1st or 2nd. |
| Text, a space, hyphen, another space, and then text. | Changes spaces and hyphens to an en dash (–). |
| Text, two hyphens, and more text. | Changes the hyphens to an em dash (—). |
| An asterisk followed by text and then another asterisk. | Turns the text between the asterisks to boldface (by applying the built-in character style named Strong). |
| An underline followed by text and then another underline. | Turns the text between the underlines to italic (by applying the built-in character style named Emphasis). |
| An Internet, email, or network address. | Formats it as a hyperlink. |
| A plus sign, a series of hyphens, another plus sign, a series of hyphens, and so on, then press Enter (looks like: +-----+---------------+--------+). | Inserts a table, putting the column borders where the plus signs were. The number of hyphens determines the width of the columns. |
| A list item that starts with a | Applies the same |

| | |
|---|---|
| bullet or asterisk, followed by bold, italic, or underlined text, followed by a period, colon, hyphen, em dash, question mark, or exclamation point, and then followed by a space or tab and then plain text. For example: *John:* Marry me, Mary, and make me merry! | formatting to the lead text of the next list item. Available only on the **AutoFormat As You Type** tab. |
| An outline while in Outline view. | Applies styles Heading 1 through Heading 9 to your outline headings. |
| Text formatted like a heading (for example, bold, centered, no punctuation), or text formatted like body text (for example, left-aligned or justified, multiple word-wrapped lines, or punctuated). | Creates a new paragraph style based on the formatting you apply, and applies the style to that paragraph. Only works if **Define Styles Based on Your Formatting** is checked. |

# Work in Different Languages

Install Office's multilingual features

Set the user interface language

Add new keyboard settings in Windows

Turn on automatic language detection in Word

Add a custom language dictionary to use multiple language proofing tools

# Know Your Multilingual Options

**Before you start installation**

Before you embark on the installation process, read this chapter carefully. You may need to purchase and install another language version of your operating system, the Word Proofing Kit, and a language dictionary for your language in order to successfully edit in multiple languages in Word.

**Not a universal translator**

Office's Multilanguage Support does not translate documents for you. It gives you the tools to open documents in other languages, edit them if you know the language, print them, and save them. You have to purchase translation programs or hire a translator if you don't understand the language of the document.

Microsoft Office 2000 provides support for multilingual users so you can view and edit documents in many languages. Dialog boxes and menus appear in the language of your choice. Plus, Word has a language autodetect feature that immediately detects a different language (or you can mark text as being in a different language) so you don't get a lot of erroneous red and green wavy lines. It's even possible to have proofing tools (spelling, grammar, thesaurus, and AutoCorrect) for more than one language.

However, all of this does not come without some work. There is an additional process following your installation of Office 2000 that includes several steps:

- Install Multilanguage Support.
- Enable Office Language Settings.
- Add keyboard layouts in Windows.
- Add the foreign language dictionary.
- Install the Microsoft Proofing Tools Kit.
- Set Word to automatically detect languages.

After you have completed all these steps (explained in more detail later in this appendix), here are some of the benefits you'll see in working in Word:

- *Fonts.* Many of the standard fonts (Arial, Courier, Times New Roman) used in Word have expanded character sets so you don't need the Greek version of Arial to type a Greek letter in Arial. This is actually a feature of Windows, but certainly a program such as Word makes it a very useful feature.
- *Dialog Boxes.* Multilingual text now appears in your dialog boxes. For example, the author of a document created in Greek will appear in Greek in the document's Properties dialog box even though all the other language in the dialog box is English.

- *Symbols.* To access language-specific symbols and letters in the Symbol dialog box, you select a font subset. For example, switch the font subset to Russian to see Cyrillic characters.

- *Dates.* The dates you insert can be set in the format required by the language you are using; such as entering dates as 16-09-98 for some European countries but as 9-16-98 in English (also a Windows feature).

- *Punctuation.* Punctuation marks differ within different languages. Word detects the language being used and switches to the correct punctuation marks.

- *Spelling.* With the appropriate language dictionary installed, you can spell check a document in that language. If your document has mixed languages and you have marked the text that is not one for which you have a dictionary, the spell checker will skip that text.

- *Sorting.* You specify the language for sorting lists and tables to sort correctly for the designated language.

- *Printing.* You can easily change the formatting of a document set up to print in one size of paper so that it prints correctly on the size paper you have in your printer. For example, you can switch a European document set up to print on A4 paper to print in the United States on 8.5 x 11-inch letter size paper.

- *Keyboard Switching.* When you switch your keyboard to another language, Word automatically switches fonts in your document to fonts appropriate to the language of the keyboard.

- *Correct Language Display.* Except for bidirectional versions such as Hebrew and Arabic, you can open a document created in another language version of Word provided you have the correct fonts.

**SEE ALSO**

➤ *To learn more about printing on different paper sizes, see page 264*

**Localized Version**

The term "localized version" is used frequently in Office documentation about multilingual support. This is the language you have chosen to set up as your basic language when you installed the Language Pack. You generally use that language for menus and dialog boxes. What you establish as your basic language may be different than what someone else may use as their localized version. For example, You may choose English for your localized version of Word, but a person in Germany may use the German version. The beauty of multilingual support is that regardless of the localized version that was used to create a document, another user with a version in another language can still open the document.

## Install Multilanguage Support

The first step in the process is to install the Multilanguage Support package for Office 2000.

### Install Office 2000 Multilanguage Support

1. Close all open application programs.

2. Insert the Language Pack CD in your CD-ROM drive.

3. Click Start and choose **Run** from the Start menu.

4. In the **Open** text box, type **D:\Setup.exe** (substitute the letter for your CD-ROM drive if your drive is not D:).

5. Choose **OK**.

6. From the Choose the language version of Office you wish to use drop-down list, select the language you will be using for most documents when you work in Word—such as, German, Greek, Hebrew, Japanese, and so forth. For example, if you generally do your work in English and would prefer English to appear on your menus and dialog boxes, select English even if you plan to work frequently in German.

7. Choose **Install**.

8. When the setup program is complete, click OK. If the setup program prompts you, allow it to restart your computer.

## Enable Office Language Settings

Now that you have installed the Multilanguage Support, you have to enable it for the language you prefer.

### Enable the Office Language Settings

1. Click Start and then choose **Programs**. From the submenu, select **Office Tools** and then **Microsoft Office Language Settings**. The Microsoft Office Language Settings dialog box appears (see Figure B.1).

---

**Additional System Support Required**

Some languages require additional system support for entering characters specific to that language, such as Chinese, Japanese, or Korean. For these languages you also need to install a program called an *Input Method Editor (IME)*. The IME is available on the Language Pack CD, in the IME subfolder of the Extras folder. Open the IME subfolder and select the folder for your language (use Global if you don't have that language version of Windows 95, Windows 98, or Windows NT installed). For Japanese and traditional Chinese run Setup.exe by double-clicking that file; for simplified Chinese run Pvertsp.exe.

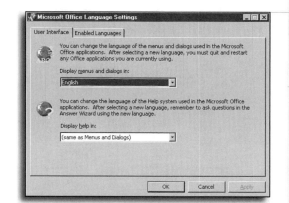

2. On the **User Interface** tab, select the language for your menus and dialog boxes from the list under **Display menus and dialogs in**. If you decide to change this language later, you must exit all Office programs, change the setting, and then restart your applications.

3. To have help displayed in the same language as your menus and dialog boxes, select **(same as Menus and Dialogs)** from the **Display help in** drop-down list. Otherwise, select another language.

4. From the **Enabled Languages** tab (see Figure B.2), select the languages you want to use for editing documents from the list under **Show controls and enable editing for**.

5. Click **Apply** to apply the language setting without closing the dialog box, or choose **OK** to apply the language setting and exit the dialog box.

6. A dialog box appears noting the update to the language settings will not take place until you start your Office applications. Choose **OK**.

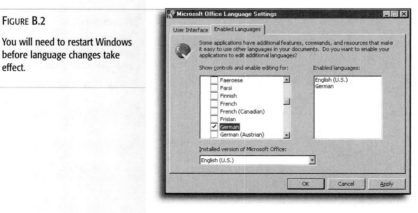

## Add a Keyboard Setting

For languages that include characters not on your current keyboard, you need to configure Windows to work with additional keyboards. To do this, you need to change the settings for Keyboard in the Control Panel. Second, you may need to change the Regional Settings properties in the Control Panel.

### Add More Keyboards

1. Click Start and choose **Settings** from the Start menu. Select **Control Panel** from the submenu.

2. Double-click the **Keyboard** icon.

3. When the Keyboard Properties dialog box opens (see Figure B.3), click the **Language** tab.

4. Choose **Add**.

5. In the Add Language dialog box, select the language you want from the **Language** drop-down list. Choose OK.

6. Under **Switch Languages**, select the keyboard shortcut keys you want to use to switch between keyboards—**Left Alt+Shift**, **Ctrl+Shift**, or **None**. Select **Enable indicator on taskbar** so you double-click that indicator and change keyboard settings.

7. Choose **OK**. You may have to insert your Windows CD to complete the set up of the keyboard.

Regional settings control how numbers, currency, time, and dates are formatted.

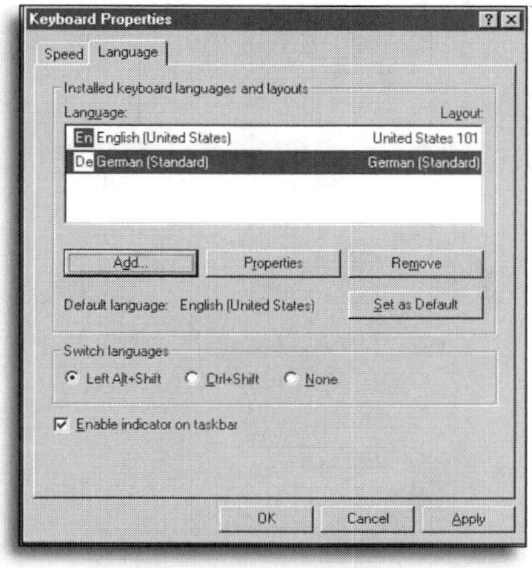

FIGURE B.3

Choose **Add** to add a keyboard setting for another language.

### Change Regional Settings

1. Click Start and choose **Settings** from the Start menu. Select **Control Panel** from the submenu.

2. Double-click the **Regional Settings** icon to open the Regional Settings Properties dialog box (see Figure B.4).

3. On the **Regional Settings** tab, select the language for which you want to specify settings.

4. Click the tab for the settings you need to change to select currency symbols, decimal characters, negative number formats, time formats, and date formats for the language you specified.

5. Choose **OK**.

# Add a Foreign Language Dictionary to Word

In order to check spelling for another language, you must install a dictionary for that language. Follow the directions that come with the dictionary to install it and then do the following to activate it.

**Euro Support**

Your operating system may not have support for the new Euro currency, although Office 2000 does. If you need more information about getting Euro support, check the following Web site: `http://www.microsoft.com/windows/euro`.

**FIGURE B.4**

Select the appropriate settings for number, currency, time, and date that your language uses.

**Where to get the dictionary?**

For information about purchasing a supplemental dictionary, contact your local Microsoft subsidiary or Alki Software Corporation at (800) 669-9673 from within the United States or (206) 286-2600 from outside the United States.

### Activate a Supplemental Dictionary

1. Open the **Tools** menu and select **Options**.

2. In the Options dialog box, click the **Spelling & Grammar** tab.

3. In the **Speller Type** box (which doesn't appear unless you've installed a supplemental dictionary), select **Normal** or click the name of any other supplemental dictionary you want to activate.

4. Choose **OK**.

## Install the Microsoft Proofing Tools Kit

You will need to install the Microsoft Proofing Tools Kit for advanced editing. In the kit are the fonts, localized templates, spelling and grammar checkers. It also contains the AutoCorrect lists, the AutoSummarize rules, and the Input Method Editors (Asian Languages Only). Then Word will be able to automatically detect the language in documents and apply the correct proofing tools.

## Set Word to Automatically Detect Languages

When you first open Word after installing the Multilanguage Support and making your language settings, a dialog box may appear asking if you want to install additional language features. Insert the Language Pack CD and click **OK**.

The language you are currently using appears in the Status bar of Word (see Figure B.5). As you begin typing in another language, Word automatically detects that language and the Status bar reflects that change. In Figure B.5, the language of the first paragraph is German, which was one of the languages enabled in Language Settings.

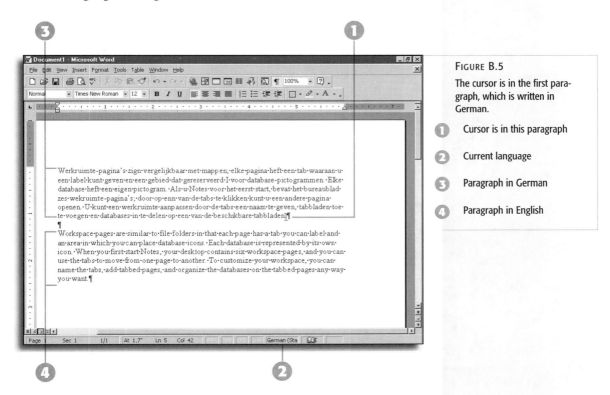

**FIGURE B.5**

The cursor is in the first paragraph, which is written in German.

1. Cursor is in this paragraph
2. Current language
3. Paragraph in German
4. Paragraph in English

Word won't automatically detect every language, so if another language is added to the document that wasn't enabled in language settings, you may see the wavy red and green underlines that indicate possible spelling and grammar errors. You need to mark the text in that language so Word ignores spelling and grammar, or enable that language so Word will automatically detect it.

### Enable the Language in Word

1.  Select the text involved.

2.  Open the <u>T</u>ools menu and select <u>L</u>anguage. Select **Set Language** from the submenu. Alternatively, double-click on the language notation in the Status bar. The Language dialog box opens (see Figure B.6).

3.  From the **Mark selected text as** list, select the language of the selected text.

4.  If you've installed the spelling dictionary for the selected language, Word will automatically use it to check that language's spelling. If not, you should select **Do <u>n</u>ot check spelling or grammar**. Otherwise, you'll always see spelling and grammar errors when you write in that language in your document.

5.  To have the selected language automatically detected in the future, select **D<u>e</u>tect language automatically**.

6.  Choose **OK**.

FIGURE B.6

Disable spelling or grammar checking or enable automatic detection of the language.

### Default

To have the language you selected in the Language dialog box become your default language in Word, choose **Default**. Changing the default does affect all new documents based on the Normal.dot template, so be sure you want to do this. After this, all new documents will start with the default language being the selected language.

### SEE ALSO

➤ *To learn more about the Normal.dot template, see page 344*

# Glossary

**.doc**  The default file extension for Word files (documents).

**.dot**  The default file extension for a Word template.

**.gif**  A file extension for graphics saved in the Graphics Interchange Format.

**.html** (also **.htm**)  A file extension for documents saved in HTML format, needed to publish documents on the Web. See also **Hypertext Markup Language**.

**.jpeg** (also **.jpg**)  A file extension for graphics saved in the Joint Photographic Experts Group format.

**.pcx**  A file extension for graphics saved in PC Paintbrush format.

**.rtf**  A file extension for rich text files, which are text files that retain their formatting.

**.tif** (also **.tiff**)  A file extension for graphics saved in the Tagged Image File Format.

**.txt**  A file extension for text-only files, such as those created in Notepad.

**.wbk**  The file extension that Word assigns to backup copies of files that it creates during saves when **Always Create Backup Copy** is activated in the Options dialog box.

**.wmf**  A file extension for graphics saved in the Windows Metafile Format.

**.xls**  The default file extension for Excel files.

**accelerator keys**  Keys used as shortcuts in lieu of accessing menu commands. Also called shortcut keys. These keys are identified by underlined letters in the menu command, such as **File**, **Close**, and are used in combination with the ALT or CTRL keys.

**alignment**  The arrangement of items on a document, or on the screen in relation to the margins. (See also **horizontal alignment, vertical alignment, indentation, center-aligned, right-aligned,** and **justified.**)

**antonym**  A word whose meaning is the opposite to another word. Hot and cold are antonyms.

**ascenders**  In a typeface, the portion of letters that extend above the "x" height, which is the average height of most lowercase letters. This includes the top of most uppercase letters, but also lowercase b, d, f, h, k, l, and t.

**AutoComplete**  A word feature that automatically inserts items such as AutoText

**AutoComplete**

entries when you type the AutoText entry shortcut.

**AutoCorrect**   A Word feature that automatically corrects typos—spelling errors and grammar errors—as you type.

**AutoFormat**   A Word feature that automatically applies styles (such as headings, bullets, and so forth) as you type a document.

**AutoRecover**   A Word feature that periodically saves a temporary copy of a document while you are working.

**AutoShapes**   Drawing objects provided by Word and accessed on the Drawing toolbar.

**AutoText**   A text (name and address) or graphic (logo) entry stored for frequent use. AutoText entries are assigned shortcuts—when you type the shortcut the entire AutoText entry is inserted in your document. In previous versions of Word, AutoText was called "Glossary items."

**background printing**   A Word feature that enables you to continue to work in Word while a Word document is being printed.

**boilerplate**   Static text or graphics that don't change and are used over and over again in different documents. Examples of boilerplate text include contracts, logos, and so forth.

**bookmark**   A placeholder that references a selection of text or a location in a document.

**border**   The frame of a Microsoft window, table, cell in a table, document, Web page, or drawing. Window borders cannot change, but object borders (such as tables, cells, and so forth) can have formatting applied that includes colors.

**browser**   See **Web browser**.

**callout**   A text label identifying an object. Often applied to identify sections of a drawing, picture, or graph.

**caption**   A label applied to a table, figure, equation, listing, or graphic to identify it or describe its contents.

**category axis**   An axis in a graph. In a graph such as a line, bar, area, or column chart, data is generally plotted in reference to two axes. One contains the values and is called the Y-axis or value axis. The X-axis, or category axis, shows the different categories into which the data falls, such as months, dates, cities, brand names, and so forth.

**cell**   The intersection of a row and a column in a worksheet or spreadsheet.

**center-aligned**   Paragraph formatting in which all lines of text appear to the left and the right of a center point. The center point is user-defined and may be the center of a document, table, paper, cell, column, and so forth.

**character styles**   Attributes assigned to a font. Character styles include such attributes as bold, italic, and underline.

**chart**   A graphic representation of data or relationships between data.

**client**   In a network, a computer that uses programs or data files located on the server.

**Client/Server**   The relationship between the server computer, which controls the network and stores files and programs, and the workstation computers that are part of the network and access files and programs on the server.

**clip art**   A collection of prepared drawings, diagrams, and graphic images that are available to the general public, or that can be purchased as a software package for your personal use.

**Clipboard**   See **Windows Clipboard**.

**collapsed**   An outline view of text, usually displaying header information. Clicking the headers expands the view and displays additional content.

**column**   A layout arrangement that displays information in vertical alignment. Table columns consist of cells; newspaper columns consist of text wrapped within a vertical area defined by margins.

**column break**   Word symbol that instructs the program to begin a new column.

**concordance file**   A list of words from a document and the context in which they appear in the document, generally used in creating indexes.

**condensed**   A font format in which the characters are more narrowly spaced. See also **expanded**.

**context-sensitive menu**   A menu that changes according to the current task the user is performing.

**copy**   Duplicate.

**copyright symbol**   ©.

**cross-reference**   Text that refers to (points to) a different location in a document or to a different document where additional information on the topic at hand can be found.

**cut**   To delete or remove.

**CV**   Curriculum Vitae—a résumé.

**data source**   In Word, the original file containing data to be used for merging.

**database**   A collection of information stored in fields and records that can be sorted and manipulated or merged with forms, letters, envelopes, reports, and so forth.

**datasheet**   A spreadsheet-like window in Microsoft Graph used to enter the data and labels needed to generate the chart or graph.

**default**   The direction or choice made by a program unless intervention is made by the user. Many program features require values, such as a font size, and defaults are set by the program but can be changed by the user.

**delete**   To cut or erase.

**delimited text file**   A text file whose contents are set apart by a symbol that separates the values of fields. The symbol used to separate fields is called a *delimiter*.

**descenders**   In a typeface, the portion of letters that hang below the "x" height, which is the average height of most lowercase letters, as in the letters g, j, p, q, and y.

**destination file**   The receiving file when information is sent to a file from a **source file**.

**directories**   A container (also called folder) that lists filenames and is used to organize files on a computer hard drive. Directories created within directories are called subdirectories. See also **folder**.

**Document Map**   A view in Word that displays an outline view of a document in a separate pane. Documents can be navigated using the Document Map.

**document properties**   A listing of an object's characteristics. Document properties include size, author, number of pages, and so forth.

**document summary**   Part of **document properties** that stores information concerning the document contents. Document summary information is indexed and can be searched.

**dot leader**   A special tab setting in which the whitespace that precedes the tab stop is filled with dots. This type of tab setting is frequently used in a table of contents.

**drawing**   An object or graphic inserted into a document. Typically used to define user-created objects such as boxes and lines.

**ellipsis**   Three dots (…). Commonly found in menus of programs designed to run in Windows and used to indicate that a submenu or dialog box will appear when the user selects the menu choice followed by the ellipsis. Also used in quotations to note that the full text isn't shown.

**em dash**   A long dash (—) that is as wide as the uppercase M in the specific font being used. It's often used to express a parenthetical thought.

**embedded object**   Data from one document that is placed or *embedded* into another document. After it is embedded, it becomes a part of the other document, but still retains a separate identity for editing.

**en dash**   A regular dash (–) that is as wide as the uppercase N in the specific font being used. It is often used to separate numbers or dates, to indicate that the numbers or dates between them are also included (such as "pages 10–25").

**endnote**   Numbered note appearing at the end of a document that provides information on the source of certain text in a document, or that explains or comments on that text. See also **footnote**.

**expanded**   (1) A font format in which the characters are more widely spaced. See also **condensed**. (2) In the Outline view, displaying heading information and the body text accompanying it. See also **collapsed.**

**export**   Save a file in a different file format for use by another application.

**facsimile**   See **fax**.

**Fast Save**   A method of saving a document that only saves any changes made to the document (as opposed to saving the complete revised document) by appending them to the previously saved file. It's usually used with large documents to save time.

**fax** (also **facsimile**) Transmission of a document or picture over a telephone line that is received as a copy of the document or picture.

**field** A container, or location, that stores a particular type of data, such as number fields or text fields. Fields can be a part of a record in a database, or act individually to store or display information on a document, such as a Date field. Field information may be filled in by the user, or calculated by the program, depending on the form or database design.

**field code** A placeholder for field information. Field codes are surrounded by brackets {}.

**field label** Text that identifies the purpose or content of a field and that appears as static text on a document or screen, even when the field has not been populated.

**file server** The computer in a network where the files are stored for access by other computers in the network.

**filter** A set of criteria that determines which of the database information to display. For example, a filter can cause a database to display only records that contain a certain area code or zip code.

**filter criteria** Parameters used to determine which records a filter will display.

**flowchart** A diagram of a process or procedure using specific symbols to indicate decision points and alternate paths.

**folder** A container (also called directory) which lists filenames and is used to organize files on a computer hard drive.

Folders created within folders are called subfolders.

**font** A character set that has a typeface, size, and style (bold, italic) in common.

**footer** Information printed at the bottom of a page. Footer information is determined by the document creator and can contain page numbers, document names, logos, and graphics.

**footnote** Numbered note appearing at the bottom of a page that provides information on the source of certain text on that page, or that explains or comments on that text. See also **endnote**.

**footnote separator** A line that separates the body of a document from the footnotes.

**form** See **online form** or **printed form**.

**form letter** A standardized letter that differs only in a few pieces of data, such as the name or address of the person to whom it is addressed.

**Format Painter** A Word feature that enables the copying of formatting options from one selected object to another, or to many throughout the document.

**frame** A rectangular object that can be moved anywhere on a Word page. It can contain text or graphics. Text on the page wraps around it. In Word 2000, it has been largely replaced by the Text Box object. Alternatively, a boxed section of a Web page. A Web page can contain several forms.

**gradient** In the Fill Effects dialog box, gradient is the section in which you can define the background shading of an object in which the background color *gradually* changes from light to dark or from one color to another color.

**graph**   A picture of the relationship between two or more variables.

**graphic**   A drawing or picture created by a graphics application or scanned and stored in a file.

**gridlines**   Optional lines that extend from the tick marks on an axis across the plot area of a chart. Gridlines make it easier to evaluate data values when reading the graph. Also, the nonprinting lines used to define cells in a table.

**group objects**   Create a single set of objects from two or more individual objects.

**gutter**   The area of a page that is lost in the binding of a book.

**hanging indent**   Paragraph alignment in all lines of a paragraph are indented except for the first line.

**hard page break**   See **page break**.

**hard-copy forms**   Forms created for the purpose of being filled in by pen or pencil as opposed to online or user forms intended to be completed using the computer keyboard. An example of a hard-copy form is an employment application.

**header**   Information printed at the top of a page. Header information is determined by the document creator and can contain page numbers, document names, logos, and graphics.

**heading**   A main topic in a document that is followed by body text; for example, outline headings, column headings, headlines, and subheads.

**horizontal alignment**   Controls the location of text between the right and left margins of a page.

**HTML**   See **Hypertext Markup Language**.

**hyperlink**   A block of text (usually colored and underlined) or a graphic that represents a connection to another place in the document or a separate document. You usually can open the other document or jump to the other place in the currently open document simply by clicking on the text or graphic.

**hypertext**   See **hyperlink**.

**Hypertext Markup Language (HTML)**   A collection of instructions or tags that tell a browser program how to display a document as in when to bold or italicize. HTML tags typically appear embedded within a document, set apart from the document text by angle brackets. For example, <B> means display the text that follows as boldface; </B> means turn off boldface for the text that follows.

**hyphen**   A dash that marks where a word at the end of a line of text has been broken and then continued on the next line. See also **nonbreaking hyphen** and **optional hyphen**.

**import**   To insert or copy information from one program into another.

**indent**   Paragraph alignment in which additional whitespace is inserted between the margin and the paragraph text.

**index**   A listing or set of topics derived from document or book text. An index includes the page number of the document or book on which the topic is discussed. An index usually appears at the end of the document or book.

**index entry**   A topic or word marked and identified as belonging to the index.

**Internet**   A worldwide conglomeration of computer networks that can communicate with each other.

**intranet**   A company's computer network which stores HTML documents and serves HTML documents to clients running Web browsers.

**justification**   Aligning the ends of lines of text so that each end is flush with the left or right margin, or both. See also **alignment**.

**justified**   A paragraph alignment in which the text in the paragraphs are even with the right and left margins, except for the last line of the paragraph. The amount of space between words varies to facilitate this balance of text.

**landscape**   Page orientation in which text runs parallel to the long edge of the paper.

**layer objects**   To place objects in a document on top of other objects.

**leaders**   Characters used to fill otherwise blank spaces between an item in the table of contents and its page number. Most commonly used leader is a period.

**left-aligned**   Paragraph formatting in which the left ends of lines of text are an even distance from the left margins and the right ends are uneven.

**legend**   An area on a chart that displays a set of symbols or color boxes that represent each set of series data displayed in the graph. It helps the reader understand what the elements of the chart mean.

**line spacing**   The vertical distance between lines of text, usually measured as the number of lines (such as single, one and a half, or double).

**link**   A pointer to a block of data located in an external file. A linked object appears to be in one file but really exists in a second file. The first file only has a pointer or link that tells the first program where to locate the object pointed to.

**linked object**   Data that is created in one file and then connected to another file. Although the data appears to be part of the second file, it really remains part of the first file.

**Local Area Network (LAN)**   A network that connects a group of computers that are within an immediate area, such as the same building, and are connected to each other by network cable.

**macro**   A set of program commands and instructions that are recorded and played back on request. Macros can contain lengthy strings of commands that can be played using a single menu command or set of shortcut keystrokes.

**macro recorder**    Records the steps involved in a task so they can be played back when you run the macro.

**macro virus**    A program that is hidden within a macro. It is designed to destroy files or programs, or at least disrupt computer operations. Using a template or document containing such a macro may cause damage to your document files. See also **virus**.

**mail merge**    An operation that extracts data from a data source and inserts it into fields on a main document to create form letters, envelopes, and labels.

**mail server**    In an email system, the server that stores email messages for pick up and sorts incoming messages into the mailboxes for delivery to the correct individuals.

**main document**    The document that contains the information in mail merge that does not change, for example, the return address on an envelope.

**margin(s)**    The distances between the text on a document and the edge of the paper.

**master document**    A document that acts as a binder for other documents, facilitating the creation of a table of contents, index, headers and footers, and uniform formatting for all documents it binds.

**merged document**    The third document that results from a merge of a main document and a data source. See also **mail merge**.

**metafile**    A file that contains information from which a program can create a desired result. A graphics metafile contains a set of vectors from which a graphics program can draw a picture. In Windows printing, an *enhanced metafile* (EMF) is an intermediate file that the Windows Graphical Device Interface (GDI) creates when you use the Print command in Word. It allows you to more quickly return to working in Word after sending a graphics print job.

**Microsoft Graph 97**    A program used for creating simple charts and graphs.

**mirror margins**    In a document that has facing pages, the right margin on the even page is equal to the left margin on the odd page, and the left margin on the even page is equal to the right margin on the odd page.

**monospace font**    A font in which each character takes up the same amount of horizontal space on a line.

**multilevel list**    An outline.

**newspaper column**    A page format in which more than one column appears on a page and text flows down one column, then wraps to the next column and flows down it, and so on, down each column on the page, similar to the way text flows in a newspaper or magazine.

**nonbreaking hyphen**    A type of hyphen that you should use when you want to keep hyphenated words from splitting apart at the end of a line. Word does not insert a line break at a nonbreaking hyphen. Use Ctrl+Shift+hyphen to insert a nonbreaking hyphen.

**nonbreaking space**    A type of space that you should use when you want to keep two words from splitting apart at the end of a line. Word does not insert a line break at a nonbreaking space. Use Ctrl+Shift+space to insert a nonbreaking space.

**nonproportional font**   A font in which the horizontal space occupied by each character is the same, so the letter m takes as much space as l. The space between words and letters cannot be stretched or reduced to fit within margins.

**Normal.dot**   The default template that Word bases a document on if you don't tell Word to use a different template. Normal.dot is a *global* template in the sense that its features are always available to all documents, even documents that are primarily based on another template.

**numeric keypad**   A block of keys on the right side of the keyboard set up like a calculator, used to enter numbers, that has keys for performing mathematical functions.

**Object Linking and Embedding (OLE)**   Allows different applications to share and copy information by either linking two files, or by taking selected data from one file and copying or embedding it in another file. Also known as OLE, Microsoft has released two versions of it. Word 97 supports version 2 of OLE.

**ODBC**   See **Open Database Connectivity**.

**OLE**   See **Object Linking and Embedding**.

**online form**   A form that you can fill in while working on the Web. The form designer decides, when you save the form, whether only the variable data or the whole document is saved or printed. Note: Microsoft also uses this term to refer to forms that you fill out onscreen, but not on the Web.

**Open Database Connectivity (ODBC)**   An industry standard that defines how databases and other programs can share information even though they store the information in different formats.

**optional hyphen**   A hyphen that is used between syllables when a word is broken at the end of a line.

**orientation**   The direction the lines print on a piece of paper. See also **portrait** and **landscape**.

**orphan**   When the first line of a paragraph is at the bottom of one page or column and the rest of the paragraph is continued on the next page or column, that single first line is called an *orphan*.

**Outline view**   A view that shows the various levels of a document by using indentations for headings and text.

**page break**   A break in the text of a document where a new page is started. *Automatic* or *oft* page breaks automatically occur when the amount of text reaches a specified maximum. To change the spot where the text breaks, a **hard page break** can be manually inserted.

**paper source**   The source where paper is taken from when a document is printed, such as lower tray, upper tray, or manual feed.

**paragraph spacing**   The distance between the end of one paragraph and the beginning of another, generally measured in points.

**paragraph style**   A predefined set of formats that are stored together under a name. By applying the style to a paragraph, you apply all the formats at once. You apply a style by picking its name from a list of styles.

**password**   A word or phrase that must be entered to open or edit a protected document. A password is used to give a document greater security.

**paste**   A function that takes data that has been cut or copied from one document and places it into another location.

**pattern**   In the Fill Effects dialog box, a panel in which you can choose from a set of background designs for an object.

**plot area**   The area in which Microsoft Graph plots your data. This area includes the axes and all markers that represent data points.

**Plug and Play**   A feature of Windows 95, Windows 98, and to a limited extent, Windows NT, that automatically detects new hardware devices and configures the system to work with them.

**point**   A unit of measure used in specifying type size. One inch is equal to 72 points.

**populate**   Use already existing information from another file to supply data for a database.

**portrait**   The orientation in which the text runs parallel to the short edge of the paper.

**print device**   (1) A device for making paper copies of documents. (2) A printer.

**Print Preview**   A view that shows all the pages of a document in the form in which they will be printed.

**printed form**   A form intended to be filled out on paper. See also **online form**.

**printer driver**   A program that provides the operating system with the language and information necessary to run the printer.

**printer font**   A font that resides in a printer but not in the computer. When you use a printer font in your document, Windows must display the document onscreen using some other font because the printer font is not available in the computer for display purposes. Windows would normally substitute a **screen font**.

**properties**   The attributes belonging to an item—file, object, picture, text, document, and so forth. See also **document properties**.

**proportional font**   A font in which the horizontal space occupied by each character varies, so a letter such as i or l takes less horizontal space than a letter such as m. The spaces between the letters and words in a proportional font can also be stretched or reduced to make the font fit within margins.

**ragged-right**   The lines in a paragraph do not end evenly at the right margin.

**raster format**   A graphic format, also called a *bitmap*, in which each pixel in a graphic is individually colored.

**record**   A collection of related fields in a database (a row of information on a client, person, and so forth).

**registered trademark symbol**   The uppercase letter R enclosed in a circle ®.

**revision mark**   An editing mark that shows where changes, such as deletions or substitutions, have been made.

**right-aligned**   Paragraph formatting in which the right ends of lines of text are an even distance from the right margins and the left ends are uneven.

**route documents**   A function in email that enables a document to be sent to several people, one after the other, instead of to all of them at once.

**row**   Items arranged horizontally in a table or spreadsheet.

**ruler**   Bars at the top and side of the document that display measurements, such as inches, and indicate the location of margins, indentation, column width, row height, paper size, and tab settings.

**scalable font**   A font that can be changed to allow different character sizes instead of being restricted to a few specific sizes.

**screen font**   A font that is used for display on a computer monitor to represent the font as it will be printed.

**ScreenTip**   Helpful pop-up text that appears when you position and hold your cursor over an icon, menu, or screen component.

**script**   A program that consists of a set of instructions that use the syntax of the application.

**section**   Division of a document that allows different formatting to appear in the same document.

**section break**   An editing mark used to delineate the end of a section in a document.

**series data**   A row of data in a datasheet that produces a line on a line chart, a set of columns or bars that share a color on column or bar charts, or an area in an area chart.

**Server (Web, Network, file, and mail)**   A computer that stores information or programs for access by other computers.

**Service Provider**   An organization that offers a service (such as Internet connection) that users may subscribe to and then access. Internet Service Providers are often called ISPs.

**shading**   A background color or shade of gray that you can apply to a block of text, cell, row, or column in a table, or an object (such as a frame or text box) inserted in a document.

**share**   To allow computer resources (files, printers, folders, and so forth) to be used by other computers in the network.

**shareware**   Software that you are allowed to use for free for a trial period. If you decide to continue to use it, you are supposed to send a payment to the author of the program.

**shortcut keystroke**   A keystroke or combination of keystrokes that allow a task to be performed more quickly and simply, without using a mouse.

**side-by-side columns**   Columns that are parallel to each other on the same page, but whose text flows to the same column on the next page instead of going to the top of the next column on the same page (usually accomplished in Word by using tables).

**sizing handles**   Small hollow boxes that appear at the endpoints of lines or arrows, or on the sides and corners of objects. The appearance of these handles means that a line or object is selected. Dragging the handles changes the size of the selected item.

**source document**   The document that contains the information that is either linked or embedded into another document.

**source file**   The file that contains the information that is either linked or embedded into another file or a document.

**spike**   Stores text so that it can be moved without using the Clipboard. Items can be appended to the spike so that the spike grows until you empty it.

**static text**   The nonvariable parts of a form. The labels that identify what should be filled into the blanks.

**style**   A collection of formatting specifications that have been assigned a name and saved. Styles can be applied to other paragraphs or characters to give them the same formatting.

**subdirectories**   Directories that are contained in a directory. Beginning with Windows 95, Windows refers to directories and subdirectories as folders and subfolders.

**subdocument**   A document that is contained within a master document.

**subfolders**   Folders that are contained in another folder.

**subordinate text**   Text that is nested beneath a heading in an outline.

**summary information**   See **document summary**.

**synonyms**   Words that have nearly the same meaning as each other.

**tab**   A keystroke that moves the cursor to a set position on the ruler, where the next text entered will align, or to the next cell in a table. Also, the name of the set position on the ruler.

**table**   Organizes information in a row and column format.

**table heading**   A column or row title.

**table of contents**   Lists all the main topics in your document, and the page on which the topic starts. It appears at the beginning of the document. The topics are generally listed in page order.

**template**   A Word document, usually having the extension .dot, which includes features such as boilerplate text, styles,

AutoText entries, macros, and custom toolbars and menus that are available to any document based on that template.

**texture**   In the Fill Effects dialog box, a panel in which you can choose background patterns that simulate real-world textures such as marble, granite, wood, or cloth.

**themes**   Predefined templates supplied with Word 2000 for designing Web pages quickly. Themes include backgrounds and fonts that work well with Web browsers.

**thesaurus**   A book or file that provides a list of synonyms and antonyms for the selected word in a document.

**trademark symbol**   The letters TM, capitalized and superscripted, appearing next to a trademark to identify it as a trademark ™.

**TrueType**   A type of scalable font developed jointly by Apple and Microsoft, in which the characters are described mathematically within the font, and a rendering engine interprets the description to draw the characters on your computer screen, on paper, or wherever the text is to be displayed.

**Uniform Resource Locator (URL)**   A pointer to the location of an object. URLs conform to a standard syntax that generally looks as follows: `[protocol]://[host].[domain].[superdomain]/[directory]/[file]` such as `http://www.microsoft.com`.

**Universal Naming Convention (UNC)**   A standard syntax for naming paths to servers, directories, and files.

**value axis**   The axis in a graph such as a line, bar, area, or column chart that contains the values (also referred to as the Y-axis).

**variable**   A placeholder that will be replaced by information to be supplied at a later time. For example, a template might include a field code as a variable that will be replaced by the creation date of a document based on the template.

**versioning**   A feature of Word that permits you to save succeeding versions of a document all within the same file on disk, and to review and revert to earlier versions.

**vertical alignment**   Controls the location of text between the top and bottom margins of a page.

**VIM (Vendor Independent Messaging)**   An industry standard that allows different applications to interact with different mail messaging systems.

**virus**   A program designed to destroy files or programs or at least disrupt computer operations. It can be included or attached to an innocent program, file, or disk, and carried from one computer to another. See also **macro virus**.

**Visual Basic Editor**   An optionally installed component of Word (or Office) that enables you to do basic programming in Visual Basic, an object-oriented programming language used to create and change programs that use a graphical user interface (GUI). You use the Visual Basic Editor when editing Word macros.

**WAN**    See **Wide Area Network**.

**watermark**    Text or a graphic that is layered either on top of or behind text in a document. For example, a lightly shaded logo may appear in the background on each page of a document.

**Web**    The World Wide Web (or just Web) is a component of the Internet. It is a collection of HTML documents accessible through the Internet.

**Web browser**    A program that enables users to read and download documents on the Web, use hyperlinks, receive email, and access newsgroups.

**Web page**    One of the HTML documents that makes up the World Wide Web.

**Web server**    A server that makes Web pages accessible to users of the Web and maintains Web sites.

**Web site**    A group of related Web pages.

**What's This?**    A type of Windows help that identifies objects that you click with the mouse.

**Wide Area Network (WAN)**    A network that connects computers over a large geographical area, such as a city, state, or country.

**widow**    When all the lines of a paragraph except the last one are on one page or column, the last line of the paragraph that appears at the top of the next page is called a *widow*.

**Windows Clipboard**    A Windows function that allows data to be cut or copied from one file, stored on the Clipboard, and then transferred to another file.

**wizard**    An interactive "mini-program" designed to assist users in a particular feature or function of the software program, such as Word's Letter Wizard.

**word wrap**    The automatic break of lines of text by a word processing program to fit text within the boundaries set by the user, such as the margins.

**WordArt**    A program that creates special effects for text, such as creating shadows, skewing, and stretching.

**workgroup**    People who are working together and sharing computer data and resources, often over a company intranet or network.

**worksheet**    One page, or sheet, of an Excel workbook. A worksheet can contain one or more spreadsheets, as well as charts. If the worksheet contains a single spreadsheet, it is often simply referred to as a spreadsheet.

**workstation**    A computer in a network from which the user can access other computers.

**World Wide Web**    See **Web**.

**WYSIWYG**    An acronym for What You See Is What You Get, which means that the appearance of your document on your screen is the same as the printed document.

# Index

## Symbols

## A

**tables**

# Get **FREE** books and more...when you register this book online for our Personal Bookshelf Program

*http://register.quecorp.com/*

Register online and you can sign up for our *FREE Personal Bookshelf Program...*unlimited access to the electronic version of more than 200 complete computer books — immediately! That means you'll have 100,000 pages of valuable information onscreen, at your fingertips!

Plus, you can access product support, including complimentary downloads, technical support files, book-focused links, companion Web sites, author sites, and more!

And, don't miss out on the opportunity to sign up for a *FREE subscription to a weekly e-mail newsletter* to help you stay current with news, announcements, sample book chapters and special events including sweepstakes, contests, and various product giveaways.

We value your comments! Best of all, the entire registration process takes only a few minutes to complete...so go online and get the greatest value going—absolutely FREE!

## Don't Miss Out On This Great Opportunity!

QUE®is a product of Macmillan Computer Publishing USA—for more information, visit: *www.mcp.com*